ALSO BY NANCY MILFORD

Zelda: A Biography

SAVAGE
BEAUTY

SAVAGE BEAUTY

THE LIFE OF
EDNA ST. VINCENT MILLAY

NANCY MILFORD

RANDOM HOUSE

NEW YORK

Copyright © 2001 by Nancy Winston Milford

All rights reserved under International and Pan-American
Copyright Conventions. Published in the United States by
Random House, Inc., New York, and simultaneously in Canada
by Random House of Canada Limited, Toronto.

RANDOM HOUSE and colophon are registered trademarks
of Random House, Inc.

Owing to limitations of space, acknowledgments of permission to quote
from unpublished materials and previously published materials will be
found following the Index.

Library of Congress Cataloging-in-Publication Data
Milford, Nancy.
Savage beauty : the life of Edna St. Vincent Millay / Nancy Milford.
p.   cm.
Includes index.
ISBN 0-394-57589-X (acid-free paper)
1. Millay, Edna St. Vincent, 1892–1950.   2. Poets, American—20th century—Biography.
3. Women and literature—United States—History—20th century.   I. Title.
PS3525.I495 Z72 2001
811'.52—dc21
[B]   2001018598

Random House website address: www.atrandom.com
Printed in the United States of America on acid-free paper
2 4 6 8 9 7 5 3
First Edition

Frontispiece photo: Doris Ulmann

All interior photographs not otherwise credited are part of
the Steepletop Collection in the Library of Congress. All rights, including copyright,
to these photographs are owned by The Edna St. Vincent Millay Society,
and they are used with permission.

Book design by Victoria Wong

For Nelly
and for my mother, Vivienne

I am waylaid by Beauty. Who will walk
Between me and the crying of the frogs?
Oh, savage Beauty, suffer me to pass,
That am a timid woman, on her way
From one house to another!

—Edna St. Vincent Millay

PROLOGUE

I played a hunch in the winter of 1972. I drove up Route 22 to a farmhouse called Steepletop in the Taconic Hills of Austerlitz, New York, sat down in the kitchen of that house with Norma Millay, and told her I wanted to write about her sister's life. Both of us knew that any serious work about Edna St. Vincent Millay had been blocked for almost a quarter of a century. Norma was Edna's only heir, she controlled her estate, and she thought she might write what she called The Biography. But as we sat there eating and drinking and talking, it became more and more clear to me that I was going to write the biography of Edna Millay, that I would write it with her sister's help and permission, and that I would resist her influence as best I could. "All right," she said, raising a tumbler of Dewar's to mine as if it were a toast, "I've waited long enough. It's yours!"

But that wasn't the hunch. It was that within the dining room, library, bedrooms, woodshed, and front hall files of Steepletop, beneath the damask tablecloth and under the piano benches there would be a collection of papers, letters, snapshots, notebooks, and drafts of poems that had not been destroyed or lost, as Norma sometimes hinted, that even if in disorder had been carefully kept. They would provide the fresh ground from which a life could be found and shaped.

During the summers of 1975, 1976, 1977, and 1978, I brought thousands of pieces of paper out of that farmhouse. I tried to make a list of what I was removing. This turned out to be difficult, for as I began to read among Edna Millay's papers, Norma would stop me. She intended to read each piece of paper before I did and to hand it to me. In order, she said, to tell me what it meant. Or might mean. We sat crouched over a letter written in a cascade of inky curls from Georgia O'Keeffe, postmarked Lake George but with the year smudged, telling Edna she wasn't ready to see her yet; or a scrap of paper from Edmund Wilson reminding her she'd left her rings on his piano and imploring her to let him see her again before she left Greenwich Village for the Cape in the summer of 1920. "Oh, poor Bunny," Norma said.

I made the list because I anticipated that at the very last minute, at the moment of removal from the grounds of Steepletop and therefore from Norma Millay's control, she might balk. She did. We dickered. I reminded her we had an agreement drawn up by lawyers according to which she was obliged to release these papers to me so that I could begin to work. I told her she would receive a hefty percentage of whatever I earned *after* the book's publication. I told her we were not adversaries and that I admired her caution. Then I handed her the list. She barely looked at it, waved her hand, and I drove off with the goods.

Was it my luck that this extraordinary collection was in no university library? Can luck strike twice? Just as no one had Zelda Fitzgerald's papers but her daughter, Scottie, who handed them to me in shopping bags, so no one had ever seen this collection. Except, of course, her sister. For who but a Norma Millay or a Lavinia Dickinson, the younger sister of Emily Dickinson, each of whom in her day was considered eccentric, neurotic, and difficult, if not downright ignorant, would have cared with such intensity to have cherished the past so carefully? And with such mixed motives?

To be a biographer is a somewhat peculiar endeavor. It seems to me it requires not only the tact, patience, and thoroughness of a scholar but the stamina of a horse. Virginia Woolf called it "donkeywork"—for who but a domesticated ass would harness herself to what is recoverable of the past and call it A Life? Isn't there something curious, not to say questionable, about this appetite for other people's mail, called *Letters*? What does it mean to be mulish in pursuit of someone else's life, to be charmed, beguiled even, by the past, if not held fast to it? It isn't true that it provides insulation from the present. On the contrary, it impinges upon it, for while it is from the terrain of my own life that I work and mine hers, biography is the true story of someone else's life, and not my own.

But certain lives—the "rich, dim Shelley drama" Henry James wrote about, the Fitzgeralds—are cautionary tales of high romance upon which entire generations feast. There is almost the same period of time, sixty years, give or take, between the Romantic movement and James's generation as there is between our own and the writers of the 1920s. It is our own past, it is just within reach, and Edna Millay is our lyric voice.

Edna St. Vincent Millay became the herald of the New Woman. She smoked in public when it was against the law for women to do so, she lived in Greenwich Village during the halcyon days of that starry bohemia, she slept with men and women and wrote about it in lyrics and sonnets that blazed with wit and a sexual daring that captivated the nation:

> I shall forget you presently, my dear,
> So make the most of this, your little day,
> Your little month, your little half a year,
> Ere I forget, or die, or move away,
> And we are done forever; by and by
> I shall forget you, as I said, but now
> If you entreat me with your loveliest lie
> I will protest you with my favourite vow.
> I would indeed that love were longer-lived,
> And oaths were not so brittle as they are,
> But so it is, and nature has contrived
> To struggle on without a break thus far,—
> Whether or not we find what we are seeking
> Is idle, biologically speaking.

It wasn't only that she was the first woman to win the Pulitzer Prize in poetry or that Thomas Hardy once said there were really only two great things in the United States, the skyscraper and the poetry of Edna St. Vincent Millay. It was that when she published "First Fig" in June 1918, her cheeky quatrain ignited the imagination of a generation of American women: she gave them their rallying cry. A wild freedom edged with death.

> My candle burns at both ends;
>   It will not last the night;
> But ah, my foes, and oh, my friends—
>   It gives a lovely light!

But it wasn't all play or sexual glamour with her by a long shot. She stood by the editors of *The Masses* when they were up against charges of treason in 1918. She marched for Sacco and Vanzetti in 1927 and was arrested for protesting their death sentence, a protest she took all the way to the governor of Massachusetts. She fought the Lindberghs when Anne Morrow Lindbergh published *The Wave of the Future* in 1940, advising that we capitulate to fascism. When the Nazis razed the entire Czech village of Lidice in 1942, Millay wrote a verse play for radio called "The Murder of Lidice," which was broadcast throughout America when a third of the country was willing to accept a separate peace with Germany.

—

In October 1934, Edna Millay read at Yale. A young graduate student, Richard Sewell, who forty years later would become the biographer of Emily Dickinson, never forgot the impression she made that night. Walking to the center of Woolsey Hall, wrapped in a long black velvet cloak, her bright hair shining, she "stood before us," he remembered, "like a daffodil." Looking at her wrist, she told her audience that the poems she was about to read were from her new book, *Wine from These Grapes,* "Which is coming off the press just about now." That night she read with the zeal of a young Jeremiah, her words burning the air as she closed her reading with a sonnet from "The Epitaph for the Race of Man." Tickets for her readings were wildly sought whether she was in Oklahoma City or Chicago, where the hall seating 1,600 was sold out and even with standees an extra hall had to be taken for the overflow of another 800 who listened to her over amplifiers.

There were other writers who read in America in her time. Gertrude Stein was touring in the United States precisely when Millay was, and somewhat before Millay there had been Carl Sandburg and Vachel Lindsay, popular poets who were unacknowledged models for Robert Frost's readings. But Millay's was an entirely different sort of performance. Stein was a coterie figure, self-published until her *Autobiography of Alice B. Toklas;* she was immensely admired but very little read or bought. Lindsay and Sandburg were part of a pattern of performance that went back to James Whitcomb Riley, that old Hoosier the Millay sisters adored when they were little, back even to Emerson and Twain.

Deep into the nineteenth century there had been literary gentlemen who filled lecture halls and athenaeums with their deft recitals of poems and sermons. But Millay was the first American figure to rival the personal adulation, frenzy even, of Byron, where the poet in his person was the romantic ideal. It was his life as much as his work that shocked and delighted his audiences. Edna Millay was the only American woman to draw such crowds to her. Her performing self made people feel they had seen the muse alive and just within reach. They laughed with her, and they were moved by her poetry. Passionate and charming, or easy and lofty, she not only brought them to their feet, she brought them to her. In the heart of the Depression her collection of sonnets *Fatal Interview* sold 35,000 copies within the first few weeks of its publication.

Norma was as generous as she was possessive. When I arrived to do research—for the papers I had taken turned out to be only a fraction of the entire collection—I was to have breakfast in bed, as her sister had, with freshly squeezed orange juice and hot coffee in a silver carafe with heavy cream. I slept in the north bedroom that had been Edna's husband Eugen's. On the wall next to the bed was an oil painting by Charles Ellis, Norma's husband, of Norma, nude, swimming in a pool while a man holding a drink was watching her. Norma slept in her sister's bedroom on her linen sheets. Even then I knew these were not regular research trips. I would work in Edna's studio, away from the farmhouse just on the edge of a field of blueberries. I drove a dark green Morgan roadster in those days, and I would take Norma for a spin across those rough fields while she hollered with delight, her long blond-white hair flying out behind her.

There was always some young person, most often a woman, sailing into her orbit and sometimes being flung out again. She called them her myrmidons. These relationships were never casual: some people stayed for years. If they'd come because of their love of Edna Millay's poetry, they stayed because of Norma. Norma was seductive. She exercised her considerable powers not primarily for sexual attraction, although that was certainly still a part of her charm—that she flirted with being sexual—but to ply her will and to get others to do her bidding. She could be merciless.

There were hilarious scenes when guests from distinguished universities and others hoping to secure her papers were brought to their knees by Norma's sly willfulness. She told one such gentleman he would look adorable without his glasses. No one had told him he looked adorable for a long time, and he seemed to swell with his new handsomeness. Norma suddenly leaned over, took his glasses from his face, and said, "There! Don't you look splendid?" He laughed winsomely. Then she brought out the nude photographs of her sister she'd used as bait to lure him to Steepletop. He couldn't see of course without his glasses. Might he have them back? "Oh, la!" Norma said prettily. "Did you think I was going to let a stranger gaze upon the naked body of my sister?"

There were only three things she said she'd destroyed. One was a letter returned to her by a no-longer-young man to whom Edna had written. Norma said it was indiscreet. Edna described his physical beauty in detail and made what she wanted clear. He was homosexual. Norma said, "Maybe she didn't care. Anyway, he turned her down. We can't have that." There was an ivory dildo, which Norma admitted was difficult to burn, but she'd managed. And there was a set of pornographic photographs, taken, she thought, about the same time as the nude photographs from Santa Fe in 1926 or 1927, when Millay was writing her libretto, *The King's Henchman,* for the Metropolitan Opera. These were of Eugen and Edna, she said. Some were taken down at the pool, perhaps shot by Eugen using a timing device on his camera. Norma guessed that Arthur Davison Ficke had a hand in shooting them. "Vincent was already a famous poet, how could she have let these photographs of her be taken? Well, she did. Naughty Vincent Millay! I found them, and I destroyed them. For her own good! You can put that down!"

Edna St. Vincent Millay, whose very name her mother said was song, was shy and small and intense, almost prim. Her hair was her glory—it was the color of fire. Thick and curling, it fell to her waist. Her skin was as pale as milk. She was the firstborn, the eldest of three sisters who were as unalike and yet as close as the fingers on a hand. They had to be, for there was nothing and no one behind them but their mother. Their parents had separated in 1900 in Maine.

> I remember a swamp . . . that made a short-cut to the railroad station when I was seven. It was down across that swamp my father went, when my mother told him to go & not to come back.
>   (Or maybe she said he might come back if he would do better—but who ever does better?)

This book begins at home, where all family romances start. There were in the Millay family certain stories that rose out of the past with a power and thrust that was felt through three generations of women. These were tales of romance and hardship, but, even more crucially, of female infidelity and freedom won at high cost. They were as much of a shared legacy as their red hair. Bargains were struck between mother and daughter, and acts were committed with no knowledge of the consequences that would befall them.

What I had not counted on was that creature for whom there is no name, the American Eve, dead at fifty-eight.

CONTENTS

BOOK ONE

THE LYRIC
YEARS
1892–1923

One realizes that even in harmonious families there is this double life: the group life, which is the one we can observe in our neighbour's household, and, underneath, another—secret and passionate and intense—which is the real life. . . . One realizes that human relationships are the tragic necessity of human life; that they can never be wholly satisfactory, that every ego is half the time greedily seeking them, and half the time pulling away from them. In those simple relationships of loving husband and wife, affectionate sisters . . . there are innumerable shades of sweetness and anguish which make up the pattern of our lives.

—Willa Cather, *Not Under Forty*

PART ONE

THIS DOUBLE LIFE

CHAPTER 1

Camden, with its ring of mountains rising behind the white clapboard houses facing Penobscot Bay, made the most of its view. Nowhere else on the coast of Maine was there such dramatic natural beauty. The houses were like weathered faces turned to watch the sea. The upland meadows of ox-eyed daisies, timothy, and sweet fern, the dark green woods of balsam and fir swept to the gentle summit of Mount Megunticook, and the rock face of Mount Battie rose from the edge of the sea as if to hold it. But it was a far less generous time than the early days of shipbuilding, upon which the town's wealth had been founded. Now even the great woodsheds along the wharves were mostly abandoned, permanent reminders of the long death of shipbuilding. The wool mills looming behind the town offered scant wages and long hours. Later in her life Edna St. Vincent Millay would say she was "a girl who had lived all her life at the very tide-line of the sea," but in the fall of 1904, she moved with her family into 100 Washington Street on the far edge of town, in a section called Millville because it was near the mills. It was the smallest house in the poorest part of town, but it was one their mother could afford when she brought her girls to Camden after her divorce.

Their brown frame house was set in a large field, and just beyond it flowed the Megunticook River, into which the mills sometimes spilled their dyes. The house, on low ground, could be reached only by walking down a long, rickety wooden sidewalk from the street. When the Megunticook River overflowed and the weather turned cold with no heat in the house, the kitchen floor flooded and froze and the girls gleefully ice-skated across it. The house was close enough to their mother's aunt Clara Buzzell, a large, easygoing person who ran a boardinghouse for the mill hands, that she could keep an eye on the girls while their mother worked. Cora wrote to her daughters often; the three little sisters felt her presence even when she was absent, which was almost all the time.

> Have the baker leave whatever you want at Aunt Clara's. . . . I can pay him when I see him and it will be all right. Have your washing done every week now and have some system and regularity about your work. . . . You can do it and you must do it . . . for Mama who has her heart and hands full.

She told them to make up a song to sing while they did dishes, "and think 'I am doing this to please mama,' and see how easy the dishes will get clean."

"We had one great advantage, I realized later," Norma Millay wrote. "We were free to love and appreciate our mother and to enjoy her because she wasn't always around, as most mothers are, telling us what to do and how to do it. . . . when mother was coming home, that was an occasion to be celebrated, and we usually celebrated by cleaning the house."

They invented games to make play out of work. "Dishes were handled differently," Norma remembered. "This game was called 'Miss Lane' for miscellaneous: here one of us washed, another dried, and the other did miscellaneous pots and pans, milk bottles, whatever. Vincent was mostly responsible for the songs we sang as we worked." This one was written the first year they were in Camden:

> I'm the Queen of the Dish-pan.
>   My subjects abound.
> I can knock them about
>   And push them around,
> And they answer with naught
>   But a clattering sound;
> I'm the Queen of the Dish-pan,
>   Hooray!
>
> Cho.
>
> For I've pots and pans
>   And kettles galore.
> If I think I'm all done
>   There are always some more,
> For here's a dozen
>   And there's a score.
> I'm the Queen of the Dish-pan,
>   Hooray!

But they missed their mother and longed for her return. "At night, sometimes, we would lie in bed together, huddled against the cold, pretending to be brides, and little Kathleen would call out, 'Goodnight, Cherest!' in the direction we thought our mother would be."

Not everyone in Camden agreed with the way the Millays lived. When their neighbor Lena Dunbar came to visit, she was dismayed: "For instance, they had shades at their window and nothing else. I don't think they cared much. Well, once they stenciled apple blossoms, painted that pattern down the sides of the window. Or, for instance, they had a couple of plum trees in their backyard and they never waited for the plums to ripen, but would pick them green, put them in vinegar, and call them 'mock olives.' Well, no one else did that sort of thing in Camden, don't you see?"

Emma Harrington, who taught eighth and ninth grades at the Elm Street grammar school, where Vincent enrolled that fall, never forgot her. "She was small and frail for a twelve-year-old. . . . Her mane of red hair and enormous gray-green eyes added to the impression of frailty, and her stubborn mouth and chin made her seem austere, almost to the point of grimness." She kept her after school after reading her first composition to find out if someone had helped her with it. Tactfully, she asked if her mother had seen her excellent work. Vincent interrupted her: "Excuse me, Miss Harrington, . . . but I can tell that you think I didn't write that composition. Well, I did! But the only way I can prove it will be to write the next one you assign right here, in front of you. And I promise it will be as good as this one, and maybe better."

It was her determination to excel that drew attention. That first winter, she clashed with the principal of the school. He was a good teacher but quick-tempered. Vincent questioned him whenever something he said puzzled her, and she was often puzzled. He felt she was challenging his authority and began to mangle her first name. He called her Violet, Veronica, Vivienne, Valerie, any name beginning with a V but her own, which he considered outlandish. Unshaken, Vincent would respond, "Yes, Mr. Wilbur. But my name is Vincent." One day he erupted during an exchange and shouted that she'd run the school long enough. He grabbed a book from his desk and threw it at her. She picked the book up carefully, took it to his desk, and walked out of the classroom.

That afternoon Mrs. Millay marched to the school and demanded an explanation. Trying to conclude their heated interview, Wilbur pushed her away from his door sharply enough that she nearly fell down the stairs. Dusting herself off, Mrs. Millay strode into the office of the superintendent of schools, who quickly agreed with her that Vincent should not return to the Elm Street School. He transferred her to Camden High

School, midway in the first term. She was "The Newest Freshman," the title of her first composition to be published in the school paper, *The Megunticook,* and the youngest. Though they misspelled her last name—Milley—they would learn to correct it, for by her senior year she was editor in chief.

"She was supposed to be a year behind, you know," Henry Pendleton, who was in her class, said. "But her mother had—well—she had a downright fight with the principal of the school, and she took it upon herself to put Vincent ahead. Yes, she did. Now the girls associated with her more than the boys did. Their circumstances were very poor. They were a very poor family. Oh, neatly dressed and all, but their home looked . . . ah, well, they didn't have, let's say, the things that most people in Camden enjoyed."

What began to disturb, even offend, the local worthies, was the way Millay's mother treated Vincent. "You see," Henry Pendleton recalled, "sometimes people felt a little . . . oh, well, for instance Father—my father was a farmer—and Mrs. Millay would be bragging about her daughter, Vincent, and my father couldn't get a word in edgewise. He had a daughter, too, you see, and he'd come home fuming. He said to Mother more than once, 'I would say my daughter is outranked!' And people didn't like that."

Vincent's birthday that year was noted by her mother as "an unpleasant day." As Cora totted up its costs, she said she'd paid $30.00 for a set of books for Vincent and $3.00 for a subscription to *St. Nicholas,* a children's magazine. She said there were

> 1 cross little girl
> 1 grieved little girl
> 1 satisfied little girl
> 1 tired and discouraged mama.

The satisfied little girl was Vincent. She wrote to *St. Nicholas* and asked to join its League:

> We have just been reading your interesting stories and poems and Norma, Kathleen, and myself wish to join your League. We think you are very kind to devote so much valuable time and space to your readers. Norma was ten years old last December. Kathleen, seven last May, and I shall be twelve Washington's birthday. Please send three badges of membership to three very interested little sisters.
>
> —Vincent, Norma and Kathleen Millay

What Millay called her first "conscious writing of poetry" was done that year. "Mother sent it to the St. Nicholas League and it received honorable mention." Published in New York, *St. Nicholas* was a monthly illustrated magazine for children. It was begun in the 1870s by Mary Mapes Dodge, the author of a children's classic, *Hans Brinker; or, The Silver Skates,* who was able to bring authors such as Mark Twain, Rudyard Kipling, Christina Rossetti, Louisa May Alcott, Rebecca Harding Davis, Lucy Larcom, Sarah Orne Jewett, and Jack London—writers of distinction who might not ordinarily have written for children—to young readers throughout the country. But what truly distinguished the magazine was the St. Nicholas League, which each month gave out not only prizes—badges in silver and gold, and cash—but the gift of publication. *St. Nicholas* confirmed and gave voice to a generation of young writers: Ringold W. Lardner, the Benét children—Laura, William Rose, and Stephen Vincent—even the young Scott Fitzgerald, who won a prize for a photograph.

"When I was fourteen," Millay wrote, "I won the League's gold medal for a poem, and there was an editorial commenting most flatteringly on my work." The poem was called "The Land of Romance," signed E. Vincent Millay. The League addressed her as Master Millay until she was eighteen, when she bothered to correct them. While the title and length of the poem were assigned by the editor for its March 1907 competition, Millay made it the story of a child's quest to find romance. The child (who always speaks as "I" and is never identified as either a boy or a girl) first asks a man to show the way. The man, described as thin, trembling, and uncertain, says he does not know the way, then that he can't remember it. Next the child turns to a woman, who does not respond at first but continues to work at her spinning wheel, until impatiently:

> "Oh! Why do you seek for Romance? And why do you trouble me?
> "Little care I for your fancies. They will bring you no good," she said,
> "Take the wheel that stands in the corner, and get you to work, instead."

What is most interesting about the poem now is the difference between the man's inability to give any direction or help at all and the woman's fiercely practical advice: get to work.

On the same page as the poem, the editor of the League cautioned young writers, "Very sad, very tragic, very romantic and very abstruse work cannot often be used, no matter how good it may be from the literary point of view, and while the League editor certainly does not advocate the sacrifice of artistic impulse to market suitability, he does advocate . . . the study of the market's needs." It is hard to know how seriously

E. Vincent Millay took any of this, but she did correctly judge what was and was not suitable to the needs of *St. Nicholas,* for by the time she was eighteen and too old to enter their competitions anymore, she had won every prize they gave.

"The Land of Romance" was considered good enough for Edward J. Wheeler, the editor of *Current Literature* in New York, to select it to reprint in his April issue. He said that although he couldn't tell from the signature whether the author was a boy or a girl, "the poem seems to us to be phenomenal."

ے ے ے

Norma remembered that publication in *Current Literature* confirmed their belief that "Vincent was a genius." Although each of the sisters had sent things in to *St. Nicholas,* "we never got a bite. Vincent got everything."

ے ے ے

Vincent began her first diary in the spring of 1907, when the snow was so deep it drifted over her knees. She was fifteen. She was walking home in the evening from a Glee Club rehearsal when a man called to her and, turning, she saw a sleigh drawing close to her house. "The sleigh was coming to take mama to Rockport on a consumption case. How I hate to have her go! Have to keep house all through vacation." Five days later, her mood had lifted considerably:

> I am going to play Susie in *Tris.* . . . I have the stage all to myself for a while and I have a love scene with the villain. The villain is great.

Triss; or Beyond the Rockies was a melodrama in four acts, and Vincent Millay was cast as Susie Smith, "all learning and books."

> My part is going to be great,—at least they all told me how well I did. I am awfully glad for this will be my first appearance. I want to make it a dazzling one. I get rather sick of having Ed Wells forever hugging me while he is showing Mr. Keep how to do it. Mr. Wells seems to understand the performance all right. He has evidently had experience in that line.

The play went off without a hitch, or nearly. Everyone said that it was the best home talent performance ever given in Camden, and some even considered it better than the productions of the traveling companies.

My part isn't very large, but it is important and rather hard. I hope we will get as good a house in Rockland as we did here. The Opera House was crowded full and everything went off finely except when Allie Eldredge lost his wig. Of course something had to happen. But what of it?

Four years later she stuck the following note in the margin of her diary: "I have just read through to this part and I wish to remark that I consider myself at this point of my life an insufferable mutt and a conceited slush head." By then she was nineteen and hard on herself.

She pasted the flyer from *Triss* in her memory book, which she called *Rosemary,* and within it is one sort of record of her Camden girlhood: the three postcards from the St. Nicholas League announcing her prizes and the newspaper clippings reprinting her poems. There are pressed wild-flowers and snapshots, a thick copper Indian-head penny kept from a canoeing trip upriver to Lake Megunticook, and the programs of the girls' clubs to which she belonged, the Genethod and the Huckleberry Finners.

What is most striking about her scrapbook is the record it provides of the amateur theatricals, concerts, and readings in which she and her sisters took part. The first program she kept was from the Town Hall in Union, Maine, February 3, 1897. Her mother sang with a quartet and E. Vincent Millay had a solo: "The little maid milking her Cow." She was not quite five years old.

She began to perform at the same age she began to write, and her early involvement was prompted and sustained by her mother's passionate interest. That encouragement and its purpose cannot be stated any more clearly than by Norma Millay.

◌ ◌ ◌

"She was not like anyone else's mother. She made us—well, into her per-formers. I remember Vincent and I doing the cakewalk down between aisles of people. I don't remember where it was or even when it was any-more. But I'd bend down—all of this in rhythm to the music Mother was playing on the piano, or the organ maybe—one! two! I'd tie Vincent's shoe. Then we'd throw back our heads, take arms, and strut and cakewalk down.

"Yes, she was ambitious for us. Of course she was! She made us—oh, not ordinary."

◌ ◌ ◌

But who was Cora Millay that she dared to instill such ambition in her daughters? She gave one sort of answer in this interview printed under the title "Mother of the Millays":

The hardships that bound the children together made them stronger, and banded them together in self-defense against the world. If you touched one you touched the whole of us. That was our safety. It strengthened anything in me. I had a chip on my shoulder for them. It is a vicarious thing to live on the edge of everything, but with the parent against the world it is stronger yet. . . . They always had a line out to the beautiful and the tragic realities of life. . . . Their mother's battle increased their nervous tension. Anything mother said was their criterion of all life.

We did keep our appearances, and it made the struggle inside themselves all the keener. . . . I let the girls realize their poverty. I let them realize what every advantage cost me in the effort to live.

Isn't there something hazardous at play here? For hardship can as easily crush a child as fire her ambition. What was Cora that, penniless, without formal education, with three little girls to support alone, she could sustain such fierceness? I asked her surviving daughter, who was offended by the question.

"How do you dare to question us—my mother, or Vincent Millay? You! What do you know of the love between sisters? Or of hardship?"

In an undated poem that exists only in draft in a workbook, Edna Millay gave another answer, which Norma chose not to include in *Mine the Harvest,* the collection of poems she published after her sister's death.

THOUGHTS OF ANY POET AT A FAMILY REUNION

Would I achieve my stature,
I must eschew the *you* within my nature,
The loving notes that cry
"*Our* mother!" and the "*I, I, I*
Name you, claim you, tame you beyond doubt my creature!"

Cool on a migrant wing, if I sing at all,
Down-gliding, up-carried,
Free must be over mountain and sea my call,
Unsistered, unmarried.

Unsistered, unmarried. But what she did not say—what she never said—was unmothered. For locked in the stories of her mother's life and her grandmother's past lay clues to her own future.

CHAPTER 2

If Cora looked more like her father than her mother—her hair was a deep brown like his, and her eyes were gray—she was very like her mother in temperament. She was impulsive and possessed what one of her sisters, in an unpublished memoir, would one day call "a driving force that carried all before it." Even as a child, she flamed. From the first mother and daughter were more like sisters, united by a special bond of intimacy that only strengthened during Cora's adolescence.

Cora's mother, Helen Clementine Emery, was the baby of her family of twelve. Spoilt and pretty, she was a redheaded scamp with a sweet, clear voice and a wealth of bright auburn curls piled high on top of her head in the puffs and lovelocks of the Civil War era. When Eben Lincoln Buzzell, a handsome giant of a man, came to Belfast, Maine, to hire out as a field hand at haying time, she fell in love with him. He was fifteen years her senior, and her parents did not approve of the match. But although she was only seventeen, Clementine (that is what she was called) married him anyway. When Cora was born seven months later, the sharp-eyed neighbors slyly checked the baby's fingers and toes to see if the nails were fully formed.

The Buzzells eventually left Belfast, where they had two sons, Bert and Charles, and moved to Camden, where twin girls, Susie and Clem, were born in 1873. Eben Buzzell, who had become a cooper in Maine, had not prospered, and when the twins were several months old the young family moved again, this time to Newburyport, Massachusetts, where Clementine's older sisters lived. There was the promise of work in the rich mills along the Merrimac, and with a large, young family to support, Buzzell took what he could get. He became a night watchman in the mills. In Newburyport they soon had another child, Georgia, but all did not go smoothly after that. The Buzzells quarreled. One of the twins, Clem, later wrote in her memoir that their conflict was due to a difference in religious beliefs, but she was only five when the split occurred. Cora, who was fifteen, knew the real story because she had played a part in it.

When the newborn baby needed special medical care, Clementine turned to a young doctor, Gard Todd, for help. Soon Todd, who was her sister's brother-in-law, was with her every day, offering counsel, helping even to ease her household duties. The trust and confidence she felt for him, his gentleness and his learning, turned to love. And the only person she confided in was her oldest daughter, Cora.

One unhappy day, when I saw her grieving in a desperate hopelessness over the maelstrom she was being sucked into, I asked her why she did not leave him. I told her, her little girl for once the older woman, that I knew it must be hell for her to have him as a husband to her, to wait in bed for him mornings, when she loved this other.

At first she said she couldn't leave him. Then she asked, as if to herself, how she could leave him with all her little ones. They would be adrift and motherless. Cora told her to take only the three little sisters; she would stay at home with the boys and her father.

The astonishing thing is that her mother took that advice. She fled in the night. Years later, Cora called it her martyrdom; in letters and in peculiar fragments of a memoir she wrote about it again and again:

My mother was gone from the house at the head of the wharf. It was evening. My father was at his work for the night, watchman at the mill. . . . I was alone in the house . . . save for the two little boys, my brothers, who were crying for their mother.

I wasn't crying for my mother. I was too much buoyed up by what was happening, and what was coming in the morning, when my father would come home; too much buoyed up by the part I was taking in this tragedy, my responsibility in this breaking up of a family, I was keyed up to this sort of martyrdom, by my love for my mother.

She thought it was "prostitution" for her mother to remain with her father; she was fired with a sense of self-importance:

My mother was young, she was only thirty-three; she was very beautiful . . . and she had long since ceased to love [our] father. Further than that, he was often very unkind to her, even to being abusive in his talk and more than that. . . . More still, she was deeply in love with another man. All this I knew.

When her father returned, he asked where her mother was. Cora was merciless. "I did not try to soften the blow," she wrote. "I told him baldly, with what I now know was an hysterical strength and coolness, that she had left him."

Dazed, he glanced around the room. He heard his sons weeping, looked into Cora's face, and began to cry.

Eben Buzzell returned to his kin in Maine without much fuss. For a while it looked as if Clementine and her little brood were going to succeed. She established a thriving hairdressing business. It was said that her own lovely red hair was the only advertisement she needed, and her business flourished. Soon she was making regular trips to nearby towns, taking orders for the frizzes, bangs and coils, puffs and switches, with which women transformed themselves. Cora quit school in order to help. She and her mother would hire a horse and buggy and set out to gather hair combings, returning home to wash the hair for the real work, which was fashioned on hand-operated equipment, a hackle and a header, through which the combings were unsnarled and made over. Her mother's hands flew, weaving the fine strands of dead hair, locking it into place, literally weaving the hair on the instrument that looked like a harp.

Later Cora wrote that she cut her father completely out of her life. She remembered that her mother was madly in love and now she was free to become engaged to Gard Todd. "Not that she ever neglected us, we had our place, but all the thwarted years of her mis-mated life had to be made up for in the little time she had him for her accepted lover. I have never seen anyone so much in love as my mother was with this man." They would meet in the late afternoon at a spot called The Laurels because of the lovely wild pink laurel that bloomed there.

One warm day in May 1882, Clementine was driving alone in her open buggy along a country road when something startled her horse. It shied and bolted, and she was thrown to the ground. Her head struck a rock. On June 3, one week before Cora's nineteenth birthday, her mother died of wounds from that fall. She was thirty-seven years old. As she stretched her arms out in the darkened room, her last words were "I cannot leave my babies!"

Cora suffered such wild remorse that the family thought she would be harmed by her grief. All her life she remembered her mother lying in the downstairs room, where the funeral was quickly held:

> her hands quiet for almost the first time in my memory, clasping some white lilies, after all that . . . she was forever locked away from me, from us all, from the daylight and the sunlight . . . from the lover who was now making a heaven on earth for her, from the life she was too young to leave; from the life she was too beautiful to leave . . . they shut her away, and I knew I should never see her face again, never, never, it could not be shown to me again . . . when they were closing her little last house away from me and my loving, adoring gaze.

The twins, who were nine, were immediately adopted by her mother's sister Susan Todd and her husband, Gard Todd's brother, while Cora, Bert, and Charlie set up housekeeping with little Georgia. They took an apartment in Newburyport and filled it with their mother's fine old furniture. One night, shortly after they'd settled in, a fire broke out and destroyed the building and with it every memento of their past. All Cora could remember was running through the smoke with Georgia in her arms, holding her rag doll.

After the fire the family was finally broken. Georgia was taken in by a childless couple in New Hampshire, and the boys, young as they were, were put to work. Cora wandered stricken from relative to relative, first in Massachusetts and then to Maine.

Cora finally settled in West Camden with Joe and Marcia Keller, cousins of her mother's with three sons and no daughters, who took to her as if she were their own. They were generous, kind, and even-tempered. Their seventeenth-century farmhouse was painted a fresh white, with an attached barn and a larger cow barn out back, and apple orchards. Beyond the farmhouse were fields of herbs Marcia gathered for home remedies, and beyond them the sea. The Kellers gave Cora a distance from her past and provided her with a link to her mother's kin.

But she had to work to earn her keep. She began to practice the hair work she'd learned from her mother. When she shut her eyes, she could still see her mother pulling and combing and weaving the silky strands of hair; she could almost hear the humming sound it made as it was worked into place.

Among her keepsakes was a bright pink flyer. "To the Ladies," it read, "CUSTOM HAIR WORK! On short notice, in the best and neatest manner, in the latest styles and at the cheapest rates." Below it said that Miss Cora L. Buzzell, formerly of Massachusetts, would be in Lincolnville Centre, Maine, on Monday, September 13, 1886, "For a short time only." While she lived with the Kellers, she canvassed the surrounding countryside, from the small towns and villages of Warren, Union, Hope, Appleton, Searsmont, and Lincolnville to Camden.

All was not work, however, for among her flyers were tickets for "Miss Buzzell's Concerts." One night she met Henry Millay at a dance sponsored by the local grange, where she was chief musician. Henry Tolman Millay was the sixth of seven brothers of a farming family in Union, Maine. Tall, handsome, and broad-shouldered, he was a year younger than Cora, as fair as she was dark, as easygoing as she was intense, and there was never a time when he could not make her laugh.

Henry loved to fish in the ponds that lay like cups of sweet water between the hills surrounding Union. And he played a mean hand of poker. His blond hair was short, his face smooth and wide and open, with a fine mustache and blue eyes that rarely darkened. He had a knack for wearing his clothes with a nonchalance that distinguished him. He was generous to her: from the beginning he bought Cora presents of books she adored and that he rarely read. He was not uneducated, but he lacked her appetite for self-improvement. Henry Millay was a charmer, and he liked to loaf.

On January 1, 1889, Cora began a diary (adding an "e" for elegance to the end of Buzzell). She was writing to Henry almost every day now; when she was not writing to him, he was likely to visit her on horseback. Marcia Keller made them molasses candy as they sat in the parlor playing High-low-Jack with the Keller boys. On January 9, Henry brought her an engagement ring. Five days later, the diary broke off. Two months after that, on St. Patrick's Day 1889, they married in the Kellers' parlor.

They settled at first in an apartment in Rockland, a small city on the coast of Maine. Henry took a job selling men's clothing and worsteds. Within the year they'd moved into a smart two-family cottage with mahogany sliding doors between the parlor and dining room. In the parlor were Cora's piano, a smoking set for Henry's cigars, and an over-stuffed chair big enough to hold them both. Cora had hemstitched and cross-stitched linen pillow shams and antimacassars in bright red to adorn every available surface. Henry's contribution was a set of deer antlers. They both agreed their new place was entirely "D.E."—damned elegant!

On November 1, 1889, Cora began another diary, this one given to her by Henry. She called it a "journal," and on the first page she quoted her beloved Tennyson:

> Break! break! break!
>   On the cold gray stones, O sea!
> And I would that my tongue could utter
>   The thoughts that arise in me.

In her first entry, she mentioned that *The Maine Farmer* had come with one of her poems in it, and that she did not feel very well and was taking iron medicine. From the beginning of her marriage she suffered constantly from those small illnesses, headaches, and fatigue. She recorded in her journal:

> I do not enjoy taking it: but will for the sake of health; and to please Henry.

Cora was still troubled by the loss of her family. She yearned for Charlie's company and fretted over Clem's welfare at the Todds'. In that stuffy household no one danced or played fan-tan, pitch, or poker, and she knew that Clem, who was not yet eighteen, felt stifled there. Shortly after their move into their new home, they invited her to visit. Henry had to be on the road during the week, and Cora, who could go along only sometimes, wanted company. By the time Clem arrived, their adored brother Charlie had shipped out on a cargo boat, bound for adventure.

Henry, with no sisters of his own, was suddenly surrounded by women. Clem adored him, and he came to think of her as his own sister. Together he and Cora taught her the reel dances they loved, the Portland and the Boston Fancy. Cora turned into a crackerjack card player. Her only flaw, according to Henry, was that she loved to win and couldn't help but show it, whereas Henry played with an ease that appeared to be indifference. On weekends friends came to call for cards, or for sing-alongs. Henry's specialty was a parody of "Down on the Farm." His thumbs tucked into the armholes of his vest, his feet planted far apart, he would glance slowly around the room, grin, and sing. Clem, who'd come for a week's visit, stayed with the young couple for eighteen months.

While Henry was gone, Cora and Clem would visit Marcia and ramble with her along the country roads and through the fields, harvesting herbs and wildflowers. They learned when to pick pennyroyal, tansy, camomile, yarrow, and boneset, and how to dry or soak and steep the great leaves of the mullein plant and the hairy stems of alkanet for their curative properties. They made ointments, decoctions, oils, and syrups carefully and kept them even more carefully. Marcia Keller, having no daughters of her own, took Cora out into the fields in the mornings when the air was clear and taught her all she knew.

Cora remained ambitious for her writing. She had poems in *Judge* and *The Maine Farmer,* and although she was not able to place her stories or poems outside New England, it was not for lack of trying. When she sent her story "Whippoorwill" to *Frank Leslie's Magazine* in New York, her note of rejection came from Mrs. Leslie herself. She said it was "very pretty and well-written, but on account of its length" they could not take it. That was rejection blunted with praise. Cora kept the letter all her life.

Then, in the summer, she found she was pregnant. She was terrified: "I was sure I was going to die." Eventually she and Clem began to make baby clothes and to embroider the soft flannel garments and bedding, but Cora grew restless and found it hard to stay indoors. Local convention almost prohibited pregnant women from being seen. If after the fourth month the mother was startled, it was whispered that the baby was sure to be disfigured for life. Bad news was kept from expectant mothers for fear of its effect. So Cora did not know, until she found a telegram stuffed in Henry's jacket, that her brother Charlie was in grave condition in New York at St. Vincent's Hospital.

After shipping out on the *El Monte* while it was loading a cargo of grain in New Orleans, Charlie either had an attack of fever (which is what he said at the time) or was (as he later admitted) drunk. He lay down on a bale of cotton in the hold of the ship and fell asleep. When he awoke, he was trapped. Between the last day of January and the tenth of February, he lay pinned belowdecks; he couldn't move, and his shouts went unheard. He had given up all thought of being rescued when, suddenly, a light began to grow in the blackness of the hull, "& I could see through the ship as though it was made of clear glass." He felt free of his body and could see himself from a distance. It was not, he felt sure, delirium or a dream. "I was compelled to accept the fact that I had been in touch with the spirit side of nature," he later wrote.

He was found unconscious and rushed to St. Vincent's Hospital, to the care of the Sisters of Charity in New York City. Newspapers around the country carried the story of the incredible man who had lived to tell the tale of his imprisonment. The varying accounts of his entrapment said he'd gone nine to ten days without food or water. They said he had died and been reborn.

His family knew no more than that he was working as a stevedore aboard the *El Monte* when, on the fifteenth of February, a Western Union telegram was sent to Henry Millay in care of Spear & May in Rockland:

CHARLES BUSSELL IS WELL ENOUGH TO LEAVE HOSPITAL.

SISTERS OF CHARITY.

When Cora found the telegram in Henry's pocket, she fainted. Six days later, on February 21, Charlie wrote to them himself: "O Henry you don't know how I long to see you all again for its something that I had given up all hope of doing but I am feeling all right now and will be at home as soon as I get through with this engagement. . . . it's hard to kill yours truly." To Cora he added a separate note, using her childhood nickname: "My Darling Sister Nell don't worry about me I'm all right and at work be at home as soon as I get through here."

But by then Cora had gone into labor. Restlessly pacing the floor, she complained of indigestion and asked Clem to call for Henry's aunt Lucy, who was a practiced midwife. Henry ran next door to tell their neighbors and raced through the snow to fetch the doctor.

It seemed like hours before they heard a sleigh draw up to the house. When the doctor finally arrived, he told Clem to stay with Cora while he and Henry had a cup of coffee with Aunt Lucy. Clem tried not to show her fear as she passed a wet cloth across her sister's lips. Meanwhile, Henry and the doctor fell asleep. After ten hours of labor, just before first light broke, the doctor told Cora to push while Clem and Aunt Lucy climbed onto the bed to hold her legs down. Then, as the moist little head with a thatch of red hair plastered down like wet feathers crowned, the doctor stepped toward the tiny body as if to receive it and made a curious gesture with his hand to wipe something from its face.

A few minutes past six o'clock in the morning of February 22, 1892, exactly as the baby was being born, bells began to peal wildly. For a moment, everyone was startled. The baby reddened and howled. Then they realized that it was George Washington's birthday as well as hers.

Clem wrote to Charlie three days later, "We have named the little one Edna Vincent Millay. Don't you think that is pretty? . . . the Vincent is for the 'St. Vincent' Hospital, the one that cared so well for our darling brother. Nell would have called it 'Vincent' if it had been a boy." They called her Vincent anyway.

She was born with a caul, which was why the doctor acted swiftly to slip the thin membrane from her face so that she could breathe. But that caul, considered a good omen by midwives, confirmed their belief that this child was gifted with eloquence and promised a long life of riches and fame.

CHAPTER 3

In the spring, when Vincent was a few weeks old, the Millays moved inland to Union, where Henry's parents still lived. The move was suggested by the senior Millays, but why their suggestion was taken is not clear. There must have been some resistance, at least on Henry's part, for he had said he would never consent to live on a farm again. His parents offered him a house in the center of town, close to the common. Around the leafy green were the single general store, the livery stable, the Masonic Temple (to which Henry's brothers belonged but he did not), the common school, and two Congregational churches.

If Rockland was a small city, it was nevertheless a real city, with a certain bustle. There were people on the streets after eight o'clock—there were even sidewalks. Whereas Union, with a population of seventy-seven souls in 1892, was something less than a village. They rented a spacious old white frame house within an easy stroll of the common.

On a sunny day in May, Cora and Clem, with Vincent bundled in Clem's arms, drove an open Concord buggy the several miles inland to Union.

They ambled along the dirt road, following it as it wound past the railroad tracks away from the coast toward the fresh green meadows in the west that marked Union. A freight train whistled as it sped by. Their mare snorted in fear and began to shimmy in the braces of her harness. Cora stood, bracing her feet against the buckboard, to gain better leverage as the skittish horse tossed her head and began to prance. Clem clasped the baby closer. Suddenly the mare reared. Cora licked the whip down across her rump as she skittered and reared again. She whipped her once, twice, and the mare bolted. Cora was thrown back into her seat, but she held fast to the reins and within moments brought the horse under control. It had been a close call, and each of the sisters, fraught with the memory of their mother's fatal accident, was tearful and trembling when they reached Union. History, Henry told them blandly as he lifted each down from the buggy, does not repeat itself. Vincent slept soundly throughout the entire drive.

They were settling into their new home when Charlie came to visit. He had been appearing at the Globe Museum down on the Bowery in New York City, where he was advertised as "The Adventurer and Evangelist":

Chas. A. Buzzell The New Orleans Stowaway, will relate his Awful Experiences while on board the Steamer El Monte for nine days and nights without food or water!

He swore he'd seen the spirit side of nature firsthand.

Charlie was still recuperating from his devastating entrapment, and Cora and Henry wanted him to stay with them until he had fully recovered. Now he, too, joined their family—it was a band of Buzzells, they joked among themselves. That summer and fall, Charlie and Cora, who had hundreds of songs by heart, sang together at the outdoor fairs—"Bold Jack Donahue," "The Bride's Lament," and "These Hard Times." Vincent would be placed in a hammock hung from the lowest branch of a tree in their yard, where she would croon or doze while they sang.

The Millays were a French Huguenot family who had come to America just before the Revolution from the north of Ireland, where they'd changed their name from Millais, or perhaps Millet, to Millay. William King Millay, Henry's father, had married a black-eyed dot of a woman named Mary Jane Pease and bought a farm in Union, where they settled down to raise a family of seven sons to pick the rocks out of the fields and pile them into the walls that still surround their pastureland. "That," Cora guessed, "is why Henry preferred not to farm." Nevertheless, the Millays raised tons of blueberries, and from Millay Hill on a clear day looking west you could see the White Mountains of New Hampshire. Due east lay the Atlantic.

William Millay was a converted Methodist and, Cora remembered, "as hard-shelled as any Baptist that ever braved the water." Although he had enjoyed a glass in his youth and knew how to deal a deck of cards, "He never took another drink, was a solid and esteemed member of the church he joined at Union." Henry was nothing like his father; neither he nor Cora joined the church, and what he liked best was to fish. "I can remember when he rowed me around some of the ponds in Union," Cora wrote, "while I gathered armfuls of water-lilies." It wasn't much fun to go fishing with him because he wouldn't let her talk, but she remembered all her life the time he took her with him to his favorite fishing hole "and put me far enough away from him not to disturb his sport, and I caught the biggest trout of the morning." She said that in all fairness he was as pleased as she was, "though he did say, as he always did on the rare occasions when I won from him at cards, that it was beginner's luck." They were so different "that any crank on Eugenics would have said we were perfectly mated for the propagation of a family."

Cora wrote a poem for her firstborn and called it "My Comforter," a "Song to Vincent alone because she was all I had!"

> Sometimes, when the day is dreary
>   Filled with dismal wind and rain,
>   Sometimes when the frame is weary,
>   Filled with nervous ache and pain;
> Then, across Earth's darkest shadows,
>   Comes Life's dearest sweetest bliss
> As with sweet red lips uplifted,
> Baby whispers: "Onts a tiss."
>
> Sometimes when no sun is shining,
>   And my head is bowed with grief
>   . . .
> Someone comes on weak feet toddling,
>   Someone gives my sleeve a tug,
> And with eyes and arms uplifted,
> Baby whispers: "Onts a hug!"

What is striking about the poem is not only that the mother admits to emotional bad weather so early in her marriage but that the baby, not her husband, provides what comfort she needs.

Three days after Christmas 1893, their second daughter, Norma Lounnella Millay, was born, taking her mother's middle name for her own. She
was as fair as her father and very like him, her mother always told her—
except that Norma could sing before she could talk, while Henry couldn't
carry a tune in a bucket.

When the weather turned warm again, Cora took her two daughters to
Newburyport for a visit. The girls were put to nap in an upstairs bedroom
while the grown-ups went downstairs to talk. Before long they noticed the
sound of racing feet, and Cora called up to Vincent, "Are you in bed, darling?" to which she answered, all too quickly, "Yes, Mamma."

There was a horrible noise, and although no one could quite place what
sort of sound it was, it sent a mother and three aunts flying upstairs. Facing them as they entered the room was the large bay window, into which
Aunt Sue had placed an immense geranium plant. Now it was stripped of
leaves, a trail of which led to Vincent, who sat astride two pillows, innocently humming and not looking at her mother. Norma was nowhere to
be seen. Soon the throne of pillows began to heave and wobble. Cora
raced to lift Vincent from the pillows, under which lay Norma, her mouth
stuffed with geranium leaves. It became a family story—for soon the little
girls were inseparable.

Henry did not seem able to keep work, although he remained well enough
liked in Union to have been appointed its superintendent of schools during 1896 and 1897. But he wasn't so good about supporting his wife and
children. The Millays' house was sold out from under them, and a neighbor across the street made room for them in one side of her house. Cora
gave music lessons to help pay the meat bill.

Kathleen Kalloch Millay, their third daughter, was born on May 19, 1896.
Cora had had three children in four years. Just three weeks shy of her
thirty-third birthday, precisely the age her mother had been when she had
fled from their father, Cora noted in her diary, "Henry not there when I
am taken sick. . . . The doctor is there long before Henry is. Mr. Gales
comes to Union at about this time."

From the moment of his arrival in town shortly after Kathleen's birth,
there is more of Mr. Gales, the minister at the Congregational church, in
Cora's new diary than there is of Henry. Her small dark red leather notebook, the first diary she'd begun since 1890, the year after her marriage,
was all about the weather and the Reverend Mr. Gales.

Sat. May 22. . . . Mr. Gales in just as we were eating dinner. Our dinner was real late. He was on his wheel and had a cap on, and looked real cute and boyish and happy.

The children had colds, the weather was foul, and Henry was beginning to grow stout.

Although Cora had not been a regular church member since Newbury-port, she was asked to fill in as an organist in the Congregational church, which had a splendid new pipe organ. It was a rarity in a rural community, and Cora loved to play it. Soon not only was she involved on Sunday, but she was made director of the church choir. But her diary records another sort of absorbing interest: Mr. Gales.

Sunday, [May] 23
    Sermon on the threefold attitude of Christ: toward his enemies; toward the hypocrites; toward those who believe in him. It was good. . . . It was grand. Oh! he is a brave man, and a good one. God bless him and his work. . . . He spoke this morning before his sermon of a certain something that attracts people toward each other and causes them to seek the society of each other; of scholar for scholar, artist for artist, etc. I think it is true friendship. He called it elective affinity. I think there is such an attraction between us. He is my very dear friend.

Mr. Gales had begun to stop at the Millays' every day. He asked Cora at first for suggestions for his sermons, then for her help in writing them. She was pleased to give him what assistance she could—it buoyed her spirit.

I told him how much good he had done me here. . . . I am beginning to think that it is not too late for me to commence anew and study and be something yet. I have started in on Logic. He lent me his. I'm afraid my mind is not adapted to it. *Henry says it isn't.* He thinks everything of Mr. Gales, too. *So do the babies, dog and kitten.*

But not everyone in Union did. They said Mr. Gales dressed like an Englishman, which meant he wore dandified clothes, and although he was forty, he was still a bachelor. Local talk had it that the woman who laundered his shirts had noticed chewing tobacco in his pockets. There were even those who thought Mr. Gales was a sham and that Cora Millay wrote all his sermons. At last the church decided to call a meeting to decide whether his contract should be renewed. Cora was worried:

I am all excited up over this Church Meeting. It seems to be more than I thought! . . . Mr. Gales will have a hard chance to stay. . . . They can go to the Old Nick as far as I am concerned in it. Of course I am not the whole choir; but I'm the "Power behind the throne," all right. . . . If I knew I'd lose every friend I've got in Union (outside of Henry and the babies) by standing by him, I wouldn't budge.

Cora was going too far. She had no voting power in the church because she didn't belong to it. However, a paper was drawn up by those who wanted him to stay, and Cora was asked to write it. Henry was late for supper one evening when the Reverend Mr. Gales came by. "I was a sight and so was the house," Cora notes in her diary. "He looks as if he had been sick. He has a bad cold. He looks wretchedly, and I know he is feeling so. . . . I tried to keep him but he went about nine. I hated to have him go, he seemed so blue." When Henry came home, he told her he thought the paper supporting Gales would work.

I got so worn out I had to take my case to a higher court. . . . I stole off upstairs long enough to pray about it. And I have felt better ever since. I prayed to God to strengthen him and not to allow him to go back one point on the high standards he has maintained, even if he has to go. But I can't bear to think of his going.

The battle between Gales and those who wanted him ousted did not let up. "Henry says Mr. Gales enemies are making a hard fight. I've prayed until I would have tired anyone but God out," she noted in her diary. Mr. Gales had come to represent to Cora all that was worthy and refined. If Union could not recognize his qualities, then it was the town that was at fault. "Went over to Choir Meeting . . . and acted like a fool. I was so dead tired I could hardly sit up. And I kept my tongue going like a madwoman. . . . If this church lets Mr. Gales go now. . . . I've told everyone I've talked with that I should not sing if he went, and I won't."

Cora was losing her head. She stormed, she railed, at last she prayed. She felt charged with passion.

Then I went up into the pulpit, his pulpit, and knelt there and prayed for him. And as I knelt there it seemed as if I could see him standing there beside me, his earnest eyes and strong resolute face, and his uplifted hands. . . . and then I prayed for myself and for my friend and that he might be left to me.

The vote was taken, and Mr. Gales was dismissed. Before leaving, he gave her a book of poems, *The Poetical Works of James Russell Lowell;* "To Cora Buzzell Millay from Thomas Gales" was all his inscription read. She kept the book her entire life.

Her last two diary entries were unhappy ones:

June 5:
   Don't feel very well. Henry home late. Went back to play cards. I went
to bed.

Sunday, June 6
   An unsatisfactory day.

Then she quit her diary completely. She had not bothered to make an
entry for Kathleen's first birthday, nor had she marked the anniversary of
her mother's death on June 3. Maybe, as her sisters came to think, Mr.
Gales had preyed on a kind of discontent in Cora; his interest had suggested a life that was nothing like the one she shared with her husband,
who favored cards and fishing. The Reverend Thomas Gales offered her
solace and appealed to her intellect and to her restless and dormant faith in
herself. It proved a dangerous awakening. It also sounds disturbingly like
her mother's doomed love affair with Gard Todd.

Edna Millay, who was five years old, knew none of this directly, but indi-
rectly children know everything there is to know. They just don't know
why. They don't even wonder why. Her mother taught her to read at five
by studying poetry. She would always say, "Mother gave me poetry," as if
it had been a Christmas present.

   What she called "My first encounter with Poetry" was a curiously physical experience: "I know that it knocked the wind clear out of me, and left
me giddy and almost actively sick . . . when, on opening at random my
mother's gargantuan copy of Shakespeare, I read the passage from Romeo
and Juliet about the 'dateless bargain' and Death keeping Juliet as beautiful as she was in life, to be his 'paramour.' "

   She called it delight. She fastened on the mysterious word "paramour."
Was it foreign? Was it *French*? Her entire little body felt itchy. The
encounter was "truly terrifying. . . . It grew and grew in both my mind and
my body until I became so giddy that I must surely have fallen had I not at
the time been lying flat on my stomach on the attic floor."

   We can imagine her secretly climbing upstairs into the attic, for once
without her sisters, where no one could reach her. As she reads she forgets
time, holds her breath; she feels, she said, an

   unearthly happiness which opened suddenly outward like a door, before
   me, revealing through the very tangible radiance in which I stood as if I
   stood in the path of the sun . . . even to the edge of nausea and over it, and

dropping directly before me a bottomless abyss in which every colour of ecstasy moved like a cloud, now drifting close, now inexorably drawn away, and a wind from depths unthinkable puffing out my pinafore, and the tops of my doll-size slippers sticking out very black and conspicuous from the brink of the precipice into the air above the conscious void.

This is not, of course, a simple little girl; this is a woman remembering what she chose to recall of an encounter that left her stunned by beauty, sickened by loss.

Soon Vincent could read music as easily as poetry. "I was eager to learn," she wrote later, "for I loved music more than anything in the world except my mother." Since there was no piano but an organ in their home and she was too small to reach its pedals, her mother had to help her. They would some-times spend hours together at the keyboard. "There was one chord in a piece which my mother taught me, which I could not get right," she recalled.

We did not have the notes of it, it was something she knew by heart. I called her to help me with the chord, and she came in. She had been doing washing, and her hands, as she placed them upon the keys were very pink, and steam rose from them. Her plain gold wedding-ring shone very clean and bright, and there were little bubbles on it which the soap suds had left, pink, and yellow, and pale green. When she had gone and I was sure that she would not hear me, I laid my cheek softly down upon the cool keys and wept. For it had come into my mind with dreadful violence as she bent above me and placed her fingers upon the keys . . . that my mother could die; and I wanted to save her from that, for I knew she would not like it; and I knew that I could not.

Later she would also remember her mother sitting beside her bed after supper, in her black dress with its smooth tight bodice, her cuffs and high collar trimmed with black jet, reading to her from *Hiawatha* or *Evangeline,* or reciting it from memory, "for she knew the whole long poem by heart, the beautiful 'Snowbound' of Whittier, and quite unconscious that I was doing so, I learned much of it by heart myself."

But where was her father in all this? What did she learn in his company? She didn't seem to remember him at all.

౼ ౼ ౼

"That's not quite true," Norma said. "I remember him coming from the back of the house through a door in Union. And I remember his presence,

which is nice. That the house was not just a house of women, then. . . .
And I remember some of his samples—of wool and of worsteds. Scratchy.
And hiding behind the door when Papa comes. And that he sang to Kathleen. There! That's something, isn't it? And Vincent said that he used to
make Mother laugh."

ه ه ه

In a notebook Vincent kept in the cabin where she worked late into the
night when she was older, she remembered him:

> Yet, he was the one who made her laugh, for he was witty, out of a
>   bland face;
> He could send her into gales of laughter, and never crack a smile.
> But his eyes—his eyes were very blue—would show a deep light
> Suddenly, like sapphires.

In the early spring of 1900, just before Vincent Millay turned eight,
Cora sent Henry away.

Grace Whitten Thurston, who was then the Baptist minister's daughter
and a playmate, remembered when he left: "It made me feel bad that they
didn't have a father and I had. And I never heard them, any of them, mention his name after that. All I remember was he'd gone."

Vincent wrote about his departure only once:

> All my childhood is in those bayberry-bushes, & queen-of-the-meadow, or
> maybe you called it hardhack, & rose-hips. And cranberries—I remember
> a swamp of them that made a short-cut to the railroad station when I was
> seven. It was down across that swamp my father went, when my mother
> told him to go & not come back.
>
>   (Or maybe she said he might come back if he would do better—but
> who ever does better?)

What made Cora Millay send her husband away? Almost thirty years later
she would write this brief note of explanation in a series of sketches she
was making about her life:

> I left him in 1900. And all my people were dazed. Why? Because unlike
> most people, I kept my mouth shut about the man I was living with.
>   I had not gossiped with them, or my neighbors. His brother Fred, one
> of the finest men I have ever met . . . told me he did not know how I had
> stood it for so long.

When Cora met Gales, she was thirty-three, the age her mother had been when she had fled from their father. Now, in May of 1900, she would turn thirty-seven, precisely her mother's age when she had died. Her mother's death stood as a benchmark in Cora's life. Emotionally, it had locked her. But it had also charged her with an urgency that had nothing to do with being equitable, or careful, and everything to do with her desperate sense of loss. Did she fear that if she did not break with Henry Millay then, she never would?

Her sister Clem never stopped seeing this as a disaster:

> Separation was Nell's goal, and she told Henry to go and not return; this was a one-sided affair. . . . I was rebellious about this, and Nell never was allowed to lose sight of the fact that my loyalty to Henry was first, last, and always and that we, of her family, were firm in our opinion that she had . . . thrown away a life-time royalty of happiness, and deprived her little girls of their birthright of happiness, good cheer, and wealth of unselfish interest from him to them.

Clotted though her prose is with righteous certainty, Clem is clear: Cora *intended* to be separated from Henry, and he was powerless before her determination. Certainly her decision was also about money; he gambled, he didn't provide.

2

By the end of May, Henry was writing to Vincent from a remote town called Kingman in the northern wilderness of Penobscot County, Maine, asking her not to forget him. She had written to him first.

> Your papa ought to be ashamed of himself for not answering your nice letter sooner and I guess he is. . . . How does Norma get along at school I suppose she is getting to be a pretty good scholar and Wump I suppose is awful busy making mud pies. I want you to kiss them both for papa, and mamma too. Tell Mamma that papa . . . has got started to earning money at last.

By July his news was less reassuring: "Tell Mama she must not kill herself with work because her little girls are going to need her for a long time & Papa is earning quite a lot of money only he can't get it very fast yet." In letter after letter now, addressed only to his eldest daughter, E. Vincent Millay, he promises her that he'll come back soon, for Thanksgiving perhaps or for Christmas, surely for her birthday in February. She was eight years old in November 1900 when he wrote the following letter. Norma and Kathleen were six and four.

It seems an awful long time to Papa since he saw his little girls, but he could not help it. If your Papa gets some money that he expects soon he is going to see his babies but he can't stay with them long for he has got lots to do and he is not sure that he can go this fall. But he wants to O, so much.

He never came. Her father's letters would remain the same throughout her childhood: he is far away and misses her. He does not write, and he is sorry. He is beginning to make money, but he does not have it yet. And he is sorry. The break between Henry Millay and his family was all but complete by the end of 1900, when Cora turned to the Kellers for refuge. They refused her: Marcia was too old, Joe said, to take on three little girls.

Cora left Union for Rockport, a village built on the steep edge of a cove on the Atlantic coast, where she managed to rent the upper half of an old house overlooking the harbor. She began immediately to look for work as a practical nurse, using the notes Clem had made while studying nursing in Newburyport. It looked as if she would succeed. Vincent began to write a novel, certain it would be published, although Norma, who was six, said skeptically, "I wish I thought it!"

Cora even found someone to help care for the children while she was away on cases and kept a working notebook that first year detailing her cases. She worked night and day wherever she could find work—in Rockland, Camden, and Rockport—usually for a dollar a day. Her cases ranged from recuperation from surgery and childbirth to several cases of typhoid fever, mysteriously plentiful in the coastal area.

She changed bandages and dressed wounds; she watched while her patients' temperatures shot up to 108 degrees and their pulses raced. She dosed them with milk—warmed, iced, or laced with brandy. She gave them raspberry shrub, blancmange, powders, and tablets, and when she had to, she called the doctor. Some died, most lived. The single note of relief in the notebook is her entry on the reelection of the president: "McKinley. Rah! Rah! Rah!" Otherwise it is a record of unremitting hard work. She did not keep the news from her oldest daughter, who tried to write her the cheering little notes from home she asked for.

I thought I would write to you and tell you how I am I am getting along all right in school but in my spelling-blank I had 10 and 10 and then 9 and I felt auful bad because I thought I would have a star I am getting along all right and so is Norma and Kathleens cold is better now I went to practise and a boy called me a little chamipion and I asked him what he ment and he said because I was the best singer and I thanked him.

———

On February 13, 1901, just before Vincent's ninth birthday, "Cora B. Millay of Rockport, County of Knox and State of Maine, respectfully" became a "Libellant against Henry T. Millay of Bangor, in the County of Penobscot and said State of Maine Libellee" and began divorce proceedings. She charged that he had "cruelly and abusively treated your libellant; that being of sufficient ability, or being able to labor and provide for her, grossly or wantonly and cruelly refused or neglected to provide suitable maintainance for her." She asked to be divorced from him, to be given care and custody of their children, "and that he may be ordered to pay her a specific sum of money for the support of said children."

On March 6, Henry was served with the divorce charge. In September, "the Libellee though called did not appear but made default." Once again, Henry did not oppose Cora.

The girls were now their mother's "little women," and she cautioned them again and again against being or causing anyone trouble. There are no stories of their pranks or escapades when they were young. They didn't get into scrapes for fear of upsetting their mother. Instead, she told them to be tidy, clean, and responsible, and they took her admonishments seriously. They were careful among their relatives, mostly aunts, not to reveal how they felt or what they in fact desired. The burden of this restraint fell most harshly upon the eldest.

"Keep your things in the box, so they will not be in the way. Keep your dresses hanging up," Cora wrote to Vincent on a visit to her aunt Marcia Keller. "Don't stay too long, for Marcia is not well. Of course you will be a little lady, and make your little visit one of pleasure to each one, if you can. Don't make Marcia nervous. . . . Take good care of your clothes, for it is such hard work to get them."

In August 1901, Cora was on a difficult case in Vinalhaven. She didn't know how long she'd have to stay, but she promised that this time when she returned home she'd stay put

and do hair-work, for you will all be at school soon, and I can canvass for work if I need to. Be nice little girls while mama is away, and it will please her so much to hear it when she comes home all worn out for her little girls to love her and get her rested. Didn't mama send home some nice shoes? Keep yourselves neat and tidy, and wash and change your clothes after dinner. Don't go down town looking dirty.

That September, while Cora was still in Vinalhaven, Vincent wrote her a plaintive letter. She didn't feel well; Norma and Kathleen didn't either.

Exasperated by her vagueness, Cora fired off this note: "You said you were almost sick, and that made me anxious about you. I cannot write much now as I am very busy; but I want you to write me at once and tell me if you are well. . . . I am working awfully hard night and day, and cannot stand it if I have to fret about you."

Cora raced home to find that all the girls had typhoid. She knew better than anybody how ravaging the disease was—there was no medicine that could touch the fever, nothing but alcohol baths and the desperate constant watching that Cora now began.

She sat by their beds in a vigil that lasted day and night. She dozed sitting up beside them, stroking their burning faces with wet towels, rubbing down their feverish bodies with ice. She was completely alone with the children, for the neighbors were afraid of catching the disease. She watched helplessly as their fevers raged from mid-September until the eighteenth of October, when each of the little girls was given up by the local doctor. It struck Kathleen, the youngest and most delicate, the hardest. All Cora could think of during the long vigil was the tiny starched dresses, "freshly ironed, three sizes, hanging there; and all the little petticoats, three sizes . . . starched and sticking out. Typhoid!—"

Their hair fell out, and at last, fearing their deaths, she summoned Henry, who did come, pleading with her to take him back. She promised to consider it, and later the girls remembered that he had been in the house. Then the fever broke. Cora wrote, "They lived, and that was all." Exhausted, floundering, with winter coming on and without the stamina or the resources even to pack, Cora fled to Newburyport, Massachusetts.

3

It was Uncle Charlie and Jennie, his new young wife, who took them in and helped bring the girls back to health. It wasn't easy. Kathleen had developed chorea, a disease of the nerves that left her five-year-old body in spasms of uncontrollable muscular twitching. Cora turned to Clem for help, but her nursing skills proved useless; the little girl was wasting away. In desperation, Clem later wrote, "We studied herbs, talked of herbs and dreamed of herbs," for it was only with their use that the two sisters finally halted her disease. In a school photograph taken on Ring's Island, across the Merrimac River from Newburyport, the recovered sisters stand among schoolchildren. Their cropped hair has just begun to sprout. A somber Vincent leans her head against another girl's shoulder for support, while Norma, round-faced and smiling, alone looks nearly well. Kathleen, staring fearfully into the camera, her round eyes circled with dark shadows, her small mouth ajar, looks permanently damaged.

In Newburyport it wasn't easy to find a landlord willing to rent to a woman without a husband or a job, with three small children in tow. But by the summer Cora had found a house of their own within sight of Charlie's. Called the Coffin House, it was an old square frame house built in the 1800s on the banks of the Merrimac where Charlie clammed. Once elegant, it was now shabby and run-down, but it was there Cora brought what little they had from Rockport. To Vincent, however, the house and grounds seemed grander than anything they had ever had

and very romantic. The yard was infinite; in the back it ran right down to the marches; but in the front, it was infinite with something else . . . the pheasants eye narcissus, which I had never seen, and which I suddenly came upon in the grass there, was as much like a voice as a flower. . . . Years later I learned it was called *narcissus poeticus.*

～ ～ ～

Norma remembered the house with a spacious attic full of her mother's books, "and Mother allowed schoolchildren to walk in and up to the attic to read," a real privilege because Mrs. Millay had a larger and finer collection than the local library. But Norma remembered, too, that a local woman refused to permit her son to go to the Millays' to read because she thought it improper for a child to enter a household where a woman lived without a husband.

"My mother began to have very bad headaches. We used to rub her head and put folded hand towels wrung out in vinegar and water, lovely and cool, over her forehead." The little girls, young as they were, began to work folding and boxing Seidlitz Powders—a patent medicine for headache—to help their mother out. Sometimes, however, instead of sending the boxes on to be sold, Mrs. Millay used them herself. Norma said quietly, "Mother took lots of them because she had lots of headaches."

～ ～ ～

In the fall they moved again, to 78 Lime Street in Newburyport proper, closer to their great-aunt Susan Todd, and to Clem, who had been adopted by the Todds. It was on Lime Street that Mr. Gales once came to call. The only evidence of his visit is an angry page in Clem's unpublished memoir. The aunts were sitting in the living room at the Todds' when they heard Cora and Vincent's voices laughing at the door, "but the third, evidently a male voice, was baffling. I opened the door just as Nell was reaching for the knob. . . . I recognized the man instantly." Cora hesitated as she introduced him, and Clem leaped forward angrily.

> I explained that he was the sanctimonious cheat who had violated all rules of decency by trading on Cora's love for music and her equal love for deep literary research, easing his duties on to her narrow shoulders, robbing the children and their father of her time and attention, for he was the very one of whom Henry spoke, when he said that the minister and the church were destroying his peace of mind and breaking up their marriage.

Clem stopped just short of the charge of infidelity.

Vincent stood behind her mother, watching silently. As Cora tried to speak, one of the Todds took Gales aside and told him he was not wanted in their home. They walked him back to Cora's house, retrieved his bags, and put him on the evening train.

If there was any question that Vincent hadn't known, or had been protected from knowing, her aunt's suspicions, she certainly knew them then.

Newburyport, where the family would remain for the next three years, was no ordinary Massachusetts village. It had been a hotbed of reform and religious revivals in the nineteenth century and the seat of the abolition movement, which had begun there.

In the first decades of the nineteenth century, when women were supposed to be pious and submissive, when their primary energies were expended on domestic duties, the women of Newburyport had formed the first female associations in the country. A cross between benevolent and voluntary organizations, they fed the lives of the women who ran them not just with notions of being good but of doing something specific, of keeping accounts, of being involved with other women for the good of women. Newburyport had an orphanage, founded and managed by women, which decreed that only a single woman, twenty-one or older, could be its treasurer, thereby avoiding a husband's legal right to control his wife's money—no husband, they figured cannily, no control.

Imagine how this atmosphere of doing, being, and making affected the Buzzell family or the Millays. For while these women were domestic enough to have six children, as Clementine had, or even three within four years, they were clearly neither submissive nor weak. Clementine Buzzell did not minister to household peace—no matter what *Godey's* magazine or *The Ladies' Companion* advised; she was out in her buggy scouting for hair work immediately after her divorce. When Vincent Millay heard the stories of her grandmother's lover—and her aunt's accusations about her mother's friend Mr. Gales—she knew the women in her family had been headstrong, that they had had the courage or the grit to achieve their independence at whatever cost to themselves and their children.

There was one quality in Vincent's nature that was left out of almost every family description of her childhood. It was not her talent, nor her ability to absorb the hardship she faced alone with her sisters, nor the balancing act she performed with her aunts. It wasn't even that in her mother's constant absence she must be good or that because others were helping them she must be grateful.

Only Norma talked about her sudden rages. Norma remembered having her mouth stuffed with geranium leaves, suffocating under the pillow Vincent had placed over her and then sat on. It hadn't felt like a prank. Now, in Newburyport, she remembered Vincent in a fury: "I don't remember why. But she ran outside and stuck a kitchen knife in a tree. We watched." She remembered, too, a conflict of wills between Vincent and their mother. Vincent was banished to the basement until she would apologize. She refused. After what seemed like days to Norma, with no apology forthcoming, she and Kathleen stole downstairs to send her little boats with food and messages tucked inside. It was their mother who finally relented. "We used to say of Vincent that she had a bee chasing her. When she was bewildered by what she . . . I have to be so careful what I say. We had to calm her down a bit. Once in a while, when reality would hit her— something she couldn't handle in her lovely way, then she was wild."

Cora was ready to leave Newburyport behind her and head for Camden. She won her divorce that January, and Henry's brother Bert Millay, who testified for her, told her if she went back to Camden, she might be given alimony. They stood in the courtroom while the judge asked Bert Millay if his brother Henry had abused her. "He has, shamefully," he answered.

She was granted her divorce in an uncontested suit on January 11, 1904, "for the cause of cruel and abusive treatment" and awarded custody of the three children and a sum of five dollars a week for their support.

CHAPTER 4

Vincent began a diary she called *Rosemary,* in which she charted the upheavals of her domestic life and of her struggle to surpass the lim-

its of a Camden girlhood. If *Rosemary* provides the mementos of that girlhood, it also bears witness to Millay's passionate interior life, which was
never entirely bound to her family or at ease within her community. She
started the diaries innocently enough at the suggestion of Ethel Knight,
whom she'd met through the St. Nicholas League. But whereas Ethel kept
her diary without missing a day, Vincent rarely kept hers with any regularity. From the beginning she felt her lapses signaled a lack of self-respect,
and she chastised herself for them. She intended to be worthy of her own
self-respect, and worthiness was linked to God. At sixteen she was serious,
severe even, and somewhat self-important. She attended the Congregational church and was part of a girls' Bible study group, the Genethod, the
Welsh word for "daughter." New England Protestant though she was,
Millay was not much interested in self-surrender, either to God or to convention. Her greatest praise was reserved for the "God of Life."

The Genethod was founded by her friend and Sunday school teacher
Abbie Huston Evans. Abbie's father was Welsh, the pastor of the Congregational church that the Millays attended. "Abbie," Martha Knight, Ethel's
sister, remembers, "must have been about ten years or more older than
Vincent. She was tall with chestnut hair and . . . fragile. She had an awful
funny gait; she sort of sidled. I remember Ethel once saying this rhyme at
one of our meetings of the Genethod: 'Do little souls go upward / when
little bodies die?' It was just a silly little rhyme she'd made up, and we all
laughed. All but Abbie, that is. She didn't like it. She was not frivolous. Oh,
but Vincent could be. She had lots of spark and spunk; she fairly snapped."

> June 29 [1908]
> I guess I'm going to explode. I know just how a volcano feels before an
> eruption. Mama is so cross she can't look straight; Norma's got the only
> decent rocking-chair in the house (which happens to be mine); and Kath-
> leen is so unnaturally good that you keep thinking she must be sick. I sup-
> pose this is an awful tirade to deliver. . . . But it is very hard to be sixteen
> and the oldest of three.

That same day Cora promised her girls a picnic with their friends, with
sardine and salmon sandwiches, bananas, fancy cookies, chocolate, and
strawberry shortcake. Millay noted in her diary that she no longer felt as
explosive as she had: "Scribbling must be wholesome exercise."

By late June, the grass left uncut in the field behind their house was
lush and high, and the Millay girls made up another game to play. They
would run waving long, colored silk ribbons high above their heads and
try to guess who held which color. From a distance all that could be seen
was swirling ribbons above the tall grass.

At ten that night Vincent made her last entry about the party; it was important to her that it had gone well. It was not only that her mother didn't often have the time or the money to give them; it was also that Vincent sensed the resentment in Camden toward her family's way of doing things.

"For instance," one of her friends recalled, "giving parties is a lot of work for—well, for the somebody that gives them. So she didn't have parties. Not our sort, anyway. And the point is, there was just no money. What they did was to make everything fun, I guess; make a game out of it. . . . I suppose their mother was responsible for this in them, too."

In the face of tacit disapproval, they fortified themselves by pulling their family ties even tighter about them. They had no lights when their mother was away unless they trimmed and filled the lamps, no heat unless they tended the fire, and all that time Vincent drifted into another life in the world of books and dreams.

Ethel Knight remembered one night in particular when

Vincent opened the front door to three of her friends who had come to spend the evening. She wore a blouse of white muslin with cuffs and boned collar made of rows of insertion edged with lace. A full gored skirt came to the tops of her buttoned boots; a patent leather belt circumscribed a wide equator around her tiny middle; and a big blue bow spread its wings behind her head where her hair was fastened in a "bun." Books were piled on the floor from a table Vincent had cleared for games and in the center was a plate of still warm fudge.

All too soon it was twelve o'clock, and the Knight girls had promised their mother to be home early. Still, they wanted just one more song.

So the girls gathered around the organ and the little room was filled with song. They retreated with "The Spanish Cavalier," they saw "Nellie Home" and ended with an old favorite—

> "There is a tavern in the town, in the town,
> And there my true love sits him down, sits him down"—

With a lighted lamp in her hand Vincent went to the door with her guests. Going down the walk they sang:

> "Fare thee well, for I must leave thee."

Ethel remembered how her slim figure stood in the doorway, her red curls shining from the lamp held high in her hands, her clear deep voice taking up the refrain that followed the girls down the hill:

> "Adieu, adieu, kind friends, adieu."

—

The plate of warm fudge, the glow of light around the slender girl, her rich voice ringing out against the Maine night, seem more properly the stuff of sentimentalized fiction than of real life. And fiction larded with autobiographical detail is exactly what Millay was writing in a novel she called *The Dear Incorrigibles*. The story begins with the mother, Mrs. Randolph, hanging up the telephone after a summoning call from a sick relative:

> "I don't know what I'm going to do! I'm sure, I don't know what I'm going to do!" . . . "Well, neither do we," Margaret remarked. Margaret was fourteen and accustomed to taking things cooly.

Mrs. Randolph is around only long enough to set the scene and leave it. "Of course I'll have to go. But who will stay with you while I'm gone?" she asks. Katharine, who at sixteen is the eldest, solves the dilemma handily:

> "Now, Muvver," she said, cheerfully. "There's not a thing that I can see to scowl about. What got you into trouble in the first place was your supposing right off that we couldn't be left alone. Imagine a great big sixteen-year-old girl like me not being big enough to keep house for a little while. I should be ashamed if I couldn't. Besides it isn't as if we were all sole alone. Aunt Cass lives right next door. . . . Goodness knows we've aunts enough."

This is the familiar Millay family scene recast only as to motive: Mrs. Randolph must leave her daughters not to earn money but to help a family member in need. It is a slender piece of fiction with a light, domestic charm and no great urgency. Katharine, the eldest, is somewhat bossy and prim, a little unsure of herself and vulnerable to being hurt. Margaret is a good deal like Norma—pretty and vain, lazy and good-natured. She is the only person who challenges her older sister. In chapter 4, Vincent introduces a fairy tale, the telling of which serves to bribe her youngest sister, Helen, into doing the dishes. It began:

> Once upon a time there was a very beautiful princess who lived with her father in a palace surrounded by a lovely garden.
> She had a gold plate to eat from, a gold mug to drink from, a gold chair to sit in and a gold bed to lie on . . . all the flowers in the garden to smell.
> And yet she was not happy.

Why not? Because her father wants her to marry a scary old king whose kingdom "joined theirs on the left." Stamping her foot in defiance, she refuses. Outraged by her disobedience, her father summons his wise men to decide upon a fair punishment. Her chin is to turn green. But the king, whose daughter's beauty reminds him of his dead wife's, cannot bear their penalty. A subterfuge is worked out. The princess is to be *told* her chin is green, when in fact all the mirrors in the kingdom will be broken and no one, under penalty of death, is to tell her it has remained pink. She is given a week to reconsider her defiance. When she does not relent, her father suddenly realizes that she no longer considers herself his daughter. The novel breaks off here, abandoned and incomplete.

As a child Vincent had been told fairy tales by her mother, who spared her daughters whatever was disagreeable or frightening by changing unpleasant endings to happy ones. It's a form Millay would turn to again and again when she was grown. The power of the fairy tale is that through magic or enchantment, through trials and clever guessing, one's life can be utterly altered. Quick as a wink, the ugly are made beautiful, the poor become rich, the stupid clever, the powerless powerful. It works transformations outside the realm of the real world.

Millay's princess, who is motherless, is not passive as the princesses in fairy tales usually are; she does not wait, asleep or enchanted, to be rescued—she's defiant. If the irreconcilable facts of life were glossed with the gold dust of fairy tale—green chins and gold plates, princesses and kings—nevertheless *The Dear Incorrigibles* was her first small act of protest against loss, anger, grief, and fear. No wonder she couldn't finish it.

Only once in her life would she write directly about what it was like to live with her sisters and without her mother in the small house by the Megunticook River. In this strange passage from a notebook she kept when she was grown, nowhere does she say "we," "our," "my," or "I":

> To live alone like that, sleep alone at night in that house set back in the field and near no other house and on the very edge of Millville, the "bad" section of town where the itinerant millworkers lived,—this was the only way they could live at all. For the house was the cheapest to be found, and their mother, when fortunate enough to get a case, which indeed was most of the time, for she was a very good nurse, competent & resourceful, was obliged to be away from them almost all the day and all the night.
>
> But they were afraid of nothing, which was important,—not of the river which flowed behind the house, coloured with the most beautiful and changing colours,—dyes from the woollen-mills above—and in which they taught themselves to swim; nor afraid of that other river, which flowed past the front of the house, and which, especially on Saturday nights, was often very quarrelsome and noisy, the restless stream of mill

workers, who never stayed long enough anywhere for one to know them even by sight. . . . And once it took all three of the children, flinging themselves against the front door, to close it and bolt it, and just in time. And after that, for what seemed like hours, there was stumbling about outside, and soft cursing. And after everything was quiet again the children lay awake for a long time, listening, and not making a sound, and thinking sometimes of the inconspicuous little path at the back of the house which they could follow in the blackest of nights without making a sound, through the tall grass of the field to the banks of the river, & how there, if it should seem unsafe to cross the corduroy bridge a little further upstream, they could swim across as quietly as water-rats to the further banks, & . . . hide themselves in less than a minute in any one of ten places where nobody on earth—no, not even with a dog and a lantern!—and the mill hands never went about with dogs and lanterns—could possibly find them.

Her fear is everywhere clear. The girls weren't safe. There was no one to protect them.

2

Vincent was supposed to make breakfast for her sisters while their mother was away, but it was early morning and she wanted to write in her diary instead. Above her desk she'd pinned Abbie's Christmas card:

Let us give thanks. Nature is beautiful, friends are dear, and duty lies close at hand.

"In this case," she wrote wryly, "duty lies very close at hand and is slumbering in the kitchen where she may lie and snooze until I get this entry written." Her diary was not only her duty, it was also her "confidante, (that *e* on the end makes it feminine. It would be out of my power to tell all these things to a mere confidant)." Besides, it was the only one of her friends who could keep quiet long enough for her to unburden herself,

and talk I must or my boiler will burst. . . . It's Sunday and therefore it's Sunday School, and I don't want to go one bit. It looks like rain, and I hope it will rain cats and dogs and hammers and pitchforks and silver sugar spoons and hayricks and paper covered novels and picture frames and rag carpets and toothpicks and skating rinks and birds of Paradise and roof gardens and burdocks and French grammars, before Sunday school time. There!

She didn't go; she baked beans instead. "Beans are cheap, and we must have them at least once a week or we will be bankrupt. It will be real original to have beans baked on Sunday, and originality is my long suit." Almost everything that could go wrong had. She fretted about setting a good example in her mother's absence, which seemed almost constant now. But that night, after her sisters had fallen asleep, she turned to her diary again and made a remarkable entry: she gave her diary a name.

> I think I'll call her Ole Mammy Hush-Chile, she's so nice and cuddly and story-telly when you're all full of troubles and worries and little vexations. It's such a comfort to confide in her and let the cares roll off your mind. After this I'm going to talk right to her and not be content with a proxy.

For Mammy was there whenever she needed her, as her mother was not. She was doing what she always did now; she took what she needed from books, she made up what she could use. And she was careful to admit no ambivalence; not a touch of anger or resentment surfaced—she reassured herself that her real mother was a treasure.

> I make two cups of tea in the little blue china teapot, and we sit opposite each other and drink it nice and hot while we watch each other's faces in the fire-light of the crackling stove. It makes up for all the time she's gone, Mammy Hush-Chile; I forget all about the things that went wrong and she forgets all about the doctors and the patients and the surgery and the sleepless nights.

Now, for the first time in any of her diaries, she mentioned her poetry:

> I've written so many verses and keep on writing so many more, that I became afraid that if I didn't write them into one big book I might forget some of them. . . . I love my verses so that it would be like taking my heart out if I should wake up some morning and find that all I could remember of one of my most loved—was the name. O, mammy, I mustn't let it happen, you mustn't let me, you dear old white-souled, black-faced cuddle-mammy. . . . I haven't neglected it; there are fifteen poems in it already.

If her mother had given her poetry when she was a child, now in the summer of 1908, when she was sixteen, she gave her mother the *Poetical Works of Vincent Millay* and dedicated it to her:

To My Mother,
   Whose interest and understanding have
been the life of many of these works
and the inspiration of many more, I lovingly
dedicate this little volume.

               E.V.M.
               July 10, 1908.

During the two years that she kept the *Poetical Works,* she wrote out sixty-one poems in her clear slant hand in a brown copybook, with an alphabetical index at the back carefully noting the age at which she had written each poem. Forty of these poems were written before she turned sixteen; another ten would be added that year. She placed her gold-medal poem, "The Land of Romance," first.

In these poems she is serving her apprenticeship, and her themes are those of a Victorian, albeit New England, girlhood. Winter is king, rain-drops sing, gardens drip with loss. There are moonbeams and fairies in abundance, and love is either lost, dying, or dead. There is a great deal of loneliness. But there is very little renunciation for its own sake, and there are few poems devoted to duty or to domestic accomplishment unless they are treated with rebellious humor. None is pious.

If she has not yet broken clear of the nineteenth century—it was, after all, only 1908—she uses the first person with ease, her language is usually simple and direct, and her rhythms swing clear. She doesn't yet have her own voice, but she is working to acquire it, and even a simple poem such as "Homing" begins to sound like her own.

Homing bird and homing bee;
Nest and hive in the apple tree;
Sweet song, sweet honey,—but sweeter to me
   The homing.

Nest where two crooked branches meet;
Hive in the hollow trunk's retreat;
Sweet song, sweet honey,—but far more sweet
   The homing.

You who drowse on weary wing,
You who sleepily, sleepily sing;
Tell me, sweeter is anything
   Than homing?

There is only one sonnet, written at seventeen, "To My Mother." But there are other poems written to her mother; she called this one "Song."

Dearest, when you go away
   My heart will go, too,
Will be with you all the day,
   All the night with you.
Where you are through lonely years,
   There my heart will be.
I will guide you past all fears
And bring you back to me.

It is striking that it is she who protects her mother, who shares her loneliness, who guides her rather than being guided by her.

What is most remarkable about the *Poetical Works of Vincent Millay* is that at sixteen she had a sense of vocation. Her title placed her squarely in the company of Burns, Wordsworth, Tennyson, Longfellow, Whittier, Holmes, and Lowell, each of whose *Poetical Works* lined her mother's bookcases. It would be a mistake, however, not to notice that the *Poetical Works* of the wildly popular nineteenth-century poets—James Whitcomb Riley, Eugene Field, Mrs. Felicia Hemans, and Jean Ingelow—let alone volumes of fairy tales and copies of songs her mother had written, as well as Scottish border ballads, Irish and old American ballads kept in her family for more than two generations and sung to her as a child, were just as prominent. She was grounded in two very different traditions; the nineteenth-century worthies were as familiar to her as popular ballads and songs.

In her senior year, Vincent was made editor in chief of the school paper, *The Megunticook*. She had a role in every play put on that year. She gave her first piano recital. And she continued to work on a poem she'd begun that summer. It was her most ambitious and longest work, intended to be delivered at graduation, when she was sure to be made class poet. By Christmas the Millays had moved into a larger house in the center of town at 40 Chestnut Street that overlooked the bay. The girls even had a window looking out onto the water.

In the early spring, Cora was on a case in Rockland. One of her letters home to Vincent was the first indication that something was wrong. She told her she just might be able to run up "for an hour's stay some evening," but what she really wanted was for Vincent to take thirty cents, "and get you some oranges. Now be sure to do it." She continued, "When I get home I'll see to things and I'll take care of you till you are in school again bright as a button."

Cora cautioned her against overdoing: "Don't read anything but trash or play anything but rag-time. Eat all you can, get you some beef-steak. . . .

O! I'm dying to get home. . . . I've got a cure all planned out . . . it's a dandy. I've got some sherry for you."

No one in the family would talk about it, but Vincent had suffered a setback at school that hurt her deeply. Her classmate Stella Derry remembered:

> In her class at Camden High School . . . she wasn't very popular. They felt she was way beyond them. . . . She was the type to exclaim over things and make a lot of almost nothing. Her family made so much of everything she did that I guess the class was a bit envious.

George Frohock, president of their class, son of the Baptist minister, and captain of Camden's first football team, was the leader of the boys devoted to mocking her. They laughed at her and mimicked her until the peak of malice was reached at class elections. Vincent, whose every attempt to speak inspired thirteen heroes to stamp and catcall until she stopped, was nominated as class poet, but she withdrew when the boys nominated Henry Hall. Worse, the girls hadn't stood up for her.

She made only two entries in her diary for the year 1909, both marked by longing: "I've come back to you, Mammy Hush-Chile." For she had suffered what she called

> the first big disappointment of my life: I graduate in June—without the class poem. You wouldn't have believed it, would you, Mammy? But it's true, all too cruelly true. . . . There is a boy in my class who, when we were Juniors, used to amuse himself by writing to me queer rhymeless, meterless things which I suppose he meant for poems. This year I was Editor-in-chief of our school periodical, the "Megunticook." I was at a loss for material for one of the issues and someone suggested that he write a poem. I thought that perhaps with care he might produce some funny verses. But when it was almost time for the material to come in he came to me and said that he had it partly done and could not possibly finish it. So I, about crazy for my paper, took the thing, finished it, changed it all over, rhymed lines that didn't rhyme, balanced the shaky meter of other lines, named the thing, and had him sign his name to it.

When it was published, everybody loved it. They even told Vincent how much they admired it. Of course she didn't tell them she'd written the poem.

> When the time came for the writer of the class poem to be elected, the boys had an idea that Henry Hall was a poet and he—oh, he'll make a manly

man some day, didn't have stiffening enough in his great fat sluggish stolidity to get on his feet and tell them that the only poem he ever had printed in his life had been half written, wholly made over, and published by me. *Oh* it makes me white when I think that it was my own fault. And I did it just for the paper. Oh, Mammy, Mammy, Mammy, how can he sit there in front of me in school and smile at me with his round, red face! How can he speak to me with his great fat voice! . . . I've helped him take away from me the only thing I cared anything about, and now . . . I despise him as I despise a snake. I shiver when his coat sleeve brushes against me. I hate the sight of his fat white hand,—his pretty, lady-like white hand, that copied and copied in the symmetrical, self-satisfied writing that stole my poem, my class poem that belonged to me.

Her fury turned into disgust, then physical revulsion:

Our class had a play this winter. He was my father. I put my arms around his neck and kissed him every night for weeks. Oh, I could strike my mouth! I can feel the touch of him now. I laid my head on his knee and clasped his hand. Oh, I loved him dearly in the play, but if I had known what I know now, my mouth would have burned him when it touched him. Oh, Mammy, I can tell it all to you, for it won't hurt you, it won't sadden you, except as you know it hurts and saddens me. I can't tell it all to mama. She knows all that happened, but she doesn't know the way it feels to me. Only it worried her that I didn't cry about it. . . . But I couldn't cry even to please her. I cry when I'm angry, not when I'm hurt.

Thwarted and angry, finding her rival repellent, she fell ill. No amount of oranges, sherry, or milk would cure her.

When the class photos were taken, Martha Knight remembered, Vincent wasn't there. "She was absent a good deal her last, her senior year, as I recall. I don't know if she was ill or somehow discouraged about her future—I just don't know. We did not discuss it. But she missed the class picture, and Mrs. Millay called me up and got irate. . . . She said that if I had told Vincent, she could have come up. But I hadn't thought to tell her. I mean, I didn't intend not to, I just hadn't thought to tell her."

Instead Vincent had her photograph taken in town, wearing her graduation dress. Seated on a Roman bench, she is wearing two great white hair ribbons, one at the back of her neck, the other perched atop her head like a white moth. Her bright hair is swept back from her face, caught up behind her ears. Her dress is of flowered Persian lawn, with a deep V bodice trimmed with lace, the long puffed sleeves caught just below her elbow, her tiny waist cinched with ribbon. She looks weighed down with bows and ruffles. Her gaze is direct and unsmiling.

The graduation exercises were held the evening of June 16, 1909, in the Camden Opera House. Martha Knight gave the first essay, on Scottish folklore, while Stella played a piano solo. Then the boys recited their talks on "The Value of Higher Education" and "The Uses and Values of Electricity"; near the close of the commencement ceremonies, Henry Hall, who stumbled out of nervousness, read his class poem, "Our Destiny."

The final speaker was Vincent Millay. Jessie Hosmer, who was sitting in the audience that night, said she would never forget the small girl with her bright red hair, her chin lifted, her head thrown back, who seemed almost to sing out her essay, the poem "La Joie de Vivre": "Well, she spoke it just as if she was doing what she was doing. She was stealing thunder."

All the heat and urgency of being young was in her poem, and it began like an anthem to youth:

> The world and I are young!
> Never on lips of man,—
> Never since time began,
> Has gladder song been sung

Her writing vindicated her. "Oh, Mammy," she wrote in her diary, "they gave me the prize!" With that ten dollars she went to visit her aunts in Massachusetts, alone, for the entire summer.

CHAPTER 5

In October, Vincent won the lead in a traveling stock company's production of *Willowdale,* in which each of her sisters had a small role. Vincent, playing the prim Milly Bassett, "who loves Tom" and loses her primness, stole the show. When the company left Camden for their next stop, the ingenue there fell ill and Vincent was summoned from Camden to play the role. Throwing her clothes into a suitcase, racing to catch the steamer and then the train, she wrote in her scrapbook, "*Spree!* Lunch & Bath at Midnight." Kerosene lamps were lit in the train stations along the way and stoves were banked with coal, for in November it was already winter in the North.

She'd played amateur roles before at home, but this was different: "—oh, this was life! It was more than life,—it was art." While at home, "I might pretend to myself as much and as long as I liked,—until the deep-vibrant-note I had discovered in my voice . . . out-Hedda-ed Nazimova—yet was my native village unthrilled and unconvinced; I was asked to serve ice-cream at church socials, and the grocer-boy called me by name." But no longer. The costumes had not been altered since she'd worn them, and the other girls in the company "hooked me up the back and pinned me together in a dozen places, one knelt and put on my shoes while I balanced with my hand on her shoulder, one went to find the frilly sun-bonnet I was to carry on in the first act."

When she heard the silky swoosh of the curtain rising, she glanced in the mirror, took a deep breath, and ran onstage

with my sun-bonnet over my arm and held out my hands to Danny; there was a sudden hush all over the house, more pleasant to me than would have been the most enthusiastic hand. For this was genuine, the result of keen and unfeigned interest and curiosity. Probably every person in the house knew that I was the girl who had been sent from out of town. . . . Not that there would have been any pains to conceal it; on the contrary, because of its unquestionable advertising advantages.

Flushed with excitement, she calculated her effect: "There, away from home, I was under no restraint from loving friends in the orchestra seats or hated rivals whose talent and time had not been solicited. For the first time in my life I could, from rise to fall of the curtain, unstintedly play the part."

She let her voice fill to its most vibrant; she knew her voice was becoming a remarkable instrument that she could use to draw the audience to her. "I did not hurry with my lines. . . . I made my pauses tell. I felt that the audience liked me, and I did my best to make it love me. I did little wistful things, made little forlorn gestures, and once or twice smiled piteously. It seemed to me I could hear the lumps come into their throats."

Afterward, the company's producer and director, Van Duzer, offered her a position in his permanent company—if he should ever bring it together. She never heard from him again. Instead she received an autographed photograph of his wife, a middle-aged woman holding a lorgnette and wearing a flat straw hat like a plate of salad greens.

Then she returned to Camden, and the winter turned to iron.

Throughout the fall and winter, her father's letters to her remained the same as they had always been. In September, he inquired about their mother's health, sent five dollars, promised to "send you some more the first of the week if possible," and closed fretting about his own health: "I am having a bad time with my stomach but I guess it isn't going to be any thing serious." One week later he sent two dollars: "I have got money coming in soon and will keep you going somehow." How that seven dollars would keep any of them going is hard to tell. Still, he assured Vincent, "I think there is no doubt I will get to see you this fall. I intend to, if possible." Seven dollars within three weeks was very unlike him. But the assurance of his own arrival—"I *think* there is no doubt. . . . I *intend* . . . if possible"—was just like him. By December 11, the reality was clear:

> My dear girl; I cannot possibly go to see you just now. I haven't the money but I am going just as soon as I can. I haven't been able to do much for two months I have a very bad cold now but I always expect it this time of year. I would like to go now so much. But I will get to see you this winter sure.

But he didn't come. He sent them a little money for Christmas presents instead, a dollar each. "I wish I could make you some Xmas presents but it don't look like it now." It's hard to imagine a more forlorn, defeated man than Henry Millay must have seemed to his daughters.

On Christmas Day, alone in the house with her sisters, Vincent wrote to her mother, assuring her that they were having a "beautiful Christmas." She put the best face on their being without her. She'd had a quarter ton of coal put in; she'd bought a pound of "nice butter"; she told in exact detail what each of the girls had done to make their presents for one another. Only one of their gifts appears to have been bought. Then she enclosed a copy of her next *St. Nicholas* poem, "Friends." "This is all I can think of now. We must dress for dinner. Good-bye, Honey. With love, Vincent." Her letter was dutiful, as if she were working to muster the details. Within six months of graduation she had taken over the running of their household. Only her poems began to tell how she felt under the weight of that domestic burden.

The last poem she sent to *St. Nicholas* (because after eighteen one could no longer contribute) won its Cash Prize, which was the hardest to get. The editors spent half their editorial praising it, calling it "a little gem," pointing to its "striking excellence" in the use of double rhymes.

She wrote the magazine a farewell letter:

> Dear St. Nicholas:
> I am writing to thank you for my cash prize and to say good-by, for "Friends" was my last contribution. I am going to buy with my five dollars

a beautiful copy of "Browning," whom I admire so much that my prize will give me more pleasure in that form than in any other.

Although I shall never write for the League again, I shall not allow myself to become a stranger to it. You have been a great help and a great encouragement to me, and I am sorry to grow up and leave you.

Your loving graduate
Edna Vincent Millay

"Rosemary," a poem she'd written earlier that same year, was shot through with longing for childhood, a perfectly acceptable convention although at seventeen she was a little young to long.

> The things I loved I may go to see.
> I may lie in them no more.
> But I stand at the door of the used-to-be,
> And dream my childhood o'er.
>
> . . .
>
> I sit at my window alone.
> I hear each voice, and I know
> That I miss through them all the sound of my own
> As it rang in the long-ago.

Becoming a woman meant more than the loss of freedom and playfulness, it meant loneliness. Worse, it meant the loss of her voice.

Truly homebound now, she turned inside. Her diary entries fell slack. On February 24, she waited to catch sight of Halley's comet but didn't and began to embroider a corset cover for her mother. "Mama said today, that if she dies before we do, Kathleen is to have her wedding ring and I her mother's ring though she formally expressed a wish to have that buried with her."

Her father, who had not written since Christmas, wrote now, telling her a fire had destroyed most of his belongings. His letter ended with a postscript: "I am going to see you just as soon as I can get any money ahead and I mean for it to be this spring. Papa." Ten days later he enclosed three dollars—it might not buy "many Easter hats but will get you a dinner"—and described the fire:

The Hotel that was burned was run by an old man (and owned) and was paying him over $2000 per year besides all expenses without selling a drop of liquor. And if it had not burned I should have had a lease of it this spring. . . . I might have known something would happen, but I didn't. I really thought I was going to get hold of a business that my health would stand and that would pay more than well. I had visions of being able to do a whole lot for some girls that I think about a great deal although I haven't seen them for eight years. But I mean to see them this spring. I know Vincent I am a poor correspondent and I can't explain why. I only know that when I have said a few words to tell you how much I inclose, my pen stops.

This was the saddest letter he had ever written. The way he described his losses that spring suggested how constant and expected they were. Even in his letters he was distant, a solitary man of small ambitions and dashed hopes. His life had settled into small and constant illnesses, which he told her about—long winter colds, asthma, and stomach trouble. The only dream he ever admitted to his eldest daughter was this one, and he told her only after it had burned to the ground and his hopes were reduced to ashes.

Henry Millay never contributed the five dollars a week for child care that he was supposed to. In Camden, Vincent mentioned him only once, soon after she'd arrived, when a girl in her class asked what had happened to her father. "She was quite upset and said they'd lost him, and didn't like to talk about it. She gave the impression that he wasn't even alive." She didn't mention him in her diaries, except to note that once a month she wrote to him. Why she wrote is clear enough in this poem:

> Dear Papa, I am puzzled sore
> To think why you don't send some more
> Of that nice stuff you sent before.
>   . . .
> Now, Papa darling, will you tell
> When ham is fifty cents a smell
> And cold soused trype is quite too swell
>   To view,
> How in the world your daughters dear
> Can keep alive—or anywhere near—
> Unless from time to time we hear
>   From you?
> But, Papa, this is not a fluff,
> I've lived on sawdust long enough:
> 'Tis quite unsatisfying stuff.
>   And so
> Your hat in deepest mourning drape—
> Send me some pinks tied up in crape,—
> Or send me something in the shape
>   Of dough.

—

Boys did not loom large for Vincent, at least not in the world of her diaries. When they appeared, it was to limit her unfairly or to hurt her. In July 1909, with her mother away working, she noted that she had gone to a ball on the fourth in Lincolnville in her pink muslin dress. "I was the only red-headed girl in pink at which I was not surprised. Red-heads are supposed to wear blue." She hated blue. From July 6 to 25, we begin to hear of a young man named Russell Arey. "He's the only man I know who is as Rubiyat-mad as I am," she wrote in her first entry. He began to drop by every day. On the eleventh they went canoeing and took along the *Gold Treasury of Verse.* "Went ashore over on the beach and read." On the sixteenth she made him wipe the dishes after supper. On the twenty-fifth they went for a walk down by the lily pond and had a falling-out. "Oh, what a fall was there, my country man!" she scribbled in her diary. She never mentioned him again.

Their mother had been gone for six weeks, the better part of their summer vacation, and although she kept writing to them that she'd be home shortly, she wasn't. "If your father sent you the rent, you will be all right now till I get home. Be saving; but have enough to eat." On August 3, she wrote again, "Save what you can toward the rent for I want it paid right away. . . . Can I hear from some of you, I wonder? I am the dearest mama you have." On the fifth, sticking three dollars in her letter and reminding them again to "hang on to it for the rent," she finally left for home.

On July 20, with her mother still in Newburyport, Vincent began a journal separate from her diary. In a small brown copybook that had been her sister Kathleen's, filled with colored pencil sketches of birds and flowers, a fishing cat, and a blind dog, she began her "Journal of a Little Girl Grown-Up."

> I'm tired of being grown up! Tired of dresses that kick around my feet; tired of high-heeled shoes; tired of conventions and proprieties; tired, tired and sick of hair-pins!

At eighteen, she constructed a protective retreat through recollection:

> There is a little spicy-smelling yellow flower growing in clusters on a bush, in old-fashioned gardens—I think they call it "clove" or "flowering currant." The smell of it never fails to take me back into a little play-house I made once under such a bush, just this side of the church-yard fence.

On a hot summer afternoon, the air is heavy with the fragrance of sweet-smelling flowers, and, except for the droning of bees, there is no sound. She is hidden.

I am pains-takingly trimming a rhubarb leaf hat with white-clover and butter cups, with which my lap is filled. Beside me are two long, slender white wands from which with primitive implements of sharp teeth and nails I have been peeling the bark for ribbons. I taste again the sweetness of the smooth round stick in my mouth. I see again the moist, delicate green of the living bark. And into my nostrils I breathe the hot spicy fragrance until my very soul is steeped in it.

What is it that propels her so fiercely into the past—if it is her past—at any rate into childhood or fantasy and away from being adult? It is as if she were in a bower, within which a romantic past might be remembered and her own youth kept, savored, a past from which she felt herself severed by having become a woman.

I am homesick for that little girl. . . . I like the old white house and the vivid grass around it. I loved the blackberries and the hill—And Auntie Bine! Why, I was Auntie Bine's little girl! O, Auntie Bine, if I might just come back and be your little girl again!

If there was a real Auntie Bine in Union—or anywhere else in her childhood—no one, not even Millay's sister Norma, remembered her. What is real is the need Millay gives voice to again in her writing for a female figure, a maternal person who will recognize her, love her, and comfort her. In piece after piece, whether it's the poem "Rosemary," her diary *Mammy Hush-Chile,* or this journal, Millay is after two things. She wants to remain a child; she wants a woman to comfort her. With the single exception of *The Dear Incorrigibles,* her mother is either absent or dead or has abandoned her.

Cora Millay seems to have had no idea of her daughter's sadness. During one of her everlasting absences, Vincent made a schedule to reassure her mother that their topsy-turvy household would be run efficiently and cheaply. "*Do it Now*" was signed by each of the sisters, like a promissory note, but gleefully using their childhood nicknames—Sefe was Vincent, Hunk was Norma, and Wump was Kathleen.★ It ended with a notation that Kathleen was to bring in wood for the breakfast fires, Norma was to feed the cat, and "Vincent kills flies."

★Of their family nicknames—Sefe and Hunk—Norma said, "It was an old college song Mother used to sing:

> There was a man who had two sons
> And those two sons were brothers.
> Josephus was the name of one
> and Bohunkus was the other."

SCHEDULE*

Do it Now

	Kathleen	Norma	Vincent
6 A.M.	Arise	Arise	Arise
	Fire	Bath	Lamps
6:15	Bath	Breakfast	"
6:30	Table	"	Bath
7:00	(Breakfast)	(Breakfast)	(Breakfast)
7:45	Dress	Dress	Dress
8:00	Garden	Garden	Garden
8:15	Beds	Dishes	Dishes
8:30	"Corner"	"Corner"	"Corner"
9:00	Study	Wash, Iron or Cook	Write
		Sweep or Get Dinner	
11:00	"	Get Luncheon	"
11:30 to 12	(Luncheon)	(Luncheon)	(Luncheon)
12:30	Dishes	Dress	Dishes
1:00	Dress	Mend and Mail	Dress
1:30	Garden	Garden	Garden
2:00	Study	Sew	Write
3:30	Leisure	Leisure	Leisure
5:00	Table	Supper	Supper
6:00	Dishes	Dishes	Pick up
6:30	Bath & Dress	Bath & Dress	Bath & Dress

Bed at <u>8 P.M.</u>, <u>posilutely</u>.
Kathleen brings in wood for breakfast.
Norma feeds Wuzzy.
Vincent kills flies.

Signed—Sefe—Hunk—Wump

*Note from Norma Millay: "Copy of Vincent's 'Schedule'—in her writing—as to how the Millay girls were to conduct and occupy themselves throughout the days. This I remember well but don't know the date. It must have been in summer when there was no school for any of us; since Kay is to 'study' she is doubtless in school still,—I wouldn't have studied anyway so I might still be in High School. Vincent is through school,—in Camden, at least—; No, I'm through school, too, and we are at 82 Washington Street,—could this be after my graduation in 1918 and before I went to Whitehall: the lovely bathroom seems still to enchant us and the garden is the flower garden there and perhaps my little veg. garden, too. I'll find out when for certain somewhere."

CHAPTER 6

It began in April 1911, though no one knew, not her mother or her sisters, because she confided only in the back pages of her diary, where she recorded her "Consecration." It would last for nearly two years. She met him on the third of every month, usually at night but only if there was no one else in the house, when she would light a candle as if casting a spell to enchant them both. She even had a tin ring to kiss. "I am," she wrote, "as surely betrothed to you as if your ring was on my finger." If from the first there were doubts, she intended to transcend them: "Sometimes I'm afraid that I love too much and expect too much in return. Maybe men can't love as I want to be loved. But I mustn't let myself think that."

On their first night together she said she was going to put on her prettiest nightgown and braid her hair just as he liked it. But she couldn't bear to leave him alone in the room reading, so she "parted the curtains and peeped through"; did he like her hair, she asked?

> Now, I'm coming out to see you. I am wearing a fluffy lavender thing over my night-dress. It is very soft and long and trails on the rug behind me. My bare feet sink into the rug. My hair is in two wavy, red braids over my shoulders. My eyes are very sweet and serious. My mouth is wistful.
>
> You watch me from your chair.
>
> I come slowly to you over the rug.
>
> I drop at your feet and lay my head on your knee. My braids touch the floor.
>
> You lift my head in your two hands and look deep into my serious eyes.
>
> You lift me from the floor in your two arms. You rise to your feet and hold me straight before you, flat across your arms. The lavender thing falls soft about my feet. My braids sway slightly. My eyes are closed.
>
> You kiss my wistful mouth.
>
> - - - - - - - - - -
>
> Oh, Love! I feel your arms about me. I feel—!
>
> Good night, sweet-heart!

He was perfection, her comforter and her ballast: "You are strong, clean, and kind. I know I am weak. But I will grow strong thinking of you, never forgetting that I am not mine but yours. . . . I will keep myself clean. Even the smallest of my favors I will keep for you." Just the thought of him steadied her, and when she was most in need of him she would kiss her ring and feel his strength flood through her. "I could weep with the love that does so hurt my heart. Oh, I adore you!"

There was only one thing wrong with him. Having established all the rules of their vigil, all the terms of their secret love, "Confident," she wrote at the start of her "Consecration," "that you are seeking for me even as I am waiting for you": seeking for her? *waiting?* She had made him up! Her extravagantly adored beloved was imaginary. How could he possibly disappoint her?

Whereas a real young man was nothing but trouble. At nineteen she was unsure of herself, and her defense was to take on a superior tone with any man who crossed her path. When a man who was no more to her than a pen pal apologized for owing her a letter, she reprimanded him sharply: "Dear Delinquent,—You don't deserve so amiable a correspondent as I. You are not worthy even to wield my pen-wiper. But you made a very nice apology. And, moreover, you groveled gracefully." While she did scrawl on the top of her copy that she hadn't sent it exactly as it was written, she was apt to be dismissive, coy, and prim. That summer she wrote that there wasn't a chance that anybody was going to call her up to take her out for a spin or even an ice-cream soda:

> Boys don't like me anyway because I won't let them kiss me. It's just like this: let boys kiss you and they'll like you but you won't. . . . But I'd be almost willing to be engaged if I thought it would keep me from being lonesome. . . . if I was engaged I would be going to the play tonight instead of sitting humped up on the steps in a drizzle that keeps my pencil point sticky. I'd be going out paddling tomorrow instead of practicing the Beethoven Funeral March Sonata. And I'd like to have something to do besides write in an old book. I'd like to have something happen to give me a jolt, something that would rattle my teeth and shake my hairpins out.

When nothing did, she returned to him. But what a world of difference there was between the way she imagined a relationship should be and the way she conducted herself among the boys her own age in Camden. By July 3, 1911, she no longer wanted to tuck her entries about him into the back of her *Ole Mammy Hush-Chile* diary, so she began another, "Vincent Millay—*Her Book.*" What these different diaries were beginning to show was the increasing division within her between the unrelenting duties of her domestic life that weighed her down, which she kept for her *Ole Mammy Hush-Chile* diary, and the ardent life of her imagination: "Sometimes I don't mind so much the uncertainty which envelops you, but tonight I wish we were quite, quite sure of each other, and I knew all your nicknames, and what kind of pipe you smoke. It would give me such a feeling of security and comfort."

It is only when she begins *Her Book* that we grasp how much she needs this idealized male. At once resolute, understanding, and silent, he is comforting and permanent as no one else in her life has been. Her book begins with a poem:

> My life is but a seeking after life;
> I live but in a great desire to live;
> The undercurrent of my every thought:—
> To seek you, find you, have you for my own
> Who are my purpose and my destiny.
> For me, the things that are do not exist;
> The things that are for me are yet to be. . . .

For her, all was future, destiny, and him:

> In perfect understanding I shall come
> And lay my hand in yours, and at your feet
> Sit, silent, with my head against your knee.

What was more conventional for a girl to think, or to dream, than that a man would come and rescue her from her lonely life? She sought him as if he were a part of her: "It is as if I had been cut in two and ached for the rest of me." Inventing him was her effort to be whole, to regain some part of herself that was imperiled. Who knows why she thought it was love that would alter her life—and yet, for a girl in Camden, Maine, in the early years of the last century, what else could it have been?

Cora was away most of the summer, caring for four young girls in Rockland who were sick enough to all be placed in quarantine. Writing home, even her pencil had to be wiped in alcohol and the letter baked before it could be sent to her daughters. Although she was earning twenty dollars a week, very good pay for her, it was never enough. "I cannot stand it," she told them, "and it must be different. I thought earning what I am now I might get caught up a little." They must "plan for mama's interest, which is nothing but your own interest as all I get is what I eat."

When almost a week passed with no word from her girls, she pressed them more sharply: "Just a few words, as you don't seem to have any spare time. . . . I thought my last letter would make it very easy for us all . . . but, suit yourselves." She was out of quarantine and fumigating the household. The room she had been cloistered in with the sick children retained the strong odor of formaldehyde, and her head ached terribly. "I think these little girls would write to their mama if she were alive. Mama."

That did the trick. Receiving the letter in the morning mail, Vincent wrote her mother and posted it by noon. This letter was different from her others; it was full of the small reassurances and affectionate baby talk that assured her mother of her devotion, as well as her continuing dependence on her:

> Where'd you get the penny-royal, honey? Isn't it sweet? Always makes me think of Aunt Marcia and Uncle Joe and the old place. It grows so abundantly on the hill above the brook, you know.
>
> Doesn't it seem good to be out of quarantine? I should think you'd be just hopping joyful. Unless you're too tired even to hop, you poor dear. Binnie's sorry!

Mother and daughter were engaged in a sort of duet of need. Cora, hurt, found fault, and Vincent, prodded, flew to respond. Everything at home was fine, she wrote: "We serve three meals a day at 'Millay's Cafe,' if you please. . . . come home quick as you can to your 'free bad tids.' Lovissimusosso, Vincent."

The baby talk was never a good sign. A poem (this one would later be titled "The Suicide") was slashed in pencil across the back of one of her mother's letters:

> Curse thee, Life, I will live with thee no more!
> Thou has mocked me, starved me, beat my body sore!
> And all for a pledge that was not pledged by me
> I have kissed thy crust, and eaten sparingly
> That I might eat again, and met thy sneers
> With deprecations, and thy blows with tears,—
> Aye, from thy glutted lash glad crawled away,
> As if spent passion were a holiday!

Then she returned to him. She lit her candle and kissed her ring, but the flame guttered out and she now called her ring "a ghost ring."

> We have been betrothed just half a year tonight. I have been very faithful to you. I have loved you more and better every day. Six months is quite a long engagement, I think. . . . I do so ache to be taken care of. How I shall glory in your strength—I who am not strong. . . . With you I shall be complete and wonderful, but without you I am nothing.

But she did not set foot outside her home. She didn't seek a permanent job. She didn't venture forth with any of the young men who came to call. Mostly they came to call on Norma, anyway. Vincent stayed put. She wrote.

In the working draft of a poem she called "Interim," the death of a wife is personified by language:

> Dark, Dark, is all I find for metaphor;
> All else were contrast;—save that contrast's wall
> Is down . . . where night
> And day, and frost and thaw, and death and life,
> Are synonyms.

It was a fine piece of writing, but if she sent it out, no one took it. She had not been able to publish anything since *St. Nicholas.* She'd begun to work on a long poem that was entirely different from anything she had tried before. A dramatic monologue written in the first person, it began as simply as a child's counting-out rhyme. But there was nothing childish about the poem itself; it was luminous and wild and—so far—incomplete. Only her mother knew she was working on it.

Only once did she come to her love without need of his comfort. She linked her giving to what she called "The mother-heart: there is no strength like it":

> I want not to be comforted, but to comfort;—to hold your head on my lap, and love you, and fuss with your hair, and cry over you; not stormily, not hysterically, but tenderly; and quietly, lest you see and be grieved. I want to find things for you, to pick up things after you, to straighten your tie and brush your coat, to fill your pipe,—all the little things so many women have done and that I long to do.

Domestic, devotional, almost, the pull for her was always back to being good at home.

That fall and winter she came to him more than she ever had before. Soon she didn't want a boy anymore, she was too tired. "Two girls," she wrote, "are enough for me." She wanted a man. But why didn't he come? What was all this hard work for, if not for him?

> I looked out of the window a minute ago and saw the mountains. . . . They are so beautiful they almost kill me. The color—oh—there is never anything like their color in the fall! And I want to climb Megunticook before the leaves are all gone.

But she couldn't; she had to work, "Sweep the floor, and sweep it again tomorrow and the day after tomorrow and the day after that and every day of your life;—if not that floor, why then—some other floor." Very few young women have ever put it more clearly—or more fiercely—than Millay did when she was nineteen:

> I'm getting old and ugly. My hands are stiff and rough and stained and blistered. I can feel my face dragging down. I can feel the lines coming underneath my skin. They don't show yet but I can feel a hundred of them underneath. I love beauty more than anything else in the world and I can't take time to be pretty. . . . Crawl into bed at night too tired to brush my hair—my beautiful hair—all autumn-colored like Megunticook.

Then she stopped. She'd promised him she "would never let go again." But she hadn't really broken her promise. "No one else knows how I feel. I am keeping up before everybody else." Now she imagines him as her husband. "My husband," she writes again and again and again, "I am ashamed to think I didn't know why Megunticook is there! It is to look at! . . . to lift your eyes to!" Beauty was the only thing that sustained her. Except him.

On January 3, 1912, snow and ice covered everything in Camden; even the bay was icebound. No matter where she was, she couldn't get warm.

> Honey, I don't feel good a bit. I've a tooth-ache and I think I'm going to have a cold. I've been freezing all day and now my nose feels all squizzled up. Does your nose squizzle up when you're about to have a cold? Mine does, and my conscience with it. . . . I'm dissatisfied with everything,— myself first of all. I'm egoistical and self-analytical. I suffer from inflammation of the imagination and a bad attack of ingrowing temperament. I don't believe in anything. I am morbid and miserable. My mind must be rotten, I think. I need a man who has been somewhere and done things to graft his healthy ideas into my silly brain. Truly my head is in dreadful condition. I don't know what to do.

It didn't let up, and her writing became more frenzied, more desperate. On February 3, when she returned to him again, she simply wrote, "This is another death—this night." A week later it was darker. She felt she was suffocating, as if she were being buried alive. She would be twenty in less than two weeks, and still he had not come for her.

> I do not know what will become of me. . . . I know that I am in a dreadful condition. I know that the thoughts that fill my mind are fearful thoughts. . . . I do not think there is a woman in whom the roots of passion shoot deeper than in me.

CHAPTER 7

She was alone in the house when the telephone rang—a long-distance call from Kingman, Maine. The voice of the operator was scratchy and faint, but at last Vincent made out "Mr. Millay, your father, is very ill, and may not recover." Stunned into silence, she just stood there. "After a minute she asked me if there was any message . . . I managed to stutter something and to say that I would send a telegram. Then she said, 'Is that all?' And I said, 'Yes' and hung up the receiver." Quickly, Vincent called her mother in Rockland, and they decided Vincent would start for Kingman in the morning, for she'd just missed the noon boat. She borrowed a suitcase and threw some clothes together. On March 1, she caught the boat to Bucksport, traveling from there by train to Bangor, where she took another train and arrived in Kingman at 6 A.M. Dashing down a cup of coffee, she hurried to the house where her father boarded.

> The minute we came in I heard from upstairs the sound of a man's coughing, and it was then, for the first time, that I realized how long it had been since I had seen my father,—eleven years!

His nurse met her downstairs and told her he was expecting her. The owners of the house as well as her father's doctor, Dr. Somerville, and his daughter, Ella, stood watching her. "They kept telling me to brace up, and be calm, and things like that, which was really funny, as I was not the least bit nervous and everybody else seemed very much upset. . . . Perhaps I wasn't so calm, tho, as I was numb." As the doctor guided her up the stairs, he told her she could stay only moments and that her father had very little time to live. She entered the room.

> It didn't seem to me that the man on the bed was my father, but I went over and stood beside him and said, "Hello, papa, dear," just as I had planned to say only that my voice seemed higher than usual; and when he heard me he opened his eyes—the bluest eyes I ever saw—and cried out "Vincent! My little girl!" and struggled up in bed and held out his arms to me. . . . I put my arms around him and made him lie down again. Then I sat on the side of the bed and talked to him a little, not of anything in particular; I remember saying that I wished my eyes were blue, too, so that they'd match my hat, and that he whispered back—he couldn't speak at all—"You can't very well change your eyes, Vincent, but you might have got a green hat." Then I laughed, and he smiled a little, with his eyes

closed. He had difficulty, I noticed, in keeping them open and somehow that made me all the more certain he was going to die.

That night she wrote to her mother briefly to tell her that Dr. Somerville had given her "very little hope." Cora wrote back by return post:

> My dear little daughter:—
>   Such a hard experience for my little girl to meet all alone. If mama could only help you darling and help him too.

She urged her to tell Henry he had to get better, "to enjoy his dear girls for years yet."

But seeing his daughter had done him more good than any of them had counted on. On Friday, March 1, the doctor hadn't expected him to live out the night. By Monday, March 4, Vincent wrote home excitedly, "Papa is better and they think he will get well." By then her mother's anxious letter had crossed with hers. Cora didn't know Henry was improving, and while Vincent didn't know exactly what was the matter with him, she tried to waylay her mother's fears: "He's had pneumonia I guess, and asthma and a bad heart," but now he was clearly on the mend.

Dr. Somerville, who looked, she told her mother, "exactly like Andrew Carnegie," took her driving every day and sleighing miles upriver, where she saw a deer hanging in a tree, killed by a bobcat. "Papa says that now a bob-cat is the only thing that can legally kill deer. He seemed rather skeptical. . . . I have to run on like this because I'm in a hurry." What had begun as an ordeal for Vincent was becoming an adventure. She promised her mother she'd tell more later, and she closed admiringly with this:

> I see Papa twice a day. We can't talk very much but he loves to have me with him. . . . I have never in my life heard so many people inquire for one man. All festivities here are post-poned until he recovers. An M.D. and an L.L.D. from somewhere around here came in on the train today just to see him a minute—great friends of his.
>   I'll write later, home,
>
> Love,
Vincent

Cora regained more than her composure with the news of Henry's recovery. She said it was "nice" that Vincent was having a good time after all—"I am glad your papa has so many good friends. He was always very popular and made friends wherever he went." But now she asked pointedly how much Vincent's trip had cost and reminded her, "It is hard for those left at home sometimes and they want a letter. Write often." Then she sent Vincent a photograph of herself in her nurse's uniform, looking stern and competent, her face more deeply lined than it should have been for a woman just shy of her forty-ninth birthday. It was a telling gesture, and it was intended for Henry. Vincent, after all, had just left home; she knew what her mother looked like. "Give my best wishes to your papa, and tell him to get well and do the best he can for his nice big girls I've kept so well for him."

Her mother continued to press her not only for news but for her return. Norma needed her help with French. "I can get along without you when I'm away; but home misses you awfully." But Vincent wasn't thinking of Norma's French or her home duties, and she didn't respond to her mother's letters. The next letter came with an enclosed note from Norma that flashed with anger:

Sister Millay:—
I am exceedingly ashamed of you for not letting us hear something from you. . . . You have been up there almost three weeks and you haven't exerted your self in writing letters to your family. What is the matter, dear? Are you sick yourself? Just because you have found your father must you forget all about your mother and us kids?

She closed in a voice very like the one Vincent used when she was trying to reassure her mother that she loved her: "I can't help scolding you for I am disgusted wif youse."

In that inevitable tug between parents, especially those who have divorced, one parent wears the mantle of the victor and the other becomes the vanquished. Henry was clearly the vanquished. But there is a peculiar susceptibility children have to the fallen, to the not victorious, particularly if it is the father and they are girls. Henry had been irresponsible. He hadn't supported them, and Vincent knew it. But now, for the first time since she'd been very young, she was in his world, and she was thriving. She found him as charming and winning as her mother once had. However, her lengthening absence, with very little word home, made Cora excruciatingly anxious. And Norma was acting her part in a family drama long established among them. She wrote not only on her mother's behalf, but on her own.

Cora tried to telephone Kingman, but the line above Bangor was out. She told Vincent that if she didn't hear immediately she would telegraph, which was costly. Still Vincent didn't write. Her mother would write ten letters to her four.

She wasn't sick, she was having fun. The gloom that had engulfed her at home was lifting. She began a letter to her sisters on St. Patrick's Day (the date of her parents' wedding anniversary), but as she became more and more drawn into the social life of Kingman, she let it slip. She even forgot to write to her beloved on March 3, "because . . . I don't care a snap about you. I don't even think of you. No, these are lies, I adore you, but yesterday was the 3rd and I didn't know." In fact, she only once again turned to him on the third. The intensity of her need was over for good.

She told her mother and sisters that there was only one thing the King-man boys were good for, and that was dancing. "And they certainly can dance, not contras, but waltzes and schottisches, and they waltz their two steps. Whodathunkit!" She and Dr. Somerville's daughter, Ella, spent every night that week at a show that had come to town; she called it "a Kickapoo medicine-show, an all-the-week, Kickapoo, Sagwa, vaudeville, medicine show," where they "queened in."

And say,—It's great to be the new girl in town when there's a dance on. Everybody fell over himself to get a dance with me, and every dance I had was lovely.

At home she had not been a girl sure of her powers; now she was a hit for the first time in her life. It did wonders for her, as did her renewed contact with her father.

I pop in and out all the time and we just love each other. Sometimes when I'm coming upstairs I call out, "Hi papa!" like that, and sometimes I just say, "I bet a cent my dad knows what's a-coming!" And then he'll laugh and tell me to hurry up.

Maybe it was inevitable that she would find him, even in illness, a charming and sunny man. Certainly it was clear from her letters home that he was enviably well liked. Then, too, he was impressed with her—he loved to hear her read Burns and Kipling, and he praised her highly. He thought her singing voice was superb.

I will say right now that I sang the "Ave Maria," which is a very dramatic, operatic thing, after the manner of a dramatic, operatic star. Up here, where no one knows but that I have taken lessons for years of Madame Marchesi, I am not afraid to howl.

And sing she did, standing by the church's open window, just across the yard from where her father lay listening to her.

Consequence—Papa thinks I have a voice with a future, said he thought it was Schumann-Heink a-bellering next door, had no idea I could sing like that, did I call that a little parlor voice?—etc. etc. Lud! How I do fool 'em all!

She was old enough to know that his praise was excessive, but how welcome it made her feel. What a delight to be taken care of, to be praised, flattered, and danced with when she'd thought she'd come for death.

But she knew her mother well, and even if it had taken her three days to finish the letter she didn't ignore her mother's feelings. "Tell Mother, *be sure to tell* mother, that I worship her cap-frill," she wrote back to Norma. "Goodnight, you bad tids! Vincent."

Cora was no fool. When she summoned her daughter home this time, there was bait on the hook. "Dear Vincent," she wrote on March 21, "I . . . am going to try to catch you now with something that may interest and encourage you." She'd been sent a sample copy of *The Magazine Maker* in which there was an article announcing a grand contest for poets. One thousand dollars in prize money would be awarded to the three best poems submitted by June 1, to Mitchell Kennerley, the New York publisher. One could send in as many poems as one wanted. One hundred American poems would be published on November 1 in a single volume to be called *The Lyric Year.* The judges were Edward J. Wheeler, editor of *Current Opinion;* William Stanley Braithwaite, poetry editor of the Boston *Transcript;* and the editor of *The Lyric Year* itself, who was anonymous.

"Here is your chance," Cora scrawled across the top of the letter. "Think what Wheeler said of your *Land of Romance.*

"Come home," she wrote urgently, "and make a good try."

Vincent raced back to Camden. She helped Norma with her French, and she helped her mother move into their new house at 82 Washington Street, across from the high school. By May 27—in less than two months—she had finished her long poem "Renaissance" and sent it in to *The Lyric Year.*

At the same time, but in separate envelopes, she sent along other poems, "La Joie de Vivre," "The Suicide," "Interim," and probably three others, each of which she signed E. Vincent Millay. Into the return envelope of each she placed a note "of consolation and encouragement," thinking that if they came back, the blow of no comment or a printed rejection slip would be softened.

It's hard to know exactly when she began to write "Renaissance," the spelling she used when she wrote it. According to notes her mother made much later in life, the poem was begun in 1911, when Vincent was nineteen. It was then put aside and was not finished until the late spring of 1912. But her mother, for whom there was more at stake than she ever acknowledged, put it variously, and sometimes clearly inaccurately, this way:

> Renascence was partly written in 1911, when Miss Millay was in Kingman, Maine, on a visit to her father. . . . I saw the advertisement of Mitchell Kennerlys for The Lyric Year in which a hundred American poets would be represented. I at once recognized a fair chance for her to receive recognition and wrote her to come home and finish the poem and get it into the contest—This was in the spring of 1912.
>   She did this with little enough time in which to accomplish so great a work, and just get it done in time.

Nowhere did her mother mention that she, too, had sent poems in to the contest that spring, placing herself in direct competition with her daughter.

☙ ☙ ☙

"If I'd thought that would occur to you, I wouldn't have told you!" Norma Millay said to me almost seventy years after the contest was over.

"You didn't tell me," I said carefully.

"Of course they were not competitors. Mother would never have competed against Vincent. She was competing. As Vincent was." Norma paused, her head bent down, and then, softly, watching me closely through her filmy glasses, "She was competing *with* Vincent. Was she not?"

CHAPTER 8

> —You inquire my Books—For Poets—I have Keats—and Mr and Mrs Browning. . . . I went to school—but in your manner of the phrase—had no education. . . . But I fear my story fatigues you— I would like to learn—Could you tell me how to grow—or is it unconveyed—like Melody—or Witchcraft? . . .
>   Is this—Sir—what you asked me to tell you?
>   —Emily Dickinson to Thomas Wentworth Higginson, April 25, 1862

Vincent had gone into a nearby meadow to pick blueberries for supper, and when she had a pailful she came home to find her mother waiting anxiously on the doorstep with a letter in her hand. It was addressed to "E. Vincent Millay, Esq." and it was from the editor of *The Lyric Year*. On July 17, 1912, he accepted "Renascence" as one of the best one hundred poems in the contest. Addressing her as "Dear Sir," he told her just how much he liked it and asked for a biographical sketch. He signed himself, "Yours faithfully, The Editor." He did not give his name. She waited less than a week to answer, addressing her letter to Mitchell Kennerley, the New York publisher under whose aegis the prize had been announced: "It may astonish you to learn that I am no 'Esquire' at all, nor even a plain 'Mister'; in fact, that I am just an aspiring 'Miss' of twenty."

It wasn't unusual, she told him, for people to be "deceived" by her masculine name, "and it was in the hope that you, too, would think me a man, that I signed my name as I did, with its feminine *Edna* just initialed."

What would any seasoned editor make of that sally? Rapid-fire she told him when she'd been born, quoted her first poem, told him, even, how she'd felt when she'd seen that Edward J. Wheeler, who'd reprinted and commented on her gold medal poem from *St. Nicholas,* was one of the judges: " 'Mitchell Kennerley' and 'William Stanley Braithwaite' were formidable enough . . . but 'Edward J. Wheeler' was the name of an old friend. It was the fact that he had once been pleased with my work which gave me courage to enter the competition."

But if she was stumped when he asked her for "characteristics," she soon rallied; she told him how she looked:

> If I were a noted author you would perhaps be interested to know that I have red hair, am five feet-four inches in height, and weigh just one hundred pounds; that I can climb fences in snowshoes, am a good walker, and make excellent rarebits. And if I were a noted author I should not hesitate to tell you . . . that I play the piano;—Grieg with more expression than is aesthetic, Bach with more enjoyment than is consistent, and rag-time with more frequency than is desired.

She was crazy about Ibsen, knew *The Rubaiyat* by heart, paddled stern in a canoe. "But, since I am not a noted author,——and since, without telling you these things, I have so skilfully acquainted you with them——I will be silent lest I bore you."

Her style in this opening letter is playful, even cheeky. She's clearly having fun, beckoning her editor. She even sent along a photograph, which she asked that he return, but that snapshot as well as this letter were bound to provoke a response, and two weeks later, on August 6, the editor replied. He asked to keep her photograph. But he kept her guessing as to his identity.

Dear and true Poetess!
    You have indeed astonished me through and through—a *lassie* o' twenty—is it possible?

He said he hadn't been alone in finding her poem "very fine, original, strong, impressive." But he'd had certain reservations about it. He'd come upon other poems by "Mr." E. Vincent Millay, and they had been so unequal to "Renascence" that he'd suspected "some sort of forgery was being palmed off on 'The Lyric Year.' " He hadn't liked the other poems, so he'd taken "Renascence" to a friend of his, "author, critic and attorney, to see if he could detect a clue. . . . The next day I came across a strong short piece—'Then why the appetite—Why the fruit.' "

The strong, short piece he was referring to was her mother, Cora Millay's, not Vincent's, but he didn't know that—and no one was about to tell him.

Furthermore, RENASCENCE itself is at the same time very finished and very crude. What am I to think!
    Certainly I did not suspect that a fence-vaulting, Bach-mad, ninety-nine-pound mite of a girl was causing all the hubbub!
    Sometimes I think that *Renascence* is the most interesting poem in the selected Hundred of The Lyric Year.

Signing himself "The Editor," he told her that it might add "zest" to her anticipation to know he was not Mitchell Kennerley.

She answered him by return mail. She said nothing about her mother's poem. Instead she told him more about herself: "I am to some extent self-educated, having read ever since I could read at all everything I could find. . . . I could almost say with Simple Simon, 'Please, sir, I haven't any.' I want, and have always wanted—dreadfully—to go to college."

She turned the last sentence in her letter in such a way as to flatter him:

When, in my old age, I compile my real autobiography, entitled "Wild Editors I Have Met," you, a rare type, and strangely tame, will have a chapter all to yourself; and the frontispiece will be your photograph,—if I can get it.

Rare or wild, she said, he must tell her who he was. "You aren't a girl, too, are you? You can't be Edward J. Wheeler, can you? *Please* tell me." And she wanted to know why she couldn't call her poem "Renaissance" "in the French way? I see you used the Anglicized *Renascence.*"

They began writing to each other now by return mail. The guessing game continued as he told her he was not Wheeler, "nor," he wrote on August 14, "anybody of importance. Just 'a lover of poetry,' and of plump babies, and of skis, blizzards, Bach, kittens and embroidery"; but he did give her his summer address, engraved on the top of his stationery, "Vindrholm, Monroe, New York," and told her that address in care of "F.E." would reach him. It was a remarkably coy response. He had conceived of *The Lyric Year*

> to reach just such budding geniuses as yourself. . . . I am indeed proud and happy to have discovered you. . . . And although nearly old enough to be your <u>grandfather</u> . . . I am not ashamed to caper with delight over "Renascence."

It was Kennerley, however, who was English and who preferred the English spelling, not he.

After receiving this letter Vincent decided her editor was *Mrs.* Mitchell Kennerley.

> But it makes no difference who you are. You are perfectly charming, and I am crazy about you. There! Such a relief to be able at last to confess it, without indiscretion; or, if not without indiscretion—all confessions are indiscreet—at least to confess it.—This is not a crush; don't be alarmed; I never have them. It is purely an intellectual enthusiasm.

She thought it was sensational to be anybody's discovery. Cora, who was working in Rockland that summer, and who was privy to Vincent's guesses, wrote:

> Isn't it dear about your poem and your Editor? I think it is real sweet that way, don't you? She may be a great help to my girl. I must say goodnight.
>   Lots of luck to my other girls. Yours—
> > "The Mother of A Poet."

By the end of August, though she was hot in correspondence with her editor, there was still no word of the contest itself. What she could not have guessed was that her editor was trying desperately to attract other poets into his competition. By September 5, after Ridgely Torrence, to whom he had appealed, had sent his revised poem "A Ritual for a Funeral," the editor assured him that "Mr. Wheeler and *all* your friends are very anxious for you to take the Lyric Year prize." This was far more than angling for distinguished talent.

❧ ❧ ❧

As High Street rises away from the center of Camden, there was, and still is, a large white frame summer hotel called the Whitehall Inn. It sprawls across a broad lawn rimmed with fir trees and wild roses, its long porches sleepily watching the bay. It was there in the summer of 1912 that Norma Millay took a job as a waitress.

Since she'd never worked as a waitress before, I asked her why she had taken the job.

"Mother said I could go. And, well, I guess as always, it would be nice to make a little money. And, too, it was just as a sort of lark. . . . The guests got interested in me. What beautiful hands I had, when I served from the tray, or the way I spoke. Anyway, soon they asked me about myself and my family. I said I had a sister who was a poet. I said she had a poem in *The Lyric Year.*"

Norma remembered that at the end of August there was to be a staff party, a masquerade dance. "And they said, will your sister be there? and I said I didn't know. But I got the feeling that they were . . . what? well, interested in us. I made up my mind that Vincent was going to come.

"You understand, Vincent had been out of school a long time. And we *knew* she was a genius. She was shy. She went with her girlfriends. So, I . . . I . . . Why should I go to a party for the help? Oh, God, yes, it just sounded ridiculous. But I decided I would go and I would bring Vincent up. I had to work to bring her. I told her it would be kind of fun. Kind of a lark. And we loved to dance well together. So, *Come on! Vincent!*"

❧ ❧ ❧

But Vincent balked. From the moment Norma mentioned the party, she dug her heels in. Norma said it would be good for her to see people, to be drawn out of herself. She didn't want to see people, she didn't think it would be good for her. Years later Vincent would write, "Norma was . . . carefree, gay, gregarious and unselfconscious; I was thoughtful, intense, involved, reticent & retiring." Vincent was also mulish. But Norma was unrelenting.

"Then *Okay!* It was—let's see some of these funny people who come summers. I made her a little Pierrette costume, and in it with her long red-blond hair she looked about fifteen."

Vincent wore a tiny black velvet mask with rosettes of red crepe paper at the sides where the tie was fastened. Her costume had a short, full skirt made of yards of white cheesecloth fitted smartly at her waist, with a low-cut sleeveless bodice with black pompoms down the front. She won the prize for best costume, and Norma got the prize for best dancer. Afterward, everyone, guests and help, went into the music room for ice cream and cake. Norma continued, "And for us to perform. . . . I said, 'Ask Vincent to sing some songs, ask for "The Circus Rag!" ' Vincent gave me a dirty look, the look that meant—you've been tattling! What are you up to? Then she played the piano and sang, jazzy and bright and quick." Norma closed her eyes and began to sing Vincent's song:

> "You must have heard that circus rag
>   Years ago when you were a kid!
> Now the same old wag gets the same old gag
>   Off, just as he always did. . . .
>   . . . .
>   —Chorus—
> Right this way, ladies and gents!
> Just a quarter of a dollar, only twenty-five cents!
> Step right up! Tickets here!
> We make it just a quarter to a pretty girl, dear. . . ."

"Vincent had a deep contralto voice, you know, completely different from my own. And then she sang, 'Who Will Go a-Maying?' which was sweet and light. Finally, after she'd sung her songs, I said, 'Ask her to recite "Renascence." ' She turned around on the piano stool and said this poem. Then it was absolutely still in that room.

> "All I could see from where I stood
> Was three long mountains and a wood;
> I turned and looked another way,
> And saw three islands in a bay.
> So with my eyes I traced the line
> Of the horizon, thin and fine,
> Straight around till I was come
> Back to where I'd started from;
> And all I saw from where I stood
> Was three long mountains and a wood.
> Over these things I could not see;
> These were the things that bounded me. . . .

"Well, yes. Now things were happening very fast. The next day they had her up to lunch and I waited on her. Then they began taking us out sailing. That sort of thing. And Mother, who was nursing one of the guests upstairs at the hotel, came down and did the silver for me, so I could leave to sail. You see, we were different. We were different from all the others."

☙ ☙ ☙

One of the guests in the audience at the Whitehall Inn that evening was Caroline B. Dow. She was stunned by Millay's poem, but even more by this provincial girl's assured performance. In a diary Vincent called "Sweet & Twenty," "Being The Extraordinary Adventures Of Me In My Twenty-first Year," she wrote, "If I had known then how much was to happen to me this year I would have started a diary that night."

> Wed. morning . . .
> Miss Dow (Caroline B.) called;—dean of New York Y.W.C.A. Training School. Wealthy friends in New York who might send me to <u>Vassar</u>.

☙ ☙ ☙

"Miss Dow wanted to come up and talk to Mother, privately," Norma recalled. "And, of course, Vincent had to go to college. I remember Miss Dow as tall, about fifty-five maybe. As Vincent said, 'She's the hull ting.' And, of course, she was."

☙ ☙ ☙

On September 3, Vincent's editor sent her two snapshots, but he was still teasing her, for on the reverse of one he wrote:

> (to Miss Edna Vincent Millay
> from The Editor of
> The Lyric Year.
> with her—(his?)—best compliments!)

A tall, narrow man with thick straight black hair, sharp dark eyes, and a crooked grin is standing with his wife; in the other photo he holds their baby daughter. By the middle of the month he said that if he were a sport, "I should wager odds on Renascence for first honors"; and he returned a carbon copy of "Renascence" with his comments in red pencil. Too much, he felt, happened *"suddenly."* He left it entirely to her judgment but asked if the effects of the poem wouldn't be stronger by "allowing <u>some</u> of them to dawn quietly." He closed by saying, "What a wonderful person—to have written this poem. I envy you!"

Her responses to these letters exist only in pages of undated pencil drafts, but pieced together they are clear enough to tell us how she felt. For one thing, she paid careful attention to his advice about "Renascence" and replaced the first "suddenly." She also seems to have reworked several lines—in other words, she was able to accept his criticism. On the twenty-first, she received proofs of her poem. It was not until September 25 that he revealed he was Ferdinand Earle and assured her she would be pleased with the results of the contest. "Several have prophesied that you have the best chance for the first prize." Which, unbeknownst to her, was exactly what he'd suggested to Torrence three weeks before.

What was she to make of this man? What did he mean "by betting on my Pegasus?" she asked. "I know now, of course, that you meant I have a big chance to win." But now that her hopes were high, "the disappointment, if I am disappointed, will be terrible."

Their letters flew back and forth, and every other day Earle seemed to have some fresh delight to offer her. Would she come visit them? Would she be their friend "until you become so grand and famous that you would have no time for small fry." He tempted her with his word pictures of New York City, of gleaming high buildings, museums, and theaters. But what he truly admitted was that

> if I could believe that I have encouraged and helped you with my big clumsy venture. . . . And when your name is pronounced only with whispers of awe, it will be my secret pride to believe that I had the privilege of discovering your worth, before anyone else.

Would she come to New York? She shot back, "Why, bless yuh heart, sir, I *shall* come to New York!" As for his venture, he must never call it clumsy. "Say, rather, your big, splendid venture. O, but it's great to be a man! You made this year so . . . miraculous to me!"

Savoring her spunk, he wrote to her as his "Dear Tom Boy," admitting that "the big, central thrill of the whole affair was digging you out of oblivion." His single note of caution fell in this letter of September 29:

> I have no right to promise you a prize, as that depends mostly upon Mr. Wheeler. Aren't you bursting to learn the November decision?—I am.

" '*Bursting* to learn the November decision'! My dear man, I shall *bust* long before then!" But why, she asked in all innocence, did he leave the "Saint" out of her name? "It really belongs there, and—please, sir, I need to be reminded of it!"

It was audacious of her to flirt with him this openly. She was summoning him to her, and something she'd written to him—it may have been a letter that no longer exists among her penciled drafts—caused him to realize that far more was at stake for her than he'd understood before. Their exchange wasn't just about the contest anymore. "I realize that you are a woman, and not the mere elf-child I let myself imagine. I am half very sorry and half very glad. . . . And yet, should I write to you so much? . . . Yes: until the fateful decision! . . . And then I hope to see you."

That last phrase he put in brackets, as if the punctuation would lessen the impact of what he was telling her.

The poems had gone to the other judges that morning; he expected to know the decision in about two weeks but was honor-bound to hold his tongue. "What you read between the lines, I should not be responsible for? . . . Should I?" This was exactly the tone he took with her, coy and flirtatious. If it was a pity she wasn't "an elf-child," with whom he could tramp the city, nevertheless "you are a wonderful young woman, and a gifted poet: that is still better, even if that leaves us a little less free." He lamely added that she was still "very welcome here by at least one member of the household, if not by the trio." But that last phrase was a clear note of caution. She'd had two: he'd said he had no right to promise her a prize because he was only one judge among three. Now his wife had begun to read Vincent's letters. Earle said that while he was left "glowing with wild, uncontrollable delights" by her letters, someone else "did not glow one bit!" But he couldn't leave it at that; he wanted more.

> Now, to be serious, dear Miss Millay: may I ask you, how you came to write Renascence? . . . How could a charming young woman of a quiet New England village write a stupendous poem, that threatens to carry away spoil from the midst of our established singers—booty they are making mighty efforts to capture?
> How did you do it?
> How, O how?

Millay had told him a great deal about herself, but she said remarkably little about "Renascence" itself. Only this once. And even here she said more about his effect on her:

[I]f it will make you the least bit happier to know just what your friendship has meant to me, then please understand this: the sky had to cave in on me, of course, before I could write Renascence, and I dug my man up because it wasn't pleasant to leave him there, not because I had come up too. It was you who, in your enthusiastic "discovering," accidentally exhumed me. Now, we won't talk about *that* anymore.

Two days later he sent her proofs of several of the other contesting poems. But again he cautioned her, "You must promise me, dear, dear Tom Boy, never, never to write to a strange man as you have written me." He didn't say what she'd written that had disturbed his wife, and he admitted later in the same letter that he wasn't really a stranger to her, that he was, even, attracted to her. He was writing to her, he said, for the sake of his own part in her future development and to protect her from herself. Couldn't they go back to an earlier point in their correspondence, she asked, "a little bit shocked and a little bit shamed. . . . and—talk about the weather?" Otherwise, not only would he never meet his provocative little elf, she would never hear his Cremona.

(If you could know how—almost annihilatingly I want to hear you play that violin! Or how I would come straight back home again and be *tamed* for the rest of my life, if just for one evening I might listen to Wagner music with a man who *knew how* to love it! Savage passion! There could be no savage passion in you that would not find itself again in me! I am not big enough to love things the way I do!)

If that didn't jar Mrs. Earle's sense of propriety, it's hard to imagine what would. Poor Earle. He had no idea what he was up against in trying to restrain Edna St. Vincent Millay. "But there," she sweetly assured him,

I had not meant to say so much. It is shockingly bad form to be so unreserved. Dear me!
    What will you do with me now, Mr. Ferdinand Earle,—scold me, or shake me, or—pat me on the head? (don't *dare!* O, I *have* to giggle!)

Her letters to Earle are the most amazing mix of girlish bravado and cunning innocence. She wanted to be the wonderful young woman he'd said she was. She also wanted to be tamed, and that was something else again—something Mrs. Earle might well object to. Millay was practicing. She wanted her match in a man she could admire—a man who could dominate her and fire her imagination. But the very notion relies on the ideal of a man superior to herself, and if Ferdinand Earle was a silly, he was also, crucially, the first to try.

What he wanted, he told her on October 14, was to "flame back into silence, leaving a trail of fire across your dreams. . . . I would leave you a mingled peace and unrest." He closed this letter by asking her to remember a title, "Golden Pastoral Horn," for "Last night it seemed to me *the* prize winner. The judges have Renascence. Would you hate me . . . if they snubbed you?"

Stunned, she began a letter on the fifteenth which she left unfinished in midsentence. It was wild and nearly incoherent, as she faced for the first time, after all his assurances, the fact that she could lose.

> My Editor,—
>
> I shall not hate you, no. But I shall cry. I shall cry all night long the night I get that letter, and I hope that all night long you will lie awake and know that I am crying. I wished once to make you glad in return for the gladness you had given me, and now, by the same token, I would make you wretched. I desire that you can not sleep that night for thinking of my wretchedness.

It was not just the difference between "Renascence-Honored and Renascence-Snubbed," she told him, or between "Vincent glad and Vincent sorry"; it was the difference between five hundred dollars and nothing: "You had not thought of that, had you? I would choose not to think of that myself if I had any choice."

This is the most telling letter in their correspondence. With crossed-out patches and paragraphs of screed, Millay moved from a diction that was almost imperious to that of a child. She was hampered not only by the immense disparity in their roles—the young poet at twenty, competing for a national honor against a judge whose contest it was (and who had the cash to put up the prize money)—but because she had believed him. Her anger and dependence are everywhere in this letter, and by its close the child voice is the dominant one:

> Then what if you wrote an indiscreet letter (partly because you . . . didn't know whether you dared or not, and partly because you wanted to see just what your editor would say, and partly—oh *lots* because you were only twenty) and Your Editor wrote back an indiscreet letter that made you want to baby him—tho you really couldn't *help* it—and at the very end of it said, "Will you hate me if you don't get any prize?"—then, why then you wouldn't *hate* him, of *course* but wouldn't you want to cry on him? (Please, that isn't wicked is it? It's just that men are so much more comfortable to cry on,—and you're the only man-friend I have. . . . I haven't in all the world one friend who is stronger than I. I need someone to make me do things, and keep me doing things, and keep me *from* doing things.

I guess I shall never see you in all this world. O, dear, I feel so l'l' an' small an' all shrunkd up, I guess you couldn't see *me* if you were here.—I'm honest 'fraid you' have to use a big nifying glass!—I—Please, sir, I'm sorry for my badness, and will you write me a letter purpose to cry on?

> V.M.

What she couldn't have known was that Earle had written to Kennerley on the fifteenth, just after he'd written to her, placing "Renascence" second. But even then he had equivocated, "Renascence could easily deserve first honors."

On October 15, he wrote to her again:

Feel nervous and restless, do!—*Do* keep me company! The poems are almost "judged"—the decision hangs in the balance. . . . I ache to know.

> Faithfully,
> F.E.

On October 25, 1912, Earle delivered his final choice to Mitchell Kennerley. He championed "Renascence":

The most astonishingly beautiful and original poem in the *Lyric Year,* the poem most arresting in its vision, the poem most like a wonderful Pre-Raphael painting, is surely *Renascence* by Miss Edna St. Vincent Millay. To me it is almost unthinkable that a girl of twenty could conceive such a work and execute it with such vigor and tenderness. . . . And it is with no small pride that I give it my first vote for the prizes.

In second place he chose Orrick Johns's "Second Avenue," with Ridgely Torrence's "A Ritual for a Funeral" third.

Then he wrote her a peculiar letter, cut and pasted together, telling her that most "friendships, relations, acquaintance-ships are bloodless, frigid, and stark, with no becoming drapery in the form of mystery and romantic atmosphere, with no bared elbows and throats." He did wish he could tell her "about the prizes—the question, however, is still an open one, (shut at the outside ends!)"

She didn't write to him for three weeks. Or, more precisely, she drafted three letters and sent none. She kept them, and she waited. Her drafts tell us how she felt as she waited:

I am asking you to return to me a letter which I, a short time ago, wrote to a friend of mine, and which you, a complete stranger, seem to have received by mistake. The letter can mean nothing to you, as you are incapable of understanding it; but to me, who wrote it in all sincerity and candor, it means much—and it annoys me to think of its being in your possession.

She gave him permission to read all of her letters to his wife, "unexpurgated. Yours to me I will return, if you like, and them, also, you can read to her,—at your discretion." She had not been obscure in her letters to him; "possibly your translation has been purposely a little free." Had he thought of that? He, with his "advantage over me that fourteen years have given,"

Are you trying to tell me not to make a fool of myself? Believe me, such advice could only be *needless* or *useless*.

She boiled on:

And I did *not* mean to tell you anything whatever about "bloodless friendships" as opposed to the "romantic atmosphere" of "bared elbows and throats,"—tho I am sure that bared throats are not half so indecorous as bared hearts; and I shall not forget again, have no fear that I shall. I told you I always make mistakes in men. I always do. But never the same mistake twice.

Indignantly, relentlessly, she pressed on:

I am wild, if you like; but I stayed in my burrow a long, long time,—nibbling your straws and snapping at your fingers, but always just a little out of reach. Until at last I got to trust you so much that one day I ventured out for a minute,—and you threw rocks at me. And I will never come out again.

Before she could send her letter, Earle wrote to her again: "I say: the Prizes have been awarded. . . . Can you see anything by the tone of this letter? Would you feel satisfied with a very honorable mention? Would you hate me if RENASCENCE is entirely out of it?"

He had said she would win; he had nearly promised. They had corresponded for months now. He'd suggested very few changes in the poem—the title Anglicized, a word overused or overstressed—and she had been grateful for his attention. She'd made the changes. She'd provoked his correspondence, she'd sent him snapshots, and she wanted, she needed his attention and his support. What she had done was to seduce that support. Now she had not won first prize, or second or third. She was steeled for anything but loss.

Camden, Me. Nov. 5, 1912

This, then, is what I have been waiting for, from day to day . . . in such
an agony as I had not known I could experience. This is the answer; this is
the end. I wonder why I am not crying. My mother is crying. Did you ever
hear your mother cry as if her heart would break? It is a strange and terrible sound. I think I shall never forget it.

I cannot realize what you have done. I am numb, I think. I read your letter, and read it again, and I neither cried out nor fainted. I can sit and write
quite calmly. I do not understand myself. I shall not try to understand you.
I will try to keep from understanding you. I will not let my mind admit you
as a possibility. And I would not be in your place, with my own capability
for remorse, for anything in earth or heaven that I have ever heard of.

Her letter breaks off, incomplete and, again, apparently unsent. On the
fifteenth of November, she received another letter: "What have I done to
make you so silent?" Was she punishing him? he asked. He told her that
there was something better than a prize: Jessie Rittenhouse, a force in
American poetry, who was an officer of the Poetry Society of America and
"perhaps our most distinguished critic," had written Earle to tell him that
Millay's "Renascence" was

"the best thing in the book . . . in fact one of the freshest and most original
things in modern poetry. If it doesn't get the prize, I pity your
judges." . . . Think of it!

Earle added, irrepressibly, "O, what more can you hope for! You might
as well retire and rest on your laurels the rest of your life."

Ruefully, after entering Earle's reassurances in her "Sweet & Twenty"
diary, she added, "But it didn't get the prize! Everything but money!"

Two weeks later, in the Holiday Book number of *The New York Times*,
Jessie Rittenhouse—while praising Earle's and Kennerley's effort and
commitment to modern American poetry—singled out and saved for the
conclusion of her full-page review Millay's "Renascence":

The "Lyric Year" has, however, a poem so distinct . . . that it seems to me
the freshest, most distinctive note in the book. This is "Renascence," by
Edna Vincent Millay. . . . Miss Millay's defects are the healthy defects of
youth, time will take care of them; but that so young a poet should have so
personal a vision of humanity, nature and God, such a sense of spiritual
elation, of mystical rebirth, and present it to us with the freshness of first
view—is certainly worthy of recognition and one could wish that the
judges had seconded Mr. Earle in his choice of this poem for one of the
awards.

2

Miss Caroline B. Dow had not forgotten Vincent. "You might easily think that I had," she had written to her in October, "if you did not believe that I was serious when I said I wanted to help." After hearing her recite "Renascence" at the Whitehall Inn, she had decided to marshal whatever support Vincent needed to go to Vassar. Precisely what work had Millay done in Camden High School?—What had she read, what was her standing in the class?—and while Vincent had sent her some poems that she had welcomed, she cautioned her "not to deal much with metaphysics & philosophies but keep yourself and your expressions simple & spontaneous." It was advice Miss Dow would give often and in a variety of ways, for she assumed a far greater simplicity in this young woman than her poems, letters, or diaries suggested.

Since mid-September Millay had also been in correspondence with a woman named Charlotte Bannon (a friend of a Mrs. Esselborn, who, with Miss Dow, had also heard Millay recite at Whitehall). On November 15, Miss Bannon had taken "Renascence" to the head of the English department at Smith College, who now asked to know exactly what Miss Dow wanted to know, and for the same reasons. Miss Bannon sent Vincent a catalog to the college, telling her that if she could get admitted, Smith College would take care of her after she was there. It was as close to an outright commitment as anything Millay had yet heard, but she didn't feel she could enter into any sort of relationship with Smith until she knew what her chances were at Vassar.

"I have always wanted dreadfully, and until now hopelessly, to go to college," she wrote to Miss Dow. "I would far rather go to Vassar than anywhere else. . . . but even more than I want to go to *Vassar*,—I want to go to *college!* So that if anything should happen that I couldn't go to Vassar, I wouldn't want to have spoiled my chances at Smith." She hoped Miss Dow understood, and even more that she wouldn't "be obligated to say, 'By all means, Smith.' For I am already, at heart at least, a Vassar girl."

Miss Dow hedged. She was uncertain if there was a vacancy for the year, and while she assured Vincent of her own impartiality, she said there were some very good reasons why Smith might not be as "helpful to you as Vassar." But she gave only one: "the country life." Her best news she saved for last: "I have about $400 promised for your first year, and feel no doubt about getting the rest."

Two days later, Miss Dow advised Millay to apply to both Smith and Vassar and see what happened. Vincent did just that. Meanwhile, Miss Bannon was not only working to have her admitted to Smith, she was telling her that whether she chose Vassar or Smith was "a question of what is best for you entirely—and I think you have a right to choose your own college—even if we all *do* want to be kind to you." Vincent's position was delicious. From having had no chance of going to college, she was now close to being fought over.

On December 18, 1912, the president of Smith College offered her a full scholarship for the following year. When Miss Dow learned of Smith's offer, she wrote immediately, "I have on hand enough money for the first year at college and it seems to remain for you to decide whether you will go to Smith or Vassar." Vincent wrote to her mother in Rockland:

> Isn't this *fierce?* . . . She puts in her little word about the country life at Vassar, but leaves the matter entirely in my hands. . . . Mother, I *knew* it would come to this! . . . My head is a howling wilderness. And every once in a while I have to *shriek* with laughter over the *dead funny* side of it!

Two days later, Miss Dow made her condition clear: "Since three of the largest gifts for your education came from people who expected you to enter Vassar I shall have to write them and find if the gift wld. still hold if you went elsewhere." In other words, she continued to press for Vassar, while Miss Bannon advised Vincent to take the first and best offer, from Smith. She even told her how:

> I would write and explain to your Vassar friend that President Burton of Smith has offered you a full scholarship here and . . . that you feel you ought to accept what is a definite certainty. . . . You can explain it in your own way—of course with gratitude & appreciation for all they have done for you.

In closing she told Vincent, "I want to be your great friend and I will be, if you will let me."

That was a remarkable note of affection, and it would not be the last time Edna St. Vincent Millay would win to her side an older woman who was in a position to help her. They were *taken* with Edna Millay. They wanted to assist her in any way they could, perhaps because in the careful structure of their lives they felt diminished. Her life would be grand, sweeping, urgent. Incapable of this themselves, they would help her.

In the end, when Vincent had chosen Vassar, the grace and generosity with which Miss Bannon took her news was a signal of the attachment she had developed for her young poet. It was ardent:

> I do not want them to conventionalize your spirit—One can learn anywhere—but I want you to learn to think and dream for yourself—Do not

think everything that is told you is necessarily true—because what you want is freedom to think & freedom to range among dreams.

This was from a woman she'd never met, who knew her only through her poems and their correspondence. "I shall always be interested in you—if anything happens that you cannot go to Vassar write to me at once and I shall be your friend again—and again."

Vincent told her mother she was picking Vassar because it would be great to know girls from Persia, Syria, Japan, India, and "one from Berlin, Germany"; besides, she wrote her mother, "There isn't one 'furriner' in Smith." But the real reason was "Lots of Maine girls go to Smith; very few to Vassar. I'd rather go to Vassar."

3

Her copy of *The Lyric Year* arrived the day before Thanksgiving. The next day she received a joint note from Arthur Davison Ficke and Witter Bynner, who were also in the collection:

> This is Thanksgiving Day: we thank you. If we had a thousand dollars, we would send it to you. You should unquestionably have had the prize.
> All three prizes!

The two young men had been friends since their days together at Harvard. Ficke, who was married and had already published four volumes of poetry, was a lawyer, practicing in his father's law firm in Davenport, Iowa, and hating it. Bynner, who was visiting them for the holidays, had published two volumes. Arthur Ficke was tall and narrow and wore a carefully trimmed stiff black mustache to hide his tight lips, whereas Hal (Bynner's nickname) was softer, with silky fair hair and languid airs. Arthur's voice was high, clipped, and nasal; Hal's was deep. Both lived in large part on trust funds established for them by their parents. Arthur had written to Earle that "Renascence" was

> a real vision, such as Coleridge might have seen.
> Are you at liberty to name the author? The little item about her in the back of the book is a marvel of humor. No sweet young thing of twenty ever ended a poem precisely where this one ends: it takes a brawny male of forty-five to do that. Don't, however, fear that Bynner and I are going about bud-mouthed with dark suspicions; if it's a real secret, we respect the writer of such a poem far too much to want to plague "her."

Earle passed along the letter to Vincent, who told them she simply wouldn't be a

"brawny male." . . . I cling to my femininity.

But, gentlemen: when a woman insists that she is twenty, you must not, must not call her forty-five. That is more than wicked; it is indiscreet. . . . P.S. The brawny male sends his picture. I *have* to laugh.

This teaser was the beginning of an exchange that would mark all of their lives in ways they never could have imagined.

Arthur was keen to understand just how Millay's poem had come into being, and he went about finding out just as a lawyer would—with innumerable probing and somewhat patronizing questions. Had she read Coleridge or William Blake? he asked. "How did you come by the image—'Washing my grave away from me'? Did you *see* it, or was it a happy accident of composition, or did you get it from a book." That last was nearly too much for her; she thought there were

vastly fewer "accidents of composition" than one might think.

As to the line you speak of—"Did you get it from a book?" indeed! I'll slap your face. I never get anything from a book. I see things with my own eyes, just as if they were the first eyes that ever saw, and then I set about to tell, as best I can, just what I see.

As for William Blake, she'd never heard of him. Ficke was so astonished he wrote, "O, Wonder-child!" and sent her a copy for Christmas.

By then there was mounting controversy about the prizes; Ficke, Bynner, and Jessie Rittenhouse weren't alone in finding "Renascence" more exceptional than the poems that had won. Louis Untermeyer wrote in the *Chicago Evening Post* that "Mr. Earle may be extolled to the stars" as the patron of struggling poets, but "as the editor of 'The Lyric Year' he should be hailed with more modified raptures." Here was all the stir Earle and Millay could have wished. Among all that old deadwood, Untermeyer had found a poem to like, and he praised it to the skies. "Renascence" was, "without doubt, the surprise of the volume."

For her loss of the prize there was the balm of the publicly stated, clear injustice of the judges' inept decision. By the winter of 1912, at twenty, Edna Millay understood just what it meant to become a cause célèbre.

It was her talent that enabled her to transform the airless life she'd led into a poem that freed her from it. "Renascence" was the culminating poem of her apprenticeship, the shaped instrument of her release. It began as simply as a child's lament, with words of mostly one syllable, moving in rhymed couplets, four ringing beats to a line. If it harked back to Whittier's "Snowbound," that great favorite of the nineteenth century, which her mother had read her to sleep with when she was little—she would remember all her life the shiny jet beads on her mother's bodice as she bent over her, reciting the poem from memory, until she felt she too had it by heart—"Renascence" transcended it. She had found the three major themes in lyric poetry and made them her own: nature, love, and death.

On February 3, 1913, with no warning at all, Millay received a telegram from Miss Dow telling her to come to New York immediately. While Millay's work at Camden High School had been inadequate to the standards of admission to Vassar College, she could be accepted if she successfully completed one semester of preparation at Barnard College in New York City. She boarded the train the next morning with a single suitcase, her initials painted on it in gold, E.St.V.M. But before she left, she turned to *Her Book* and made her last entry to her Beloved:

> Some people think I'm going to be a great poet, and I'm going to be sent to college so that I may have a chance to be great,—but I don't know—I'm afraid—afraid I'm too—too *little,* I guess, to be very much, after all. I'm not joking a bit. I don't want to disappoint people, and perhaps tomorrow I won't feel like this, but it seems to me that all I am really good for is to love you,—and that doesn't do any good. Perhaps I could be a great poet or nearer to it—if I had you, and if you wanted me to. I have some big thoughts . . .
>
> *Darling, Darling, Darling.* I could *kiss* you *now,*—and *now* I could kiss you,—and *now,* and *now!* . . . Dear, I think if I once *saw* you I could write and write and write! If I once could just *hear* you over the phone wire—and know it was you.—I could work and work and write and write!

For the first time she linked loving and writing—if she had *him* she could work, she could write. But no man had come to rescue her from Camden, Maine—she had rescued herself through her poetry. Now she took her tarnished ring and, pricking her finger for "a drop of red, red blood," she sealed the book into a small white box with the hot wax from a candle. It was her last vigil. Her life in Camden was over.

RENASCENCE

All I could see from where I stood
Was three long mountains and a wood;
I turned and looked another way,
And saw three islands in a bay.
So with my eyes I traced the line
Of the horizon, thin and fine,
Straight around till I was come
Back to where I'd started from;
And all I saw from where I stood
Was three long mountains and a wood.

Over these things I could not see;
These were the things that bounded me.
And I could touch them with my hand,
Almost, I thought, from where I stand!
And all at once things seemed so small
My breath came short, and scarce at all.

But, sure, the sky is big, I said:
Miles and miles above my head.
So here upon my back I'll lie
And look my fill into the sky.
And so I looked, and after all,
The sky was not so very tall.
The sky, I said, must somewhere stop . . .
And—sure enough!—I see the top!
The sky, I thought, is not so grand;
I 'most could touch it with my hand!
And reaching up my hand to try,
I screamed, to feel it touch the sky.

I screamed, and—lo!—Infinity
Came down and settled over me;
Forced back my scream into my chest;
Bent back my arm upon my breast;
And, pressing of the Undefined
The definition on my mind,
Held up before my eyes a glass
Through which my shrinking sight did pass.
Until it seemed I must behold
Immensity made manifold;
Whispered to me a word whose sound
Deafened the air for worlds around,
And brought unmuffled to my ears
The gossiping of friendly spheres,

The creaking of the tented sky,
The ticking of Eternity.

I saw and heard, and knew at last
The How and Why of all things, past,
And present, and forevermore.
The Universe, cleft to the core,
Lay open to my probing sense,
That, sickening, I would fain pluck thence
But could not,—nay! but needs must suck
At the great wound, and could not pluck
My lips away till I had drawn
All venom out.—Ah, fearful pawn:
For my omniscience paid I toll
In infinite remorse of soul.

All sin was of my sinning, all
Atoning mine, and mine the gall
Of all regret. Mine was the weight
Of every brooded wrong, the hate
That stood behind each envious thrust,
Mine every greed, mine every lust.

And all the while, for every grief,
Each suffering, I craved relief
With individual desire;
Craved all in vain! And felt fierce fire
About a thousand people crawl;
Perished with each,—then mourned for all.

A man was starving in Capri;
He moved his eyes and looked at me;
I felt his gaze, I heard his moan,
And knew his hunger as my own.

I saw at sea a great fog bank
Between two ships that struck and sank;
A thousand screams the heavens smote;
And every scream tore through my throat.
No hurt I did not feel, no death
That was not mine; mine each last breath
That, crying, met an answering cry
From the compassion that was I.
All suffering mine, and mine its rod;
Mine, pity like the pity of God.

Ah, awful weight! Infinity
Pressed down upon the finite Me!

My anguished spirit, like a bird,
Beating against my lips I heard;
Yet lay the weight so close about
There was no room for it without.
And so beneath the weight lay I
And suffered death, but could not die.

Long had I lain thus, craving death,
When quietly the earth beneath
Gave way, and inch by inch, so great
At last had grown the crushing weight,
Into the earth I sank till I
Full six feet under ground did lie,
And sank no more,—there is no weight
Can follow here, however great.
From off my breast I felt it roll,
And as it went my tortured soul
Burst forth and fled in such a gust
That all about me swirled the dust.

Deep in the earth I rested now.
Cool is its hand upon the brow
And soft its breast beneath the head
Of one who is so gladly dead.
And all at once, and over all
The pitying rain began to fall;
I lay and heard each pattering hoof
Upon my lowly, thatchèd roof,
And seemed to love the sound far more
Than ever I had done before.
For rain it hath a friendly sound
To one who's six feet under ground;
And scarce the friendly voice or face,
A grave is such a quiet place.

The rain, I said, is kind to come
And speak to me in my new home.
I would I were alive again
To kiss the fingers of the rain,
To drink into my eyes the shine
Of every slanting silver line,
To catch the freshened, fragrant breeze
From drenched and dripping apple-trees.
For soon the shower will be done,
And then the broad face of the sun
Will laugh above the rain-soaked earth
Until the world with answering mirth

Shakes joyously, and each round drop
Rolls, twinkling, from its grass-blade top.

How can I bear it, buried here,
While overhead the sky grows clear
And blue again after the storm?
O, multi-coloured, multi-form,
Belovèd beauty over me,
That I shall never, never see
Again! Spring-silver, autumn-gold,
That I shall never more behold!—
Sleeping your myriad magics through,
Close-sepulchred away from you!
O God, I cried, give me new birth,
And put me back upon the earth!
Upset each cloud's gigantic gourd
And let the heavy rain, down-poured
In one big torrent, set me free,
Washing my grave away from me!

I ceased; and through the breathless hush
That answered me, the far-off rush
Of herald wings came whispering
Like music down the vibrant string
Of my ascending prayer, and—crash!
Before the wild wind's whistling lash
The startled storm-clouds reared on high
And plunged in terror down the sky!
And the big rain in one black wave
Fell from the sky and struck my grave.

I know not how such things can be;
I only know there came to me
A fragrance such as never clings
To aught save happy living things;
A sound as of some joyous elf
Singing sweet songs to please himself,
And, through and over everything,
A sense of glad awakening.
The grass a-tiptoe at my ear,
Whispering to me I could hear;
I felt the rain's cool finger-tips
Brushed tenderly across my lips,
Laid gently on my sealèd sight,
And all at once the heavy night
Fell from my eyes and I could see!—
A drenched and dripping apple-tree,

A last long line of silver rain,
A sky grown clear and blue again.
And as I looked a quickening gust
Of wind blew up to me and thrust
Into my face a miracle
Of orchard-breath, and with the smell,—
I know not how such things can be!—
I breathed my soul back into me.

Ah! Up then from the ground sprang I
And hailed the earth with such a cry
As is not heard save from a man
Who has been dead, and lives again.
About the trees my arms I wound;
Like one gone mad I hugged the ground;
I raised my quivering arms on high;
I laughed and laughed into the sky;
Till at my throat a strangling sob
Caught fiercely, and a great heart-throb
Sent instant tears into my eyes:
O God, I cried, no dark disguise
Can e'er hereafter hide from me
Thy radiant identity!

Thou canst not move across the grass
But my quick eyes will see Thee pass,
Nor speak, however silently,
But my hushed voice will answer Thee.
I know the path that tells Thy way
Through the cool eve of every day;
God, I can push the grass apart
And lay my finger on Thy heart!

The world stands out on either side
No wider than the heart is wide;
Above the world is stretched the sky,—
No higher than the soul is high.
The heart can push the sea and land
Farther away on either hand;
The soul can split the sky in two,
And let the face of God shine through.
But East and West will pinch the heart
That can not keep them pushed apart;
And he whose soul is flat—the sky
Will cave in on him by and by.

PART TWO

THE ESCAPE ARTIST

CHAPTER 9

She arrived in pigtails at seven in the morning of February 5, 1913, having forgotten her hair combs in the rush to leave Camden. "Fancy!" she wrote in her diary. "After all these years to strike New York in braids!" She wore a brown suit and hat, with shoes, ribbons, and bag to match. She looked, she hoped, elegant.

She looked, in fact, about twelve. Mary Alice Finney, an aide to Miss Dow who had come to meet her, never forgot Millay standing in the middle of Grand Central Terminal awestruck, like a little girl, and "wearing a broad-brimmed hat not at all in the fashion of the day, totally unaware of that fact." Finney whisked her off to Huyler's for an ice-cream soda before taking her to the National Training School for the YWCA on Lexington Avenue and Fifty-second Street, where she was promptly put to bed and told to rest. But how could she when from her eighth-floor window the entire island of Manhattan seemed to rise before her, sun-shot and shimmering? She wrote home at once that she could "see *everything*":

> . . . buildings everywhere, seven & eight stories to million and billion stories, washing drying on the roofs. . . . Children on roller skates playing tag on the sidewalk, smokestacks *and* smokestacks, and windows and windows, and signs way up high on the tops of factories and cars and taxi-cabs,—and *noise,* yes, in New York you can *see* the noise.

That first afternoon, she registered at Barnard College, where she was to prepare for Vassar because her high school courses had been woefully inadequate. She took two courses in English, one in French, and another in Latin. When asked on the application what her occupation had been since leaving high school, she wrote, "Typewriting."

Miss Dow had not been idle. There was more than $1,200 deposited in Millay's account at Barnard, and she had persuaded Dr. Talcott Williams, the director of the new School of Journalism at Columbia University, to write to the registrar at Barnard presenting Vincent Millay as a nonmatriculating student in his school, so that her entrance exams had been waived. "You see," Vincent wrote home later, "thanks to the pulls I had, I am a very, very irregular *Special.*" The week before her arrival, Williams had written to the dean of Barnard, Virginia Gildersleeve, "Let us by all means have Miss Millay here and handle her gently." Earlier he had written Miss Gildersleeve that not only had Miss Dow already raised $400 toward Millay's education, but "my experience has been that Miss Dow uniformly completes what she undertakes." There was no doubt at all that she had undertaken Vincent Millay.

Caroline B. Dow was stout, proper, and generous; unmarried and childless and now in her late forties, she respected order and believed in restraint and self-discipline. She cherished the arts and was deft at organizing people on behalf of the things she believed in, whether the YWCA, the Poetry Society of America, the MacDowell Club, or Vincent Millay. Having no use for disorder, extravagance, or wastefulness, she was a natural administrator.

From the beginning, Miss Dow suspected a certain instability or wildness in her young charge, which she felt was due to her environment as much as to her immaturity. It was, she said, "in a certain sense . . . an asset, but it must be offset by very careful plans as to her personal surroundings." In other words, Vincent Millay was to be cautiously nourished. Miss Dow felt that to have just missed *The Lyric Year*'s prize was good medicine for her character: "She will be distinctly more on her mettle to reconstruct and polish her work. . . . Successes are not always the best tonic for young authors or artists."

Within a week of Millay's arrival, Miss Dow was writing to the registrar at Barnard with a certain proprietariness:

> I appreciate keenly the kindliness which you have shown my little protegé; she needs guidance, and I am glad to have my responsibilities shared.
> I am so anxious that she should not be spoiled of which I think there is some danger.

Yet she had far more than she'd bargained for in Vincent Millay, who that same week was writing gleefully, "Well, here I am in New York! at last! I have heard a Philharmonic concert, I have ridden in the subway, I have bought a tie on Fifth Avenue. . . . I have been so very good that I haven't yet been sent home."

The only person Edna St. Vincent Millay was dependent on was Caroline Dow, and with Miss Dow she intended to be careful. "Miss Dow," Vincent wrote her mother, "is going to start right in getting me everything I need." She would provide for her charge, and she would orchestrate her introduction.

> Well, now I've come to yesterday. We bought everything at Lord & Taylor's, and this is what we bought. . . . a pair of black satin pumps with eleven story heels (New York slippers you see) and big rhinestone buckles; rubbers to fit (it was sort of wet and I would have to cross the pavement to the cab, and back later), white kid gloves, sixteen button length way up ones, and a scarf, a beautiful soft big white silk one with pale yellow roses in it— didn't I *drape* it tho!—as it wasn't an *awful* dress affair, we decided that Non's yellow would do if I wore the scarf all the time to cover where it's too big in back.

Then she listed and described in detail three tailored waists, two shirts, two collars, six plain linen handkerchiefs, "a perfectly heart-smashing loose coat of dark grey chinchilla with a rolling collar of a lighter plush," a hat of grey velour, "when I get them both on I look like pictures you see of Senator Thing-umbob's daughter"; a black leather handbag, and, for dress, two muslin waists with "Robespierre collars," more handkerchiefs, silver cuff links, "and a silk (or near silk) umbrella, with a little silver maple-leaf on the handle, warranted sterling."

No wonder her mother wrote right back, "O, it seems too wonderful to be true to have Miss Dow take such a dear interest in my girl. Still," she added cautiously, "I hope this out-put now cannot hurt the Vassar fund; but, of course she would not allow it to do that would she?"

Miss Dow understood clearly the importance of introducing Vincent to people who could help her. She was supposed to impress them, and she did. She wrote in her diary after one such event, "I think Miss Dow may have been pleased with what they may have said of me after we had talked a little while,—for, later, she let me have two cups of tea, Russian tea, lemon tea, Samovar tea." In her letter home she was even clearer:

> I met two of *the* Vassar people, a Mr. Babbott and his daughter, Miss Babbott. . . . They of course were not introduced as *the* Vassar people, but from

the way Miss Dow carried me off to meet them I knew they were important. I made a *decided* impression on them both, I flatter myself, but more especially on Mr. Babbott, who just simply fell in love with me. . . . I guess you needn't worry about the money giving out. And anyway Miss Dow knows what she's about.

Norma could hardly believe Vincent's luck:

Isn't it perfectly dear and just-what-I-hoped-for the way Miss Dow is taking you around with her. She is certainly wonderful alright. Perhaps she had some little pride, don't you know, when she was the one to present you to Monsieurs Class, Society, and Brains. . . . More Notes on the volume
Early Life in the City

Edna St. Vincent Millay.

Only Norma asked the one question that struck home: "Does Miss Dow like you for yourself yet? Better all the time?"

On the evening of February 11, Vincent was taken to the MacDowell Club by Miss Dow, who was its treasurer. "Only you, my family," she wrote conspiratorially, "must ever know the whole truth" of what had happened that night. She'd nearly fainted and had to be helped out. "Some people think today that it was the too-warm room, Miss Dow thinks it was the excitement of New York, the maid who spread me out on the window-ledge in the (I think) smoking-room, thought that perhaps my corsets were too tight,—but it was none of these causes." Her shoes pinched.

Don't try to imagine it, you never *could imagine* your slippers hurting you so that right in the middle of a speech all at once your head flopped right over and the sweat started out on your upper lip and the dear grey-haired lady in black who sat next you put her arm about you and led you out of the room.

After a swallow of whiskey to revive her, she lay on a sofa near the entrance to the room, where she could hear what was being said. "I sat on my right foot and stuck my left foot down on the floor where it would look cunning if anybody should happen in." Just then Miss Dow asked if she felt well enough to meet Edward Wheeler,

A tall, rather slim, dark man of about forty-five, with hair slightly greyed and perfectly beautiful eyes—one of the handsomest men I ever saw in my life, simply glorious in evening dress, came trotting up with Miss Dow. O, dear, he didn't trot! He—he appeared!

Miss Dow said, "Mr. Wheeler, Miss Millay." I didn't get up—I was an invalid, so I just *leaned* up and held out a long arm—*you* know the way, and he held out a lovely warm hand and looked down at me and said, "Is this Edna St. Vincent?" And I said, "It is. Is this Edward J.?" Of course that's what I said.

And after a minute or two of more-or-less talk, he said——and mother dear, don't let this make you regret anything, much—just be glad of the glad part—

"Miss Millay, my conscience has troubled me not a little since the *Lyric Year* came out. I fear that if the awarding was to be done again I should have to include *Renascence* among the first three. I'm afraid I wasn't in just the right mood the first time I read it,—or the second time. It grows on me. It's a wonderful thing."

Mother dear, I know just what you can't help thinking, and especially if you're not having nice things to eat—I *worry* awfully about you all sometimes—but you *do* want me to tell you just what Edward J. Wheeler said to me the first time I met him, don't you?

Then she wished them all good night, "Brer Bear, Brer Tenapin, ad Brer Fox,——Brer Rabbit sen his lub."

Cora felt only pleasure at Vincent's triumph, "only rejoiced that our own Edward J. at last sees the light. A little ready money would have vanished like dew; but this outcry for justice for Renascence is the dearest thing that could be and means much for your future. . . . Regret nothing dear." For, as they all knew, "Brer Rabbit always did get the best of it."

The day after Millay's arrival in the city, she had written to Louis Untermeyer, who had reviewed "Renascence" as a triumph, "Here I am! . . . If you sent me a note some morning, would I get it in the afternoon?" By return mail she heard not only from both Mr. and Mrs. Untermeyer but also from the poet Sara Teasdale, whom they had alerted of her arrival. "Whaddayouknowaboutthat!" Vincent wrote Arthur Ficke sassily. "The news of my arrival has *sprud clean* from here to East 29th Street! . . . I have been here since Wednesday and I am become a hardened citizen of a heartless metropolis."

Ficke answered her by return mail: "Loose in New York! How did your mother come to let you do it?" He said he could see her now, "your hair disheveled, your face slightly grimy, your eyes heavy, but your soul burning—as you recite over and over again your complete works," and then he asked her if she had a dollar to spare, not for himself but to subscribe to the *Chicago Evening Post's Literary Supplement.* He called it "the most brilliant literary sheet published in America," and Louis Untermeyer was its literary editor. In closing he warned her against the perils of becoming a bohemian.

When she replied, she assured him that she was "not so Bohemian by half as I was when I came. You see, here one has to be one thing or the other, whereas at home one could be a little of both." She was now

> prudent to the point of Jane Austen. I left all my bad habits at home,— bridge-pad, cigarette-case, and cocktail-shaker. I brought with me all my good habits,—diary, rubbers, and darning-cotton. . . . I run in my rut now like a well-directed wheel. Sometimes, it is true, I feel that I am exceeding the speed-limit. But I seldom skid, and when I do there is very little splash.

Sara Teasdale invited her for tea, asking that Vincent meet her at the Martha Washington, a hotel for women, where she stayed when visiting from her home in St. Louis. "And in order that I may know you in all the crowd of women in this unlovely place, sit as near as possible to the desk. . . . As for me, I wear glasses and have red brown hair."

Teasdale, eight years older than Millay, was tall, slender, and pale—even her eyelashes were colorless and gray was her favorite color—and suffered from ill health. But if she lacked what Jean Starr Untermeyer would, in her autobiography, later call Vincent's "bewitchment," she was a woman quick and generous in her enthusiasms. She had also written "I shall not care," one of Vincent's favorite poems in *The Lyric Year,* and Vincent was eager to meet her.

They took to each other from the first, and after tea they rode up and down Fifth Avenue on the top of a bus. Sara then gave Vincent a copy of her new book of poems, *Helen of Troy,* and they had dinner together and "talked & talked."

They met several times that spring, and each time they shared their work with each other. By April, Vincent told her mother, "I call her 'Sara' and she me 'Vincent.' . . . I love her. . . . *Here's one of Sara's little things.*

> I hoped that he would love me,
> And he has kissed my mouth,
> But I am like a stricken bird
> That cannot reach the south.
> For tho' I know he loves me,
> Tonight my heart is sad;
> His kiss was not so wonderful
> As all the dreams I had.

Isn't that perfect? . . . All her little songs are like that. You think they're going to be like something else you've read, but they never are.

Millay took tea with the Untermeyers in the library of their large, elegant apartment on upper Broadway. It was a spacious square room with sturdy, highly polished mission oak tables, the latest magazines displayed on top, and books neatly ordered behind glass bookcases. Vincent seated herself beneath a large table lamp. "The light made a nimbus around the little head with its loosely coiled mass of red-gold hair," Mrs. Untermeyer observed. "We—or to be precise—they, she and Louis, talked eagerly."

When they asked her to read, her voice held them spellbound. "I was terribly moved, almost in tears," Jean Starr Untermeyer remembered; she had to excuse herself from the room. When Vincent left with Louis to be taken home, Jean felt that "some deep chord had been struck and vibrated still to the sheer enchantment of the verse I had been hearing." She found herself at her desk, writing her first poem, which she called "Deliverance." She said it had been "husbanded" by Edna Millay. It was not the first time the striking intensity of Millay's voice or the force of her poetry had been felt, nor was it the last time she would make a woman feel both attracted and indebted to her.

Louis Untermeyer remembered Millay that first evening as "absolutely artless. She was not going to show off before me. She didn't fawn, she wasn't servile. I asked her to read and she did. Again, artlessly. I remember her reading, reciting, 'God's World' and 'Renascence.' She recited beautifully. With nothing forced; she simply gladly read."

His vision of her haunted him—her tawny, russet, sorrel-colored hair. "I had no sense of the fame she was going to achieve. I thought she was a poet for the elect. There was no other voice like hers in America. It was the sound of the ax on fresh wood."

Vincent told her family that the Untermeyers had a "lovely home,— three or four maids, I guess, perhaps not more than two." She also noted that she didn't much like "those black velvet suits that button up the front and are always partly unbuttoned" that Mrs. Untermeyer wore. By April, she was sure enough of her relationship with Untermeyer, or maybe just plain sure of herself, to write of an essay he had given her, "Has it ever occurred to you that besides writing fairly credible verse you write rather good prose?"

Feb. 21.
    Shall be grown-up tomorrow,—oh, dear! I *loved* being twenty! Good bye to this beautiful year. I somehow feel that twenty-one will be different.

Miss Dow left for a holiday at Atlantic City, and Vincent, broke and afraid to ask for money in her absence, passed her birthday at the Y dressed as Martha Washington.

Two days earlier, Miss Dow had arranged for her to attend *Madama Butterfly*, her first grand opera. "Wish I could hear it again tomorrow night & the next night," she wrote afterward, the last time, in her "Sweet & Twenty" book. "Memo. I did not weep. The lady who accompanied me and whom Miss Dow warned that I *might* weep, *did* weep! Well, well! I never cry at the theatre. It seems to me that I feel things far too deeply, too deep down in my heart, to—to splash on top!"

The next night, she went to the dining room wearing her hair down in a long curl. "I *won't* be grown-up even if I am twenty-one," she wrote in her diary. "I *love* my little black satin slippers with the rhine-stone buckles. Wonder if Witter Bynner will be at the Poetry Society meeting Tuesday night."

She was not wondering if Ferdinand Earle would be there; she knew he would be. Millay had not given him her address in New York, but his letters were forwarded to her from Camden, and she knew he was living in New York with his mother. As early as December he had written her, "Such a heap o' trouble. . . . Someday you may know. But not now. Please tell nobody—I'm losing my beautiful home." He told her nothing more, but his hints were pretty heavy, and by now she had good reason to be wary of him.

She met him for the first and only time in her life on the afternoon of February 25 at the Poetry Society, and although she recorded in her diary that she met "Miss Rittenhouse, Miss Anna Branch, Mrs. Edwin Markham, and some others," there was not a word about Earle.

He wrote her that night at eleven o'clock:

I felt that it was hateful!—I could not exchange a few sober words with you. Did they fear I might eat you? You are truly charming and lovely enough to eat—slowly and cautiously, lest one atom escape.

Hip, hurrah, I'm off. And so you are safe. . . . What dull and soggy folk *"poets"* are! They need ginger and dynamite. . . . I wanted awfully to say goodbye, but felt I had already damaged your reputation quite enough.
Your Editor.

She said nothing to anyone about meeting him, until her mother wrote across the face of a letter to her,

What about Mr. Earle!
What about Mr. Earle!
What about Mr. Earle!

Then Vincent explained their meeting clearly:

Mr. Earle I saw and talked with only once and then only for a few minutes, at the February meeting of the P.S. of A. He sailed for Europe a day or two later. For reasons which I am sure you can understand I preferred to meet him for the first time at the Society meeting. I preferred saying "I am *very* glad to meet you, Mr. Earle" to saying "O, *we* know one another!" That is why I let him keep writing to Camden instead of giving him my address here. But in the last letter he sent me before the meeting he told me how anxious he had been to see me, so I sent him a note telling him I would be at the P.S. of A. meeting. He doesn't know now where I am in New York. . . . Don't you think I managed that rather skilfully?

I am getting a great deal more sense than I ever had before. A year ago I would have called him up in some desperately lonely fit while Miss Dow was away and had him come down. Which wouldn't have been so very dreadful, but which isn't the way I'm running things now.

Mama, *pat* me!

"Witter Bynner is tall and rather thin and dark with lovely eyes and a comical whimsical mouth and a nice voice, and—whisper! a wee bit o' a bald spot!" she wrote in her letter home. She met him at a Poetry Society luncheon and then at a party given for her by Jessie Rittenhouse. "Sunday—*My* party at Miss Rittenhouse's"; "just a small party," she wrote, and listed fourteen people.

Yes, I have seen and talked with Witter Bynner. He has said to me "Do you mind if I smoke?" and I have said to him, "Not in the least." He has proffered me his cigarette case and I have said, "No, thank you." He has raised his eyebrows and said, "O, you don't smoke?" And I have replied, "Not here, certainly."

The day after her party, sitting in the library at Barnard, she wrote two poems, "If I should die tomorrow," which, she noted in her diary, "is not as bad as it sounds" and "I'll keep a little tavern below the high hill's crest, Wherein all gray-eyed people may sit them down and rest." She sent only the first one home with a note to her mother that she was not to "take it too seriously."

> If I should die tomorrow
>   Perhaps I should not care
> Whether today had brought me beads
>   Or bells or a kiss to share.
> It may be that the twilight
>   Has never a tale to tell,

And I shall love the silence
That have loved song so well.
Yet, since I may remember,
—And how could I forget!—
This day will I keep watch for Love
Until the moon has set.

Do you like?
Are there parts you don't like? Do you know what I mean by "beads,"
and "bells?"

Here's another.

I brought my little song
And laid it on his knee;
He smiled and shook his head,—
"What has this to do with me?"

I took my little song
And laid it on my breast;
It stirred and 'gan to cry,
But I hushed it back to rest.

Do you see anything in that?

She wanted her mother to like her poems, but even more than that, she
wanted them to be clear, not puzzling or obscure.

There wasn't much time for her own work; there were themes to be
written, translations of Horace's Odes to be worked out, and what she
called "a merciless amount of Milton & Marvel"; her diary entries on
March 20 were typical:

Did a lot of easy mending & read about 120 pages of *Paradise Lost*. . . . Wrote
Dean of Vassar. Letters from home; wrote Norma. . . . Conference here
today. A great many conventional people. (Don't anybody laugh) Finished
reading *Paradise Lost*. Somehow *Paradise Lost* at three gulps makes one long
to spring hysterical puns. I say "one." The one is I.

Overloaded with schoolwork, she sometimes cut classes, stayed in her
room, and slept.

If, within the family, Norma was the most likely to tease her, to use baby
talk to express her love for her, she was also capable of striking back if she
felt Vincent was getting too high-handed. As she did when she got Vincent's postcard about a certain tan dress. Considering the ample lists of
clothing Vincent had been writing home about, it seemed to Norma "Sort
of funny" that she should demand it back, "but guess if you need it you

can have it." The dress was being made over for Norma now because Cora had thought "that you were perfectly well provided for and I really needed it. What have you done with the $10 your dad sent for your birthday? Not all squandered I hope. Think you might have bought some little dress with it. Why didn't or don't you? Things are supposed to be cheaper in New York than here." Then, too, Norma was "Sick of staying in Camden Burg *all* the time meself. Bah. (graceful gesture here.) . . . Do you ever feel like you wanted to see Muvver, Wump & Hunkus? Don't believe you have half time enough to get lonesome do you? Gorry I do & don't care one dam who knows it."

At exactly the same time, Vincent was writing to her, "I am *dying* to come home for Easter. . . . This is the first time I've been the least bit homesick, except for scattering minutes, and I'm *dying* to come home. For one thing, I haven't heard a word from you for a solid week (minus a few hours) and I think you might write." For another thing, she'd had a quiz in French and her professor hadn't asked anything she knew. "Why don't you write, old top? You don't like me any more now you've got Wump to live wid, do youse?" Their letters must have crossed.

"I wish I hadn't said a word about coming home," Vincent wrote in her next letter home. "I didn't know you'd think I really could. I wouldn't ask to for anything. It isn't as if the Vanderbilts were sending me to college, you know. There's quite a lot of money, but it's not unlimited. My opera *cloke* isn't new. It was somebody else's I don't know and was fixed over for me. But it is lovely, just the same." Then she told her sister exactly which dresses she had, which had been fixed over, and which had fallen apart. "Kathleen's pink I'm going to send back to her. It is really too babyish & too short for me. . . . The tan dress, tho, dear, I really don't need at all. I was piggish about that. I didn't think."

When she signed her letter "Love," Norma came around in a rush:

Po' ole Sephus—
    Hunk didn't mean to 'buse him. Please make up—Squeeze & make up? Yes?

At the same time as she was telling Norma about her scrupulous economy, she was writing in her diary that she'd gone to look at dresses with one of her chaperones:

Everything that is pretty is too expensive. I am *cursed,* and I know it, with a love for beautiful things. I can't *bear* anything that looks cheap or feels cheap or is over-trimmed or coarse. I hate myself all the time because I'm all the time wearing things I don't like. It's wicked & it's ungrateful, but I can't help it. I wish I had *one* <u>graceful</u> *dress.*

And then she did: "I've got it. O, my heart! The *sweetest* thing. Makes you think of summer & iced tea on the lawn & men & girls & once in a while a breeze. I am—I am languorous in it."

On the morning of April 8, Millay received a check from Mitchell Kennerley for two of her poems, "Journey" and "God's World," which he had taken for *The Forum.* "$25.00!!! O, girls!!!!!" she crowed, "O,—Glory!" It was the first money she'd earned from her writing since *St. Nicholas,* and she sent the money home.

She'd initially sent the poems to William Rose Benét at *The Century,* who had returned them, telling her that although he hated to lose them, "there were several obscurities in them" that she'd have to clear away. Writing home that "some of the obscurities happened to be the best things in them, I sent them off just as they were to the *Forum,* so the *Century* has lost them for good." The victory was delicious. She asked her mother:

> Promise me, please, that with some of this you'll do something to make something easier for yourself. Shoes, dear,—or have your glasses fixed if they're not just right. Please, please, do something like that. And I'd like it so much if each one of you would get some little tiny silly thing that she could always keep. But that's just a whim; the other isn't.

Cora wrote back that she'd use that "dear money" to pay off old bills, but the last dollar was hers. "I want to be a pig; I want the 'Lyric Year' for my own out of it."

But the academic load at Barnard made Millay edgy about finding any time to do her own writing. What was it going to be like at Vassar for four years if this one term was any example? "Here register I my first doubt." By the end of the month she was even more despondent: "I am going crazy with the poems that I simply can't get time to write. It isn't a joke. I can't study now, I'm too old; I ought to be through college at my age, and I know it, and I have other things to think about, and *I can't study.*"

Yet that spring, when Mitchell Kennerley offered to bring out a volume of her poems, she balked. To her family she wrote that she didn't think it "a very wise thing." In her diary, she said plainly, "I don't think it feasible." It was one of the canniest decisions she could have made. Other than "Renascence" and two or three lyrics, she didn't have a strong selection of poems on hand, and she knew it.

Both "Journey" and "God's World" were begun in Camden, and "Journey"—at least in the pencil draft that exists—lacked the final six lines that made it her own. Midpoem the voice changes abruptly; she returns to the natural beauty of the Maine landscape to draw sustenance from it. If the poem had stopped short there, it would have lacked the conviction she brought to her published version: that only through the senses could she transform and take possession of a world rightly hers.

> Ah, could I lay me down in this long grass
> And close my eyes, and let the quiet wind
> Blow over me—I am so tired, so tired
> Of passing pleasant places! All my life,
> Following Care along the dusty road,
> Have I looked back at loveliness and sighed;
> Yet at my hand an unrelenting hand
> Tugged ever, and I passed. All my life long
> Over my shoulder have I looked at peace;
> And now I fain would lie in this long grass
> And close my eyes.
>
>   Yet onward!
>   Cat-birds call
> Through the long afternoon, and creeks at dusk
> Are guttural. Whip-poor-wills wake and cry,
> Drawing the twilight close about their throats.
> Only my heart makes answer. Eager vines
> Go up the rocks and wait; flushed apple-trees
> Pause in their dance and break the ring for me;
> Dim, shady wood-roads, redolent of fern
> And bayberry, that through sweet bevies thread
> Of round-faced roses, pink and petulant,
> Look back and beckon ere they disappear.
> Only my heart, only my heart responds.
>
> Yet, ah, my path is sweet on either side
> All through the dragging day,—sharp underfoot
> And hot, and like dead mist the dry dust hangs—
> But far, oh, far as passionate eye can reach,
> And long, ah, long as rapturous eye can cling,
> The world is mine: blue hill, still silver lake,
> Broad field, bright flower, and the long white road;
> A gateless garden, and an open path;
> My feet to follow, and my heart to hold.

When "Journey" appeared in the May issue of *The Forum,* she heard nothing from home about it. She wrote plaintively:

It isn't anything great, I know. But Miss Rittenhouse says it is nothing I need be ashamed of even tho it does come after *Renascence,* that some of it is wonderful and a lot of it is lovely and it's all good. So there now. . . . I'm joking. I know you read my poem before I came out here. But you might have said something. Bincent is "coldin'."

That prompted a quick response from her mother; of course she liked it, it was "beautifully written, but at first it hurt me as it seemed to me that it told of how very much you had always been deprived."

She received the proofs of "God's World" on the heels of the publication of "Journey," and she was glad Kennerley was rushing them right along "because this is the better poem," she wrote her mother. "This poem, the one with the 'burning leaf' in it, you know, looks lovely in print."

> O world, I cannot hold thee close enough!
>   Thy winds, thy wide grey skies!
>   Thy mists, that roll and rise!
> Thy woods, this autumn day, that ache and sag
> And all but cry with colour! That gaunt crag
> To crush! To lift the lean of that black bluff
> World, World, I cannot get thee close enough!
>
> Long have I known a glory in it all,
>   But never knew I this:
>   Here such a passion is
> As stretcheth me apart,—Lord, I do fear
> Thou'st made the world too beautiful this year;
> My soul is all but out of me,—let fall
> No burning leaf; prithee, let no bird call.

2

William Tenney Brewster's composition classes were a legend at Barnard, where he was professor of English and provost of the college. Tall and lean, he would sit with his feet coiled about the wastepaper basket, his fingers toying with a rubber band as he read his students' papers in a flat, dry voice. His comments about Millay's work, which were written in a cramped hand on the back page of her themes, were guarded and almost always on mark. He'd given "Laddie," about the death of the family dog, a B and said it verged on sentimentality. When she trotted out one of her old *St. Nicholas* poems, "Friends," he wrote "Browningesque" and gave her a B. And in one of her less inspired themes, when she wrote, "Why *should* it be imperative for me to write a theme? System is a fine thing. . . . But even if I were a literary genius (which Heaven forbid) *would* I be able to—er— give, as it were, whenever System might choose to wiggle her finger at me? Decidedly not," he marked "coy" and added to his B, "Pretty good for the sort; but capable of improvement." But he continued to encourage her, and when he admired her short-story writing, she was "elated."

> Yesterday I got an A on an English theme . . . [he] says there's no reason why I can't make a living writing short stories, if I keep at it.—I have imagination, humor & a *wonderful* command of language (which he doesn't see where I ever *got,* if you please. . . .)

She was thus all the more disappointed on May 13 to get a B for a long story called "Arline," which she had written immediately after he had praised her so highly. Strangely, he made no critical remarks on her paper at all. The story was laden with autobiographical detail, direct and without the coyness or sentimentality he sometimes found in her work.

It opens with a young girl falling asleep in her room when she overhears the voices of her mother and a male friend talking about her. Her mother calls out, asking if she's asleep; she's not, and the man enters her room to give her a good-night kiss. It's clear that she does not like him, but she lies on her back obediently, pursing

> her soft child-mouth into the pout which had always seemed to bring satisfactory results. She did not wish this man to speak of her afterwards as a little girl who did not know how to be kissed.
> A groping hand fell on the pillow, then on her hair, but Arline did not move. The bed creaked as the man sat down, and the clothes, dragged down by his weight, tightened across her body. Still she did not stir. Hot lips touched her cheek, the corner of her mouth, then—

In fury, Arline forces his face from hers. She screams for him to get out of her room, slaps him twice, and, slamming the door behind him, locks it. Then she hears her mother talking to him. " 'You know Arline *isn't* just your style,' she heard her say in a soft, ironical drawl."

After he leaves the house, her mother tries her door and, finding it locked, calls to her to open it. Arline refuses. Her mother says she's sorry. She warns her mother, "If you ever let another man into my bed-room I'll kill him. And after this anybody who wants to get in will have to knock. You too."

The second chapter begins with the arrival of Arline's father, Jim, whom she adores. He calls her "Nuisance," and she tells him she loves him, but she will not kiss him.

> In fact, she never kissed anybody. Sometimes, rather than hurt or embarrass a visitor whose osculatory intent was unmistakable, she would lift her

face and submit passively. But this had never been and would never be her form of greeting.

Her mother calls her cold-blooded because of her reserve, but she isn't. "Her seeming coldness was always either one or the other of two things,—intense repression, or passionate reserve. Never, in anything, for one instant, would she be indifferent."

The father in the story has been away for some time, and Arline wants him to tell her what he's been doing.

To her mind he was composite of all manly virtues and graces. Because he was a little inclined to be stout and had light hair, she disliked thin, dark men. His broad, good-natured laugh prejudiced her invariably against a man who cackled. And because he was "in the insurance business" the insurance business was the only business in which to be. He was a good-looking man, with a boyish fairness of skin and clearness of brow which gave him the appearance of being younger than his wife, though he was in reality a little older. . . . Also, he was possessed of an unusually keen brain and a disinclination to exert himself. Men who knew him well spoke of him as "a man who might be most anywhere if only he were not so damned lazy."

It is hard to imagine a clearer assessment, or a more affectionate description, of Henry Millay. Later, Arline would grow "to deplore" her father's lack of energy, but she never ceased to adore him. Whereas the mother, who compromises her daughter, is judged far more sharply:

Her mother was not lazy. She was indeed, in her own way, exceedingly energetic. True, she never rose before ten, often not before noon, and always had her first cup of coffee in bed, prepared and served by Arline, who was always up by seven, and whose coffee was excellent.

This was a story Vincent never sent home. But what was really going on here? Did any of this actually happen to Edna Millay when she was a girl?

꘠ ꘠ ꘠

Gingerly, I mentioned the story to Norma Millay. Had she read it?

"Mother should have been more careful."

"Is it true, then?"

"Oh, my dear, it's one of Vincent's stories."

"But you just said—"

"What I said and what I know are two very different things. I read the story up there in the study just as you did."

"It would make a world of difference if she—"

"If she what? Vincent was a little prig, you've seen that by now."

"This isn't about being a little prig."

"No, it most certainly is not."

There was a long pause. Norma asked me to put another log on the fire.

"Of course Mother must have had visitors, she was still a young woman." The wood caught fire. "I don't know. How would I know?"

"You were there."

"I wasn't there all the time."

∽ ∽ ∽

That spring, Vincent received her first invitation to visit Mitchell Kennerley in Mamaroneck. ("They are in the *country!*—I can eat grass!") Mrs. Kennerley formally invited her to spend Sunday, May 18, with them,

> and guess who are going to be there, she thinks,—Witter Bynner & Bliss Carman!—. . . . I wish I had something ravishing to wear, something heart-smashing, you know. . . . But there! I wrote a poem once. Which is why they're inviting me. How stupid I am!
>
> Love,—Vincent.

Although she rode with Witter Bynner on the train to Mamaroneck, not a word about him surfaced in her diary. "Met another man, Mrs. Kennerley's cousin, I think," she wrote. "Stayed all night. Mrs. K. brought me in the machine this morning & called for me this afternoon to take me out again. . . . Saw the other man again."

She returned to New York just long enough to take exams in English, French, and Latin, and the following weekend she returned to Mamaroneck. At one on Sunday morning, after dancing all night at the Kennerleys' country club, she wrote in her diary, "I have not yet begun to regret this day & night, but I shall be sick about it in the morning. I have been intemperate in three ways, I have failed to keep, or rather to fulfil an obligation, and I have deliberately broken my word of honor." She didn't say what the third intemperance was.

She returned to the city for a day, but when Mrs. Kennerley called and asked her to come back to Mamaroneck, she went back to the country. "She really did insist. And I came. Fool! *Fool! Fool!*" This time she stayed for nine days.

The "other man" was Arthur Hooley. Elegant, dark, and slender, he was seventeen years older than Vincent; he was English, and he was married. He was also the editor of *The Forum,* for which he wrote under the pseudonym of Charles Vale. When they met, she realized it was he who had published "Journey" and had taken "God's World." And the previous January, reviewing *The Lyric Year,* he had quoted almost all of "Renascence," calling it "a remarkable production for a girl of twenty,—remarkable for its freshness, its spirituality, its renunciation of artifice, and its unmistakable power."

Soon she was calling him "My Englishman" in her letters home.

> He's the dearest thing. But I'm not in love with him. He says the cutest things sometimes. This morning he was late to breakfast & I stayed with him while he finished. He sits almost across from me. And all at once he began to look around for something & I said, very seriously, "Is there anything up at this end you want?"—And he answered, very gravely, "Nothing I can have."

Then she did not write home or make an entry in her diary for three weeks. When she returned to it, it was full of him: "Borrowed a black silk bathing suit which made me glad I'm red-headed. Stretched out on the beach and talked to Him."

They had quarreled, but "We are made up. He says I have been damned nasty. I suppose I have. I *hope* I have." Now it was even more delicious to be together. "Tonight was lovely. I wore my white dreamy dress and walked under the trees with Him."

This was not what Miss Dow had in mind for Vincent Millay, and on June 1 she called Mamaroneck to tell her so. "She's heard some new cussedness about me and is about heart-broken. Damn 'em, I wish they'd keep their mouths shut."

Still Vincent didn't rush back to New York. She stayed another three days. "Didn't rest much last night. Came down to breakfast looking like a ghost. Felt like dying and couldn't do anything. He came over this afternoon. He felt like dying and couldn't do anything. So we went off into the woods together."

On June 4, she "Left Mamaroneck forever. . . . He stayed until I started. O, well!"

But it was not the end of her relationship with Arthur Hooley. *The Forum* would publish all of her poetry for the next three years, from May 1913 until May 1916—other magazines would sometimes reprint her poems, but *The Forum* would always be first.

Finally she wrote home, in a letter full of baby talk and marked by the male pronoun.

Dearest old neglected Muvver & Wump,—

Bincent he's going to be good again once more like he used to be. . . . But I've been having such a good time that I've just been selfish. Besides I've been in love. . . . His name is Arthur Hooley and he's the *Forum*'s "power behind." So help me I *was* in love with him, for a week, and I've written some lovely poems which the *Forum* will never see. It's all off and all over, since I left him wringing his hands in the station yesterday, but it was all the more acute for not being chronic (forgive it). Mother, all the people in Mamaroneck, *he* especially, think I have a beautiful voice, just talking, you know, wonder and ask if I haven't studied voice culture, think that my voice would have been lovely on the stage,—it's so low and yet so clear and carries so easily. . . . [H]e says . . . I'm like the English girls in a lot of ways,—my *beautiful* voice, you see, American girls don't have 'em.

Isn't that fun? But its all over, don't worry.

Cora was glad to learn that "the affair with His Majesty's subject flunked in the pram. We must keep you American, in America, even if we permit and admit the English voice is faultless."

On the twenty-third of June, Vincent at last returned to Camden. She still had entrance requirements to prepare for Vassar in the fall, but she couldn't resist playing. She and Kathleen spent an entire day on the Perrys' yawl, *The Comfort,* bound for Great Spruce Head Island. There were thirty-one in the party, and they built huge fires of driftwood along the beach to make coffee and bacon sizzle, and sang until the moon was high.

George Perry, whose father's boat it was, remembered Vincent that summer reciting "God's World" in their living room before the fireplace: "She had just come up from swimming on my cousin's shore and had her hair in two pigtails down her back. It gave her a childish look, an elfin look. We'd been in grammar school together, you see, and although my aunt said there was a lot of talent in that room, I wasn't smart enough to think it. She was just Vincent Millay wearing red pigtails and reciting her verses."

On another afternoon at the Perrys', Vincent turned to Norma at one point when the others had left and said quietly, "Sister, don't smile so much." It was her first sharp reminder that she was moving into another world from the one they had shared as children.

By the end of June, it was clear that as a nonmatriculating student at Barnard who had not passed her entrance examinations, Vincent couldn't count her courses toward a Barnard degree, and she couldn't offer them for credit to Vassar, either. Once Barnard had made that plain, Ella McCaleb, dean of Vassar, wrote back immediately:

> Thank you for the statement about Miss Millay's work. She seems to be a problem to her friends, some of whom are very anxious that she should have a regular college course in a country college before she takes up the definite work in the School of Journalism. She is surely an interesting and promising young woman, but just what she should do next year is truly an open question and one upon which I am seeking light.

When Miss McCaleb wrote to Vincent in mid-July, she said she had a larger problem in her entrance work than most of the other girls. She had to work up Latin prose composition, mathematics, the equivalent of a third language, and some ancient history. She couldn't possibly do it all in one summer. She suggested that Vincent focus on American history and mathematics or Latin. Vincent must have written back to her in desperation or panic, for a month later Miss McCaleb replied:

> Did I fail to make clear the situation about your election of courses? I gave you a choice between Latin and mathematics for the coming year because I thought you could get ready for only one. . . . You see it is not because of any hatred of you that this summer work is demanded but because every Vassar girl has to take certain subjects in her first year, and there is no justice or pleasure in admitting a girl if she is not ready to go on with the required work. . . . If you are really so desperate and ill-prepared as your letter suggests, then perhaps you have no right to try for Vassar this year— the disappointment of those who are interested in you would be nothing compared with the possibility of your attempting too much. No one wishes you to endanger either your health or your best development, but this is only a college, with pretty much the same regulations for every body, and not a great university with all sorts of *different* chances for different people.

Nevertheless, she was anxious to have Millay come to Vassar and closed by asking, "What can I do to help?"

But "only a college" was hardly the way Vincent Millay considered Vassar. A lifeline would have been more accurate. Whatever she may have felt in response to Miss McCaleb's letter, she wrote nothing in her diary. But in the course of their correspondence, she won a crucial ally in Ella McCaleb. By September 4, when Miss McCaleb wrote to her again, Vincent had become "My dear child." Two weeks later, Vincent was dining in Main Hall at Vassar College, a member of the freshman class of 1917.

CHAPTER 10

In some ways I'm sorry you are going to Vassar. But I guess you've too much sense and humor to be much hurt, and it is a fine opportunity to learn a lot of things that I daresay are of value. I am so ill-educated myself that colleges are always a bit of an affront to my self-esteem.

—Sara Teasdale to Edna Millay, September 2, 1913

She lived off campus in a rooming house called Mrs. McGlynn's Cottage. The first thing she did was to take entrance examinations in algebra, geometry, and history. She wrote home immediately afterward:

It's all right. I belong here and I'm going to stay. I'm sending Kathleen the geometry examination. Perhaps she can pass it. I couldn't. But Miss McCaleb says it doesn't matter. I'm admitted *anyway,* if I flunk 'em all. . . . So you can send my snowshoes.

At last she met Miss McCaleb. After the exams, all of the girls were to tell her how they thought they'd done.

I waited in line till my turn came and then I went in, and she looked at me a minute and then sort of smiled and said, "Well, my dear, what did you do?" And I answered, very solemnly, "Miss McCaleb, I did my darndest." . . . She's a darling, and I love her.

She had won Miss McCaleb to her just as surely as she had Miss Dow. But when classes began on September 22, Vincent learned that although she had passed geometry, "I flunked—*just* flunked" both algebra and history. She'd been certain she had passed history, "but Miss Thompson was funny & didn't like the way I did it. She told me so. We stood on the campus an hour day before yesterday, swapping insults. We are born enemies."

Her history exam now lies in the vaults of Vassar's rare books library, where C. Mildred Thompson gave it a 1–, with the following comments: "No understanding of history, grand epithets." Millay had begun by writing "I was prepared in American History at my home in Camden, Maine, in the hammock, on the roof, and behind the stove." That was not guaranteed to win a serious young instructor of history to her side. Her examination paper was six pages long, marked by cheek and ignorance. At its close she added this note:

At precisely that point the pleasant lady in an Alice-blue coat, who I wish might be my instructor in History, requests us all to bring our papers to a close. As I know a great deal about American History which I haven't had a chance to say, I am sorry, but obedient.

There was every reason to doubt her. Thirty-eight years later, C. Mildred Thompson, who had saved the examination and was then the dean of Vassar College, explained why she "reckoned it as a Failure. The answers were 'at large,' . . . and did not bear any particular relation to the questions asked." That attitude, with its saucy insolence, was signal of the success and failure that would mark Vincent Millay's entire career—with both faculty and students—at Vassar.

Among the first girls Vincent met was Agnes Rogers, "my sopho-more . . . the most wonderful Sophomore there is, they say," she wrote home. In August, Agnes had written to welcome a number of freshmen to Vassar in the fall, wondering "what sort of girl each one is from her name"; but in Vincent's case, not wondering at all.

I am writing to you with real pleasure having just read your "Renascence" in "The Lyric Year." It is yours isn't it? . . . How very proud Vassar and 1917 will be, and how you will be pounced upon by "Miscellany" people— the "Miscellany" is the college Magazine you know.

When they met at McGlynn's, Agnes remembered, "She was one of the celebrities. And, well, I think she liked it. She had done something. She was special. She wasn't really pretty, she had pale red hair—but there was a quality—she was luminous, as if there were a light behind her. That must sound corny. But she was magical and luminous. I felt it. Everyone did."

When the English department arranged for her to take a sophomore course in Old English with the distinguished scholar Christabel Fiske, Fiske started right off by lending Vincent the edition of *Morte d'Arthur* she had edited. Her German teacher, Florence Jenney, never forgot the first moment she saw her that fall: "Running footsteps overtook mine on the path between Rockefeller Hall and the Quadrangle, and a slight figure paused beside me. I had noticed especially that pale, eager face and gold reddish hair in a large section of Beginning German, and remembered that she signed her papers 'Vincent Millay.' 'I just wanted to say something to you,' a rich, vibrant voice began. 'I am going to love German. I know my work has not been very good yet, but it is going to be. By Christmas I shall be the best in the class.'

"She was, easily. And by Thanksgiving, not Christmas."

But Miss Jenney also noticed that Millay had what she called "a star-tling . . . instinct for self-protection." To survive at Vassar, she would have to do well. It wasn't only that she was twenty-one years old among girls four years her junior or that she had more academic conditions to work off than anyone else. While she was rich in talent, nerve, and ambition, they were rich in everything else. That mixture of self-assertion and her need for acceptance was apparent from her first letters home.

> All the girls here at McGlynn's, about 30, like me, I know. . . . they all want blankets like mine, and—and, fo' de Lawd's sake listen——they *make fun of me because I have so many clothes*!!!!
> Shan't you die.

What mattered was not just that she belonged at Vassar—despite flunk-ing two exams—but that she was not being outclassed. Even her voice was shaped to distinguish her, for while she was one of only two New Englanders at McGlynn's, Vincent said, "She talks just like everybody in Camden, you know. *And I don't.*" It wasn't the first time an ambitious, poor girl was careful that her accent not betray her.

One of her classmates, Lydia Babbott, whose mother had been Miss Dow's roommate at Vassar, remembered quite clearly that Miss Dow had asked her father to help the young poet go to college: " 'Frank, you've got to send her. She is superb and Vassar will be proud.' Well, my father lis-tened, and she entered college when I did." Lydia Babbott remembered, too, that her father spoke to Charles Pratt, "but I've no idea if Uncle Char-lie paid any of her board and tuition. It was only five hundred dollars then." That $500 would have broken the Millays.

In a fundamental sense Millay was in disguise. The strain was apparent in her correspondence home. Lunching at the president's house on one of Miss Dow's early visits, Vincent again stressed, "Miss Dow doesn't give anything away.

> Miss McCaleb knows. . . . but you're glad of that, aren't you. I am. She kissed me Hello right before 'em all, to show 'em she loved me, and then she kissed me good-bye just only before me, to show *me* she loved me. She's a perfect darling. But my mother needn't be jealous.

When Norma asked if she was writing, she told her she had very little time, "but the fear is quite gone that college will spoil me for the desire to write. You see I am really too old to change very much in essentials." Mostly she was too tired to write, and she admitted their letters to her were "about all that keep me here. You see I miss you all as much as you miss me, and while you have some of us, so to speak, I haven't any of us. . . . Perhaps I oughtn't to admit that everything isn't just perfect,—but you're my family, and I don't know who else I'd say it to, or could."

The previous spring at Barnard, she'd been so uncomfortable at a luncheon, "let in by a butler & ushered & announced!," that she could barely touch her food:

> I was so nervous that I couldn't hold anything in my fork, but I could manage a knife real skilful so I buttered my muffin & ate that . . . and so help me that's all I could get, but I strategized & "toyed with my food," and anyway its classy not to eat any-thing.

She depended on her voice to cover her uncertainty. She called it "wonderful voice control," and she spoke, she said, "in a soft, slow way that was not the least bit hysterical." But the strain of constant performance sometimes made her ill. When she got home, she was "weak as a kitten, had to go right to bed." This was close to panic.

When Arthur Ficke sent her his new book, *Mr. Faust,* she told him she was kept so busy studying she couldn't even open it until Christmas break. "So Vassar College has won!" he teased her in verse. "It has tamed the wild spirit of Vincent Millay!"

> Now uttereth she no more little songs with wings,
> But trafficeth with wisdom only.
> O melancholy days of Vincent Millay's downgoing . . .
> The mighty have fallen.

That was too much for her to bear:

> Don't worry about my little songs with wings. . . . I hate this pink-and-gray college. If there had been a college in *Alice in Wonderland* it would be this college. Every morning when I awake I swear, I say, "Damn this pink-and-gray college!
> It *isn't* on the Hudson. They lied to me. It isn't anywhere near the Hudson. . . .
> They trust us with everything but men. . . . a man is forbidden as if he were an apple.

But girls were not. They were there in abundance. Vassar was more like an operetta than Lewis Carroll, with plots and counterplots among girls who were rivalrous, homesick, secretive, passionate, and four years younger than she.

One of the girls was teaching Vincent to dance the newest and most fashionable steps: "I let her lead me & do just as she wants me to & she will never know just how little I did know to begin with about the Fish-Walk & the Horse-Trot & the Figure-Eight & the Open Boston & the Heavenly Rest." They were to have a Halloween ball at McGlynn's. There were about twenty girls, of whom ten would have to go as men. "Lucky I'm little, and *have* to be a girl!"

Flirtation was a practiced art, and Millay was adept at handling the girls. Her room was at the head of the stairs, and as she was dressing,

> I heard a masculine giggle & looking down saw *Jack* . . . watching me. The *best* looking boy.
> "You horrid thing," said I. "I shall close my door at once."
> "No, you don't," said he, "I'm coming in."
> "You can't," I screamed, "it's not proper!—All right then, come in, and see if I'm all hooked up."

"Jack," who was Margaret, stood there gazing at Millay—who wrote home that without either her petticoat or her corset, "Honestly, you *don't know* how cute & slim I look."

The girls dressed like men tucked their hair in their collars and posed with chocolate cigarettes stuck jauntily in their mouths. Millay refused the chocolate, afraid she'd give herself away. "They give themselves away, all right. . . . Catherine Filene, who took the flash, is in the middle of the other picture. Doesn't she make a wonderful boy? —Had two dances with him and he wanted another. Really almost convincing. Just look at the way she's standing. She ought to have been a boy."

When Millay sent the snapshots home, she concentrated on Catherine Filene: she was bossy, she was domineering, she was "too executive"; "Catherine can't do a thing with me . . . because I don't let her see that I resent her manner of Authority, I just plain do as I like and don't notice her. She'd give a lot, I think, to have me chase her round. I don't go near her." But that wasn't entirely true. She paid close enough attention to the intrigues among the girls at McGlynn's to test her own powers, and she was becoming masterful at these skirmishes.

> You see I interest her. And she's so jealous of me really and of my friendship with Katharine Tilt that she isn't quite smart enough to keep it to herself.
> Katharine T. has a darling room on the third floor. The stairs begin right at Catherine Filene's door so she's pretty likely to know when I go up there. If she sees me in the hall she watches to see if I turn towards my room or towards the stairs. One night I came along in my blanket bathrobe with some books in my arms and started down the hall.

"O-*ho!*" said Catherine Filene. "Where are *you* going?" "Where do you s'pose?" said I. And tramped up stairs. You see, it bothers her. Sometimes she comes up when I'm up there—knows I'm up there—and says, "O, I *beg* your pardon! Perhaps I interrupt. *You two <u>turtle-doves</u>!*" And there you are. She's a handsome thing, very boyish, deep rough laugh, but the sweetest, most charming smile when she wants to be decent for a while. Really a fascinating type. Isn't she *wonderful* in that picture? Couldn't you die in her arms? —Fancy two dances with her in that rig and a third one *begged* and almost sworn about right after we'd finished the second! She actually made love to me, the devil, in her uninterested, insolent way.

But although Vincent insisted in this letter, which is to Norma, that she finds the girl completely resistible, she was intrigued—challenged, even— by her directness as well as by her insolence, which was provocative. When Millay's friendship with Katharine Tilt began to falter, she was not above flirting with Catherine Filene to make Tilt jealous. She did it consciously, and she knew exactly how.

If in her letter to Norma there was a sort of begrudging respect, the tone in her diary, "Lest We Forget," where the following entry was made just three weeks later, was entirely different: "People, my friends & hers, are very much interested in a seemingly new friendship which has sprung up between Catherine Filene & me. Handsome great big child! . . . People are very disturbed."

The following day, her entry was even clearer: "Went down town with Katharine Tilt. . . . Told her about Catherine Filene purposely to make her jealous, because she's been telling me how much she likes somebody else. It worked beautifully."

The next day was Sunday, a "Horrible day" she wrote in her diary. And why? She and Katharine Tilt gave a tea, and Agnes Rogers, her "sophomore," among others, came to it. Afterward, "I just came home & howled over a little thing Katharine did. However, Catherine Filene came in & consoled me beautifully."

The following day, December 8, she said that Katharine felt "nervous" about what she'd done, and although whatever it was goes unsaid, this doesn't: "She will feel nervouser before its over. And it will be good for her."

When the girls at McGlynn's put on their last dance before the Christmas break, Vincent wrote in her diary, "Wore my tan satin with the train & not much of anything else & felt just like dancing. Danced with Catherine Filene most of the time. Katharine Tilt came upstairs with me & asked to unhook me. I let her. It's all working wonderfully."

The next night they danced again, this time in Catherine Filene's room—four of them, and no Katharine Tilt: "Heaps of fun. Love to dance. And Catherine makes a wonderful man. She was *swell*-looking & swell *feeling* last night!"

Then it was over—a dash home for the holidays with an invitation in hand to visit the Kennerleys. There's barely another mention of Catherine Filene. But it was a crucial test of her power to attract, and she was willing to provoke jealousy as an antidote to a crush.

Christmas break provided her with another chance to sharpen her wiles: Witter Bynner and Arthur Hooley would both be spending part of the holidays with the Kennerleys in Mamaroneck. This time, meeting Bynner's train, she arranged herself against the door of the Kennerleys' car— "sort of leaning out & when I caught sight of *Him* I leaned out taller & just looked at him & when he caught sight of me he—he—he just *gusp* & lunged right at me &—oh, it was wonderful—he didn't take his eyes off me a minute,—I apologised for my decolleté"; by which she meant she hadn't worn a petticoat.

It was nearly time to dress for dinner when they arrived, but Bynner asked her to stay and talk to him. He asked her if she didn't have a book of her poems for him to read. When she said no, he said:

> "To think that *every* thing you do is good, I wish you'd write something ordinary," & I told him Oh no he didn't.
>
> I *have* got a beautiful speaking voice & somehow I knew I could really interest Witter Bynner with *that* quicker than with almost anything else. He really was fascinated listening to me. (Sounds so silly, but gosh! its [*sic*] dead earnest.) . . . Oh, girls, I have *wanted* Witter Bynner to really—*put down his paper & look at me*—& now he has.

On her last night, Arthur Hooley, who had stayed up after everyone else had gone to bed, delighted her with a compliment. "I'm not in love with him, exactly," she wrote home. "I love him, he's such an old dear, & half the time such an old bear . . . but I'm really in love with Witter Bynner, & not quite so hopelessly as I used to be."

2

"The *Miscellany* is offering four prizes of fifteen dollars each for the best poem, best story, best essay, & best play," Vincent wrote home on her return to Vassar in January. She was going to send them "Barbara-on-the-Beach," a short story she'd written at Barnard,

&, in order to be almost sure of the prize, if you don't think I oughtn't,— *Interim*. It might help me to get a scholarship next year. . . . & anyway it would undoubtedly smooth things out for me here. On the days when I didn't have my lessons people would think,—instructors especially—"O, well, she's been writing a poem."

Vincent Millay was a canny young woman, for that was exactly what was said about her throughout her college career.

A month and a half later, on February 23, she wrote her mother again about "Interim." This time she'd made up her mind: "It would make a bigger hit in a college full of women than anywhere else in the world and might do a lot for me, help to get a scholarship for next year, you know."

She seemed to need to justify her decision both to her mother and to herself—"If you don't want me to do it, mother . . ."—she was angling for her approval. And although the fifteen dollars was not much, it was better than nothing, "& I want to be sure of getting the prize. . . . After all, I shall write other poems, better than that, or I'm not much good."

She became so absorbed in college life that her family began to feel neglected. When her mother didn't hear from her for weeks and wanted to know why, Vincent finally wrote:

Don't worry about your bad, bad run-away child. . . . All that keeps me from writing long, long letters about Vassar is that I'm getting so crazy about Vassar & so wrapped up in Vassar doings, that I don't have so much time as I used to have when I just liked it well enough. . . . But oh, I love my college, *my* college, my *college!* Last night by the light of the moon we ran into a band of Seniors & a few others whom we knew out in the athletic circles on the bleachers, strumming the mandolin & singing, & we got boosted up along o' the rest & sang, too,—& the moon shined bright as day & the warm wind blowed, & oh, didn't we love our college! —I thought— Lord love you—"If Mother could only see me now!"

Now, lemme go, I gotta study,—or they won't let me stay.

Miss Dow was keeping her on a fairly short shoestring, but the relationship continued to be warm, and Vincent began to call her Aunt Calline, as Lydia Babbott did. Just before exams, Miss Dow had sent her another box of clothes.

If she's trying to spoil me utterly, to turn my mind entirely from academic pursuits, & make an absolute butterfly of me,—why, she has struck the way to do it. . . . and so it is perhaps a blessing that this last exquisite yellow chiffon & heavy silk embroidery thing is hopelessly large & will have to be all made over.

. . . .

> O, girls, I have saved the best for last! It is what I needed more than any-thing else in the world, perhaps,—an afternoon dress. Sweller than any-thing you ever saw, simply regal in every scrap of material, unquestionably this season's. . . . O, *girls!*
>
> It is made of very soft taupe satin (must be just about the shade of that suit I had, violetish-gray) the skirt is Frenchily long, tho perfectly manage-able—made with very soft panniers at the side which end in a row of but-tons. . . . Its very clingy. I've been draping myself around without any petticoat & with one bronze shoe on to get the effect.

She inked in the long sleeves in a sketch, with their "purple plushy vel-vet" bands. "With my hair at one end & my bronze shoes at the other it is rather nice." But the very best she saved for last: Wanamaker's department store sent four women to McGlynn's parlor to model its spring styles, "& I have paid $10.50 for a tan linen, tailory, cutey, *so* becoming, with a white muslin collar, spring dress, that I really need, to wear to college. Yes, I know. And I'm going to, from now on." She was a girl who wanted to be beautiful, and well liked and powerful in her class. And she set out to be just that.

At the Kennerleys' in Mamaroneck that spring, Arnold Genthe took a photograph of her standing among the blossoms of a magnolia tree in full bloom. Wearing that linen dress, she just touched the branches of the tree, her glance away from the camera and slightly downcast, her long curling hair caught in a knot at the nape of her neck. She looked winsome and young and fragile, as if at any minute she might become a wood nymph.

Back at Vassar she told her mother she had remarkable news:

> This I must tell you. Don't get any false hopes, but she never speaks idly, does Aunt Calline. Lately Aunt Calline has shown interest several times in Kathleen. One day at lunch someone was asking me if I had a sister still in school. Then I bragged about Wump for all I was worth, exclusively *to* the person who had asked me, but *at* (Heaven forgive me) Aunt Calline. . . . — I had to be sort of calm & yet very earnest & sensible, & not stupid, & yet not too grateful. It was terribly hard. But Aunt Calline doesn't forget. Maybe nothing will happen at once but Wump will be only eighteen, & I was twenty-one when mine came. She ought to go to college if any girl ever ought. I told Aunt Calline that *whatever* she did she excelled in,—

that as far as little things like brains, & will-power, & perseverance, & endurance, & thirst for knowledge are concerned, Wump's dust is too far in front of me even to get in my eyes.

Don't get too excited, dears, but you know what she's doing for me. And she's rather fond of me. And if there's one thing about me she *does* like, it's the way I like my family.

It was only this once that Cora indicated how beyond mere indebtedness to Miss Dow she felt herself to be. "I shall be on my knees crawling around after Miss Dow, yet."

But the news in the last letter of Vincent's freshman year was the best. On May 21, 1914, she was notified that "Interim" had won the Miscellany Prize Contest for best poem. She sent the prize money right home.

Please, please don't feel bad that I've let it go for so little. I shall do more, much better, or it won't matter. And it will mean a great deal to me here, both with the faculty & the girls. Please don't *mind*, dear.

That she had to apologize at all to her mother shows how highly they both regarded her talent. And her future.

3

Latin prose was not going to be a snap. When Elizabeth Hazelton Haight, who was in charge of helping Millay prepare over the summer for her exams, suggested she needed a Latin tutor if she was to pass them in the fall, Millay asked if she herself would tutor her. Surprised but flattered, she agreed. Haight was forty-one, an associate professor of Latin with a passion for the classics, who was capable of being sentimental over her favorites. Millay soon became one of them.

Helen Sandison, a brilliant young instructor in the English department at the time Millay was there (and later the beloved teacher of Mary McCarthy), remembered Miss Haight as "an enthusiast": "She was tall and spare and homely with a long face. She didn't do her hair well or dress well; she was not impressive looking. Her whole manner of dress just lacked shape."

Sandison felt that Vincent's association with the Latin department had an effect at Vassar: "Vincent just stood for the classics, you see. There was no question at all about it. They were important to her.

"And Vincent seemed devoted to Hazel. It was odd, because you could see through her in some ways. But I never got any indication that Vincent looked at her with critical judgment."

The opening sentence of Haight's memoir *Vincent at Vassar* is "Once I taught a genius and she became my friend." She explained more precisely than anyone else what Vincent faced in her course work:

> The college then set exacting conditions for the B.A. degree: required year courses in English, one Classical Language, one modern (French or German), History, Mathematics, Physics or Chemistry, half a year of Philosophy, and students had to take 14 or 15 hours of class work for three years, 12 to 15 in the last year. Vincent fulfilled all these conditions and then built her course around her own interest. English studies were its foundation, and they included a wide range and great teachers: Old English and Chaucer with Christabel Fiske, Nineteenth Century Poetry, and Later Victorian Poetry, an advanced writing course with Katharine Taylor, English Drama with Henry Noble MacCracken, The Techniques of the Drama with Gertrude Buck, who started the Vassar Theater. Then she enriched her knowledge of literature by many courses in foreign languages: both Greek and Latin, French, German, Italian, and Spanish.

She also took courses in introductory psychology, economics, and art, in all of which she got C's. She got her only D in social psychology. But she did superbly in all languages except Greek, in which she did not so much do badly as barely do it at all.

On her return to Poughkeepsie in the fall, Vincent stopped in the city to see Mitchell Kennerley, who took her to the Plaza for breakfast and afterward for a smoke in his private office. Vincent had refused a cigarette at the hotel "because someone might be there 'who knows I do not smoke.' " Kennerley thought that very funny indeed. Then he called up Arnold Genthe, the photographer who had taken the stunning photos of her the spring before in Mamaroneck, whose studio was at Fifth Avenue and Forty-sixth Street. His single shot of her standing among the magnolia blossoms would become the blaze that marked an era in American poetry as her own. She found his studio glorious, with tapestries, colored divans, mysterious cabinets, "& photographs, photographs everywhere of beautiful women & famous people, Paderewski, & David Belasco, & Billie Burke. . . . To think that he wanted to take *me*!"

But her modesty had its limits. "Besides having beautiful hair, an extraordinary good forehead in spite of the freckles, an impudent, aggressive, & critical nose, and a mysterious mouth," she wrote, "I have, artistically, & even technically, an unusually beautiful throat." Genthe draped her in a heavy deep-blue cloak to reveal it "& made me lean forward & lift back my head,—and photographed my throat!" Afterward they went out and had dinner together, because Genthe told her in his deep German accent, " 'to eat . . . is the best little thing we do.' "

Being on campus was more expensive than McGlynn's. Vincent's twenty-dollar-a-month allowance from Miss Dow went like water, but it made "such a difference in knowing people, and North is *full* of the best people in our class . . . and some awfully nice Juniors." One of those Juniors was Elaine Ralli. From her first mention of Elaine, her diary entries are full of ambiguity. But the crucial note will be her use of the masculine pronoun—Elaine has become a boy.

> Elaine is jealous when Bad Vincent loves anybody but hisself. He is almost even jealous when Bad Vincent loves *him*, because that is his nature.

She doesn't explain who the jealous Elaine is until her next letter home, on November 4, 1914.

> She's Elaine Ralli, a Junior, another hockey hero, cheer-leader, rides horse-back a lot, very boyish, & makes a lot of noise, not tall, but all muscle.

The two girls could not have been less alike. Still, Vincent told Norma,

> She's just naturally taken me, for better or for worse, and Lord knows why. And the way she treats me is killing. I'll be talking, in the middle of a crowd of people, and if Elaine wants me for anything, the first thing I know she has come and got me, just plain lugged me off to another part of the field. Everybody recognizes the situation, and accepts it unquestion-ingly, and there's no fuss about it. They just go on talking. And I say, "Hello, Elaine."

What situation did everyone recognize and accept? "Vincent was very definitely a person to whom others formed crushes, and attachments," Virginia Kirkus, one of Elaine's classmates, explained.

> And these were both obvious and intense. I was not among those girls, but there were a great many of them. . . . They simply trailed after her. And I do think she enjoyed it largely. . . . She was a natural subject. She was different from others, from the rest of us. She had an elusive, physical charm which we didn't associate with our own sex in those days. I think I was naïve. I was matter-of-fact. Vincent was not matter-of-fact about any-thing.

But it was not that *she* formed the attachments. She was reserved, not aloof exactly, but deeply reserved. Elaine Ralli was almost the opposite of Vincent. She was very aggressive in her human relations.

In a snapshot taken of them on the lawn in front of Main, Elaine is swirling Vincent, holding her aloft in her arms, their eyes locked in hilarious laughter. Vincent's hands are clasped tight around her neck, holding on for dear life.

Elaine Ralli was a year ahead of Vincent at Vassar but three years younger, nineteen to her twenty-two. Her family was Greek, and their fortune had something to do with the East India Tea Company. They lived in a grand apartment on the fashionable Upper West Side of Manhattan. She'd had a luxurious childhood with European travel and French governesses. "She had this confidence or early assurance," a friend of hers remembered, "that comes from having money early. She was freer. She was made free by it. She hadn't had to buckle under, because she'd had this absolutely glorious childhood." She was not pretty—she was short with a broad, flat face—but her skin was a pure olive, and her hair, which she wore in a braid around her head, was thick and glossy and black. Elaine was as direct as her gaze. They were good enough friends that Vincent spent Thanksgiving with the Rallis in Manhattan and stopped there again during the Christmas holidays before she went home.

4

Around the time she met Elaine, Vincent won the lead role in Vassar's Sophomore Party Play. The college set great stock by its plays, and she was to be the princess. She wrote home, "You don't know really how important it is to be a big thing in Sophomore Party. All the Freshmen will know me as the Princess afterward. And some of the Juniors are ushers, so they'll be there. And all the faculty." At the end of October the rehearsals were almost over and "I'm the whole show!—Guess if I enjoy myself!" she crowed. She'd seen her costume, all white cheesecloth with glittering golden ornaments, but in the end she didn't have to wear the skimpy cheesecloth; someone gave her a swath of white satin from which she made her own Maxfield Parrish dress.

After it was over even the *Faculty* congratulated me, and the girls,—I can't *tell* you the things they said, but its been a wonderful thing for me. Everywhere on campus now I meet people who say "Hello, Princess!" & yesterday, actually, in the laboratory, with many girls experimenting all around us, Professor Saunders came up to me & said, "How *is* your Royal Highness this afternoon?" And then he said, "I want to thank you for what you did for us Saturday. It was very lovely."

The news from home now was always in striking contrast to her life at Vassar. When Norma wrote to her that fall, she said Camden was "dead, worse than it ever was before." Their bills haunted her, and the only good news was Vincent's. "You must keep your great long name before the public all the time, dear. Now's your chance."

> You must be about as important as any thing around there about now, with your big poem and everything else they know about you. Oh Hon, don't think I don't appreciate everything about it, even the title you are to have. Princess!! Please have your hair down. Of course you will any way. Unless it's done way up—ever so high and all bound around some how. . . . Then there will be all those wonderful tall girl-boys for you to abuse as suitors.

Around this time, Vincent's good news began to include Kathleen. It looked as if Miss Dow would become actively involved in securing a fellowship for Kathleen. In a postscript to one of Vincent's first letters home that fall, she said Miss Dow had asked to see Kathleen's work and, referring to her drawings, suggested that Kathleen send her "two or three of her best things. . . . Aunt Calline is really awfully interested." If only, she said, things might "come true for her as they have done for me!"

The next month, after a pitiful letter from Norma, Vincent said that Kathleen, at Vassar, would "probably make more out of it than I ever shall here. I get too tired,—not *get* too tired, but *remain* too tired—to have any ambition or any gratitude, or any enthusiasm for other people's plans."

Although Miss Dow was still sending her boxes of other people's clothes, they weren't in style, and Vincent quickly complained of feeling "shabby." "Who ever is seen now in a corduroy suit,—for best?" But when Miss Dow wanted to know if they'd do, "of course all I can say is that they *will* do. What wouldn't I give for a good-looking *new* suit and a winter dress!"

Deprivation was of course a question of perspective: no other undergraduate at Vassar was having her poems printed in *The Forum*. Arthur Hooley had taken two. "The Shroud" appeared in the October issue and "Sorrow" in November. Her sisters wrote a parody of the latter's last stanza. Vincent had written:

> People dress and go to town;
>   I sit in my chair.
> All my thoughts are slow and brown:
> Standing up or sitting down
> Little matters, or what gown
>   Or what shoes I wear.

Kathleen called theirs "Hunk's & my latest efforts in your line":

> Guess I'll dress and go to town,
>   Not sit in my chair.
> Shall I wear my suit of brown
> Or my flimsy woolsy down?
> Little matters or whose gown
>   Or whose shoes I wear!

By February, after almost the entire winter without a word from Vincent (except for a quick stint at home after visiting the Rallis at Christmas), Cora wrote:

> Let's have a cup of tea and talk it over. . . . Kathleen has had word from two of the three people about the . . . scholarship, asking her what she had decided, and the poor child does not know what to write them. I don't see how it could be managed yet when the scholarship covers nothing but tuition.

When there was still no word from Vincent, she wrote again, just before Vincent's twenty-third birthday, "Why have we not heard from you? Kathleen can have the Coe fellowship, if I could manage the rest of it. We are trying to see some way out, but she must let them know very soon."

Then she closed her letter with a "Goodbye for the twenty-two and howdy to the twenty-three girl I love. Mother."

Finally, Vincent wrote to her "Dear darling adored Family" on March 8, 1915. Her news was entirely about her performance as Marchbanks in Shaw's *Candida:*

> A great many people said I made them cry. And certainly in other places I made them laugh.—It's a queer part, you know, of a boy of eighteen, a poet, terribly sensitive to situations and atmosphere, in love with the wife of an English clergyman. . . . I had a dark blue Norfolk coat and dark blue trousers that fitted me perfectly and a tan soft shirt and black tie tied in an artist bow—long ends, you know—and those old brown rubber-soled shoes I had last summer & black silk stockings. Everything fitted me perfectly and I felt *perfectly* at home in the clothes. People told me I reminded them of their brothers the way I walked around and slung my legs over the arms of chairs, etc. Instead of a wig I had my own hair bobbed. There's a girl who does it wonderfully . . . just a little long in the back like a poet's— and it grows beautifully like a boy's around my face, you know.

On her birthday, Elaine had sent her a great armful of roses, "big tan-pink roses mixed with pussy-willows," and for the play she'd filled her room with daffodils and given her a corsage of pansies so that it seemed always in bloom even in the deepest winter months. Then Vincent told them what everyone else had said about her acting:

> Somebody never saw a girl before who could act so much with her mouth and neck and hands—somebody thinks I'm the best amateur actor she ever saw—somebody never knew anybody before to hold the facial expression so beautifully all the way through—(I suppose she meant I didn't *sag* out of my part, or laugh when people at my side cracked jokes and the audience roared)—somebody hates me because I made her cry.

She saved the best for last: "Somebody says my voice was wonderful and has in it the quality that makes the audience pay absolute attention to what I'm saying—(I *know* that. I can always *hold* them when I speak, I find.)" That last somebody was Elaine, about whom she added, lightly, "Elaine & I have been living at the Inn lately, it seems"; she closed this letter, her first in months, by asking, "How is Mother?—Please tell me in detail."

Norma would have none of it. She wrote sharply to Vincent on March 16, "Dear Vincent, please pay a little attention to this in spite of all your *busyness*. Mother is sick. . . . I have to wash her face & hands & comb her hair & help her up stairs to the bath-room and every little thing like that."

She was, Norma said,

> the most impatient of her illness of any one I ever saw. Talks about it all the time and really I don't think she thinks we do anything for her. . . . I'm not doing this to frighten you 'cause she is lots better and has no temperature and her pulse is alright but you must write her a letter once in a while. . . .
>
> When we *did* get a letter from you Mother made the remark "All she said about me was to ask how I was—no other special message—and the letter wasn't even to me." Please address your letters to her once in a while. You might as well know what she says—Wump and I get it all the time. . . . Mother said it seems as if you have gone right out of her life . . . and if Kathleen goes next fall she will probably be the death of me. . . . You will remember when you went back you were going to send Mother some of the money she lent you. I believe she gave you all she had but you have never even *mentioned* it. How easily you forget.

That was harsh. But since Cora wouldn't hear of Kathleen's working—she was to study to have her chance—that left Norma holding the fort. She'd asked her aunts to help her find work in Boston as a milliner, but they wanted her to stay closer to home. "I'd go anywhere I got the chance. Mother is over her nursing I guess—We will owe three months rent the first of April and they have been making a deuce of a fuss over it."

She was happy to type Vincent's poems, and she suggested very firmly that Vincent must send them out if there were any chance of having them taken. Then she told her what to do: "Write Mother once a week whether you do anything else or not. Burn this letter please and don't hate me for writing it. Much love, Norma."

That did the trick. Vincent wrote to her mother as soon as she got Norma's letter, defending herself against her sister's accusations, in a letter which is as revealing for what is withheld, as for what is not:

> Beloved, beautiful, sad, sick Mother,—
> I love you. I love you. Don't be sad any more. I'll take care of you, way from here. I remember how you used to rock me and sing to me when I was sick and sad. And now I'm going to make you better by telling you some lovely things all about yourself.
> *First:*—Of all the songs I sing,—and I sing often now to crowds of people who love my little songs—the one they seem to love best is your beautiful "I may not dream again."

But she did not promise to come home, or to write more frequently. The following fall would be Vassar's fiftieth anniversary. Plans were under way for "a tremendous celebration. And your daughter has made the part of Marie de France in the pageant, a lovely part. . . . Give my love to my sisters, my mother. Your daughter, Vincent."

She told her mother she was trying for a scholarship for the following year, and she thought she'd get it.

> If I don't get it I can't come back here, very likely. But if I don't come back I can get a good job somewhere and help at home. One reason why I've been doing so many plays and things here is so that the college will want to keep me. The faculty were all crazy about my *Marchbanks.* . . . So, just now, I am notorious, the best known girl in college. It all helps, too.

But if she was notorious, it was not just because of her acting or her poems.

On April 12, 1915, with only eight more weeks of school, she wrote her mother:

> Elaine is going to ask her mother if she can come to Camden in the summer and *board with us!!* She knows all about us. Her people don't, but she does. And I told her like as not she wouldn't get anything to eat. But she

says she can live on grape-nuts and salad. She would hire a sail-boat and have a real time. Of course it's a crazy idea and probably her mother wouldn't let her anyway.

But she did. "The two of them seem to have made all arrangements without consulting the mothers about it," Daisy Ralli wrote to Cora,

and I am wondering whether it will be convenient to you to keep Elaine for the length of time she wants to stay. I feel that it will be an imposition on you unless you will allow me to pay her way. I know that she is a spoiled child and an extravagant one, in the bargain, and every additional member of a house-hold adds to the expense. So please let me know how much I ought to contribute.

Elaine would come as a paying guest, and while it would be a mistake to suggest that money lay at the heart of their relationship, it did enrich it. When Kathleen wrote to Vincent earlier that spring and said, "I think Elaine is a perfect dear—we'd die if it wasn't for her, and so would you, I guess"—she'd meant money.

In June, her exams behind her, Vincent stopped by the Rallis' in New York, waiting for Elaine to accompany her to Maine. She wanted to be sure that Elaine's first impression of all of them in Camden would be exceptional.

Girls, I want you to be all beautiful when we get home. Not too gorgeous, you know. Just shirtwaist & skirt,—simple, you know, and your hair all *simple,* Non, not frizzed & false. You see at college, no one ever *hears* of false hair. And don't be *too* powdery. Please excuse me. Wump, you see to it that Non is not too artificial, and Non, you see to it that Wump is not too much in earnest about anything. And both see that Mother is particularly beautiful. Fix her hair lovely, Non, & have everything she wears just as *dainty* as possible, because I want Elaine to fall in love with her, & first impressions mean so much.

She even fretted about the smell of the house: "Burn something so it will smell all *homey,* coffee or a cigarette, you know. And if you have *anything* <u>Djer-Kiss</u>* about the house or anything that even remotely suggests it, <u>drown</u> it!!! This is no joke. It makes me sick to vomiting."
Then she asked that they not hate her for all of this. She wanted only that Elaine should love them as she did, and that required careful staging.

---

*Djer-Kiss was a heavily perfumed bath powder.

In a snapshot taken that summer, Elaine is sitting at the helm of her little knockabout sloop, *Watch Your Step,* hunched and absorbed, her left hand steady on the tiller. They're sailing directly into the sun. Norma looks away from the camera, while Vincent gazes directly into it, smiling wanly. Elaine's gaze is absorbed and level; her right arm is draped nonchalantly over Vincent's shoulder, her hand just grazing her breast. Vincent tilts her head slightly, leaning into the crook of Elaine's arm. "She's one of the strongest girls I ever saw," Kathleen said of Elaine, "can pick Vincent right off the floor & carry her around and can make her muscles wiggle." She and Vincent, Kathleen entered in her "Good Times Book," "had packs of sport—She's dear."

But whether or not she was dear, she was very much in love with Vincent Millay. And Vincent knew it. When Elaine left at the end of August, it was with the promise that Vincent would visit her summerhouse in Bellport, Long Island, within the week. "It won't be long now until I see you," Vincent wrote to her just after she left, and then she broke into the French they used when their messages were more intimate:

> Mon ami, je ne t'oublie pas. Il ne faut pas avoir peur. Tu es encore mon enfant. Tu le sais bien. Et je t'aime. Tu le sais bien.★
>
> —Vincent

In any relationship between two women there is never just one child to be loved. There are two, and their roles are shifting.

Before Elaine left, Vincent turned to Arthur Hooley. He had written to her the previous fall, after he'd published both "The Shroud" and "Sorrow." It had been a queer letter in which he told her that although he wanted to see her, he didn't know when. "It is merely a matter of my mental condition,—which is rather rotten." Nearly everyone he'd left in England was now "on the firing line. And I am not. It's a funny world." His was almost the only mention of what would be called "The Great War" to surface in her correspondence during her years at Vassar.

In the spring of 1915, Hooley had published another one of her poems, "Indifference," so they were in contact. While his letters to her were consistent from the beginning—he pined for his return to England, for the Derby, even for her—her own letters to him did not begin in earnest until the summer. Certainly she was never unaware that he edited one of the finest literary publications in America, but while she played him just as

---

★My friend, I do not forget you. Don't be frightened. You are always my child. You know that well. And I love you. You know that well.

much as he played her, that summer her equilibrium was disturbed, and she let him know. Not *why;* that she cloaked.

My Dear,—

I want to write to you. I have nothing to say,—except a thousand things which I may or may not have said when this letter is done. But I am sick of never speaking to you any more. Once I knew you, and loved to be with you, and I would love to be with you tonight. I shall live quite comfortably to the end of my life—after tonight—without you, without ever seeing you again; I shall marry one of the three men that I love, and have a wonderful time; but tonight I would rather write to you. Tonight, of these three men that I love, one would bore me, and one would frighten me;—and the other one is you. The last time I saw you, when I was a little girl, I told you quite simply that I loved you. And you tried to hush me. Do you remember? Why did you do that?—Didn't you want me to love you? Don't you now? Would it please you or grieve you or not interest you at all. . . .

Arthur, don't say to me, "Child, child," . . . I am not a child in love with you, to be patted and sent away, or to be scolded and shaken. I am an almost reasonable human being, who has not spoken to anyone for a long time. . . . People fall in love with me, and annoy me and distress me and flatter me and excite me and—and all that sort of thing. But no one speaks to me. I sometimes think that no one can. Can you?

Edna

But the letter was a ruse. There weren't three men she loved; there was only one girl in love with her, in Camden, Maine. The striking note here is that she reaches out to him, summoning, needing his response. That is just what she'd done with Ferdinand Earle.

CHAPTER 11

Like all truly intellectual women, these were in spirit romantic desperadoes. They despised organizational heretics of the stamp of Luther and Calvin, but the great atheists and sinners were the heroes of the costume picture they taught as a subject called history. Marlowe, Baudelaire—above all, Byron—glowed like terrible stars above their literature courses.

—Mary McCarthy, "The Blackguard," from *Memories of a Catholic Girlhood*

The Pageant of Athena was held outside on October 11, 1915, in a great open-air theater built by the trustees especially for the performance celebrating the fiftieth anniversary of the founding of Vassar. Vincent played Marie de France, the twelfth-century Breton poet and the first woman to write poetry in France. The *Poughkeepsie Eagle* called it a "Wonderful Spectacle" and concentrated on Millay's performance:

> Into a scene of courtly beauty, where stately ladies and gallant cavaliers are dancing the minuet, came a dainty little figure, slight and dainty even in a dress of white satin with a train so big that two pages were needed to carry it. . . . Her grace was as great as her learning. So noble ladies and great lords listened . . . as the girl from France told her stories of love and hate and fighting.

It was a triumphant beginning to her junior year. She sent home lots of snapshots, and when she wrote on October 27, she told her family "how sweet Aunt Calline has been to me, loving me more than ever, & how I met Inez Milholland, the great suffragist." Then her letter broke off abruptly, and she did not pick it up again, or at least mail it, until November 1, 1915.

By this time she'd received a stern, daunting letter from Miss Dow, enclosing her allowance with advice. Millay was working on a draft of a poem called "The Suicide," which Miss Dow didn't like one bit. She linked her own—and her friends'—continued support of Millay to "high ideals not only of womanhood but of what woman produces." She was not referring simply to the poem.

> Of course you are mistress of yr. own productions and as always I do not want to . . . make unreasonable demands, but tho' I am not a literary woman there are some ways in which I might be of help thro' various friendly avenues. It seems important to me that the next year or two you should guide yr. self & yr. products pretty carefully if the future brings what I believe it should. More of my friends have seen you now and their influence is to be had—if—your trend is in the right direction.

She made herself even clearer: "It will be easier for me to finance the next two years with their sympathetic support. . . . their influence can radiate pretty far into the future, if it is once held."

She then suggested that Millay was unaware "of your dangers both from physical & temperamental conditions." She did not mean by this that she should guard herself against illness: "Absorbing attentions from individual students are a hindrance in spite of the pleasant things they bring. Those very things are not the best for yr. nature."

Millay had missed meeting a distinguished friend of Miss Dow's who'd come to speak during the pageant. "I was impressed by your anxiety lest you disappoint some girl who seemed to have a claim on you for the evening." She had heard about Elaine Ralli.

> Because of yr. gifts, Vincent, life will present some complicated problems for you—I believe you have both courage & strength & yet I see such pit-falls. . . . I want you always clean, sweet & pure & ready to return your talent to the world enriched by an idealism which means ennobling the lives of others. I want you different from the usual type of poet who claims a freedom bordering on licence, & who thinks she can touch pitch without being soiled. How much the world with its sordidness & selfishness and now mourning needs the word that brightens, that strengthens, that illumines a path to the great fundamentals.

While she did not define those great fundamentals, it was clear that neither "The Suicide" nor Elaine Ralli was among them. "This may sound like a sermon," she continued, "but it is not so intended; it only means love and interest in a great gift and its setting."

Millay didn't change a word of her poem, but she was shaken. And if she wouldn't budge about her work, she did alter her friendship with Elaine. When she picked up the letter home she'd begun on October 27, she wrote:

> You know neither you-all nor Aunt Calline nor any of my older friends were very pleased to have me with Elaine all the time, so I decided I would see if it was too late for me to make new friends or renew old ones. And I haven't really had to do a thing, because all at once people began to come to see me & now people don't say any more that I'm with Elaine all the time, & better still its so nicely come about that nobody says either that Elaine & I have had a row,—because people see me still with her, too.

Then she told them exactly the way it happened.

> One day I was going over to pageant rehearsal & as I came out of Main I met Fran Garver going in. "Come on back," she said, "& get some fudge. I've made some in the candy-kitchen, & I give it to the people I love." So then I said, "Oh, do you love me?"—And Fran said, "Yes; I always have."—Now that wasn't wildly exciting, because Fran loves a great many people. But then, so do I,—and what I was after was particular friends, & I have always liked Fran a lot anyway—she has perfectly beautiful eyes—so *that* was nice. Fran's roommate went to New York the next week-end to march in the Suffrage Parade, & I spent Saturday night with Fran,—but every-

body knew I had just come back from Mohonk, where I had spent Friday night & Saturday at the hotel on the lake, with *Elaine.*

Her aim seemed not so much to lose Elaine's friendship as to loosen its grip. The problem was that these young women were apt to fall in love with her. "Beloved!" Fran Garver's letter to her that winter term began, "if I could only see you for a second I'm sure this chronic ache would go away.

> I think no feeling, ever, has come so strongly over me as the all-gone chok-ing sensation I have when I'm in your room,—when you're gone. The only time I ever felt anything like that was when my mother, whose breath I had been watching for half an hour, smiled at me happily & closed her eyes. I knew she was dead. . . . Vincent dear, it was because you had the same beau-tiful expression in your eyes as my dying mother did, that I couldn't bear to have you look at me the night you were so tired. I didn't write to you Thurs night because I knew I'd make love to you. . . . Everything that was danced or sung or played had an undercurrent of you. You haunt me beloved— beloved Vincent. I love you—. . . . If you don't marry when we're out of V.C. I shall earn a million and you shall write & we'll divide the money & when it pleases you you'll visit me and do exactly as you wish—

Elaine was struggling with her own feelings about Millay. In an undated and unsigned, but initialed, letter she began:

> You will excuse the paper I know—You see I must find some common way to begin altho' why I cannot say for certainly you are the most uncommon of people. . . . How I want to come back to you—yes I know I have just left—but the longing in me never leaves and this is a night that seems for you and me. Do not worry—we are friends but I am still in love—that is a characteristic of you [she then slipped into French] et je suis encore un enfant—la tienne? ah! dit "oui." If I am not careful I will be covering this paper with words that make a poor endeavor to tell you I love you—the reason I repeat so often those words is because I can really find nothing to express the hunger, the yearning and oh! the love for you—and you are so small! . . . You have not spoken to me for so long about your poems and I dare not ask—will you not say something—surely some day you will find time to say something to me. Have you heard the rain? It is cold to-night and I'm too restless for rain—only for the touch of you—will I ever not want that.

The letter, with poems slashed in ink across the back page, ends with "If ever I can see you, will you come—mes bras vous attendent—et mon coeur ne pense qu'a toi. . . . oh! Why can't I go to you—?" It was signed E.P.R.—Elaine Pandia Ralli.

But the chill in their relationship, especially after Thanksgiving, was undeniable. Elaine saw Millay turning to other girls for friendship that seemed to her to lessen, even to supplant, her own. She didn't know why. "Dearest little old sweetheart—miss you dear—Gee!" she began lightly but awkwardly, with none of the ease she could express when she was confident: "I want you just as much as I've always wanted you, with all my heart—You know that I never could feel towards anyone the way I do towards you—it is more than true—remember what we've said—yes and done."

She told her, again and again, in a tone that became increasingly desperate, not only how much she loved her but that Vincent must never doubt her, that she was the only person in the world for her. And that she was Vincent's child.

A friend who knew Ralli much later in her life said that after a while Elaine "knew Vincent had dropped her. She had, then or shortly thereafter, but while at Vassar . . . a serious crack-up. She was in the infirmary, and then she went home, and her mother cared for her. I remember her telling me stories of her mother feeding her, sitting her in the sunlight on the porch, that sort of thing. I don't think Daisy Ralli ever knew how much Elaine cared for Vincent. She, of course, knew she cared, but how much, or how deeply, she would not have known. And she could not have guessed.

"They were lovers. Elaine told me that they were. . . . Certainly Elaine did not know why Vincent had thrown her over, she just knew that little by little she became distant. Remote. . . . But she felt she had been loved by Vincent and surely she had loved her.

"Millay was a seductress. Oh, I should think so! You have only to look at those poems. I see nothing wrong with that in her. She drew people to her. She liked to draw people to her. . . . Elaine felt there was a ruthlessness about Vincent. That her work came first. . . . She always thought Vincent had an eye on herself, her future. . . . She felt it was her first love, and perhaps her only one: her poetry."

While Millay had still not seen Arthur Hooley—it was nearly two years now—she began to write to him with more regularity, usually twice a month, eighteen letters in all, until the end of her junior year. She was always "Edna" in her letters to him, and perhaps she wrote to him for no other reason than what she'd admitted in her letter the summer before—that although people loved her or desired her or annoyed her, no one spoke to her. And she needed the sound of a man's voice in her life. He had answered her desperate letter of July, wondering if she wrote such interesting letters to anyone else. Warily, perhaps stung by the memory of her correspondence with Earle, she had said, "Not anymore."

In early October she wrote him an extraordinary letter from Vassar, one in which she revealed what she felt not only about him but about herself.

> My dear,—
>
> Do not think that I am sorry for anything that I have ever said to you, or for any mood of mine that I have ever let you see. I am not sorry for anything at all that has to do with you.
>
> Indeed, if you love me, it is your own affair. I shall never try to make it mine, Arthur.—But if my letters sometimes hurt you, I am glad. You shall not have me vaguely with you,—but clearly.—I want to be all that I can be to you, in a letter.
>
> But more than that I do not wish to be. . . . You said once that there are so many beautiful possibilities in me that you would be loath to leave with me any memory that I could wish to obliterate. God knows, I wish no such memory of you.—But no memory that any man could leave me could really touch me.—I am sure of this. And why I am so sure, is because none has. . . . —Although I have been faithful to you—in my fashion. (Not that you have desired my faithfulness; or that faithfulness is in any way a virtue,—It is oftener a stupidity, I think.) But nothing has ever hurt *me*. Nothing can. In that respect, surely, I shall always remain a child.

Then she told him an anecdote with a point: a friend of the Kennerleys had once watched her and another woman together and come to the conclusion that if the other woman should marry she would stop writing, "but that under the same circumstances I would not. As far as I am concerned, that is true. No man could ever fill my life to the exclusion of other things." She was, for someone as young as she was—twenty-three to Hooley's forty—entirely clear about her yearnings. She was as accurate as it was rare to acknowledge.

A little more than a week later she wrote to him in an entirely different vein, marked by what was her real need for him:

> Arthur—Arthur—Arthur—why am I writing to you, when I am so tired, and have so much to do before I can sleep? . . . My dear, do you think of me, sometimes?—What do you think?—Tell me, Arthur—just for fun.—I should really like to know.—Will you? . . . Why not?—*What do you think of me?*

It was as if she wanted to discover who she was by her reflection in his eyes. She never gossiped with him about people they both knew—she told him only about herself, what she felt, or thought. One would barely know, from her letters, that there was a war in Europe or that women were marching for suffrage in New York. The drama she described was entirely interior.

When she received his response she wrote, "I shall be glad until the day I die that you wanted me, and that you told me so." It was a sort of literary snare. "Nothing has changed, in spite of all the things you said, my dear,—only that now I am more accustomed to it, and can get on quite nicely without you." Then her lines loosened: "—except sometimes, when I cannot get on at all."

If it was a seduction, it was a chilly one. "Wouldn't you just *love* to see me again for a minute, sometimes?—I should think you would.—I would you." The week after her birthday she made what she called "an observation, & not a confession":

> It really isn't necessary that I should be a man, Arthur, in order to know what the word *girl* sometimes means to you.—What do you suppose the word *man* sometimes means to me?—In a place like this? . . . This is a strange place. I had known, but I had not realized, until I came here, how greatly one girl's beauty & presence can disturb another's peace of mind,—more still, sometimes, her beauty & absence.—There are Anactorias here for any Sappho.—And I am glad . . . that I have never felt moved to say harsh & foolish things about an ancient Greek philosopher or a modern English poet, whom the world has condemned & punished. . . . For up here, while some of us are thinking of the rest of us, the rest of us are thinking of you, & men like you.

It was as close to a confession as Edna Millay would ever make in writing. Arthur wrote back immediately:

> Edna—Edna—
> Even if you *had* cared for a girl, & even if you had given yourself (so far as you could), I do not think I should care, greatly. No. I should not. For everything would have been beautiful, to you. As to Sappho. And so, to me.
> *Arthur*

That note drew blood—or he may have written something more that was not saved—for on March 10 she wrote him a savage little note:

> Indeed,—I will be very careful from this day,—for of course you must not really love me. That would spoil it all,—& we have had such a beautiful game.—It is "no fair," as we say, to love me.

As for myself,—God forbid that I should give my heart to a dyspeptic Englishman!

_____

Edna.

Three days later she withdrew her mocking words:

Arthur, promise me that you will not go away . . . without seeing me. . . . Promise me.—

—Sometimes as it is, with you there, & myself here, I want you very much,—want just to feel you touch me again, you know.—I am not willing to have the sea between us and not have been very near to you, just once more.

_____

I am glad that you have wanted me terribly. I am very glad that some-times you think of me at night, and suffer. You have made me suffer, too.

_____

Last night we gave the play of which I once spoke to you, *Deirdre of the Sorrows.* It was very real to me, as always. In the last act I stood beside the grave of the man I loved, who had been killed in battle, and with his knife killed myself.—I did it with all my heart,—and when they picked me up from the floor after the fall of the curtain, I found that I had actually driven the knife right through my little leather jacket.

Her self-dramatizing here is extraordinary, and it lay at the heart of her character; her fierce instinct for self-protection was the iron in her blood. She wrote these two final sentences:

Why would it be absurd for me if you should really love me?—The absurd-ity would be, would it not,—for me to really love you?

_____

—Edna.

2

Vincent wrote home immediately after *Deirdre* but said very little about it because she'd just received the news that they would have to leave their Washington Street house. "Never mind," she wrote Norma,

dear old loved. . . . Of course I could just weep all day at the thought of leaving the house,—but I'm not going to let myself. . . . I can't ever let myself *think* of that hedge of morning-glories, & the morning air coming in the bath-room window.—But we can't help it, dear. So never mind. It doesn't really matter at all,—if you just think of it that way.—Dear Sister, I love you very much,

———————

Vincent.

But of course, it did matter. Being asked to leave is not the same thing as choosing to.

Money was always short at home, whereas at Vassar, Millay, who was spending her spring break at Miss Dow's in New York, was exposed to people with more wealth than she'd ever known, and she moved among them as their guest. "I came down Friday," she wrote home just two weeks after her previous letter, "& Arlene Erlanger met me & took me to lunch at the Biltmore,—then her chauffeur picked us up & took us to several art galleries where we saw beautiful pictures & statues." Her letter went on like that for pages, operas and theaters to go to, breakfasts in bed, meeting her hostess's husband's mother, "who *lives,* not just visits, but *lives,* at the St. Regis. . . . Judge if I enjoyed myself over the week-end."

"Vassar was *not* a college for rich girls, then or now," one of Millay's classmates told me many years later. It was for the intellectual girl with a social conscience. "You see, we all wore middies, which were a sort of leveling uniform. Although it is true that one knew, if one were at all observant, that certain middies were from Wanamaker's. Or they might be from Filene's. And we were not permitted to board our horses on campus."

Now imagine this girl—without a cent to spare—among the rich girls at Vassar, all of whom were preparing for the annual ball. Vincent weighed ninety-five pounds, stood five feet one inch, and, in her made-over yellow chiffon gown with its butterflies of gold and fur at her shoulders and her flaming hair, must have looked like a demented fairy out of Rackham. The astonishing thing is that she invited Elaine Ralli's brother to be her date. Victor Ralli was no one's idea of a prince—he was shy, hardworking, short, and swarthy—and he agreed immediately. He told her he had had to read her letter of invitation several times to make sure she meant him. He apologized in every note to her for being inarticulate. He said to be her "suitor" he'd be happy to bunk with a janitor. He was, in other words, modest to a fault. He could not have interested her at all. Although she gave her mother and sisters every detail of her dress and of the dance itself—who said what to whom about her and how many times she danced which dances with which men—she mentioned Victor Ralli only twice. The first time was to say with "relief" that he agreed to come, the second that he brought her orchids.

That May of 1916 she won the Intercollegiate prize for "The Suicide," the writing of which had become a piece of drudgery, she wrote home ("I was so discouraged about what those critic friends of Aunt Calline said that I didn't feel like trying to do anything else with it"). And Mitchell Kennerley published three of her poems in *The Forum*. When he enclosed the check, he told her that while the next issue would be his last, he hoped she would let him publish her first book of poems, with Arnold Genthe's photograph of her standing among the magnolia blossoms on the dust jacket. "Then I think I shall publish no more books of poems by anyone else."

The short lyric "Witch-Wife" was the most delightful of the poems she gave to Kennerley, and clearly something of a self-portrait.

> She is neither pink nor pale,
>   And she never will be all mine;
> She learned her hands in a fairy-tale,
>   And her mouth on a valentine.
>
> She has more hair than she needs;
>   In the sun 'tis a woe to me!
> And her voice is a string of coloured beads,
>   Or steps leading into the sea.
>
> She loves me all that she can,
>   And her ways to my ways resign;
> But she was not made for any man,
>   And she never will be all mine.

Yet the sonnet "Bluebeard," a grim parable about female disobedience, was far more revealing. Millay wrote in the first person, in the voice of the murderous king, but there are no murders here. Hers is an innocent, maligned Bluebeard, a melancholy man of secrets. It is the girl whose villainy is her intrusiveness and greed. In the original fairy tale Bluebeard is often a king and always a husband, who marries one after another of three or more beautiful young women who are sometimes sisters. He hands each young wife the keys to his castle, telling her that in his absence she may unlock any room except one. Incapable of overcoming her curiosity, she opens the forbidden door only to find a room full of clotted blood from the heads or corpses of her murdered sisters. The key is indelibly marked with blood, and upon his return Bluebeard discovers her disobedience and kills her. Sometimes she is saved by a passing knight, in other versions she is able to fool Bluebeard into not knowing she has opened the door to the forbidden chamber. But in all versions Bluebeard is a murderous husband. Yet Millay's is not:

> This door you might not open, and you did;
> So enter now, and see for what slight thing
> You are betrayed. . . . Here is no treasure hid,
> No cauldron, no clear crystal mirroring
> The sought-for Truth, no heads of women slain
> For greed like yours, no writhings of distress;
> But only what you see. . . . Look yet again:
> An empty room, cobwebbed and comfortless.
> Yet this alone out of my life I kept
> Unto myself, lest any know me quite;
> And you did so profane me when you crept
> Unto the threshold of this room tonight
> That I must never more behold your face.
> This now is yours. I seek another place.

She has transformed the classic tale of Bluebeard into a story about intimacy and privacy. Here the wife's greedy intrusiveness has violated Bluebeard's necessary secret. Not only is he no murderer, all he seeks is a secrecy in which to hide, "lest any know me quite." His penalty is swift and severe. But it isn't death—"I must never more behold your face. / This now is yours. I seek another place"—it is withdrawal.

That summer, short of money as always, Cora was barely home. She was canvassing for hair work on the islands off the coast of Maine. It was a tough season; most of the summer people had plenty of hair of their own, so instead she washed it. Then the news came that Kathleen had not passed her entrance examinations to Vassar. Plucky in the face of such a blow, Cora said she was reconciled to what had happened; it just meant "another year of systematic well arranged study." While washing the hair of a girl who turned out to be from Vassar, Cora told her she had a daughter there and invited her to visit Vincent. "She must be made an acquaintance and friend," Cora suggested in her next letter to her daughter.

But Vincent no longer saw herself as a girl who had to win the good opinion of everyone at school. When she answered her mother, the tone of her letter was almost icy. Not only did she not know the girl, but "You must not think that just because a girl goes to Vassar I want her to visit me." Her letter was fierce:

And it doesn't make any difference whether you wash their heads or their floors, they have nothing on us, unless we give it to them. As long as we consider ourselves their superior & they can't get the idea out of our heads, they have nothing on us, & can't get anything, you see. The girl is a nonentity at Vassar,—*I am not.*

You haven't got me into any mess, dear. But you must <u>never</u> again invite anybody to see me unless I have said it is somebody I want to see. People can say anything they like about me & my family conditions, but they can *not* visit me unless I want them.

Cora kept this letter all her life.

3

She had a fine time senior year. She took two courses in Spanish (and became president of the Spanish Club), took English drama with President Henry Noble MacCracken and the technique of the drama with Gertrude Buck. Her play *The Princess Marries the Page* was written for that class and performed on May 12, 1917; she was the princess. She even took one term of Italian, having taken every other language course Vassar offered. And, in what was a great honor at Vassar, she was asked to write the Baccalaureate Hymn for her class of 1917, which was to be sung at commencement. She did not, however, hear it sung.

In the spring she was invited down to New York for a night at the opera and stayed overnight even though it was the end of spring break and she knew she shouldn't. She was campused, which meant she was forbidden any additional nights away from the college. But come May, when the weather warmed up, one of her roommates, Charlotte Babcock, and some friends invited her to join them in their little red Saxon for a trip up the Hudson. She didn't give it a second thought: she went along for the ride. It was late, and in the end they spent the night at the house of one of the girls. The next day they stopped at the Watson Hollow Inn near the new Ashokan Reservoir, where Vincent playfully signed her name in the register. One of the college wardens lunched at the same hotel and saw Vincent's name in the register, directly below that of a man. She thought the worst and reported her. "The faculty," according to Elizabeth Haight, "voted to suspend her indefinitely. . . . This meant the loss of her degree." It wasn't because Millay was suspected of staying overnight with a man that she was so harshly disciplined; she had broken almost every rule at Vassar, had thumbed her nose at the school's authority or, worse, ignored it. Now the faculty was set to punish her, and they were in no mood to relent. Some felt she'd been excused once too often and dug their heels in.

Henry Noble MacCracken had become president of Vassar in 1915. He later recorded that Millay cut classes regularly, and while some faculty members excused her, others did not. He called her in to reprimand her but was none too persuasive. "I . . . told her, 'I want you to know that you couldn't break any rule that would make me vote for your expulsion. I don't want to have any dead Shelleys on my doorstep and I don't care what you do.' She went to the window and looked out and she said, 'Well on those terms I think I can continue to live in this hellhole.' . . . What could you do with a girl like that?"

But this time she'd overdone it. Even President MacCracken sat tight.

On June 6, Millay wrote home; as it turned out, only Norma was there to receive her letter. "Dear Mother & Sister,—In a few days now I shall write myself A.B." She had, however, to tell them that something "unpleasant but quite unimportant" had happened:

> Because I was absent-minded & stayed away out of town with three other girls one night, forgetting until it was too late that I had no right to be there because I had already lost my privileges for staying a couple of days in New York to go to the Opera,—the Faculty has taken away from me my part in Commencement.—That doesn't mean just what it says, because my part in Commencement will go on without me,—Baccalaureate Hymn, for instance, or the words of Tree Ceremonies, which we repeat—& all the songs & our Marching Song. . . .
>
> What I mean is this,—I can't stay here at all for Commencement: I can't graduate with the class,—my diploma will be shipped to me, as I told Miss Haight, "like a codfish"—& it all seems pretty shabby, of course, after all that I have done for the college, that it should turn me out at the end with scarcely enough time to pack and, as you might say, sort of "without a character."

Her class was behind her, sending in petitions and brewing up a splendid row. "I always said, you remember, that I had come in over the fence & would probably leave the same way.—Well, that's what I'm doing."

She asked them not to tell Kathleen until after she was finished at the Hartridge School, where she was preparing. "This will make no difference about her. If she passes her exams she has next year here sure." She closed with good news: Edith Wynne Matthison, an actress who was a friend of Miss Haight's, had written to her that there might be a place for Vincent for eight weeks in summer stock, in Milwaukee.

Norma was left to tell Cora. On June 10, writing from Belfast, Maine, where she'd been born fifty-four years before to the day, Cora addressed herself to the college board at Vassar, Miss McCaleb, and Dr. MacCracken:

Dear Friends

I am Vincent Millay's Mother, and I am here a supplicant before you. . . . The last I heard from Vincent, directly, was that she should graduate next Thursday. . . . I have looked forward to this time as a culmination of a wonderful dream. To see my girls thru High School was a feat, thought by my family and friends an utter impossibility, as I have been alone with them seventeen years with nothing save what I have earned.

She had always hoped to see Vincent graduate, she wrote, but the plan was not possible. However,

she assured me, that everything would be most simple because of the war. That she should be allowed the benefits of your institution has seemed so wonderful to me. That the same field seems to be opening to Kathleen seemed almost too much to believe. . . .

But now, this awful thing seems more than I can bear. It does not seem that it can possibly be true that my girl will not be with her class-mates on Thursday. You cannot realize what it means to us. Such a possibility never occurred to us, and it is a terrible shock. If it must be, if your decision is final, it is a blow from which I shall never recover.

It didn't seem right to Cora that "the class for which she has won so many honors, for whose ceremonials she has originated so much, should sing her very songs while she is weeping outside." Then she asked, "Must I give up the picture of my girl in her graduation exercises? . . . You are taking the very bloom from the best thing that ever came into my life."

On June 7, MacCracken sent a letter out to the faculty telling them that 108 members of the class of 1917 (somewhat less than half the class) had sent him a petition asking that "Vincent Millay be permitted to remain for Commencement, insomuch as she has contributed largely to our Commencement activities and we feel that the penalty inflicted is too great." It was accompanied by letters from eighteen individuals urging that the penalty imposed was too severe, particularly "in view of the leniency shown to Miss Millay before the spring recess; second, that false rumors regarding her reputation" would be stopped by allowing her to take her degree with her class.

Millay had met with him before the petition arrived. The only record of this encounter is two letters of hers, which he kept.

You told me once that if I ever needed a friend to let you know.—I need one now. And I want to see you. May I?—If you don't want to see me, I shall understand. But there is nobody else I want to go to.

Mayn't I see you this evening.—Sunday?—If not, don't tell me that it is because you are too busy; I shall know quite well why it is.

Her tone here was extraordinary for any undergraduate, let alone one in trouble. She told him that if she were to sleep on the letter she was about to write, she would probably destroy it.

But I'm not sleepy.—and I remember that you chided me a bit for never telling people who are kind to me how kind to me I think they are and it occurred to me that if I should die tomorrow it would be rather shabby of me not to have blessed you just.

_____

I shall remember till I am very old—if I live to be old—your great gentleness with me.

Vincent Millay

Then she heard from her mother:

What are they thinking of dear? Is it absolutely final? . . . Is there nothing that can move them so that I may not be robbed of that proudest day I have ever dreamed of seeing? I may not live to see Kathleen graduate. Tell them so, those people. Forgive me dear for turning the knife in the wound. . . . I'm so sorry for Vassar, for you, for the girls and Miss Dow and your class and myself.

Ella McCaleb wired Mrs. Millay on June 12 at one o'clock that she had just seen Vincent get her diploma with the rest of her class. On the thirteenth, McCaleb wrote to Cora, apologizing at first for not having written to her the week before, when it had all begun, "but," she said honestly, "I really did not know what to say. I was rather dumbfounded by the action of the faculty when it decided that Vincent would have to withdraw last week and not be allowed to take her degree with the class." The petition from part of her class had helped, but "All the way through college Vincent has found it extremely difficult to live according to college regulations, and she had been forgiven possibly too often."

In other words, it wasn't only that she'd calmly stayed in New York to go to the opera instead of returning at the end of spring recess; it was that "when the impulse came to go off for a lark, she yielded as any little child might have done, hoping that she would not be found out." The entire experience had been both "bitter and trying for her friends as well as for herself," and McCaleb hoped that Kathleen would take a different attitude from that of Vincent. "If I did not believe this I could not work to have her come here." A full scholarship for her first year was promised, but beyond that nothing was assured.

After commencement, Vincent fled to Miss Haight's apartment in New York, from which she wrote to Norma:

> Tell Mother it is all right,—the class made such a fuss that they let me come back, & I graduated in my cap & gown along with the rest. Tell her it had nothing to do with money;—all my bills have been settled for some time.—Commencement went off beautifully & I had a wonderful time. Tell her this at once if you can.

After graduation Vincent went straight to New York to look for work. Maybe she could return home with Kathleen after her graduation from the Hartridge School.

> You see I have to start right in working as soon as I can get a job,—& I may not be able to come home at all. We mustn't be foolish about these things. . . . But I *can't* come home unless I have something sure here to come back to,—you understand.
>
> —I sent Wump a pair of silk pajamas & a neck-tie & a large white silk handkerchief & a pair of arm-elastics for a Commencement present,—"To my dear brother, Kalloch."—! . . . Please write me, darling, darling, darling, sister.
>
> Vincent.
(Edna St. Vincent Millay A.B.!)

But Norma did not understand. She did not understand why Vincent could not be home with her and their mother. She grasped only that she had begun to lose her—and she held on fiercely. She wrote her a letter, which she didn't send:

> Highly Esteemed Edna St. Vincent Millay, A.B.
>
> Oh—My baby, cute thing—How things are changing—I realize now that you don't really belong here any more. You belong in New York. It hadn't been that way through college but it begins right now to be so. It's lovely and it's dreadful. How childish minds like mine hate to admit a change, things were always so nice "as they used to be."

At six in the evening, sitting in an old red string hammock on the front lawn "(unmowed because I have no lawn mower and no way or means of procuring same) I don't in the least care whether or not it is ever mowed," she had exactly nine cents in the house.

The next morning she wrote to Vincent again, trying to explain why she felt such despair, coupled with such longing: "I have really no interest outside—concerning myself I mean. You are interested in your affairs—Kathleen in hers . . . Mother has *her* interest—her work."

Norma was the only one of her sisters who was exempt from her mother's expectations. She remained alone, at home. Yet of all the family she was perhaps the sharpest about Vincent. "Mother—listen—" she wrote to her,

> I think it would have been one mighty good thing for *Edna St. Vincent Millay* if this thing had gone thru. . . . They have been wonderful—Simply wonderful to her all thru her College career and she has done exactly as she did so please. . . . She thinks it rather cute to stay out to go to the Opera just because she *dares* and wants to. She has done things like that all her life. It is not part of the genius which prompts these things in her; it is *because* of the genius that she *dares* do everything she pleases.

☙ ☙ ☙

I found a small green leather case upstairs in Norma's bedroom which I brought to her, sunk into the long sofa in front of the fireplace. We opened the box. There was a thin gold chain with a baroque pearl in the center. "Mother gave each of us one, because the other girls in Camden had jewelry and we had none." She also had three identical rings made for the little sisters, with real scarabs—ancient fat bugs—set in the center. We found the one Norma had once urgently sent to Vincent. "Hunk" is engraved inside the band, but the scarab is missing. Lying next to it, wrapped in chamois, is Vincent's gold Vassar class ring of 1917. It's as tiny as a kitten's eye. Norma slips it on her little finger. "Vincent was free now, while I was the one at home, you see. Looking back at my life, I felt . . . I might have done something else. Oh, something with my life. I was keeping house, that's all. But I had nothing. Having no way, no control of yourself, of your life. I was just a girl in a lonely house."

PART THREE

GREENWICH VILLAGE: BOHEMIA

CHAPTER 12

Millay had been in New York only a week when she decided to go home, "in time for baked beans" on Saturday night, she wrote Norma. "I am enclosing $2. to make sure of the baked beans." It was the wrong time to find a job in the city: it was expensive, and it was hot. She would go home with Kathleen, do a big wash, get to her writing, "and then come back in the fall, whether I have a job or not. . . . I wish you could come back with me. But that would leave mother alone.

> We could have such a good time if we had some tiny dirty uncomfortable room somewhere down in the disreputable district . . . that's where I'm staying now,—way down on West 4th Street. . . . Darling, I wish we could arrange it so that you could be here with me next winter. Don't you suppose we can? There's nothing for you there at all, and I've always wanted to bring you out here with me. . . . Don't you suppose mother could get a job editing some dum page in some newspaper?—she might. She writes such beautiful English and she's so funny. She could try. At least there's no reason for sticking in Camden.

The convention of leaving one unmarried sister at home to care for an aging mother was not going to become a pattern in their lives. If one got out, they all would. That was the tacit bargain struck within their family. But the burden of getting out depended entirely upon Vincent. How would she manage?

One of her plans was to try the stage. Edith Wynne Matthison, the actress and friend of Miss Haight's whom Vincent had met at Vassar that spring, had promised to arrange an introduction to a theatrical manager in New York. She and her husband, the English playwright Charles Rann Kennedy, invited Vincent to their summerhouse in Connecticut. "I shall ultimately be able to find something for you," Miss Matthison assured her.

> Don't be downhearted; and *do* keep in touch with me, and let me know where you are, and everything you are doing. I hold out my hand to you in love and fellowship. Take it in full belief of my sincerity.

Edith Wynne Matthison had a majestic beauty and an imperious style. With dark hair, full breasts, and creamy skin, she looked at forty-odd like a dark duchess. Her voice, rich and passionate, won audiences to her. Within the year Millay would write in tribute to that voice:

> If I should lose my hearing, I
> Two senses would have lost thereby,
> There having passed beyond my reach
> At once my hearing and your speech.

Little is more flattering or more seductive to an ambitious girl than the interest and help of a successful older woman.

The previous season, Edith Wynne Matthison had starred on Broadway in *The Spy*. She told Millay she was afraid of nothing but fire—and Vincent was as attracted to that high-handed confidence as she was to the offer of friendship. That Matthison might promise more than she could deliver, or that she might make such promises out of an expansive and theatrical disposition, did not occur to her. She wrote to her that summer as she had never written to Miss Dow or Miss Haight:

> You wrote me a beautiful letter,—I wonder if you meant it to be as beautiful as it was.—I think you did; for somehow I know that your feeling for me, however slight it is, is of the nature of love. . . . nothing that has happened to me for a long time has made me so happy as I shall be to visit you sometime.—You must not forget that you spoke of that,—because it would disappoint me cruelly.

> Listen; if ever in my letters to you, or in my conversation, you see a candor that seems almost crude,—please know that it is because when I think of you I think of real things, & become honest,—and quibbling and circumvention seem very inconsiderable.

Edith Wynne Matthison took three weeks to answer Vincent's letter. She told her to beware:

I am terribly demanding of those whom I love. . . . I am beautifully tolerant of the failings of those whom I do not love, but my poor friends I treat in the same way I treat myself. Do you think you can stand it? Anyway you can make a trial. If you can't stand it, I shall not blame you, I shall only become "tolerant" and "kind."

This letter she signed with love, and Vincent answered her by return mail. Twice within her letter she told her that she would do whatever Edith wanted her to do, whatever Edith told her to do, and then this:

Love me, please; I love you; I can bear to be your friend. So ask of me anything, and hurt me whenever you must; but never be "tolerant," or "kind." And never say to me again,—don't dare to say to me again—"Anyway, you can make a trial" of being friends with you! Because I can't do things in that way; I am not a tentative person.

Mrs. Kennedy backed off a little after that, and she was careful to mention another "rare child" she wished Vincent to meet: "It is such as you and she, that must hold the banner of the spirit up to the coming generation. I am so glad you can come to me; and more glad that you love me." If it was to be love, it would be shared with other rare girls.

The August 1917 issue of *Poetry* magazine ran three of Millay's lyrics: "Kin to Sorrow," "A Little Tavern," and "Afternoon on a Hill." None of them had been written that summer; Vincent was kept too busy tutoring and typing in Camden to write. Miss Haight wrote to ask if she could help: she offered a check for twenty-five dollars, as a gift or loan, and asked if she needed more. Vincent admitted she did want the money: "I could use seventy-five quite as easily. But I don't want it to be given me, I want to *borrow* it."

By return mail Haight added something else useful: she had a fall prospect for her: "My friend at Greenwich, Mrs. Hooker, (a perfect dear), motored up last week for the night with me and she has promised to have you out there for two or three readings." Vincent would help her daughters and do a reading of *The Princess Marries the Page* for their young friends, which would be followed by a reading of her own work in the evening to the adults. "So there's a dramatic engagement for a beginning!"

Miss Haight asked about her sister Kathleen, advising Vincent to "see to it that she writes Miss McCaleb at once. . . . Tell Kathleen I should like so much to help her with the Latin Prose if she will write the exercises I send her. (Do you remember our first correspondence, Brilliant One?)"

But Vincent had prospects of her own: "Did I tell you I am probably letting Mitchell Kennerley bring out my book this fall—*Renascence and Other Poems*? Are you mad or glad or indifferent. I think I am indifferent." Her nonchalance was, of course, feigned. She was delighted to find that Miss Haight was glad, for she wanted Millay to have her "heart's desire," and if that was sentimental, it was also generous. Vincent needed her older women—Miss Haight, Miss Dow, and Edith Matthison—for the support they gave her. And they, suspecting or guessing that her life would be larger and her talent more enduring than their own, needed her to dream upon.

Miss Dow's response to Vincent's decision to publish with Mitchell Kennerley was typical. She began by pointing out how worthy it was for Vincent's developing character to work for the good of others, rather than for herself. Self-sacrifice was a tonic.

> I am sorry about your decision as to your publisher—it is not wise for me to write what many wiser people than I have said to me about your being launched thro' him. He is not working this matter for altruistic reasons; and he does not appeal to the clientele which I wish might be yours. $500 is not very much money to weigh against a long future. When you have located yourself in a certain class in the literary world, it is hard for others to feel that you have anything they want.

What, precisely, was the matter with Kennerley as a publisher? And why, since Arthur Ficke and D. H. Lawrence were being published by Kennerley, shouldn't Millay be also? Kennerley's publishing house was conspicuous for being one of the most dynamic in New York. But his business practices were shabby, and Lawrence had to set Amy Lowell on him before he was either paid or published. "There were good publishing houses, of course," Alfred A. Knopf recalled, "Houghton Mifflin, Scribner's, Harper's, but it was Mitchell Kennerley who was setting another and more adventurous course." The young Knopf, who would one day found what was arguably the finest publishing house in America, was employed by Kennerley, from whom he learned an important lesson.

"We worked in a large, open floor, and his office was tiny and bitterly cold, as I remember. The only thing in it besides his desk and chair was a full-length nude photograph—or perhaps it was a painting?—of Emily Grigsby, who had been the mistress of Charles Gerkes, about whom Dreiser wrote *The Titan*.

"Kennerley was a pink-complexioned man of medium build," Knopf remembered. "Very English, very hauteur, and a ladies' man." His business life and his publishing acumen were by all accounts directly affected by the conduct of his private life.

"As he would leave of an afternoon," Knopf said, "he would tell Bel Greene, his assistant, 'I'm off to the Biltmore Baths,' and I can still see him, putting on his bowler hat, rather carefully pulling on his gloves, picking up his cane, and off he'd go. But of course he was not going to the Biltmore. He was going to meet a woman!

"But, oh, the manner of his books. The way they were bound and produced. I remember them clearly, still, in their rich black cloth bindings with gold stamping. The man had extraordinary taste and certain judgment, but he was dishonorable. It was not infrequent that someone from the sheriff's office was sitting in the front office. He never seemed to be bothered. Had Kennerley been an honest man, I don't believe I would have become a publisher."

Vincent dismissed Miss Dow's advice. She was coming close to ignoring her old adviser.

At the end of August, Millay visited Edith Matthison and her husband, Charles Rann Kennedy, at "The Rafters," their summerhouse in New Hartford, Connecticut, where they were trying to arrange readings for her later in the fall. She was charmed by the Kennedys—Edith, working in the garden in her blue linen smock and bloomers; Rann, as she now called him, writing in his hut in the field.

> He is a great big gruffey man with a childlike smile & eagerness,—he wears an enormous yellow smock which reaches to his knees,—& that is *all*— excepting a pair of sneakers, & drawers whose cunning hems sometimes show when he puts a book on a high shelf. Imagine—bare legs—long, grey hair—& a face like a child's! Oh, he is so sweet!—and she is beautiful— . . . . We have a wonderful time together.

By mid-September she was back in the city, staying at the Kennedys' apartment on West Eighty-sixth Street. It was not the bohemia she had dreamed of, but it was free. She hurled herself into life in the city. There were luncheons and teas with Edith, who arranged for her to see George C. Tyler of the New Amsterdam Theatre and Winthrop Ames, another theatrical manager. She almost got a part in the new play of "Mr. Carpenter, who wrote last season's success, *The Cinderella Man*," she told her mother, "& who says he would give me a secondary part in *his* play except that my hair is too near the color of the lead's." And she gave a reading of her poems at Mrs. Blanche Hooker's in Greenwich, "a very wealthy woman." Because her trunk hadn't arrived yet from Camden, she'd had to dress in one of Mrs. Hooker's gowns "with a train & hanging about six inches on the floor all around, made out of three rainbow colored scarfs. And, family, I discover that I have nothing to give readings in, I *must* have long dresses, trailing ones." She looked best in such gowns, "very long & drapy—more like a negligee than a dress, really—very graceful & floaty." By the end of September, Mrs. Hooker sent her fifty dollars for her reading that evening.

The *Literary Digest* reviewed the three poems she'd published in *Poetry* magazine, saying that they were "of the same charm and simplicity which struck the world in this writer's unforgettable Renascence. . . . Much of Miss Millay's strength lies in her colloquial directness." She had seen the title page of *Renascence* and was delighted with it; she'd asked Mitchell if it weren't going to be too expensive to print it on that sort of paper and he'd said, " 'Oh, well,—you *promised* me, Edna, it was to be a very small book!'—and so it is—lovely & thin—only the very best—& bound in black with gold letters."

She thought it would sell at Jess Hosmer's store in Camden, and of course in Poughkeepsie; it might seem peculiar to her family for her to be thinking of the business end of it, "but I want it to be read—it's that more than the disgusting money—the dirty necessary money."

Vincent was offered an opportunity by Mrs. Thompson, who'd helped put her through Vassar, to be her social secretary. She refused: "she believes in me as a poet & would even pamper me in order not to interfere with my writing & she would pay me a salary & her place is out in the beautiful country & everything would be lovely & Aunt Calline is exceedingly anxious to have me do it—but I just *don' wanna!*"

She was very clear about why. After all, Edith Wynne Matthison had been good to her, too, and she wanted a chance at the theater. She wasn't going to "break all my dates & say 'I'm going up to Sparkhill to be private secretary to a beautiful woman of fashion.' "

By October 12, she had reversed her decision. She was at Mrs. Thompson's, she explained to Charlotte Babcock Sills, her Vassar friend:

> I came thinking I was to be a sort of unofficial secretary. But I find she just did it, bless her, to get me out into this wonderful place & rest me up & give me a chance to write. She is concerned for my future, & rather afraid, I think, of what I may do, if left indefinitely in New York alone.

She'd been at Mrs. Thompson's for the better part of three weeks without telling her family. Finally she wrote home. Norma had mixed feelings about her sister's prolonged silence:

You bring new life to Mother and me for we thought of you as settled at Mrs. Thompson's forever, doing something you "donwanna" do. We talk you over so often and wonder and wonder about you and hear so seldom. I, of course, stand it a great deal better than our Mother does. . . . Just a postal twice a week would keep things easier here. . . . Mother *has* to know where to picture you or she is very unhappy. 'Course *I* don't care where you are. I couldn't picture you any where any way 'cause I've forgotten absolutely how you look! What color is your hair?

Millay grasped that Mrs. Thompson didn't want her to lift a finger except to write, so she stayed three weeks; her pleasure in the delicious care that was being taken of her is evident in every line of a letter home:

It is eleven o'clock in the morning. I am still in bed. At nine o'clock Anna, my personal maid—(for all I ever see her doing for anyone else) awakened me with my breakfast. She came in with the tray—silver coffee-things, & fruit, & bacon and an egg—(God forgive me if you are even now hungry!—I will send you five no, *one* dollar I wish I could send ten)—and little sticks of toast rolled up in an embroidered napkin, & a vase of hot-house flowers. This she set down on the bed. Then she closed the windows, saw that the register was open, brought me my negligee & helped me into it, propped pillows behind my back, brought two hair-pins from the bureau for me to pin back my hair with, put my cigarette-case, holder, & matches within easy reach—all this without a word from me except Good-morning—then asked if there were any-thing I would like, & left me, softly closing the door behind her.—I swear to you I am not inventing a word of it; & that is the way it happens every morning!

Mitchell Kennerley was going to publish her just as handsomely as he had promised. Fifteen copies of the first edition were printed on Japan vellum, a thick, creamy handmade paper whose edges had been trimmed to look as if they had been torn. The jacket copy is worth quoting: it reads like a declaration of Kennerley's feelings about her:

Miss Millay's poems have a remarkable freshness, sincerity, and power. They do not depend upon curious and involved artifice, upon wayward-ness of method and metre, upon the presence of what should be absent, or the absence of what should be present. They do not avoid rhythm and music as dangerous intrusions in modern poetry. They do not present uncouthness, or mere triteness, as strength. They are not the facile outpourings of one form of shallowness, nor the curt trivialities of another. They deal, as poetry should deal, primarily with emotion; with the sense of tears and of laughter, in mortal things; with beauty and passion; with having and losing.

He gave her, however, only $25 of the promised $500 advance. By now she was becoming desperate for funds.

Only Caroline Dow would have given Edna Millay a personal account book—"Five cents put aside every day will amount to $182.50 in ten years"—and expected her to keep it. She did, for one month. The first entries in the mud-colored book are arduously recorded in her most careful script.

At the beginning of October 1917, she had $75 on hand, the $50 from Mrs. Hooker and $25 from Mitchell Kennerley. But her expenses mounted quickly; there were roses for Mrs. Hooker, $10 for lingerie, another $10 for velvet for a skirt she intended to sew, and a few dollars for Hunk and for Kathleen. Since there was always a discrepancy between her balance and what she actually had, she added a column of her own, "Lost in the Shuffle." She began November 1917 with $55.05 and never made another entry.

At the close of the book was a record keeping of another sort, far more crucial to her than money saved: she began to detail the long list of poems sent out again and again to the magazines she hoped would publish her: *McClure's, Pearson's, Harper's Monthly Magazine, Scribner's, The Century;* she even tried *St. Nicholas* with her two plays. By the turn of the year she had sold only one poem, "Time does not bring relief," to *The Century,* and that was a sonnet Burgess Johnson, her journalism professor at Barnard, had helped her place the summer before.

How did she manage at all? It helped that during her first two and a half months she paid no rent. She was with the Kennedys in Connecticut and then at their New York apartment until the end of September and went from there to Mrs. Thompson's in Sparkhill for the greater part of October. Now she had no choice but to spend November under Miss Dow's wing at the YWCA.

That autumn Vincent went to a costume ball in Greenwich Village with Miss Dow and some of her friends. "They were great events in those days," Charles Ellis, a young painter from Ohio, recalled. "There was a group of elderly people who were not in costume up on the stage watching the dancers, and in their midst was this little girl. She had made her-self a costume, a Turkish outfit of some sort of pajamas, and there she sat among these older people. She just seemed to sit there for hours, and she looked to me as if she wanted to dance. So I walked up to the stage and held out my arms and said, 'Wanna dance?' "

Ellis had come to New York from Ohio because he wanted to paint. Soon he was designing sets and painting screens for the Provincetown Players and was acting in their productions. "We were all little boys from the Midwest," he would recall years later, "Jimmy Light and Kenny Burke and me. And that winter of 1917–1918 was a wonderful winter.... We knew everyone ... Stuart Davis, John Sloan, O'Neill, Jack Reed, and Max Eastman—we all knew each other. And the two things that drew people together were *The Masses* and the Provincetown Players."

They read everything that was fresh and innovative. Every one of them had read Edna St. Vincent Millay.

"I knew her name," said Ellis. "She'd been in *The Forum* magazine, and her first book was out. Afterwards I asked her did she want to come to a party. It was at our place on Macdougal Street—Jimmy Light and Suzie and Kenny Burke and me—& we were sitting in front of our fireplace drinking mulled wine. It was an extremely cold winter, one of the coldest in the history of the city, I believe. We'd burn anything we could find, wooden street signs, anything. Then we'd put the poker in the wine to heat it. Little Vincent was sitting there with us and had a couple of glasses and we were all talking intensely.

"I suddenly looked up at her and she was green, positively green. I took her to the bathroom and told her what to do and she did it, and she was all right after that. She was such a shy little girl, right out of Vassar."

On the twenty-fourth of November, Vincent wrote Norma and asked her to come share her life in New York:

> Am sending you twenty dollars. If you can't make that do all right, tele-graph me, or, no, Hunk, I'll just send you twenty-five instead, & let you save all you can of it. It's going to be hard, baby,—we'll probably want money pretty bad pretty often,—but no unworthy girl ever had so many friends as I have, & we shan't starve, because we *can* borrow.—I'm as crazy to see you as if I were going to be married to you—no one is such good pals as we are—I want you to bum around with—to cook breakfasts with.

They were, she told her, with an optimism that was young and high, "bound to succeed—can't keep us down—I'm all enthusiasm & good courage about it. So come on out, my dear old sweet Sister,—& we'll open our oysters together."

2

On Sunday morning, December 2, 1917, Vincent and Kathleen met Norma in Grand Central Terminal and had breakfast together. "She was so pretty," Kathleen wrote their mother, she "looked blooming." Now, with Kay having been accepted at Vassar, they were "Three New Yorkers," Norma scribbled on the face of their mother's envelope. Years later Norma would describe her entrance into this new world somewhat less glowingly than Charles Ellis had:

> It may have been a wonderful winter to you, Charlie Ellis, but we nearly starved to death that first winter in New York. Or froze. Vincent had this little hall bedroom on West 9th Street. Well, the gas main froze. She put a bouquet of violets on the window sill and they froze. We stayed in bed together for two days once just to keep warm.
>
> And, then, this boy I knew from Maine came in to town and came upstairs and told us to get up. He was taking us to dinner. The first thing we asked him was how he got by our German landlady. He said, "I told her I was your brother." "And what did she say?" Vincent asked. "She said, 'Ya! and my Brudder, too!' "
>
> But up he came and took us to Tom & Jerry's, and it was our first good meal in I don't know how long.

Less than two weeks after Norma's arrival, Vincent had bound copies of *Renascence* in her hands. The book was published on December 17, 1917. She sent her first copy home, inscribed *"To my Mother,"* and quoted these stanzas from "Tavern":

> I'll keep a little tavern
>   Below the high hill's crest,
> Wherein all grey-eyed people
>   May set them down and rest.
>   . . .
> Aye, 'tis a curious fancy—
>   But all the good I know
> Was taught me out of two grey eyes
>   A long time ago.
>
>   Edna St. Vincent Millay
>   December the fifteenth
>   1917

Millay received one letter that pleased her more than any of the superb reviews. It was from Edward J. Wheeler, one of the three judges who had voted against her winning the prize in *The Lyric Year*. "It has just come, and it is wonderful," he wrote. "It gives me a sort of choky feeling in my throat. I had not known that there was so much beauty in the world. . . . I don't know how you could do it,—you a mere school-girl. I can't say anything, as yet, of any critical value. I don't want to. I am just feasting."

But Miss Dow's note stung:

> I have wondered why some of those poems I had heard most praised were omitted, probably for some good reason. Of course I am happy to have an "author's copy," and hope it is only the beginning of better things. . . . If I had not heard from several sources how bored you have been in the atmosphere of our home, I would have been glad to have you bring Norma up to dinner some time—but I hesitate to suggest a return to a place which seems to have been dull.

If that weren't clear enough, she added that Vincent would always be as welcome as she was when "we were all you had."

At an audition for the Provincetown Players in December Edna Millay met Floyd Dell, who was casting his play *The Angel Intrudes*. He needed an ingenue, someone who was fresh and quick and bright, about whom it could be said, "Annabelle is little. Annabelle's petulant upturned lips are rosebud red. Annabelle's round eyes are baby-blue. Annabelle is— young."

He waited impatiently one snowy afternoon at the tiny theater on Macdougal Street to listen to the young woman who had come to read for the part.

Floyd Dell was thirty when he met Edna Millay that December and gave her the part of his ingenue. He was divorced, an apostle of the shocking new Freudian school of psychoanalysis, and he was one of the editors of *The Masses,* a radical new magazine, which had been indicted by the government the previous October under the Espionage Act. "Which was being used not against German spies," he would write in his autobiography, *Homecoming,* "but against American Socialists, Pacifists and anti-war radicals." He faced, along with the founding editor, Max Eastman, Art Young, John Reed, and other editors, cartoonists, and writers, a twenty-year imprisonment.

In the fall of 1916, George Cram Cook brought the Provincetown Theatre on Cape Cod to New York, where a theater was made in the parlor floor of a brownstone on Macdougal Street in Greenwich Village. Floyd Dell's play *King Arthur's Socks* was on its first New York bill—along with Louise Bryant's *The Game* and Eugene O'Neill's *Bound East for Cardiff.*

Now, with *The Masses* forced to suspend publication, Dell had no job, and the novel he was writing was stymied. He decided to get involved in Cook's production of his play.

The morning of the first rehearsal, Millay knew all her lines by heart. Dell observed her closely. "Without demur or delay she did whatever she was asked to do. She was eager to please; and it appeared she especially wished to please me."

In photographs Floyd Dell looks bland and milky, with lank pale hair drawn like a wing across his wide brow, eyes as pale as his skin. Norma remembered him wearing soft flannel checked shirts, "and always with his shirt-tail out. You have to understand that Floyd Dell was special to us in those first days in New York," she continued. "Oh, he could introduce Vincent to so many things she'd missed and didn't know about. She was impressed by all these people. She never took me to rehearsals. And I'd been in everything in high school."

The play opened on December 28. Edna was pronounced "delightful as Annabelle" by the author and the others in the Provincetown Players. In celebration, she was invited to join the troupe.

The Provincetown Players planned to produce *Sweet & Twenty,* another one of Dell's one-act plays, at the end of January 1918. There was a good part in it for Edna, if she wanted it, and Dell asked her to read the script and decide. She said she'd rather have him read it to her. And so, a little stiffly, for they were on somewhat formal terms with each other, Dell invited her to the basement dining room at the Brevoort Hotel. When he arrived to pick her up, her landlady stopped her and demanded the over-due rent. Dell quickly intervened and paid it. "Edna," he remembered, "was much humiliated but unable to refuse." But neither let that spoil their dinner, and soon they were talking eagerly. Then, rashly, Dell told her he'd dreamed of her the night before. She watched him quietly and said that she had dreamed of him, too. He'd tell his dream if she'd tell hers, he said shyly. But she refused, "coldly," he remembered.

He had dreamed that he was sitting beside her on a sofa in her room watching her hand on her knee. He wanted to clasp it in his but was afraid to and hesitated. Then suddenly he did take her hand and kissed her. "It was," he wrote, "a simple wish-fulfillment dream. But I hadn't known that I had any such wish." After supper Dell walked her home.

We went on to her room—where I had never been before. There was a big iron-framed bed, a small fireplace, and among other furniture a battered old sofa. In the fireplace blazed a cheerful fire, lit by Edna when we came in; it was chiefly of newspapers. I sat on the sofa with my play in my lap. Her hand lay on her knee, just as in my dream the night before. I wanted to take her hand, but was afraid to. However, encouraged by that dream, I did venture to take her hand—and the next moment we were in each other's arms, kissing; and then she said, in a husky, vibrant violin-like tone that I had never heard before except in my dream, "I'm so glad you wanted to kiss me, Floyd."

Then she mumbled something about her own dream, and they drifted into another kiss. "She talked as if she were breaking a long silence," he remembered, "as if now, in my arms, she was free to speak her mind without fear."

Soon, to Dell's delight, they were seeing each other every day. But even this early in their relationship, Dell was anxious. When Edna wanted to know why he was in analysis, he spoke about certain "faults of character." His inconstancy and fickleness with women troubled him. Edna was unconvinced. She said she'd noticed that his girls remained friends after they had stopped being lovers. Dell laughed and said that at thirty he had had enough love affairs. Edna didn't think romantic love could last long in any case—she wanted to be in bed with him now, but she also insisted that their relationship continue "platonically."

He watched her undress in her little room while the fire died down, carefully folding her clothes and placing them on a chair, before she slipped into bed. As they lay in each other's arms, they kissed and talked, and he thought to himself that if she really wanted their companionship in bed to continue without going further, "I would conform to her wish."

And it appeared that this was just how she wished it to be. Lying in my arms, not beneath but always above me, she kissed me with kisses that were for the most part sweet and dreamy but were sometimes fierce and agonized.

At first he considered it some peculiarly New England form of "bundling." He fully expected that his "patience and devotion would be rewarded in the natural course of events." But it wasn't.

Dell was living in a basement room on Charlton Street. It was large and comfortable and bright with the Japanese prints Arthur Ficke had given him. He had built his bed in such a way that it resembled a low divan, and when Vincent admired it, he offered to build her one when she moved. Dell remembered one night turning out all the lights save one, over which he draped a colored silk scarf. Undressing slowly, admiring each other, they lay in bed, again kissing tenderly and chastely. They talked, and they argued.

She attacked my Freudian views and I defended them. I argued somewhat reluctantly and awkwardly, for a Freudian defense could not be conducted in amusing phrases—and besides, I felt that she wasn't listening to anything I said. I had a notion that she was using intellectual argument as a means of cooling off my erotic feelings, and her own, too. In this earnest debate we would now and then sit up in bed, she with her lamp-lit torso and small firm breasts confronting me with impudent audacity while she defended platonic love against Freud.

To her (so far as I could make out) the Freudian program required woman's complete sexual surrender to man—which might be inevitable but which brought an inescapable penalty; for when a girl gave herself completely to her lover, he would soon stop being in love with her—and then she could pine for him forlornly or turn lightly to another lover.

Dell thought this was nonsense and told her so. She thought it was entirely true and that he ought not to be impatient with her. She would keep their love the way it was, in its beauty. They had then known each other less than a month.

Dell helped Vincent find new rooms at 139 Waverly Place, "a fairly large room on the second floor, at the back. It had a corner washbowl with hot and cold taps." The following day he built her a wooden frame for her bed just like his. Then he put up shelves around the washbasin and brought her some colored dishes from Vantine's and hung a Hiroshige print of Arthur's.

> Norma, one evening, made a witty remark, and Edna said to me, "Give my little sister a kiss for that." Norma came and put herself in my arms, our lips met in a kiss—and together we floated off in a blissful trance. . . . and clung together in that dreamy kiss, which went on and on until we were at last wakened by the sound of Edna's sobbing. Norma, filled with remorse, ran to her. Edna was apologetic about her outburst. And I went away.

After this passage (which was left only in an unpublished manuscript), Dell records that none of them ever mentioned the incident again.

ᴥ ᴥ ᴥ

Norma insisted it hadn't happened. When I pressed her—why would Dell invent such a scene? It wasn't really about him, it was about the relationship between the sisters, wasn't it?—she said, "I don't know. I don't remember. You'd have to ask Floyd, wouldn't you?" Since Floyd Dell has been dead for years, the only record left was Norma's memory.

Years, not weeks or months, but truly years have passed, and we were talking about their other sister, Kathleen—about the enmity that can grow between sisters like a malignancy—when Norma did remember that kiss: "Well, yes, okay! I do remember Vincent's asking Floyd to kiss me. Why should she? But why should I not? So I suppose I gave him everything I got. I suppose we got caught up in some long lovely kiss. I don't mean anything vulgar. And, then, yes, she was crying. You see, there was this change in Vincent. In Camden, *I* was the girl all the boys wanted to take out. Well, things had changed in New York, she'd published *Renascence*. That made quite an impression in New York. They'd heard of Vincent."

√ √ √

"One day it occurred to me to wonder what was the Freudian explanation of her persistence in 'platonic' behavior in bed," Dell wrote, "and the answer came to my mind instantly." The next time they were in bed together, Dell told her he'd guessed her secret: "You pretend that you have had many love affairs—but the truth, my dear, is that you are still a virgin. You have merely had homosexual affairs with girls at college."

Dell says she was astonished and defensive about her behavior. "No man has ever found me out before!" she said. He "lectured her, instructively, affectionately, scornfully. I felt that it was my duty to rescue her from her psychological captivity." But he refused any longer to take part in what he later called their platonic "performances."

Shortly after that confrontation, he came swinging into her place with a bag of groceries for dinner, only to find her "sitting adoringly" at the feet of a college friend. "Edna told me that she had forgotten to tell me that she had a dinner date with Imogene [as he called her]. I went to the kitchen corner and unpacked the groceries, and went out. Something ailed me, and at first I didn't know what it was. I was stricken, confused, shattered." (In an earlier draft of this memoir Dell added another sentence: "It was in fact a violent attack of jealousy.") He felt he could never see Edna again.

Norma came to him at last and asked what had happened. He could not tell her. But he went back to Waverly Place to say good-bye to Edna. At first he couldn't speak. Edna asked him to tell her what was troubling him. "I managed with great difficulty to say a few words about her lies."

She listened to him gravely and told him she had not lied to him, she had simply forgotten. She was not in love with the girl, she never had been, and she would not lie to him. He believed her.

After their reconciliation, Floyd awoke one morning with the feeling of spring, though there was still snow on the ground. He felt that he had a rare girl waiting for him, and he dressed quickly and ran to her.

> I rang her bell (with my special ring), and, after a brief interval, the door clicked to admit me. I ran up the stairs and opened the door. She was alone

and in bed. I locked the door and went and sat on her bed. She put her arms about me, and we kissed. . . . and then [she] closed her eyes and seemed to sleep. I took off my clothes and got into bed with her. Was she really sleeping, or only pretending, as my love-making began? Anyway, there was nothing platonic about it. She was yielding herself to me, sweetly and completely.

Her sleepy dreaminess went on until she seemed to awaken "with an air of being surprised at what she found herself doing"; but she did not stop him, and she was no longer simply yielding. Afterward, stroking his pale silky hair as he curled next to her, she said—almost to herself, it seemed to him—"I shall have many lovers."

CHAPTER 13

Dell felt that their happiness together was "paradisal." He noticed that she continued to see her college friend, but it no longer bothered him. When he told her this, she smiled and said it was because now they were lovers. "This was said in her occasional hard-boiled or down-to-earth manner," he wrote. But when she added, "Now that you are having a normal sex-life you are not so sensitive and easily upset," that did bother him: she hadn't said "we," and she hadn't said "love."

But she was no longer shy or hesitant, and at his apartment they were free from interruption by Norma, who after all shared Vincent's room on Waverly Place. Dell remembered placing a long gilt-framed mirror

on chairs alongside our divan and [we] lay there naked in each other's arms, so that we could see what we looked like when we made love; we had read that the spectacle was ludicrous and ugly—but we saw that that was a lie, for the spectacle was beautiful and charming.

Dell wanted to know everything about her and pressed her relentlessly. When he said he wanted to marry her, she deflected him. She told him, playfully at first, that she was not the girl to cook his meals and iron his shirts. When his importuning became unbearable, she cautioned him, "Never ask a girl poet to marry you, Floyd." Finally, she said point-blank, "I am not so hopelessly besotted with you as that!" Which didn't mean she was no longer interested in him sexually.

‿ ‿ ‿

One night after Norma had gone to bed, she heard Vincent in the hall. "I remember her coming in and passing my bed. I was sleepy and almost asleep when she came and sat down on the edge. Without any conversation that I can remember, she told me that I had this little piece of flesh between my legs and that I should rub it back and forth. And when I thought I couldn't stand it anymore, then I should keep on rubbing it. I'm sure it was Floyd Dell who taught her that. And it was like Vincent to share the news with me." Norma's roguish gaze caught mine. "And now I'm sharing it with you. I'm sure you won't believe it, but I had no idea what a clitoris was."

Leaning forward in my chair, I asked her the only thing I could think of. "What did you do?"

"Oh, naughty Normie. I tried it!"

‿ ‿ ‿

When Cora had heard nothing from her daughters by the turn of the year, she was frantic. "My dear, dear girls," she wrote, "I am all at sea, and so far away from any knowledge of how you are faring . . . as if I were on some other planet." She pictured them having a terrible time, "alone and penniless in the biggest city in the world, in the hardest year in history." Did they have friends they could call on? They needed to find jobs and to find them at once. "For the first time in our history I feel myself pushed entirely out of things." Her letters continued in this vein from week to week as the girls' silence deepened and her fears increased. She'd enclose a few dollars and then ask if they'd received the cash. "I used to be a sort of chum. . . . I shall think I'm an old woman pretty soon and not capable of standing real things."

Finally Norma wrote back on January 24, 1918, the day before Floyd's *Sweet & Twenty* opened at the Provincetown. Both of the sisters were ill, Vincent with a sore throat and Norma with a toothache, but they were hardly friendless. "Floyd Dell is at the moment sitting on the edge of the bed holding Edna's hands and telling her funny things. . . . Floyd is the dearest man on earth and a wonderful friend to us." He'd awakened them at noon with his arms full of breakfast. "He is just like a wonderful brother to me and a bit more than a brother to Vincent." Vincent's note, tacked on the tail end of Norma's letter, gave her mother the only acceptable reason for her silence: "I've written some quite good poems lately,—a few excellent ones,—and one that you will love."

When she wrote to Harriet Monroe, the editor of *Poetry,* a few weeks later in a letter which was really about her need for money—"Would you mind paying me *now* instead of on publication for those so stunning verses of mine which you have"—she identified the poems *Poetry* would publish in June: "First Fig," "Second Fig," "The Unexplorer," "Thursday," and "The Penitent." They were stunning: witty, flippant, defiant, and fun. "First Fig" would change her career utterly.

> My candle burns at both ends;
>   It will not last the night;
> But ah, my foes, and oh, my friends—
>   It gives a lovely light!

If "Renascence" had suggested Saint Theresa of the Illuminations, as Wilbert Snow had called her, or the saintly girl poet treasured by Louis Untermeyer and Sara Teasdale, these lines did not. They would, however, help make her the most widely read poet of her generation. In fact, this single stanza, what Norma in her sister's published *Letters* called "the candle one, surely the most quoted and mis-quoted quatrain in America," became the anthem of her generation.

But at some cost to Millay. For while these poems would win her a larger audience, she risked alienating those who wanted their poetry serious and inspiring. It is a chancy business for a poet to straddle the licentious, but especially for a woman, when the very fact of her writing at all makes her either a figure of awe or suspect. Here was a quatrain that people, young women especially, took to heart. They took it even further; the Jazz Babies, as they would soon be called, took it as their rallying cry.

Curiously, these poems expressed an ideal as ancient as the Latin poets Millay knew and loved: Life is impermanent and in the face of that impermanence, cavort! Look death in the eye, tell him you're as cute as a button, flash a little defiant guile his way, and tell him to go feast on somebody else's sweet flesh. For just as there are no happy rustics in Edna Millay's work, so in these merry verses there were no repentant women.

> I had a little Sorrow,
>   Born of a little Sin,
> I found a room all damp with gloom
>   And shut us all within;
> And, "Little Sorrow, weep," said I,
>   "And, Little Sin, pray God to die,
> And I upon the floor will lie
>   And think how bad I've been!"

> Alas for pious planning—
>   It mattered not a whit!
> As far as gloom went in that room,
>   The lamp might have been lit!
> My Little Sorrow would not weep,
> My Little Sin would go to sleep—
> To save my soul I could not keep
>   My graceless mind on it!
>
> So I got up in anger,
>   And took a book I had,
> And put a ribbon on my hair
>   To please a passing lad,
> And, "One thing there's no getting by—
> I've been a wicked girl," said I;
>   "But if I can't be sorry, why,
>   I might as well be glad!"

She had the audacity to call this "The Penitent." "Thursday" was even cheekier:

> And if I loved you Wednesday,
>   Well, what is that to you?
> I do not love you Thursday—
>   So much is true.
>
> And why you come complaining
>   Is more than I can see.
> I loved you Wednesday,—yes—but what
>   Is that to me?

But there was something else in "First Fig" besides cheek. For while Millay was able to flaunt the brevity of her own life, she had written a poem that would defy the brevity of life itself.

Norma took on the role of writing to Cora, and at the end of February her news was all about Charles Ellis, "A young artist whom I really love just now and who really loves me. He loves Vincent too but they feel more 'sister & brother' than we do. He *is* just like a real brother to us both though. You would love him he is so *nice*." When Charlie got his check from Mrs. Whitney, who helped support the young artists she believed in, he would take Norma and Vincent to the National Lunch on Sixth Avenue and Eighth Street. "You could eat for forty or fifty cents," he said, "and that was with a good cup of coffee with real cream." Norma and

Charlie described themselves as "a silly little blond girl from Maine and a kid from Ohio." They went everywhere together.

Greenwich Village was a little republic set apart from the rest of Manhattan, bounded on the north by Washington Square, with its gracious redbrick town houses that had seen better days, and on the south by the seedy boardinghouses in which lived young and not-so-young artists, political writers, cartoonists, playwrights, poets, and novelists of the era they were inventing. These scrappy young women and men, often living together just a few blocks shy of the Italian families to the south, came from another America, and not just for cheap rents and free love. The Provincetown Players were in a stable on Macdougal Street right off Washington Square. When John Reed moved into a dilapidated apartment at 42 Washington Square on the south side of the park, he paid a jaunty tribute to their way of life:

> We are free who live in Washington Square
> We dare to think as Uptown wouldn't dare
> Blazing our nights with arguments uproarious
> What care we for a dull old world censorious
> When each is sure he'll fashion something glorious?

Close to the flower markets, iced-clam wagons, and fish stalls of poor Italian families, the Village was called the Ninth Ward in New York City, but it was bohemia to the young writers and artists who found their rooms and studios there. The offices of *The Masses* were at 91 Greenwich Avenue, right around the corner from Frank Shay's bookshop on Christopher Street, where the newest books and quarterlies were in his windows, as well as the first blue-paper-wrapped copy of James Joyce's *Ulysses*. There was a spirit of carnival where no one said good-bye to the flesh, and where even the masquerade balls were called "Pagan Routs." Uptown men wore suits with vests and high starched collars, and women wore corsets. In the Village, men wore corduroy shirts and tied their neckties around their waists as belts. Greenwich Village women smoked and didn't wear corsets, and as Art Young, the brilliant cartoonist for *The Masses,* wrote, "Here a woman could say damn right out loud and still be respected!"

They ate together, played and drank and talked together. "I'd never seen a place like the Hell Hole in my life," Norma said, "people leaning over and standing and drinking, and everybody talking—about what? about labor, and the theater and Rimbaud and politics and philosophy—and then a lovely hand, Charlie's, just came through the crowd, and I just took it. A look of horror and despair on my face. Those were terrible nights at the Hell Hole—anarchists, Wobblies, with Hippolyte saying 'Bourgeois pigs!' and he always took taxis!"

One of the first things Vincent explained to Norma was that there was a certain freedom of language in the Village that mustn't shock her. It wasn't vulgar. "So we sat darning socks on Waverly Place and practiced the use of profanity as we stitched. Needle in, shit. Needle out, piss. Needle in, fuck. Needle out, cunt. Until we were easy with the words."

2

On February 7, 1918, Major Arthur Davison Ficke wrote to Edna from the War Department in Washington, D.C., where he was stationed prior to carrying dispatches to General "Black Jack" Pershing in France. If she could bring herself to meet "a reformed poet who is now a soldier," he would be in New York shortly, awaiting embarkation to France and the front. He wanted very much to see her before he left. Floyd Dell took Major Ficke to her on Waverly Place.

Arthur cut a dashing figure in his officer's tunic with its high, snug collar and a Sam Browne belt strapped smartly across his chest. He was, Dell wrote forlornly, "tall, handsome, elegant, rich, a distinguished poet, intelligent, kind, gentle." Floyd knew he was no match for Ficke. They all sat on the floor, eating sandwiches and pickles that Charlie Ellis had brought from a local delicatessen, when Norma raised a pickle to her lips and said, "This pickle is a little loving-cup." Arthur, his eyes glittering with mischief, scrawled effortlessly across the lid of the pastry box a sonnet to her pickle:

> I raise it to my lips, and where you kissed
> There lurks a certain sting that I have missed
> In nectars more laboriously put up. . . .

Soon they were all giddy with laughter and talk and planning pranks. "Oh, Arthur was witty and quick, and debonair," Norma remembered. "He was everything Floyd was not."

Ficke expected to be in New York for several weeks, but the following day his orders came through: he was to sail for France at noon. In a wild scramble, he wrote, "I had time only to rush to her apartment, kiss her good-bye . . . as I ran and barely caught the ship on which I was ordered to sail. That night, in the darkness of the muffled ship . . . I wrote my sonnet, 'Sea Midnight,' and sent it to her." That was not the only poem he wrote to her. Although she did not hear from him until March 5, when his letter at last arrived it was filled with poems. At sea with thousands of men in a vast fleet of troopships with no one to talk to, he wrote her sonnets. In closing he asked for her photograph and told her to write to him "like a good child."

He signed the letter "Major Arthur D. Ficke, Ordinance Dept N.A., Headquarters, Lines of Communications, American Expeditionary Forces, France." Stamped across the face of the envelope was "PASSED AS CENSORED."

Ficke did not hear from Millay for eight months. When he did, he destroyed her letter. It was too ardent. He was afraid his wife would find it among his personal papers if he were to die in France.

Vincent was as shaken as he was. She had dreamed of meeting him since that Thanksgiving Day in Camden in 1912 when he and Bynner had been the first to welcome her triumph with "Renascence." "My time, in those awful days after you went away to France," she later wrote, "was a mist of thinking about you & writing sonnets to you."

She sent him two sonnets: one "about you & about myself—we were both like that—but are not anymore." She would not reprint this in any book, for its conclusion was a little too easy, but there was this single line that rescued the entire poem: "There is no shelter in you anywhere." The second sonnet was extraordinary. She was writing in full command of her voice and talent.

> Into the golden vessel of great song
> Let us pour all our passion; breast to breast
> Let other lovers lie, in love and rest;
> Not we,—articulate, so, but with the tongue
> Of all the world: the churning blood, the long
> Shuddering quiet, the desperate hot palms pressed
> Sharply together upon the escaping guest,
> The common soul, unguarded, and grown strong.
> Longing alone is singer to the lute;
> Let still on nettles in the open sigh
> The minstrel, that in slumber is as mute
> As any man, and love be far and high,
> That else forsakes the topmost branch, a fruit
> Found on the ground by every passer-by.

After Arthur had left, Vincent—who again had not been writing home—told her mother, "You will forgive me when you read my sonnets." The only person who had a hard time forgiving her was Floyd Dell. "A generous-minded lover," Dell wrote, "would perhaps not object to his girl's having a poetical long-distance romance with another poet." But he was possessive, "and this girl poet would always be falling in love with someone else."

3

On the morning of April 15, 1918, the trial of Max Eastman, the editor of *The Masses;* Art Young, an artist and cartoonist; Merrill Rogers, their business manager; Josephine Bell, a poet; and Floyd Dell began. In June 1912, Congress had passed the Espionage Act, making it illegal to obstruct recruiting or to interfere with the operation of the military. Woodrow Wilson, who had won an election by promising to keep America out of the war in Europe, committed the country instead to war with Germany. *The Masses,* which Floyd said stood for "fun, truth, beauty, realism, freedom, peace, feminism, revolution," was the first journal of any significance to be refused the U.S. mails, upon which its existence depended. It was accused of being against recruiting, and it couldn't afford to continue publication if it couldn't be mailed. By December 1917, four months before the trial began, *The Masses* was out of business.

On the bench that spring morning in the mahogany-paneled chambers of the old Post Office building opposite City Hall sat Augustus N. Hand. He was reputed to be more conservative and less genial than his cousin, the famous Supreme Court justice Learned Hand, but his integrity was unimpeachable. The charges the government brought against the defendants were reduced to a single issue: conspiracy to obstruct recruiting or enlistment. For the first time in American history since the eighteenth century, words as well as deeds could be treasonable. If convicted, the men could look forward to twenty years' imprisonment.

For Dell, once war had been declared against Germany, Americans "who had just voted for peace were exhorted, clubbed, censored and when necessary lynched into acquiescence. . . . and the I.W.W. [Industrial Workers of the World] leaders were arrested. The respectable leaders of the pacifist movement counselled doing nothing in particular." Business was grafting millions onto war contracts, and even labor got what he called "its slice of the boodle." Political cartoons and drawings, poems and news articles were linked in protest and shaped by social passion. "The Masses became," Dell wrote, "against that war background, a thing of more vivid beauty."

But what had it done to incur the wrath of the American government?

It wasn't only its editorials and articles that spoke out against military intervention—some of its cartoons were fiercely antiwar. Henry Glintenkamp, who drew a cartoon of a handsome young man standing naked before rows of coffins, being measured by a skeleton and called "Physically Fit," fled to Mexico rather than stand trial. What had once been provocative was now alleged to be treasonous.

As the trial began on the third floor of the old Post Office building, a Liberty Bond band struck up the tune of "The Star-Spangled Banner." Every time the tune floated into the courtroom, tiny, stout Merrill Rogers sprang to his feet and slapped his hand upon his heart. If the trial was to be a show, with brass bands playing patriotic tunes, the editors of *The Masses* would show their spunk.

Edna Millay swept into this pandemonium at Floyd Dell's side. "Don't worry about the *Masses* trial," she wrote reassuringly to her mother. "I cannot possibly be mixed up in it." But the truth is she was with Floyd every day.

"One morning," Dell remembered,

Edna and I overslept; dressing hastily, we took the subway down to the federal court building. . . . The courtroom was silent as I walked down the aisle with the girl at my side. The room was filled with the Socialist, liberal, and radical intelligentsia of New York; they all looked at the girl and me, and I felt that they all knew why I was late. She, walking demurely by my side, slipped into an empty seat, and I hurried to take my place at the defendants' table. The judge in his black gown looked stern, but he did not rebuke me. Edna afterwards said to me: "It really does not matter if everybody knew that we were in bed together."

The trial lasted nine days, and the jury was out for forty-eight hours. When they returned they were deadlocked, and the defendants were free. But they had not yet been acquitted.

With the trial over, Edna's interest in Dell waned. When he was suddenly drafted, she invited him to a farewell dinner, just the two of them in her backyard. The air was soft and blue at dusk, and as the wind blew up from the Hudson, she put candles in a tree to brighten their supper. The dripping wax looked like icicles, "and those blossoms of fire that dripped ice seemed to me," Dell later wrote, "symbols of the heart of this girl poet."

The Army, however, had blundered. Dell was still indicted under the Espionage Act and was therefore sent packing back to New York with an honorable discharge, where he found nobody had expected him back so soon. "Somebody else had my job," he wrote forlornly, "and my girl seemed to have fallen in love with somebody else."

Millay was not in love with Walter Adolphe Roberts, but she did like his devotion to her poetry. Roberts had just become the editor of *Ainslee's, The Magazine That Entertains,* published by Street & Smith in Brooklyn, a firm that exploited the dime novel in the nineteenth century and adventure and detective stories at low prices at the beginning of the twentieth. There was always a girl on the cover of *Ainslee's,* and she was inevitably sporty or flirty. When Roberts became its editor after his return from France, where he had been a war correspondent, he was given a free hand. While the publishers were indifferent to poetry—verses were used to fill up spaces left blank at the ends of stories—he was resolved "to make the poetry in *Ainslee's* among the best printed in the United States." On August 15, 1918, he wrote to Edna Millay, asking her to contribute to his magazine. He paid fifty cents a line and wanted to meet her.

"I looked up and saw a slim . . . girl with sea-green eyes, finespun reddish hair and remarkably small hands." He thought she looked like a tiger lily. She agreed at once to become a contributor, and when he asked her if she'd brought anything with her, she promptly gave him a batch of poems. A week later, he wrote to tell her, "Yours is real genius, a fine and delicate gift. Your 'Daphne' in particular is exquisite. It is a long time since I have read so beautiful a lyric." He bought it, and three others: "Fugitive," "Lord Archer,—Death," and "A Visit to the Asylum," for twenty-eight dollars.

Within a month he told her not only that "Daphne" would be in the November issue but "I want, if possible, to have a poem by you in every number thereafter. You are a *real* poet. There are not many such."

He kept his word to the letter. From November 1918 until October 1920, Roberts published twenty-three poems and eight pieces of her fiction; *Ainslee's* had become the first major outlet for her work.

Having been forced to close *The Masses,* Max Eastman and his sister, Crystal, founded the *Liberator.* Fifty-one percent of the stock was theirs. This time the magazine would not be a collective as *The Masses* had been. They would edit it, and Dell would be managing editor. They would pay themselves a salary, and they would have final say over the material they published. Max had raised $2,000 to send John Reed to Russia in 1917 to write an eyewitness report of the revolution. Reed's testimony from Petrograd would become *Ten Days That Shook the World*. His reports were at the heart of the *Liberator*.

A second trial was scheduled to start, with charges that were remarkably the same. The cast of defendants was too, except for Reed, who was now back in New York. The trial provided a homecoming for the radicals of Greenwich Village, with friends and contributors hailing each other in the bustling courtroom. As soon as it began, Millay returned to Dell. "I was again in danger, and her place was at my side. She was my companion all through the trial."

Eastman spoke daringly in defense of socialism and even more eloquently in defending himself and his colleagues against the charge of willfully opposing America's right to conscript. When the offending articles for which he and the others were held responsible were written, America had not yet begun to fight. The president had even pledged, he reminded them, not to go to war. Wasn't freedom of speech at stake?

Max Eastman addressed the courtroom for three hours as if giving a lecture on American history. When Art Young was asked what a particularly pointed cartoon meant—in which a capitalist, an editor, a politician, and a minister were dancing a war dance while the Devil directed the orchestra—he said, "Meant? Intend? I intended to draw a picture." When he was asked for what purpose, he slowly said, "Why, to make people think—to make them laugh—to express my feelings." Did he intend to obstruct recruiting and enlistment with such a savagely mocking picture? the prosecuting attorney asked. "There isn't anything in there about recruiting and enlistment, is there? I don't believe in war, that's all, and I said so." Young had been drawing a caricature of the chief prosecuting attorney, Earl Barnes, and the jury had noticed. Now he slyly asked Barnes if maybe some of the jurors thought he was trying to discourage Mr. Barnes from enlisting. As the courtroom burst into laughter, Young returned to his seat, settled in, and snoozed for the remainder of the trial.

Jack Reed, whom *The New York Times* had labeled "the Bolshevik agitator," hesitated and then equivocated on the stand. But by then the defense of *The Masses* was plain: criticism of the government didn't amount to a desire to overthrow it. If all hostile opinion were suppressed, how could Americans believe they lived in a free country? Dissent was a safeguard to freedom, not an impediment. Max Eastman again stood to take the stand at the closing of the trial. He said that a prominent member of his own family had asked a long time ago whether or not conscription was consistent with a free government and civil liberty:

> Where is it written in the Constitution, in what article or section is it contained, that you may take children from their parents, and parents from

their children, and compel them to fight the battles of any war in which the folly or the wickedness of Government may engage it?

That member of his family was Daniel Webster, and those were his words. Eastman said that for himself, "I am not afraid to spend the better part of my life in a penitentiary, if my principles have brought me to it. . . . I am more afraid to betray my principles." The courtroom was silent as the handsome, eloquent editor of *The Masses* quietly took his seat. They called him the Byron of the Left.

The second trial was even shorter than the first. After five days the jury was again unable to agree and deadlocked. Once again, the defendants were free.

Jack Reed, husky, snub-nosed, and rumpled, looked like a shaggy, massive boy. He had helped organize the Patterson Silk Strike in New Jersey and had been arrested and jailed for it. He had been a war correspondent with Pancho Villa in Mexico, and he had written the first eyewitness account of the Russian Revolution in English. At the time of the trial, he was at the height of his powers. When he told Dell he had secret news that negotiations for an armistice to end the war were under way, Floyd believed him. They celebrated with Edna Millay one night by crossing on the Staten Island ferry. The fog was thick, and as they walked along the beach, Reed told her about his adventures as a war correspondent and in Russia. She was charmed by him and lightly said, "I love you for the dangers you have passed." And he replied, "Yes, I thought there was something Desdemona-ish about this."

"And the third person present," Dell wrote of himself miserably, "would rather be elsewhere. . . . so that her new romance may go on unimpeded." Dell was convinced that Millay and Reed had a brief affair. He also believed that her sonnet "Lord Archer,—Death" was written to Reed. Roberts had purchased the sonnet in August, by which time Reed was back from Russia, but there is no evidence that he and Millay met before the second *Masses* trial in October, well after the poem was written.

It's hard to know now if Dell should be taken as a credible witness. Again and again, both before her death and after, more than thirty years after their love affair was over, he kept returning to the issue of her fidelity—or infidelity. In his unpublished memoir he insisted that her sonnet "Oh, think not I am faithful to a vow!" had been written during their first winter together on Waverly Place. He said she read it to him with "a mischievous air which was intended to give me liberty to believe that this was about us."

> Oh, think not I am faithful to a vow!
> Faithless am I save to love's self alone.
> Were you not lovely I would leave you now:
> After the feet of beauty fly my own.
> Were you not still my hunger's rarest food,
> And water ever to my wildest thirst,
> I would desert you—think not but I would!—
> And seek another as I sought you first.
> But you are mobile as the veering air,
> And all your charms more changeful than the tide,
> Wherefore to be inconstant is no care:
> I have but to continue at your side.
> So wanton, light and false, my love, are you,
> I am most faithless when I most am true.

In a long letter written to her at the time, Dell describes standing outside her apartment on Charlton Street waiting for her to return. He says it has been a vain boast for him "to being equal to being in love with you": it is beyond his strength to endure his changed status. He remembers things that have passed between them that she has forgotten. "The only decent thing to do," he asks her, "is for you to bid me also to forget. . . . I am asking you to end a one-sided love relationship."

At the end of his letter he sounds just like Elaine Ralli, only he asks her "again to marry me." His hurt and his manipulativeness were intended to press her into making a decision. She did. Their relationship as lovers was over.

In their happier days together, a friend remembered seeing Millay running around the corner of Macdougal Street, her hair flying out behind her, "flushed and laughing like a nymph," as Floyd Dell, stretching out his arms to catch her, raced after her. It was like a scene from "Daphne":

> Why do you follow me?—
> Any moment I can be
> Nothing but a laurel tree.
>
> Any moment of the chase
> I can leave you in my place
> A pink bough for your embrace.
>
> Yet if over hill and hollow
> Still it is your will to follow,
> I am off;—to heel, Apollo!

The problem with nymphs is that they are so changeable, let alone inhuman.

4

By May the sisters had moved to the top floor of 25 Charlton Street, a lovely old redbrick town house with a stoop out front and a tiny garden at the rear. On the parlor floor was a milliner's shop run by Avril Unger, for whom Norma sometimes worked. With room enough at last, Vincent invited Cora to join them. "Dearlings," Cora wrote on May 24, "I'll come just when you want me. . . . I can stand any heat or anything else you can. I can sew, nurse, or do the heads to match those hats next fall." They would sink or swim together. Four days later she wrote again: "I can't believe it, and I don't; but I'm coming." Vincent warned her not to budge from the waiting room in Grand Central Terminal if they were late. It had been such a long time since they'd seen each other, she thought of wearing a gardenia.

Cora arrived on June 3, 1918, one week before her fifty-fifth birthday. Now Vincent had brought her entire family out of Maine, and they were all, at last, together again. Only this time they were under her wing— except for Kathleen, who was at Vassar because of Vincent's efforts on her behalf.

While Poughkeepsie was only a couple of hours north of New York, Kathleen was feeling sharply the contrast between her life and the life her sisters were living in the city. "Edna," she'd written that fall, at the beginning of her first year at Vassar, "I love the poems, dear. . . . but you *don't* know how I love to have them." Was it, she asked,

> nasty to say that I was so surprised to get it that I was sad to think I should be so surprised. It just happens that you and Hunk never did write any, you know, and it made me feel funny. I wish awfully this year that I knew you two girls better than I do. I really don't know much about you, I guess, and it makes me lonesome. I just don't "belong" up here.

This letter is the first evidence in her own hand that Kathleen felt left out of her sisters' lives.

A woman who knew Kathleen at Vassar said, "She was really out of her depth. And one knew it, felt it. She was always striving to be more than she was." What was particularly noticeable "was this trading on Vincent's reputation and standing at Vassar. For Vincent was greatly regarded, as something quite special. Kathleen was not."

Within another year Kathleen would leave Vassar and join her sisters in New York.

——

Malcolm Cowley, who would later write *Exiles Returned* and become a discerning critic rather than the poet he intended to be, remembered coming into New York while still an undergraduate at Harvard. He had a head of russet curls and a cherubic grin, and visiting the Millays in their rooms on Charlton Street was a delight: "When the sisters appeared it all tripled—if there is one pretty woman, and then there are three pretty women—well, it is simply heightened beyond the belief of a very young man.

"I would go up into that room, I remember the big bed in the corner, and lie on it. Norma had undertaken to rescue us. Oh, from the cold! from the everlasting human cold! They were each lovely girls. But Edna had something more than that. She'd break your heart. There was something wild and elusive about her.

"It was something to hear the sisters singing," he continued. "They sang easily together, in three-part harmony, and sometimes they'd sing their own songs, too. Oh, it was a treat." Cowley threw back his head and sang lustily, " 'Have a little sniff, Have a little sniff on me.' But," he said, "of course, the great drug was alcohol."

Everyone who knew them then remembers how gaily they sang parts together. Kathleen would take the air, Norma the tenor part, and Vincent the baritone.

Song to Men

Let us sing a little song
To the men we've loved so long—
And to those we've only loved
 A little while
TENOR SOLO: A lit-tle while
Ti de dee and ta dee da,
We must take them as they are—
 Let them spoof us
For they love so
To beguile.
BARITONE SOLO: Let them beguile.

Chorus
 Oh, darling men!
BARITONE: Oh, men, men, men.
Oh, men alluring,
Waste not the hours—
TENOR: Sweet idle hours—
In vain assuring,
For love, though sweet,

TENOR: Love though tho thweet—
Is not enduring.
Ti de da! Ti da dee da!

Cowley found Edna and Norma most intriguing. "Now people often describe Edna as elfin," he recalled. "But it was Norma who had a sort of pixieish, naughty look to her face. With Edna it was something more like Titania—the Queen of the Fairies."

Actually, not quite everyone was charmed by them when they sang. When Floyd took Edna and Norma to meet Max Eastman for the first time in the Village—Eastman was living with Eugen Boissevain, the handsome, broad-chested Dutchman whose extraordinary wife, the suffragist leader Inez Milholland, had died tragically in 1916—"it really didn't take at all, for any of us," Norma remembered. "Vincent and I sang together, but somehow it just didn't work out that night. And I think Floyd was rather disappointed. He wanted to show us off."

Eastman called it "skillful—their harmonies were perfect, their rhythmical sense exact—but I did not find it pleasing. They seemed a little school-girlish, almost simpering, to me."

By this time, Walter Adolphe Roberts was taking Millay out to dinner as often as she would agree to go. He recalled the "flickering" way she talked about herself—"I had been thinking of the poet as fragile and unearthly; suddenly I perceived that she was strong."

He knew the fifty cents a line he paid her for her poetry wasn't going to help solve her financial problems, so when she hinted that she'd like to write fiction, "I gave her every encouragement." "Young Love" ran in the May 1919 issue under the pseudonym Nancy Boyd, her great-grandmother's maiden name. It tickled Roberts to be able to send her a more substantial check, and whenever possible he slyly placed one of Edna St. Vincent Millay's lyrics in the space left at the bottom of a Nancy Boyd story.

Four of Millay's workbooks survive from this period in New York; she worked quickly and in longhand, writing poems on the right-hand side of the page and then sometimes reworking them on the left-hand side. It was a pattern she followed most of her life. Sometimes the poems are dated; most often they are not. The dates are of entry, not necessarily of composition, and never of publication. A workbook was just that. She said later in life that she might write a poem down anywhere, on the back of a telegram for instance, but usually she worked them out in her mind, and when she had something she liked, she wrote it down in these paper composition books.

The dated poems seemed to come in clusters: July 17, 1918: "Lord Archer,—Death" (not published in *Ainslee's* until December). July 18: "I do but ask that you be always fair," which waited a year and ten months before publication in a remarkable group of twenty sonnets in *Reedy's Mirror*. But many of her finest poems were left undated, scrawled hastily across the page in pencil. Reading in those workbooks now, one can feel, even see in the dashes of thick lead strokes across the pages or her hesitant crossing out, a poet trying to seize and shape on paper the work that would distinguish her a half century after her death—the intensity and excitement are palpable.

While she was spending her time with the Provincetown Players, Roberts kept his distance. He knew the Provincetowners provided her with what he called an "effervescent social life," but he wouldn't join in "because I was jealous of its influence over Edna. . . . I was enamored of such communion as she gave me, and more deeply than she guessed or probably cared, I wanted it to be an exchange between us only." What he treasured were their times alone together when they talked about poetry, and love.

She told him "it was impossible for a poet not to be influenced by the work of those he venerated as artistic ancestors—that this was in fact desirable, for it assured a continuity and development of the general stream of poetry." When he asked whose influences she recognized in her own work, she acknowledged Housman and Tennyson. "The former for his emotional attitude and spare poignancy of expression; the latter for narrative power and technical innovations." He thought it "singular" that she credited Housman, for he ranked her a far better poet. And while he admired Tennyson, he was puzzled that she regarded him as a technical innovator. He insisted that Swinburne was far superior. Edna looked at him quizzically and asked him to read favorite stanzas. When he began to quote

> I hid my heart in a nest of roses,
>   Out of the sun's way, hidden apart;
> In a softer bed than the soft white snow's is,
>   Under the roses I hid my heart,

she said he could have his Swinburne; the passages he quoted were " 'but sound'; the debt she recognized was to Tennyson." Her true generosity was toward contemporary American poets, praising them, in Roberts's estimation, beyond their worth.

By March 1919, Roberts was under her spell. He had taken to writing to her in French, because, he told her, he could think of nothing but her, her marvelous poetry, her splendid sensibility, her tragic and beautiful mouth, her arms, her breasts, her throat, all that was her, whether or not she loved him. It was a play on one of her own lines in this sonnet, which he did not publish:

> I shall forget you presently, my dear,
> So make the most of this, your little day,
> Your little month, your little half a year,
> Ere I forget, or die, or move away,
> And we are done forever; by and by
> I shall forget you, as I said, but now,
> If you entreat me with your loveliest lie
> I will protest you with my favorite vow.
> I would indeed that love were longer-lived,
> And vows were not so brittle as they are,
> But so it is, and nature had contrived
> To struggle on without a break thus far,—
> Whether or not we find what we are seeking
> Is idle, biologically speaking.

Edna, who had begun just one year before as an actress with the Provincetown Players in Floyd's one-act plays, now had her own play, *The Princess Marries the Page,* on the bill to open their third season in New York. She wrote it, directed it, and played the role of the princess. She had moved from being an ingenue to one of the Players' major creative forces.

The Players had outgrown the old front parlor in 139 Macdougal Street and moved a few doors down into 133, a four-story house that had been used as a stable. They left the hitching ring attached to the wall of the auditorium, inscribing above it "Here Pegasus was Hitched." It was their playfulness as much as their spirit of adventure and innovation that kept them a lively force in New York. They took risks with the plays they chose. They didn't court the press. Tickets to their performances could be obtained only by subscription. The roster of names of those who wrote plays for them was sensational. They were the new figures in American writing: besides Dell and Millay, John Reed, Eugene O'Neill, and Susan Glaspell, there were William Carlos Williams, e.e. cummings, Wallace Stevens, Djuna Barnes, Alfred Kreymborg, Michael Gold, Harry Kemp, Maxwell Bodenheim, James Oppenheim, Wilbur Daniel Steele, and Sherwood Anderson. Those who came to act, design sets, or do odd jobs included Marsden Hartley, Alexander Berkman, Lawrence Vail, Lawrence

Langner, Margaret Anderson, Jane Heap, Art Young, Rollo Peters, Harrison Dowd, Mina Loy, and Boardman Robinson. Some even brought their mothers into the theater: Cora Millay was about to enter the fray; also George Cram Cook's mother, Ellen Cook, who sewed costumes; and Christine Ell's mother, who helped her cook sixty-cent dinners in the tiny kitchen on the second floor of the theater, where everyone gathered to talk and to celebrate. Cora became an active part of Eugene O'Neill's *The Moon of the Caribbees,* in which she sang and in which Charlie Ellis was cast as Smitty, one of the seamen on the S.S. *Glencairn.*

"Edna and all of the Millays were involved in this extraordinary production," said Susan Jenkins Brown, who was then the wife of James Light, one of the Playhouse's founders. "It was a mood play, and the Millay family provided the background music, which set the mood. The Millays, with Ma Millay, too, had this special musical ability—it was their own, the first of its kind really—a crooning group. As I remember, they stood behind the scenery—it was all swooping vocal harmonies—they weren't seen, and . . . well, it was unearthly."

5

In February 1919, the Millays moved again, this time into a neighborhood they thought was Chelsea. It was, in fact, farther west, in the poorer Irish district. "The new Millay home was a ground-floor flat at 449 West 19th Street, in the colorless, rundown block between 9th and 10th Avenues," Roberts wrote. "It was an incongruous setting for the family, but . . . Strong personalities create their own atmosphere, and this did not apply only to the poet."

Roberts had just met Cora Millay. It's fascinating to see him stumble about, trying to pin her down: "Mrs. Cora Buzzelle Millay was not beautiful, and she looked workworn, gnarled. . . . Her conversation was pithy and the ruggedness of her character salient."

"I have never come across a more devoted mother and daughter," Susan Jenkins Brown recalled. She felt there was something odd and forced about their relationship. "This might have been, what, *Little Women*? They were together the perfect picture postcard—the Christmas postcards—of the family. Edna was, however, the least effusive.

"But"—and with this Susan Brown wagged a cautionary finger—"the important thing to remember is that the whole family were devoted to each other."

☙ ☙ ☙

I decided to discuss this with Norma. It had crossed my mind that I, too, was being drawn into a spell. By now I had an inkling of the furies that drove the Millays, and I was wary of their enchantment. I didn't know then the strength of that pull on women, or that one cannot be wary enough.

Norma was poignant when she described Cora's first months in New York with her and Vincent:

"We realized now that we were not in Camden, Maine, anymore. We wanted to live in our own way—and now we were with people who did. Oh, I don't mean just people you had sex with or who used dirty words. I mean interesting people. We were either going to include Mother in our fun, or we were not. And I remember Vincent and I sitting down and talking about it, deciding what we were going to do—were we going to leave Mother behind? Mother could say quite startling things. . . . [We decided] that we would not just put Mother on the shelf; that we would continue to share our lives—as we grew up.

"We were pals, companions, and we were trying to get on, make a living, to get on to better things. So we'd always stuck together; and now we were branching out."

"Did you worry that would hurt her?"

"Yes. Damned right!"

"Did it hurt her?"

"No, I think she handled it marvelously."

ھ ھ ھ

They handled it by making of their lives a theater piece, a family romance. It was their story of triumph over adversity, one of the best women's stories there is in America: hopeful, enduring, centered in family, and fraudulent—not especially because it was deceitful but because it was built on so much unadmitted pain that it was impossible to sustain. By now that air of plucky resilience was as much a family routine with the Millays as singing in parts. But Vincent's role was an increasingly tough one, for now *she,* not Cora, was their caretaker. She sustained all of them. One solution was for Cora to go visiting relatives or friends from time to time when Vincent couldn't muster the cash to support her.

We're not going to let you stay away from home much longer, little old Irish devil! . . . Financially, dear, I need to get bucked up a bit before I can send you the money to come home with. I've been giving all my time to this play, you see.

The play was *Aria da Capo,* and she knew it was "a peach,—one of the best things I've ever done." Alexander Woollcott, the drama critic for *The New York Times,* announced on December 13, 1919, "You should see this bitterly ironic little fantasy by Edna St. Vincent Millay. . . . this is the most beautiful and most interesting play in the English language now to be seen in New York."

But there was more going on in her life in 1919 than writing a superb antiwar play. She'd fallen in love with a young engineer who was working for the Bureau of Construction of the American Red Cross in Washington, D.C., whom she had met through Norma. His name was James Lawyer, and he was married.

All that remains of their love affair is a tarnished silver identification bracelet inscribed "James P. Lawyer" and eighteen letters, which began with a special delivery letter dated November 27, 1919:

> Dearest Girl, My Own,
>   This is just a scrawl to let you know . . . that I adore you. . . . I'm already planning to see you again so soon. Love me I need your love so. I am writing this at a corner cigar store I don't dare write it home. . . . Oh love me girl, love me. Mrs. Lawyer is quite ill and . . . she knows something happened.

He wrote to her every day, sometimes two letters in a single day, not wanting to, "for I am so afraid that we will burn our love by being [too] feverish." From the beginning of this correspondence he was troubled by thoughts of his wife's response to his deception. "That is the hardest part for me for I hate deceit.

> God knows, Edna, that I adore you. My love for you has certainly been tested very thoroughly. I feel so sorry for my poor wife and I really love her you know. Next to you there is nothing in the world I love better. She just suspects something she doesn't even know herself what. . . . Those things make it so much harder to hurt her but I simply cannot give you up. Not even if I tried for in my heart I would always love you. What a pity that we could not have met long ago.

That was the first ominous note struck in their correspondence, but four days later he was back with her in New York. Each time now it was more difficult to leave her: "I felt so badly today when Norma and you both cried. . . . You were right when you said that I would come back to you unless I died and I don't believe even death could keep me away from you."

ഛ ഛ ഛ

At first Norma didn't want to talk about him, but she had already acknowledged his importance by admitting one of her sister's letters about him to their mother into the collection of Vincent's *Letters:*

> I carry my typewriter all over the world with me, the little Corona Jim gave me. He was a sweet boy, mother. I loved him very much. And still do, whenever I think of him, though it was all nonsense, of course, and I wouldn't want him back. Only I like to think about him sometimes. You were wonderful, mother, about him and me. I realized afterwards how terrible it must have been for you. But you never hurt me in any way.

This was written well after the fact. What Norma hadn't done was to identify him or give any description of their affair. When I discovered a tiny snapshot slipped into the soft leather fold of Millay's first passport wallet, I guessed it was Jim, and Norma relented:

> Jim was a beautiful boy, you must understand that. He was tall and slim and blond. Godlike, really, a lovely man. And, yes, he was married— although I don't think Mother knew it, certainly she didn't at first—and, yes, Vincent loved him. Well, you know, it can happen that you can feel quite a lot for someone who is not in any way your equal.

But she left me to guess for myself in what way Jim was unequal to Millay. At first I thought it might have been because he was not literary. I should have realized that would have been to his advantage.

ഛ ഛ ഛ

Jim was going to try to return for the opening of *Aria da Capo* on December 5, 1919. He hoped she had finished the costumes "and that you are not dead, dead, tired. You were not meant to live in a big city anyway. You were meant to live in the beautiful out of doors somewhere with me. You do need someone to take care of you too."

By December 22, he referred to his wife no longer as Mrs. Lawyer but as Louise, and by January 2 Louise knew "that I love you more than anyone else and that we intend to live together." The rest of the story was not pretty. His wife wanted to be absolutely certain they loved each other "before she gives me up." She was not nearly as upset as he'd thought she would be; she treated him with contempt and was hurt that he'd spent so much money when they were together in New York—"She keeps telling me that I never spent so much on her." And she was reading Millay's poetry. On January 6, he wrote to tell her that his wife was treating their affair as a joke and telling people about them. "There is a great difference though when we happen to be alone." Four days later he wrote to assure her that within three days they would "have all of the things both of us have always wanted all of our lives. . . . I adore You, Darling. . . . Your own Jim."

Then his letters broke off. When they resumed twelve days later, it was with the news that Louise had tried to kill herself. "Oh, Girl, Dear," he wrote Vincent, "things are hard very hard just now but they won't always be this way. God will let us be together soon if we can stand all we have had to stand nothing can keep us apart." At the close of this letter he added, as if it might be reassuring, "God Bless You and help us to do the true right things."

There was only one true right thing to do. And Jim did it. In an undated letter that began, "My Own, My Darling," he used the past tense for the first time: "I loved you more than I ever have before and I realized what I must do." There would be no terrible scene. He was "writing instead of calling You because if I should hear Your voice I might weaken." He asked that they not see each other again. He told her that he would love her always, and on February 10, 1920, he returned everything he had of hers. "Your letters I have always destroyed. . . . The memory of you no one can ever destroy."

Two weeks later, in a burst of anger and hurt pride, Edna told Norma she'd wired Jim from Cincinnati, where she was giving her first professional reading outside the East: "If I can earn my way lecturing I'm going from here right around the world, & he'll never see me again,—tell him." That was sheer bravado.

No one knew then that Jim, having broken with Vincent, had turned to Kathleen and that Kathleen had agreed to see him.

ᘐ ᘐ ᘐ

I had found a single undated letter, a fragment of a letter really, from Jim to Vincent, apologizing for something about Kay, as Kathleen now liked to be called:

> I guess my mind just snapped and "K" who is very sweet filled the place that I needed you for so very much. . . . I know you will all hate me now even "K," but it isn't quite so strange to believe that I should really be insane, when you stop to think that the terrible things we have been through. . . . I don't know what is to become of me now. I love you not "K" and I have lost you.

What, I asked Norma, had happened? Norma gazed away from me for only a moment and said, "Vincent did care about him very deeply, deeply. I don't believe I knew that at the time. Not as far as it had gone. And then he dated Kathleen for a while, and that was terrible and I remember telling Kathleen so. It was just because he couldn't be with Vincent."

᎐ ᎐ ᎐

Within nine months Millay had published this sonnet, found in draft among Jim's letters to her. It is one of her first great sonnets, and it was as sharp with loss as an epitaph:

> Pity me not because the light of day
> At close of day no longer walks the sky;
> Pity me not for beauties passed away
> From field and thicket as the year goes by;
> Pity me not the waning of the moon,
> Nor that the ebbing tide goes out to sea,
> Nor that a man's desire is hushed so soon,
> And you no longer look with love on me.
> This have I known always: Love is no more
> Than the wide blossom which the wind assails,
> Than the great tide that treads the shifting shore,
> Strewing fresh wreckage gathered in the gales:
> Pity me that the heart is slow to learn
> What the swift mind beholds at every turn.

One month after its publication, on December 17, 1920, Kathleen married Howard Young in a private ceremony at the Brevoort Hotel. Norma said that both she and Vincent were there. "I no longer remember how she met Howard, nor where. He was in the theater. And he looked like the Prince of Wales. She wanted him, and she got him. Poor, poor Kathleen."

CHAPTER 14

Millay had made fun of her reading in Cincinnati when she quipped that the year before they'd had Amy Lowell, "wherefore I deduce the system as being: one year a fat girl, next year a thin girl," but this was the beginning of a crucial aspect of her career. She was a superb performer.

She had a reputation of being sexually free, and her work was assumed to be daringly autobiographical. People wanted to see this girl poet of the new bohemia. She teased and charmed the Cincinnatians with poems like "To the Not Impossible Him":

> How shall I know, unless I go
> To Cairo and Cathay,
> Whether or not this blessed spot
> Is blest in every way?
>
> Now it may be, the flower for me
> Is this beneath my nose;
> How shall I tell, unless I smell
> The Carthaginian rose?
>
> The fabric of my faithful love
> No power shall dim or ravel
> Whilst I stay here,—but oh, my dear,
> If I should ever travel!

This heartland city took her in; it even gave her a party for her twenty-eighth birthday. Hubertis M. Cummings, head of the Ohio Valley Poetry Society, described Millay's theatrical appeal:

The slender red-haired, gold-eyed Vincent Millay, dressed in a black-trimmed gown of purple silk, was now reading from a tooled leather port-folio, now reciting without aid of book or print, despite her broom-splint legs and muscles twitching in her throat and in her thin arms, in a voice that enchanted.

When *Aria da Capo* opened in December, Millay insisted that Mitchell Kennerley come see it. Afterward he wrote telling her how much he liked it. "Aren't you about ready for a new volume of poems? It will be a pity to let too long a time elapse between 'Renascence' and its successor." He said the day she brought in a manuscript there would be a check of $150 ready for her.

She answered immediately: "You, dear, I thought, were entirely out of the publishing business forever. Everybody says so." At the close of her letter she asked if he was going to bring out another edition of *Renascence:* "There's not a copy to be had in town."

Kennerley assured Millay that *Renascence* had never been out of print. "At this very minute there are 800 bound copies in this very building. I will send you six copies tomorrow. It is sweet of everybody to say I am not publishing any more and pleases me very much."

By March 1920, reassured that Kennerley was about to publish, Millay sent him a letter full of business suggestions, including adding a preface about *Aria da Capo,* which was about to be produced, to the volume. Kennerley's response was dead silence.

Norma, who played Columbine with Harrison Dowd as "a playful, graceful, disenchanted" Pierrot, opened the play. To describe *Aria da Capo* as a one-act antiwar play based on the commedia dell'arte in which two sweet young shepherds kill each other out of greed is to give scant hint of its power. It is a deadly little play. Norma described the first performance:

> Charlie did the sets at the Provincetown Players. He had black screens on which he painted mushrooms of different sizes in white, and these were set at angles through which the actors made their entrances and exits. And he painted a proscenium border of coloured fruits & flowers, cut as though they were hanging down—very effective it was. . . . Vincent was very good directing her play because she knew exactly what she wanted.

The play ran for two weeks and was completely sold out. Millay did not explain the play in her preface; she gave a description of how it was to look. She was precise.

The two shepherds, Thyrsis and Corydon, were to look like happy rustics in sandals, with rough cloaks flung about their shoulders. Edna wrote, "There must be no red or blue used anywhere in the entire play excepting in the blue and red of these two cloaks." Pierrot wears a lavender or lilac silk smock with wide trousers and a wide white tarleton ruff. Columbine's costume is a tight black satin bodice "cut very low, with straps over the shoulders, quite like the modern evening gown; very full tarleton skirts of different shades of pink and cerise"; "Hat should be small and very smart—not a *shepherdess* hat."

When Edmund Wilson saw *Aria da Capo,* he wrote, "I was thrilled and troubled by this little play: it was the first time I had felt Edna's peculiar power. There was a bitter treatment of war, and we were all ironic about war; but there was also a less common sense of the incongruity and the cruelty of life, of the precariousness of love." It began as a caprice:

> COLUMBINE: Pierrot, a macaroon! I cannot live
>   without a macaroon!
> PIERROT: My only love. You are *so* intense! . . .
>   Is it Tuesday, Columbine?—I'll kiss you if
>   it's Tuesday.

These frivolous lines are returned to at the close of the play, after the savage deaths of the shepherds, whose corpses remain onstage, tucked beneath the long table upon which Columbine and Pierrot lean, ignoring them as they begin again at the top, *Aria da Capo*.

Edmund Wilson, Jr., whose mother's nickname for him as a little boy, Bunny, had stuck, had been at Princeton with F. Scott Fitzgerald and John Peale Bishop. When the war began, Wilson enlisted and served with a hospital unit as a stretcher bearer in France, until he couldn't stand the carnage and asked his father, who knew Woodrow Wilson from his days as attorney general in the state of New Jersey, to intervene. He was transferred to Germany in the Intelligence Corps and returned to America in July 1919.

Wilson was short and stout; his fine red hair, neatly parted in the middle, was already, at twenty-five, beginning to thin. His speaking voice was high, "harsh and light," Edna Millay described it. He wore brown suits that matched the color of his eyes, carried a slim Malacca cane, and performed sleight-of-hand and card tricks to calm his nerves. When Scott Fitzgerald caught sight of him in the Village one evening, he found Wilson enviably urbane, no longer the "shy little scholar of Holder Court" he'd been at Princeton. A small legacy permitted him choices that Edna Millay did not have: a Chinese manservant who cooked for him, for instance.

Wilson had fallen in love with Millay's poetry well before he met her in the spring of 1920. The March issue of *The Dial* published her sonnet "To Love Impuissant," which Wilson "got by heart," reciting it in his shower:

> Love, though for this you riddle me with darts,
> And drag me at your chariot till I die,—
> Oh, heavy prince! Oh, panderer of hearts!—
> Yet hear me tell how in their throats they lie
> Who shout you mighty: thick about my hair,
> Day in, day out, your ominous arrows purr,
> Who still am free, unto no querulous care
> A fool, and in no temple worshiper!
> I, that have bared me to your quiver's fire,
> Lifted my face into its puny rain,
> Do wreathe you Impotent to Evoke Desire
> As you are Powerless to Elicit Pain!
> (Now will the god, for blasphemy so brave,
> Punish me, surely, with the shaft I crave!)

He felt himself "worthy to deal her the longed-for dart." He had been reading her since the spring of 1916, when his cousin Carolyn Crosby Wilson, who was in Vincent's class at Vassar, gave him a copy of *The Vassar Miscellany Monthly,* in which "The Suicide" had appeared. When later in the year she sent him *A Book of Vassar Verse,* including both that poem and "Interim," he decided to review it in the New York *Evening Sun,* where, just out of Princeton, he was working as a fifteen-dollar-a-week reporter. The following year, that same cousin sent him *Renascence* when he was in France with the AEF, and he was even more impressed. Now he longed to meet her.

At last he did, at a party in Greenwich Village to which she came late and tired after the theater. That night her beauty overwhelmed him, but it was not only her beauty that was arresting: he found her speaking voice thrilling. Unsettled, he felt for the first time "her power of imposing herself on others through a medium that unburdened the emotions of solitude. The company hushed and listened as people do to music—her authority was always complete; but her voice, though dramatic, was lonely.

"She was dressed in some bright batik, and her face lit up with a flush that seemed to burn also in the bronze reflections of her not yet bobbed reddish hair. She was one of those women whose features are not perfect and who in their moments of dimness may not seem even pretty, but who, excited by the blood or the spirit, become almost supernaturally beautiful."

Wilson decided to cultivate her favor precisely as Walter Adolphe Roberts had. He would publish her in *Vanity Fair,* on whose editorial staff both he and John Bishop then worked. "She had," Wilson later wrote, "at that time no real market for her poems; she sold a lyric only now and then to the highbrow *Dial* . . . or to the trashy *Ainslee's.*" This was an exaggeration that served to place Wilson far more centrally in her career than he belonged. Wilson and Bishop took over when Roberts had been forced to withdraw. *Ainslee's* would publish only one more short lyric of hers, "To Kathleen," that summer, and two of her Nancy Boyd pieces in the fall. For by 1921, Roberts was no longer on the masthead as editor. "Walter, dear," Edna wrote him that summer, "What in the world happened?—But never mind—so long as you are out of there—you were getting so tired of it all, I know. . . . *bon voyage,* dear friend, wherever you go & whatever you do."

Wilson moved in to acquire her work. In July 1920, *Vanity Fair* published "Dead Music—An Elegy" and in the following month "Prayer to Persephone," part of the elegies she was completing. It wasn't only *Vanity*

Fair that picked up the slack from *Ainslee's*. William Marion Reedy of St. Louis, whose *Reedy's Mirror* first published her *Aria da Capo,* began on April 29, 1920, to publish in batches of five her "Twenty Sonnets." These remarkable sonnets were seized by the crusty old midwestern editor, who published only what he liked. Luckily, what he liked was absolutely first-rate.

Reedy had met her at the Kennerleys' house in the country, and he told her how much their "gab-fest" had meant to him: "I remember we didn't even mind the 'skeeters.' Next morning I lost my hat, but that was the odds. I'd lost my head the night before, and, honestly, a bit o' my heart too, in the glorious talk."

Kennerley had shown Reedy *Second April* in proof, and he stayed up all night reading it. "It's splendid work—all shot through with brightness; the air of the open world in it too. The Elegiacs, fine. The Sonnets, superb."

But that spring Kennerley's entire publishing process simply halted. Edna sent off the dedication, which was to Miss Dow. She pursued Kennerley with polite questions. She offered to help: "If you will send me some circulars, and envelopes and things—things meaning stamps!—I will mail them to thousands of people, about two thousands." She tried being deferential:

> Do you want me to give you some clippings?
> I am very unhappy today.
> I am sure that you dislike me.

But nothing worked to prod a response from Kennerley. On June 22, Millay's tone was no longer deferential:

> Mitchell, dear,—
>   You are behaving disgracefully to l'il' Edna, whom you love.—all the time her mother keeps asking her questions which it is impossible for her to answer, & it is all very awkward & horrid, & you ought to be ashamed.
>   Write me at once, giving me some nice, plausible, mendacious-as-hell reason why you have not yet published my pretty book.

But this note, too, was met by silence. She wrote Arthur Davison Ficke, "My book isn't out yet. It's dreadful. I write Mitchell all the time, and he won't answer my letters; and every time I call up the office they tell me he's out, and I know dam well he is so near the telephone . . . that I hear his breathing." She wished she'd gone to Knopf, as Witter Bynner had suggested, "Although I don't see what he could do." That last was a puzzling remark—what he could do was publish her—but it signaled her own uncertainty, for she had already tried to place *Second April* with another publisher.

The only clue that remains among her papers is a letter from Horace Liveright as early as December 1918, reminding her that she'd promised to show him her new book of poetry if Macmillan didn't make a prompt decision. In the summer of 1919, Macmillan was promising a clear answer; by the fall it made it. It didn't take her book because of its theme of death. The editor pointed directly to the "Memorial to D.C.," a group of five poems written about Dorothy Coleman, a girl from Vassar who had died suddenly in the flu epidemic that swept the country in 1918. Coleman's death was the stimulus for lyrics that were among the finest Millay was writing. And she knew it. She would cut only one poem from that group, and even this single poem, "Elegy Before Death," with its ringing Virgilian irony and longing, she replaced in the body of the book.

> There will be rose and rhododendron
>   When you are dead and under ground;
> Still will be heard from white syringas
>   Heavy with bees, a sunny sound;
>
> Still will the tamaracks be raining
>   After the rain has ceased, and still
> Will there be robins in the stubble,
>   Grey sheep upon the warm green hill.
>   . . . .
> Oh, there will pass with your great passing
>   Little of beauty not your own,—
> Only the light from common water,
>   Only the grace from common stone!

The publishers were right: death moved through these poems like a morbid fever. They didn't care that Millay was echoing her beloved Latin poets in "Prayer to Persephone" and "Epitaph":

> Heap not on this mound
>   Roses that she loved so well;
> Why bewilder her with roses,
>   That she cannot see or smell?
> She is happy where she lies
> With the dust upon her eyes.

Or the jocund fop Herrick in "Chorus":

> Give away her gowns
> Give away her shoes;
> She has no more use
> For her fragrant gowns;
> Take them all down,
> Blue, green, blue,
> Lilac, pink, blue,
> From their padded hangers;
> She will dance no more
> In her narrow shoes
> From the closet floor

Death scared them off, as it had neither the Elizabethans nor the Romans.

2

> As for John Bishop and me, the more we saw of her poetry, the more our admiration grew, and we both, before very long, had fallen irretrievably in love with her. This latter was so common an experience, so almost inevitable a consequence of knowing her in those days. . . . One cannot really write about Edna Millay without bringing into the foreground of the picture her intoxicating effect on people, because this so much created the atmosphere in which she lived and composed. [It was a] spell that she exercised on many, of all ages and both sexes.
>
> —Edmund Wilson, *The Shores of Light*

In May, when Millay learned there was a chance to rent a cottage on Cape Cod that Jig Cook and Susan Glaspell had just bought, she seized it. They warned her it was really no more than a beach shack, and Jig listed the drawbacks: "remoteness, mosquitoes, no running water, etc., etc.," while Susan added that the mosquitoes would bear mentioning twice. They did want her to come but fretted that she'd like Provincetown better, for "P-town is gay and Truro is in the country—So there you are." But the little house, with a hedge of wild roses out front, set in a pine hollow just back from the dunes on the outermost reach of Cape Cod, behind the wild and lovely Longnook beach at Truro, delighted her, and she took it at once. The Millays moved out of their apartment in the Village, boxed what they needed to take, and stored the rest.

In July, Edmund Wilson was pleading with Edna to let him come to see her: "I don't know how to write you letters now. . . . I love you. E.W." The next day he was desperate: "*Please* be decent and call me up. Otherwise you'll leave me pretty flat." Millay had already left for Truro, where she wrote him:

> I don't know what to write you, either,—what you would like me to write, or what you would hate me for writing.—I feel that you rather hate me, as it is.—Which is false of you, Bunny. . . . I don't know just when I shall be in New York again. I am going to the Adirondacks . . . & after that to Woodstock. . . . I don't suppose you can get away from the office during the week, & especially now that John [Peale Bishop] is away. But could you get away . . . do you think?

It wasn't much of an invitation, but, pressed so intensely and unhappily by him, she offered it in the best faith she could muster. "I have thought of you often, Bunny, & wondered if you think of me with bitterness." Then she warned him, "My sister is amused & disgusted by my lewd portrait of myself. At her suggestion, which I now feel to be a wise one, I beg you not to circulate it." One evening in the spring, Edna, Wilson, and Bishop had playfully decided to write their self-portraits. This was Edna's:

E. St. V. M.

Hair which she still devoutly trusts is red.
Colorless eyes, employing
A childish wonder
To which they have no statistic
Title.
A large mouth,
Lascivious,
Asceticized by blasphemies.
A long throat,
Which will someday
Be strangled.
Thin arms,
In the summer-time leopard
With freckles.
A small body,
Unexclamatory,
But which,
Were it the fashion to wear no clothes,
Would be as well-dressed
As any.

Wilson's was marked by the same regret that surfaces in his letters to her. He is misunderstood, and his playfulness turns wooden:

E.W.

What devil sowed the seed of beauty
In the brain of this *raisonneur.*
He could have been happy in the XVIIIth century,
Before the Romantic Revival:
. . .
But now Byron has spoken
And the damage has been done;
. . .
You say that it is an Encyclopaedist
That lurks behind that respectable exterior.
I tell you: no! it is a Byron,
A Byron born amiss:
. . .

Later Wilson would admit that these poems were an embarrassment. "John Bishop used to say that it always made him nervous when I resorted to a high romantic vein." But Wilson was beside himself. She hadn't taken him into her life. He was desolated when he wrote:

I who have broken my passionate heart
For the lips of Edna Millay
And her face that burns like a flame
And her terrible chagrin.

The chagrin, of course, was his.

On a hot August night, a sweaty Edmund Wilson came trudging out to the Millays' Cape Cod house, dragging his suitcase, cutting through fields of scrub oak and sweet fern because the old man who'd met his train had for some surly reason dropped him off some miles shy of Truro. Wilson had begged her to let him come. Now, stumbling and lost in the dark, when he at last saw a light and found the Millays, it's hard to say whether he was more stunned by the cottage or by the women sitting inside.

They gave me dinner on a plain board table by the light of an oil-lamp. I had never seen anything like this household, nor have I seen anything like it since. Edna tried to reassure me by telling me that I mustn't be over-powered by all those girls, and one of the others added, "And *what* girls!"

It was as if he'd fallen into the enchanted world of a fairy tale, in which a crone and her three pretty daughters cast spells upon the innocent young traveler who has lost his bearings in the black night. Inside, in the flood of light and warmth, after he was loosened by a tot of whiskey, they began to work transformations on him, and he was bewitched:

> Edna was now very freckled. All were extremely pretty. But it was the mother who was most extraordinary. She was a little old woman with spectacles, who, although she had evidently been through a good deal, had managed to remain very brisk and bright. She sat up straight and smoked cigarettes and quizzically followed the conversation. She looked not unlike a New England schoolteacher, yet there was something almost raffish about her. She had anticipated the Bohemianism of her daughters; and she sometimes made remarks that were startling from the lips of a little old lady.

In his first version of this memoir Wilson remembered Mrs. Millay saying that she "had been a slut herself so why shouldn't her girls be," a statement Norma asked him to cut. Such a word from the lips of anyone's mother so shocked him that he remembered it all his life. "But," he continued, "there was nothing sordid about her: you felt even more than with Edna that she had passed beyond good and evil . . . and that she had attained there a certain gaiety."

Soon the sisters were singing songs they had made up in three-part harmony to entertain him. But Wilson had come with a purpose, and he was not to be diverted.

> Since there were only two rooms on the first floor, with no partition between them, the only way for Edna and me to get away by ourselves was to sit in a swing on the porch; but the mosquitoes were so tormenting— there being then no mosquito control—that we soon had to go in again. I did, however, ask her formally to marry me, and she did not reject my proposal but said that she would think about it. I am not sure that she actually said, "That might be the solution," but it haunts me that she conveyed that idea.

While he said it was clear to him that proposals of marriage were not a source of great excitement for Millay, he could not acknowledge that it was *his* proposal from which she shied.

The next morning Edna sat just below the stairs and recited some of her new poems. Then they walked to the sea. "Coming back from the beach, I kissed her behind a bush . . . her grin and summer girl-smile." But when Wilson told her, " 'By the time we're fifty years old, we'll be two of the most interesting people in the United States'—she said, 'You behave as if you were fifty already.' "

He didn't use these entries, which are from his diary, when he wrote his memoir, and he certainly hadn't known about the description in Alexander McKaig's diary for September 28, 1920. McKaig, who had been a Princeton classmate of Wilson, kept a diary in which he recorded the upheavals of their lives, and his own:

> One of the younger Millay girls told this anecdote of his [Wilson's] visit to them last summer—Offered coffee, Bunny declared he never drank coffee, a cigarette, Bunny said he never smoked—offered a drink, Bunny said he never drank. Other guest at dinner—a stranger—said—"Ah—he must write the minor poetry." (Bunny has never told this anecdote about himself.)

Wilson was in love for the first time in his life. Edna Millay was the first woman he'd ever made love with. Afterward he remembered her saying, "I know just how you feel: it was here, and it was beautiful, and now it's gone." He couldn't believe she wasn't in love with him, since she had

> ignited for me both my intellectual passion and my unsatisfied desire, which went up together in a blaze of ecstasy that remains for me one of the high points of my life. I do not believe that such experiences can be common, for such women are not common. My subsequent chagrin and perplexity, when I discovered that, due to her extreme promiscuity, this could not be expected to continue, were rather amazingly soothed by an equanimity on her part which was also very uncommon.

Their sexual relationship was over.

That summer Millay learned to drive and to ride, and she had her hair bobbed. "I look, when I am blessed with health, approximately twelve years old," she wrote to her mother from Lake Placid, where she was visiting Mrs. George Mixter. Then she left for Woodstock, where she began to learn Italian from a handsome Italian baritone she'd met there. "From the point of view of character and personality, he is just a sweet and friendly fellow, not so deep as a well nor so broad as a church-door, but oh, how he doth sing!" Cora asked Norma pointedly, "Who is Edna killing now? Is he almost done for?" Norma and Charlie had come to stay with Vincent in the Birdseye Cottages in Woodstock.

ಲ ಲ ಲ

Norma hooted with delight as she remembered that summer with Vincent: "Our little house was swarming with bees that August; they were there in abundance—when we bathed, when we cooked, when we ate. Finally Vincent and I decided to let them have just one sting. You know, one says to the bee, 'There! If that's what you want! If this will satisfy you!' And we held out our arms, heads turned away, eyes squeezed shut. Of course they never stung us. There was this Swedish writer among the artists who were there, and he looked wonderfully at ease in country clothes. He was talking to us about the bees. It seems they had swarmed about his little house, too. He'd been in the bath, he said, when a bee alighted on the tip of his penis. He remained, shall we say, perfectly still. And quick as a wink Vincent said, 'Where the bee sucks, there suck I.' You see," Norma said, "she could say such things, and did say them, immediately, without a moment's thought.

"One afternoon we'd gone for a walk up Mount Overlook, and on our return two boys were following us. At first we paid no attention to them. We'd always liked to walk, and there we were, two—I daresay pretty—girls striding along, enjoying ourselves. And these two callow youths, calling out to us, trailing behind, but trailing, still, if you follow me, threateningly. Suddenly Vincent turned around and, crooking her finger, beckoned them. Well, they came right up pretty quick. And she said, looking them directly in the eye, 'It is true that we have vaginas and breasts, but we are walking alone together because it pleases us to and that is our right. We have selected to be alone, and we intend to so remain.' The boys just stood there, bug-eyed, truly stricken. We turned on our heels and continued our walk, unimpeded. They were quite simply appalled. And that, too, was just like Vincent. She could be direct and graphic when she needed to be. They took off like rabbits."

Norma handed me a snapshot taken that summer in Woodstock. Vincent is standing with Norma, who looks a little dim and uncertain. Jimmy Light and Vincent's black-haired Italian baritone stand scowling behind them. She gazes directly into the camera, self-possessed, unsmiling, one hand nonchalantly on her cocked hip. She is astonishingly full-breasted, and her lips are slightly parted, as if about to kiss. She looks ripe, voluptuous.

☙ ☙ ☙

"Between John Bishop and me relations were . . . becoming a little strained," Wilson wrote. "Frank Crowninshield was complaining that it was difficult to have both his assistants in love with one of his most brilliant contributors."

Bishop was just as much in love with Millay as Wilson was. Even their letters to her were remarkably similar, except that Bishop was far more analytical even as he tried to shake her from his mind:

My dear dear girl, . . .

I am still restless with desire to feel your cool white hands against my temples. O Edna, why do you have power to torture me so? . . . I wonder, sometimes, if you do not hurt for sheer pleasure in hurting. . . . And yet I think with me, you have tried not so much to hurt as to save me from later and more desperate pain. Edna, I love you because you are passionate and wise. And if your passion had been less than your wisdom I should not have felt you so cruelly. . . . To come to me from someone else and to leave me for someone else. I don't care whom you loved last year or even last month—but now—well—what am I that I should hope to keep you. . . . I think really that your desire works strangely like a man's. And that desire has few secrets from me.

But by the fall Bishop was too much in the thick of it even to want to slake his desire for her:

For god's sake, Edna, don't forbid my coming to see you this week—I can't stand it—really. I don't want you to spend any great amount of time with me, if you feel you can't without hurting your work. I'm reasonable. . . .

Only let me see you, and touch you for a moment sometime—very soon. . . .

McKaig, their Princeton classmate, was now charting Wilson's conversations with him about Millay:

September 11: . . . Bunny W and I at dinner bewailed the misconception of his character (the omission of his Byronic trait which he claims but no one else sees except Edna Millet).

Met Edna Millet for a minute at Bunny Wilson's, light dim. She seemed pleasant and better looking than I had been led to believe. Bunny evidently much in love with her. Not much chance to get impression from her myself though I think from her verse she must be a genius. Modern Sappho. 18 love affairs and now Bunny is thinking of marrying her.

Five days later he notes:

Bunny Wilson and Edna Millet in intolerable situation. He wants her to marry him. She tempted because of her great poverty and the financial security he offers (he has private income). However, in addition to curse of Apollo she has curse of Venus. While her heart is still in the grave of one love affair she is making eyes at another man. It nearly kills her but she can't help it.

September 20: Bunnie has repeated to Edna . . . things John [Bishop] said about her. . . . John is very distressed. I've come to think he's damn stupid—interested only in himself, poetry, & women, and loves most the sound of his own voice, & liquor, & adulation (when he can get it).

October 7: Bunny came for evening—we discussed John's lack of ideas & borrowing them. Bunny, being under stress & strain, did parlor magic tricks. Says he does them for hours in front of glass to quiet his nerves, instead of smoking. . . . Regrets lack of will power lately to work nights— since meeting Edna. She certainly has played hell with him.

When Edna returned to the city in September, she decided she was going to live alone. It would be the first time she would live without any member of her family since she had brought Norma out of Maine in December 1917. Explaining the decision to her mother, who had remained in Truro, was going to be tough. Her mother had written to her in Woodstock telling her and Norma "to do just as you want to, and have just as good a time as you can, both of you. . . . I am all right and am not too lonely."

In an undated fragment of a letter, Vincent tried to tell her mother why she must live alone. The thrust of the letter was her need to break free from Norma:

. . . we're all going to have to put up with a lot of things this winter. Norma will have to shift for herself, & find a place for herself. It's only right that she should. And I'm not going to worry about her.—I hope you wont be displeased or disappointed by any of our plans, dear.—Please write & tell me what you think. I am sure I am right in believing we should all have separate rooms this winter. For myself, I know it has to be, or I shall lose my reason. It is a practical matter, of common sense & efficiency & has nothing to do with my great love for you & the girls.—Your loving daughter, Vincent.

P.S. I cant rid myself of the feeling that you will be displeased. And it makes me feel dreadful. You know that I love you, sweetheart, dont you? And dont you understand?—You see, I am a poet, & not quite right in my head, darling.

It's only that.—Vincent.

Millay included with her next letter a batch of clippings about her from her friend Franklin Pierce Adams's★ popular column "The Conning

---

★Adams was a columnist and a humorist who had begun in Chicago before starting his famous "The Conning Tower" in 1913, which he signed with his initials, F.P.A.

Tower," which was running in the New York *Tribune*. There were more than a score of couplets and quatrains written about her, in which the trick was to use her name in the final line, rather like a limerick. "It is certainly wonderful publicity for me," she told her mother.

> Laurel is green for a season, and love is sweet for a day;
> But love grows bitter with treason and Edna St. Vincent Millay.

Cora wrote back quickly, thrilled "with the Tribune craze." She didn't sound at all distressed, but written in pencil and dated October 15, 1920, on the back of the envelope in which Vincent's letter and clippings had been sent to her, she wrote:

Put this in your collection:—

> We all know the poet who shot into fame
> As Edna St. Vincent Millay,
> But who was the poet who gave her the name
> Of Edna St. Vincent Millay?

Then, perhaps dissatisfied with those four lines, she wrote:

A POET TO A POEM:—

> I am a poet, I have had my day
> For I have written one immortal line;
> Nor Greek nor Latin ever wrote more fine—
> The Poem: Edna St. Vincent Millay.
>> With love to the Poem,
>>> from
>>> The Author.

By October 20, the intensity of guilt in Vincent's letter to her mother had reached a new pitch. It was peculiar: they had been apart at most seven weeks.

Dearest beloved Mother,—
    I am so worried about you that I don't know what to do. I think about you all the time in the daytime, and lately I dream about you at night, I am so worried. I am afraid you are sick or something, out there in that cold old shack all alone. And I miss you so it's terrible.

After all her brave words about Norma fending for herself, she describes the two of them having a tea party "to which you were the only guest." They placed her snapshot on the table and pretended to give her tea, and "talked to you and everything, and then we both cried, we were so homesick for you." If either one of them could afford a telephone, they would call her every night, "just to say goodnight to you, no matter how much it cost." Vincent would even return to the Cape, except for the prohibitive cost. "I want to go terribly. But both the girls think it's silly to think of it, because you have much more need of a warm winter coat and to have the grocery bill paid . . . and to have your fare out to Aunt Clem's." But her questions to her mother follow hotly: Is she sick, is she cold, is she stinting on ordering kerosene at the expense of her own comfort?

> Please don't do that, sweetheart. Are you lonely, my own darling? Oh, please, dearest mother, let us know how you are! We are about crazy. There is nothing in all the world I love so much as you. We all love you better than anything, just as we did when we were little kids, you know. Tell us exactly what you are feeling about being out there all alone, please, oh, please!
>
> *Vincent.*

What is going on here? Did Millay feel she had abandoned her mother to exactly what she and her sisters felt when they were young and defenseless: isolation, coldness, and a desperate thrift?

Wilson remembered her on West Twelfth Street saying to him suddenly, "I'll be thirty in a minute!" He felt she was even

> more accessible and exposed . . . to the importunities of her suitors, who really besieged her door. . . . She had one or two depressing illnesses. Her apartment was poorly heated, and I brought her an electric heater. I remember how miserable she seemed—though she never lost a certain liveliness—wrapped up in an old flannel bathrobe and bundled in shabby covers.

We learn from him that she'd hung Charlie's painting "Directions for Using the Empress" above her bed. The Empress was a mechanical dress form, operated by a series of screws that used would make the form plumper or more slender, remembered clearly not only because Charlie had painted it but because one of Edna's suitors had given it to her in the vain hope of freeing her from being Norma's model. Edna became pregnant that winter, and, according to Norma, who did not know by whom, she suffered a "botched abortion," which left her bleeding and weakened.

⋐ ⋐ ⋐

"Don't ask me," Norma said warningly.

"I wasn't going to ask, you said you didn't know."

"There were things we didn't talk about."

"Of course."

"But I'll never forget the name of that goddamned abortionist!"

⋐ ⋐ ⋐

Toward the end of December, John Bishop invited her along with Wilson to dinner, "à deux—à trois—as you wish and then come to the apartment where I shall provide a stuffy air, cigarettes and a manuscript." Wilson remembered the night as festive. In his notebook for the twenties he described a hilarious scene where, after their dinner, "sitting on her day bed, John and I held Edna in our arms—according to an arrangement insisted upon herself—I her lower half and John her upper—with a polite exchange of pleasantries as to which had the better share." He said she called them "the choir boys of Hell," and complained, according to Wilson, that their both being in love with her hadn't even broken up their friendship.

To consider it from her point of view, these men, who were themselves best friends, seemed to relish being in love with her at the same time. Hal and Arthur were acting out roles similar to Wilson's and Bishop's. It seemed to cement their relationship rather than break it. Their love for her was something they shared. It brought them even closer together. But it did not bring them closer to Edna Millay. In these jolly triangles, she was the conduit for their affection for each other.

Wilson told her that her many admirers should form an alumni association, "to which she answered with promptness and point: '*On en parle toujours, mais on ne le fait jamais.*' "

Beginning with the three poems published in *Poetry* in 1917 up until the end of December 1920, Edna Millay had published seventy-seven poems, thirty-nine of which were sonnets. She had published a volume of her poems and had written eight prose pieces under a pseudonym for *Ainslee's*. She had also written and directed a play, *Aria da Capo,* and although her second book, *Second April,* was stalled in proofs, it was complete. A first edition of *Figs from Thistles* made up in pretty, brightly colored paper was brought out by Frank Shay, in the windows of whose bookshop at 4 Christopher Street in the Village they were displayed. They sold like hotcakes.

Millay was not languishing; she was in full command of her powers. That she was able to be consistently productive during a period of such disarray in her personal life is something of an achievement. Edmund Wilson has described this period as the beginning of her "immense popularity." She would from time to time point to her popularity and mock it, a little pleased and a little puzzled. "Also, I am becoming famous," she wrote to Hal, who'd gone off to China with Arthur.

> The current Vanity Fair has a whole page of my poems, and a photograph of me that looks about as much like me as it does like Arnold Bennett. And there have been three reviews of something I wrote, in New York newspapers in the last week alone. I am so incorrigibly ingenuous that these things mean just as much to me as ever. Besides, I just got a prize of a hundred dollars in Poetry, for the Bean-stalk. And I'm spending it all on clothes. I've the sweetest new evening gown you ever saw, and shoes with straps across them, and stockings with embroidery up the front. I wish you were here. We'd all go on a swell party together.

Yet this girlish delight in her fame wasn't the whole story. "There was something of awful drama about everything one did with Edna," Edmund Wilson remembered. "Her poetry, you soon found out, was her real overmastering passion." Wilson came to believe that other than her mother and her sisters, people were in some sense unimportant to her—except as subjects for poems. She was impartial, Wilson said ruefully. And so her lovers did not quarrel with one another, or even much with her. What she was interested in was "her own emotions about them.

> In all this, she was not egotistic in any boring or ridiculous or oppressive way, because it was not the personal, but the impersonal Edna Millay—that is, the poet—that preoccupied her so incessantly. But she was sometimes rather a strain, because nothing could be casual for her; I do not think I ever saw her relaxed.

Trying to put some distance between herself and her family had not worked. That fall, Kathleen took the room in front of hers on West Twelfth Street. And Norma stayed. Finally, just before Christmas, she made up her mind to escape:

Dearest, beloved Mother,—

The reason why I have not written you for so long is because I have been sick. I am all right now, but I have been quite sick, almost ever since I moved in here,—bronchitis for a while, & another small nervous break-down after that. I didn't want you to know, for fear you would worry.—but now that I am all right again I have decided that the thing for me to do is to have a change,—change of everything,—so I am going to travel.

She was going to Europe. Frank Crowninshield, the editor of *Vanity Fair*, had asked her to write two articles a month for the magazine: one she'd sign her own name to, the other Nancy Boyd's. "Technically," she said, she would be a foreign correspondent for *Vanity Fair*.

This is the thing I have always wanted to do, you know how much, dearest,—& my work, more than anything else, my poetry, needs fresh grass to feed on. I am becoming sterile here; I have known it would be, & I see it approaching if I stay here.—Also, New York life is getting too congested for me,—too many people; I get no time to work. . . . And I need to be alone for a while. I shall come back a fine strong woman. . . . Mother, dear, this is the whole thing, just as I've told it. It has nothing to do with any love affair, past or present. What the future may bring I don't know, maybe something more satisfactory than I've had so far. But that is not even on the horizon. I'm going as a free woman, a business woman, & because I want to travel.

She wanted very much to see Cora before she left on January 4, 1921, on the *Rochambeau*. She would cross with some friends. "But after I get to Paris I shall be alone. And I shall be perfectly happy, & perfectly safe, because I speak French, & because I am a very capable & sensible woman, when left to myself. You know that, dear."

But there was neither enough money nor enough time to bring Cora to New York. "I shall bid you God Speed," Cora wrote to her daughter,

just the same here as if I were in New York, and our spirits will often speak to each other on the way and after you get over there. There can be no real separation for two like us, who love each other so well, and you do not have to come here to tell me so, and I don't have to go there to hear it.

Only in her journal, it was a different voice that cried out on the day Vincent's ship left New York harbor: "My baby! My baby! My baby!"

Edna Millay may not have known she had to break the relationship with her mother, but that grip was now a stranglehold, and she was prying free.

SCRUB

If I grow bitterly,
Like a gnarled and stunted tree,
Bearing harshly of my youth
Puckered fruit that sears the mouth;
If I make of my drawn boughs
An inhospitable house,
Out of which I never pry
Towards the water and the sky,

Under which I stand and hide
And hear the day go by outside;
It is that a wind too strong
Bent my back when I was young,
It is that I fear the rain
Lest it blister me again.

It was not going to be an easy separation. Cora, too, had written a poem for her daughter. It was as prophetic as it was ominous.

HEALING, A PLAY IN TWO ACTS

ACT I.

Unlike as Life and Death they met.
The younger spake: Who are you, mother?
The older: A little, lone, old woman, gathering herbs. And you, daughter?
The younger: I gather flowers.

ACT II.

Less unlike again they met.
The younger spake: Where are your simples, mother?
The older: What would you, daughter?
The younger: Forgetfulness.
The older: Gather herbs.

C. B. Millay

PART FOUR

"PARIS IS WHERE THE 20TH CENTURY WAS"

CHAPTER 15

Vincent raced through the snowy streets of New York on January 4, 1921, just making the ship as the French porter, slapping a sticker on her trunk, "Mis à bord au dernier moment," hurried her up the gangplank of the *Rochambeau*. Even her mother joked with Norma about Vincent's "getaway," as if she were fleeing the scene of a crime. She was fleeing. But while her stomach had roiled with excitement for a good week before she left New York, once on the wintry Atlantic she didn't get sick and took no seasick remedies. "Whatever it might be," she wrote Cora, ". . . —I wanted the whole of it.—I wanted every bit of the experience, & no dope. (Like you, when I was going to be born.)"

Now, after nine days at sea, they were in the English Channel. She was too exhilarated to sleep, and, wrapping herself in the great white Hudson's Bay blanket she'd brought along, she went up on deck to see the dawn break over France. A steward, pointing to a rising gray bluff off the starboard bow said, "Voilà, Mademoiselle, la terre de France!"

By January 18, she had settled into her room at the Hôtel des Saints Pères on the Left Bank. It was a pretty, old hotel with a tiny winter garden filled with palms; it was cheap, and it had steam heat. Outside, the rain didn't let up; Paris turned the color of grisaille. She made her first diary entry that week: "It is so damp this afternoon . . . that the wall-paper of my room is dark and bubbly with it. I have given orders that my breakfast be brought me at eight o'clock after this, it being my notion to work in bed until noon."

Millay didn't know that on the rue de Varenne, within hailing distance but worlds away from the Saints Pères, the elegant Mrs. Wharton was keeping the same schedule, writing in her bed—although she was propped up by goose-down pillows, her little dogs tucked in beside her.

Each morning two American girls in the room next to Vincent's began their French lessons. The walls were paper thin. As soon as their tutor left they would break into a torrent of American slang, "all in a rather pleasant drawl which might mean Memphis," Edna mused. But they had only three topics of conversation: "Clothes; How many Francs does one get for a Dollar; and How Well One has done in a Week to see all One has seen." Her diary read as if she were collecting material for *Vanity Fair* pieces, and of course she was.

Frank Crowninshield had tried to persuade her before she left New York to sign her own name to her prose pieces. He'd proposed a series of twelve glimpses into "the social life of our day." Dialogues,

> apropos of divorce, and, in successive sketches, you could touch on The Debutante, The Perils of Domesticity, At a Dance, Social Climbing, The Honeymoon, Art Exhibitions, The Flirt, The Jealous Woman, First Love . . . Bridge, (if you play it), Golf (if you play it).

His point was to make the series notable, not only to please *Vanity Fair* but—and here Crowninshield was no fool—because it would give Millay material for a book: "only, I want your name on the sketches, even if you have to elevate the moral, intellectual and literary tone of them to a height level with your lofty position as an artist." He would pay her a hundred dollars for each, which was as high as he'd ever paid for a play or a dialogue, but, he persisted doggedly, "Your name really ought to be on them, in order to make us pay you this money willingly and gladly. If your friend Miss Boyd were to sign them, I would pay this money a little grudgingly." Still Millay continued to refuse, and Crowninshield continued to pay.

"Did you see *The Implacable Aphrodite* in the March *Vanity Fair*?" she wrote Norma, "—it reads rather amusingly." After that she managed a Nancy Boyd piece, alternating sometimes with a poem, about once a month until the October issue, when the magazine published nine of her poems.

Vanity Fair was providing her with an income, just as *Ainslee's* had, and again the most substantial portion of it came from her prose. "The Implacable Aphrodite" was set in Greenwich Village. Tea is about to be served by Miss Black, a sculptress, to Mr. White, "a man of parts, but badly assembled." As she bends down to prepare the tea, her robe falls away, clinging "to her supple limbs." Mr. White is soon beside himself. Other men, he tells her, may importune her to marry, for they do not understand her need to be free to create her art. It is her beauty that attracts them, " 'your extraordinary grace, your voice, so thrillingly quiet, your ravishing gestures.' *(He is silent, breathing hard.) (She, delighted by his understanding, leans back wearily and closes her eyes, exposing a long and treacherous throat, full of memories.)*" What fun Millay must have had writing this. It's hard to tell who she is twitting the most, herself or the men drawn to her. At the end of the story, Miss Black announces she's about to sail for Europe:

" 'It will be of infinite value to me in my work.'

" 'But what about me?'

" 'I don't understand you.'

" 'You say you're going because it will help your work—but think of me! What will happen to me?' "

She replies that it hadn't occurred to her to consider him.

"He *(shouting)*: 'No! Of course not! Oh, you're cold, you are—and cruel, my God! Your work!' *(He laughs scornfully.)* All you think about is those damn little putty figures!' "

Here *he* is, flesh and blood: " '—and what do you care?'

"She *(icily)*: 'Less and less.' "

Millay was not unaware that certain men in her life, particularly the literary men who would later leave written records—Floyd Dell, Edmund Wilson, and John Peale Bishop among them—found her refusal to continue her affairs with them a stunning rejection. They wrote to her about their desperate hurt and anger; they waylaid her on the street. To a man they felt that her leaving them meant far more about her inability to be faithful than it did about their need to secure her exclusively for themselves. They talked about her chagrin, even when it was clearly their own; they talked about her promiscuity and her puzzling magnanimity. They failed to acknowledge the pull she felt between the excitement and energy of her sexual life, where she was a sort of brigand who relished the chase, and the difficult, sweet pleasures of her work. But Millay did seem irresistibly drawn to relationships that were doomed to fail. Maybe she couldn't bear the weight of a permanent attachment, in which she had no reason to believe. The love of her life remained her mother, and until that tie was broken it held her fast.

You know, mother, the quaintest thing. All around Paris in public places, where we have a sign up saying *toilet* (a word we took from the French, of course) they have signs up saying *"Water Closet"* or just the letters *"W.C."* Isn't that killing? Of course they think it very grand. They pronounce it, naturally, a little like this:

"Vatair Closette"

Well, enough of this Paris gossip, dearie!—Isn't it racy, though? So far my note seems to be all about . . . public toilets.

Cora was overjoyed at Vincent's simply being in Paris; any news was part of *their* triumph: "How we used to think and dream and plan and work and give up one thing and reach out for another. Hasn't it been a big wonderful, terrible, triumphant, old haul up the hill? And if it had been smooth and less steep, we would not have gotten so much out of it." She cautioned Vincent against making it too hard for herself now:

> The other night after I went to bed I lay for a long time thinking of the terrible winter you had last year—one thing piling upon another to the breaking point, and the getting away last spring, and all the demands upon my little girl. I hope you will be able to recover from it all during your stay abroad, and come back when you get ready to come all saddled and bridled and fit for the fight again; but not the same fight, ever again. Other burdens may come, and will, of course, but never the same ones . . . again.

Some of those burdens lay at home. A man in New York told her he was keeping in touch with Norma and Kathleen "so that through them the memory of you . . . shall keep fresh. Our few weeks intimacy was & is one of the bright spots in my life." He told her how blooming Kathleen looked, and he confided about Norma that although she was playing in *Matinata,* the curtain-raiser to *Emperor Jones,*

> I don't think she's overly satisfied or contented. She's a queer child & not satisfied with what she can do well. . . . I think she misses you a lot; but that's natural, so do I. She one time said she was going to Europe, & I said & live how? & she said Oh Edna always looked after me. Well, I said, she's a fool if she does again.

The week before her twenty-ninth birthday, stricken with homesickness, Vincent wrote her mother:

> February 13—
> Two o'*clock in de* mo'nin'
> *In bed*
>
> Dearest Muddy,—
>   Jus' a lil' note to say goodnight to my muddy afore I goes to sleep. I've written a lot today—just got through—& am tired.

Then she lapsed into excessive guilt: Had she forgotten to return the five dollars she'd borrowed from her mother just before she'd left for

France? "Oh darling, if I did, I shall never get over it! . . . It makes me cry when I think I didn't send it—& I'm crying right this minute, all of a sudden, like a nut, just for thinking I forgot, simply *forgot,* something my dearest wanted."

She circled a tiny spot on the paper: "Tear-drop, see? I had to do something ridiculous, to shake me out of it, darling. . . . I'll send you some money soon, dear. . . . Goodnight, my dearest thing in the world. *Vincent.*"

This was a pattern in their correspondence now that mirrored a new pattern in real life: Millay fled, embarking on something of her own rather than staying with her mother. Then she felt guilty. Her guilt was almost always linked to having abandoned Cora, but she assuaged it only with money, not by returning.

Up until then, Cora had been spending the winter and early spring in Newburyport with her sister Clem, where she had been deeply unsettled by a visit from her youngest sister, Georgia. Swanning about in her splendid black Packard, with her boys wrapped in bearskin next to her, Georgia asked Clem why Cora didn't work, as she was able. "Clem told her she supposed it was because the girls didn't want me to," Cora wrote to her daughter. "I'm tired of Georgia and her ways and talk and coarsenesses and selfishnesses and do not think I shall trouble her very much more or let her trouble me." But for all the grief and jockeying for position among those sisters, Clem and Susie, Georgia and Cora could not do without one another.

The Lamp and the Bell was a play that Millay was commissioned to write while she was in Paris, for the fiftieth anniversary of the founding of Vassar College. It was in five acts with a cast of forty-eight, not counting musicians, cupids, pages, and children. Freighted with the heavy cargo and paraphernalia of mock Elizabethan drama, it listed but stayed afloat because it was centered in the remarkable love between two young women who become stepsisters. Nothing could have been cannier for Vassar. It was lavishly produced outdoors on the greensward, where Vincent had often performed, and it was a ringing success.

What was disturbing, almost chilling, was the letter Edna Millay wrote to her mother from Paris after the play was finished: "I have a curious feeling that someday I shall marry, and have a son; and that my husband will die; and that you and I and my little boy will all live together on a farm." This is nearly a reprise of the central theme of the play: that the enduring love between women is the only bond that lasts.

"Lovéd," Cora wrote back, dismissing the notion with an air of parental good sense, "the idea of living with you and a grandson cannot tempt me into hoping his father will have to forego that privilege, unless he may be someone you will not want, which heaven forbid." How disingenuous this was coming from a woman whose own mother had chosen to forgo that privilege, as had she. Leaving a husband was mother's milk to the Millays.

Vincent's homesickness was for her mother. Even as she teased Norma

Dearest Darling Baby Sister 'Loved Hunk,—it does seem a long long time, little sweet sing, since us heard from each other! . . . Sweetheart, this is a silly letter for one grown-up sister to write another grown-up sister, but maybe it will express . . . how much I love you, & how often I miss you.

But it was her mother for whom she longed:

It is nearly six months now since I saw you. A long time. Mother, do you know, almost all people love their mothers, but I have never met anybody in my life, I think, who loved his mother as much as I love you. I don't believe there ever was anybody who did, quite so much, and quite in so many wonderful ways. I was telling somebody yesterday that the reason I am a poet is entirely because you wanted me to be and intended I should be, even from the very first. You brought me up in the tradition of poetry, and everything I did you encouraged. I can not remember once in my life when you were not interested in what I was working on, or even suggested that I should put it aside for something else. Some parents of children that are "different" have so much to reproach themselves with. But not you, Great Spirit. . . . If I didn't keep calling you mother, anybody reading this would think I was writing to my sweetheart. And he would be quite right.

Between this letter, written on June 15, and her next, sometime in the last week of July, when she was going to the seashore, Vincent invited her mother to come to Europe

and play around with your eldest daughter. . . . We could go to Italy and Switzerland, and to England and Scotland, and, if there are not too many riots and street fights there at the time,—mavourneen, we would go to Ireland! . . . and then, my Best Beloved, you and I will just have ourselves a little honey-moon.

Before she left Paris, she mailed Cora a poem. She told her mother she could show it to her sisters. "P.S.—Do you suppose, when you & I are dead, dear, they will publish the *Love Letters of Edna St. Vincent Millay & Her Mother*?"

She hadn't said why she was suddenly leaving Paris, and she certainly didn't tell her mother she had had to borrow travel money from Edmund Wilson, who had just arrived there. "You told me that if I got into desperate straits you could raise some money for me," she wrote to Wilson. "Well, I am there now. That's just where I am.—I will pay it back very soon,—that is to say, in a month's time.—If you can't do it, will you please wire me that you can't."

There was considerably more going on in her life than she admitted in any of her letters to her mother or to her sisters: in the spring she had fallen deeply in love with the young English journalist George Slocombe, from whom she was about to flee.

When Edmund Wilson arrived in Paris, he immediately looked up Edna and found her at the Hôtel de l'Intendance, "a very first-rate hotel on the Left Bank and better dressed, I suppose," he wrote John Bishop, "than she has ever been before in her life." She was sitting at her typewriter with a pile of manuscripts on her desk, wearing a little black dress.

> But she looked older, more mature—at least she has on the occasions when I have seen her; she assured me that perhaps the next day she would be like a little girl again. She was very serious, earnest, and sincere about herself—inspired, I suppose, by my presence, . . . and told me that she wanted to settle down to a new life: she was tired of breaking hearts and spreading havoc.

Then he told Bishop about Slocombe:

> Unfortunately, he had a wife and three children at Saint-Cloud and a very cruel situation had arisen. She did not know whether he would get a divorce or not, but if he did, she would marry him, go to England to live, and have children. She was very happy, she said. I am sorry to say that, when I first talked to her, I was inclined, with the memory of my own scars still giving out an occasional twinge, to jeer at her seriousness and be sarcastic at the expense of the pain she expressed at having wrecked another home. . . . She . . . has a new distinction of dress, but she can no longer intoxicate me with her beauty or throw bombs into my soul; when I looked at her it was like staring into the center of an extinct volcano. She made me sad; it made me sad, curiously enough, that I had loved her so much once and now did not love her any longer. Actually, of course, I would not love her again for anything; I can think of few more terrible calamities; but somehow felt that, impossible and imperfect as she is, some glamour and high passion had gone out of life when my love for her died.

He must have realized how inflated his own rhetoric was, for he added, "Well, these are old Dr. Wilson's last words on the chief maelstrom of his early years. Preserve them carefully, but do not publish them until all parties are dead."

Wilson was far more uncertain of how he felt about Edna than he admitted to Bishop; in fact, he seemed to friends to have pursued her to Paris. While she had not invited him, he nevertheless took a hotel close to hers, where he felt uncomfortable because she was "very much allied with the Bohemians of the Left Bank, with whom I was not much at home." Millay liked and admired Edmund Wilson, but she never again considered him as a lover.

CHAPTER 16

In the spring of 1920, George Slocombe had come to Paris from London, where, at twenty-six, he was already a political reporter for *The Daily Herald*. He was rumored to have brought the czar's jewels out of Russia in the confused aftermath of the Revolution. He stood just over six feet, and, with his mahogany hair and bright red beard, which he wore full at a time when men were clean-shaven, he looked like "a radiance," one of Edna's lovers, Griffin Barry, said in envy. Slocombe had married a Russian girl who was the daughter of the *homme d'affaires* of the Grand Duke Michael, for whom he'd been a tutor.

Slocombe led a daring life as a young journalist and went to Paris when it was the most promising city in the world. The hotels were still filled with the journalists and small fry of the diplomatic corps who had remained in residence after the Versailles Peace Conference was over.

That spring the city seemed caught in a spell, the creamy white blossoms of the chestnut trees perfuming the air while tiny red taxis, their drivers wearing boiled-leather top hats, took Americans into Montparnasse, which was still a village. "The Café du Dôme, not yet internationally celebrated, was a small, dark and modest establishment," Slocombe wrote. Inside, foreigners played chess and a small group of American writers and artists played poker. The Rotonde hadn't yet swallowed up the little narrow Café Vavin, "at which Trotsky was frequently seen, and Lenin more rarely."

No more extraordinary state of affairs had existed on the Continent since the Congress of Vienna. . . . Civil war in Russia and Hungary, D'Annunzio and his toy cannon manning the walls of Fiume . . . famine in Austria and Germany, typhus in Russia, revolutionary agitation in France and Italy.

It was into this world in the spring that Edna Millay began to move with Slocombe, until sometime in early July, when he told his wife. By the night of July 19, only two weeks after Wilson had written to John Bishop, Edna and Slocombe quarreled.

The next morning Slocombe wrote her a long letter, in which he began by calling her David: "The name I first called you by, I will call you by last." He was leaving her, he explained,

not because I don't love you any longer, but because I love you too much. I leave you before our love becomes less than the perfect thing it has been to me: & because I want to love you all my life as I love you now. . . . I know that if we had been married I should have tried to master you. . . . I must master those I love [and] I could not succeed in mastering you without making you something less than you are. . . . If I had been sure . . . that you would be happy in subjection, I might have been forced to do the ignoble, but still inevitable & even necessary act of leaving my wife & children.

This self-serving, peculiar explanation went on, "Edna, David, I kiss your lips and your eyes and God help me your little round knees." He asked only two things of her: if they met in the street, she should not be afraid to talk to him. "I even think I shall not be happy without seeing you sometimes, if only at a distance." And could she write him a letter, since he had "never had a letter of yours & I would like one to keep with the picture of you." The man's caution combined with his arrogance was stunning; no wonder Edna fled. As for Slocombe, once he'd made his decision to leave her, he was unable to keep it. He wrote her every other day until she escaped to Dieppe.

When he hadn't heard from her by mid-August, he pressed her: "If you are forgetting me, there is no harm in a friendly little note once in a month is there?" This time she did weaken, telling him how strange it was to be without him in her life. He jumped at her reply; he was "eager & crazy to see you again." He asked her to return to Paris by September 1, because "on Sat. Sept. 3rd I take my family to . . . Italy."

The mails from the States were irregular and slow, and Vincent asked again and again why she hadn't heard from home, chiding Norma, "Rise on your legs, you poor piece of imitation Camembert, and write your sister a little note. See? And that's that. As ever, your childhood's friend, Sefe." When not even bantering seemed to work, she wrote her mother, "I do hope it is not the best reason,—that you are ill and can't write"; because months before she'd sent her

> a lovely poem of mine, called *The Ballad of the Harp-Weaver*. . . . & I think if you had received it you would surely have spoken of it.—I send you another copy of it now. It is practically the only poem I have written since I left America.—That was just what I wanted, you know, not to write a word of poetry for a year. When it begins to get a little *easy*, or one begins to write in certain forms almost from habit, it is time to stop for a while, I think, & almost forget that one is a poet—become a prose-writer, for instance—& then let it all come back to one later, fresh, & possibly in a newer form.—The next thing I hope to do is to finish the long sonnet sequence about the New England woman. . . . I hope you will like this poem, darling. It is dedicated to you, of course, as may be seen at a glance.

No matter where or with whom Vincent was—in Paris, at the seashore, or in England—this poem, sent to her mother and "worshipfully" dedicated to her, loomed as something more significant than anything, with the single exception of "Renascence," that Millay had yet written.

Wilson didn't much like the poem when it appeared in *Vanity Fair* and told Millay so. He thought "it verged on the sentimental." To his surprise she defended it "strongly." "I had known that it was about her own mother," he wrote in his memoir of Edna, "and I knew how devoted she was to the debonair hard-bitten old lady who worked for her and educated her."

He hadn't felt at first how profoundly moving the poem was. Then it seized him: "the loneliness, the poverty, the undervalued Irish heritage, the Spartan New England self-discipline, the gift of artistic creation and intellectual distinction . . . that the mother had been able to transmit." It was a record of "the closest relationship that Edna, up to then, I suppose . . . had ever known."

THE BALLAD OF THE HARP-WEAVER

"Son," said my mother,
    When I was knee-high,
"You've need of clothes to cover you,
    And not a rag have I.

"There's nothing in the house
    To make a boy breeches,
Nor shears to cut a cloth with,
    Nor thread to take stitches.

"There's nothing in the house
    But a loaf-end of rye,
And a harp with a woman's head
    Nobody will buy,"
    And she began to cry.

That was in the early fall.
    When came the late fall,
"Son," she said, "the sight of you
    Makes your mother's blood crawl,—

"Little skinny shoulder-blades
    Sticking through your clothes!
And where you'll get a jacket from
    God above knows.

"It's lucky for me, lad,
    Your daddy's in the ground,
And can't see the way I let
    His son go around!"
    And she made a queer sound.

That was in the late fall.
    When the winter came,
I'd not a pair of breeches
    Nor a shirt to my name.

I couldn't go to school,
    Or out of doors to play.
And all the other little boys
    Passed our way.

"Son," said my mother,
    "Come, climb into my lap,
And I'll chafe your little bones
    While you take a nap."

And, oh, but we were silly
    For half an hour or more,
Me with my long legs
    Dragging on the floor,

A-rock-rock-rocking
   To a mother-goose rhyme!
Oh, but we were happy
   For half an hour's time!

But there was I, a great boy,
   And what would folks say
To hear my mother singing me
   To sleep all day,
   In such a daft way?

Men say the winter
   Was bad that year;
Fuel was scarce,
   And food was dear.

A wind with a wolf's head
   Howled about our door,
And we burned up the chairs
   And sat upon the floor.

All that was left us
   Was a chair we couldn't break,
And the harp with a woman's head
   Nobody would take,
   For song or pity's sake.

The night before Christmas
   I cried with the cold,
I cried myself to sleep
   Like a two-year-old.

And in the deep night
   I felt my mother rise,
And stare down upon me
   With love in her eyes.

I saw my mother sitting
   On the one good chair,
A light falling on her
   From I couldn't tell where,

Looking nineteen,
   And not a day older,
And the harp with a woman's head
   Leaned against her shoulder.

Her thin fingers, moving
   In the thin, tall strings,
Were weav-weav-weaving
   Wonderful things.

Many bright threads,
　　From where I couldn't see,
Were running through the harp-strings
　　Rapidly,

And gold threads whistling
　　Through my mother's hand.
I saw the web grow,
　　And the pattern expand.

She wove a child's jacket,
　　And when it was done
She laid it on the floor
　　And wove another one.

She wove a red cloak,
　　So regal to see,
"She's made it for a king's son,"
　　I said, "and not for me."
　　But I knew it was for me.

She wove a pair of breeches
　　Quicker than that!
She wove a pair of boots
　　And a little cocked hat.

She wove a pair of mittens,
　　She wove a little blouse,
She wove all night
　　In the still, cold house.

She sang as she worked,
　　And the harp-strings spoke;
Her voice never faltered,
　　And the thread never broke.
　　And when I awoke,—

There sat my mother
　　With the harp against her shoulder,
Looking nineteen,
　　And not a day older,

A smile about her lips,
　　And a light about her head,
And her hands in the harp-strings
　　Frozen dead.

And piled up beside her
　　And toppling to the skies,
Were the clothes of a king's son,
　　Just my size.

A ballad is the simplest four-line verse we have in English. With its clear rhymes and even beats, it tells a plain story as simply as a song or a nursery rhyme. But it is never an exercise in innocence, for it is almost always a tale of violence ending in death. Millay's is no exception. Although "The Ballad of the Harp-Weaver" may be read to bear two messages, both are fraught with peril. Millay is using the story of her own childhood and her mother's, each with its iron poverty and maternal self-sacrifice, to equip her child for a grander life than any she would ever know without her. She is a daughter transformed into a son—and no ordinary son of a poor mother but a king's son, a royal. It is *he* who writes the poem; when the mother speaks,

> "Son," said my mother,
>   When I was knee-high,
> "You've need of clothes to cover you,
>   And not a rag have I."

there is nothing in the house but a heel of bread

> "And a harp with a woman's head
>   Nobody will buy,"
> And she began to cry.

That single phrase, "a harp with a woman's head," which will be repeated four times in the ballad, is the key to the poem. A ballad works by repeating certain phrases, charging them with such increased feeling that an almost unbearable tension is created. The third time Millay uses that phrase, she varies the stanza to lead us into the center of the poem, which is about the mother, the Harp-Weaver.

> Looking nineteen,
>   And not a day older,
> And the harp with a woman's head
>   Leaned against her shoulder.
>
> Her thin fingers, moving
>   In the thin, tall strings,
> Were weav-weav-weaving
>   Wonderful things.

In her hands the harp is transformed into a magic loom upon which she will weave not simply dross into gold—but bright "gold threads whistling

> Through my mother's hand.
> I saw the web grow,
>   And the pattern expand.

What web? Where else in Millay's life have we seen a mother who weaves to earn a living for her brood? In fact, we've seen it twice. The harp with a woman's head is the lap loom upon which Cora wove hair, a skill she had learned from her own mother, but which she refused to pass down to her daughters.

⊘ ⊘ ⊘

"She didn't want us to know how," Norma said matter-of-factly. "There's no more to it than that. But look what Mother made for us," Norma said as she lifted out of a trunk three identical porcelain-faced dolls—identical except for their hair. One was dark, and one was blond, and one was fiery red. Norma asked me if I wanted to hold them, and I didn't. They seemed to me spooky, lying in their old muslin clothes, but their hair was real, all right, and richly colored, and dead.

When I said that I found the dolls macabre, Norma thought I meant dirty. "No, Nancy, the hair was washed. Mother washed our hair before she used it." Here was some fragment of their real bodies, and Norma wanted me to touch them as she fondled their hair, as if they were relics. I recoiled from them as if they were tiny pieces of flesh. It was an odd moment—I felt flushed. It was just a little too close for me, in the library at Steepletop. Vincent's bright red hair was bristling with color, as shiny as a fox's pelt.

"I must wash their clothes, then you won't be afraid to touch them."

"I'm not afraid."

"Yes, you are."

"What am I afraid of?"

"I don't know. Oh, maybe I have a little tiny hunch."

⊘ ⊘ ⊘

Even accounting for the slow transatlantic mails, Vincent didn't hear from Cora until very late in the fall. "Mother has been a terrible woman for a time in not writing her sweet lovely one," she began. So it wasn't the slow mails; she hadn't written. "I guess I thought you must know how I loved that wonderful poem"; she called it "that wonderful poem" twice, as if she were uncertain how to praise it. Then she told Vincent that she'd given it to Kay, who had returned it to her via Norma (whose nickname she uses here),

> and we all love it. Charlie and Non were mad about it, and Non told Charlie a little more so that he had a little better idea of what it might mean to us. But I should never think of mentioning anything like that to Howard, and Kay would not want to do so. And it is just as well.

Astonishingly, Cora, Kathleen, and Norma had decided not to tell Kathleen's husband about the poem because it was so centered on their own past.

None of it mattered at that moment, when Vincent was thinking of George Slocombe, to whom she'd just written. He wrote back quickly that he would try to be "to you what you would have me be . . . in any case you are the only woman I love, or want to love." He said her letter broke his heart. "Do you remember a walk back through the woods to Blois, when you picked flowers, & told me of your mother's cupboard & kitchen? Do you remember anything?"

She remembered far too much. For all his declarations of love, she did not hear from him again until the end of November, when she was traveling with Griffin Barry to Italy.

CHAPTER 17

Millay had been in Rome less than a week when the American ambassador, Richard Washburn Child, suggested it would be an adventure to travel to Albania, which had just been opened to the West but whose borders, in the aftermath of World War I, remained unfixed and in dispute. The young John Carter, whom she'd met in Paris and who was connected to the embassy, would accompany her.

The rugged isolation of tiny Albania, with its rival clans and religions, was as legendary as its beauty. Its coastline, with the ruins of old Venetian fortifications set among fields of wild dill, black mountains rising from the sea, was ravishing. But after five hundred years of Ottoman domination Albania remained backward, fiercely independent, and desperately poor.

They began the first day under starlight, before dawn, riding through mountains from the capital city of Tirana to Elbasan. Edna spent ten hours in the saddle because it was the only way to get there; it was the second time she had ever ridden. In a snapshot taken halfway between Tirana and Elbasan, she is sitting uneasily astride a dark bay, squinting into the bright light. Two armed guards are in the foreground. Standing next to her is their young Albanian interpreter, Abdullah, holding a rifle with a clip of ammunition in his hand, a cartridge belt around his waist. He is dressed in a Serbian uniform. "They wear the uniforms of anybody they can catch & tear it away from," Millay noted in her journal; "—their army on the march must be a sight. This boy followed us everywhere just out of pure affection & wept when we had to send him away. He cared for us like a mother & like [a] dog & like a hen with ducklings."

Although there is never any direct mention of John Carter in her journal, there are always "you" and "we." The intimacy of this entry suggests that they were traveling as lovers.

> Rain on the Adriatic and on the Moslem tower.... Sleepily from the chalk-white minaret an hour before daybreak the dark young muezzin calls the town to prayer—Only you & I, alarmed from slumber, listen, staring into the darkness, Ah—Ah—Ah—husky & shrill the bodiless voice in the sky climbs/mounts the wide, uneven steps to the folded feet of Allah. . . .
>
> Let us tear apart the tough thick skin of the ripe pomegranate & split the seedy fruit in two—ah, how wet & good to the love-parched mouth—how cool on the naked breast & knees drips now the clear bright blood of the crushed pomegranate—suck up & spilt—wipe the wet mouth & chin on the warm smooth shoulder—there are six pomegranates in this basket—shall we eat them all—hurl now the empty shells to the corner of the room—Ah, how stained & drenched we are!—Let the wind dry us if it will.

They vowed never to tell anybody about their trip, "which sounds awful," Carter later wrote Norma, "but wasn't at all."

In another photograph taken in Albania she is standing with her hands on her hips, showing off the fragile lace at the wrists and throat of her long-sleeved blouse against a heavily embroidered red velvet cloak with its stiff silk sash—embroidered with real gold, she told her mother. The image is nearly that of another poet—a man with auburn curls and a surly mouth who sat for his portrait by Thomas Phillips wearing a native Albanian costume. There is the same fitted brocaded jacket, shot through with gold threads and bright trimmings, and except for the headdress, a turban and flowing scarf flung over his shoulder, this famous painting of Lord Byron looks astonishingly like Millay. Immensely popular, his brief life a scandal, his poems memorized by schoolchildren in Albania, Byron was the beau ideal of the Romantic poet in nineteenth-century England, as Millay was becoming in America in the opening decades of the twentieth century.

"But in spite of all the hardships and inconveniences of travel in a country with no railroads or public conveyances of any kind," she later wrote to her mother from Rome, "as a matter of fact for the most part no roads at all except a bridle path through the mountains, no plumbing, no butter, no coffee except Turkish coffee which is made with sugar, and other such-like lacks, seeing Albania—and also Montenegro, where we traveled for a couple of days only—has been my most thrilling experience so far."

She said she intended to write it up for the *Metropolitan* but never did. Instead, as John Carter wrote, "She remained in Rome for a bit and then went to Vienna with Griffin Barry."

Just before leaving Rome on November 13, 1921, she totted up her expenses, listing her assets and liabilities. The latter was the longer list. She had about $53, counting everything she could lay her hands on in Italian, French, British, Belgian, Turkish, and Serbian currency. This included money in coins and paper, and postage stamps. She owed $1,085 to a wide variety of friends, not including the $450 and 250 francs she owed to John Carter or what she owed to Edmund Wilson and Slocombe. Nor did she take into account the discrepancy between *Vanity Fair*'s account and her own figures, another 3,000 francs. She tried to calculate the difference in rates of exchange among francs, pounds, and lire but gave up with a note to herself: "It is easily seen, without transposing this all into dollars, that it means a great deal of money."

Four days after drawing up her list, she invited her mother to Europe. Indebtedness was a state she was accustomed to. It would not stop her; it never had.

Sweetheart:

There is one thing, of course, which must be done before you come abroad. So I want you to write and tell me as soon as you can get together the evidence just how much it will take for you to go to Camden, pay up all our debts there, get the furniture out of hock and stored in some more congenial place, or sent to New York to help furnish for the kids, and live nicely while you are there. . . . So make me a real estimate, and don't get scared if it looks pretty big, and remember that I want you to do the whole thing like a grand lady, travel in the Pullman even in the daytime, stand Flora Harris to a couple of drinks in the Bay View House—(I had a dreadful feeling just then that maybe Flora Harris is dead; but if she is, you know what I mean). I repeat, don't get scared even if it looks pretty big, because I've got to make a lot of money anyway, and I might as well make a little more, and do the thing as it ought to be done. Also, it would be rather fun while in Camden to tell anybody who might be interested that as soon as you get your business straightened out you are coming abroad to be with me. See, dear? So don't go trying to help me out by steaming apart stuck postage-stamps, returning cream-bottles, or picking up cigarette-butts in the street and trying to sell them to Benson & Hedges. We're going to do this here trick nonchalant, or we ain't going to do it.

To Norma she joked:

Whadda you think about my bringing the little old Irish devil over here? . . . I'm going to drag her up to the top of the Eiffel Tower the moment she gets to Paris & let her crow one good long crow, & then I'm going to waltz her up to the *Rotonde* & get her drunk, & if she wants to crow all the way home, well, I'm going to let her.

But the real news in all those fugitive letters that at last began to arrive in Rome was that Norma had married Charles Ellis.

Now I have two bruvvers! And two such nice bruvvers. I couldn't have picked me nicer ones. Charlie knows I love him, unless he has lost his memory, but tell him anyway that I love him very much, and that I think he is a great actor and has a very handsome nose, and that I am proud and happy to have him in my immediate family.

She couldn't help noting that she, the eldest, remained unmarried: "Well, both my little sisters are young married women, and me, I am just about three months from being an old maid. My Englishman, honey, is, as you might have guessed, a married man, this time with three children. Oh, well. (Who the devil told you about him, anyhow?)" Then she sent them both her love, "and I do hope you'll go ahead and have a baby. If you can't support it, I will.*

As ever, the companion of your middle age, the friend of your declining years, the old woman who'll sit before the fire with you fifty years from now and knit the left stocking while you knit the right.

In her own life there was still nobody she cared for as she had Slocombe, to whom she had written while she was in Albania. His letter awaited her

*In Millay's published *Letters,* edited by Norma Millay, there is a typo that remained uncorrected. It read, "If you can't *suppose* it, I will." Whereas the key word was "support."

in Rome. "I had thought you lost," he wrote on November 19, "having no other news of you than a message from Griffin saying you were gone off into the Albanian wilds." Then he played the remembering game that lovers play when they've lost each other for good. It was like licking a sore tooth to see if it still hurt. He had asked her if she remembered telling him about her mother's cupboard filled with the healing herbs of her childhood. "Darling . . . I remember you too vividly & personally for me ever to forget," he wrote. "Anyhow I am working hard afternoons & evenings in my office. The Rotonde sees me once a week on an average. My wife sees me most of the other nights. And for the rest, I have your photograph in my table drawer, & dreams of you two or three times a week, and daydreams almost all the time." He sounded just like Jim Lawyer or Arthur Ficke: full of yearning but married and utterly unavailable.

It was to Arthur that she admitted that first winter in Paris how lonesome she was: "Oh, if only you were there now,—just around the corner from me!—Shall I never see you again, my dear?"

Arthur wrote back on Valentine's Day, telling her to pick up a Japanese print he'd left with his French dealer, as well as a few thousand francs the man was holding for him. The money was his gift to her, and she was to spend it on the same kind of riotous living they would have spent it on if they had been together. Instead, she bought a Poiret gown of silk the color of her eyes. When he asked if she minded that in his next book he'd publish a group of sonnets dedicated to her, she wrote that she couldn't care less what the world thought. At the close of her letter she asked offhandedly about Witter Bynner, "Dear, does Hal know how much you care for me?—I have wondered, idly wondered."

The mention of Hal galvanized Arthur's pen. Their letters began to answer each other, with the intimacy of a conversation held in secret thousands of miles apart. For of course Arthur was not going to come to her in Europe. "Yes, Hal knows that I am perfectly mad about you," he replied, "whether he knows *how* mad, I don't know." That was in August. By late fall, their letters had turned urgent.

Edna wrote to only three people from Albania: her mother, George Slocombe, and Arthur. "I must write you," she told Arthur. "But when I start to write you all I can think to say to you is—why aren't you here? Oh, why *aren't* you here? . . . Dear, when I come back to the States, won't you come east to see me?— . . . you could come to New York, because you often do, to see Hal . . . and don't you love me most as much as you love Hal?"

It was striking how often their thoughts turned to Hal. But Edna was drawing Arthur to her.

I think we might have a few days together that would be entirely lovely. We are not children, or fools, we are mad. And we of all people should be able to do the mad thing well. If each of us is afraid to see the other, that is only one more sympathy we have. If each of us is anguished lest we lose one another through some folly, then we are more deeply bound than any folly can undo.

————————

Doubtless all this reasoning resolves itself into one pitiful female cry,—what ever happens, I want to see you again!—But oh, my dear, I know what my heart wants of you,—it is not the things that other men can give.

Do you remember that poem in *Second April* which says, "Life is a quest & love a quarrel, Here is a place for me to lie!"?—That is what I want of you—out of the sight & sound of other people, to lie close to you & let the world rush by. . . . Arthur, it is wicked and useless,—all these months and months apart from you, all these years with only a glimpse of you in the face of everybody.—I tell you I must see you again.—

Edna

On November 22, Arthur, who had not yet received this last letter, wrote to her from Iowa, where Hal, who was visiting, had given him the astonishing news that he "has gently and politely asked you to marry him." Arthur's own advice to her was that since he couldn't, they should and then adopt him. "Do you know, I'll bet I am more interested in this damn marriage than either of you two are!" Hal added:

What about that?

I am beginning to think there is no such go-between as the Atlantic Ocean.

Why have you never answered? Is there no answer?

Hal

Hal, not Arthur, had asked her to marry him. Except that Vincent had not yet received his letter. She wrote to him just before Christmas:

Dearest Hal,—

I never received your letter of which Arthur speaks.—So that his crazy card-index note, and your post-script, are all I have to tell me what is in your mind.—Do you really want me to marry you?—Because if you really want me to, I will.

As if that were not a remarkable enough acceptance, she amplified it for him:

I have thought for a long time that someday I should marry you.

Of course I can't write to you about it, you must see that, my dear, not knowing what was in your letter. Whatever I say would be perhaps the wrong thing to say.

. . . You have known me since I was a little girl. It is curious to think of that. As little as we have seen of one another, yet you are bound in the memories of my childhood.

If, she told him, it was just a dream he'd had a month ago and now regretted or had forgotten, then she was sorry.

I wish you could come here. It is not so very far, and I feel I must see you, and I can't come there. But I suppose you have duties now from which you cannot be released—even for me. (It is amusing and pleasant to say to you: even for me.) In any case, I wish you could come, and wanted to.

―――――

You will let me hear from you at once, Hal, won't you? Oh, if you knew the comical state my mind is in! What a *ridiculous* person you are!

Edna

Then suddenly, still having heard nothing, on December 30 she cabled him: YES HAL. One week later, precisely, she cabled him again. This time the single word YES.

On the first of January, he wrote to her at last in response to her first cable—a letter she could not have received by the time she sent her second. It was an eleven-line note with which he enclosed six poems:

Beloved Edna:

Your cable with its breath of you, stirs through my days.—Instead of going to China in the spring, I shall come to Europe, and we'll talk deep. Perhaps for either of us marriage would be jolly. Perhaps not.—Uncannily I feel the beckon to be rather for Arthur than for

Hal

Again their letters crossed. When Vincent read Hal's next letter, there was no mistaking his uncertainty:

Dearest Edna:

. . . I didn't know what to say. . . . First of all I wrote, half merry, half sad, half hoping, half doubting,—that we ought to see each other some time and talk over this possibility of our marrying. To be frank, I thought you would hoot, albeit in friendly fashion. But you said nothing. So I put far away from me the flicker of a thought and returned to my content. Presently I told Arthur, lightly. And he urged it. And he wrote you; and I, still lightly, added the postscript. You know the rest of the events.

As to what is going on inside me, it wobbles and wobbles. I have very important things to say to you, even before I can let myself be serious. . . .

Arthur, with no word from me except the bare news of your cable (forgive me), rapidly changes his mind, gives in, reasons, comes to N.Y. and sweetly expostulates, for your sake, for mine and, I think, for his. All I know is that for the first time in my life I am a coward. But, darling Edna, you'll understand it all and laugh with me. We're alike a little. . . . You frighten me. But you inspirit me. You also awe me—which is necessary!—was there ever such a fool as

> Your friend from childhood
> Hal

On January 24, 1922, in Vienna with Griffin Barry, with whom she had traveled for convenience, she received two of Arthur's letters, forwarded from Rome. Outside the window of her hotel there was only a gray wall; she kept the lights on all day just to have the sense of light somewhere in her world. "I smoke too many cigarettes, and the German food nearly kills me," she wrote, "hot bread and cabbage and grease, when what I want is a bowl of plain rice and an apple." But far worse was living with Griffin Barry. She explained for the first time to Arthur the circumstances of their being together:

> I am living, chastely and harshly, with a man with whom I once had a love affair, a man whom I breathlessly and ruthlessly abandoned for somebody else, and whose consciousness of the wrong I did him is always boiling in his mind. We do not want to be together; . . . we have almost no tastes or opinions in common; but except for each other we are entirely alone in a strange city, so that we are constantly forced back into each other's society; he is irascible and sarcastic; I am hard and pugnacious; we spend all the day and half the night in quarreling, or in abstaining from quarreling with an effort which whitens his face and makes my back ache; then we separate, either with a make-shift amiability or with the sublime insult of the encounter, and go to bed; I lie awake until four o'clock in the morning, at times desperately getting up and turning on the light, smoking a cigarette, trying to read, then lying down and making another try of it; finally I fall from entire exhaustion into a succession of little dozes, from each of which I am slowly, chokingly awakened by a glimmering and malevolent nightmare.

She was not writing. "I might as well try to work on a ship-wrecked raft. . . . I think I am going to marry Hal," she wrote. She told him that Hal was going to come over to Europe in the spring. Clearly, she had not received Hal's last letter.

Of course we may do nothing about it. But I rather feel that we shall. Would you be sorry or glad if I did? Tell me seriously, dear, what you feel about it. Of course, there is every geometrical reason why I should. We should make such a beautiful design, don't you see,—Hal and you and I. Three variable and incommensurate souls automatically resolved into two right angles, and no nonsense about it.

She knew it wasn't quite so simple. Hal, she said,

is very troubled about my feeling for you. . . . he feels I care more for you than I do for him. I just got a note from him, in which I saw that plainly. . . . Well, there's no denying that I love you, my dear. I have never denied it for a moment, since the first time I saw you, either to myself or to anybody else. . . . When people ask me if I know you I say, "Yes, I know him." Then if they ask me if I like you, I say, "I love him." And that's all there is to that. And they can shut up, or go on asking questions, or talk it over among themselves. . . .

No one can ever take your place to me. We know each other in such a terrible, certain, windless way. You and I have almost achieved that which is never achieved: we sit in each other's souls.

But she thought that was no reason why she couldn't marry Hal "and be happy with him. I love him, too. In a different way."

By January 19, Arthur raced to New York to Hal. Years later, he explained exactly what he'd done: "I at once took every letter I had received from Miss Millay . . . and forced him to read every word of them. He saw at once that I had not been guilty of duplicity toward him, and that my relation to Miss Millay was of a very remarkable kind, which, in spite of its passional elements, had its real center quite outside of the usual realm of human love. Nothing, I think, except my frankness to him could have saved our friendship from a catastrophic wreckage."

Millay had no idea what he'd done. She had become the exquisite link between the two men, neither of whom could afford to have her, for it would threaten their connection.

What no one mentioned, but what Edna would not have been insensitive to, was Hal's money: he had inherited a small fortune. It may have been his homosexuality that troubled him after he proposed to Edna, and not her relationship to Arthur. Whatever it was, Arthur couldn't let up. Wouldn't Hal grow jealous

of the fact that you write better poetry than he does? And then there is another thing: I don't suppose marriage would put an end to your having "affairs"; and though Hal thinks now that he wouldn't mind, I'm not so sure of that. . . . You ask me, would I be glad or sorry? And all I can tell you is that I don't know. There is a stab for me in the idea, somehow,—perhaps in the dim sense I have that <u>this</u> is the one sole precise way in the world by which I might really lose you.

But by the time she received Hal's letter of January 19, she'd understood and fled to Budapest, from which she wrote him on her thirtieth birthday:

> Poor boy,—*did* Edna write him solemn letters from German cities and frighten him almost to death?
>
> ————
>
> Oh, Hal, you abysmal nut!
>
> ————
>
> As I sit in my small but costly apartment looking out upon the Danube, the thought of you hits me on the head like a piece of lead pipe.
>
> ————
>
> Oh, Lord—oh, Lord—Oh, *Hal!*
>
> Apoplectically yours,
Edna
>
> I am now going under the divan and have a fit.

The day after her birthday, she wrote home that she was happier than she'd ever been. There was no reason to believe her: the rest of her letter except for the following note was sodden with depression.

> I was interviewed the other day by a reporter for a Budapest paper—they printed about two columns about me. And the Hungarian fiancé of my friend Dorothy Thompson is going to give me a lot more publicity, & try to get *'Arry de Cop* translated into Magyar & presented here. Well, we shall see. I sign myself in full,—Your loving niece & nephew,
>
> Esther St. Nonsense Millwheel

Dorothy Thompson had a prodigious talent for journalism and boundless vitality. She would soon marry the first man she'd made love to, Josef Bard. Unfortunately, he was as unfaithful as he was cosmopolitan and suave. In a diary entry Thompson made years afterward, she retained the fury she must have felt in 1922.

> She was a little bitch, a genius, a cross between a gamin and an angel. In Budapest she had two lovers . . . both from the embassy. Keeping them apart was a *kunst,* an art. And we sharing a room. . . . She sat before the glass and combed her lovely hair, over and over. Narcissan. She really never loved anyone except herself. Very beautiful, with her little white

body and her green-gold eyes. "Dotty, do you think I am a nymphoma-niac?" she asked. Then she comes in a Grecian robe and reads aloud to the Ladies Club, "Such lips my lips have kissed . . ." And what a sonnet that one was.

I had to go back to Vienna and I left her the toast of half the town. . . . Handed her all I had because she was an angel. A bright angel. She might have left Josef alone, but not that, either. When she came back to Vienna, she twisted a little green ring on her finger. "Josef gave it to me," she said absolutely brutally. "But he really cares for you." "It's all right Edna," I said, "I know he does." And I was full of furious tears.

In the midst of what Edna would call being "panic-stricken, and con-fused," she canceled her mother's trip to Europe. Her letter is nowhere to be found among her papers, but Cora's wire is. She sent it precisely on Vincent's birthday, telling her she "understood." Norma's response was to tell Vincent sharply how sick their mother was, how Cora could not keep from crying with disappointment as she walked the streets of New York.

"Beloved Sister," Millay wrote back in the next post, "if ever a girl needed a letter, I was that girl, and yours was that letter." She said her mind had been cluttered, but now she knew

that nothing in the world is important beside getting mother over here with me. . . . nothing in my life, at least, is important in comparison to this thing. A possible marriage, for instance, is not important beside it. Any-body can get married. It happens all the time. But not everybody, after the life we have had, can bring her mother to Europe.

Kathleen was married, and Norma had married, whereas she had been rejected by Slocombe, and now almost certainly by Hal.

As for my getting married, I may and I may not. You know who the man is, Norma. At least you could guess. Do you remember one day in Truro, you and I were walking to the station together, and I had a letter with me which I was reading, and I said, "I think I shall marry this man some day"—do you remember? Well, if you don't remember, you don't deserve to know. And if you do remember, don't breathe it to a soul. Because it very likely will never happen. But it may.

Then she cabled her mother to come. "Bon voyage, sweetheart! . . . I shall find out where your boat docks . . . and of course I shall be right there to catch you when you jump. Please wear a dandelion. I shall be wearing a corsage of small spruce-trees."

CHAPTER 18

No matter what café in Montparnasse you ask a driver to bring you to . . . they always take you to the Rotonde.

—Ernest Hemingway, *The Sun Also Rises*

Both John Carter and George Slocombe warned Edna that the Latin Quarter had changed since she'd left. It had become "mean, monotonous, vicious," George wrote her. "So I am glad you are out of this silly Rotonde crowd." It was precisely that crowd to which she returned at the end of March 1922, to await her mother's arrival. She'd been gone more than a year, but even with this complete change of scene from Vienna and Budapest, she couldn't shake her sense of despair. Nothing seemed to be working out as she had hoped—not Hal, not even Griffin, with whom she'd never been in love. "My dear," Slocombe wrote, "how you must have suffered at that priggish, arrogant & ignorant boy's hands."

John Carter, who'd been cautionary about Paris but not hurt or angry, wrote her now:

For the first time since I left you I have wanted you so badly that I almost cursed you, and myself for loving you. It started fairly innocently with a remark by Norma concerning a rumor that you had lived with Griffin in Vienna. So I wanted to slay Griffin for two days. Then I wanted you.

But it wasn't Griffin's hands she'd suffered at; it was her own.

PARIS APRIL 1ST, 1922

A mile of clean sand.
I will write my name here, and the trouble that is in my heart.
I will write the date & place of my birth,
What I was to be,
And what I am.
I will write my forty sins, my thousand follies,
My four unspeakable acts. . . .
I will write the names of the cities I have fled from,
The names of the men & women I have wronged.
I will write the holy name of her I serve,
And how I serve her ill.
And I will sit on the beach & let the tide come in.
I will watch with peace the great calm tongue of the tide
Licking from the sand the unclean story of my heart.

. . .

Allan Ross Macdougall had joined the staff of the Paris *Evening Telegram,* where he began a new column called "The Merry-go-Round." On April 2, he wrote, "Late up and to the Dome to break my fast and happening in by accident to the other Tavern across the way who should I see to my great joy but fair Margaretta Schuyler whom I have not seen this year and more. Then came . . . Edna Millay and sat with us saying things that were witty and gay."

Macdougall had in fact arranged for Margot (Margaretta's nickname) to meet Edna, and it was not quite as he described it in his column. "Remember," Margot wrote him years later,

> that rainy April afternoon in the Rotonde when we had a rendez-vous with her and she came in looking like a little New England school teacher with a touch of the Candy Box. . . . What fun we had. What laughter and that inner throbbing of excitement that always affected everyone who met her. . . . Vincent with her gamin and Princess Lointaine qualities, her freckles and her romantic hair.

More than a half century later, this tiny woman, her glossy hair cropped close like a silver helmet, remembers Millay; her voice breaks as she speaks: "I *did* call her my Candy Box girl. Do you remember those elegant boxes of American chocolates?—Well, they always had a portrait of a pretty girl in a lace blouse on the cover.

"I was staying at the Hôtel des Saints Pères, and we were to meet at last at the Rotonde. . . . I was delighted. So I shined my shoes. And she was late, of course. Dougie and I sat and waited and chatted and waited, when a girl in a velvet dress with frills at the throat walked across the room and came to our table. Dougie stood up and said simply, 'Now two of my dearest friends meet.'

"Certainly she did not look at all as I had expected her to look. We took hands. We talked. And later that afternoon we went to bed together."

When Margot didn't hear from Vincent that night, she sent this note up to her hotel room in the morning:

> I hope this won't wake you up.
> I hope you are already awake.
> Dear lady . . . please let me come up a moment. I want to tell you something.
>
> Margot—

Millay didn't reply. "I was terribly in love with Vincent from the first. Did she know? Oh, yes! There was very little she did not know. But after we were together and then I didn't hear from her, or see her, for two or three days—I suppose I was afraid. I *was* afraid. I thought maybe she was just promiscuous." She wrote to her again:

> For goodness sake telephone me or send me a petite blue. I'm most awfully low. . . . Don't practice your sadistic tendency on me now I need some moral support. This is a hell of a town tonight and I want to talk to you.
>
> Margot

"I have no idea why I wrote 'sadistic'; you must understand that there were a great many other people who rushed after Vincent. And she was exclusive. She was not promiscuous, which she easily might have been. But, oh, she could make it very clear."

The only trace of this encounter Millay left behind besides a white lace hankie embroidered with her initials, which Margot kept all her life, is a provocative glimpse in a fragment of a poem of a woman in a café. It may not refer to Margot Schuyler, although its date suggests her. It is untitled and was never printed.

> You are most like some pale, impersonal
> Small flower, that has no color for the bee,
> Only a potent fragrance. Quietly
> Turning your eyes to none, troubling us all,
> (Even the anxious waiter, even me)
> You sit before the cafe in the heat,
> Rendering the heavy air too deadly sweet.
> Drawing your puff & powder from their case,
> Dusting with pollen your small, serious face.
> Paris   April 26, 1922

"Then one morning she called me and said her mother was arriving," Schuyler said. "I asked if I could go with her to meet Cora and she said, 'No, I want to be with her alone.' "

Vincent met her mother's boat, the *Rochambeau,* which by coincidence was the same ship she'd crossed on the year before, then whisked her off on the noon boat train to Paris, where she'd booked a front room across the hall from her own. In her room Cora found "a beautiful bouquet of lilacs and iris, from a girl friend of V's, from Margaret V. R. Schuyler to Vincent's mother, on *her* mother's birthday, the 6th of April."

"And in she walked with this old woman in a Buster Brown bob, steel-rimmed glasses, and the minute we shook hands I loved her. She was very plainspoken, Cora was. She called shit shit, and not feces. She was not an ignorant woman, not by any means. I was with her all the time, for weeks on end. And she always had an idea. It was: *Let's go!*—to the Tuileries! to the Louvre! Let's bum around these backstreets! There was very little she was not game for."

That first night they went to the Rotonde Grill for dinner, "and then we all went to the Boeuf sur le Toit—and they danced, but it was so crowded they went to a cabaret called Zelli's, and that was lovely," Cora wrote home.

A young poet, Harold Lewis Cook, remembered meeting them at Zelli's, "that wicked, wicked nightclub in Montmartre. But the striking thing was that Edna was there with her mother. And this rather elderly, to me, then, little woman had cut her hair in the short bob of those days. I danced with both of them. . . . [Edna] was wearing a black satin dress—I remember the feel of the silky fabric against my hand as it slipped across her back."

Café de la Rotonde
Tues. Apr. 25, [1922]

Dearest Kids,—

Here are your mother and sister sitting with Margot Schuyler at the famous sink of corruption (see above) of the Latin Quarter.—Mother has a cold & is imbibing a Grog Américain, which is to say a hot rum with sugar & lemon.

Me, I have been sick in bed about all the time since mother came—the weather is frightful here, it has rained every day for nearly three months. But in spite of hell, we have had a swell time together.—Mother is so wonderful, & she enjoys every minute of it. I take her everywhere, on all my rough parties, & she is always the best sport present—everybody loves her & is crazy about her. . . . (Margot now says I must eat my noix de veau braisé aux endives while it is hot.)

At the beginning of Cora's stay in France, mother and daughter went everywhere together, most often with Margot. Cora began meticulously to list to her "Dear girls" at home where she'd been, with whom, and what they'd seen. This was just one weekend in May:

I saw Bernhardt, went with Margot and Sefe, Sat. night, saw the Russian Ballet at L'Opera. Margo Schuyler . . . and Sefe and I, went out to Pere Lachaise, the great grave-yard where Abelard and Heloise are buried in one grave, saw Chopin's tomb, and Oscar Wilde's. Sat. P.M. with John, Margo and Curtis Moffitt, to the Eiffel Tower and to the top, in four stages by elevator and then a short flight of stairs. Sat. Ev'g. with Margo and Sefe to Russian Ballet. Yesterday, we three girls, and John and Max Eastman, to the country. Not much time to write.

Vincent said she was saved from total exhaustion only by the "fact that she has just acquired a small blister on her heel. . . . Isn't it wonderful, sweetheart, that I really did it & here she is!—And it was all due to you, Normie, that I had her come so soon. She is the sweetest looking thing, & you have no idea . . . how everybody loves her."

The handsome Max Eastman, who knew Millay's work but knew her only slightly from that single evening in New York during the *Masses* trial, drifted into her life in Paris that spring, having decided to fall in love with her. "The idea of loving someone more like myself . . . a companion of my ambition as well as of my mind and body, had always intrigued me. And so much the better if she was famous—for I like to admire those whom I love. I like to love those whom I admire."

Eastman was in Genoa, where he had gone to cover the postwar conference; he was traveling with George Slocombe. Then he went to find her in Paris.

> We dined together, making conversation successfully, and after coffee, I asked her to come to my room on the rue des Beaux Arts and read me some poems. I was not, alas, falling in love with her, but still only hoping I might. She did come, and as my room was infinitely narrow with only the bed to sit on, we sat, or rather lay, on the bed together with our heads propped against a pillow. She read to me, after one or two less personal poems, a sonnet which defends, or pays its respects to, a love that is momentary and involves no complications. But by that time . . . though we were almost in each other's arms, we were not together. We were still making conversation.

If by the early 1920s Edna Millay had become a romantic figure— someone to make love to as a mark of one's own increased stature—she was not about to become that for Max Eastman.

That June, when Millay sat for a photograph by Man Ray, she looked desperately unhappy. Her face was drawn, her shoulders hunched; she was wrapped in a woolen shawl, hugging her arms across her stomach. Cora wrote Norma:

> She is not at all well, and would have seen a doctor here about her stomach, but thought it would be more sense to wait till we get to England. . . . And it is more than probable that the food here, with no cream and nothing but boiled milk had a great deal to do with her trouble, which a French doctor would not understand, and which a change of food might correct with the help of out-door life and quiet.

In a carbon copy of another letter to Norma dated June 30, 1922, Cora told her that "Tess Root, and Mrs. Townsend, [new] friends of ours," were going ahead to meet them in England.

"She [Vincent] was sitting across the table from me. Someone had given her a bunch of violets," Tess Root later recalled. "We started chatting and she suddenly said, 'We agree about so many things. Take these violets.' And then we were friends forever."

Dwight Townsend left an extraordinary record of her own in a remembrance she wrote years later:

> She dropped into our hotel room wearing a childish blue gingham dress with a white apron attached. Now, girls go about cities like that. Then it seemed very unconventional—no hat, no gloves, no purse. She looked like a schoolgirl as she might wander around a small town.
>
> Edna was so bright and gay and vibrant. Such a totally bewitching sort of person that you just looked at her and loved her and thought, this is the most wonderful girl that ever was. You see, you must remember there was no sense of smallness, or evil in any way attached to Edna. You must know that she was—well, she was splendid.
>
> I think Edna's mother was rather, was a little bit in awe of her. That she had created such a creature. She was willing and eager for Edna to work out her own life, and yet I was sure there was a sadness. I could be wrong. But a sadness on Mrs. Millay's face—of what?—that Edna had gone overboard.

One scene in particular stood out in her mind, and when she told me about it her breath seemed to catch: "We were sitting in the Dôme in Paris—the whole lot of us sitting around a table. Edna and her mother and a strange young man, a very attractive man, whom she must just have met. I don't recall ever having seen him before. Well, they must have made an arrangement, for he would keep looking over at her, as if to say, 'Come. *Come.*' And Mrs. Millay must have noticed, for we all noticed.

"Well, at last Edna said, 'We'll see you later,' something like that. And the two walked off. There was a silence. Mrs. Millay sat with her head down— this may be entirely my own imagination. Surely it was very romantic in its way. But it did seem to me, then, that Edna's mother accepted this. But had she a choice, you see? . . . And all that time Mrs. Millay was sitting at our table, passed over in conversation—& here's this man; this man who means nothing to Edna. She never saw him before and she never will see him again. I felt a real sadness radiated from her mother."

That Millay would expose her mother to her sexual life in this way, with no effort to protect her or even to consider her own privacy, seemed punishing.

On June 28, 1922, Millay applied for and received through the agency of the American consulate general in Paris two documents. The first was an affidavit testifying that she was a citizen of the United States residing in Paris, that her name was Edna St. Vincent Millay, that she was the legitimate daughter of Henry Tolman Millay and Cora Lounnella Buzzell, that she was born in 1892 in Rockland, Maine, and that she had never been married. The second was a longer legal document, a "Certificat de Coutume"—which Norma Millay, whose French was sketchy, thought was a permit to bring costumes out of France to America—assuring the French government of all that the affidavit had, as well as that she had attained her legal majority, so that she could marry in France without her parents' consent.

These two legal documents were drawn up by an American attorney in Paris and stamped with the raised seal of the American vice consul. Edna Millay had gone to considerable trouble to secure permission as a foreigner to marry in France. Who was it she was suddenly so intent to marry? Did she think her mother would try to stop her? There was only one person alive, who was in Paris then, who might know.

"His name was Daubigny!" Margot Schuyler remembered. "It was the name of a great painter of the nineteenth century, I believe. I thought he was a fop! A hanger-on! He was a gentleman, insofar as breeding was concerned, and for some reason that I shall never understand he swept Vincent off her feet. Completely.

"He was a pseudo-aristocrat who did nothing. He was tall, rather tall, immaculately dressed, he was French—oh, he had a delightful accent. But, no, he did not belong to our group. Nor to any other that I could tell; he insinuated himself into our group—there were other eligible men—I don't understand it and I didn't then. He was suave, oily, I thought—Thelma Wood, Djuna—none of us liked him. And, of course, I was extraordinarily jealous. Because Vincent showed very plainly that she didn't want me. She wanted Daubigny."

Cora loathed Daubigny. Her fury at being displaced by him was astonishing; it was virulent. In a prose fragment, which is the only record we have, she whips herself into a rant as she pits herself against her daughter's lover. "The dirty panderer!" she exploded.

If he had not been kept by some rich wanton! If he has not been a runner-in for some whore-house, I am mistaken—Borrowing money from her—making her borrow money from her friends, because of him she cannot get a chance to do her work, and spending the money on him—people at the Quarter must think that this devotion to "Mummie" was easily broken, and for a very little in exchange. The gradual, sure, insidious taking

her over away from me. . . . even leaning over her, his head between us—
she can hardly get a chance to eat—in the street, running on ahead with
her, leaving me to get along as best I may. . . . [not] appreciative of her
wonderful powers, but lustful, greedy, full of evil possession——each
glance almost an orgasm . . . his snake-shaped head and fish-eyed—carp-
mouthed face—his head darting out like a snake till you look for a red
tongue to flash out and strike her—for a wound on the sweet, tender
face—each glance seemed to corrode the gold in her hair, and leave it tarnished. . . . she swore she would drive him out of the Quarter.

Then the she who rages becomes the I who agonizes at this violation of
her daughter:

He slinks like a whipped cur when he sees me. He acts as if he had shit in
his breeches, or pooped at meetin', as my good wholesome New England
ancestors would have said. Of course he knows how I feel toward him. He
has even acknowledged that he does not blame me, the slithering whelp!
The spineless jelly-fish! But how anyone, favored of a goddess could slink
from the gaze of an ordinary mortal, I cannot see. He should be so uplifted
by her favors that he should transcend me and my attitudes, and be able to
laugh in my face. I could like him more, or rather, dislike him less if he
did, for I could have some respect for his taste. . . . She has stooped infi-
nitely toward him, and she has not in any way raised him by it, not one
atom.

She loses control completely; her physical revulsion is relentless:

She knows he makes me ill near to death—I can see his hands on her sweet
flesh—when she is with him she is not even a woman—she has no right to
consent—she cannot be in her right mind—she is a child being violated! O
Christ! Why am I her mother! Why must I, of all the world, wish to spare
her? Why am I so near that I must know? And I cannot be away from her
and live, and if I stay I shall die. When he is with her my heart is hurt physically, it aches like a sore, and cries out against this outrage to my womb,
and the nine months I waited for her. I would kill him if I had the
courage. . . .
    My God! Why is she so child-like! With all the appeal to me of a little
girl, adolescent—and why is she so lustful? . . . I wonder if his hands are
profaning her child-like structure now. . . . It is as if I were in the room.
She does not always lock her door—I have blundered in there more than
once and surprised her in his embrace—God damn his soul! . . . My baby!
If I had let myself go freely, might it not have been better for her now?
O Christ! Is she bearing what I had not the courage to bear, openly
and unashamed? What my mother had not the courage to proclaim from

the housetops, the burden of my premature birth—and God! How do I know what my grandmother did! And what she wanted to do and dared not. And he—is he but an instrument to work this out? Am I—my mother—her mother—her mother—to blame for him? To save her reason? Her balance—to prolong her marvellous gifts—Must it be? Let me be honest—I wonder if he brings back to me some of my own indiscretions— I wonder if she can remember, could she not picture some no more attractive who were allowed to fondle me—when she may have known—How do I know that some of the lovers I had hanging about me in the days of my breaking loose, and, before the re-adjustment had given me new balance—were not even more repugnant to her virgin young soul? How do I know? Does she remember? Is she bigger, and more generous than I am? Stumbling along, alert, alive never half satisfied, they may have seemed ugly quagmire, the man-holes I just skimmed over—I wonder if the real difference between us is that the added generation has given her a courage I never had, to be honest, even with myself—and all my feelings, temptations, appetites denied or gratified might not be declared to them— my babies—*Now* they need keep nothing from me—and I had no one who could help me, and understand.

After this remarkable outpouring, in which Cora tries to find some common ground for reconciliation among her own generation, her mother's, and her daughters', she jams back to her fury against this man, unabated: "I sent word to him to keep out of my way, and he had self-preservation enough to do it. The snake-headed fish."

This is peculiar, even perverse. But the very excessiveness of Cora's tirade reveals how damaged, how unbalanced their relationship has become.

Within two days, all was cast in a different light. On June 30, 1922, Cora wrote Norma, "Sefe . . . is lying down as she is very tired. . . . We have our tickets for London for Monday noon, July 3rd. . . . We expected to have been there some time ago, but several things have held us here."

Millay was not simply tired or ill, she was pregnant. In less than a week she fled France with her mother for England. Daubigny—whatever Edna may have hoped for from him—remained in Paris.

2

As Edna and Cora crossed the Channel, they made plans to meet Dwight Townsend and her small daughter in London. Tess Root, Dwight remembered, would follow. "The weather had been cold and rainy. . . . The Millays were both tired and sick; we could not wait to get to the country."

They arrived in a downpour, "but after lunch the sun came out and there was Shillingstone, exactly what we were looking for. A winding, unpaved street, a few shops and small houses, many with thatched roofs. The downs around the town reached up to the sky."

They were driven across the fields in a tiny roadster to Shillingstone the following morning. "We packed in and Mrs. Millay sat up on the back of the rumble seat. We drove all day through south Dorset towns and the children shrieked at that witch-like figure sitting up there, her cropped gray hair blowing wildly."

Tess Root and Dwight Townsend found a house that delighted them, with a garden and a fireplace and a piano. "And so we were settled in the perfect spot. Edna found a 'hay shed' at the foot of the downs and rented it to work in. Afternoons she came for tea or we walked up the downs. She and I had bicycles and rode and we talked by the fire, all the evening." Now that they'd spent time together, Dwight found Edna even more astonishing than she had in Paris; "she had Latin poetry by heart, Shakespeare and a great deal of modern poetry at her fingertips."

But in spite of the relaxed living in Shillingstone, Edna was not well. She was worried about finances and unhappy with her publisher. She had accepted a $500 advance for a novel which she was quite sure she would never write.

"I have been sick as a dog for months," Edna wrote to Edmund Wilson,

and so entirely convinced of the elaborate uselessness of everything, that there was nothing in the situation to get dramatic about and make a poem of, even. But little by little now I am getting back my health. . . .

Bunny, is it only when you're tight that you want to be friends with me? I suppose so. And I don't complain. I have no rights in you. But I do solemnly offer this pious pagan prayer: that one of these days you'll become a dirty inveterate souse and bully your wife and beat your kids and kick your dog, and think of me with steadfast love.

Having heard of John Bishop's wedding from "ye fatte Bunnye," she sent Wilson these celebratory Chaucerian lines, ironic but no less true:

> The poet synges and spylls abroad hiss breth
> In prayse of prettye friends brought lowe by dethe;
> Ah, me!—to lose a friend bye lyfe, I gesse,
> Holds lesse of songs and more of bitternesse!
>
> Prithee, in future houres, cher Bunnye,
> Think on thy distant friend withe charytee,
> That hath of thee, I sware bye the swete sonne,
> No evyll thought, but many a wystful onne.

Edna told Norma she was getting better, but that she had been very sick. "Mother is wonderful," she wrote. "Every day we go for a long walk, either climb one of the downs or walk to some other little village and back." She had become once more her child.

> Mother and I have dandelion greens all the time. And you'd die at mother. This is what she cooked one day all in a pot together and served up to be et: dandelions, mustard, dock, pig-weed, clover, nettles and thistles. I put the clover in myself, making fun of her for cooking nettles and thistles. Some of the neighbors had told her nettles were good, boiling takes out all the sting . . . and the kind of thistle she gathers is called milk-thistle, it's much gentler than the other kind, but that's not saying much.

Edna didn't tell Norma what was truly at stake in her long walks, her rides on horseback, her feasts of "greens" that Cora searched for and brewed for their supper: Cora had found *Culpeper's,* a seventeenth-century herbal guide, in Dorset, from which she took pages and pages of extraordinary notes: "Willow Tree . . . under the dominion of the moon. Leaves, bark and seed, used to staunch bleeding of wounds . . . to stay vomiting—Leaves bruised and boiled in wine *stayeth the heat of lust in man or woman,*" Cora underlined, "and quite *extinguisheth it, if it be long used.*" Henbane, or caraway, under the influence of Mercury, all-heal and heart trefoil, hedge hyssop, and gentian, the leaves of which, either steeped in wine or bruised, were, "(*not to be* given to women with child)."
Cora was reading carefully and with a clear purpose, listing hundreds of herbs and flowers and their healing medicinal properties, searching for something—jotting down which time of year was best for brewing their seeds or roots, bark or blooms, under what signs, planets, and conditions they were most useful. The herb alkanet is mentioned again and again. In her notes, *Culpeper's Complete Herbal* carried this description:

> It hath a great and thick root of a reddish colour; long, narrow, hairy leaves, green like the leaves of bugloss, which lie very thick upon the ground; the stalks rise up compassed round about, thick with leaves. . . . It is a herb under the dominion of Venus, and indeed one of her darlings. . . . If you apply the herb to the privities, it draws forth the dead child.

Alkanet was the abortive Cora was searching for. Once she found it in flower in July, she was able to use it to cause Vincent to miscarry in the first few weeks of her pregnancy. Her mother, in other words, country-wise nurse that she'd been, aborted her own daughter.

———

There is a snapshot of Vincent from that time, standing in a wide meadow, eating an apple. Her hair is bobbed, curly, thick, and wild in the wind coming up from the downs. She wears the same striped jacket she wore in Woodstock, except this time the jacket will not close in front.

"I cannot say that she had a miscarriage in Dorset," Dwight Townsend says slowly, recalling events that took place half a century ago. "I cannot say that she did not. Edna and I would talk in the evening in front of the fire in Shillingstone. She would tell me more or less why she was promiscuous. I was so fond of her. And I tried to make sense of her, of it—this quality—of what she was saying. But it didn't make any sense to me.

"I had never had a lover. Oh, yes, I had married. I had a child. But I had never had an affair. And it seemed, it just seemed to me, that is Edna—I just felt as if this kind of life produced such an entrancing person. . . . she tried to give me instructions. Once I remember her saying, 'When a man looks at you you simply look back. Or ask him for something, for a match.' And I said, 'Edna, men don't ask me for a match or for the time. And if I am going to the post office for a stamp, I come home with one. I am not met by a man.' I did not have whatever it takes, whatever it is to arrest men. But she did. Oh, yes. She did! And could. And did!"

⤏ ⤏ ⤏

"Norma."

"Yes, darling?"

"The envelope you showed me, the one your mother marked with 'Shillingston/the fits of the mother,' with all those tiny pages of tissue-paper notes about herbs and witchcraft—that's from *Culpeper*, isn't it?"

"I suppose so."

"I asked you whether or not Vincent told you she had an abortion in Dorset."

"She didn't tell me. Mother did. Vincent drank a potion Mother had concocted and walked and walked and walked. Later Vincent said, 'How did you know?'

" 'Mother told me,' I said. Vincent seemed surprised. 'Mother told you?'

"Well, sure. Mother and I were pals."

"That's not an answer."

"That's all I know. Oh, yes, and she said the Frenchman looked like our father."

⤏ ⤏ ⤏

In Millay's "The Ballad of the Harp-Weaver," the emotional intensity builds up as one waits for something dreadful to happen. In the penultimate quatrain the mother dies equipping her son for life. That is, in fact, the second theme of the poem. The first is maternal self-sacrifice. The ballad could have been resolved in any number of ways, but the mother's death, while seeming to be sentimental, is so charged with feeling that instead it serves perfectly to resolve the poem:

> A smile about her lips,
>   And a light about her head,
> And her hands in the harp-strings
>   Frozen dead.

Sainted, maybe, but dead, surely. Matricide, cloaked in sentiment. It's no accident that Millay wrote the poem in Europe, in her mother's absence, for only in that situation could she transform the grip of *Duty! Duty! Love! Love!* into a work of the highest achievement of her career so far. Just as none of the Millay daughters would weave hair, none of them would become mothers. To do so was to risk this deadly devotion.

Early in September, after her pregnancy was over, Vincent went to London with Tess. From London she wrote her mother, who remained in Shillingstone, to tell her that she hadn't felt quite up to doing certain things. "Not that I've been sick, but I've been uncomfortable until today. Now I am done menstruating & all right." She enclosed a pound for her mother, whom she seems to have been writing to every other day. When three days passed without a letter she wrote, "I've been such a bad girl. It comes over me all of a sudden that I've not written you for days, & it makes me sick to think of it. I've just this minute telegraphed you."

She told Cora she had motored with Tess to a summer cottage on an island in the middle of the Thames. She was going to work on one more article for *Vanity Fair*, and she included two more pounds in her letter.

"Sweet darling, I didn't even write you that I got the rest of the money all right!—I suppose you're worried!—Maybe, oh of course, you need money, too! Oh, I could kick myself!—Don't ever forgive me, Mummie!—Your bad, Vincent."

She visited Doris Stevens in London. "Edna, Doris felt, was again getting ready to take off," Doris's husband, Jonathan Mitchell, recalled, "and she really had no idea of what she would do. She might remain in England, she might not. She wanted to go to Italy. She wanted to go back to Paris. It was a time of mustering of forces."

She did try to tell Doris what had happened. "And it was an incredible story," Jonathan Mitchell remembered, "of her mother, of rolling in the fields! Well, they produced a miscarriage, and it made Edna frightfully sick. There were doctors in London to whom she might have turned, you understand, and Miss Stevens would have helped her. But instead the two of them went off like two animals—off together in the hedges of Dorset!"

By the middle of October Edna wrote Norma, "just to break the silence between us, baby." She had caught sight of the poet A. E. Housman in Cambridge

> and chased his retreating tall, thin figure and cotton umbrella for about half a mile through the streets . . . till he turned in at Trinity College, where he is professor of English, and was lost in the gloom. I caught just a glimpse of his face, a nice face. They say nobody ever sees him, that he goes along like a shadow and is lost before he's found.

She enclosed the photograph Man Ray had taken of her in Paris, "pretty rotten, but never mind," and described an enchanted dinner with the sculptor Constantin Brancuşi in his studio:

> It's the greatest, barest studio you ever saw, all white beams and white blocks of marble and everything covered with white dust like a flour mill, and we ate our dinner off a great round marble thing like an enormous mill-stone, and all full of little depressions and bitten-out places where he has pounded and banged at his work—no cloth on the table, and in the entire room not a square-foot of fabric of any sort, no hanging tapestries, no kimonos flung over easels, no pictures, nothing—only some beautiful, pure curving figures standing on pedestals, looking like nothing on earth that you ever saw, things complexly wrought into a simplicity that fools one,—and little Brancusi with his fine, shaggy, grizzly-dark head and beautiful black eyes, dressed in loose trousers and a shirt rather like a smock, and heavy rough shoes, which either *were* wooden sabots or looked exactly like them—a little Roumanian peasant and a great sculptor all at the same time, shuffling in from the kitchen with bowls of soup, and chicken that he had broiled himself, and poking up the fire in the big, rough, white-stone stove, like a stove you build on the beach, that he had made himself, and the two of [us] chattering at each other in two different kinds of French, and eating big white radishes sliced across like turnips, and drinking sweet white wine.

She admitted to her family she was not writing "much poetry" but said she had sent on to her new agents a short story called "The Murder in the

Fishing Cat. I tell you, me and Eddie Poe,—there's no stopping us Americans. As for HARDIGUT, it's really going to be published next spring." Horace Liveright, who had advanced her $500, was now pressing her agents for the novel. "Now little Ediner is hopping to the south of France to write the dam thing. But don't tell anybody; Liveright thinks it's all ready but the numbering the chapters."

Not long after Edna's letter to Norma, Cora wrote to tell Norma that they were sailing at midnight for Le Havre. "A friend of Sefe's wrote of a little place called Cassis, about 8 m. from M. on the R.R. and the Mediterranean, not a resort, which is what we want for the winter."

Millay remained ill. Her illness, her discomfort, her colds, stomach, or digestive problems only intensified after her mother's arrival. To Norma and Charlie she tried to take a jaunty note: "No, I've never tried Kellogg's Bran. . . . If Mr. Kellogg has invented something that will move my bowels, I will marry him."

They arrived in Cassis on November 17. Walking from the railroad station to their hotel, they saw vineyards everywhere and gray-green olive trees that had just been harvested. Soon they were eating the "Bouille-a-beisse," as Cora wrote, so flavored with saffron and garlic that even the coins Vincent got at the post office reeked.

And everywhere they stepped, it seemed to Vincent they crushed wild thyme underfoot. Within two days of their arrival she dove into the still-warm Mediterranean, and when she surfaced the beads of water sparkled like tiny green jewels on her throat and shoulders. She looked like Ondine.

Cassis
Dec. 12

Dearest Hunk—

Now the real winter has come even here. . . . Never did two people flee before the cold as we are doing.

But Vincent was no longer fleeing simply the cold. "Of course, . . . the real trouble is me. I've been so dam sick I can't stand anything.—I'm weak as a kitten,—every time I hear the mistral blowing up I can hardly keep back the tears."

Her last letter from Cassis was to Arthur. She congratulated him about Gladys Brown, the woman he'd fallen in love with in New York: "My God—it's marvelous." She told him she had known, "in my way, just as well as you know in your way, how nice she is. . . . I knew it the first moment I set eyes on her in Prunier's. You can't fool me. And you didn't think we'd like each other!—men don't know very much." Still, she said, "I shall love you till the day I die." As for Hal, since Arthur was still fretting over their possible marriage, she teased, he wasn't to give it another thought: "There's not the slightest danger that I shall marry him: he has jilted me!"

Within two weeks of her last letter to Norma, they left Cassis for Paris. On January 17, 1923, they boarded the S.S. *Rotterdam,* bound for America. Margot Schuyler saw Vincent before she left, "And she looked so ill and worn. I just looked at her, and I remember the last thing I said to her: 'You go home and you find the most marvelous man in the world, and marry him!' " That must have stung, coming from a woman she'd made love to and dropped for Daubigny.

It was hard to tell from the copious notes Cora kept during their crossing whether it was the rough seas or illness that kept Vincent in her room in bed for most of the trip. But the phrase "Vincent not feeling at all well" was frequent. The last night at sea, while the orchestra played "Ain't We Got Fun," Vincent remained alone belowdecks as the black Atlantic heaved.

BOOK TWO

STEEPLETOP
1923–1950

All the time there is this split in the American art and art-consciousness. On the top it is as nice as pie, goody-goody and lovey-dovey. . . . Look at the inner meaning of their art and see what demons they were. . . . The deliberate consciousness of Americans so fair and smooth-spoken, and the under-consciousness so devilish. *Destroy! destroy! destroy!* hums the under-consciousness. *Love and produce! Love and produce!* cackles the upper consciousness.

—D. H. Lawrence, *Studies in Classic American Literature*

PART FIVE

LOVE AND FAME

CHAPTER 19

The younger generation forms a country of its own.

—Edna St. Vincent Millay

Ice and snow were frozen to the rails and rigging of the *Rotterdam* as she docked in Hoboken, New Jersey, on January 26, 1923. Millay returned just before her thirty-first birthday. "Poor me!" she'd written one of her aunts from Rome after Norma had married, "I'm the only old maid in the family! but I'm so busy just now writing a novel that I can't be bothered getting married." In fact, she would abandon *Hardigut* within a month of her arrival.

Norma remembered her as looking tired and listless and not being able to write at all. Even Edmund Wilson, who had what he called one magnificent evening with her, felt that Europe had provided no better environment for her than New York. "She must," he wrote, "have continued to live with considerable recklessness, for, at the end of two years abroad, she was in very bad shape again."

During those years abroad, her career had not languished at home. Frank Crowninshield had written her in Europe that when *Second April* had at last been published in August 1921, it had outsold *Renascence* four months after publication. "They have printed three editions ... more than 3000 copies and [it] may mean 5000."

A reporter who called himself Young Boswell talked to her just after her return to the States; he said that he had to meet her because, he wrote, "All young men left flowers at Edna St. Vincent Millay's door and then went home and wrote poems to her." He rang timidly at a house in Greenwich Village. A young woman with bright red hair cut like a medieval page's answered the door. She gave him coffee, and they began to speak of her reaction to New York after having been away.

"The younger generation," she said, "forms a country of its own. It has no geographical boundaries. I've talked with young Hungarians in Budapest, with young Italians in Rome, with young Frenchmen in Paris, and with young people all over. . . . These young people are going to do things. They are going to change things."

Flashing her slender fingers through her hair, she paused just long enough for him to ask her eagerly if that meant there would be an artistic awakening in America, too. "I think that America is already artistically awake," she said, fixing him with eyes he was sure were the color of the sea. After which, Young Boswell said he would go home and write poems to Edna St. Vincent Millay.

In November, Millay had written to Horace Liveright, who had advanced her $500 for her novel, that *Hardigut* would be ready for spring publication in New York. She described in her letter the theme of the novel: "people, otherwise perfectly sane and normal, do not eat in public, or discuss food except in innuendos and with ribald laughter." She assured him that the book would be not only amusing and satirical but "an unmistakable allegory" about sexual hunger. But while she'd certainly learned in her *Vanity Fair* experience how to craft short prose pieces with wit and considerable skill, *Hardigut* was not a short take. Among the many scenes in her notebook or on odd scraps of paper, there's no sense of an integrated story moving smartly forward. She seemed unable to sustain a novel.

Millay had been considering a satirical play on sex as early as her notebook in 1918–19, when she had drawn up a cast for "Figs from Thistles / An Unmorality of the Seven / Deadly Virtues." Her characters were "Vice, a very young girl" and her maiden aunts, "Humility, Abstinence, Thrift, Self-Sacrifice, Piety, etc." The character called "Life" was "a lovely boy, dressed in green." But she did no more than list their names.

Roughly three years later, in the black notebook where she had made her first Paris entries, she began a sketch for another one-act play called "Food," and she was again having fun with her characters' names: Matrix,

Utera, Aphrodisia and Venerea (daughters of Matrix), Erotic, son of Utera, Semen, husband of Matrix, and Lascivia, "a neighbor who wears French clothes." Later she added "Master Bates, their little son." As broad as these characters' names are, it's impossible not to link the play to *Hardigut,* for they share the same theme: secrecy about sex, and food as its allegorical equivalent.

We must eat to remain healthy; we must have sex to remain fully alive. It should be openly engaged in, Millay thought, and not hidden by taboos. But she was not able to complete these sketches: neither play was written, the novel was never finished. In her poetry sex surfaced constantly, sometimes ironically and sometimes sensuously, but in such a way that the reader thinks it is about Millay's own sexuality, about her own life. The reader is encouraged, invited even, to suspect autobiography. It may be a naive way to read, but it is as enduring as human curiosity. This confusion between what an author imagines and writes, and what she may actually do, would help earn Millay a small fortune—and a large audience.

There was a summer colony at Croton-on-Hudson, where a cluster of charming old frame houses on Mt. Airy Road formed the center of a group of friends who knew each other from the Village. It was a politically radical, socially unconventional, jolly group who liked to play together and were not given to bourgeois tidying up. "The houses," one wrote, "have no gardens, the grass grows long and the rose bushes are weed tangled." But they shared a glorious view of the Hudson River, and it was a green refuge from the city, only an hour away.

Behind the Boardman Robinsons' house was a clay tennis court where Max Eastman and Eugen Boissevain, who were sharing a house that summer, could be seen playing tennis in their white flannels. "It was as though Greenwich Village in summer array had been dumped down with almost deliberate pageantry upon the grass," one of them wrote. Doris Stevens, who had met Millay in London, and Dudley Field Malone, with whom she was then living, had taken a house. Max's sister, Crystal Eastman, and her husband, Walter Fuller, had too. Even John Reed had had a house there before his death in the Soviet Union. And Floyd Dell had been invited to stay that summer by several intense young mothers who Dell thought might send their children to Russia for an education.

In this festive community Edna Millay found herself playing charades one April evening, paired by chance with Eugen Boissevain. She was a houseguest of Dudley Malone and Doris Stevens. Floyd Dell was also there, watching.

Eugene and Edna had the part of two lovers in a delicious farcical invention, at once Rabelaisian and romantic. They acted their parts wonderfully—so remarkably, indeed, that it was apparent to us all that it wasn't just acting. We were having the unusual privilege of seeing a man and a girl fall in love with each other violently and in public, and telling each other so, and doing it very beautifully.

Floyd, who had been disappointed by Eugen Boissevain and Max East-man when he had first taken Edna and Norma to meet them, was now prepared to be more generous. "The very next day she was all in; Eugene took her to his home, called the doctor, and nursed her like a mother."

A far less generous interpretation of Eugen came from someone outside that charmed circle of Village comrades. Jonathan Mitchell, who would become Doris Stevens's second husband, said, "As soon as she returned to America, Doris asked Edna Millay to Croton. Gene was visiting Max at the time. The story was that Gene appeared that weekend at Doris's with a blooming tulip and wanted to know which room the lady poet was sleeping in. And he never left her side again.

"Gene had an ability to get on with anybody. Like a cruise director. He did decorative things. . . . And my guess is that he had all those qualities of kindness and graciousness and tenderness. . . . But he behaved like a male nurse to her, always going around saying, 'Hush, hush!' And of course Edna was taken with him. Well, why not, eh? In the first place, he was big and handsome—and Edna had gone through this frightful humiliation.

"He used to call her 'the poetess'—I mean, literally! He would say, 'What would the poetess like for luncheon?' She *was* always something very special—not one of us, you see. And Gene was the keeper of this marvel."

According to Arthur Ficke, who had taken a house in Croton right next door to him, Boissevain came to see him "in a frenzy" after having met Millay. "He said that Vincent was the most fascinating person alive—where did she live, and how could he see her again?" Ficke offered to arrange a lunch date with her the next day, and a delighted Boissevain insisted he come, too.

He was out of his head. Finally I said to him that Miss Millay was nobody's fool, and that he was one of the most attractive men alive—why didn't he just take the Millay by the horns and invite her to come out and spend a week at his country place? "Hell, Arthur," he said, "I don't want to have a *dirty little love affair* with her; I want to marry her!"

He was that certain that quickly. After their lunch "Eugene sent for a grand open car with a grand liveried driver, and we went up Fifth Avenue, stopping at the important street-corners long enough for Eugene to rise in the car and bow to the astonished spectators." Once he jumped out of the car, reached into his pocket for an imaginary gold piece, and gave it to an imaginary beggar woman. "Of course, we were all drunk as owls—but it was not with champagne only. Terrific emotions were in the air, for all three of us; and we were half mad with the conflict of them."

Arthur seemed to be working himself into the relationship between Edna and Eugen from the beginning. He was more passionately attached to the idea of loving Edna Millay than he was to anyone or anything else. His own attachments, whether to Hal or to Gladys Brown, his new wife, paled before his sense of wanting to be in on the love of the century. He was a peculiar fellow, possessive of a woman whom he had elected not to have—or was afraid to. "Oh, maybe a one-night stand with Arthur," Charlie Ellis said with a wink. "But it couldn't have been much more." With gallant Eugen Boissevain, however, it was about to be everything more.

By May 2, 1923, Vincent was using a Croton return address with her agents, Brandt & Kirkpatrick, and advised them to write to her in care of "Eugene Boissevain, Mt. Airy." She was living with Boissevain.

On April 30, 1923, Edna received a letter from Columbia University informing her

> that at the meeting of the Advisory Board of the School of Journalism, held on April 26, you were nominated for the Pulitzer Poetry Prize of $1,000 for the best volume of verse published during the year, based on "The Ballad of the Harp-Weaver," "A Few Figs From Thistles," and eight sonnets published in "American Poetry, 1922, a Miscellany."

She was asked to keep this news confidential until the full list of the awards was released to the papers, on May 14.

That spring, Millay became the first woman to win the Pulitzer Prize for poetry. In her first interview in the New York *Evening Post,* "A Fireside Afternoon in Croton Hills with Girl Winner of $1,000 Pulitzer Poetry Prize," she said she would use her prize to return to Maine. "My mother is on her way there now and will find a house by the sea for us to live in together."

Eugen's farmhouse, where his maid brought them salad and dandelion greens, where the rooms were filled with flowers, where even the little wire-haired fox terrier, Jerry, whom she'd trained to bring her a box of cigarettes between his teeth—all were given to her by Eugen. As she talked with the reporter she began to shiver, and she pulled her green silk wrapper closer around her shoulders, telling her that what

> lies deepest of all is my love for this silly old America of ours. Why does it do what it sometimes does? Why does it think so foolishly sometimes? It is because life is brown and tepid for many of us. I want to write so that those who read me will say . . . "Life can be exciting and free and intense." I really mean it!

She saved the more private news for her mother, to whom she wrote on May 30:

> Dearest Mother:
> I have been a bad girl not to write you, or send you any money. . . . But you will forgive me when you know my excuse. Darling, do you remember meeting Eugen Boissevain one day in Waverly Place?—It was only for a moment, & possibly you don't remember. But anyway, you will like him very much when you know him, which will be soon. And it is important that you should like him,—because I love him very much, & am going to marry him.
>
> *There!!!*

"Will you forgive me?" she wanted to know. "—My mind has been pretty much taken up with all this, & I have neglected my mummie." They planned to marry in the summer; just when depended on when she got well. She wanted, they both wanted, to visit Cora in Maine.

> We are going to motor up. Gene has a beautiful big Mercer,—at least he had, but now he has given it to me, so I have one. Won't that be fun?
> You must need money dear. . . . Let me know as soon as you get this & I will send you some—I haven't at the moment a great deal (except my thousand bucks, which I ain't going to bust for god or hero,—. . . .)

She wrote again two days before her mother's birthday: "Darling Mother: I am in town just for a few days, motoring out to Croton again this afternoon. At last I am doing what I should have ages ago, having an excellent diagnostician examine me thoroughly." She was being sent to all kinds of specialists. "For the last three days I have been going to an X-ray man two or three times a day, having my stomach and bowels X-rayed." She told her not to be alarmed, because it didn't "mean that I feel any worse than I have done for the last two years; it just means that at last I am going about getting cured in a reasonable way." But the truth is, she was terribly sick.

> I am allowed to work only one hour a day now, and I have to be lying down fifteen hours out of the twenty-four, and I must be pretty quiet and see almost nobody. These are severe instructions, severely enforced. I must tell you again not to worry about me; I don't feel bad at all; I am just being helped to get perfectly well, you see.

It was, she knew, not much of a birthday letter,

> all about me and nothing about you, but I know that nothing would be so nice a birthday-present for you as to know that I am being taken care of, and am going before long to be well and strong again. Eugen has been taking me to these doctors; probably by myself I would never have done it. You will like him, mother.

ᶜ ᶜ ᶜ

I'd just turned to Charlie and asked if at that time he had thought it likely that Vincent would marry Boissevain.

"Yes, I think I did. He was the solution to a lot of problems for her because he was obviously the mother type."

I asked him what he meant.

"Just in the complete attention, at all times, to her needs." Then Norma pinched him quiet. She was irritable, intimating that I should have asked her opinion first, which I usually did. Now she commandeered the conversation. She had a point to make, and it was not about Eugen's caregiving.

"I went up to Croton before the marriage. I was making some things for her to wear. I remember a lovely pink-and-lavender chemise, mauve it was, of beautiful silk. She gave me a job to make it for her. It was never done, finished; she couldn't stand to have it fitted.

"She was working on *The Harp-Weaver* then, and I—Arthur was up there helping her work to put the book together—And I wanted to help. Anyway, I went up. And we were just sitting there. They [Edna and Eugen] decided they were going to get married. Jan [Eugen's brother] was there, and he told me they were going to be married. . . . They were getting married right away, like the next day.

"I remember being in the living room and she opposite me. He, Gene, suddenly said to me, 'I'm not marrying the family, you know!'

"It came out of nowhere. She said nothing. Well, that's not very pretty.

" 'You wouldn't want to say that again!' I said.

" 'Yes. I'm not marrying her family.' He repeated it! I'm giving them both every chance—giving Vincent a chance to say, 'Please don't say it, Gene.'

" 'Are you really going to marry this low, cheap son of a bitch? Can you really go on? Sister, think it over. Is this what you want to live with?' And finally, then, I burst into tears and ran upstairs. And she hadn't said a word.

"I went up to the bed and threw myself on it. Suddenly everything cleared. What am I doing? You don't *have* to see her.—If she's happy. You love her enough. Then he came up, put his arms around me, and said he was sorry. He told me, 'She made me come up. She's never scolded me before,' he said."

Norma said pensively, "You know, we'd written these things together— 'Sentimental Solon' for *Ainslee's,* and 'The Seventh Stair'—But it *had* been up to her, financially. Vincent was responsible."

⊘ ⊘ ⊘

On Tuesday, July 17, Vincent and Eugen were in New York consulting with her doctors, who now insisted she enter the hospital the next day. The operation was scheduled for Thursday. Eugen wrote Arthur and Gladys urgently from the city: "We get married tomorrow morning at 12 at Croton. . . . You cannot be there?" Then he dashed off "God bless us all" as they raced back to Croton to prepare.

July 18, 1923, was a brilliantly sunny, hot summer day. In a photograph, Vincent, in a dark dress, is standing in the sun, looking down. She is clearly dazed and ill, her thin arm through Eugen's, leaning into him, her head barely touching the top of his shoulder. Strapping, beaming, and anxious, with a cigarette in his hand, he seems almost to be holding her up. Norma was Vincent's maid of honor, and Jan, Eugen's brother, was his best man. Charlie was there, as well as Arthur and Gladys and Floyd Dell, who took the only snapshots of the wedding. It was a hastily assembled gathering of brothers and sisters and—with the exception of Gladys and the justice of the peace—lovers. Norma remembered that at the last minute she took mosquito netting from around the porch, and "I made her a lovely veil and train from it. Then we all stood up outside on the lawn before a great big house. And they married."

Standing on the broad, grassy lawn behind Boardman Robinson's house on Mt. Airy Road, Eugen slipped a ring on Edna's finger. Someone placed a single red rose behind her right ear. "Then they got right in Gene's Mercer and left for New York and the hospital. The point being that the only way Gene could be with her was by being married to her."

—

Five afternoon New York newspapers covered the story of her marriage, and three put it on their front pages.

"Edna Millay Goes Under Knife"
"Famous Love Lyricist Belies Her Own Philosophy by Marrying"
"Honeymooning Alone in Hospital"
"Poetess Bride to Go Under Knife"

The newspapers stressed three things about her: that she'd married a "Wealthy New York Importer"; that she'd been successfully operated on for appendicitis at New York Hospital on West Sixteenth Street; and that her husband was "Considerably Older than Bride."

Just before she was operated on, Arthur came to see her, and she said, "If I die now, I shall be immortal."

The day after Eugen knew she'd survived the operation, he wired his mother in Holland: "MARRIED YESTERDAY EDNA ST VINCENT MILLAY GIVE ME YR BLESSING."

Vincent's first letter was to her own "Dearest Mummie," and Eugen wrote it for her "because though I'm getting big & strong, I'm still very lazy and do very little cooking, scrubbing, writing and other dirty chores."

It was just the sort of letter to reassure Cora. She described her scar as a "transverse incision directly parallel with my waist line, about 7 inches long, above and an inch to the left and about 6 inches to the right of my celestial belly-button." It would be, when she healed, scarcely visible. "So I can still be an oriental tummy-dancer, if I like and get you and me a lot of shekles in our respective old ages." Eugen, she noted, was having trouble spelling. "That is what occurs when a plain business man marries a literary lady of colorful vocabulary and insubordinate intestines." She kept up her banter: "Well I'm happily married to a kind and thoughtful man, a little bit slow in the head but all the steadier for that . . . (The hussy! don't believe her. E.B.)"

She said she'd close now that Eugen was beginning to call her names. She signed herself for the first time Edna St. Vincent Millay Boissevain. But she couldn't resist adding to her mother, "I hasten to sign myself as ever your devoted son, *Sefus.*"

She had not been operated on simply for appendicitis. Four days after her operation, Norma wrote to Cora to explain: "They not only removed her appendix but straightened a prenatal twist in the intestine. . . . The intestine at this place near the appendix had . . . twisted and grown together in one place—or grown to the appendix, I don't know which—but it was straightened and fixed."

Cora had asked "Two sweet questions about Gene," which Norma now hastened to answer:

Well—he is an importer of sugar and a speculator or broker of same. He has a business of which he is the name and head—importing business. If he goes to the office once in a while—this is a joke he is with Edna so much—he will be able to support our Ed St. Bincent in the manner to which she is not accustomed but which she damned well deserves. He is quoted in all the papers stories of this marriage as "a wealthy Dutch importer" but that, between us, isn't true—he has had several fortunes in his life and will doubtless make another, but he has enough to do anything they will want to do, keep a maid and a couple of cars (he just paid $600 to have the Mercer overhauled) and travel or buy a country place etc. *And I think* be able to pay the hospital and surgical expenses for his wife—which will be no mean item, my dear. This information is for you—he can pass as a "wealthy importer" if you want him to, I guess. His name is pronounced *Bois*-se-vain and the Bois is the French word for woods and is pronounced like bwa. . . . accent on the first syllable. It is a French name anyway but really everybody says it as "bwa-se-vain" so you had better too. Now you can say it over many times and get in practise. Haven't you a cat you can name for Gene or something you can address once in a while?

It was a charming letter and certainly belied whatever tension had existed between Norma and Eugen just before the marriage. Cora was so relieved she immediately wrote to her sister Susie, repeating to her exactly how to pronounce her new son-in-law's last name and adding that Vincent not only had a private room and two private nurses but "a beautiful car, a big Mercer Gene gave her."

Within a month of her operation Edna was recuperating back in Croton, where Tess Root Adams sent her a bouquet of wildflowers.

Tess, darling,—

No, they were not withered & I did not laugh,—all my childhood is in those bayberry bushes, & queen-of-the-meadow, or maybe you called it hardhack, & rose-hips. And cranberries—I remember a swamp of them that made a short-cut to the railroad station when I was seven. It was down across that swamp my father went, when my mother told him to go & not come back.

(Or maybe she said he might come back if he would do better—but who ever does better?)

It's striking that at the moment of her own marriage, what she remembered was her parents' failure.

CHAPTER 20

He is forty-three years old but it isn't necessary for you to say anything more than he is "around forty." He acts like a kid and is really
marvelous looking. Handsome in a distinguished way with a beautiful smile. He is far from white—a dark tan where he has worked the
garden in a batik cloth only about his loins has seen to that. He is the
only man in whom Edna has ever been interested who will stand a
show of making her a bully good husband.

—Norma Millay to Cora Millay, c. July 1923

Eugen, drawn by Vincent's fragile loveliness as she regained her health,
photographed her again and again during those first few weeks of her
recovery. She lay back against soft pillows, sunk indolently into a chaise
longue on the sunny porch of his Croton house, her abundant hair curled
fetchingly away from her cheekbones, her long slim arm outstretched as
cigarette smoke played around her lips. The silk kimono Arthur had given
her fell away from her breasts as she posed in the garden. In another snapshot, perhaps taken by Arthur, she looks grave and utterly beautiful as she
poses against a batik throw. But in early October she was still weak enough
for Arthur to have to help her correct proofs for her book *The Harp-Weaver
and Other Poems,* which her new publisher, Harper & Brothers, would
publish at the end of November.

Cora, who had remained in Maine during the entire period of Vincent's
marriage, operation, and recovery, was desperately anxious to see her.
"Darling Mummie," Vincent wrote, "Just a little tiny note to tell you that
I love you.—Sweetheart, how are you? . . . Write me about yourself. I have
so many things to talk about with you. . . . —I can't write much, because
it still tires me, but I can love you just as much as ever, sick of well." Her
little spelling slip was telling, for Edna Millay never made spelling mistakes.

That fall Eugen found a tiny three-story brick house in Greenwich Village
at 75½ Bedford Street, which he rented for a year and ten months at $200
a month. It was a princely sum to a young woman who earlier in the year
was deeply in debt and staying with friends to economize. Then they
managed a trip to Camden, where Edna repaid all her family's debts. She
wrote to Cora, telling her the enclosed $75 was to tide her over until she
could visit them in New York.

It is <u>wonderful</u> to have the Camden bills paid,—but of course it has made quite a hole in my bank account, which I must get busy now & fill. Of course my lecture trip in January & February will do wonders for me. I shall clear nearly two thousand dollars, which will come in very handy. . . . I suppose it is a mean pride in me, but oh, I wish I could have done this before I got married!—because of course everybody thinks it is my rich husband who has done it, when in fact it is really I myself, every cent of it, with money that I made by writing,—nearly a thousand dollars, in all, since you went to Camden.

Oh, well, it doesn't matter.

But of course it mattered enormously—enough that Edna forgot to send her mother the money she said she'd put in the letter. One month later she told her, "Of *course* I want you to come!—I am getting pretty anxious to see you again, as a matter of fact, old sweetie.—And you *must* be here for Christmas.—This time I am enclosing the enclosure.—What a silly thing to have done!"

After the New Year they were settled enough to see people. She wrote to Edmund Wilson, teasing him:

Am I a swine?—Oh, but such a little one!—Such an elegant and distinguished one!—So pink & white! A truffle-sniffer, not a trough-wallower!

I love you just as ever. I would go driving with you in Central Park in an open Victoria in a howling blizzard in a muslin frock.

But, since there is so little snow-fall as yet, won't you come to see me here instead—at 4 o'clock next Monday?

I will offer you a cigarette, just to be playful; and then I will give you a fine, sound, rosy-cheeked apple,—because my heart is really in the right place.

Not many women ever had played him so lightly, or ever would. Then she said, "Do come, Bunny, or suggest some other time. Wire me. Soon I shall depart this life or leave for Pittsburgh & points west on a reading-tour. I want to see you before I go. Let not the light tone of this communication put you off. I do want to see you."

Immediately after seeing her, he wrote to John Bishop about it:

I saw Edna the other day for the first time since her marriage. . . . The operation she had during the summer on her intestines—for congenital stoppages—was apparently really rather serious and she doesn't look terribly well yet. I found her drinking gin and reading William Morris on the top floor of her house, all alone and with really an air of having allowed herself at last to be attended to and put away and forbidden to see people. Her husband takes good care of her and her lousy rout of followers has been banished.—She is calmer than she used to be—and I really felt for a moment as if I were visiting a sort of voluntary prisoner who had crept away and given herself up to other people's kindness.—Then she told me she was about to start on a month's reading tour which, so far as I can find out, is to take in all the important cities east of Chicago! And she is going all alone. "I must keep clear of the people I know," she said, "in the cities that I visit"—but—! She can never be caged for long, I know—never, never. . . . Her husband came in before I left. He seemed a very nice honest fellow—he is a Dutch importer, you know, a little older than she and not, I think, overwhelmingly clever. She was at pains to tell me, as if she were on the defensive at having married a businessman, how irresponsible he really was—"just like me"—but I am sure he is the steadiest importer in the world.—We are planning a grand party for her and you and me, detached from our respective husbands and wives, when you come back.—She left today on her tour.

She read in Washington, Louisville, Springfield, Pittsburgh, Evanston, Cedar Rapids, and Chicago, where she gave six lectures. In Minneapolis she gave two separate readings and, according to the local newspaper, *The World,* "on the last visit had to have the hall changed three times to accommodate the crowd." She continued on to Omaha, Milwaukee, St. Louis, Columbus, Cleveland, Buffalo, and Rochester.

Millay's reading tour was an immense popular success. She was described in headlines throughout the country as the "poet-girl" of American writing:

> The distinguished young poet is slender, [has] bobbed hair and resembles more the shy little undergraduate than a successful poet and playwright. She is wistful, appealing, and in every way lives up to the image of the poet-girl of fiction.

The reporter described how she was dressed before he described how she read:

> Last night she wore a simple blue dress, with a scarf of brilliant yellow silk around her shoulders. At times the reading of her verses was as quiet and simple as the blue dress, at times as flaming as the flame-colored scarf that clung about her.

It was as if the press couldn't quite make up its mind how to describe a woman who was both accomplished and small.

During pauses in her readings, the poet chatted informally with her audience. In her reading, however, she withdrew herself entirely within the poem. She read expressively and enthusiastically, but with nothing of artificial rhetoricism, and the fine lyric quality of her verses was allowed to stand forth unobscured by posing and affectation.

Millay spoke publicly for the first time about marriage, calling it

one of the most civilized institutions in the world. . . . But . . . swimming is one of the most wonderful of sports, and yet there are always some people who cannot swim who insist on going into the water and getting drowned. Many people spoil marriage in a like manner. One should be sure she knows how to be married before rushing into it.

The press coverage continued with the same flattering, but troubling, attention. When, for example, Edna arrived in Rochester from Indianapolis, a wearying nine-hour trek, the reporter focused again on how she looked: "Seated in one corner of the taxi . . . she looked so frail and appealing and so very little in her big fur coat and small cloche hat of Periwinkle blue with her auburn hair peeping out from under it, that one hesitated to ask too many questions." He managed only one. "Recalling the universal interest displayed last summer when she was married to Eugen Boissevain, the question, 'Are you terribly in love?' was inevitable."

She refused to answer, but "her smile," the reporter waxed broadly, "made an answer superfluous."

Millay was aware, from the start of the tour, that she was being characterized, and not only in the press, in a way that compromised her as a poet. For, as she wrote Eugen,

I got through my two readings yesterday well enough—the one in the afternoon in Evanston was a great success—a crowded house, large audience, etc.—But the one in the evening was in a private house in the next town—& God! how I hate reading in a private house!—A bunch of wealthy Jews, come together to see what I looked like, & bet with each other as to how many of my naughty poems I would dare read.

There were even, she remarked wryly, a few women who liked poems that were not from *Figs,* and there was a man who had driven her back to Chicago who "seemed to know all my books by heart.

—But on the whole—oh, Jesus!—If ever I felt like a prostitute it was last night.—I kept saying over & over to myself while I was reading to them, "Never mind—it's a hundred & fifty dollars."—I hope I shall never write a poem again that more than five people will like.

By February, writing to Eugen from Cedar Rapids, Iowa, where "all your letters came, even the ones that forgot to say *Iowa*," she was bone-tired, and her readings were flat-out performances.

> Once a day my keepers come & drag me forth, "with all my silken flanks in garlands dressed," to the miniature sacrifice.—That is all. . . . I give my reading still with charm & spirit, though with an ever-increasing nervousness if a door bangs or a train goes by. . . . I do not even miss you very much. And I haven't wanted you to be with me these last days. . . . I don't want anybody, not even you, maybe least of all you, to see how foot-sore & dusty I am.

There was only one exception, and that was in Milwaukee, where Edna met the parents of Dorothy Coleman, the Vassar girl whose death in the 1918 flu epidemic had occasioned her tribute "Memorial to D.C." In the summer of 1920, after Millay had published one of the five lyrics, "Prayer to Persephone," in *Vanity Fair,* she had sent the entire group to Mr. and Mrs. Coleman. Certain phrases in the poems had distressed Mrs. Coleman, who had written to her:

> My emotions are very mixed—I want to thank you—and I also want to reproach you. I thank you with all my heart for the loveliness of the poems. . . . But *why, why* spoil it all by those unkind, *untrue* lines in the second verse of "Dirge"!?! . . .
>
> I learn from her diary that you had a bitter quarrel and said many unkind things to each other but you must remember how young she was—not even twenty-one when she was graduated.
>
> You are endowed with brilliant talent and genius, she was just matter of fact perhaps with the gift of good common sense.
>
> You are bound to mis-understand each other. I know that she was greatly attracted to you, that she was very happy in having gained your love but in the end she seems to have been a little frightened by your genius.

Then she asked her if she couldn't either rewrite "Dirge" or leave it out completely.

A fragment in a notebook Millay kept in 1919 in New York set the scene for the "Memorial"—although it would never be published:

> It might have been today, although
> You died about a year ago,
> Somebody dropped her voice & said,
> "You knew that Dorothy is dead."
> It might have been this very day.
> I lied & told her that I knew,
> And wished that she would go away,
> So I might sit & think of you.

Later in the same notebook is a draft of the poem that became the "Chorus"; here she called it "Epitaphia":

> Slip her pretty gowns
>   From their padded hangers,
> She will dance no more
>   In her narrow shoes
> Just a rainy day or two
>   In a windy tower;
> That was all I had of you,—
>   . . .
> I remember three or four
>   Things you said in spite,
> And an ugly coat you wore,
>   Plaided black & white.
> Just a rainy day or two
>   And a bitter word,—
> Why do I remember you
>   As a singing bird?

It's interesting here to watch the way she transformed what she knew about Coleman by linking it to herself. It was Millay who had an "ugly coat . . . Plaided black & white." Even the image of the singing bird is one that would remain potent for her—she would use it again when she wrote of Elinor Wylie after Wylie's death. So that by the time "Dirge" had been worked and reworked, the pronoun was "me" rather than "her"—which it would become in the published version. This is the unpublished draft version:

> Boys & girls that held me dear
> Those of you that held me dear
>   Do your weeping now:
> All you loved of me lies here.
> Brought to earth the insolent brow
> Quenched the withering tongue. . . .

In the late fall of 1920, Millay wrote to Mrs. Coleman, promising to leave out "Dirge." Mrs. Coleman said she was grateful, as she was afraid of "the lines being misunderstood. However if you cannot change them we will let the wonderful tenderness of the poem comfort us." And it must have, for there is no evidence that Millay either left out "Dirge" or made any of the cuts Mrs. Coleman had suggested. What she did leave out of the

"Memorial" but not the book was "Elegy Before Death," with its extraordinarily lovely closing quatrain:

> Oh, there will pass with your great passing
>   Little of beauty not your own,—
> Only the light from common water,
>   Only the grace from simple stone!

At the end of her tour Edna wrote Eugen that if only he were there in the chair beside her how "*totally,* ABSOLUTELY different everything would be." There was only one thing that sustained her: "Oh, it will be so lovely when we go around the earth together!—I told some people yesterday that we are going to Java & China in March.—Why not?—For we are, we are!—Aren't we?"

2

Just before their departure for the Far East, Eugen drew up a "Personal Account." According to this ledger, he'd been taking regular loans from his company of $800 or $1,000, beginning early in 1923, just before he met Millay. His debits from the close of 1922 to March 1924, were $7,833.41, while his credits were $4,115.16. In other words, he was $3,718.25 in debt to himself.

The truth was, Eugen wasn't much of a businessman. A favorite nephew of his, Tom de Booy, tried to give an idea of what he was like in the early 1920s. There was a strain in the Boissevain family, marked, some thought, by their Irish blood. "The Boissevains are," Tom said, "some of them, like rare flowers that bloom once and do not endure. And Eugen was not a good, a successful businessman. He would go off; he did not care deeply enough."

Before they left, Vincent gave her mother a rough itinerary, with dates where and when she could be reached:

> Hotel Imperial, Tokio, Japan—Cable till 20 May—
>   write till April 30—
> c/o Nederlandsch Indische Handels bank, Hongkong,
>   Cable 15 June Write—May 20
> c/o Nederlandsch Indische Handels bank, Singapore
>   Cable 10 July Write June 10
> c/o Mercantile Bank of India, Ltd. Colombo, Ceylon—
>   Cable till 30 July write till July 1st—
> After that c/o Morgan Harjeste Co. Place Vendôme—Paris

Still exhausted from her reading tour, Edna must have felt ill when they left because their first letters, written from San Francisco, assured both Arthur Ficke and Cora that she was feeling better. Eugen stressed just how well she was:

Dear Mother Millay,
. . . Your great little girl is much better. She stood the trip wonderfully well. Tomorrow we go aboard the Tayo Maru and will arrive in Yokohama the 5th of May. I'm sure the sea trip is going to make her a strong husky brute. I will send you a line from every port so that you will know how things are with your little daughter.
You were such a darling the day we left. I don't know how we ever would have got packed without you. Edna had only her black suit case with her in the dressing room and EVERYTHING was there and easily to be got at. We both blessed you and sang your praises several times a day.—And bless you for fixing the socks for my huge Trilby hoofs.—You *are* a darling and with all your faults I love you.

Vincent added only three words at the bottom of his letter: "Love from *Sefe*."

As they arrived in Honolulu, Eugen wrote one of what he called his "bulletins" to Cora about Vincent: "She is doing fine. She had a lovely rest, and is feeling much stronger. There is a beautiful marble swimming pool on the top-deck. We swim in it twice a day." Since the boat had only sixty passengers instead of the more than three hundred it was equipped to carry, it was like being on their own private yacht.

"The old lady is in wonderful trim," he told Arthur and Gladys. "She has rested and rested and now is full of pep"; to which Edna added, "Hello, kids! Where will you be when you get this? I wonder. Paris, maybe.—I know six Japanese words."

In Japan, Edna began to keep a journal of their trip. She told her mother that they planned to spend only a day or two in Tokyo and then travel by train to Nikko, "then *on foot* from Nikko to Fujiyama, a pilgrimage to the sacred mountain.—(Do you remember Shillingstone to Romsey?) Love, darling, from Vincent."

The following day, May 5, they docked at Yokohama and took the train to Tokyo, where they stayed at the huge Imperial Hotel, which looked like a frosted cake. Their room was expensive, and the service was deplorable: "ring for it, clap for it, whistle for it, shout for it, then go get it."

By May 9, they'd begun their walking trip, fourteen miles the first day, twelve the second to Kirifuri waterfall, where they climbed a steep hill to an unfrequented Buddhist shrine. There were "candles, tin swords, paper prayers, paper fringes hung at entrance. Picnic here, silence, butterflies.

Names of Europeans scratched in stone of temple—Charlie Brown, 1918, sort of thing. . . . image of cats just inside entrance in grey stone."

On Sunday, May 11, they went with their guide on an eighteen-mile walk to Ashio and found a Japanese inn with matting on the floor, a hibachi with charcoal fire, a tea tray, two cushions, and a bowl of azaleas. They had supper on the floor before a table that was, she noted, five inches high; they dined on salmon and poached eggs shirred with rice and soy and an "awful stinking root called *daiko*. Now I know what it is that gives Japanese villages their peculiar stench."

There were hot springs in Ikao, Japan, their next major stop, where they stayed at a little hotel very like the Hotel Panorama in Cassis, she told her mother,

> except that here there are mountains instead of sea. We are about a week out on our walking trip—have a coolie along as a guide and to carry our pack. We have been spending the nights so far in Japanese inns, sleeping on the floor, eating on the floor,—rice, tea & fish; rice, fish & tea; tea, fish & rice, etc.

They were walking now between twelve and twenty-two miles a day. By the end of their trip in Japan, they'd walked 114 miles. "But," as Vincent wrote Cora:

> the moment we struck the cities again we got the flu. We went to Peking— a two day train trip from Shanghai, where our steamer docked—because we were crazy to see the place; it is the old capital where the emperor lived, where the young dethroned emperor still lives, in a little walled Forbidden City within the city. And when we got there we went to the hotel & went to bed with the flu—picked it up on the train, probably,—& stayed in bed ten days.

When they recovered, they took a steamer to a small seaside village on the Yellow Sea called Chefoo. There they chartered a Chinese junk and sailed every day "to some island or other & build a fire & make coffee, & swim & lie in the sun. So now we are feeling pretty fit again."

But the most curious thing, she said, was that no one who had ever been in a Chinese seacoast village could grasp how she'd managed to build a fire; they

> would say, "Of what?"—for there *is* no drift-wood. They are the cleanest beaches in the world. There are no forests to send logs down river to the sea, there are apparently never any wrecks, & wood is so scarce in China that if a drifting spar appeared on the horizon, I am sure that the entire village would swim out to it, yelling & beating each other off, to drag it in. It

is my boast that there does not exist a beach where I can't gather wood enough for a fire, & so far I have just held my own. I gather the fire-wood in my bathing-cap! A dried walnut shell!—I see it from afar & make for it. This is not a joke—it is the truth,—dried shells & the corks of bottles & bits of bark no bigger than my finger—these make the drift-wood fire. I have never yet found a piece of drift-wood as large as my hand.

Vincent lies curled against Eugen's naked chest in the prow of their small boat, her dark straw bonnet in her lap; his sarong is slung low around his hips; they smile into the bright sunshine, a line of hills rising just beyond his shoulders as they sail the Yellow Sea.

Hong Kong, she said, was the most Chinese of all the cities they'd seen. On July 14, they were in Hong Kong bound for Singapore, "having the most <u>wonderful</u> time." They were three days out of Shanghai when their ship had gone aground in the yellow Yangtze mud, freighted down with her cargo of eggs. That night, as they slept in the heavy wet heat, the ship pitched "like a floating cork," sending Vincent's perfumes and salves crashing onto the thickly carpeted floor. In the morning she learned

> (a.) That I was about the only passenger aboard who had slept a wink, & (b.) That we had during the night passed unscathed through the whiskers of a healthy typhoon. Oh, mummie, you know, day before yesterday all day almost, first on the starboard & then on the port side, the spray of the ship was full of beautiful bright rainbows! & last night the phosphorus made the edge of the waves all like green electric light,—& there was heat lightning, & I said, "Oh, Eugen, rainbows by day & phosphorus by night,—I can hardly bear it!"—& he said, "If you should see a rainbow at night, I don't think you *could* bear it." And just at the moment he finished speaking there was a flash of lightning, & across the phosphorescent crest of the wave at which I was looking, a beautiful perfect rainbow appeared bright for a moment, & instantly was gone.—And I *did* bear it. Little Vincent big strong girl now.—I think not many people have seen a rainbow made by lightning on phosphorus. It was marvelous beyond words.—Oh, mummie, I am having the most <u>thrilling</u> time!

Two weeks later they had reached Java. In mid-August, they stopped for a spell in the foothills of the mountainous interior of Java, where they stayed in the house of a friend of Eugen's. Writing from the interior of Java, Eugen said they were keeping house together and that Edna "gives instructions and scoldings as fluently as any Baboe." Her note explained that this was how the word was pronounced in Malay and that it meant a Javanese Malay woman servant. The house was at 4,500 feet. "The air is wonderful, and Edna is as strong as a horse. We climbed the other day a high mountain 11000 feet high."

Edna put in her own two cents:

It is true about the mountain, mother. From the top of it, after we had got there, after many groans and sighs from the weaker vessel, meaning me, we could see the whole world nearly, only not quite Camden. We take a lot of exercise, and I am feeling awfully well. We live on stuff from the garden here, spinach and carrots and rhubarb,—and rice, if not from our garden, at least, from the gardens of our neighbors, as you might say.

Eugen added that he wished Cora

could see your girl now. You would not know her: she is so strong and husky. We get up at six and then she eats a breakfast as is a breakfast. We walk and climb a young mountain pretty nearly every day, or otherwise ride horses. She eats for dinner and lunch mountains of spinach, salade, and lovely vegetables, and twice a day plate fulls of rhubarb and three times a day buttermilk. She has just had the curse, and during all that time we went for big walks every day and she only once layed down for half an hour! She had no gin, no asperine or other dirty poisons and not even a hot water bag! The time before last just the same. What do you say about that.

Eugen could hardly finish crowing about his care of her.

They stayed well throughout their sometimes arduous and exciting adventurous journey through the Dutch East Indies, where it was steaming hot, or in the mountains, where it was extraordinarily chilly. But by the time they reached India they were both seriously ill, Vincent with a form of dysentery and Eugen with such a severe tropical fever that he had to spend a week in a hospital in Bombay. It wasn't until early October that they left India bound for Marseille. And even at that, he wrote Arthur,

We left the hospital too soon, to catch the boat to Marseilles and on the boat I got flebitus. I had to be taken from the boat to the train in a stretcher and ambulance and the same way in Paris from the train to the hotel. Edna arranged everything wonderfully, although she was still very weak. We are now 14 days in this hotel. I have not moved and must lie perfectly quiet on my back. Vincent does everything for me, which is a lot.

Eugen's illness put Millay in the position of taking care of him, when from the first hours of their meeting, let alone their marriage, he had been nursing her.

He thought he was doing pretty well now, and they were planning to visit his family in Holland within a week or so, "And then for New York, where with the help of God we hope to be in your arms before the end of

November, about 14 days after this letter reaches you." But two weeks later, they were still in Paris.

3

The Boissevains were, on their father's side, descended from an old French Huguenot family that had gradually achieved a certain degree of wealth; they had become shipowners and prominent members of the Walloon church. Eugen's father, Charles, was the editor and later director of the *Algemeen Handelsblad,* a leading Dutch newspaper. He was for many years an immensely popular journalist.

The Boissevains were, in the words of Hilda von Stockum Marlin, one of Eugen's nieces, "a teeming family." She was seventeen when Vincent and Eugen came to visit. "I was only one—truly only one—of the lesser members of our family. There were eleven children and scores of grandchildren and even great-grandchildren.

"When she first came, we all stood at the entrance to Drafna, on the great front portico, to greet her. I seem to remember her in some slight, frail, gauzy long frock. And what did she do before the great assembling of Boissevains? In front of Granny, Eugen's mother? She came running directly to me with her arms outstretched. She said something to the effect of—'You, too, write poems!'

"Well, it was such an embarrassment to me! You must understand my position in this family, and to be singled out in such a manner, at such a time. I did not turn from her so much as I withdrew into myself. I no longer remembered, if I had ever known, that one of my fond aunts had sent her a poem . . . perhaps some translations of mine. And yet there I stood singled out by her. It was completely undeserved.

"Perhaps she felt my aloofness, which was really only shyness and puzzlement. I had no idea what to say, or what to do, or where to look. I remember, later, Eugen trying to tell his mother—and Granny was a difficult, wonderful, artistic woman herself, with—it must be said—the Irish gift for malice. He would try to say how wonderful this Girl Poet was. And Granny would narrow her eyes, and smile, and wave his words aside, and say: 'And Eugen? What about Eugen!'

"He may not have been her favorite, but he was surely—among the younger brothers and sisters—*among* the favorites. And then he would carry her, Edna, up those long flights of stairs at Drafna to their rooms."

Tom de Booy described Eugen's father, Charles: "emotional, romantic, warmhearted, and intelligent and always defended his liberal principles. His column, 'From Day to Day,' became famous. . . . In January 1900, during the Boer War, he sent an impressive open letter to the duke of

Devonshire, in which he fiercely attacked Great Britain's aggression." His letter had been persuasive and eloquent enough not only to draw the attention of the head of the Labour Party in England, which had distributed copies to the working classes of Great Britain, but also to be sent to the president of the United States. His emissary was the eighteen-year-old Eugen, who personally delivered it. Charles Boissevain had also staunchly defended Dreyfus. "We," Tom said, "the grandchildren, admired him; he was a very remarkable man. Of course he had his weak points: vanity, but it was a disarming vanity."

In 1865, when Charles was in Dublin reporting on the International Exhibition, he met and fell in love with Emily Heloise MacDonnell, whose father was provost of Trinity College, Dublin. "They were never well off (like Charles's elder brother, Jan, a prominent businessman and cofounder of big shipping companies), but thanks to several legacies they were able to bring up their eleven children in good style and were accepted as equals by the patrician families of Amsterdam. But they were never considered entirely ordinary by Dutch standards." For they had on the one hand a certain French *esprit* coupled with an Irish quality that de Booy charmingly called "happy-go-luckiness." Several of their children never quite adapted themselves to the Dutch style of respectability. And three of the sons, Eugen and his brothers Jan and Robert, lived abroad their entire adult lives.

Although Eugen had been born in Amsterdam, when he was seven his parents had moved their brood to Drafna near Naarden, an old fortress town that lay close to the inland edge of the Zuider Zee.

Drafna was a three-story half-timbered chalet built entirely of wood, with great open porches and summer awnings above them. It sat upon forty acres of woodland with its own pond, meadows, stable, and tennis court. In the glass negatives of the surviving photographs and snapshots taken of the family, there are wonderful scenes of the eleven children with their English nurse, Polly. These are tableaux out of the nineteenth century, the children astride ponies and bicycles or riding gray goats, with geese and large brindled dogs, their tails like plumes, bounding among the children, the tiniest of whom are tucked within wood carts.

The little boys are in bloomers, the older ones in knickers and soft-billed caps; the older girls in mutton-sleeved white starched blouses, with cocked hats festooned with snowy egret feathers. At the seaside, the women would step into great curtained bathing machines, which were pulled by the servants into the water while the women delicately undressed and donned their bathing outfits of caps, tunics, and long skirts as gaff-rigged catboats beat away from shore.

What they all remembered was Eugen's first wife, Inez. Tom de Booy, who was only fourteen, said, "I remember the intense excitement at Drafna when, in the summer of 1913, a telegram had arrived from Eugen announcing his first marriage.... 'Have married Inez Milholland; are coming home Thursday next. Please postpone criticism till after our departure.' But when they arrived everyone fell in love with Inez.

"She was devastatingly beautiful and charming," Tom recalled. "We had never seen a woman like her, and I fell in love with her immediately. She smoked cigarettes. Eugen and Inez kissed each other incessantly, even at table, and she won the hearts of almost every brother-in-law, although some were a bit shocked by her un-Dutch behavior! I'm sure several of my aunts heaved a sigh of relief when Eugen and Inez left Drafna."

It was Edna's intensity and her loveliness that Tom remembered, whereas Hilda could not shake the impression Inez had made with Eugen: "They were both splendid physical specimens, they were a match for each other. And then here was this frail, small person, this poet—whom, one instinctively felt, much had been made over. In her family she was the wunderkind! Among us she was simply one of many talented family members. There were singers and actors; there was this sense of an extraordinary, perhaps even overwhelming family of gifted and artistic people. And Eugen! Well, he was the most artistic of the brothers. His gift was, I suppose, for life and for intimacy. And for play, of course.

"But ours was such a distinguished family. It was not only that our grandfather was the editor of the largest, most prestigious paper in Amsterdam, but he wrote poems, and whole issues of the paper would be mocked up and devoted to an anniversary, to a family celebration, a birthday or a marriage, a masque, a theatrical that we had ourselves written the songs for, the music, the poetry, everything. It was their great gift; they appreciated whatever in life, or art or poetry, had beauty and grace.

"Edna was, you see, walking into another world, and she was what?— bewildered, I felt. She hadn't a clue. She was the great outstanding person in her own family. But among us she was just one, and one of many."

Eugen and Edna were home in time for Christmas, and they would never visit Holland again.

CHAPTER 21

That February, after attending a concert of Deems Taylor's "Portrait of a Lady," Millay wrote a letter to the anonymous music editor of the New

The Buzzell sisters (above, left) in
Newburyport, Massachusetts:
Clem (top), Cora and Susie,
and Georgia. Cora Buzzell (above,
right), the Minstrel Girl.

Henry Tolman Millay. Tall, handsome, and broad-shouldered, he
was a year younger than Cora, as
fair as she was dark, as easygoing as
she was intense.

Two little sisters: Edna St. Vincent Millay (left), the firstborn, on her sleigh in Union, Maine, and Norma Millay (right), also in Union, reaching out.

Sunday school in Union. Norma is at the far left in the second row and Vincent is next to her (with ribboned braids).

"Ring's Island, 1901–2—After children had typhoid. CBM"
The above is Cora's caption for the photo. On the reverse, Norma tells the story: "We had each nearly died of Typhoid fever in Rockport, Me. Mother nursed us through. When we were well enough she took us to Uncle Charlie's at Ring's Island, Mass.—just across the river from Newburyport. Our hair has been cut short. Vincent, in the top row, has her head on girl's shoulder. Kay is farthest left in middle row; I am second to the right of her. N.M."

High school graduation, 1909, Camden, Maine. White bows on bright red hair.

Cora Millay, nurse. "Show this to your father . . ."

Vincent (second from the left) with friends on Penobscot Bay.

Girls in the grass, Camden (Vincent is second from the right).

The sisters: Vincent and Norma (top), Norma and Vincent (below, left), Norma and Kathleen (below, right).

E. Vincent Millay, the Girl Poet,
around the time of *Renascence*.

Vassar College,
freshman year,
1913–14,
Halloween
Ball. Vincent is
in the center, in
a dark dress.
"Lucky I'm
little, and *have*
to be a girl!"

In the Pageant of Athena, celebrating
Vassar's fiftieth anniversary, October 11,
1915, Millay played Marie de France, the
twelfth-century Breton poet and the first
woman to write poetry in France. "Into a
scene of courtly beauty . . . comes a
dainty little figure . . . in a dress of white
satin with a train so big that two pages
were needed to carry it."

"She's Elaine Ralli, a Junior, another hockey hero, cheer-leader, rides horse-back a lot, very boyish, and makes a lot of noise, not tall, but *all* muscle" (Edna Millay, November 4, 1914).

In the summer of 1915, Elaine Ralli came to Vincent's home in Camden as a paying guest. Here Vincent, Elaine, and Norma are in the helm of *Watch Your Step,* the little sloop Elaine rented.

This is the famous photograph taken in the spring of 1913 by Arnold Genthe at the Kennerleys' estate in Mamaroneck.

Luigi Mario Laurenti, Norma, Ida Rauh, James Light, and a sultry Edna Millay in the summer of 1920, in Woodstock, New York. "I have met a handsome and perfidious Don Giovanni of an Italian baritone and am learning to speak Italian. . . . From the point of view of character and personality, he is just a sweet and friendly fellow, not so deep as a well nor so broad as a church-door, but oh, how he doth sing!"

Floyd Dell was thirty when he met Edna Millay in December 1917. He was divorced, an apostle of the shocking new Freudian school of psychoanalysis, and one of the editors of that radical magazine *The Masses.* (© Bettmann/CORBIS)

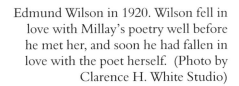

Edmund Wilson in 1920. Wilson fell in love with Millay's poetry well before he met her, and soon he had fallen in love with the poet herself. (Photo by Clarence H. White Studio)

Witter Bynner, her dear "Hal," who asked her to marry him. She said Yes! And he withdrew.

Alan Ross Macdougall in 1920s Paris, where Millay wrote "Blessing on the Head of A.R.M. (on the occasion of his going abroad a-minstrelling)."

This photo was slipped into her leather passport wallet. The signature is George Slocombe's.

Dressed in a red velvet cloak, embroidered with real gold. She told her mother that seeing Albania in 1921 "has been my most thrilling experience so far."

Playing on the shingle near
Shillingstone, in Dorset.

"When all I want is an apple . . ." Pregnant on the
fields and downs of Dorset, 1921.

On July 18, 1923, Edna St. Vincent Millay married Eugen Boissevain in Croton-on-Hudson, New York. She was ill and looked worn as Norma took the mosquito netting from the porch and, pinning roses from the garden on it, made her wedding veil.

Except for Gladys Ficke and the justice of the peace, there were only brothers and sisters and lovers at the wedding. Left: Norma, her dog Jerry, Arthur Ficke, Floyd Dell, and Gladys Ficke.

As soon as the ceremony was over, Edna and Eugen left for the hospital in New York. "If I die now, I shall be immortal," she told Arthur Ficke. But she didn't. She won the Pulitzer Prize instead.

Recovering from her operation on the porch of Eugen's house in Croton.

Honeymoon: "Oh, it will be so lovely when we go around the Earth together!
. . . For we are, we are!—Aren't we?"

In Burma (above).
A happy couple in the
bright sun of Java.

York *World,* who had criticized it roundly. He'd said the audience had been so enthusiastic, it must have been packed with the composer's relatives, which Edna hotly denied: "Sir, I was a member of that audience. I heard with close attention and deep pleasure an unusually good program unusually well performed." Last night's audience, she wrote, far from being composed of Mr. Taylor's relatives, "was made up of discerning and honestly delighted strangers." The joke was that Taylor *was* the music editor, a job he quit at the end of the season in order to compose.

Deems Taylor and Mary Kennedy had first met Edna in Paris, when they had been on their honeymoon in the early summer of 1922, just before she had fled to Shillingstone.

When the Metropolitan Opera Company commissioned Deems to write an American opera, Mary suggested that Edna Millay write the libretto. "I thought she was extraordinary. She had something to say that I wanted to hear. And I knew that from her first poems." However, there was a snag: "She had written just this one act of *The Casket of Glass*—which turned about the Snow White fairy tale of the beautiful girl who when she takes an apple which is poisoned and it lodges in her throat—well, it was one of the classic versions of Snow White. And it could not be done. There was one entire scene where the heroine had to sing with her face covered with a cloth! And that was impossible for a singer."

So Edna abandoned it. And then all three waited.

In May 1925, Millay was invited to read at Bowdoin College for the college's centenary of the class of 1825, which had included Longfellow and Hawthorne. The other speakers were Robert Frost, Carl Sandburg, and Professor Irving Babbitt of Harvard. But it was Millay who garnered the attention of the press. The reporter for *The Christian Science Monitor* began by describing how she looked, the lights of the stage playing on her "cropped hair as Miss Millay trailed up two steps to the platform, smiling like a little girl anxious to please neighbors."

> She made no attempt to explain her poems, to point to them as good examples of what one, if one chose the imagists—the visual imagists—would do in order to gain fame as a poet. Nothing about how she became a poet.

But the students stamped their feet in approval when she'd finished. Then the reporter described what she'd worn:

> a robe of gold and bronze and green and her voice was a bronze bell as she read. Back and forth she moved, slender, by turn gay and grave, pompous

and flippant. Her robe, because it was traced with gold threads woven into its pattern, whispered and chimed faintly against the floor. If Miss Millay had not been a poet she could easily have been an actress. . . . And Miss Millay ended her evening, leaving the platform not as a great poet but as a girl, quite young, of Maine who had done her best.

It was so successful a performance that it was hard to tell whether the students or the reporter had been more "fascinated by the swift moving bronze-gold figure, so slender, so competent, at times exquisitely unreal." In the morning this vision was gone, "and in its place a straight boyish person in lilac tweed and a tricorn. . . . striding fast like a boy, not at all formidable or unreal." In other words, being a hometown girl, anxious to please, was not the same as being a great poet—and being like a boy was at least being real. This is peculiar stuff. But it lay at the heart of her increasing fame. And it continued.

What the Bowdoin students really wanted, wrote John Hurd, Jr., in the *Boston Sunday Globe,* was a good look at the poet

> as a married woman with a residence in New York City. It was a remarkable thing the way their faces lighted with joy. And no wonder, she was exquisitely beautiful to look at. She is 33 years old. You would not have said she was 21. She wore a loose flowing gown of gold and bronze without a semblance of a girdle. Her sleeves, bound at the wrist no larger than a ring, flared above the elbow. But what is the use of trying to describe the way her gown fell to the top of her gold slippers and her trick of flicking her train in back of her?

In fact, two of the young men were so smitten they wangled the job of serving her breakfast. However, they were "too fussed" to make the most of the situation. They noticed that Mr. Boissevain wore striped pajamas, "but neither of the boys dared to look at Miss Millay and so could give no description."

The chance to compare Frost's work with hers—it would be the only time they shared a platform—was not of the slightest interest to the press. There were only anecdotes pointing up the differences in their style. Robert Frost was represented as curmudgeonly and surly; Millay was girlish, elfin, and seductive. The first evening, both were the guests of President and Mrs. Sills of Bowdoin, who thought it would be pleasant to have the governor of the state meet Frost for dinner. "But Mr. Frost refused to be lionized. He asked to be excused on the ground that he never would attend a dinner on the evening he was going to speak."

The following morning at ten, Frost, scheduled to be interviewed, had overslept. When the reporter returned at eleven, he came down sleepily.

"His complexion had none of the New England ruddiness, and actually had a yellowish tint. Mr. Frost was not feeling well and said so." Frost then launched into a description of his past:

> "I earned only $15 a week until I was 35 years old. . . . And I had a wife and children to feed."
> You wonder what they ate.
> "O, we scratched along somehow," he replied. "Part of the time I didn't make $15 a week. It is difficult to determine just what you get on a farm."

When the reporter told him that it was "heroic" to have survived such a beginning, Frost would have none of it: "With me it was . . . an animal passion. That's just what it was, an animal instinct—more than instinct— a passion to write poetry."

His victory—and here he winked at the reporter—was that the University of Michigan, "a State institution in the Middle West," had just offered him a lifetime appointment with

> absolutely no demands upon his time except that he live near the college. He does not have to teach any classes, although he may conduct what they call a seminar the last few months of next year, and his full professor's salary goes on just the same.

Millay had not overslept, for the next morning the reporter quoted her.

> "I am not writing poems any more," she said. "I have become terribly interested in the drama and I want to write plays. Yes, I am writing one now, a four-act play. I have finished the first act. Then I want to write a sonnet sequence of about 150 sonnets based on psychological experiences in my life.
> "No, I cannot write in New York. It is awfully exciting there and I find lots of things to write about and I accumulate many ideas, but I have to go away where it is quiet.
> "We have bought a farm, which we are not going to farm, in the Berkshire Hills, and I hope to work on my plays there."

Next to Frost's remarks about his lack of a living income, this must have seemed like girlish flummery. What is happening here is a refashioning of herself after her marriage. She would better be able to write in the country. She would dress well. She would no longer cuss like a trooper. She was redefining herself publicly.

But she was an amateur compared to Frost's performing self. Frost called it "barding around," and he would supplement his income for fifty years by giving such readings, at which he was eventually, if not this time at Bowdoin, canny and masterful. He performed his poetry for $50 at first, but by 1950 he was finally getting $1,000 for each appearance. He'd given forty readings in 1922 alone—grueling schedules of trains and discomfort and sleepless nights in strange hotel beds. Just the year before this reading, he'd been asked who might be willing to read at Amherst, where he was then teaching. He recommended Millay without reservation. According to his most recent biographer, Jeffrey Meyers, he was wry about Millay, "whose notorious sexual life and highly charged verses," he said, "had won her a large audience. Miss Millay is a great audience killer. . . . She loses nothing of course by her reputation for dainty promiscuity. . . . She is already a love-myth. I don't have to tell you how much I admire her less flippant verse."

On May 24, 1925, Eugen, who had already taken over a good deal of Vincent's correspondence (sometimes even to her mother, whom he called "Mother Millay," or "M.M." for short), had very good news indeed: Edna was to be given an honorary doctor of letters degree by Tufts College in Boston. "So," he wrote Cora, "after the 15th of June, you will have to address your letters to your daughter: Edna St. Vincent Millay, A.B. Litt.D."

On May 21, 1925, Edna St. Vincent Millay was deeded a property of 435 acres, "two roods and twenty-five rods of land more or less," for a consideration of $9,000 in the town of Austerlitz, in Columbia County in New York State. They'd found an abandoned farm through an advertisement in *The New York Times.* By July she named it Steepletop, after a common wildflower that grew everywhere on the hills and meadows around the house. A tall single-stemmed plant with a cluster of pale pink flowers at the top that forms a plume, it's more often known as hardhack. The place had been a dairy farm.

"Here we are, in one of the loveliest places in the world," Edna wrote her mother. The house was not, however, quite in the "really splendid condition" they said it was. In fact, by June 22 she was telling her mother that they were "working like Trojans, dogs, slaves." Still, they were "crazy about it." But their expenses mounted: "The furnace & bathroom alone come to a thousand dollars. It's terrible. But it's going to be a sweet place when it's finished—and it's ours, all ours, about seven hundred acres of land & a lovely house, & no rent to pay, only a nice gentlemanly mortgage to keep shaving a slice off."

Then she fell into the sort of comical baby talk that always signaled something was wrong: "We're so excited about it we are nearly daft in the bean—kidney bean, lima bean, string-bean, butter-bean—you dow whad I bean—ha! ha! ha!"

One month later they were still at it. Gene's nephew Freddie, his brother Robert's son, was a landscape gardener; he'd given them help and fresh courage because they were just about spent in the exhausting labor of the renovation.

> You see, we have had living with us for three weeks now six masons, four plumbers, two carpenters, two ineffectual and transient servants, and fifteen insubordinate and mischievous berry-picking children. They don't spend the night here, but they might as well, for they appear in the morning before we are dressed, and tramp through the bedrooms without knocking, bearing ladders and bricks and trowels and buckets of cement.

There wasn't "a spot within a quarter of a mile where I can stand and brush my teeth except in full sight of some of them."

She wanted to show her mother everything, not just write to her. But she'd even had to stop writing because "I have a headache all the time lately and spots before my eyes, and, as mother used to say, I don't feel so darned well myself. I have no idea what the trouble is. . . . I imagine I got too tired just at first. I worked frightfully hard."

She tried to make the renovation sound like a romp, but the constant disorder and the hard work were taking their toll:

> I am going to Pittsfield . . . to have my eyes examined. I went to a general practitioner in Great Barrington, a very good man, I think, who assures me there's nothing the matter with my heart, lungs, kidneys, liver, lights, etc., so I imagine it must be my eyes. I've had a headache for two months now without an hour's respite, and dark spots before my eyes all the time, so if it isn't something else, it damn well must be my eyes, for it's damn well something.

Then she told her mother that if she needed more money than she was enclosing, "I can always go out and gather a few dollars for you; but it's been a very wet spring here, and it will be late in October before the dollars are really ripe enough to drop from the bough."

2

In June 1925, just as Arthur Ficke was leaving for Harvard to read the Phi Beta Kappa poem at commencement, he was diagnosed with pulmonary tuberculosis. He went anyway, but immediately afterward the Fickes left for Saranac Lake in the Adirondacks, the location of a famous sanitarium for tuberculosis. Eugen, who maintained the correspondence, wrote to them from Austerlitz in the fall:

Darling children,
  —I'm writing in Vincent's bed room. She is feeling rotten. But the fire is blazing away in the fireplace and the hot water spouts out of the spigot in the bathroom, and things are getting to look like something. . . .
  But we are homesick for you two. The couch is in front of the huge big fireplace in the living room, but we want to have you sit on it, and we want to discuss many things with you. We haven't had a discussion with you for so long that I'm afraid poor Arthur will have so many wrong ideas about God and Coolidge and cheese and automobiles and books, Poor Artie. Come quickly to Vince and Ugin and we will tell you what's what in this world and the next. . . . We are planning to fetch the Mercer next week and will come over to see you and rest and drink gin and talk too much and smoke too much. That is provided we can gather enough money to get the Mercer out of hock.

Vincent added:

Darling Artie and Gladdie,
  Vincent can't write a letter 'cause she's so tired and sick, and got a headache, and got the curse, and you know, and all that—but she loves you both desperately, desperately, and longs to see you . . . & oh, Artie & Gladdy, we miss you so! Please, please love us always, & we'll love you always, & then, anyway, there'll always be that!—

                                                            Vincent

Not long after this they received a letter from Gladys telling them that they were going to Santa Fe for Arthur to recuperate. Eugen wrote his third letter that week trying to talk them out of going. As for Vincent, she was beside herself: "I am speechless with despair. Just when we're beginning to see the end of the tunnel. Oh, what's the use. I suppose you'll be gone a year."
  They would try to see them before they left, "but," she wrote, "suppose we can't—& suppose you can't come here—it's *Separation,* by God, that's what & nothing less."
  Gene admitted in another letter that Vincent had been sick for the past three months, "pretending not to be sick and would work and then have to stay in bed for days." He was, he said, dreadfully unhappy about her. "What is the good of the house, the scenery, the beauty, the apples and pears and the ripening tomatoes if Vincie is feeling rotten? What's the good of anything?"

By November they were in New York, where they had systematically begun to search for a doctor

> who would cure Vincent. We went everywhere and saw every kind of specialist, from a pedicure to a sinecure (I hope you get my jeu-de-mots). Finally a specialist in Boston who had examined her sinuses sent us to N.Y. . . . She has been X-rayed all over and all kinds of tests taken in the most unromantic way, and now they know that she has been suffering from toximia, which has finally got her dreadfully weak and she was having now a nervous breakdown.

Bed rest and isolation were required. "Just a little of me, but not much. She has a nurse who does funny things to her at 8 a.m. and keeps it up until 4 p.m."

He had to close Steepletop. "All the beautiful, expensive water put in with such heart-breaks, and so much money, is going to be cut off. . . . And then Eugin is going to walk the lonely streets of New York, with a lump in his throat. And Vince in bed, and Artie and Gladdy way down south and everything.————"

While his letter bounded gaily on for nineteen pages, there was this: "Gladdy, will you come and have some fun with Ugin in New York. I will ship my sick poet to yours. And then we'll pick them up later. Whatyer-say?—Let's park them for a while." It was the first sign that Eugen was tiring of all the illness.

3

By the fall Millay had sent only two scenes of the last act of *The Casket of Glass* to Deems Taylor. The third scene remained in her handwritten draft. Having made that beginning in the midst of the pandemonium of construction at Steepletop, now she tossed it. She began fiddling with a new idea. By November, Eugen said she had it: "Vincent now has a theme for her opera. She is crazy about it.

"My poet," he continued, "is doing fairly well, but it is a slow business." They were staying in New York briefly and then spent a week in Atlantic City, "waiting until she can come to a sanatorium in Stockbridge. . . . Then she stays two or three weeks and/or months, and then she must come to New York to see whether they want to take her tonsils out."

Edna was really no better in Atlantic City. Eugen put her to bed, tucked her in with a hot-water bottle at her feet before a wide-open window:

> She looks over the ocean, she drinks in soft mild salt sea air; her nostrils quiver with delight, like full blooded Arabian steed.—And twice a day

Ugin pushes her in a chair on wheels, miles & miles along beautiful sea
and pretty shops.—And we are indecently happy.

Eugen remained cheerful. It must have been hard to remain always the
cheerful one. Only once in the drifts of letters he wrote, early in December, did he admit

God, but it will be wonderful when Vincent is on her feet again and can do
what she likes, and may be, once we all four get roaringly, indecently, hilar-
iously, indiscretely and indiscriminatingly drunk. I'm sick of medicines
and doctors and carefulness. Well, that's off my chest.

At last, instead of going to the sanitarium in Stockbridge, in December
they returned to Steepletop. "We saw the last dozen specialists last week,
and it was agreed and decided by them that what we had done for Vincent
so far was all wrong, and now she must have good air and exercise and we
must go back to Steepletop."
Eugen had been offered a job; "and," he told Arthur,

as soon as Vincent is strong enough that I can leave her alone with Mother
Millay, I intend to get my nephew here to look after things and go to New
York and take that job. Jesus, how I'm longing to have her well.—We are
beginning to be sick of it.

Then he added, "Oh, and I forgot to tell you that I love Vincent. No, I did
tell you that some time ago, I believe."
Cora was now with them. "Mother Millay and I do some splendid
team-work and are giving Vincent a cure of rest, exercise, good food, fresh
high dry air, and funny inside treatments," Eugen wrote. "We have read all
about her trouble in learned books and I think she is gaining weight and
will soon be strong enough to get well."
Now she had them both caring for her.

CHAPTER 22

Kathleen wasn't up to snuff, either. She had begun to write fiction, and
she was mired in a novel centered on her mother's life. While Vincent
had invited Cora to come to her, she didn't want to separate her mother
from Kathleen in Camden. Eugen added that it would be wonderful if

Kay could come with her, "because the workmen will have left by that time, and you & I could look after the two little Millay kids." But Kathleen didn't come, and by the fall of 1925 Cora was living at Steepletop. That winter Cora hired Helen Nitkoski, the young daughter of the farmer who owned the caretaker's house across the road from Steepletop.

Cora did the cooking and all the hard work, Helen recalled. "All I did was get the vegetables ready and wash the dishes. . . . I came only in the morning, about nine or nine-thirty. She never cared what time I came. Edna, I never saw. Cora was the housekeeper. She was a hardworking woman. Edna just looked tired. She seemed fragile. Every single morning she'd go do her writing.

"Cora was very affectionate, very warm, but very lonely. . . . She talked a lot about her husband; he had been abusive, she said. Edna had decided not to have children. Cora told me that, and, yes, I think it disappointed her."

Just before the turn of the year, Eugen told Arthur that Steepletop was as well equipped as a small country. It had to be; it was twelve degrees below zero, and they were snowbound.

> We have 12 tons of coal in the cellar and 15 cords of wood in the shed, three fireplaces, two stoves, a furnace, a hot-water heater and plenty of matches. We have thousands of tins of everything, a huge bag of potatoes, 100 lbs. of sugar, flour, beans, peas, rice and. . . . Hanging from the rafters an enormous ham, bacon, pork, a brave brace of ducks, pounds and pounds of coffee, fresh fish frozen into a prehistoric fossil and resuscitated by Mother Millay into a glorious New England fish chowder.

They were, in fact, he said, living like "pigs in clover, i.e., a bit swinishly but with much good humored jostling and creature comforts."

Even though Vincent had the curse and was drinking her customary "anticurse" gin, she'd tied her hair in pigtails with the red twine from their Christmas presents, and they were having good times again. They'd bought an organ for ten bucks at a country auction and sang Christmas hymns. "It was lovely," Eugen said, "Mother Millay's touching tremulous little voice and my funny voice, now on, now off the key, and Vincent's pure, true lovely voice democratically mixed in the ether."

But the best news came the next week, when he told "Dear Artie, darling Gladdie" that

> Hallelujah! Vincent has powdered her nose; Vincent has put on naughtie, gauzy, gazie undies! Hallelujah! Hallelujah! She is ribbald, she's flippant.

She has a pretty, pretty dress on. Jehovah, the highest, Hallelujah! Vincent is a little bit better. Better, but not well. It is: bad, better, well. I have thrown the advice of the 12 plus x doctors to the winds, and am giving her a Eugen-ic cure (ha, ha, ha). And it is helping her—. . . . Vincent has washed her hair. Apple-jack is in my round and freckled belly and all's well with the world.

Now, he said, if Vincent would hurry up and get well he could still take the job he'd been offered. He didn't say what that job was, "but I cannot leave just now. . . . I must make money, Vincent must finish her opera and get well." Vincent added her own note: "This is me, Vince, in person, here to tell you that I eat my bran every day like a good nag."

That January there was still no manuscript, and Deems couldn't wait any longer. He wrote suggesting that they postpone the opera. On January 5, Eugen replied for Edna:

Vincent says: "Postpone, Hell," and sends you enclosed synopsis of the opera by Deems Taylor "Aethelwold."
It is going to be called Aethelwold, unless you can think of something better, which you probably cannot. . . . This is a very rough sketch and will be changed, very likely, considerably by both you and Edna, and she does not like to have unfinished work kicking around. That reminds me, will you please get hold of the Synopsis of "Snowwhite," and return it to Edna, when you come here to finish the opera.

But Edna's health was no better:

We cannot find out what is the trouble. It is not a nervous breakdown. She cannot use her eyes AT ALL now, and I must do all her reading and writing. Her headache has never stopped for a single minute, and is very often dreadfully bad. Do you know of a good doctor who will give some time to find out what is the matter, and make her well?

In precisely two weeks the first draft of Act I, thirteen pages ending with "(curtain, and about time)," arrived, typed out on yellow paper. Millay was now calling it "THE KING'S HENCHMAN or THE WARLOCK." Taylor wired her immediately:

FIRST SCENE BEYOND MY FONDEST HOPES GO AHEAD WITH SCENE TWO MY CORRECTIONS COULD BE WRITTEN ON A DIME LETTER STOP LOVE AND CONGRATULATIONS FROM BOTH

On January 19, she sent him her "Song of the Harper," which would open the opera. It was as alliterative and rolling as the Anglo-Saxon ballads it was based on, with heavily stressed two-beat lines that swung back and forth into each other, intensifying the beauty of the language with each swinging line:

> Wild as the white waves
> Rushing and roaring,
> Heaving the wrack
> High up the headland;
> Hoarse as the howling
> Winds of the winter. . . .

Eugen explained to Deems that "The Song of the Harper" was written entirely "in the old Saxon style, and will give the atmosphere much better, being a story out of the Anglo-Saxon Chronicle of an incident, which took place in the year 755, much better than a story of Eadgar's conquests."

But despite her continuing illness, one of the effects of which was like "looking at everything through a dotted veil," Edna's next note to Deems was confident:

I'm sending this with all its imperfections on its head.—It is much too long . . . & frightfully rough in places & a little silly in other places, 'n' everything. But parts of it are pretty good. And it's time you should see it. Let me know your reaction at once. Then I'll spend a week following your suggestions, or strengthening myself & my book against them,—& then go on as you suggested, to the second scene.

Love,
Edna

Warlock is an Anglo-Saxon word, which, in its original sense, meant "a traitor, a breaker of a pledge."—You may think this is too ancient & hidden to use, since that meaning is quite obsolete, but it's a grand title, & we could always explain it in the *Argument.*

E.

But since Deems didn't much like "The Warlock" as a title, she said, "I'm not at all sure that I do myself——then *The King's Henchman* is the best title so far; so let's call it that until we hit on something better, and see how it wears."

She would not, however, give in about the Anglo-Saxon names of her characters, Eadgar and Aelfrida, who would not be modernized into Edgar and Elfreda. "For who-the-hell am I writing this libretto anyway, Deems Taylor or George Gershwin?"

Then she gave him a gentle lecture:

> Honest, old bean, nobody's going to know who Eadgar was, anyway; and if you go and spell him without his remote and softening diphthong, people will only feel the more self-conscious about their ignorance. Audiences aren't annoyed by diphthongs, Deems, they're comforted by 'em; and thousands, nay, what do I say?—millions, of poor starved souls, whose lives are just one unvarnished vowel after another without even w and y, will lap up our pretty diphthongs with tears.
>
> As for Aethelwold, if he had been born in Wales instead of East Anglia, and his name were Llwwghghftrw,—why, I would have changed his name all by myself long ago, I would have *felt* somehow you couldn't sing that name. . . . As for your remarks about "Ethel,"—if you say that again I shall at once change the name of my lords Cymric, Gunner and Wulfred, to Ella, Lilla and Ida, also good Anglo-Saxon masculine names.
>
> I'm terribly sorry, Deems. But I'll be a sister to you.

There were, of course, changes he suggested that she thought were grand, and at the close of this long letter she saluted their mutual effort: "Here . . . is to the great day when we listen to the opening bars of IT." She signed it LOVE.

On April 14, she wired Deems:

> KINGS MESSENGER ABSOLUTELY IMPOSSIBLE FOR THIS REASON THE WORD MESSENGER WAS BROUGHT INTO ENGLISH BY THE NORMANS AND I AM WRITING MY ENTIRE LIBRETTO IN ANGLOSAXON THAT IS TO SAY THERE IS NOT A WORD IN THE LIBRETTO WHICH WAS NOT KNOWN IN ONE FORM OR ANOTHER IN ENGLISH A THOUSAND YEARS AGO. I MEANT TO SPRING THIS ON YOU LATER AND TO KEEP IT SECRET FROM EVERYBODY ELSE UNTIL THEY FOUND OUT FOR THEMSELVES IF EVER. IF YOU MUST TELL METROPOLITAN BEG THEM TO KEEP IT SECRET. METROPOLITAN CAN CHOOSE BETWEEN SAXONS AND KINGS HENCHMAN.

By the end of May, she was working on Act III. But she'd have to send it to him "in small doses like this. My head is terrible, and has been for weeks. After I work for a while it gets crazy." On June 10, Eugen wrote, sending four more pages by special delivery, telling Deems they were coming to town the next day "and you will be able to talk it over. Don't be nervous. She won't take much of your time, although she is coming over expressly to see you." She was desperately trying to keep the acts to less than forty minutes.

They met in New York, and Deems's wife, Mary Kennedy, remembered her own irritation at being stuck in the kitchen making steak, trying to overhear their conversation rather than being a part of it: "I remember that when she was ill—and this was during the precise period when she was to be writing the libretto—she would see us one at a time. First Deems and then me. But once when I was in the room alone, she said, 'Mary, Deems isn't going to wait for me to do it.' And I reassured her that he would, and of course he did."

2

"Vincent's illness," Cora declared to a friend, "has been the first and almost only thing in my mind, that, and what I might be able to do towards making her comfortable here this winter, and towards getting her well." It was February, and she had been living with them since November. Her devotion coupled with or even contrasted to Eugen's must have been trying. For there is always in a marriage that sense of allegiance to a parent that needs to alter as the couple's attachment to each other strengthens.

On Saturday, March 27, Cora received three letters: Abbie Evans, Vincent's girlhood friend from Camden, invited her to Philadelphia for Easter; Kathleen's first novel, *The Wayfarer,* had been accepted for publication and would be out in the fall; and Kathleen's husband, Howard Young, had written to tell her that Norma had been fired from his play *Not Herbert.*

That night, after a dinner that she had prepared for their friends, the talk drifted into a religious discussion. "Ugin and I got into an unpleasant wrangle," Cora wrote in her diary,

> which closed with his going to bed angry with me, and I with him. I had a talk with Vincent. She thinks I am all tired out, and of course I am. I am lighter in weight than I ever was since I was a child, I do not weigh as much as Vincent does—only 99 dressed—and she thinks I must accept Abbie's invitation and go and have a change, and come back for a little visit before I go to Maine this spring.

The next day was no better: "Unpleasant here today, Vincent did not come down to dinner, and Ugin had a rather stilted time of it, but he talked about my trip, insisting that I take it." In less than a week, she was in New York.

———

In New Mexico, Arthur Ficke was becoming a proficient amateur photographer. He was especially fond of nude shots. It was to one of these photographs that Eugen referred in his letter of March 20:

> We just received that beautiful picture Artie sent us. It is beautiful. No bloody amateur ever made, developed and printed that. . . . I'm going to send you these films I took of Edna: that is I will send them to you as soon as I find them. I put them away in a safe place where nobody could get them, but at the time I remember I did hope that I would be able to get them. I'm still looking for them and as soon as I catch them or trap them I will shoot them to you. In the mean time I'm sending you some films which we took the other day. . . . I'm sorry to say that there are hardly any of Edna, but she did not feel like being taken, and you know what girls are.

Edna, he said, was getting stronger,

> but is as sick as ever, if you know what I mean. Did I tell you that we are getting a chiropractor here three times a week? I got him some snow-shoes, and taught him how to use them, and now he struggles here three times a week. He has not done any harm so far. We are going to try him another month, and if he does not make her worse we are going to give him the snow-shoes.

When Arthur continued to send his nude photographs, some of Gladys, Eugen assured him that they were safe at Steepletop. His own regret was that he couldn't

> take any pictures of poor little suffering Vincent, with her head in her hands. Besides, we have been handicapped by not being alone at Steepletop, but having mother Millay with us all that time. I want to take them awfully badly. But it is difficult to be naked and abandoned with parents in the offing.

At last the opera was finished, except for revisions, and Eugen and Edna fled to Maine, to Cora's cottage, for the month of August. But Edna's condition persisted. After her stint with their snowshoeing chiropractor, Eugen wrote Arthur:

> Vincie went on strict diet of linseed and two enemas a day. This lasted also for two months. We are now . . . motoring to Augusta, Maine, State hospital three times a week, over 120 miles of the most God forsaken roads that ever were conceived by the brain of man . . . for Xraying and Ultra violet

raying of the back, front and toncils. Her head-aches are the same and her eyes are the same, and Abie's Irish Rose is still running.

"Dear, dear," Arthur wrote his "Darling Kids,"

I wonder why our darling Vincie is having so frightfully prolonged a siege of eyes and head and everything! You will think I am crazy—but are you sure the trouble isn't something with the mind rather than the body? Are you sure that psychoanalysis could do nothing for you? Maybe I'm wrong: I just wondered.

There is no record of any response to his suggestion.

Three weeks later Arthur wired "Eugene Millay":

. . . COME AND SEE YOUR LITTLE FRIENDS FOR A FEW WEEKS FREE BOARD AND RAILROAD FARE AND NATIVE BREW AND ARGUMENTS.

ARTHUR BROWN

Although Vincent had never been in the Southwest, her first order of business on arrival in Santa Fe was to ready the manuscript of *The King's Henchman* (which was slightly different from the libretto) for Harper & Brothers. "It has been a terrible job, but it's done now," she wrote in December 1926. "All that's left to do is a few odd jobs such as writing a synopsis for the front of the printed libretto, & correcting proof . . . dirty chores, but nothing more." Then she was free to explore. Arthur was too ill to go with them, but Gladys was game. They took packhorses into the Grand Canyon, camping on the outer rim, and hired a boxy Ford to motor to the Petrified Forest and the Painted Desert; later they went to an Indian dance ceremony in Zuni.

"If we have good luck we shall have some corking photographs to show you when we get back," she wrote Cora. They would also have some extraordinary photographs that they did not intend to show anyone, least of all Cora. The nude shots were not lascivious; among them were some of the loveliest photographs ever taken of Edna. In one, she is standing just inside the doorway of Arthur's adobe house, wearing only prettily beaded slippers. Her hair is falling forward, and she is lifting a cocktail to her lips. Two others have a hilarious air: In the first, she is sitting with Arthur, reading at a small table and wearing a dark frock with white collar and cuffs. In the next, they keep precisely the same posture and expressions while reading, except this time they are both completely naked.

Once they returned to Steepletop, however, the climate for taking photographs changed drastically, and Eugen wrote Arthur in a panic. Eugen's nephew, who had been minding the house in their absence, had forced the lock on Vincent's dressing table, inside of which was

> a box containing all the photos of Gladdie.
>
> Will you please destroy at once all the films containing Vincent. Also all your prints excepting 3 or 4 which you really consider artistic master-pieces. Otherwise we are going crazy. We suspect you of being a filmo-phile.
>
> We are very happy that you have taken up wood-carving. . . . Please don't send any more in letters. Often we get our mail on the way to Chatham and leave it in the car when we go shopping. Those photos become a constant care to us. We understand that you are long since beyond good and evil. You are "Der reine Thor" and cannot understand our earthbound anxieties! Nevertheless we beseech you to do as we request and write us swearing that you have done so.

3

The opening of *The King's Henchman* was set for February 17. "You will have to be in New York for that, darling," Vincent wrote her mother. "It will be a great night.—Gene & I shall be staying with Florence.* . . . You'd better write & ask Normie if they can put you up.—There will be at least four performances, the 17th, the 28th, & two later.—But of course you'll want to be there for the premiere." At the end of her letter she made one thing clear:

> I shan't be able to give anybody free passes to *The Henchman,* of course.— I'll be lucky if I get one for myself. But you're rich, you've got lots of money, & in February you'll have lots more; you can buy yourself a seat.— (Poor old sing, everybody 'fusin' her, & makin' jokes an' everythin')— Florence wanted to get a box & have Gene & me & one or two others, but we refused flat—We are going off & sit some place all by ourselves—unless for some reason it seems better to be with Deems & Mary.—You go with Kay & Howard, or Norma & Charlie—see?—You write & ask 'em about it now. I'll make you a present of the ticket, if they'll take care of you, tell 'em.
>
> Lots of love, mummie. If anybody's being mean to you, you tell me. (This is just a joke. I'm not hitting at anybody.)
>
> Vincent

---

*Mrs. Florence Mixter was a friend of Arthur Ficke's and a very wealthy woman. It was to her place in the Adirondacks that Arthur had arranged an invitation for Vincent in the summer of 1920.

Only Kathleen didn't find much humor in any of this. "Mother Darling—" she wrote,

> Here's the check for thirty five from Howard and me—I telephoned Norma today, as she had never spoken of the letter I sent a month ago when I also wrote Edna about the first of the month idea—and she said she had sent twenty five before that when you wrote her.—So I take it they paid no attention to the first of the month or any other time during the month simply because they had sent twenty five in December sometime.

It wasn't fair, Kathleen said, because Charlie and Norma were "both earning good money now—there is no reason for them not doing it." Was this friction only about money, or was it cloaking more complex differences surfacing among the sisters?

> As for the ticket, dear, Norma intends to go to the opening of Edna's opera and so I am sending Edna's check to her—for Howard and I are having to watch our step very closely now— . . . so we may not go to the opening when prices are high, but wait for the next performance—or we may go top balcony—where you wouldn't want to be.

Edna was desperate for news about the opera. "The first rehearsal must have been yesterday," she wrote Deems. "I don't suppose you were present—yes?—no?—If you were, & don't dish me the dirt, I'll be mad at you."

On Thursday evening, February 17, 1927, at eight o'clock, the heavy golden silk curtain swayed and then rose on the first act of *The King's Henchman* at the Metropolitan Opera House. The throb of a harp played the song of the harper she had written in January the year before:

> . . . Wild as the white waves
> Rushing and roaring, Heaving the wrack
> High up the headland; Hoarse as the howling
> Winds of the winter, When the lean wolves
> Harry the hindmost, horseman and horse,
> Toppled and tumbled. . . .

The story, set in tenth-century England, was based on a tale from the *Anglo-Saxon Chronicle*. It was, in fact, very like *The Lamp and the Bell*, except that this time the bond was between two men and not between stepsisters. The king, who is a widower, has sent his dearest friend and foster brother,

Aethelwold, in his stead to meet the lovely Aelfrida, whom he wishes to make his queen, provided she is as beautiful as word has it. Aethelwold, who has never been in love, says he is unfit to make such a judgment. In the first act the two men pledge their troth of friendship in an ancient Saxon rite with wine "In the cup of the Romsey nuns." And together they sing their song pledging friendship until death:

> 'Twix thee and the singing arrow with the darkened fang,
> I stand with open breast!
> Life, that is stronger than I, is not so strong
> As thou and I!
> Death, that is stronger than I, is not so strong
> As thou and I!
> Unquelled, thou and I,
> Till life and death be friends!

Aethelwold would, of course, lie and betray his king, become Aelfrida's lover, and die in the end.

The New York *Evening Post* ran a feature in the next day's issue: "Edna and Deems Call It a Night, Countless Curtains for Little Lady and All the Glory of a Metropolitan Premiere." The house was completely sold out. Spectators packed the standing room five and six feet deep along the sides and back of the house. There were seventeen curtain calls and applause lasting twenty minutes.

"Our two years' sentence is up!" cried Miss Millay to Eugene Boissevain. . . . "No one sleeps tonight. It is our New Year's," she caroled with a child's exuberance.

Miss Millay may, as she said, have felt as if she were stepping on clouds when she took her curtain calls, but to be cruelly accurate, she actually spent most of her time stepping on her train.

It was a long train, an unruly train, a train which insisted upon getting between her two little red slippers and making its owner look more like a schoolgirl than ever. But the smile never faded. It was too well earned. It lingered and grew and the little woman with the tawny bob scampered back and forth.

Gladys had come east for the opening night, and everybody was there, "My Darling," she wrote Arthur the next morning,

Tess and the Warburgs and Rebecca West.
I almost cried because you were not there. It *was* exciting! . . . Vincent and Deems appeared at the end of each act and came again and again for

prolonged applause. Vincent had a marvelous dress of red and gold but she was quite fussed and acted rather baby-girlish on the whole. But at the end of the third act people began calling for a speech and finally Vincent and Deems came forward and Deems looked at Vincent helplessly and Vincent at him. Then she spread out her hands, made a little duck of her head, and said, "All I can say is—that I love you all." Giggles and applause—then Deems—"I—I was just going to say the same thing"— laughter and applause.

There was only one hitch: that afternoon, Florence Mixter, in whose apartment Vincent and Eugen were staying, came to Gladys Ficke in a huff. She had opened the box of photographs Gladys had left with her two days earlier; inside were nude photographs of both couples. Mrs. Mixter was outraged. She thought the photos scandalous.

Gladys tried to explain to Arthur what had happened. She'd left the photographs at Florence's because carrying them around New York was risky, and she'd told Florence to give them to Edna and Eugen. Instead, Florence had looked at the photographs, ignoring the personal note from Arthur which he had put on top. "Apparently she spent two days of orgie—did not give the films to the Kids—said nothing to them and came to roast me."

When Edna and Eugen discovered what had happened, they went to Kathleen's and burned the films. Millay's response to Mrs. Mixter was icy, contemptuous, and confrontational. "Why didn't you lock it up?" she demanded to know. "It was not necessary for you to look at it! . . . When you saw the note from Arthur, why didn't you stop? And when you saw the first film why didn't you stop?" Mrs. Mixter was silenced.

Arthur gave the whole episode quite another meaning. Florence had been attracted by the pictures and felt it was wicked, he suggested, for "she was slightly in love with all four of us."

CHAPTER 23

Edmund Wilson saw Millay the weekend after the opening in New York at what he called "Our formal dinner across a too-wide table drinking Boissevain's whiskey and sauterne." He scrutinized her carefully and ungenerously, as if to make up for what he later called his adoration. "I saw her wince and the collapse for a moment of her manner: nervous, trembling, worried and dismayed—" She didn't know the new slang, and he did. She'd never heard of Hart Crane, and Wilson had. Suddenly she said to him, "I'm not a pathetic figure—I'm not!"

"Whoever said you were?" he shot back. Then he softened. "She was all burning and lit up when I came in, quite different from her paleness and brittleness when I had seen her in bed the winter before, and she put her arms around me and kissed me, leaving Boissevain behind in the bedroom, and it was I who was too stiff and unresponsive."

In the pages of *The New Republic,* Edmund Wilson continued to champion her work. "When one looks back on the American poetry of the season," he wrote in the May 11, 1927, issue, "one is aware of only two events which emerge as of the first interest: 'The King's Henchman,' by Miss Millay, and 'White Buildings,' by Mr. Hart Crane."

The King's Henchman was reviewed by Elinor Wylie on the front page of the New York *Herald Tribune*'s Sunday book section. She began by quoting Thomas Hardy's singular comment: "There were two great things in the United States: the poetry of Edna St. Vincent Millay and our 'recessional buildings' " (by which he meant skyscrapers). Wylie added that "when she and this generation are gone, the die which stamped her style will be broken." Her only hesitation had been that Millay might be more comfortable as "an Elizabethan or a Greek than a Saxon of the tenth century." That doubt vanished in the second act. When Wylie "beheld Aethelwold and Aelfrida caught in the invisible nets of love, I saw that I had been an idiot not to trust this girl Edna Millay, even into the mists of the tenth century."

On the eve of the opening, *The New Yorker,* founded in 1925, ran a profile called "Vincent." It was among its first profiles and was written by Griffin Barry. "Vincent" was Barry's first and last contribution to the magazine. In the words of Katharine White, who was then Mrs. Angell, who had helped Harold Ross found the magazine, the piece was "very meager, poor, and inaccurate. . . . Ross had not set up his demon checking department." She guessed that it was Ross's experience with this profile that decided him to set up *The New Yorker*'s legendary fact-checking department.

"In those early days we all did everything," she recalled, "and one day soon after the publication of the Profile, Mrs. Cora Millay . . . came storming into the office threatening a lawsuit." Ross told her to mollify Mrs. Millay, which was no easy matter. "I talked with her for a long time and finally pacified her by asking her to write a letter that we would run under our heading 'We Stand Corrected.' " Cora's chief complaint was in the very first paragraph:

Edna Millay's father was a stevedore on the wharves at Rockland, Maine. So was his father. Before him, certain Millays owned houses and lands— but that was long ago. Her mother appears to remember little of her own biography, but it is known that as a girl she migrated from Maine to Boston to sing in the chorus of the Castle Square Opera Company.

Barry's description of Vincent's days at Vassar was a combination of perceptiveness laced with bile: "A knowing and rather disagreeable childishness crept in." He continued, "Edna's own resemblance to an eerie child was liked at Vassar; a critic might say that she wrote poems to that." He told about her nearly losing her degree; he had her in "male disguise . . . though that is perhaps only myth," which was, of course, a way to both put it into print and disclaim it at the same time. He said that while she maintained a brave front, "it was known that in private she drooped. Social approval, high and low, then as now, was very necessary to this poor young poet from a Maine small town." He had her saved by a wealthy, "motherly" patroness, whose "keep of the poet would be met—delicately, regularly."

When Barry got to describing Paris in 1921, which was when he knew her best (and also when she left him for George Slocombe), he made two telling observations about her poetry and how she had become the voice of her generation:

> They celebrate the loves of footloose youth—of footloose girls, not men. This verse is too passionate to be called light poetry, but there is a curious omission in it, for there is no poem of abandonment to love. The only genuine surrender is to death. . . . It is the only intensity available after a love that has burned on nothing but itself—only a metaphor, perhaps, that the poet uses for goodbye.

The generation that had just gone to war, he continued, "had seen nothing so accurate about itself in print." Flaming youth "was still unnamed— spanked, if possible, deplored, unsung. The jazz age was unknown. Fitzgerald had yet to write his descriptions of moneyed, jigging youth" when "sonnets by a girl in Greenwich Village . . . began to be widely known." Barry described tables full of Americans in Paris who knew her poems by heart, but when he wrote about Millay's increasing fame, his anger stained his prose:

> Luckily, Edna Millay likes almost anybody's parties. Among people she is confiding or detached, according to her mood, and she does not demand attention. Usually she knows how to rule a situation or a group, if she wants to. If luck is against her and she loses control of the social steering-

gear, she can turn her attention swiftly to the weather or the Einstein theory or you—and have a good time anyway. Mostly she drifts and watches. She has been known to tremble when she meets a person whose literary reputation exceeds her own.

Cora's letter of detailed corrections to the editors of *The New Yorker* was published on April 23, 1927. By then, Vincent had written to her: "About that stevedore—forget it.—A stevedore is . . . almost as important to a ship as its captain. . . . Forget it, darling. It was meant for an insult.—But it isn't. And forget the s.o.b. that said it.—V."

With the triumph of *The King's Henchman* behind her, Millay returned to Steepletop to rest, "everybody worn out and dead for a little sleep," she wrote in the new diary Lawrence Tibbett, the leading tenor of the Metropolitan, had given her on the eve of *Henchman*'s opening. "Mrs. Tibbett told Ugin that everybody has told her he is known as 'the sheik of New York.' He is pleased as anything"—pleased, too, that Edna had dedicated *Henchman* to him.

The first night back, March 1, they went to bed at nine; the next night "8 o'clock, and I am already in bed." And she, who had rarely kept a diary with any constancy, was now writing every day because "I feel a little lonely at moments for the Metropolitan—the little crowded back-entrance and the enormous dark house—and the singers in their street clothes, all so simple and friendly and sweet. I miss the Henchman and so does Ugin."

They'd been back only five days when Eugen suggested they go down to New York to hear it again.

> Today on the front page of the *World* we came upon "$100 a Day for Poet of King's Henchman" and an article telling how my book has already sold 10,000 copies. Sometimes I get a kick out of things like that—oftener I don't. But this time I did. I was thrilled to death. That the amount of royalties I get for a book of poems should be of front page interest to the great New York public—well, I just sat for ten minutes with my eyes sticking out, drinking it in.—Oh, what a thrilling winter this has been! Ugin and I—what fun we've had!—how happy we are!

On the bestseller lists in New York at Brentano's and Macy's, *Henchman* was second on the nonfiction list, while Ernest Hemingway's first novel, *The Sun Also Rises,* was fourth on the fiction list.

On March 8, the New York *Evening Post* ran a column headed " 'Henchman' Leaps to Fourth Edition" with 10,500 copies in print within twenty days of publication. "Now nobody wants to intrude in Edna's private affairs . . . but still it's evident that Miss Millay's royalties in twenty days amount to $1,056.33 and possibly more if she gets more than the customary 10 per cent on a $2 book."

They went on to speculate that she had, therefore, been earning $50 a day, or about $2 an hour, since February 17, when the libretto had gone on sale. Her autographed editions were inciting "riots in the larger book stores," and the $25 Japan vellum edition was being scalped for $125. Another edition on handmade paper was impossible to buy anywhere, for any price. Her clipping service noted that even a first edition of *Renascence* was selling for $60.

Elinor Wylie wired them that she was coming for a visit. Edna and Eugen were so delighted that they raced around trying "to get things in shape before Elinor got here & got so nervous & tired—but we did save just enough time to get a bath & dress. I dumped a lot of the bath-salts Gene got in Chatham into my bath, & it left a mauve line around the tub, & the whole place smelled like a whore-house."

Edna had known Elinor since 1921, when Edna had highly praised *Nets to Catch the Wind,* but their friendship quickened after *Henchman.* Elinor and her husband arrived at Steepletop on April 2. "It is too wonderful to have them here—dear Bill [William Rose Benét]—my beautiful Elinor! . . . Elinor & I had a lovely row about Shelley—a long lovely gentle jeering row."

The next day, both couples spent their time together walking the fields and reading. On April 4, after Bill returned to the city, Edna wrote, "I lay on the couch before the living-room fire & Elinor read me from Browning things we both used to love & half know by heart—*Love Among the Ruins*—& *The Spanish Cloister,* and other things—such fun." That night their hired man got drunk and their housekeeper went home with him to make sure he didn't harm anything, so Eugen cooked dinner.

> Tonight Elinor told Gene & me from beginning to end the story of her strange & wonderful life up to the present moment, a most engrossing tale, full of tragedy.—She is the most lovely creature. Gene is crazy about her. If he weren't, I'd be furious.
>
> April 5
>   Ugin brought up breakfast to Elinor & me in my bed & made a lovely fire in my fireplace. Elinor, Gene & I drove down to Austerlitz in a snowstorm, Gene on the seat & Elinor & I tucked in on the floor, facing back—went to Columbia Inn & drank muscatel & read mail. Elinor loved it.—In the evening we discussed the relative weight of *St. Agnes' Eve* or

Epipsychidion—not as poems—but as love-poems, Elinor holding that the last twenty lines or so of it are highly sensuous & impassioned, I insisting that, except for a phrase or two, they are so much rhetorical hot air.—Later she read aloud to me from Shelley—the lovely little "If thou coulds't be as thou hast been" one, & "Less oft is peace in Shelley's mind" & "Listening to my sweet piping." Finally she read the *West Wind.* "The Best Poem Ever Written!" she cried when she finished. I did not dispute her. I do not think naturally in terms of best–next-best. I think I love the *Grecian Urn* better. But I am not sure.

This morning Elinor read to herself from *Mortal Image,* while I played first Chopin, then Bach, then Beethoven on the piano. I play so badly. But not too badly, I think, to be allowed to play them.

It sounded like a romantic idyll, these two poets together, each with her red hair, Elinor's the color of dark copper, Edna's of flame, Elinor tall and so slender that Edmund Wilson called her "skeletally thin." Her skin was so white, Edna teased her, it looked as if she lived underwater.

On April 7, the morning Elinor was to leave, they got into an argument over Kathleen's novel, *The Wayfarer,* which had been published the year before. Elinor didn't like it. Edna suggested she read the second part again—and this time she relented. "I gave it to her & made her sit down & read the part about Mother's life on the Maine farm, which is so beautifully treated. 'Why, this is lovely!' she said after a little while. 'I never read this.' "

It comes as a surprise to learn that Vincent admired her sister's novel enough to insist that Elinor read it, because there had been no mention of Kathleen's work in any of the correspondence among the Millays since 1926, when *The Wayfarer* had first been published. The only indication that Kathleen was writing and publishing came in a letter Vincent wrote to Cora on May 25, two months after the opening of *The King's Henchman.* Her letter is sharp and incisive. It's also about a different book, *The Evergreen Tree,* a book of poems published by Boni & Liveright that fall. In other words, Kathleen had now directly entered Vincent's domain. Vincent told her mother, who must have been prompting her to respond on Kathleen's behalf:

I wrote Kathleen ages ago about her book. I told you I would, & I did. And that's that.

Now will you please stop worrying.

Kathleen is about to publish a book, as thousands have done before her. A person who publishes a book wilfully appears before the populace with his pants down. And there's nothing you can do about that.

Kathleen is not a baby. She is a grown-up person quite able to take care of herself. And she has been struggling for years to be allowed to manage her own affairs. If she knew the kind of letter you wrote me in her behalf, she'd froth at the mouth & spit brimstone.

But she didn't stop there.

Kathleen is about to publish a book. If it's a good book, nothing can harm her. If it's a bad book, nothing can help her. And all your stewing & fretting will accomplish just one end: it will make you very sick & a nuisance to yourself, and a care to everybody,—so will you please forget it, & relax, & interest yourself in something else? If you don't, you're not the intelligent woman you have the reputation of being; you are just one more typical, sentimental, agitated *mother!*

Won't you please R E L A X?

Kathleen is not a baby. She is six years older than I was when my first book of poems was published. . . . I ask you to S N A P O U T OF IT and stop making yourself sick for nothing! Pull yourself together, & go to Maine, & start your garden. And I'll send you lots of plants, & help you all I can, with advice, & my own experience, & seeds, & money, & any darned thing you want. If you'll only be good, & STOP WORRYING!!!

> With a hell of a lot of love,
> Vincent

The slim black volume of Kathleen's verse looked, in terms of its design, very like Vincent Millay's, except that the stamping was in silver rather than gold. The poems were too close to Vincent's for comfort. One, "Blight," even had the same title. They are oddly self-pitying, a little lame and sorrowful.

IMMIGRANT

Nothing in this house is of my making,
No one in this place is kin to me;
They know me not in sleeping or in waking,
I am alone in this great company.

I want a fire that will be mine for raking,
I want a room that will know me for its own,
I want a love that will be mine for taking,
Strangeness and I have lived too long alone.

Or "The Spinner's Song":

> No time, no time, to sing my songs,
> But time to spin my spinning!
> No way, no way, to right the wrongs,
> But ways enough for sinning.
>
> No laugh to take, no laugh to give,
> But tears and tears for crying;
> No living worth the death to live,
> But life enough for dying.

2

In March, the League of American Penwomen had asked Elinor Wylie to be one of its guests of honor at an authors' breakfast in Washington, D.C. Elinor, who had left her first husband and their child to run off with Horace Wylie, a married man, had never been forgiven for her indiscretion. Her husband eventually became insane, her son committed suicide, and Mrs. Wylie would not give Mr. Wylie a divorce until much later. It had been a disastrous series of scandals and catastrophes. Now, thinking at last she'd been forgiven, she agreed to be honored. Then she received a second letter. "Washington is still provincial enough to object to you! I might as well tell you the truth," the hostess for the breakfast explained. "Do not think that either Mrs. Seton or I were in ignorance in our invitation . . . but we thought it of no consequence to anybody, anymore than it would be with a man." But it was. Wylie's invitation was abruptly canceled. "I wrote a letter to the League of American Penwomen, telling them where to get off," Vincent wrote in her diary. "I wish I had been a Fifth Avenue street sparrow yesterday—or in other words:

> I wish to God I might have shat
> On Mrs. Grundy's Easter hat.

Her letter was controlled, principled fury; she dropped a copy of it to Elinor in that day's mail: "My darling: . . . Please read the letter, then post it at once.—Be a good girl, & do as I tell you, & post it at once."

For Edna, too, had been invited to be the League's guest of honor, and while she had told it she regretted not being able to attend, she was "sensible to the honour you did me, and that I hoped you would invite me again." Now, however, she wrote, each word like a sting, "It is not in the power of an organization which has insulted Elinor Wylie, to honour me." How could she be a guest at a gathering of writers where honour is tendered not so much for the excellence of one's literary accomplishment as for the circumspection of one's personal life.

Believe me, if the eminent object of your pusillanimous attack has not directed her movements in conformity with your timid philosophies, no more have I mine. I too am eligible for your disesteem. Strike me too from your lists, and permit me, I beg you, to share with Elinor Wylie a brilliant exile from your fusty province.

One can almost feel the heat from the sparks flying from her pen. Elinor was delighted:

My darling—
A thousand thanks for your beautiful & noble defense. If Grattan had collaborated with Keats or Shelley they could not have contrived such eloquence. . . .

Your
Elinor

I have written you a ballad—*to you*—which perhaps you'll like. Hope so, at least.

Millay's fury was aroused not only in defense of friends but by social and political injustice. Throughout her life, as early as "Renascence," when it seems naive, to *Aria da Capo,* written in the aftermath of World War I, when it does not, Millay wrote against the folly of men engaged in the deadly game of what she called "feverish ambition" who would kill for colored glass, as they did in *Aria da Capo.*

In the spring of 1920, two Italian immigrants, Nicola Sacco, a shoemaker, and Bartolomeo Vanzetti, a fish peddler, were accused of taking part in the holdup and murder of a shoe factory paymaster and a payroll guard in South Braintree, Massachusetts. Sacco and Vanzetti were anarchists. When their judge, Webster Thayer, was overheard to say, "Did you see what I did with those anarchistic bastards the other day?" there was good reason to believe there would be a miscarriage of justice. Judge Thayer was determined from the start to secure a conviction.

What had been an obscure case—they were tried, found guilty, and, after many appeals, sentenced to death in April 1927—had during those seven years enflamed the conscience of America. For under Massachusetts law then, it was the same trial judge who ruled on the appeals from his own verdicts. Edna Millay joined the picket line before the State House in Boston demonstrating for their reprieve—along with Katherine Anne Porter, John Dos Passos, Dorothy Parker, Michael Gold, and hundreds of others, walking with placards in the hot August sun. Photographed holding her poster aloft, her jaw set in dissent, Millay was taken to the police station, where she was formally charged with "sauntering and loitering" and was bailed out by Eugen, who'd come to Boston with her to put up bail for many of their friends.

On August 22, 1927, the afternoon before the execution, Millay was able to schedule an interview with Governor Alvan T. Fuller. She hoped to persuade him to order a stay of execution. She based her appeal in part on a case in Maine, about which Cora had supplied her with the information. A man had been hanged for a crime it was later discovered he had not committed. Later that afternoon she wrote the governor:

> I suggested that, for all your careful weighing of the evidence, for all your courage in the face of threats and violent words, for all your honest conviction that these men are guilty, you, no less than the governor of Maine in my story, who was so tragically mistaken, are but human flesh and spirit, and that it is human to err. . . . You promised me, and I believed you truly, that you would think of what I said. I exact of you this promise now. . . . I cry to you with a million voices: answer our doubt. Exert the clemency which your high office affords.
>
> There is need in Massachusetts of a great man tonight. It is not yet too late for you to be that man.
>
> Edna St. Vincent Millay

For all her persuasive eloquence, Fuller, a self-made millionaire who thought a pair of immigrant anarchists would destroy the very foundations of American civilization, did not believe in clemency for these two men. He did not order a stay of execution, and they were electrocuted just past midnight on August 23, 1927. The outrage of their execution was denounced throughout the world.

Once again, Millay, who just a few months before had been called "the young sovereign of the written word," made use of her poetry to express political outrage. "Justice Denied in Massachusetts" was published on August 22, 1927, in the afternoon edition of the New York *World*:

> Let us abandon then our gardens and go home
> And sit in the sitting-room.
> Shall the larkspur blossom or the corn grow under this cloud?
> Sour to the fruitful seed
> Is the cold earth under this cloud,
> Fostering quack and weed, we have marched upon but cannot
>   conquer;
> We have bent the blades of our hoes against the stalks of them.

Let us go home, and sit in the sitting room.
Not in our day
Shall the cloud go over and the sun rise as before. . . .
Forlorn, forlorn
Stands the blue hay-rack by the empty mow. . . .
We shall die in darkness, and be buried in the rain. . . .

Evil does overwhelm
The larkspur and the corn;
We have seen them go under.

When Kathleen came to write her next collection of poetry, *The Hermit Thrush,* she devoted an entire section to Sacco and Vanzetti. "The Last Thanksgiving/Massachusetts 1927" closed the group:

. . .
And know that we have done our best
To still a Jealous God,
And paid Him well for roasted fowl
And fish upon the rod;
For did we not, a threemonths past, put souls beneath the sod—
Burn two live men and bury them
Deep down within their grave,
Because they would not thank the Lord for what He never gave?

Edna, who had been arrested in August, was one of six demonstrators who refused to pay the minimal fine in order to make a test case. Each pleaded not guilty, claiming they were exercising their lawful right of peaceful assembly. That November they were requested to appear in Boston for a trial. It was, ironically, at the same time as *The King's Henchman* was playing there. Edna wrote her mother from Boston:

I don't imagine anybody will go to jail.—It would have been marvelous publicity (not for *me!*—I mean for the Sacco Vanzetti defense people). . . .
You have been a brick through this, Mother—just as you have been through other hard things I have put you through. Don't think I forget anything of your loveliness to me, ever.

So much love to you, my darling,
Vincent.

But her letter had a troubling postscript. It was about the little cottage Kathleen and her husband, Howard, had bought for their mother in

Maine, and while it seemed to be about money, it was really about who was the more generous child.

November 16 . . .

P.P.S. Aren't you protecting Kay's feelings somewhat at my expense? It was no secret that they bought the cottage for you. Why should it be a secret that I am paying for repairs on it? I don't care a bit, dear, but it seems to me the wrong way of looking at it.

In a very few summers like this one I shall have paid out as much for the cottage & its extras as Kay & Howard paid for the cottage itself, & yet all so piecemeal & unromantically that it will never show to the eye at all. I would never write like this, mother, if we didn't understand each other so well, & if you didn't know how constitutionally incapable I am of feeling any jealousy in such matters or of wishing to publish to the world the trivial little things I do for you who have done everything for me. But I think that Kay should be glad, if the posts of the cottage were unsafe, that one of us three girls has been able to have new ones put under it, and I don't see why it should matter to her very much that I happened to be the one. Do just as you feel about it, however, Mumbles. But it seems to me that these little secrecies and evasions tend to make the atmosphere among us strained and unreal.

PART SIX

LOVE AND DEATH

CHAPTER 24

Millay's letters to her mother dwindled throughout 1928—eight lines at the turn of the year asking Cora to come for a visit, nine lines written in March: "Sefe terribly busy—writing poetries—so not writing letters—even to Mumbles—Please forgive." Cora, meanwhile, was busily writing her own collection of verses, which she called *Little Otis*. Poetry was becoming a family vocation.

Cora had begun to give poetry readings after Vincent's Pulitzer. Her style of performance, which a Maine paper described as "such a naive way of reading . . . that her audience is convulsed with laughter," was clearly modeled on Vincent's. But Cora hadn't published her poems. Now, with Kathleen's help (as well as that of her publisher, W. W. Norton), she was about to. Vincent seemed to pay very little attention to her mother's poems, maybe because she was anxious about her own writing. When she entered this note in her diary on March 31, she made the point clearly:

I seem to be driven by some force accumulated during these years when I have written no poems at all. . . . Stayed in bed as usual and worked until noon. Wrote an entire sonnet beginning "Life, were thy pains as are the pains of hell"; and the octave of a sonnet beginning "Be sure my coming was a sharp offense and trouble to my mother in her bed."

—I have never worked so furiously fast before.

What she never acknowledged was that she may have felt competitive. By July, when Vincent would again ask her mother to forgive her for not writing to her: "awfully busy—We loved Little Otis—& aren't the illustrations adorable?"—there were *three* Millay women publishing poetry. Only Norma held her tongue.

The spring turned out to be false, and although the roads were dangerously icy with frozen sleet, houseguests began to arrive on the evening train from New York: Elaine Ralli, who had gone to medical school after Vassar and had remained in touch with Vincent, came with Isabel Simpson, who was also a friend from Vassar, bringing caviar, marrons glacés, candied ginger, and cognac. Margot Schuyler and Eleanor Delamater brought roses to set out; and in the evening they all dressed up in fancy dress.

> Eleanor went as the Black Pirate; Margot as a Chinese girl in my green brocade Chinese trousers and coat and arbutus stuck over her ears, looked charming; Gene as the Maharajah of Dyokyakarta, in a batik shirt, that is to say, a sarong and a little batik tied about his head and an impeccable dinner shirt and pearl studs and black tie, and white mess jacket; I as a general houri, in an Albanian under-dress, a Turkish burnous, a headdress from Benares and a pair of slippers from Agra and a brass girdle from Paris.—We sat around the fire and told stories just like the Decameron, thrilling stories and everybody got very thrillingly intoxicated. We did not go to bed until nearly daybreak.

Edna and Eugen were as easy and playful with women who had been her lovers as they were with Elinor Wylie and Bill Benét, who arrived with Floyd Dell. It was one of the fine qualities of their starry bohemia.

"We talked before the living-room fire until Gene and I got sleepy, and said it was bedtime, whereupon a great groan went up from the more urban and nocturnal among us. We left Elinor and Floyd downstairs to make a night of it, but they didn't stay long." In the morning Elinor read Edna's new poems and told her, Edna entered proudly in her diary, that it "may be my best book." Then she said something "that hurt Elinor's feelings, but she forgave me. I didn't mean to hurt her, and I felt dreadful." Millay promised to write a poem to salve her distress, but she couldn't manage to shape the poem quite the way she wanted it. She would hold on to that poem for eleven years before publishing it in a group of poems dedicated to Elinor Wylie after her death.

Song for a Lute

Seeing how I love you utterly,
And your disdain is my despair,
Alter this dulcet eye, forbear
To wear those looks that latterly
You wore, and won me wholly, wear
A brow more dark, and bitterly
Berate my dulness and my care,
Seeing how your smile is my despair,
Seeing how I love you utterly.

Seeing how I love you utterly,
And your distress is my despair,
Alter this brimming eye, nor wear
The trembling lip that latterly
Under a more auspicious air
You wore, and thrust me through, forbear
To drop your head so bitterly
Into your hands, seeing how I dare
No tender touch upon your hair,
Knowing as I do how fitterly
You do reproach me than forbear,
Seeing how your tears are my despair,
Seeing how I love you utterly.

(1927)

In her diary, when Eugen wrote he'd put Floyd and Elinor on the train at Hudson, Vincent would later add, "I never saw her again."

There was one last exchange of letters between them. Elinor had asked Vincent to send her "your two poems about me" that spring before she left for England. Millay had not responded, except to send her a fresh bouquet from Steepletop for her voyage. Then, on September 19, 1928, she wrote:

My darling Elinor:

I have just read in the *Saturday Review* of your dreadful accident.—There was a silly story in the papers early in the summer—I didn't see it, but someone mentioned it—that you had tried to kill yourself, or some such rot; naturally I paid no more attention to that than I pay to the annual drivel of myself & Gene.—Now it seems that you really did fall & were frightfully hurt.—I can't tell you how I feel, to realize that you have been ill & in pain for months, & I haven't written you a word.—I should have answered your letter long ago, except that you asked for those two poems about you, & I wanted to finish them before I wrote again. I worked over them, particularly the one beginning, "Seeing how I love you utterly," for ages, but have not yet been able to finish them to my satisfaction. Which means that they won't be included in *The Buck in the Snow*.—But here are the lines about you in the other poem:

> Yet look to her that enters now,—
> A silver maiden leading a silver faun;
> Her eyes are fixed on you with bright intent
> Behold her, how she shines!—
> Her brow is lit with all the jewels of the mines,
> Her legs are lashed with the chilly grasses of the dawn.

. . . My dear, I am so grieved to think of what happened to you this summer.—I can see you coming down the stairs with your beautiful near-sighted eyes—for whose sake long ago I made Myopia a goddess.

2

In September 1928, *The Buck in the Snow,* Millay's first book of poetry since *Harp-Weaver,* was published. On her reading tour in Chicago, she was introduced by a young poet, George Dillon. His first book of poems, *Boy in the Wind,* had been published the year before, when he was twenty-one and an undergraduate at the University of Chicago. Now the associate editor of *Poetry* magazine, he was tall and slim, with black wavy hair carefully brushed back from his face; he looked like a modern Apollo whose glossy curls had been cut short to tame them. He was young enough, fourteen years younger than Millay, to be scared stiff at the prospect of his introduction. His voice was soft, with a slight southern drawl. He was courtly, even a little formal, as he bent down to introduce himself to her before her reading. "I'm George Dillon," he said. He remembered that she took his hand as if she were falling into him.

Later that evening, at a party in her honor, Dillon was asked to recite his poems. When someone asked Millay if she didn't think his poems were good for one so young, she said, "They're wonderful for anyone!" Then she slipped him a note inviting him to lunch the next day.

No sooner had they sat down for lunch than she handed him a sonnet scribbled in pencil on the back of a telegram—or so he would tell his cousin more than thirty years later, when she found the poem folded and refolded in the pocket of his jacket.

> This beast that rends me in the sight of all,
> This love, this longing, this oblivious thing,
> That has me under as the last leaves fall,
> Will glut, will sicken, will be gone by spring.
> The wound will heal, the fever will abate,

The knotted hurt will slacken in the breast;
I shall forget before the flickers mate
Your look that is today my east and west.
Unscathed, however, from a claw so deep
Though I should love again I shall not go:
Along my body, waking while I sleep,
Sharp to the kiss, cold to the hand as snow,
The scar of this encounter like a sword
Will lie between me and my troubled lord.

They became lovers. His lips were so soft, it was like kissing the flesh of a girl's nipple. Then she told Eugen.

Millay's letters to George Dillon began in a torrent. She told him she loved him, that he must not, cannot, doubt her, that she would bear anything—even being without him—but not his doubt of her. She wrote him four letters in thirteen days; one was eight pages long.

My darling,
     You must never doubt me again. Truly, that is the one thing I could not bear. For indeed that is the only ugly thing that ever could be between us. I remember that just for an instant once I questioned something you said: I said, "Is that really true?"—and you said in such a strange way,—"You don't believe me."—And your face was just as if somebody had blown out the candle there.

They had, she said, the two most precious things two people could possess: "that we love each other; and that we have told the truth about it." But she added something disquieting:

How easily could I cry with John Donne:

> "I am two fools, I know:
> for loving, and for saying so."

I am two fools, my dear. And I am so very happy & proud that I neither fought against this love when once I had caught a glimpse of its grave-face, nor even for a moment thought to keep it from you.——I tell you now,— and you must never doubt it again—that I shall love you always, and that I shall never let you go out of my life.

That last phrase was almost a threat. Then:

What will come of all this none of us can tell, I think. And by that I mean,—none of us three. The situation is a strange one truly: I am devoted to my husband.* I love him more deeply than I could ever express, my feeling for him is in no way changed or diminished since I met you; but whenever I think of you, and I think of you all day and half the night, an enchanted sickness comes over me, as if I had drunk a witch's philtre, and if I should never see you again, I believe that I should waste & dwindle in true fantastic style until I snapped in two.

That was her asterisk. At the bottom of her letter she told him that what she'd written "sounds so false—like something said on the stage—ugly, too. But I didn't mean it so." There was a glimpse of her high-handedness here, and no amount of warning him, or apologizing, could alter it. Unfortunately, none of Dillon's letters from this period in their lives survives.

Let me add to the strangeness of it all, this: that you like and admire Eugen, and that he likes you extremely, is fond of you. What will come of all this I can't see. But I feel sure I shall not lose you. Once I wrote, "After the feet of beauty fly my own." This is the fact. I have never once turned my back on the beautiful thing. And surely the Goddess is not offended.—Surely I shall see you again, and kiss you again.—(Oh, my darling, I must be careful how I write such words!—It sets me to remembering you too keenly. What sweet agony it is to remember kissing you, to imagine the sound of your voice.)
I am writing this just having received your letter and the poem. That you should now be writing your lovely lines to me is almost too great happiness.

She told him she had one last reading in New York before she could return to Steepletop, and she was desperate to be home.

Longing to write you from there, to read your letters in that place.
I must go now.
Goodbye.
I love you.

By then she had received his second letter. "Oh, God, what fun it is to be happy again, & to be writing romantic ardent nonsense to the only infant dragon-killer since Hercules wore didies!"
But she added a note that could hardly have been reassuring to Dillon: "And oh how proud I shall be in a month or so, stepping the streets of Paris, the only woman in the whole fashionable town with shoes & hat & handbag of genuine dragon-skin!" How could she have thought that he would share her delight when being in Paris clearly meant she would be without him? He must "not say the poem you sent is not lovely. For it is. It is I who

tell you. And I know a great deal about such matters. The last line of it nearly took my breath away forever—so beautiful—and about *me*."

3

Her last reading was on December 17, 1928, at the Brooklyn Academy of Music. As she was dressing to go onstage, somebody mentioned casually that Elinor Wylie had just died. Stunned, Millay walked onto the enormous stage, stepped downstage, and said simply, "A greater poet than I has died, and with your permission I'd like to read her poems to you." Mary Kennedy was in the audience and remembered Millay's voice as low and steady, "and when she recited those poems, that was in the realm of poetry. Her realm. Her world." Dressed in a long gown of heavy creamy silk, her hair a flame of red, she looked to a young man in the audience "incandescent."

Wylie's funeral was the next day, December 18, in the apartment on West Ninth Street where she had lived with her husband, William Rose Benét. "Young Phil Hitchborn, Elinor's son by her first marriage, was present and reminded me of a red fox," William's sister, Laura Benét, remembered. The room was crowded to overflowing. The Van Dorens were there, and Mary and Padraic Colum. "Nancy Hoyt, Elinor's younger sister, came late & went around kissing the men." Mary Kennedy recalled, "Carl Van Doren wept so that his wife Irita took him home, her arm tucked in his." Elinor lay dressed in her silver Poiret gown. Edna Millay bent over the coffin and whispered a poem to her, the poem Elinor had written to her, and placed a sprig of laurel in Elinor's hands.

> Musa of the sea-blue eyes,
> Silver nightingale, alone
> In a little coffin lies:
> A stone beneath a stone.
>
> She, whose song we loved the best,
> Is voiceless in a sudden night:
> On your light limbs, O loveliest,
> May the dust be light!

Bill Benét, distraught, wrote to her two days later, on December 20:

Dear Vincent:
    I am moved to write you because I have thought a lot about your speaking "Musa of the sea-blue eyes," and I have been sitting in her chair in her blessèd end of the apartment, drinking brandy & soda & reading "Trivial

Breath" & "Black Armour" all through. And in the copy of "Black Armour"
I picked out had been placed your original review of "Nets to Catch the
Wind." . . .

I was greatly privileged. She was a darling child & an archangel & a
genius. I am just a man. I did love her. O that I could ever have said one
impatient word to her!

She was darling to me. I wish to tell you this of her death. She died as she
was sure to die, standing up, stricken down suddenly, like a hero killed in
battle.

It was after a quiet Sunday night supper. . . . I asked her if she'd like a
glass of water. "I'd love it." I went into the kitchenette & turned on the tap,
I heard her say, "Oh my God!" . . . I called casually, "What's the matter?"
Then I heard her get up and she said in a strange voice, "I don't know!"

Those were the last words she spoke. He ran to her. "I lifted her in my
arms and began almost babbling in terror and asking her to speak to me.
But she was beyond speaking. She died as I lifted her, I know. Death was
in her throat." He thought he could feel her heart beating. He put a pillow
under her head, ran to the phone to call a doctor, then held her until the
doctor came. She had suffered a stroke.

"I wish I had been able to climb her heights with her," he continued.
"You geniuses are all the same. You strike us to awe—but how can we help
loving you humanly?

"To see you two together was beautiful. . . . I guess it is one of the things
that neither Eugen nor I will ever forget." For she was, he said, a child of
God, like Shelley.

"Darling You," she wrote to Dillon on Christmas Eve day, less than a week
after her last letter, "it seems that I have so little time for writing you—for
I can't write you unless I am alone. But as for thinking of you, that I can
do all day long, & nobody knows. Eugen, of course, does know sometimes, that I am thinking of you."

Whether or not she was longing to see him, or to dream of him, she was
busy planning her trip abroad; she and Eugen would sail on the nineteenth of January.

I feel that I must see you before I go.—I remember how I said to you that
night you drove me to the theatre; "I am sailing for Europe in January"—
how suddenly you turned & asked, "For how long?"—I knew then that I
should never be able to forget you.

———

I shall try to see you before I go. What I mean is, I cannot bear it, & I will
not have it, to go without looking at your face once more.—Oh, God, what

would I not give to have you here at this moment. . . . I am glad that it does not get easier; I am glad that I love you truly, glad that I am in for it, glad that I have no choice, glad that I am up to my mouth in love with you, and that the sand is dragging at my feet.

In a postscript she asked him to "Forgive the fuss I've made." All she wanted was to see him. Couldn't he come to Steepletop for the weekend of January 4 to 7 "(or for the whole week, if Mr. Dillon can possibly wrangle it.)—In any case, you could leave Friday afternoon, arriving in Albany Saturday, where we would meet you, & if you had to leave so soon we would motor you to Albany Sunday evening. But try to make it longer. And *do come!*"

Mr. Dillon, however, had taken a job in an advertising agency in Chicago, and spending a weekend in New York was not such a simple matter. He must have reminded her of that, for on the twenty-ninth she wrote him an eight-page letter, sent special delivery:

And do you think for a moment *I* don't know how it feels to be waiting for a letter seven days?—Big baby!—That's just what you've put *me* through, and you don't care a bit. It is true that my life is full, and full of wonder and excitement, that every day of my life is splendid. But don't you know, or did I forget to tell you, how big a part of my life you are?—And you are just as far from me as I am from you. Oh, darling, yes you are!

This, she said, brought her to the business at hand, "and the gentleman from Kentucky will please stop crying." He had to come to Steepletop.

I don't want you to mess things up for yourself; I don't want you [to] run the risk of losing your job. But I am sure that if you bring your ponderous brain to bear upon this matter, you can make him listen to reason.—Tell him it is a matter of life & death—which is the truth. (My darling, I am so gay and so matter-of-fact, because I have made up my mind that whatever happens, I am going to see you soon, and because that calls for engineering.)

Even Eugen agreed with her, she said: "Believe me, my very, very dear, that he is right. And he is so wonderful that if you know him you will surely love him. He loves you already, I think."

My lovely thing, my darling, darling—don't be apprehensive that I am trying in desperation to change your passionate beautiful love for me into something less—into simple friendship, I mean,—which is less. Someday, perhaps, we shall be friends—but I hope the day is far off when you feel only friendship for me.—I say that frankly enough, I think—I love you too much, in every possible way, to want to change in the slightest detail or degree what you feel for me.

If that disturbed him or seemed equivocal and compromising, she admitted, "You do not understand all this, perhaps." She added, "It may seem contradictory to you. Please don't try to understand, then. Just come. Believe in me. Trust me, I beg of you. Do what I ask."

This was followed by a letter from Eugen:

Vincent is writing you, asking you to come to Steepletop. I, too, want you to come: I am going to make you love me and you must make me love you.—So put on a gay tie, and pack your evening clothes and a clean, clean shirt and come and we'll drink wine together and laugh together. . . . Affectionately, Ugin.

When Edna read over what she'd written to George, she knew it was inadequate.

My darling, I shiver with terror lest in some way this letter confuse you too much.—I am afraid to send it. But I must send it. I can do no better than this just now. If it troubles you, burn it now, at once, forget all that it says, except that I love you & must see you. Believe in me, if you never believed in anything before,—and, oh, continue to love me.

She closed this extraordinary plea with an odd remark. She knew this was a desperate letter, but if he was "what I think you are, if you are what I love so dearly, you will understand, I think, why Eugen wanted to write you, too." She ended playfully, explaining again and again to him what she, what *they* meant by their invitation:

Sweetheart,—what it means is: will you please come to visit me in my crazy, unfinished, half-finished, disorderly house, where there is a place for nothing, & nothing in its place, except the only important things in the world.—I want to show you the tiny pool we built, absurd, nothing at all, & the hut in the blueberry pasture where I wrote the *King's Henchman,* I want to sit on the edge of your bed while you have your breakfast—I want to laugh with you, dress up in curtains, be incredibly silly, be incredibly happy, be like children, and I want to kiss you more than anything in the world.

Now, would he come? Would he let her hear from him quickly? "I shall not go abroad until I have seen you."

—

George Dillon did not come to Steepletop that winter. Hurt and disappointed, Edna wrote to him the day before her thirty-seventh birthday, as she prepared to leave for Europe. It was not a letter guaranteed to reassure Dillon, who was overwhelmed by Edna's demands and uneasy about Eugen's.

> My darling, forget what I wrote about feeling further away from you. . . . Perhaps I wanted to hurt you. . . . I love you terribly. Never believe that I don't, no matter what nonsense I write. Sometimes I long so to see you that I want to hurt you, I think, just because you're not there.

On March 11, 1929, Edna and Eugen boarded the *Rotterdam* for France. She wired Dillon four words: "Goodbye, goodbye, my darling." By the time she returned in May, they would not have seen each other for five months.

CHAPTER 25

Edna and Eugen returned from France in May. When Edna heard nothing from her mother after Cora's birthday that June, she began to fret. "I hope that the reason why you haven't written for so long is that you are busy and having a good time, not that you're not feeling well," she wrote. Eugen asked if they could come to Camden for a visit at the end of the summer. Vincent added:

> I have three little mountain laurels for you, tiny, but in perfect blossom. . . . The best time to transplant them, I now learn, is when they are in full bloom, like the azaleas, so I am having them taken up now and potted in buckets. They are perfectly sweet and you will love them. Next year they will blossom like anything.

At the end of August, they drove to Camden and set the laurel trees out. Cora gave her daughter a few sweetmary plants from her garden to plant at Steepletop. "She gave me some little fir-trees, too," Edna wrote to Kathleen, "tiny ones, which she dug up with her hands on Sherman's Point the day before, when we drove her out there. She stood by the car as Ugin packed the plants in the back; there was some pennyroyal, too. And she stood in the yard as we drove away."

2

That fall, a full year after their first encounter, Edna received a letter from George Dillon telling her he might move to California. She wrote back frantically:

> Darling, for God's sake don't go. . . . I shall die if you do.—It's been almost more than I could bear to have you as far away as Chicago, but I always felt that if I really couldn't stand it, by tomorrow I could be with you,—But California—oh, please don't! I shall die if you do. I mean it. They'll call it something else, but it will be that.

There was something plaintive and girlish in her letter; even her handwriting shrank and tightened.

> Do you ever want to see me? Does it ever bother you at all, not seeing me? . . . What does one do about it?—I forget, if I ever knew. It seems to me that I never knew.—No, I don't think I could just now stand the excitement of a love-letter from you—but it would be worth the risk. I wish awfully you'd conduct the experiment upon me.————
>
> Goodbye, darling. . . . I love you. Are you glad?—Or do you wish I'd stop?—Anyway, I'm glad.

Then, on November 16, just over two weeks after this letter, she wrote him angrily from Steepletop, this time by special delivery:

> *Saturday afternoon*
> Ugin & I are going to New York tomorrow. Will you please call me up at the Vanderbilt tomorrow Sunday evening at any time—otherwise Monday at about 6 o'clock—and reverse the charges?—I insist that you call me up, & I insist that you reverse the charges. And I want you to be prepared to tell me whether or not you will come to Steepletop at once. If not, Ugin & I shall leave for Chicago at midnight Monday. . . . We shall go to the Blackstone.—You cannot keep me from coming to Chicago, if you won't come here. If you think I care at all what the whole world says about me, in comparison to being absent from you at this time, you have never really loved either me or anybody else. Let them spy, let them follow, let them listen on the telephone, let every loose-tongued gossip in the country know that I love you & that I came to Chicago to see you.—I don't mean that I shall do anything at all indiscreet or reckless—I only mean that there are times when all such considerations become a lot of rot.—In any case, either

you come here, & at once, or I come to Chicago. You have nearly killed me. I won't stand it any longer. I love you and I'm going to see you.

It is impossible to know exactly what prompted this outburst, but her will is behind every phrase. She is offended, and she is determined. Four days later, having heard from him, she softened:

Thursday

Darling, I'm sending you the enclosed envelope just for fun—to show you that we were about to leave for the station when you called—the time being an hour later here.——

Poor child, how I have harassed you. I will never do it again. I should not have done it now but that I was so sure you were in trouble & was very worried. But in any case, I'll never do it again.—So breathe freely.

He had said he would come to Steepletop, perhaps even settle in New York. She assured him that if he did, she could help him find work. "Let me know what your plans are, as soon as you have time. . . . I wonder will you really come?"

From the beginning of their affair they had been separated, not only by the physical distance between Chicago and Steepletop but by her marriage, by her far greater fame as a poet—and, inevitably, by the emotional confusion and even distrust those differences were bound to engender. Dillon could be sulky, angry, jealous, and despairing. In an undated letter he gives us a clue as to how he felt when they were not on good terms with each other, when he had spoiled the little time they had together:

Darling,

I don't know what kind of depressed, drunken, insane letter I wrote you, but I can well imagine, because I haven't heard from you—I haven't heard from you at all.

Forgive me for being crude and ungrateful. It's just that I have to pay for being with you by being plunged in a worse despair every time you go away. The rest of my life seems so useless, then, that I can't bear the thought of picking it up again. So I hide away a while, and drink and read, and take long walks, and sleep. Then I'm all right again.

I'm all right now. I remember only the happiness we've had, and I know the rest isn't important. If you still love me, I'll be glad as anyone to be alive.

For all the torment they inflicted on each other, it was a remarkably productive relationship for both of them. She sent him five sonnets in one letter, twenty-six in the next. She hadn't had a comparable period of such intense productivity since her early days in New York. The longer they were apart, the more the poems seemed to come. She could even be playful to him about it:

These are samples. Enclosed is an order-blank, etc. Indicate the type you prefer and the number of sonnets on that subject which you wish me to supply. At the rate at which I am working now, I shall easily be able to meet the most wholesale demand. Oh, God, did I say "Easily"? I have never worked so hard.

She said they weren't perfect, but if she waited until they were,

you will very likely not see them for at least a year longer, and it is ... almost as if we were not so far apart, as if we were living in the same city. Except when we *are* living in the same city there never seems to be much time for reading and discussing each other's poetry, there are so many other things to be done which are so intrinsically and immediately worthwhile, such as kissing each other. If people would only just let me kiss you for as long as I want to just once, it might be different; but after two or three days somebody always comes in and interrupts.

She hoped he liked the sonnets. She hoped he'd tell her he did, but even if he didn't, she'd send him some more. "Yes, I'm as big as that." She was that confident. Then she wrote quickly again: "Darling, I'm sending you with this some more sonnets. . . . There's mountains of work to be done on them still." If they were only together, she'd talk them over with him because "Some of them were written when I hadn't heard from you for a long time, and thought maybe you didn't love me anymore." She decided to send him two sonnets "which I had not intended to send with the others. These two were written to Ugin. They are the two beginning 'Believe, if ever the bridges of this town,' and 'If in the years to come you should recall.' They are rather nice, and I'd like you to see them."

Why did she want him to have these particular poems and to know they were written to Eugen? What do they contain that she wants him to know? The first of the two sonnets seems to be an assurance to Eugen that if their marriage, which she describes within a military metaphor as a sort of fortress whose "bridges" and "towers" are built "without fault or stain," should "be taken," she would never again seek any other refuge: "No mortal roof shall shelter me again."

> Believe, if ever the bridges of this town,
> Whose towers were builded without fault or stain,
> Be taken, and its battlements go down,

No mortal roof shall shelter me again;
I shall not prop a branch against a bough
To hide me from the whipping east or north,
Nor tease to flame a heap of sticks, who now
Am warmed by all the wonders of the earth.
Do you take ship unto some happier shore
In such event, and have no thought for me,
I shall remain;—to share the ruinous floor
With roofs that once were seen far out at sea;
To cheer a mouldering army on the march . . .
And beg from spectres by a broken arch.

The second sonnet to Eugen, which would eventually become the penultimate poem in the cycle (the final poem is to George), is equally disturbing:

If in the years to come you should recall,
When faint at heart or fallen on hungry days,
Or full of griefs and little if at all
From them distracted by delights or praise;
When failing powers or good opinion lost
Have bowed your neck, should you recall to mind
How of all men I honoured you the most,
Holding you noblest among mortal-kind;
Might not my love—although the curving blade
From whose wide mowing none may hope to hide,
Me long ago below the frosts had laid—
Restore you somewhat to your former pride?
Indeed I think this memory even then
Must raise you high among the run of men.

They were strange poems to send to Dillon. They would certainly serve to alert him to the permanence of her loyalty to her husband. But her letter continued, and maybe this was her point:

Soon, I'll write you another letter to keep, a happier one, my dear, the one you want. In the meantime let me assure you that I don't in the least intend to give you up,—in fact, I dare you, I double-dare you, to escape from me. No matter what I may say, no matter how big and brave I may be on occasion, the black truth is, my lovely one, that I haven't the faintest intent of letting you go. Vide sonnet beginning "Strange thing that I, by nature nothing prone."

The poem is almost an extension of her love letter:

Strange thing that I, by nature nothing prone
To fret the summer blossom on its stem,
Who know the hidden nest, but leave alone
The magic eggs, the bird that cuddles them,
Should have no peace till your bewildered heart
Hung fluttering at the window of my breast,
Till I had ravished to my bitter smart
Your kiss from the stern moment, could not rest.
"Swift wing, sweet blossom, live again in air!
Depart, poor flower; poor feathers, you are free!"
Thus do I cry, being teased by shame and care
That beauty should be brought to terms by me;
Yet shamed the more that in my heart I know,
Cry as I may, I could not let you go.

"I've done acres of them, sweetheart. About twenty-six, I think. Isn't that terrifying? It is four weeks and a night and half a morning since I kissed you goodbye. I shall never kiss you goodbye again. There should never be hello-kisses or goodbye-kisses,—just kisses. Anyhow, it is four weeks and a night and half a morning and a minute, since you went away from me. That's long enough, I think, indeed I think it's more than long enough. I want to see you. If I don't see you soon, I shall lie on the floor and kick and howl till something is done about it."

The contrast between the tone of this letter, in which she sounds girl-ish, and the voice of her sonnets is striking. Yet we see her battling with herself in her sonnet, fighting and then giving way to her consuming desire to possess this man. In the poems she is often a queen or a goddess, at any rate immortal. Only in one, among her most achieved, does she appear as a girl, direct, proud, and generous:

Not in a silver casket cool with pearls
Or rich with red corundum or with blue,
Locked, and the key withheld, as other girls
Have given their loves, I give my love to you;
Not in a lover's-knot, not in a ring
Worked in such fashion, and the legend plain:
Semper fidelis,—where a secret spring
Kennels a drop of mischief for the brain.
Love in the open hand, no thing but that,
Ungemmed, unhidden, wishing not to hurt,
As one should bring you cowslips in a hat
Swung from the hand, or apples in her skirt,
I bring you, calling out as children do:
"Look what I have!" and "These are all for you."

She would write for him some of her most extraordinary sonnets. He could leave her, but having been loved by him, she was triumphant:

> Women have loved before as I love now;
> At least in lively chronicles of the past.—
> Of Irish waters by a Cornish prow
> Or Trojan waters by a Spartan mast
> Much to their cost invaded—here and there,
> Hunting the amorous line, skimming the rest,
> I find some woman bearing as I bear
> Love like a burning city in the breast.
> I think however that of all alive
> I only in such utter, ancient way
> Do suffer love; in me alone survive
> The blind, imperious passions of a day
> When treacherous queens, with death upon the tread,
> Heedless and wilful, took their knights to bed.

She is clear as glass. She'd struck this note for a long time in her work—certainly since *Figs* and *Second April,* and especially in her sonnets. There was always a powerfully expressed notion of her own destiny above the impermanence of mortal love, which is subject to change. Against it she places her vocation. Her theme is as ancient as the Greeks: the permanence of poetry and impermanence of love, subject to change, to loss, or to ending. She wrote with a spirited certainty that had stung Floyd Dell, as well as Edmund Wilson, taunting that they would one day wake "from dreams of me, that at your side / So many nights, a lover and a bride, / But stern in my soul's chastity." They who would "walk the world forever for my sake, / And in every chamber find me gone again!"

Against this extraordinary assurance were the playfulness and humor of her early work, through which she had also won her readers. But then there was always a hook, as there was in this sonnet, published first in 1920:

> Only until this cigarette is ended,
> A little moment at the end of all,
> While on the floor the quiet ashes fall,
> And in the firelight to a lance extended,
> Bizarrely with the jazzing music blended,
> The broken shadow dances on the wall,
> I will permit my memory to recall
> The vision of you, by all my dreams attended.
> And then adieu,—farewell!—the dream is done.
> Yours is a face of which I can forget

> The colour and the features, every one,
> The words not ever, and the smiles not yet;
> But in your day this moment is the sun
> Upon a hill, after the sun has set.

Millay had been telling her audience, both men and women, as she was cannily aware, to

> make the most of this, your little day,
> Your little month, your little half a year,
> Ere I forget, or die, or move away.

Witty and provocative, these were smart, saucy poems, and they had secured her an enormous audience. But now, nearly forty, with her young lover uncertain, she found her voice at another pitch. When she thought she'd lost Dillon, it was her art, her vocation as a poet, in which she took refuge.

3

The fall found Llewelyn Powys and his unhappy wife, Alyse Gregory, living in the caretaker's cottage across the road from Steepletop while Lulu worked on his novel *Impassioned Clay*. He would dedicate it to Eugen Boissevain, "under whose roof and in the presence of whose daring spirit this book was finished." Eugen was as rare a person, Alyse wrote, as Edna:

Handsome, reckless, mettlesome as a stallion breathing the first morning air, he would laugh at himself, indeed laugh at everything, with a laugh that scattered melancholy as the wind scatters the petals of the fading poppy. . . . One day his house would be that of a citizen of the world, with a French butler to wait on the table and everything done with the greatest *bienséance,* and the next the servants would have as mysteriously disappeared as bees from a deserted hive, and he would be out in the kitchen washing the dishes and whistling a haunting Slavic melody, as light-hearted as a troubadour. He had the gift of the aristocrat and could adapt himself to all circumstances. . . . His blood was testy, adventurous, quixotic, and he faced life as an eagle faces its flight.

Lulu needed a respite, and so did Alyse, for their retreat was tainted by his fidgeting anticipation of letters from England and his vexing indecision: he was wildly in love with Gamel Woolsey, a young American woman living in Dorset—the "little poetess," he and Alyse called her.

Alyse Gregory knew nothing of Millay's affair with Dillon, but she knew firsthand how unusual her hosts' domestic arrangement was.

She felt alien in their company at Steepletop, an awkward outsider, as she recorded one night in her diary:

> She in her long purple velvet gown with the white fur, the Elizabethan sleeves—looking like a favoured princess surrounded by her courtiers—E. trembling with love and veneration for her. . . . and I too feeling love for her—yet feeling myself like an outcast beggar.

Edna, who had after all once been Lulu's lover, was either unaware or too involved in her own troubles to breach the gap between them. Powys lavished his attention on her, avoiding the forlorn hurt that Alyse seemed to bask in:

> We discussed the difference between French and English poetry, and Edna described the feelings of a young girl at a dance—in a dance hall—as if into each dance must be packed the panic and ecstasy of her last moment of life, for underneath was death. And Gene said the saxophone was the saddest of all instruments with its wild sinking death cry. Then he talked of the difference between passion and love—his passion for little girls and his love for mature women. He was very eloquent. I saw L. sitting as I had seen him so many times when I was the centre of his life, his hands a little relaxed on his knees, wearing his Cambridge coat that I had so many times put away in a box with camphor—that I had sent to the cleaners—that I had packed and unpacked in our rooms where we had been so happy—and now he seemed so intimate to me and yet so remote—as if were we to part there would be nothing of me left to him and when I heard him read the ballads—oh, how my heart was wrung—I could hardly keep back the tears so that when Eugen shouted at me as he did several times, speaking rudely in a way that always drives me down into myself he saw that I was grave and offended and came impulsively to kneel before me saying "Darling, I have not hurt you, have I? Now kiss me" which I did, but then he went on to make more violent drunken love to me, and L. was making love to E. on the couch kissing her cheeks and neck, but without passion, without desire, or warmth because all his love is elsewhere—and suddenly I felt as if I must run, escape.

Instead, Eugen dashed outside and fired off his gun, then ran back to raise a toast to Christ, the "darling boy," while an offended Lulu chastised him. Alyse recorded one last wintry scene: swathed in blankets and furs against the cold, bundled into a sleigh, Lulu is lying beside Edna, while she and Eugen sing a German song. Altair, their German shepherd, races beside the two great steaming horses.

At the end of January, Eugen and Edna left for New York for a few days. Alyse observed that their trips had begun to have an "atmosphere of riotous nights of drinking and loud talk—We came away feeling ravished and this is sad, for Edna has always underneath an ardor sensitive and untraduced."

4

Throughout the fall and winter Millay worked on her book of sonnets. Harper made up a dummy and announced it as *Twice Required,* a title taken from a line in her fourteenth sonnet, "Since of no creature living the last breath is twice required." That December she'd written her mother, telling her there would be "about forty in all in my new book which will be published in March." One month later, she told Norma there would be "about forty-four." But now she had definitely settled on a title: *Fatal Interview.* "This is a phrase from a poem by John Donne. . . .

> 'By our first strange and fatall interview,
> By all our desires which thereof did ensue.'

"I shall quote these two lines in the front of the book."

That fall she began to publish in magazines the sonnets that would form the heart of *Fatal Interview.* Three were published in *Poetry* and five at Christmas in *Harper's Magazine,* with another five the same month in *The Saturday Evening Post.* In the spring of 1931 *The New Republic* would publish eight of her sonnets and *Harper's Magazine* two. In other words, not only would there be excellent advance notice of her work by the time of the book's publication in April 1931, but there was also a substantial market being created beyond her established audience.

Millay was being well served by her editor at Harper, Eugene Saxton. There had been, from the first, limited editions of her work: Mitchell Kennerley had printed fifteen copies of *Renascence* on Japan vellum in 1917, and even Frank Shay, after printing hundreds of copies of *The Ballad of the Harp-Weaver* with brightly colored paper wrappers, had done five copies on Japan vellum, which was about as limited as you could be. By 1924, with the printing of "Renascence" as a separate poem by the Goudys on William Morris's Kelmscott handpress, Millay's work had become a collector's prize. Still, it was not until 1928, with Harper's publication of *The Buck in the Snow,* that there were in effect three editions of a single book of hers: the regular trade edition, which sold for two dollars; a limited edition, of which five hundred would be autographed and numbered for fifteen dollars; and an ultralimited edition of thirty-six books on Japan vellum bound in boards for thirty dollars. Harper planned to call the limited edition the "Steepletop Edition" after her home and asked her for a snapshot from which a small woodblock would be cut to represent it. She must have scotched that idea, but the fact remains that by 1928, when she was thirty-six, she was being published in trade, limited, and ultralimited editions.

That was the year when Eugene Saxton, who had been Elinor Wylie's editor at George H. Doran Company, made Millay an appealing offer: that while their "present agreement includes an option for two volumes" of which *Buck* was only the first, and since her project *Selected Poems for Young People,* as a reprint of an earlier work,

> does not properly come under this option clause. . . . the royalty terms are definitely fixed under this agreement and our contract provides for a 15% royalty. . . . However, in view of the conversation we had in this office with Mr. Boissevain when he was here last, we are anxious to meet you in any way we can.

In other words, while explaining to her, as all publishers explain to all authors, that increasing her royalty might prevent the company from "spending an adequate sum for promotion," he nevertheless agreed to a 20 percent royalty on all copies sold after 25,000. This was exceptional. Harper would also pay her that royalty on all copies of the limited edition. Saxton didn't stop there. He was an inventive supporter of her work and suggested that if she was willing to write out in longhand five poems from *Buck* on her ordinary manuscript paper, "we could insert these sheets in copies 1 to 5 of the vellum edition and price them at approximately $100.00 to $150.00"; if she was willing to do that, the company would pay her one third of the price of the book. "Personally, I think it is possible we might be able to get as much as $250.00 for copy No. 1." Then he sent her some new books that he thought she might like "with a glass of apple jack at the elbow."

5

Shortly after New Year's 1931, Cora began to gather notes for a possible book about the childhood and school days of her girls. As she exchanged her annual holiday letters with her sister Clem, unhappy memories began to stir between them. It was "sufficiently wearing, emotionally," she wrote to her sister, "making notes for a sketch that will be a sort of memoir.

> It is remarkable, when I look back and have time to look back, how much my family was with me from the time I was married. . . . I am, I hope,

looking at things clearly, and if I live, Henry is going to have justice done him. You will be glad of this, for you never had a better friend. It is no wonder if people said that he had married the whole family.

Her phrase "if I live" lingers uneasily in the mind. It was in this letter of January 22 that Cora first indicated her illness: "I am much better if I were not, I could not be here alone this winter. I cannot type for very long a time without it's making my back ache, so I can not do much extra writing now, and as my handwriting since I fell is worse than ever, I type most of my letters."

But what illness was she recovering from? In the one letter she wrote in her own hand that winter, her script was peculiarly slanted; it tipped severely downward to the right and almost ran off the page. She wrote in pencil, whereas she usually wrote in ink. Her margins were wildly uneven.

On January 30, she wrote to Vincent and sent her some poems that were very different in mood from those of *Little Otis.* She said simply:

I am sending the rough copy, of one I did today. I never thought out one line of it until after I went to bed last night, and it is just as it came to me. It is just because you gave me the "Little Mountain-Laurel-trees" that I am sending it to you as it is . . . because I am so happy that I am at work again, doing I think as good work as I ever did.

My little Mountain-Laurel-trees
So sturdy, in a row;
I loved the ones who set you out
And wanted you to grow;
Of course I love my other trees
So stately and so tall———
But I loved some Mountain-Laurel-trees
When I was very small.

. . .

My little Mountain-Laurel-trees
If you should ever grow
Where I was very sound asleep,
I think that I should know.
Then I needn't dream of Cypresses
Where cold their shadows fall,
But of Mountain-Laurel-trees I loved
When I was very small.

Vincent received her mother's letter Monday evening, February 2. When she read the last stanza, she burst into tears. "It seemed I could hardly bear it. Ugin tried to comfort me, saying that I mustn't take it like that, that it meant nothing, her writing that way; and he was quite right, for she was feeling, you see, very happy. But I could not keep from crying."

Two days later, just as they sat down for supper, a taxi pulled up with a telegram:

COME MOTHER VERY SICK ANSWER IMMEDIATELY TO ME

It was from her uncle Bert in Camden. They had the taxi take a return wire saying they'd be on the next train for Boston. Then they wired Norma. When they realized that the train didn't leave Chatham until 1:30 in the morning, they decided to risk it and drive instead. Edna was afraid that they'd stall in the night with no one awake to help them; Eugen promised her he wouldn't stall the engine. "Ugin took along two bottles of champagne to celebrate her getting well. I also put in my bag at the last moment . . . a tube of Baume Analgesique, to rub her with in case she should ache anywhere. But she didn't ache anywhere at all."

It was a twelve-hour drive in the dead of night, in the middle of winter, and snow was drifting over the roads.

As we drove up the coast of Maine the sun came up, a most beautiful morning. I felt sure that she would never see the sun again. We came into Camden from Rockport by the back road, around the Lily Pond. And as we came down Chestnut Street I began to watch out for the house, just above Uncle Bert's I knew it was, although I didn't know just which one. And then suddenly I saw the door, and there was crepe on it.

She saw a mauve wreath fluttering on the door before her uncle Bert, who was still expecting them to arrive by train, could reach them to break the news. "Anyway, that's how I learned she had died," she wrote to Kathleen. "I can't go on with this, sister, I'm so exhausted writing it. I'll write again, as soon as I can."

That afternoon, when Norma and Charlie arrived by train, the two sisters immediately wired Howard, Kathleen's husband, in Paris:

DEAR HOWARD PLEASE BREAK IT TO KATHLEEN THAT MOTHER DIED SUD-
DENLY SHE WAS UNCONSCIOUS AND SUFFERED NO PAIN WE HURRIED TO GET
TO HER BUT WERE TOO LATE GIVE KATHLEEN ALL OUR LOVE

VINCENT AND NORMA

"From the moment we got there," Edna wrote Kathleen, "everything
was done for her as if she were a queen, which of course she was." A poem
was still in the typewriter Kay had given her, and Edna told her sister that
"I just put the typewriter in its box with the sheet of paper just as it was in
the carriage, & left it at the cottage for you."

The next day they wired Kathleen directly:

DARLING KATHLEEN IT IS HARD DECIDING THINGS WITHOUT YOU STOP
MOTHER WAS JUST WORKING ON LOVELY POEM HAPPILY IMAGINING HERSELF
BURIED UNDER BELOVED MOUNTAIN LAUREL STOP AT STEEPLETOP FAR FROM
HOUSE IS BIG SUNNY CLEARING COVERED WITH MOUNTAIN LAUREL NORMA
AND I WANT YOUR ADVICE WE WANT AWFULLY TO HAVE THESE FIVE ACRES
DEEDED OVER TO US THREE FOREVER AND BURY MOTHER THERE PLEASE
CABLE IMMEDIATELY WHAT YOU THINK STOP WE ARE TAKING ALL HER THINGS
TO COTTAGE WE FELT SURE SHE WOULD WANT NO SERVICES SAID BUT ARE
INVITING HER FRIENDS TO COME IN TOMORROW MOTHER LOOKS BEAUTI-
FUL DARLING IT IS HARDEST FOR YOU ALL OUR LOVE GOES OUT TO YOU SO
FAR AWAY.

VINCENT NORMA

Saturday night in Camden, Norma and Vincent decided they'd have a
wake for Cora. "We thought she would like that. Norma and I wanted to
watch up with her all night, but Charlie and Ugin wouldn't let us, we
were so worn out"; instead they dined in her regal company.

At about eight Charlie and Ugin came in with sandwiches and things for
supper. We set places for you and Howard, too, and pretended that you
were there. And we had two glasses for you and Howard, and poured into
the six glasses the champagne we had brought for mother, and drank to
her, and you and Howard drank to her, too. We always pretended that you
were with us. And everything we did we did for you, too. Every time we
went to look at her—and it was hard to keep away, she looked so beautiful,
so peaceful and asleep—we would look at her for you, too, and say "This is
for Kathleen."

That night the two sisters cut three locks of their mother's hair.

At last they received a cable from Kathleen in Paris:

AM KIND OF INSANE I GUESS IT IS TOO SUDDEN MOTHER AND I TALKED
ABOUT IT AT COTTAGE I PROMISED HER SHE SHOULD BE BURIED IN NEW-
BURYPORT WITH HER MOTHER BUT IT WAS MY IDEA NOT HERS AND AM SURE
SHE WOULD RATHER BE AT STEEPLETOP IT IS LOVELY IDEA PLEASE DO ANY-
THING YOU THINK BEST STOP I EXPECTED RETURN JANUARY BUT WAS TOO
SICK TO COME AND DID NOT WANT TO WRITE HER THAT STOP WE MUST NOT
BE TOO UNHAPPY WE MUST REMEMBER IT IS THE WAY WE ALL WANT TO DIE
PLEASE WRITE ME WHEN YOU CAN ALL MY LOVE

                                                        KATHLEEN

Now all her daughters were in agreement at last.

The snow began to fall steadily. Vincent and Norma wanted their mother
to leave Camden "not by the back way up Chestnut Street and along the
cost to Rockport," Norma remembered, "but by way of the Camden we
and she knew." They all got into the long open Cadillac.

So, our little procession, we bareheaded, snow falling in our hair and on
our faces, Charlie and I in the back seat and Vincent in the front with Ugin
driving followed our mother in the great black van back up past the last
house we had lived in, on Limerock Street, around to Chestnut and down
past the house near the Post Office where we had lived and, turning left
into Main Street, followed the street up and around the Elm Street school
house we had all attended as children and on to Rockport. There our
mother went on to Rockport where her first child had been born and so on
to Steepletop.

It was as unconventional a leave-taking as their residence in Camden
had been from the first. No one in that small seaside Maine town would
ever forget any of them.

When the hearse reached West Stockbridge, Massachusetts, just across
the state line from Austerlitz, it stalled in the heavy snow. The drifts were
ten feet deep. Eugen and John Pinnie, their caretaker, brought the body up
to Steepletop in a sleigh. Eugen wrote Lulu, who had left the little house,
"Steaming black horses, a soft, silent snowstorm, a swinging stable lantern
on the side of the sleigh, over that beautiful road through the silent hills.
Edna was on the doorstep to receive her mother's body."

The coffin was put in the large front room and surrounded with flowers. Eugene O'Neill sent an enormous spray of fiery red gladiolas and
their neighbor Bill Brann a blanket of yellow roses for the coffin. They
were going to dig the grave in the mountain laurel grove on the east side

of their property, but the grave site was on granite and it took far longer than they thought. "Four days," Eugen wrote Lulu, "as we had to blast with dynamite. Then we buried her at night."

❧ ❧ ❧

Norma was sitting in the same spacious front room at Steepletop as the afternoon light began to fail. Her voice was low and clear and somewhat formal.

"Vincent and I had our mother with us here in the living room in front of the door to the terrace, and as the blasting went on, with its always present significance, we became a little crazy, I guess."

They began to sing to her the lullabies she had sung to them when they were small, "those lilting, rocking lullabies," Norma said, closing her eyes.

"Mother had been here, by the door, for about a week . . . the blasting, blasting. Then, in the early evening, the deep rock crater was finished and the two crews succeeded in plowing our road after the last big storm. The horses were harnessed to the low sled, and, our lanterns swinging to light the road, we again followed our mother through the snow."

The woods were dark by then. The workmen stood aside while the black horses, straining against their braces, pulled the heavy casket upon its sleigh to the grave.

> First two men with lanterns, then the sleigh, then two men with lanterns, then Norma and Edna, Norma carrying a large basket with flowers, Edna with her gun. Then Charlie and I with lanterns. The grave is about 1 mile from the house. I had ten men digging a way through the snow for two days. We sent the men away, covered the coffin with flowers, and pine boughs, then I broke a bottle of champagne on the coffin, the way one does when launching a boat.

"We were," Norma remembered, "we were, well, ready to bury our mother.

"The workmen just faded back into the woods. John Pinnie was there and, oh, perhaps a half-dozen men altogether.

"We were standing alone there, it seemed, Vincent and I. And we began to sing together, she the melody and I tenor, 'Lead, Kindly Light.' "

Norma began to sing, her eyes shut now, her head down. Then she straightened and looked ahead of her.

"Our voices fit together as we sang. And then Gene, who had brought a shotgun with him, gave it to us and each of us fired off three shots into the western night. When we had each finished, Vincent asked if we would mind if Gene fired three volleys for his own mother, for he had not been with her when she died, nor to her burial. And we did that, again each of us."

◕ ◕ ◕

Then they put her down into the blasted rock.

"It seems strange to think of leaving her here," Edna wrote Kathleen, "—but she never minded being alone."

PART SEVEN

THE GIRL POET

———————

CHAPTER 26

Darlings, I knew that you were sorry. But there's nothing to say. We had a grand time. But it's a changed world. The presence of that absence is everywhere.

—Edna St. Vincent Millay to Llewelyn Powys, April 20, 1931

They fled to New York, where they stayed at the St. Regis Hotel just off Fifth Avenue and tried, Edna said, to drink themselves into oblivion. It didn't work. She was dogged by reporters. "If you love the poems of Edna St. Vincent Millay you needn't fear disillusionment in seeing her in person," one of them wrote in the *World-Telegram*. "Imagine a child with a small, pleasant body, hair still shading off into shining bronze, the levelest gray-green eyes you ever met, with a child's quickness and ready smile—above all the intense quickness of a child—and you begin to picture that elusive person who is America's first poetess, Edna Millay."

"This elf," he called her, who boasted of staying out all night pub crawling. She grinned up at him. "Don't you like that word? I wish I had invented it." She was in New York, he said, to see about her next collection of poems, *Fatal Interview*. When he asked her to tell him about it, she said, "it is very intense and very passionate. . . . Personal? Of course, everything one writes is personal. But if it were actual reporting of my own experience, I certainly shouldn't admit it."

The reporter said she had come a long way from the Vassar girl "who came down here in wartime and began battling gayly with poverty." Millay, however, insisted, "I am just the same person."

Another reporter found that unlikely. She had instead "progressed straight up Fifth Avenue from the dimmer purlieus of Washington Square to occupy, as she was doing today, a suite in the St. Regis." While there were still darkened basement bistros in Greenwich Village, such as the Vagabondia and the Pink Kitten, Millay said she didn't like the Village anymore; she didn't even like New York. "It's a swell and exciting place to come to once in a while, from her mountain farm in the Berkshires. She buys the latest gowns and frocks and shoes and hats, then retires to her mountain fastness and puts them in closets." He went on to describe her dining alone with Eugen in evening dress in their farmhouse—or working during the day in her garden in a tweed shirt and sweater. Puzzled by her contrary images he said, "At times she would seem a huge, husky woman; most of the time, however, as ethereal and wistful as Lillian Gish," the most famous film star of the era.

She said she had worked for two years on the fifty-two sonnets that made up *Fatal Interview:* "All over the rambling farmhouse she scatters notebooks—'Composition, 10 Cents.' . . . One is always beside her bed, equipped with sharp pencils. She scrawls her verses, and frequently has difficulty transcribing them after they are cold." But primarily this reporter was impressed with her self-possession and poise.

She spoke carefully. She smoked Egyptian cigarettes. She thought the best poet in America was Robinson Jeffers. Overhearing her, Eugen shot back playfully that he thought the best meals in New York were to be had at the speakeasies in the fifties. They were a pair, an enviable couple. One interview, which went out on the NEA News Service to twenty-nine papers throughout the country, was titled "Here's a Charming Double Interview in Which Edna St. Vincent Millay, Famed American Poetess, Sees Herself as Her Husband Sees Her":

> She was a sunny sight, curled up on the davenport of their hotel suite, with the afternoon light falling upon her. Healthy glowing cheeks of a child, tawny hair with a bronze gleam to it, green eyes merry . . . her small self intensely enthusiastic—like a child.

There were flowers spilling abundantly everywhere in the suite, "selected and placed by that cultivated, charming Dutch gentleman, her husband, a man who wears tweeds beautifully, is a perfect host and who anticipates her every wish." Eugen intruded into the interview only when Millay left the room, to say, "She didn't tell you what a marvelous gardener she is. . . . Vincent has a 'growing hand,' everything she touches grows." The hardest thing he did on her behalf was "teaching new maids not to bother her when she is just sitting still, curled up on a chair, without pencil or paper or even a book. She works that way. She never puts down a single word until a poem is complete."

To talk about briefing a maid in the midst of the Depression was, if not a blunder, at least insensitive. In all the interviews that spring, there was only one in which Edna mentioned her mother's death. The interview began with her story of how she had become a poet: " 'Mother gave me poetry,' she says, with a poignant wistfulness which somehow catches at one's throat. 'She wrote, too, at night after she had tucked us into bed. She published only a few of her writings—she wrote from the love of writing.' "

It was only then that she said that her mother had just died. "I've been numb . . . like a person under an anesthetic. Now I seem to be emerging from under the anesthetic and I ache terribly. I can't seem to realize it all— I keep saying 'I'll ask mother'—she always had the answer for everything."

2

At the end of March, just over six weeks after her mother's death, she at last heard from George Dillon. She wrote back at once:

> I had felt sure that you would write me, when you heard about it. But so many days went by, & still you didn't write. I was pretty unhappy about that, on top of everything else.
>
> Probably you don't know that Ugin's mother died just a week before mine did.—We're pretty sunk.—Three weeks ago we ran away from Steepletop and came here. . . . And we've been so dazed with liquor ever since. . . . I'm not sober yet, and I don't intend to be.
>
> I wish to God you'd write me once in a while, tell me how you are, tell me what you're doing,—or if you don't want to tell me that, tell me whether or not it's raining in Chicago, tell me anything, only just keep on talking to me.—It was pretty hideous thinking I had lost you too, just when I needed so seriously everything in life I had that was beautiful, to remind me that life could be borne at all. Very likely I was right to think I'd lost you, but don't let it go into effect just yet. . . .
>
> Please tell me how you are, and how you spend your time. Tell me what I don't want to hear. It's all right. I can stand anything. I really can. Except your silence.

George must have answered her letter immediately, for six days later she wrote again: "My darling, your letter healed so many wounds. Even though I'm still in the dark as to your strange repudiation of me, I'm comforted. You say that you do still love me, that you did want to see me. I don't care about the rest."

She asked to see everything he was writing and said she was sending him her book. She had wanted to send him "one of the beautiful vellum ones, but it would only embarrass you.—I called it 'Fatal Interview,'—did you know?—It's from a poem of Donne. Long ago I decided that my first book after the Buck in the Snow should be dedicated to Elinor Wylie. So I have dedicated this book to her." When she came to write "goodbye" to him, she smudged it: "(I can't seem to write that word when I am writing to you). . . . Please write to me, and send me your poems.—My darling, I love you so much."

There was one sonnet she hadn't sent him, Sonnet XLVII, which falls near the close of the sequence:

> Well, I have lost you; and I lost you fairly;
> In my own way, and with my full consent.
> Say what you will, kings in a tumbrel rarely
> Went to their deaths more proud than this one went.
> Some nights of apprehension and hot weeping
> I will confess; but that's permitted me;
> Day dried my eyes; I was not one for keeping
> Rubbed in a cage a wing that would be free.
> If I had loved you less or played you slyly
> I might have held you for a summer more,
> But at the cost of words I value highly,
> And no such summer as the one before.
> Should I outlive this anguish—and men do—
> I shall have only good to say of you.

She acknowledged that she'd lost him, but that admission was leavened by her assertion that it had been with "my full consent"—even "In my own way." Though apparently revealing, the poem remains covert; the poet has managed the neat trick of having the last word. She is both wounded and defiant. Even in her hurt, her anguish, she will survive both her anguish and the loss of him. And that, of course, is precisely what she did.

3

Fatal Interview was published on April 15, 1931. Its sales in the first ten weeks after publication were an astonishing 33,000 copies. Even before publication the demand for the first edition was so substantial that Harper appointed a three-man committee to draw lots to decide fairly who should get the limited copies. The fifty-dollar limited edition, autographed by Millay, was three times oversubscribed. At auction, a copy of the fifty-dollar edition of *Buck* went for two hundred dollars. According to one newspaper report, there was no living American author whose first editions enjoyed such esteem with collectors. In the heart of the Depression, Millay's sonnet sequence was selling as if it held secrets. And while there had always been a certain curiosity about Millay's life, now, after the publication of *Fatal Interview,* everybody wanted to know more about its author.

One reporter drove to Austerlitz to find out.

> A book of poems by a modern writer which sells a thousand copies is rated as a success by publishers. Several of Edna St. Vincent Millay's books have sold more than fifty thousand copies. . . . Millay . . . throughout the years will be a bookseller's staple, like Shakespeare and ink and two-cent stamps.

In the past, he continued, every young man in the English-speaking world had quoted Rudyard Kipling's line that "a woman is only a woman, but a good cigar is a smoke"; now young women had taken to heart Millay's quatrain as signal of their freedom in this new age:

> My candle burns at both ends;
>   It will not last the night;
> But ah, my foes, and oh, my friends—
>   It gives a lovely light!

In article after article she appeared in a consistent role. She might be photographed wearing a tailored suit with the inevitable soft collar and necktie of a gent, but she was always—whether described by a male or female reporter—a lovely, fragile child.

It is safe to say that by the late summer, with 50,000 copies of *Fatal Interview* in print and *The King's Henchman*'s becoming the most successful American opera yet mounted by the Metropolitan Opera, Edna Millay had become not simply a literary figure but a celebrity. If Scott Fitzgerald was far more than the prose chronicler of the Jazz Age, Edna St. Vincent Millay, who was his contemporary, told their generation what to say about how they felt, and she said it with wit, style, and passion. She gave the Jazz Age its lyric voice.

While Millay's poems were selling, and while she was providing the press with copy, there was something disturbing about the public vision of her that the press promoted. How would she keep from becoming that fragile child whom they adored?

Elizabeth Breuer, who'd written about Cora the spring before, wanted to do a companion piece about Vincent. She was a close friend of Norma's from New City (where as the wife of the painter Henry Varnum Poor she was called Bessie Poor), and Millay felt ambivalent about the interview. She wanted to do Norma a good turn, but clearly the inquisitiveness of any reporter, no matter how good a friend, was on her mind when she wrote to Norma:

> Say, listen, Unconscious! . . . If you want me to give any interview to Bessie Poor, you bring Bessie Poor up here. If you're going to get something out of it, I'll do it, and I'll see that she gets some exclusive material . . . of course I can't give out any dope from what you call "Ugin's angle." I can't say, "Yes, I wrote these sonnets to my husband," or, "No, I wrote these sonnets to my butler," or, "Must I be faithful just because I'm married" or "Must I be unfaithful just because I'm married?"

When Breuer arrived with Norma one afternoon, there were several guests already at Steepletop. Max Eastman with his Russian wife, the painter Eliena Krylenka, the poets Theodore Maynard and Harold Lewis Cook, as well as their neighbor Bill Brann, a stockbroker and breeder of a stable of racehorses, were all sitting in the living room gathered about a large round of Stilton. Central to the gathering was not Edna but Eugen:

> . . . he was dominating the whole roomful of people by the beauty of his sun-browned body, clad only in a pair of khaki shorts; by the vigor and gayety of his mind and person, by his quick jests and quiet courtesy. His keen blue eyes darted piercing, laughing glances; his whole body quivered with some jest. He is like Douglas Fairbanks in physical bearing and quickness, and has the patrician bearing and cast of features of a Dutch aristocrat, being a junior member of a family of international bankers of Holland.
> Soon there were sounds of a high, sweet voice in the air. The door opened, and we arose to the advance of a little figure with a delicate face and red-gold, curly hair, dressed in white—Edna, or "Vincent" Millay as her friends and family call her. She perched up on a lounge with the quick, sudden movement of a bird, and was off in a gay recital with her tall neighbor, which had to do with horses and dogs and other country interests.
> This was a pretty girl talking.

"She might be anywhere between twenty and thirty-five years old," Breuer wrote, whereas she was six months shy of forty. Millay was again made into a child, a gifted, fragile, birdlike, faery child:

> Other poets are writing in America and in Europe today, but we have to go all the way back to Byron to find one who has been, like her, so much a matter of personal excitement to her generation. Like Byron, she speaks for the young, the rebellious.

This was the *girl poet,* a treasured, pure, tiny beauty, not the swashbuckling, burly, perverse Lord Byron who had an army of creditors and lovers and who swam the Grand Canal in Venice at night holding a torch aloft with one hand. The fact that in publicity photographs taken by Berenice Abbott after her mother's death Edna had been dressed like a young man went unmentioned. To what, the reporter asked her, did she attribute her enormous popularity?

> I think people like my poetry because it is mostly about things that anybody has experienced. Most of it is fairly simple for a person to understand. If you write about people who are in love, and about death, and nature, and the sea, thousands . . . understand . . . my poetry because it's about emotions, about experiences common to everybody.
>
> Then, too, my images are homely, right out of the earth. I never went to a big city, you know, until I was twenty years old, so that I have an age-old simplicity in the figures I employ. I use the same figures that my great-grandmother might have used, and you can just sit in your farmhouse, or your home anywhere, and read it and know you've felt the same thing yourself.

People could and did memorize her poetry because "it is written in old-fashioned forms, in the very musical tradition that people have always known and loved." But how, the reporter continued, did she feel as a woman about the laurels hung on her head? Were they heavy? A burden? Millay looked stern for a moment.

> A woman poet is not at all different from a man poet. She should write from the same kind of life, from the same kind of experience, and should be judged by the same standards. If she is unable to do this, then she should stop writing. A poet is a poet. The critics should estimate her work as such. Instead they compare her poetry with that of men poets, then say condescendingly, "This is pretty good for a woman poet." What I want to know is, is it a good or a bad sonnet. That is all as a poet that I am interested in.

" 'What you produce, what you create must stand on its own feet,' she continued, 'regardless of your sex. We are supposed to have won all the battles for our rights to be individuals, but in the arts women are still put in a class by themselves, and I resent it, as I have always rebelled against discriminations or limitations of a woman's experience on account of her sex.' "

Breuer asked Edna how she managed her household, admitting late that she "was asking for myself and for all women who have children and husbands and a house to take their first energy." Millay seemed startled.

"I have nothing to do with my household," she answered quickly. "Eugen does all that kind of thing. He engages the servants. He shows them around. He tells them everything. I don't interfere with his ordering of the house. If there is anything I don't like, I tell him. I have no time for it. I want to go into my dining room as if it were a restaurant, and say, 'What a charming dinner!' "

She was quite clear about what form her insulation from the world of domesticity should take:

It's this unconcern with my household that protects me from the things that eat up a woman's time and interest. Eugen and I live like two bachelors. He, being the one who can throw household things off more easily than I, shoulders that end of our existence, and I have my work to do, which is the writing of poetry.

But I haven't made the decision to ignore my household as easily as it sounds. I care an awful lot that things be done right. Yet I don't let my concern break in and ruin my concentration and my temper. . . .

I work all the time. I always have notebook and pencil on the table at my bedside. I may wake up in the middle of the night with something I want to put down. Sometimes I sit up and write in bed furiously until dawn. And I think of my work all the time even when I am in the garden or talking to people. That is why I get so tired. When I finished "Fatal Interview" I was exhausted. I was never away from the sonnets in my mind. Night and day I concentrated on them for the last year and a half. . . . When you write a poem something begins to be a part of your thought and your life, and you become more and more conscious of it. It forms as if conjured out of steam. After I've written off the first rush of what one may call inspiration, then I really begin working on it. I begin by picking it to pieces and say, "This is awful." "That's not so bad." The rest, the final and inevitable shaping of the poem, is just hard work.

In the middle of their discussion about writing, the gong sounded for dinner. Soon the bright white dining room was festive with good talk and delicious food. Two of Charlie Ellis's paintings were hung on the walls, and the mahogany sideboard and table were laid with fine linens and china. "What gayety at the table!" Breuer wrote admiringly. "A philosopher and a social revolutionist, a painter, a singer, a poet, a writer, and a country gentleman, all engaged in sipping honey from life."

But Breuer made one observation in this interview that was unsettling: after dinner Millay quietly disappeared. "Eugen came down and joined us, saying he had just put Vincent to bed. She was tired out after such an exciting day of visitors. He had constantly to guard her against fatigue. She gave herself so intensely to every person."

Here was a woman nearly forty, a successful, productive author who now earned the money upon which Steepletop was run, being put to bed like a child. Eugen took care of her so that she might find that silence within which writers make their work. But there is a difference between that kind of usefulness, that kind of service and sheltering, and putting her to bed after supper. Listen to how he described himself to Breuer. He had been talking to her of his delight with his pheasant preserve, of their young English setter, Ghost Writer, whom he was trying to train, and of Altair, their German shepherd. He talked about their cattle and their pet black pig, Cochy. He explained that he had four men working the farm.

> I was astonished at his choice of occupation, and he countered, "Why should it surprise you? Vincent and I live like two men, bachelors, who choose their different jobs. I gave up my work in town because it doesn't interest me as much as this job, if I can smooth out things for her.
>
> "It is more worthwhile for her to be writing, even if she writes only one sonnet in a year, than for me to be buying coffee for a little and selling it for a trifle more. . . . I have had the luck to live with superior people. Inez Milholland, my first wife, was a great personality. She opened my mind to all the great questions of existence. Max Eastman, with whom I kept bachelor hall for five years, was a thrilling intellectual companion. Now I live with a person so great in mind, so beautiful in spirit and in person, that it is the most exciting, the most stimulating kind of living to keep up with her. We study together. We play together, and it's a race to keep up with her. It makes me in love with life."

The next morning he made Edna breakfast, squeezing her a tall glass of fresh orange juice; and when she did not come down until about eleven, he kept the others from interrupting her while she walked to her garden and about the grounds of Steepletop.

Millay made a point of refusing to explain or to defend her choices. She said the dilemma of a marriage and a career had no effect upon her. Still, hadn't marriage interfered with the freedom that was so necessary to a poet?

> "But we are free. I am sure I don't feel more bound than I was before I married. I have never settled down. I never could have married the kind of person with whom I would have had to settle down, or if I had, lived with him long. My husband is responsive to my every mood. That's the only way in which I can live and be what I am.
>
> "I am," she continued, "just as free as I was when I was a girl."

Marriage hadn't "dulled" her; she was as adventurous and alive as she had ever been. "I can be like that because my husband is like that. We get on so marvelously." She was crazy about music; he was crazy about music. She loved the sea; he loved the sea. He was part Irish, and so was she. They were both wild about the country, yet they both loved to get away to the city "and live in grand style," to wear evening dress and go to gay parties, to buy gorgeous clothes, and then to go home and forget all about them and wear comfortable old country things.

"I'm just terribly lucky—that's all. Why, he even loves to travel with me on my lecture tours."

It went on like that until Breuer finally muttered, "Children?"

> "Children," she echoed. "I don't know. Doubtless if I had children I wouldn't be so free, but I would try to be intelligent about it and not give every moment to them. But I don't really know. . . . I am a very concentrated person as an artist. I can't take anything lightly. After I have finished a book I am completely exhausted, and it isn't at all because I am weak. . . . I can spade a garden and not get tired, but the nervous intensity attendant on writing poetry, on creative writing, exhausts me, and I suffer constantly from a headache. It never leaves me while I am working, and for that there is no cure save not to work. Doctors advise me to go away for a rest cure, but who wants to lie stretched on one's back idle for months at a time? I might as well call it my occupational disease, resign myself to live with it and forget about it."

Millay made a striking connection here, moving from the reporter's question about having children to her headaches when she works. And if she were "just as free as I was when I was a girl," that freedom was not about being unfettered; her girlhood had been lived in a state of almost overwhelming domestic responsibility.

If she saw herself as fragile, as needing to be protected, surely having a child would severely and permanently have altered her status. Having a child suggests relinquishing being one. Not becoming a mother may leave one locked into a sort of permanent role-playing as a child. None of the Millay women had children. It is safe to say that their childhood, which they romanticized, was as much one of hardship and loneliness as it was marked by beauty. But that beauty had been achieved at a cost.

When Eugen said that they were living "like two men," what could it have meant? In the context of the interview, it was reduced to meaning simply that they shared the work equally, each according to his own abilities and needs. But they didn't. Only Edna appeared to be taken care of, protected, insulated. She was doing all the creative work; she was also earning all their income, or most of it. The balance between them had shifted. And why was it that no one mentioned that the subject of *Fatal Interview* was the progress of an adulterous love affair between an older married woman and a younger man?

4

Edna had begun work on a series of poems about her mother's death that summer, in rough draft in her notebooks.

> We said, Let us shut the coffin now, we cannot keep her always
> Like a doll in a box, arranging her hair. . . .
> She looks as if she were tired of being stared at, as if she were
>   anxious to be dead.
>
> We said, Let us shut the coffin now, this minute, and be done with it
> And promise each other we won't come in on the sly and open it for
>   a last look;
> It is morbid to act the way we do, it is wrong, it is unhealthy. . . .
> But I've often thought since that they really should invent a coffin
> Whose lid doesn't close with a click, that it would be easier afterward
>   but of course you can't tell.

That poem remains unpublished and in draft. So does this one, studded with autobiographical details:

> Lost face, never again to be seen by me,
> Where shall I go now for comfort, what door try,
> Trusting to find behind it comfort, as in the days
> When you were behind some door—the door of the sitting-room,
> The door of the kitchen, a different door from this,
> A door with a knob, a door that could be opened?
>
> I know. I know. Spring comes. Life is sweet.
> And the race goes on. Goes somewhere.
> And what has been eaten by all men I can eat.

When you taught me to play the piano,
Your hands, hot from the wash-tub, hastily dried,
Were red, & steamed above the keys,—
Clean
Bright & golden from the suds on your left hand,
    bubbled with suds
  showing me the chord,
Your wedding ring would shine.

Within a few pages this draft also stopped, and she started more certainly the poem that begins "Oh, what a lovely town were Death, / Dwelt you therein . . ." It would become, in 1934, the first of six poems published about her mother's death. Untitled in draft, she would call it "Valentine," Valentine's Day having been the actual date of her mother's burial at Steepletop.

Oh, what a shining town were Death
Woke you therein, and drew your breath
My buried love; and all you were,
Caught up and cherished, even there.
Those evil windows loved of none
Would blaze as if they caught the sun.

Woke you in Heaven, Death's kinder name,
And downward in sweet gesture came
From your cold breast your rigid hand,
Then Heaven would be my native land.

But you are nowhere: you are gone
All roads into Oblivion.
Whither I would disperse, till then
From home a banished citizen.

Here, in the first line, the earlier and weaker "lovely town" becomes the "shining town" in which her mother awakes rather than dwells. Alive, then, her hand capable of motion, it is no longer her wedding ring that shines in the light of memory; Death itself is defied.

That summer Millay met Georgia O'Keeffe in Lake George. There's no evidence they had ever met before, but oddly enough they shared a friendship with Mitchell Kennerley, who had given O'Keeffe some of Millay's books. The only record that remains of that encounter is O'Keeffe's letter to her afterward:

My dear Edna St. Vincent Millay!

I did not mean to be cold——I was surprised to see you—
and you
came so quickly and were gone so quickly that I did not recover from my surprise.

—I must tell you too what was going through my head as you stood there—

Last summer I had a very beautiful large white studio—with a very large window and a very wide double door—It was by an irrigation ditch on the desert—

—The bushes and small trees by the ditch attracted many birds—

There was no screen at the door—

—and often the birds would fly into the room——very hard against the window thinking it was the sky———

One day a humming bird flew in—

It fluttered against the window till I got it down where I could reach it with an open umbrella—

—When I had it in my hand it was so small I couldn't believe I had it—but I could feel the intense life—so intense and so tiny—

I opened my hand the least little bit to look to see if I really had it——and before I could see it at all it was fluttering against the window again—
—I caught it four times before I really had a little peep at it and let it fly out the door—

You were like the humming bird to me——If you do not understand what I mean your husband undoubtedly will—

——It is a very sweet memory to me—

And I am rather inclined to feel that you and I know the best part of one another without spending much time together—

——It is not that I fear the knowing—

It is that I am at this moment willing to let you be what you are to me——it is beautiful and pure and very intensely alive—

—I am busy with things that I wish to keep busy with right now—

But if I may feel free to go to you when I really feel free for that—I would like that—like it very much—only you must promise that if you are not ready when I am ready you will not let me disturb you——I will understand——and love you

Georgia O'Keeffe—

CHAPTER 27

On December 8, 1931, Millay wrote to George Dillon, whom she had just seen in Chicago. Crucially, it was the first time she had gone to him without Eugen. The rendezvous was fraught with conflict. "Oh darling," she wrote from the train, "I wanted to say so many things to you, not at all the things I said. Why did I have to tease us at the last moment with such painful things, leaving us both with our minds full of cruel images." Dillon had told her he'd been almost crazed in her absence, and when she'd tried to reassure him—that she, too, had had periods of what she called "extravagant depression" when she thought she'd lost "both my mother & you, & tried my best to drink myself right out of the picture"— she couldn't see, or admit, the immense difference in their situations. She had Eugen, after all.

When her train stopped in Albany, she wrote another letter from the depot. She said she couldn't stop writing to him and she couldn't believe she wasn't going to see him that night. They had both been drinking heavily in Chicago. "Can't remember taking the train—can't remember being in the station—but I do remember that you came into the train with me for one moment & that you kissed me goodbye." It had taken three full years—and the death of her mother—for their affair to develop to the point at which she was willing not only to dream of spending time with him but to make concrete plans. "Yes, I really mean it.—What's the use? This seeing you for a day or two every year or two—it's no good—it makes me too unhappy.—I love you and I want to be with you—it's as simple as that."

Of course, things are never as simple as that, certainly not when one is married. But how she felt about Dillon is perfectly caught in this note she scribbled in pencil beneath his telephone number:

> Let us be fools & love forever,
> There was a woman, if tales be true,
> Who shattered Troy for a shepherd boy,
> Less beautiful than you.

She would work to secure a Guggenheim Fellowship for him, which would give him both the money to write and the time to be with her in France. "Oh, darling, let me meet you in Paris. . . . Write me three of the million things you've been thinking about. . . . I'll write you the one thing I've been thinking about:—In the spring I shall be with you."

—

Henry Allen Moe, the president of the Guggenheim Foundation, dropped Millay a note in January, as soon as he received her recommendations: "Dear Miss Millay: . . . As I have said to you before, we are constantly in your debt for the *quality* of advice you give us." She had been asked that year about four writers: Eleanor Delamater, Abbie Huston Evans (her old friend from their Camden girlhood), Max Eastman, and George Dillon. Although Max was one of Eugen's dearest friends, she was brutally honest about his abilities as a poet: "I regretfully assure you that money afforded Mr. Eastman to enable him to write poetry is money unprofitably dispensed, since Mr. Eastman is," and here she softened her draft* from "a bad poet" to "not a good poet." She also cut this sentence from what appears to be her final draft: "If, knowing the use which he intends to make of this Fellowship, you prefer Mr. Eastman before either Miss Evans or Mr. Dillon, you will be dealing American poetry a blow on the mouth from which it will stagger for years."

Millay pointed out her relationship to Evans and gave an honest, well-mannered recommendation: "Her poetry has not and perhaps will never have wide popularity, but there is a hard integrity in it and a country-bred passion. . . . I most sincerely and without reserve recommend her to you." It was generous, and it lacked heart.

But her words on Dillon rang with passionate conviction. Millay called him "the most important poet of his age writing in America today." Her description of the nature of his needs was most revealing:

> [H]e needs a respite from the advertising business, which is as bad a spiritual environment for a lyric poet as anything I know. In the second place, he needs urgently a complete change also in his physical environment. . . . His admirers find one real danger for him, that unless vigorously stimulated and richly fed by the world about him he may come more and more to eat and drink himself.

This is a curious thing to say about someone you love—maybe it was simply a justification for her own support, for certainly she was planning to provide him with the vigorous stimulation he required in Paris in the spring.

—

*Since the Guggenheim Foundation continues to respect its own assurances of confidentiality even after the deaths of all to whom they extend their fellowships, I have quoted from Millay's drafts of letters to them.

That September, Viking Press had brought out George Dillon's second volume of poems, *The Flowering Stone,* dedicated to Harriet Monroe. Of its four parts, one was called "Anatomy of Death," another "Addressed to the Doomed." A voice of lassitude and loss underscored the entire book; even the title suggests bereavement.

The most extraordinary thing about this volume was its secret: several of the lyrics had been written to Millay, and the closing section of ten sonnets was the answering cry to her sonnet sequence in *Fatal Interview.* His sonnets, like hers, were in the Shakespearean form with its rhyming, ringing final couplet; his, too, followed the tempo of the earth's weather, except that he began in time past, which is never truly seasonal but always somewhat funereal. Such a doomed and elegiac tone for a man so young and in his prime. He must have been as difficult to reassure or to persuade as a fearful, demanding child who will insist that the kitten is lost, the dog dead, the food lumpy and cold. He was a shallower vessel than she understood. If Millay was his muse, she appears, in his poems, as uncertain and almost spent. Here is his lovely "Woman without Fear":

> How beautiful is a woman whose avarice is over.
> She is content that time should take what it will.
> She is proud to have no pride. She asks of her lover
> Love only, for good or ill.
>
> She makes of her body a strange bed till morning
> Wherein he breathes oblivion better than sleep;
> And when he wakes she is nowhere—she has fled without warning,
> And left him nothing to keep
>
> But the trace of her tears on the pillow, and a bright strand
> Out of her hair, and happiness, and a little grief. . . .

There is in this sleepy realm an eerie loveliness. Dillon's beautiful, sweet lyric "She Sleeps" is marred only by the stalling clumsiness of the Latinate opening word,

> Incipiently, the hush of death
> Lies on her limbs like early snow.
> Love, in this light-drawn tide of breath,
> Cares little whether it wake or no.
>
> As summer sleeps in autumn's arms,
> So every cry and every kiss
> And all love's laughter and alarms
> Were but a clamouring toward this;

So even the fruit forsakes the vine;
So even the heart's high branch blows bare;
So even her lips are lost from mine
Like leaves upon the flying air.

But these are odd poems in praise of love, fearful and preternaturally old. Nothing sings in Dillon's veins—there's not a bark of laughter, no gasp of joy; not a hoot, a drunken slip of decorum. We are in the high romantic lyric mode for sure, and we remember her rebuke in one of her earliest letters to him: "Will the gentleman from Kentucky . . ." What did she see in him besides his youth and beauty? Did she yearn for his languor and hesitation after years of Eugen's irrepressible élan?

George Dillon was not the only one to publish a book of poems in the fall of 1931. Kathleen Millay's *The Beggar at the Gate,* her third book of poetry, was reviewed by many of the same people who had reviewed Edna's book in the spring. Percy Hutchison in *The New York Times* said that while the poems were "Melodious, intelligent, varied and exquisite within their limitations, [they] are, nevertheless, limited." William Rose Benét was little better: "Kathleen Millay is primarily an impromptu singer. . . . There is rhythm in everything she writes, but one sometimes longs for a stricter discipline of the verse as a whole." The Boston *Transcript* said flatly that the book did not "yet lift the author out of the ranks of the minor poets." That "yet" was merciful. If the sisters were competitors for critical esteem, Kathleen's portion was stinting. Without Cora, there was no longer an intermediary to soften the critical blows.

Susan Jenkins Brown, a book editor at the Macaulay Publishing Company, the firm that had published Kathleen's second novel, *Against the Wall,* in 1929, remembered a scene with Kathleen in the very early thirties, when she had come into the office. As the conversation was drawing to a close, out of nowhere, Kathleen said defiantly that Edna's poetry had all come from her.

"I thought, 'She is a madwoman,' " Brown recalled. "I thought that immediately. I said to myself, 'Just don't say anything because it is useless.' . . . You know, we all knew, that it was because of Edna that her mother had come to New York. And it was Edna who saw Kathleen into Vassar. I knew that—so to have *this* sitting in front of me!"

Kathleen would never publish another collection of poems.

2

"Edna St. Vincent Millay Heads for Spain Aboard Freighter," announced the headline of a New York newspaper on February 21, 1932. She was quoted as saying saucily, "This trip is an impulse from which I may never return."

She called George in Chicago the night before she set sail. When he wrote to her, he said she had "the most beautiful voice in the world."

> Darling . . . I will come to Paris in April, whether I get the fellowship or not. As I told you, I shall be poor—even poorer, perhaps, if I *get* the fellowship, for then I should attempt to live on the income from that.

Then he told her just how much in love with her he was:

> In spite of the neurotic moods that come between us—in spite of my bad manners and insane behaviour. You have been sweet and patient always, and I am really grateful. If I ever amount to anything, it will be because you loved me, and continued to love me through these terrible years.

There were terms, however, to their romantic departure, and Millay set them. She was traveling with Eugen.

At the end of April, Eugen dropped a postcard to Norma and Charlie from Paris: "Darlinks, here we are. Walked in Mallorca, fought the bulls in Spain, and stopped for a month with my brother in Antibes." Later that week they were invited to a formal dinner at the American Embassy in Paris, where Millay was to be the guest of honor. They were in a cab on the way to the embassy when Eugen, tossing his cigarette out of the window, saw three men running across a bridge. Curious, he told Edna he wanted to find out what was going on and jumped out of the taxi. Leaning over the parapet of the bridge, he saw a woman's white face in the water. "Her hand was flung up for a moment," he said later, "as if in appeal to me, and then she went under."

Without hesitation, he stripped himself of his high silk hat, his overcoat, and his scarf and dropped his "smoking" on the footpath leading down to the water. Some who were watching called out to him not to jump in because she was dead. But he had seen her raise her hand. He dove in. Floyd Dell quoted Eugen about the adventure in a piece he wrote for the New York *Herald Tribune*:

> The Seine is not a wide river—or so it seems from the outside. But when you are in it the Seine is one of the widest rivers in the world, besides being

very cold, very swift and very dirty. As I swam toward the woman—who might already be dead—I wished I were not there. I was afraid that if she were alive she might grab me and drown me. Something like that had almost happened to me once, in Holland. I was afraid of her. I resented her. Why did she have to pick this time to jump into the river, just when I was passing by, on my way to a beautiful dinner? I did not feel at all heroic. I felt sorry for myself. At the same time I remembered her white face, and her hand flung up in appeal to me, and I felt a kind of personal affection for her, not as if she were a stranger, but as though she were some one whom I had an absolute obligation to save.

When he reached her, afraid of being seized, he dove under her, grabbing her neck as he came up. All he got was a cheap fur neckpiece. He plunged again. This time he held her by the back of her neck and swam diagonally to the shore. The woman was unconscious and pale but alive.

"Parisians who happened to pass about seven o'clock last night on the Pont Royal," said *L'Intransigeant,*

were witnesses of a not commonplace scene. An American gentleman in evening clothes (who afterward modestly declined to give the police his name) had leaped from the bridge and rescued from drowning a young woman who had thrown herself in despair from the Pont du Carrousel just upstream. From the American Embassy word got about that this brave American gentleman was Eugen Boissevain, who was in Paris with his wife, Edna Millay, the poet.

"Eugen Boissevain," the article continued, "is the sort of person who might turn up anywhere and do some extraordinary thing—a great, broad-shouldered, sun-browned Hollander with an enormous gusto for life, gay, laughter-loving, irrepressible and unexpected."

They raced back to their hotel. Eugen changed into the only dark suit he had, and they arrived at the embassy an hour late.

The next day they went to the Hôpital de la Charité, where the poor young woman was recovering. Her name was Pauline Venys, and she knew Eugen was the instrument of God sent to rescue her.

George Dillon had never traveled to Europe, let alone walked in Mallorca. He had no money other than the little he'd saved from his advertising job in Chicago, but he was becoming the darling of the critics, and he was about to enjoy a popular success of his own. On April 28, 1932, Dillon won the Pulitzer Prize for *The Flowering Stone,* as the best book of poetry published in 1931. In its press release, the Pulitzer committee wrote, "Of the four or five volumes which received most serious consideration, Mr. Dillon's verse seemed most original and authentic.... his poems are exceedingly beautiful. The prize is awarded to him as a young poet of very great promise."

George wrote back to the committee from Paris that the prize had never meant more to anybody than it did to him: "I feel strengthened and encouraged as never before." But, he continued, "this is my first trip abroad, and you'd have to call out the marines to get me back now!" He sounded young and jubilant, and by then he was a man who knew he'd won the Guggenheim, too.

Alix Daniels, a friend and colleague of George's from *Poetry* magazine, described the apartment he took on the boulevard Saint-Germain:

> It was one of those banal little places furnished with dingy odds and ends—a salon sparsely furnished with furniture that ran to rickety curved legs and dusty green velvet upholstery, a tiny inconvenient kitchen, a bedroom with a huge armoir. Even the concierge was impossible—a hefty dame upholstered in black bombazine.

By mid-May, George Dillon had been with Millay in Paris for just over a month. She had remained at the Hôtel Port-Royal, an elegant old hotel on the Left Bank, where Eugen wrote to her from the M.S. *Lafayette,* en route to New York, on May 10.

> Darling—
> ... I passed George's train. C'est egal, quand meme!—My love, all my love to you—I'm thinking of you as gay and happy. I'm fine.—Goodbye my courageous lion. When I come back you must be again the roaring lion. . . . Skiddlepins—the brave.

Eugen had decided to leave them alone together. The implication was that Dillon would be the tonic she needed. Just before his ship reached Plymouth, he wrote to her again:

> Uge had rainbows on the starboard side all day long. And I thought of all the rainbows we had seen together.
> The people seem of the dullest. Except one girl in a beautiful grey dress a la Louise Boulanger. She is cute. A lovely smile and she is small and dainty and reminds me of you, vaguely. I had a drink in the bar and . . . well you know, . . . I thought of you & missed you and so had to drink another and missed you more.
> I love you. More than ever you can know.—

Darling Scramoodle, sweet sweet Freckels, I love you. Be happy and without a care. Button up your over coat and be careful about booze and crossing streets. I love you— . . . —I kiss you on your soft sensitive lips. I love you. . . . Poor Bibs! Loving so much two galumps! and one is more than an ordinary girl can stand!—Never you mind. You can manage it— and you'll have a life richer than any girl, but not rich enough to scare me— Go to it Scramoodles, and no heartaches or feeling sorry for ANYBODY!—

My undying love
Sniggybus

The girl in the gray dress stands out in this letter as a hint from Eugen that he, too, is sexually alive. In the closing lines of the second sonnet in *Fatal Interview*, which she'd told George was for Eugen, she had written:

Along my body, waking while I sleep,
Sharp to the kiss, cold to the hand as snow,
The scar of this encounter like a sword
Will lie between me and my troubled lord.

Her affair with Dillon had altered her sexual relationship with her husband. If she was no longer, or rarely, making love with Eugen, this time alone with George became more weighty. Unwilling or unable to give up Eugen, Edna was meanwhile trying to decide if she needed them both in her life, and how to manage it.

3

On the morning of May 14, Edna dispatched a letter of four sentences to Eugen. She wished him a happy birthday and assured him she loved him: "Darling . . . Going to write you a biggie, biggie letter in a minute. I love you. I couldn't possibly love anybody else as much as I love you." But there was no biggie to follow. She cabled him the next week on the exact date of his birthday. Eugen told her by return post that he didn't know what he would have done without her greetings. He did note, however, that all her wires had been sent from Paris between 1 and 3 A.M., "So you are going early to bed!—Bad darling, sweet, sweet Scramoodles. But be careful of yourself.—Please look after yourself.—Please, *please,* be selfish!"

Three days after her four-line letter, she wrote again. "Darling Skiddlepins," she said, "This is another skimpy awful letter, but you know how I am about letters.—I've missed you just all the time. Everything is marvelous, but there's nobody such fun as you.—I'm happy, though,—I can't write you much because you always leave letters around so!"

Alix Daniels, who was in Paris at this time and was no friend of Millay's, thought that Edna's demands were exhausting her young lover and that she was driving him away with her sexual jealousy. "She was a woman who was sexually high-geared. She was wearing George out. He once said, 'It's too much for me.' She was forever testing him and his feeling for her. For instance, one day as the three of us were walking across the Pont-Neuf in Paris, Vincent stopped and leaned perilously over the parapet. George took her arm and pulled her back. Then she said, 'So, you don't want me to take the leap. Would you leap in after me and drag me ashore? Perhaps though you'd do the same for that poor fellow under the bridge should he leap in.' It was a *clochard*—one of those derelicts who lurk under bridges in Paris. George said, 'You are not bracketed in my mind with that tramp, and you know it.' She shrugged and treated him to one of those saberlike flashes from those little gray-green eyes of hers and we walked on.

"Well, when the evening was over and we were taking a taxi back to our hotels, Edna said she was getting out with me. I made excuses, each one more lame than the one before. She pressed. Finally I said, 'Besides, the bed is too small.' She said, 'Oh, we won't be doing any sleeping!' The idea was that if she couldn't have George, she'd take me.

"But the next day I was sent a gold Cartier heart, some silk handkerchiefs, and a bouquet of violets! That was the way she was. She was not really interested in me, mind you. She wanted George. Whether it was to dance with him or to sleep with him, she wanted him on her own terms. And when he would not or could not accept those terms, she retaliated."

                                               ❧ ❧ ❧

Norma had been listening to what I'd told her about Alix Daniels, and she was impatient. "Oh, why drag all that in? Isn't the story good enough without women?"

That night, sitting before the fire at Steepletop after we'd finished drinking our coffee with heavy cream, Norma, who had been watching *Mary Hartman, Mary Hartman* on TV, looked across the room at me. I was half asleep, dozing on one of her couches. "Naancy," she drawled in her low voice, as if it were three syllables, "haven't you ever wanted to reach out and touch . . ." She paused. "I remember standing down at the pool while ———, you know she was ———'s wife, swam toward me. Her small lovely breasts seemed to be floating on the water, and I just wanted to reach out and touch their tips." Norma made a very theatrical yawn, bringing the back of her small fist to her lips, and stretched. "People used to say that I did what Vincent Millay wrote about." Norma's eyes glowed wickedly in the firelight as she scratched the belly of her cat, Debs. "How are you going to handle that?"

❧ ❧ ❧

If Edna's letters to Eugen were scant, his to her were voluminous, abundant in their details, pages and pages telling her what he'd done, whom he had seen, how he felt. He kept telling her how beautiful Steepletop was:

> . . . the hyacinths are in full blossom, large blooms like in Holland . . . the lawn mowed and trim and neat; the drive nearly raked; the water in the swimming pool, shining in the moonlight like a real body of water. Oh, hell, I cannot describe but I know that never, even at Drafna, did I feel such delight and emotion, at coming home to the most beautiful place in creation. . . . I lit a fire and sat in the big room, naked looking at the fire, for the first time at Steepletop without you.

Here was a man trying to live by the terms they had agreed upon—an open, free marriage—yet telling her mercilessly of the loveliness that they had created together as he cut his first asparagus, took them to the summerhouse down by the pool, and ate his harvest with "melted fresh Steepletop-butter also a bottle of white wine. I am glad nobody saw me," he continued. "I felt like a traitor eating them without you. It would have been criminal not to have done it, but I hardly could swallow and I fear I had tears in my eyes. Funny if someone had seen that. Crying over an asparagus."

Couldn't she return to Steepletop? They could "go back together, or if you prefer, I'll stay here. . . . Let me know what you want to do. . . . —Let me know. But remember, I was going away for only a month or so, and here I have been away almost a year."

The next letter was just as long, just as plaintive, and just as filled with domestic details. He had done the income taxes, he would send in the renewal slip for her driver's license. He begged her at least to give him her telephone number: "I just must hear your voice again." Of course, he said, he could hear her voice by thinking of it, "but I do not get it right and it drives me crazy. Am I a nuisance? . . . I wanted you to know that I can come back at any moment. I am a nuisance, but can I help it that I love you?"

He was not so lonely without her that he did not make plans to see friends: Deems Taylor was going to stay with him, and Margaret Cuthbert was scheduled to come the following week. He'd even driven down to see Norma and Charlie in New City, where Norma had proudly shown him her flower beds and rock garden just beyond their house.

My dear she has nothing in it but the plants you gave her. . . . Next to the plants are still the little wooden markers with your handwriting on them giving the names and instructions. It was more than I could stand. I had to light a cigarette, and look at any airplane which luckily passed overhead, and tie my bootlace or else she would have noticed.

In these interminable letters Eugen is calling to his wife to return to him, to Steepletop, to the pastoral life they've created together, where he is at his fullest as husband. It is spring in the Northeast, the earth is swelling with life, the bees are swarming, the cows are coming to calf, the horses are foaling, Ghost is in heat. Even her mother's lilacs, which she'd placed near the sunken garden, are white with blossoms. Toward evening he wrote again:

I've done the things you told me to do. How long, Edna, how long must I wait? . . . I will see you soon my dear? Good-night darling Freckles. I am but half alive away from you. Never have I longed for anyone, as I am longing for you. I want you. . . . I want to see you! and SMELL you! and hear you!

All he received in return was a brief note written on his birthday:

Darling Wham-wham, I had my breakfast this morning with your little picture propped up before me on the tray. I was missing you just awfully. I do a great deal of the time.—I hope Steepletop is beautiful now. It must be, I think. Paris has been clear & very hot the last few days. Today is filthy hot.

She enclosed her license, which she'd just found, and told him to have Norma forge her signature if he could not. *"Please don't fail me,* Skiddlepins!" Clearly, she hadn't received his last letter. How dispassionate and reserved she was, especially in comparison with his outpourings.

As for Eugen, his days were beginning to have a pattern. He got up at seven, made himself a glass of fresh orange juice, worked in the garden, sunbathed and swam, and then drove to Pittsfield to post his letters to her. He had a hunch she'd left the Port-Royal. "I hate not knowing where you are," he wrote. "Is it absolutely impossible for the three of us ever to be together?—must one always hide?—Well we'll have to find out.—We'll be intelligent and courageous and we'll find out.—And then others can profit by our mistakes and successes."

He insisted that he was "pleased with our couple." But his last sentence read, "I wish I was a couple again," because there were now two couples. "Do I write too often?" he asked. Even as he mailed that letter, he wrote another, slipped into an envelope with no salutation and no signature:

What ever happens, what ever you want, what ever changes you may go through: don't be afraid.—I'll understand everything.—and I will always love you.—Always love you.—I understand you, I get in your mood, as other people only understand themselves.—no matter what you do, I'll be as clever understanding and making excuses and justifying, as if I'd done it myself.—so don't be scared about anything.—

> I love you.—
> I worship you.—
> I know you.—

She had written three letters to his twelve, one of which consisted of two sentences. On May 25, she tried to be more expansive. She told him she'd loved his cables about Steepletop and swimming and described a lavish party she'd gone to the night before, given by Elsa Maxwell:

> I wore my new white dress & red jacket & beautiful white slippers with sparkling white buckles & long white gloves & a lovely new glittering handbag: But I was all alone, there wasn't a person there I'd ever seen before except Elsa herself & the girl she lives with, and I was not at Elsa's table. And everybody knew everybody else & I felt just like a Freshman the day he arrives at college. It was awful.

People were sweet to her, she told him,

> but I had the curse (of course I *would* have—came on just as I was dressing to go) & I felt awful & I felt blue & the music was awful for dancing, Hungarians playing jazz—what you might call "weather sultry"—track slow. . . . Anyway I was shockingly lonely, and I stayed on & on long after I wanted to go, because I hated so to go alone.

For the first time she mentioned her lover:

> George has found a charming apartment, very cheap, two rooms & bath for 800 francs a month. It is on the Boulevard St. Germain just opposite the lovely old church St. Germain des Pres, by the Deux Magots,—but facing on the court, so nice and quiet. He is taking French lessons. I'm going to find an apartment too, and get out of here. It's really darned expensive here, though it seemed cheap at first. I've been, I thought, pretty careful with my money—the only extra dress I've bought is one that I got for 2000 francs because it was the model's dress and just fitted me.

She was going to take an apartment, but not with Dillon, which must have been some consolation to Eugen. Taking an apartment at all, however, suggested that she did not intend to return home soon.

"I love your letters, my darling," she wrote a few days later, "but I don't know what to say. For one thing, I don't see how I'm going to get back into the States at all this summer with all those clothes to pay duty on!" She said it might cost her as much as $1,000 just to get in. Then she gave him a list of people she'd seen:

Allan Macdougall just called me up, back from Greece & Toulon.
Mary Kennedy dropped in Thursday & took me to lunch.
Lucie Delarue-Mardrus took café-au-lait with me Thursday afternoon.
Elsa Maxwell had me to dinner at her house last night with about twenty charming people.
George Dillon is coming here to have cocktails with me at 6:30 today, after which we are going out to dine & to the theatre.
Margaret Morris, of my old Pourville (Dieppe) summer-school days— she was the head of it—called me up yesterday & I am to take tea with her Tuesday.
Pauline Venys (whom you fished out of the Seine, darling) is at a convalescent home, & doing very well. She's had a fever, but it's all gone now. She keeps in touch with me, & I write her. She's very grateful, & in better spirits.

How disingenuous of her to slip George's name into her laundry list of encounters!

Eugen was no fool. He said he felt like Sherlock Holmes trying to piece together from the scant clues she threw his way how she truly felt. "I know you love to be secretive and hate to tell things, but in a couple of months more you will be a total stranger to me and I will have to call you Miss Millay. Silly." He decided he would not write so often. "I am ashamed having bombarded you with all my letters and cables. . . . I will write you once in a while, as I know you will like to hear from me once in a while, but there will be weeks that you will not hear from me."

"I am not going to be the black shadow between you and George and make you think that you must snatch your happiness whenever the ogre is away," he told her on June 2. "Settle down quietly, Edna, take a place for a year or come back here with him, do what you like, but do not think of me as the plague of Egypt, or as a husband who with a cold hand any day can be expected to separate two young lovers."

Tell George, he said, and "tell yourself, that you're going to be together for ever and ever, or as long as you wish to. As for me, I will not do anything drastic and will live off your money for a year, unless we make some definite decision before that time. But in a year, all three of us ought to know what we want."

It was the first time any acknowledgment was made that there was a time limit as to how long this could go on. Eugen was telling friends that he'd returned to America for business reasons. "If I stay here the rest of the year, it will not be a secret any more. If you do not mind, I certainly do not. What people think and say is the least of my troubles." He didn't want to return to her until he knew she wanted him, "and further I do not want you and George to think that you are snatching, and stealing, happy moments from a cruel world. I am giving you eternity: all your life."

That afternoon, their caretaker, John Pinnie, stopped in. Eugen got some whiskey, and as they began to talk and smoke, bashful and hesitant, John said;

> "How is Miss Millay?" "She is fine." A minute's silence. Then: "That's good," another silence then: "This is the most beautiful place in miles around." Then we smoked. "It is strange here without Miss Millay. . . . it don't seem natural. I felt sure Miss Millay would be back in her garden for the spring."

Eugen said it broke his heart the way John kept saying "She'd like some more pines here." "She's going to be unhappy about the lambs."

> She, she she all the time. . . . When he was leaving and I was thinking of putting my arms around him. . . . Does he sleep in my room with the door of your bedroom open for more air? Has he got to use your bathroom with your little dressing-table with your little Elizabeth Arden bottles on it? Has he got to sit in the big-room of an evening in front of the open fire? Eat in the kitchen, walk in the garden? Weed the perennial garden? Work in the kitchen garden? I love living alone, I like it, but living with a ghost, and such a disturbing and alive ghost: that's a different story.

"You must understand that I have been absolutely alone here for several days and nights alone with your presence and all your belongings and answering your mail," he continued.

> Forgive me for my little faith, Edna, but I was sure you could not love me, I did not like myself very much . . . and then I was scared, terribly scared that you loved me sufficiently only to be afraid to hurt me and that I was a stumbling block for you. . . . and I was miserable. I made certain inquiries and I know now that at any time I can go and live by myself and be economically independent, so that is anyway an obstacle out of the way: you need not bother about that part of it.

In the corner of the last page of his letter he wrote in ink in tiny letters:

"I

do

I

do

love you."

The balance in their relationship had shifted: Edna, the sick young poet who had married the wealthy, elegant, sophisticated, older European businessman, was now receiving letters from him assuring her and himself that he could support himself without her help.

He did have a confession to make to her: he'd been in love with a girl eight years earlier and he'd just seen her again. "We spent the night together, and I just received such a beautiful letter from her. It makes me very happy. I had a few love affairs. Very lovely ones, of which I will tell you when I see you." After which he added, "Difficult to write about. You know."

Eight years before would have been only a year after they had married. Eugen had therefore then been sexually involved with other women almost from the beginning of their marriage, and it was something they discussed openly.

Yet talking about an affair doesn't necessarily imply freedom from jealousy, or from hurt. While Eugen appeared to be accepting, even encouraging, Edna's affair with Dillon, he also wrote to her in language laced with sexual possessiveness and jealousy. In a letter sent in early June, he told her he could still see her standing on the balcony of the Hôtel Port-Royal in her yellow dressing gown waving good-bye to him,

> and that desperate desolate feeling I had then, that it was goodbye, that it was the King is dead . . . that the queen-bee had left the hive with all the young bees and the old bees staid back to die silently and without complaints. . . . But I'll let things go just so far for just so long, and then I am going to think only of Ugin, and then I am going after you and get you back, even if it was only for a night.

One morning he got up early, made the fire, had a cup of tea, and, sleepily, began to think of her "wickedly. I make pictures of you and I want to have you here. I want you so badly. I want to see your beautiful body and feel all over you and smell your lovely body and play with your naughty breasts and your kitty, the only clean wicked kitty in the world." Then he told her exactly what he wanted her to do. She was to have a very good manicure, "and don't put that awful red ugly stuff on them. I took a naughty undy of yours in my bed yesterday. I miss one of them. Oh, well, I'll punish you for all your wickedness. I have thought out delicious and refined tortures. . . . I kiss your wet lips." In ink, scrawled at the bottom of the letter, he added:

> Couldn't you take a small handkerchief and put it in your kitty, before you take a bath and mail it to me. I'm longing for your Perfume.—I'm longing to smell you.—All your clothes are so washed and cleaned. I couldn't get a smell of you.—Goodbye beautiful. I kiss your exciting breasts. Ugin.

She cabled him to come to Paris. He hesitated. In a letter postmarked June 20, he wrote:

> Everything would be damn simple if I knew you really wanted me: I'd be on a steamer by now. But may be you do it half because you want me, and half out of softness to me. May be in your funny Scramoodle-mind you have a little fear, that I will be a little bit of a nuisance and a little bit of a problem.

Did she want him to catch that day's boat? Or had she been sitting one night having dinner with George, "and a few bottles of wine and you felt awfully gay and happy and adventurous and you said, 'How Ugin would enjoy this. Let's send him a cable and tell him to come.' And may be you were a little drunk. And then, bingo, there I'd be, outstaying my welcome before I had arrived."

He decided to await her next cable. "I wish I knew your plans. If I have failed you in this, I will beat myself to death. . . . But I'm going to prevent you from killing our love by kindness to Ugin. I will not be a piece of irritating, dragging piece of family."

Pages later, he suddenly guessed why she had cabled: "You are expecting a baby. And you want me to be around so that people cannot figure out who's it is." If that were true, she should come to New York. He'd come and fetch her, but she should see a doctor right away. All she had to do was cable the single word: come. What he did not want to do, "having been so Goddamn wise these last months . . . [was] to spoil everything now."

CHAPTER 28

Edna Millay was not pregnant. She was, however, having a very difficult time with George. Finally, on June 22, she wrote Eugen the letter he'd longed for. She said she hadn't written before because she knew how indiscreet he was with letters, but now

> I really don't care who knows about the three of us, so long as they don't talk to me about it. George & I have been awfully happy together, but we're bad for each other, & we both know it. Neither of us is getting any work done. I don't mind, because I don't feel like working yet & don't want to.

But Dillon did mind. He took his Guggenheim Fellowship seriously, and he wanted "to be sober & studious & live within his really almost impossible income. He got seven hundred dollars less than they usually give . . . & he had to promise not to take a job or anything while he's living on the Fellowship."

But they weren't in Paris primarily to work. They were in Paris together to enjoy each other and to figure out what their relationship would be like without Eugen. Now she explains, defensively, to Eugen that she is paying her own way everywhere. "But just being with me tends to make him extravagant, because he just can't realize that I don't mind at all eating at seven francs prix fixe places & riding on the Metro. I really don't." But when she goes on to say she is nearly broke because she has bought some model dresses at Louise Boulanger's, she is certainly undermining any claim to thrift. She sounds petulant.

Then she drops her guard and tells Eugen the truth about Dillon: "Last Sunday evening I told George we'd better not see each other any more for a while. It was pretty hard to do, because it means an entire break; we don't communicate with each other in any way at all."

It was, she continues, only three days ago,

> But it has seemed a long time because I realize we may never see each other any more. That's probably not the case, but it might turn out that way. I did it all by myself & very much against his will. He said that he would give up anything for me, even his work, & why didn't we forget everything else & just stay together & be happy & let everything go smash. Of course he wouldn't & couldn't give up his work for anybody, but to hear him talk like that made me realize how desperate he had become. And I couldn't stand it. I'm keen about his poetry, & I helped him to get this Guggenheim thing, & I'm not going to be the one to bitch it all up for him now.—Oh, I know you think he's a mess, & has no stamina, & you're probably bored by all this. But you've been urging me to write you how things are. And this is how they are. Finally I practically put him out of the apartment. It was one of the hardest things I've done.

In this letter she made one of the rare comments on George's attitude toward Eugen: he was jealous.

Of course he's known all along that I miss you & want to see you, and that keeps him upset. . . . He'd like to put me to the choice between you, but he knows that if he ever really did that I'd go back to you, although I never said so. That's why I think it more than likely that I shan't see him any more. Now that I've sent him on his way & he's alone, he's probably making a strong effort, since he can't have me all to himself, to get along without me altogether.

She was alone, and she didn't know what to do. She might go to the Riviera, she might return to Steepletop,

But of course what I'm really hoping is that things are not over between George & me, & if that is true it would be a bad idea to go so far away. For whereas you & I are never really apart, no matter how far away from each other we may be, between myself & George the distance widens very rapidly when once we're separated. And this doesn't mean that he doesn't love me, because he does. But he just is like that.

It would be marvelous if you were here. When I cabled you I was simply asking you to come, & I thought you would understand that. But since you didn't & since you were somewhat bewildered & afraid of making a mistake, so wanted to wait until you had a letter from me explaining things,—why, now I just don't know.

Edna may have wanted him to come, but she wanted the burden of the decision to rest with him. She did not want too much read into any decision of hers; she did not even appear to want to make a clear choice. She continued to equivocate:

You couldn't live with me here in this flat, because George has been with me here so much of the time, & to the concierge he's my man. She would think me pretty light, and I'm foolish & sensitive enough to be able to be troubled by that. Besides, I should still want to have a place of my own. It's been very good for me, I believe. Perhaps I shall finally succeed in thinking things out a bit & come to some conclusion. It's good for me to have to do things for myself. Even paying my own taxi is good for me. And I don't over-tip any more. And I'm not drinking very much.—But it would be marvelous to have you near me so that I could see you often, often. I long so to see you, darling. I've missed you so.

By now, June 28, their letters had crossed, and while she was telling him she had decided to do without George, Eugen was guessing that she had abandoned the better part of herself to him.

Is there any danger, Edna, that you are reverting to type, and becoming a regular woman, and losing interest in your work and yourself as a poet, and are just only interested in helping Him to be a poet and only interested in His poetry. . . . If you are going to give yourself up and your personality to be the silent power behind some man, like most women do, that would be the last straw and I'd get so disgusted with life, that I wouldn't care, oh hell I wouldn't care who got the nomination for the presidency by the Democratic Party and I even wouldn't care who became president of this great and free Republic. Do what you like my dear, but remain a poet, for Christ's sake.

It took about a week for her letter to arrive. When it did, Eugen fired off two cables, telling her he'd sail for France as soon as he could book passage. The next morning he was calmer. It was very like him to explode in certainty and then become cool. She could still change her mind and stop him, he coaxed:

It seems such a drastic measure you are taking. . . . What I always understood to be your hope, that the three of us finally would be friends and that we could go on all three of us. You have gone or rather we have gone through some pretty tough times the last two years in order to try and do that and what the world has always thought the impossible. It seemed to me so dreadful for you to think that you had to make up your mind that it could not be done. Let's make another heroic attempt. Let's try to be all three together. Let's try whether we cannot find a way out. May be we can teach him not to be jealous of me. May be we can teach him to like me.

It was a peculiar response: Eugen seemed to be insisting that Edna not relinquish George. He urged her to hold on to him; he apologizes for not liking her lover more.

I DO like him. Under other circumstances by this time I doubtless would love him. But although I don't rave and roar like a jealous man, and although I don't run around with a gun, don't think for a moment that I am not jealous once in a while, and that I haven't funny little moments of feeling desolate and forlorn and a little bit crazy. Well, that is not ideal soil for either love or friendship to grow in. But I have myself now entirely in hand.

Now was the moment the three of them should seize, and Paris was the place "for George and me to get to like each other, respect each other and with the grace of God to love each other." He cabled her twice from Hillsdale, New York, on July 1, 1932:

THANKS DARLING FOR LONG LETTER JUST RECEIVED STOP INTEND SAILING NEXT WEEK TO BE IN YOUR NEIGHBORHOOD STOP THREE OF US MUST BE

TOGETHER THIS IS IMPORTANT STOP MY LOVE TO GEORGE AND A TOAST TO
THE THREE MODERN MUSKETEERS

CABLE NUMBER TWO STOP REFUSE TO ALLOW YOU GIVE UP BEAUTIFUL AND
PRECIOUS THING WILL BE IN PARIS TO BATTLE FOR YOU AND AM COMING
PREPARED TO STAY A DAY OR A YEAR STOP HERE IS TO COURAGE AND WISDOM
TO THE THREE OF US SKIDDLES

Edna immediately cabled Eugen from Paris:

DISREGARD LETTER EVERYTHING ALRIGHT MY TELEPHONE TROCADERO
TWENTY FOUR NINETY FOUR CALL ME SUNDAY AFTER MIDNIGHT PARIS TIME.

But Eugen was mightily puzzled. On July 4, he wrote:

My own sweet darling . . . I wonder what you mean by all right and I wonder why you want me to telephone you. I cannot get you out of my mind.
I took a walk, but it is no good. . . . I know that you love me, but I long to
hear you say it or write it. Of course you said a lot when you said that if
you'd have to choose between us, you would come back to me. . . . But I
am jealous of him. For what you feel for him. Are you a little bit in love
with me? Do you sometimes think of me and want to touch me? That
would be something.

It was a reassurance she did not give him.

2

On the afternoon of June 24, 1932, Natalie Clifford Barney gave a tea for
Edna at her legendary salon at 20, rue Jacob on the Left Bank, "to introduce
a lot of French poets & people to Little Wincy-Pince," Edna told Eugen.

It's going to be awful, such a noisy crowd. Miss Barney is charming,
though, a great friend of Mme. Delarue-Mardrus, a great and famous Lesbian in her own right, & formerly a great & devoted friend of Remy de
Gourmont, to whom he wrote his "Letters to an Amazon," etc.—It will be
interesting. I'm going to wear my simple little black ensemble from
Worth's.

Goodbye,
Heaps of love, darling
From Freckles.

Natalie Barney was rich, eccentric, tiny, seductive, and American. In her
youth she was called "the wild girl from Cincinnati." One of her dearest

friends, Elisabeth de Gramont, the Duchesse de Clermont-Tonnerre, said that in her were combined the grace of the American woman "and Palestinian nonchalance." She was a Jew. Hidden in the courtyard of her small house was a temple of friendship around which Colette, as well as Mata Hari, had once gamboled nude and on horseback. The ground floor of the main rooms of the house had been covered in pink damask, but that was in 1909, when Barney first rented the property. Now the damask had paled until it was the color of silken flesh. There were alabaster chandeliers festooned with pretty glass fruits, and several dour portraits hung in the entry hall, among them friends of Natalie's painted by her mother, Alice Pike Barney, who had studied with Whistler. The entire house seemed to breathe decadence.

It was into this milieu that Millay's friend Allan Ross Macdougall brought Donald Gurney, who was "fresh out of Harvard, if one can ever be that," he said many years later. "You see, I was looking for a Proustian world—Proust had been to Natalie's—and no, that was not what I found. Natalie was already an older woman. She looked like an abbess—she dressed like one. She was very severe, a long dark cloak. She was very handsome, even then, blond and blue-eyed, clear eyes. Romaine Brooks was there, of course. . . . She looked like a good English housekeeper in her grey flannels with white collar and cuffs."

Early that June 1932, Lucie Delarue-Mardrus had written to Edna in Paris, saying "Miss Barney needs to see you. I do too." How, she asked, did she expect them to assist in her French "*gloire*" if she kept slipping away like an eel? On the twelfth of June, Millay heard directly from Natalie Barney, who invited her to dine the next night, at eight, in Millay's former *quartier* on the Left Bank. "We want you to help us choose the poems to be read on the 24th. 'Dougy' will read 2 sonnets and L.D.M. two of her translations—and Rachel one of them and one English? poem—and you?" She added this touching note: "I am glad of your dedication to Elinor Wylie. I only know that masterpiece of hers Mr. Hazard & Mr. Hodge . . . and a few poems; perhaps you will tell me more about the living poet—and not let me miss meeting you. I sometimes feel somewhat of an exile."

Millay didn't make that supper. She had begun to work on her preface to *The Princess Marries the Page,* and she was in the mood to finish it. "I can't keep Harpers waiting any longer," she wrote Eugen. "—People will be interested in what I tell them, very likely. They're crazy about That Personal Touch."

The winter before, when the reviews from *Fatal Interview* were still coming in, she'd arranged with Harper to publish what she called this "little play." She was always precise about what the format and look of her books should be. "Woodblocks won't do at all," she wrote her editor, Eugene Saxton.

> The play is too slight to be printed so seriously. What I really want—and if it is too expensive just now to bring it out in this way, then I would really rather wait, I think, until everybody has more money—what I really want is a big, flat book perhaps 14 by 10 with many colored illustrations. . . . I want the book to be a Christmas gift book and as gaudy as a Christmas tree.

Harper brought it out on October 19, 1932, with exactly the pretty, gay decorations she'd hoped for. It was stamped in gold with colored drawings and facsimiles of a sheet of music by Deems Taylor.

Millay dropped Mary Kennedy a hasty note, inviting her to dinner on the evening of June 22. She said she wanted to pump her for information about the Philadelphia production of *Princess,* in which Mary had starred, "and to give myself the fun of seeing you.—I've been to see you twice— did you know that?—My child, I live just around the corner from you, in the very next street—it was as much of a surprise to myself as it will be to you!" Afterward she invited her to the tea at Natalie Barney's.

"It was all very gracefully done," Mary recalled. "And then Edna recited some of her poems. But as she began she said that 'Renascence' was an adolescent experience . . . and I felt that she was making a little excuse for these poems."

Donald Gurney also remembered the evening well; he was curious, playful, and indiscreet:

> Rachel Berendt read "Renascence." And at this point—well, Natalie Barney was in love with her, and she *was* a glorious creature—when she suddenly threw her arm up with the line "I screamed to touch the sky"—and her dark long hair fell forward and down across her face—ah, well, all the ladies gasped.
>
> Rachel Berendt was of course a famous actress, and a rather famous lesbian, too. She played all of Giroudoux; she was dark, Jewish, I should think, and with a perfectly beautiful voice.

Of Edna Millay in that milieu:

> All I can say . . . is that she seemed at home. She was a smiling, a very American looking girl in that particular world—which was largely, but not entirely by any means, French, rather jaded, and always very well dressed. No self-respecting American woman would be seen there. Oh, no! Edith

Wharton would never have come, never! And of the intellectual world that counted, both French and American would pass through Natalie Barney's afternoons. Colette was often there, barefoot in her sandals, which did cause a sensation. Her feet were so dirty! Gertrude Stein was very self-assured.

Just before she read, Millay was drawn into a conversation with Mme. Delarue-Mardrus, who was talking about her recent trip to the States. "Wonderful country! So alive, so vigorous! But such bad food!" "Edna's eyebrow was raised quizzically as she heard these touristic clichés," Macdougall reported. "Then she began an interrogation which was at once a patriotic dithyramb and a gastronomic prose poem in praise of her country's native products and dishes. . . .

"In your travels, *chère madame,* did you ever taste the lobsters that come from the waters off the coast of my home state, Maine? Broiled or boiled and served with melted, fresh country butter, they are unforgettable. Did you have fish chowder made of haddock, Maine potatoes, onions, salt pork and rich milk?" The travelled literary lady slowly shook her head.

"Were you ever introduced to Boston Baked Beans?" Edna continued. "I mean the kind baked in an old-fashioned crock. We cook them slowly and for long hours in the oven and serve them sometimes with such brown bread as can be found in no other part of the world. Did you ever have Cherrystones or Little Necks; and did you ever, by chance, taste a Provincetown clam pie made of the deep-sea Quahogs and a liberality of olive oil and garlic, cooked by one of the Portuguese fishermen who had hauled in the clams himself? Were oyster-crabs and whitebait ever set crisp before you? Did you taste soft-shell crabs, lightly sauteed, or drink the juice of the soft-shell clam? I must say I have never met their like over here. And were you ever a happy member of an old-fashioned clam-bake on a secluded New England beach?"

"*Hélas!*" said Madame Mardrus; she had not been long enough in America to have experienced the primitive joys of a clam-bake.

"Then what of the other American dishes that are seldom to be met with elsewhere on the gastronomic globe?" Edna asked. "There's the shad roe and the shad itself, both broiled; sweet corn and sweet potatoes; pumpkin pie and deep-dish blueberry pie; diamond-back terrapin done as the Baltimoreans do it in a rich Madeira stew, or as the Philadelphians do it with egg-yolks, cream and '*sweet butter in a lordly dish.*' Then there's Philadelphia Pepperpot which has tripe in it, and that same city's surprising mixture of tripe and oysters. There's the Creole Jambalaya of New Orleans made with savory rice and shrimps almost as big as your French *écrevisses.*

"We have also our native blueberries. And there are our cranberries and our beach-plums which I used to gather on Cape Cod. We make delicious preserves from them. Oh, there are many other products and dishes native to states and regions of my country. If you have never tasted them, *ma chère,* you cannot in all fairness judge American cuisine. . . ."

As Madame Mardrus started to say something in reply we were called into the other room. I heard her there tell her friend, Romaine Brooks, the painter, that she thought Edna's defense of her country's *specialités gastronomiques* was *tres bien faite.*

ౚ ౚ ౚ

Norma was surprised when Gene, as she usually called him, told her Edna was going to call from Paris and that he insisted she be with him when he took the call in Pittsfield. "I didn't know why she'd stayed [in Paris]—or that Dillon was there. . . . Gene was terribly excited and nervous. And I didn't realize there was a chance of her not coming back. Until I got in the car. He said, 'Maybe she's not coming back, Norma.' He began to talk nervously, talked because he was nervous. He never really talked to me before. And I didn't know what he was talking about. My God! He might easily, being Gene, *not* have asked me to come along. . . . We got to the hotel, and I sat in the lobby. He went to the desk. They assigned him a room, and he went upstairs. After a while . . . he came to the top of the stairs and shouted, 'Norma! Come say hello to Vincent. She is coming home!'

"So, yes! Sure I did! It sounded as if she were underwater; it was a bad connection. . . . I said, 'I can't wait to see you. When are you coming home?'

"She seemed excited. I was very gay. Gene was beside himself."

ౚ ౚ ౚ

On July 5, the day of their telephone call, Millay had apparently decided to come home. Eugen was not to go to her in France; instead he went to New York to await her arrival. "I'm going to fetch Edna!" was how he put it to Norma.

CHAPTER 29

Edna did not leave Paris after she talked to Norma and Eugen on July 5, 1932. Alix Daniels insisted that Millay remained in Paris, but the rancor that laced her memories made her a questionable source. Millay, however, kept a series of index cards listing chronologically the crucial events of her life. In 1932, along with her walking trip to Mallorca, she made this notation: "Eugen to Paris—Veendam 3rd class Venice." Venice?

George Dillon had formed a friendship with a man called Arthur Meeker from Chicago who adored him, and together they had decided to go to Venice without Millay. Whether she was hurt or humiliated and angry is hard to know for certain; whether Dillon was more deeply involved with Meeker than anyone knew or admitted is impossible to know. But Millay decided to follow them. Eugen did come to Paris and, according to their passports, they *both* entered Italy on August 8 and departed together on the tenth. By August 11, 1932, they left Le Havre, bound for America. Eugen was bringing her home, just as he'd said he would.

There is almost no correspondence in Millay's hand from the time she returned to Steepletop in August 1932 until that Christmas. In a working notebook there is this poem, dated November 12, 1932:

> Distresséd mind, forbear
> To tease the hooded Why;
> That shape will not reply.
>
> From the safe chair
> To the wind's welter
> Flee, if storm's your shelter.
>
> But no, you needs must part—
> Fling him his release!—
> On whose ungenerous heart
> Alone, you are at peace.

Her choice of verbs is key: "Forbear . . . Flee . . . *Fling* him his release!" She is in her old high mode, imperious, if hurt, very like her voice in "Fatal Interview." But the final two lines betray a recognition more painful than loss: she needs him.

The poem will become Part III of the five-part "Not So Far as the Forest," published the following year in a magazine but withheld from book publication until 1939, when it was included in *Huntsman, What Quarry?* For *Huntsman,* she wrote later in a letter to her editor, was to be made up of "mostly love poems" composed of "what might be called the more *personal* of the new poems I have been writing."

V

Poor passionate thing,
Even with this clipped wing how well you flew!—though not so far
    as the forest. . . .

Rebellious bird, warm body foreign and bright,
Has no one told you?—Hopeless is your flight
Towards the high branches. Here is your home,
Between the barnyard strewn with grain and the forest tree.
Though Time refeather the wing,
Ankle slip the ring,
The once-confined thing
Is never again free.

"There were only two or three really important things in Vincent's life," Charles Ellis once said, "and George Dillon was one of them. He was weak, queer as a three-dollar bill. . . . He was a handsome boy, a very good-looking boy. But weak all the way through. And while she was not dominant—far from it—she could be suddenly assertive and aggressive, if she wanted to be. If she had reason to be. If it was something important to her."

On Christmas Day 1932, Millay began the first of a series of Sunday-night readings of her poems over the air on a nationwide hookup on WJZ Blue Network, arranged by Eugen's old friend Margaret Cuthbert. Cuthbert was one of the pioneers of American radio broadcasting, and according to her nothing like Millay's reading had ever been done before on air. For the first time a literary figure was on equal footing with dramatic performers and distinguished concert artists. Thousands of people heard Millay's voice. They heard her in Illinois and Michigan, in Nebraska and Texas, and once having heard her, they wrote to her. Sometimes they sent her their own poems. They told her that her voice was as lovely as her poetry. They sent in hundreds of letters, and in these letters they asked for her advice, they told her they'd fallen a little in love with her. A farm family in Missouri wrote "that the very sound of your voice transforms our country living room into a place of magic." What her listeners most seemed to like was her informality, the way she'd say, as if to herself, "Don't be nervous" when she couldn't find a poem. They told her it was as if she were in the room with them. It was her voice that they most often responded to:

It's simply intoxicating. Don't, don't ever change, and become stiff or formal or eloquent. . . . You sound so real, so natural, so—so very much alive. Even with the frightful cold you had. . . . Miss Millay—please do not stop your Sunday nights, go on and on and on. We cannot have too much of you.

It was a performance, and it was exhausting hard work. Her apparent nonchalance came from the ability that very few writers have, to seem to reach over and touch the listener with her voice.

To her friends Lulu and Alyse in England, she wrote in her offhand way, "I got a job reading my poems over the radio—eight Sunday evenings— which kept me so late into the winter and made me so tired that when it was over we just rushed to Florida to get out of the cold and into the sunshine—I needed it badly."

Of course it wasn't just a job. People who'd never given a thought to poetry or poets, who may have turned on their radios out of curiosity, stayed to listen for every Sunday night for two months. A friend of Margaret Cuthbert said she would never forget the sound of Millay's voice. "It *was* dramatic, lifting and falling without anything forced about it. She was a person who made one believe, in her presence, that there is a muse. And Edna was visited by her.

"You know, Edna did not want to record her voice, Margaret persuaded her to do it in the name of posterity. I can still hear her talking to Edna, telling her what it would mean someday, in the future.

"I remember the first time she heard the recordings played back to her. It was the first time she had ever heard her own voice. 'Is that really my voice?' she said and paused. 'Quite lovely, isn't it?'"

2

For years Edna and Eugen had dreamed of owning an island off the coast of Maine. In July 1933, almost a full year after her return from Paris, they drove up to visit Tess Root Adams, her dear friend from their days together in Shillingstone, at her summer place on Bailey's Island. It was from the Root cottage that Millay first saw Ragged Island, the outermost island of Casco Bay, four miles out to sea. The Root cottage sits directly on the shore of the Atlantic coast; to the east, seen between the wooden porch pillars, lies Ragged Island. On July 3 and 4, 1933, Edna entered just four words in her diary:

Ragged Island
Garnet Rocks.

Ragged Island consisted of some eighty acres with a single house at the head of a natural harbor, which could be entered only at high tide. There were fields of wild roses, white and pink, and wild mustard that grew to the edge of the pebble beach. Two weeks later, Ragged Island was theirs. A gleeful Tess sent them the telegram confirming their purchase: WELL BABY WE BOUGHT IT. When the message was spoken over the telephone to Steepletop, it became WHERE IS BABY WE BOARDED. Mary Kennedy, who was visiting them, remembered that Edna and Eugen, puzzled, kept asking the operator to repeat it. Finally the exasperated operator said, "It's perfectly clear, Madam, that the other party wants to know where is the *child* they left with you!"

When they told the Fickes they had just bought an island with a small shack on it, Arthur grumpily noted in his diary, "suppose we shall have to go there with them someday, but . . . I know who will have to do all the work: Gene and Gladys and I!" Arthur was not usually so peevish. He loved Steepletop. He even loved the icy, spring-fed pool they'd built in the old stone foundation of the barn where they would laze about, naked, drinking cocktails, talking poetry, and swimming.

> I don't think I'd like naked bathing with a lot of strangers, but we four have done it together for so many years that I like it very much. Don't let anyone try to tell me that it's a perfectly pure, innocent performance, though! It has its own delicately voluptuous quality. Anybody who can play around with a naked Vince and pretend to himself that it is the same as talking with his grandmother is merely lying to himself. Her breasts are the most curiously "naked" breasts I have ever seen. I suppose it is because they are rather large in proportion to her small body, and because their centers are so prominent and pink. Her middle, with its scanty golden hair, is exceptionally beautiful—and so deceptively innocent-looking.

In August, Millay's diary faltered and began to peter out. By December, in letters to both her aunt Susie and Allan Ross Macdougall, she describes being ill. Here they'd gone and bought an island intending "to spend August there, but I had to go and get flu or something like it, and have had it all summer,—and I haven't set eyes on my island since we bought it!" But she had been able to write, "and what little strength I had, has been used up in this most arduous of occupations."

However immersed she was in her own work, she did manage to take time to do the Guggenheim recommendations. In March she'd wired Mr.

Moe from Florida that the Guggenheim Foundation should grant a fellowship to Mr. E. E. Cummings. If he needed it.

> I put it this way because I know nothing of Mr. Cummings' circumstances, and because I do know that both Miss Bogan and Mr. Middleton are without exaggeration desperately in need of help, and that Mr. Dillon cannot possibly continue with the work which he is now doing in France unless he receives an extension of his Fellowship.

That was pretty helpful to a lover she'd parted from. She realized that for her to be helping Cummings was, as she put it, "really funny. For if ever I disliked a man without ever having laid eyes on him, it is this same E. E. Cummings."

She characterized his personality as "fetid." But about one thing she was abundantly clear:

> . . . here is a big talent, in the hands of an arrogant, peevish, self-satisfied and self-indulgent writer. That is to say, here is a big talent in pretty bad hands. . . .
>
> I am not one of those who stand for the untouchable holiness of the capital letter and traditional typography. So far as I am concerned, Mr. Cummings may do anything he likes with the alphabet, the English grammar, and the multiplication table, provided only the result of his activities be something interesting, and, after a reasonable period of application, comprehensible, to a reader of culture and brains. Mr. Cummings may not, however, I say, write poetry in English which is more difficult for me to translate than poetry written in Latin. He may, of course, write it. But if he publishes it, if he prints and offers for sale poetry which he is quite content should be, after hours of sweating concentration, inexplicable from any point of view to a person as intelligent as myself, then he does so with a motive which is frivolous from the point of view of art, and should not be helped or encouraged by any serious person or group of persons. . . .
>
> But, unfortunately for one's splendid hate which had assumed almost epic proportions, by no means all of Mr. Cummings poetry is of this nature. In these books which I have just been reading there is fine writing and powerful writing (as well as some of the most pompous nonsense I ever let slip to the floor with a wide yawn), and that this author has ability I could not deny; that he has more than that I gravely suspect.
>
> Mr. Cummings in love, for instance, his arrogance for the moment subdued, his spirit troubled and humbled, can produce such beautiful poems as are to be found in parts IV or V of "Is 5."
>
> If we could only trust this author to proceed along these lines, and along the line of the thrillingly lovely "Paris; this April sunset" in Part III, nothing would be clearer than that Mr. Cummings must be given anything he asks for, if it can possibly be arranged. . . .

What I propose, then, is this: that you give Mr. Cummings *enough rope.* He may hang himself; or he may lasso a unicorn. In any case it is high time we found out about this man Cummings. Let us give him every opportunity to show us at once whether he is a genius, a charlatan, or a congenital defective,—and get him off our minds.

Cummings got his Guggenheim. And Dillon got his extension.

3

On December 18, 1933, Millay gave a reading at Bryn Mawr College, the last of the year. "And it was just perfect," said a woman who had been in the audience. "After the talk—no, perhaps during it—I noticed a man sitting on the sidelines. He was very protective of Millay. But there was this strange, small, russet creature. Not pretty, mind you. Something better than pretty—an exciting creature. We wanted to meet her. So I asked, 'How would you like to come for a little drink?' And she said, 'We'd love to. But I must ask Uge.' That's exactly what she called him. Then I knew the man sitting there was her husband.

"We came back to the house, all full of her talk. And they came in our car with us. The bottles came out, and the silver, and the crystal." Why did she go to perfect strangers? "I have no idea. I think she was keen to get away. That's all. And, too, we were not *perfect* strangers," the woman said.

"There was more drinking. Again and again their glasses were refilled. She drank whiskey and soda, I remember, until about three o'clock. During this time Uge would hold her. He adored her—in the sense of worshiping her—he would hold her shoulders, trying to kiss her, and putting his arms around her knees. He finally got so drunk that he couldn't do anything. When we saw that he was helpless, Edna got on one side, and I on the other, and we took his arms and pulled and dragged him up to his bed. We just dumped him in like a sack. He was out. And then we descended into our living room. . . .

"During all of this drinking she never showed anything at all. She was what I would call cold drunk; there was a chill about her. She was very controlled, very. But she would say something and laugh, she recited parts of poems—her own and others', I think. She just sat there, drinking. And so controlled, no fumbled words, no slurred speech. I remember that she had a most special way of talking. Yes, it was a quality to her voice, and a care in her choice of words as well. I'm afraid the only way to describe it is to call it a poetic way of talking, which is a disservice to her."

The woman who recalled this looked down at her tasseled loafers and for a moment seemed unable to speak. Then she said that the drinking and talking must have gone on another two hours. "I do not exaggerate. We went upstairs, finally. I said good night to her. She went into her room. And I into mine. I undressed quickly and got into bed. Right after I was in my bed, she came into the room. She did not knock. She entered. She stood at the side of my bed and undid the clasp on her evening dress. It slipped down from her shoulders to the floor. She stood there absolutely naked. I was astonished. I didn't know what to do. She stood looking at me and said—I'll never forget her voice at that moment—'Oh, don't you like good old Elizabethan lovemaking? Oh, I like it!' There was no question of what she meant. She said it almost coarsely.

"Of course, it was the drink. She would never have behaved like that, on the first night, I think, without the drinking. I was startled. She looked so small then. She just stood there like a statue, and I—I evaded her. I tried to talk to her. I didn't want to make love to her, and we did not. I said she had to get up early for her lecture in the morning at the college tomorrow. Something like that. And I asked when she would like her breakfast. I must have sounded addled. I sort of led her back to her room. She said, 'I'd like a bottle of whiskey, please,' very politely.

"In the morning I did bring in, or saw that the maid did, the coffee and the whiskey. Uge was snoring. He was not in bed with her. And I've just now remembered that she was sitting up in bed, writing. . . . I can see her sitting there, looking down at her paper in the morning light.

"Uge had a cup of black coffee. . . . He was, I think a sort of buffer. From life, from her life, from life itself."

Millay was losing control, and Eugen, who had provided it and protected her, could no longer do so.

CHAPTER 30

In January 1934, Eugen and Edna set sail for Marseille aboard the S.S. *Excalibur.* Just before they left, she wrote to a friend that they'd rented Eugen's brother's house in Antibes, "right out on the end of the Cape, a perfectly lovely place." She wanted to be where it was warm and beautiful, "and I shall be able to keep all my energy for my work."

After twelve days at sea, they arrived at Jan Boissevain's villa, the Petite Villa Hou'zée on Cap d'Antibes, where she made this diary entry:

Furious yesterday because they wouldn't let us off for half an hour at Mallorca . . . and sat at the bar all afternoon, scolding and getting tighter and tighter. Last night and this morning terrible wind blew up suddenly, and the ship pitched and shuddered like anything. . . . Had the most awful hangover this morning, and all our packing to do, and in that sea! I must have been darned drunk last night. I don't remember leaving the bar and going to my cabin at all. But apparently I came down just before dinner and got into bed and fell asleep like a shot. I awoke about midnight when Ugin came in. I remembered nothing, but my clothes were all over the room, and I never do that. Disgraceful. Got to cut it out. Not only that the doctor says so but that I'm getting a tummy.

The following morning, with the seas still high, she forgot her resolutions and packed "with the help of seven gin-rickeys."

The Petite Villa Hou'zée sits on the rocks at the edge of the Mediterranean, where the sea is the color of fresh blue paint. Jan and his wife, Charlotte, owned two villas, the larger one just above the Hôtel du Cap, the smaller a cottage built at the edge of the sea. Beneath it, blasted into the rock, was a sort of cave with a table chiseled from the rock. The water could be heard splashing against the stone steps that fell into the Mediterranean from the tiny terrace of the cottage. The house rose from the rocky coast, with bamboo shades across the terrace and bright striped canvas awnings to keep the interior cool.

On Cap d'Antibes they began a healthy regimen: no smoking and no drinking; they got up at sunrise and went to bed early. They bought a badminton set in Cannes and played before breakfast, which they had outdoors, and took long walks, ambling along the quiet dusty lanes that bordered the sea and picking up pinecones for the open fires they made each night because the days were still wintry and overcast. Playfully they wired Jan to come for a visit in his own cottage. Within the week he was there, "bringing presents of *roggebrood* and a yellow cheese with aromatic seeds in it."

Then the violent north winds of the mistral began to blow so hard they couldn't play badminton anymore. "Had the curse and felt awful—a week overdue." In the afternoon Edna pulled herself together and they went to the casino, where "Ugin's system," she wrote, worked like a charm and he made 820 francs. Three days later they were "drinking again. . . . But my God, you have to do something to fight off the mistral." The weather stayed foul. "Haven't seen the sun for over a week, except for about an hour on Thursday. This morning icy wind blowing from the east, grey sky. Sea pale greenish blue and very handsome surf on our rocks. But I have a headache and feel nervous and irritable. Think I'll get drunk."

On February 18, they motored over to Cap Ferrat to have lunch with Somerset Maugham,

> just the three of us, Dr. Fairfield—who is a sister of Rebecca West—Mr. Maugham and the man who lives with him, his secretary, et cet, Gerald Hexton, I believe his name is. Beautiful place, up on the hillside overlooking the water, delightful gardens with the most succulent-looking green grass here and there in tiny lawns and lanes. They get the grass-seed from England, and they have to dig up the lawns and re-seed them every year. I must say it is worth it.
>> I liked S but somehow it was not very much fun, something wrong somewhere.

> February 22.
>> My birthday.—Didn't think anybody would know about it. But this morning before I was up Ugin and Jan stood outside my door and sang "Happy Birthday." And then they came in, Ugin with a beautiful bouquet of mauve stock and pink geraniums from the garden, and Jan with a great spray of almond blossoms from his little *propriété* on the hill.

The next day, her vacation was over. "I'm working like fury now on my Guggenheim Fellowship applicants. I've read them all by now, and thought about them a lot; but now I want to re-read them, and collect my notes on them, and then I must write my report.—It's a terrible job, all right. But I knew it would be."

The next diary entry wasn't until March 4:

> Slaved all day in my room on my reports from the Guggenheim Foundation. Twenty-one poets I have read and re-read and thought about and finally written about, and then re-written about. . . . I've given hardly a moment to my own work for these two months—tennis, and reading and pondering on these twenty-one writers, that's all I've done.—I'm recommending Kay Boyle, Conrad Aiken, Isidor Schneider, Walter Lowenfels. . . . —Their own pet, for some reason, seems to be Horace Gregory, who means to me, if I except certain of the bawdier among the Catullus translations, precisely not a damn thing.

She said her weight was down to 105, which meant she'd lost more weight sitting in bed writing her Guggenheim reports than she had playing tennis. The next day her reports went off, and although she was exhausted, she washed her hair, slipped into her shorts, and leaped out into the sunshine to play tennis. "Afterwards went to the Casino at Juan-les-Pins and drank buckets of champagne-cocktails."

She also danced with the professional. "He complimented me, but in a patronizing way. Thick-headed little Frenchman. I dance so much better than he does. He just knows a few little steps I'm not familiar with, that's all—and even at that I follow him like his shadow. Stupid little beast."

George Dillon had remained in Paris after their time together in 1932. Although there is no correspondence from him in her files, they must have maintained some connection, for she now sent him the manuscript of her next book of poems. He responded with a twelve-page letter and very carefully told her which of the poems he liked the best and why, and which he thought less good. His tone throughout was self-conscious and oddly precious:

> Well, my dear, this is what I really think. . . . I spent all last evening reading them and thinking about them, and writing you this ponderous batch of notes—and now I must send it off at once, or I shall become disgusted with the idea of myself as a critic of poetry, and not send it at all. . . . if it makes you angry, throw it away and forget it.

He hoped she would read it on one of the rare days when the mistral was not blowing. He sounds like a careful elderly uncle.

Two days later she made a very simple entry: "Must go to Paris tomorrow for a few days." On March 9 she left by train: "Very luxurious and elegant compartment, all to myself, very deluxe. I wanted to travel cheaper, we're so poor this year." It was raining, the mistral continued to blow, and she was testy. "I feel like the devil. And the sheets are of cotton, and I hate cotton sheets. These are particularly cheap and offensive. They feel like very old paper-covered books with dust on them—Thank heaven I have a flask of gin along."

When she arrived she met George Dillon for lunch at his hotel:

> A charming place in the rue Galilée.—Came back to the hotel and washed my hair—in water that was absolutely cold!—but absolutely!—No difference whatever in the temperature from the two fawcets. Took a bath in ice-cold water, too. . . . Had dinner with George—didn't notice where—and went to the theatre. . . . Went somewhere afterwards and had some drinks.

The next day they met again, and again they lunched together at his hotel.

> Then came back to my hotel and showed George a lot of my new poems. . . . He made one or two extremely intelligent and valuable sugges-

tions, which I shall at once try to carry out.—Had some whisky and sodas sent up.—Went out to dinner rather late. Came back to my hotel and talked some more, and read some more poems.

In the morning George left to catch the boat train for Le Havre; his destination was Baltimore. Millay wrote simply, "I did not see him." George was going home without any fresh work, and without a job.

Eugen and Jan were awaiting her at Antibes. Their welcome was to fill the house with flowers, "and in my room sweet-peas and little daisies, and a camellia."

The next day she stayed in bed working on her poems as the mistral played havoc with her nerves. Eugen, she said, "gave me a marvelous suggestion about *The Hedge of Hemlocks.*" She was uneasy: "I distrust the mood I am in, and dare do nothing definite." The poems seemed good to her, though maybe too much so: "They all look good. A dangerous state of mind."

She was still drinking too much and as a consequence had what she called "one of my old-time headaches." They managed to play five sets of tennis all the same, and she and Eugen actually beat Jan in two of the sets. "But we all played as if we were in diving-suits."

The next day she received notice that she had been elected to the Cosmopolitan Club,

and this although I . . . do not want to be a member of their club, and never did want to, and said plainly to several of their members who approached me . . . that I would rather be found shot in a night-club *cabinet* than be caught dozing over a copy of *Town and Country.* . . . Not that I have anything in particular against this particular club,—but I don't like clubs, and I'm darned if I'll join them.

March 22.
Thursday. 1934—Cap d'Antibes
    Have been working very hard these last few days on my *Epitaph for the Race of Man.* Have finished several of the sonnets which I began years ago. Am having a hard time with the one beginning "When Death was young and bleaching bones were few." The trouble is I need to have my dinosaur both a brontosaurus and an allosaurus—herbivorous in the third line and carnivorous in the seventh line!—And I'm afraid I just can't work it.— Played tennis this afternoon, and never played so well. Jan said it was for the first time really tennis. Very tired afterwards, however. Went to the Casino and drank martinis.

The following day she worked all day and finished "See where Capella with her golden kids." "Ugin read the whole series aloud to me, seventeen of them. Kept getting shivers up my spine, and at the end I found myself very shaken. A strange experience."

The next night she couldn't sleep and worked through the night on *Epitaph,* writing an entire sonnet, "What rider spurs him from the darkening east."

Jan's wife, Charlotte, arrived in Cannes from New York. "Well," Millay wrote wryly, "our peaceful bachelor establishment is invaded by the lewd presence of woman. Awoke this morning to hear Charlotte scolding Jan because he didn't have a lady's-maid waiting to unpack for her. They had a terrible row. And she's been home just one day."

In the morning of March 26, while Edna was packing to leave, Charlotte stormed into her room, "all primed for a fight, started right in without a word of preamble to say that she'd have me to know she wasn't a bitch even though I did think she was a bitch, et cetera. I was never so astonished. I simply stood there. Finally I said that I didn't know what she was talking about but if I'd said anything to hurt her feelings I was sorry."

Charlotte left the room after that. But Millay wrote, "I was horribly upset, all cold and shaky. I can't stand such things. I can't stand people who like to row and make scenes." Then she made a truly remarkable statement:

> Eugen and I have [been] married nearly eleven years, and we have never had a quarrel, but *not one.* Two or three times one of us has been irritable or spoken sharply to the other, but the other has never taken it up, so it has always stopped right there.—Uge and I left tonight on the train for Paris, and I must say we were both relieved to get away without further trouble. Women are awful, really. I have very little respect for them, with a few exceptions. They are so uncontroled and self-indulgent, and so *noisy*! I'm a stout feminist, and all that, but I do think that for the most part women are pretty awful.

   ᴐ ᴐ ᴐ

Nearly a half century after that scene, Charlotte Boissevain was reclining on a chaise longue wrapped in a white terry-cloth robe, facing the creamy light from the Mediterranean. She was nearly ninety. She was tiny, and her hair was dyed the color rich older women seem to color their hair, the color of a base metal, brass or copper, like the flesh of peaches near the pit.

She was talking about Edna Millay in the Petite Villa Hou'zée on Cap d'Antibes.

"I knew Eugen far before I met Edna. Or even before I had met Jan. This was during the First World War. I was an actress then, and doing ingenue parts." She remembered that when she first met Edna she thought, "There is a brilliant woman—there wasn't a thing in the world she didn't know about. But it was"—she hesitated—"it was like this: she looked through me and I looked through her." They were as unalike as chalk and cheese. "They played tennis every day when they were here. And I have known so many people, interesting people, people who did things well, who were extraordinary in some way—whether they were beautiful or rich or talented or whatever—and I can remember stories and conversations about all of them. And yet with Edna I cannot tell you one thing that she said, one thing that I can remember. I found her a shy person. Look at all these books. All of them with inscriptions, and yet Edna could not waste a word, could she, unless she was paid for it? What does she write here? 'For Jan and Charlotte,' or something. With the date."

But what did Millay look like? How did she dress? move? speak? "She wore very little makeup and nothing on her nails, and her hair was completely natural. She had a phobia about her hair. She washed it every day. She wore long loose robes. They were lovely, and Eugen picked everything for her—Bergdorf Goodman sort of things. He picked her clothes and her shoes, and he picked up after her, too. He cooked for her and managed the farm, the house, and her correspondence. What didn't he do! You must understand, there was never a word spoken by Jan against Eugen. Nor against Edna, for that matter. There was an attachment that was almost—oh, an attachment between the brothers, between the two men—it was beautiful and warm and completely uncritical."

Standing before her bookcase with its signed copies of first editions of novels by her friend Rebecca West and by Joseph Conrad and H. G. Wells, she began to speak, pointing to a book of Millay's poems inscribed to them both: "There. There is as much as she's ever written to me, to us—her words are precious, to Edna. And how do I see her? Edna—with a wall around her."

     ℒ ℒ ℒ

Edna and Eugen were in Paris almost two weeks, and a good deal of time was spent having cocktails with friends: "Ugin got very tight, I fairly so." They saw the Fratellinis at the Cirque d'Hiver, but "The funny little old circus stank so I was afraid I shouldn't be able to stand it until they came on. Did, however, and loved them." They saw Mae West in *I'm No Angel* and thought her awful: "She exercised no come-hither at all upon Ugin,—nor upon me, either, and I am far from unsusceptible to woman's charms."

On April 7, she described being taken by Natalie Barney and Romaine Brooks to the studio of a young painter, whose name she spelled phonetically: Chillichef. He was Pavel Tchelitchew.

> Liked some of his paintings quite a lot, but thought quite a number of them pretty silly. Also liked the young man, though this, I am sure, was purely physical. He was insufferably conceited, talked all the time and about nothing but himself, can't stand any paintings but his own, Rembrandt is awful, Vermeer is awful, except Chillichef, who is wonderful.

She'd been told that he was the great love of Edith Sitwell's life. "Well," she entered wryly in her diary,

> I can understand it, in a way. But God! what a selfish man. Still things like that never seem to stop us.
> Took Lucie Mardrus and Germain de Castro and a young French Communist friend of theirs to Maxim's for supper. Had a wild gay time. I got lovely tight. Instructed the taxi-driver to take us to a perfectly dreadful place, all naked girls walking about and sitting on your lap, and spiriting twenty-franc pieces off the table either with the *derrier* or the *devant*. Lord, I must have been plastered to take that party there!

By the following Monday they were in London. They tried to economize by staying at an inexpensive hotel, which she immediately hated. It was cold, shabby, and dreary. "Saw the forty-eight dowdiest women on earth all at the same time right here in the lounge, and the ninety-six largest feet. Must be a convention," she quipped. They went to the theater every night—to see Elisabeth Bergner in *Catherine the Great,* Sybil Thorndike, and Noël Coward's *Conversation Piece,* "charming, but not filling." Then they took Laurence Olivier and his wife, Jill Esmond, to supper at the Savoy Grill: "Champagne, lots of fun. Went home with them afterwards to their house in Chelsea." She was invited to lunch the next day but went for cocktails instead.

> Larry came in from a rehearsal of "Biography"; astonished to see me there, was very distrait, did some steps of a tap-dance, put a ship on the mantel and loved it there and hated it there, went out to get some green paint to paint the trellis, returned without it, et cet. All very droll. I felt uncomfortable, and beat it as soon as I could.

On April 14, they caught the train to Lulworth Cove "to see Lulu." Powys had been desperately ill with tuberculosis for years, but it now seemed to be in remission. It was a bleak spring day, she said in her diary, but nevertheless they walked the three miles over the downs to Chydock. "Lulu looking beautiful with his curly white hair, and a beard, and looked better than I had dared hope. Left my notebook of typewritten poems for my new book for them to read." Lulu gave her a pomander. But the best thing he gave her was the knowledge that Keats had written his sonnet "Bright star! would I were steadfast as thou art" in Lulworth before he left for Italy and his death.

2

Back in America, Edna wrote to Eugene Saxton and sent him sixteen poems "for the dummy of my new book." She wrote in her diary, "It will really be two books, I think, published together—some of the poems need a definite separation from the others." In her letter she was even clearer:

> My idea about the books is something like this: If you print them to sell separately, then they must not be called Volumes One and Two, but will be called respectively "Huntsman, What Quarry?" and "Wine from These Grapes." If you print them boxed together . . . then the entire collection might be called "Poems: 1934;" or some such thing; Volume One; Huntsman, What Quarry? and Volume Two: Wine from These Grapes. (By bad typing and sloppy punctuation I have succeeded in making both titles look awful; but as a matter of fact they are both grand titles, and will look perfectly swell.)

Huntsman was to be the more personal book, and *Wine* would be in two sections, the first

> a group of miscellaneous poems in a much harder and more astringent mood . . . the second section a sequence of related sonnets entitled 'Epitaph for the Race of Man.'
>   This book will be the more philosophical and intellectual of the two volumes; the poems in it are in no instance of a personal or intimate nature.

What she really hoped, she told him, was that Harper would publish the two books as one—Volumes 1 and 2 of "Poems: 1934." She did not want them to be sold as two separate volumes. Which was, however, exactly what Harper did.

In the summertime, after her return from Europe while she was work-

ing to prepare her new collection of poems, Charlie Ellis came to Steepletop to paint her portrait.

ॐ ॐ ॐ

"I don't believe we planned it especially. It just worked out that way,"
Charlie said. We were sitting in the front room by the fireplace, and he
nodded toward a chair by the window where Edna used to feed the birds.

"She is sitting in that corner, her legs are curled up under her, and she
is smoking a Turkish cigarette. I can see the look on her face if I look in
that corner now. . . . She posed easily; I mean, she didn't move, she
seemed able to hold still. And there was nothing in particular that I was
after or that I posed. The pose was just the way she was sitting.

"One day, well . . . I was painting, looking directly at her, when she said,
'It's finished.' 'What?' I said. And she recited this poem, which she had
apparently been composing while I painted her."

ON THOUGHT IN HARNESS

My falcon to my wrist
Returns
From no high air.
I sent her toward the sun that burns
Above the mist;
But she has not been there.

Her talons are not cold; her beak
Is closed upon no wonder;
Her head stinks of its hood, her feathers reek
Of me, that quake at the thunder.

Degraded bird, I give you back your eyes forever, ascend now
      whither you are tossed;
Forsake this wrist, forsake this rhyme;
Soar, eat ether, see what has never been seen; depart, be lost,
But climb.

In Charlie's painting Millay's breasts are full and ample beneath her
pale summer dress and her face looks composed. But it is not serene. She
looks contained, as if she's holding herself in.

"I painted Gene, too, right here on the couch in the front room. He had
been ill with the flu or a cold or something, and I don't think he liked the
picture much. There was an American Indian blanket behind him—
here—and he was just lying back on the couch with the throw behind

him. What I liked was his love of life. And he had that as much as anyone I've ever known. More so, really." And here Charlie turned away. "He could make a great thing out of anything."

There was a long pause in our conversation, as if Charlie were recollecting far more than he'd just said. "When you know someone over a long period of years, you remember—oh, you remember other things. There was a terrific threat. I don't know what it was. There were times when he loved Norma and times when he hated her. I didn't pose a direct threat. I was just a drunken Irishman. Norma did. She posed a threat to him for some reason or other."

Norma had entered the room and, overhearing our conversation, she erupted: "You never opened your mouth to defend me, not once against that son of a bitch! Do you hear me, Charlie?" Then she bent over and pinched his arm.

Charlie looked away from me, watching a baseball game on the television set. The sound was turned off. Norma returned to the kitchen. Now that I had him alone, our voices lowered as I asked if there had been one trait all of the Millay women shared equally. He answered in a flash: "Yes. They were nasty, everlastingly."

PART EIGHT

THE GREAT TOURS

W*ine from* These Grapes was published on November 1, 1934, and, as was customary for her now, Millay began a reading tour before publication. In October she was at Yale; two weeks later she reached Chicago, where a letter from George Dillon was waiting for her, telling her how much he liked her new book. Earlier that summer, having returned from his Guggenheim in Paris to live with his parents in Richmond, Virginia, he had announced to her with a certain bravado that he was at last writing again. "What marvelous news this is," she wrote back. "I'm so happy for you; and happy for myself, too. I want to read everything you'll let me read. It will be a great delight to me. But you know that." He later invited her to visit him. "Your idea that we should get acquainted," she quipped, "is as charming as it is original."

Her tour was an overwhelming success. When Eugen, writing to Norma from Oklahoma City, tried to describe her triumph, all he could say was "sold out," "standees," and "overflow. . . . We are very happy but very tired.—Your angel sister is sleeping now.—We arrived here 7 a.m. She gave a reading at 11 a.m.—And now 4 p.m. we just got rid of people, and 5:20 she leaves for Waco, Texas, where she reads to-morrow."

Millay's schedule continued unabated. By the twentieth she had left Waco for Fort Worth. Six days later, on the twenty-sixth, she would recross the country and read in Lynchburg, Virginia. It was a taxing pace in an era when travel was entirely by train, but at the end of the month she would be staying with George Dillon at his parents' house in Richmond.

—

Alix Daniels, who had kept in touch with George, said he told her he was happy and that he saw no one. He read a great deal, mostly in French, which seemed calming after a more or less stormy youth. Daniels remarked that if George's last remaining unconventionality was a passion for irregular French verbs, she never wanted to see him again.

But George didn't sound happy in his letters to Alix. He'd begun to translate Baudelaire that summer, and in a rare flush of pride he told her, "My translations are marvellous, the best ever done from French into English." By August he admitted his Baudelaire was stalled: "I begin to be worried, for I don't want to spend the rest of my life at this kind of a grind." In October he told her:

> I almost died of boredom toward the end of the summer—the air was so heavy and I had gone stale on the work I was doing. I am still stale, and I cannot at this moment bear the sight of the translations I have done. . . . Now that it is Autumn, though, I begin to feel myself coming to life again and I have begun to work a little on my own verse.

When Edna and Eugen arrived in Richmond that fall, George's cousin Missy said, his mother, who was protective of her son and had always been a stumbling block to his relationship with Millay, looked grim. She was "a steel hand in a velvet glove.

"George was an only child, as I was, and he was, you see, sort of imprisoned by those two invalids. His mother would be sitting in the corner softly weeping and reading the Bible when Vincent was on the phone— 'When will you come? I'll meet you in Chicago—in New York!' You must remember, George came from a family of southern gentlemen. He had always seen his father, who was a saint, give in. And, too, he enjoyed his mother very much. I don't know whether Vincent thought she might still get him back. I do know, because it was the talk of the family, that she came to Richmond with armfuls of roses for his mother. And that, [as she was] tired after her arduous journey, Eugen Boissevain picked her up in his arms and carried her upstairs." He also called her "my child," which did not sit well with Mrs. Dillon, who remarked lightly to Eugen that his "child" looked a tad elderly. The conversation slowed to a halt after that.

By the time of her December 31 royalty statement, Millay had sold just over 35,000 copies of *Wine*. Such sales, within eight weeks of publication and in the middle of the Depression, were phenomenal. With *Fatal Interview* she had reached the bestseller list for the first time. Her royalty was a solid 15 percent on the first 25,000 copies sold; thereafter it increased to 20 percent. Now Harper increased that already handsome royalty: she would earn a flat 20 percent on all copies sold after the first 5,000. It is on the December royalty statement that another 25,000 copies are listed at the new rate. Between January and June 1935, an additional 6,500 copies of *Wine* were sold. Her total sales after seven months were 66,500 copies.

Her reviews, however, were becoming more and more mixed. Some were downright dismissive, beginning to suggest that her celebrity had outstripped her poetry and that the younger generation was moving on. In the first sentence of Horace Gregory's review in the New York *Herald Tribune* Books section, he made direct reference to Millay's popularity:

> In reading the name of Edna Millay across the title page of a new book of poems a number of definite pictures flow through the mind. It is like unrolling a newsreel of twelve years ago. I remember a sunlit, white-columned veranda of a sorority house in a middle-Western university. A girl in a red sweater was reading aloud to me the first poem in "Second April."

He could tell from this young woman's voice that the poem meant more to her than what it actually said. It meant "Liberty, equality, fraternity." It was, he wrote, as if she had been reading a letter from a friend.

> Here was a woman speaking to other women, a poet who was a celebrity in New York's Greenwich Village, who had been an actress on the stage of the Provincetown Theater, a young woman who smoked cigarettes as she read her poems in lecture halls, rented for the evening by local women's clubs. These details, trivial as they may seem today, were then the gestures of revolt against convention; the poet was a new woman, the symbol of emancipation whose presence was acknowledged by Woodrow Wilson as he signed the bill admitting Votes for Women into an amendment of the Constitution.

This may have been the first time her life was being reviewed, her work taken to task for its reception and popularity; it would not be the last. Millay's poetry appealed to a larger public than most poets ever hope to reach. Gregory reduced that appeal to immature girls—or, as they aged, to unhappy women. It was an attack disguised as a review.

It was left for Miss Millay to crystallize an impression left upon the public mind when Sara Teasdale wrote:

> My room was white with the sun
> And Love cried out to me,
> "I am strong, I will break your heart
> Unless you set me free."

She was to recite that statement as a Bill of Rights and to give it a name, a personality, a legend. It was as though she had created a character . . . who could say with perfect freedom that she had fallen in love or out, who could be faithless as any man or as faithful. The gesture was always a bit theatrical, and one always found it difficult to discern where genuine emotion left off and a pose began. . . . Following a standard set by a crude application of American Pragmatism, the picture "worked"; it was effective, and after it had stepped from its frame into the lives of a thousand women, it began to animate a thousand lesser Millays. Hundreds of women were stirred to writing verse, to say again what Edna Millay had said the year before.

In closing, Gregory strangely chided her for no longer writing for undergraduates. Undergraduate girls distrusted her now, he claimed; "their freedom is of the kind described by Spender and Auden, that lies at the end of a road through ruin and dissolution, a map whose landmarks are 'Das Capital' [sic], the poetry of T. S. Eliot and the novels of D. H. Lawrence. . . .

"If," he said, these undergraduates "are reading women poets" at all, they "veer toward the more intense, more sensitive verse of Leonie Adams and Louise Bogan."

It was left to Louise Bogan—the poet Horace Gregory chose to compare favorably to Millay—to champion *Wine.* Bogan wrote in *Poetry* magazine that the difficult transition of any poet as she matured was to risk breaking with her past achievements:

In her latest book, *Wine from These Grapes,* Edna Millay at last gives evidence that she recognizes and is prepared to meet the task of becoming a mature and self-sufficing woman and artist. It is a task she never completely faced before. . . . The accent of chagrin and desperation, both resolved and unresolved, is there—the sound of bitter thought, of meditation, of solitude, of the clear, disabused and unexcited mind. . . . she has crossed the line, made the break, passed into regions of cold and larger air.

A month after this review, the same reporter who had mocked the desperate and uncertain Scott Fitzgerald for his *Tender Is the Night* caught Millay at the St. Regis Hotel in Manhattan. She had, he noted, grown up. "I'm forty-two; just mention it once in your story and then, please, forget it!" In boldface, the headline read, "Poetic Strife Begins at 42 for Edna St. Vincent Millay."

The press would hang on her words and then skewer her with them. The subhead of the piece in the *New York Post* was "Indignation at the Cosmic Scheme Is the Motif of Our Erstwhile Sprite."

Millay knew she was undermining herself by giving the reporters the words they would use to nail her: "I know I sound like a fool. . . . I always look like a moron in the newspapers." When she's asked to be specific, she is, and not about poetry:

> I am disgusted with the hollow talk of disarmament. Men sent to Geneva equipped with every facility. . . . Thousands, hundreds of thousands of dollars are spent. . . . There's talk of world peace . . . talk, talk, talk.
>
> And then you follow the newspapers: Italy resents German attitude . . . France ready to fight for the Saar Valley. . . . In England, Ramsay MacDonald says there shouldn't be so much freedom of speech and so many attacks on the established things. . . .
>
> Winston Churchill cries out that Britain should have an air force second to none, like her navy. . . . And then we observe Armistice Day. We put wreaths on the grave of the Unknown Soldier, who's pretty damn well known by now as the symbol of the next war . . . while Japan penetrates China.

Listening in stunned silence, the reporter asked two questions: First, should the profit system be abolished?

> Yes, I blame the system. . . . I should like to live in a world where everybody has a job, leisure for study, leisure to become wiser, more perceptive. . . . I am willing to give up everything I possess, everything I ever will have. . . . I am willing to live in the simplest life . . . to live in a hut, on a loaf a day (Oh, I do know this sounds idiotic!) to achieve it.

And: "Do you want Communism?"

> No, no, I do not. . . . Communism is repugnant to me. . . . I am intensely an individualist. . . . I cannot bear to have a thousand well-wishers breathe on my neck.

From this point on, the FBI—which had been tracking her lackadaisically since she had given one dollar to buy Soviet tractors back in 1920—became more alert.

That fall Millay's editor, Eugene Saxton, invited her to meet another Harper author, the young Frederic Prokosch, whose novel Harper was about to publish. Prokosch made no impression whatsoever upon Millay, but he observed her with curiosity. In his memoirs nearly fifty years later, he described Saxton as a lovable Pickwickian character, "like a figure in an engraving by Phiz." He found Saxton at the bar in the Vanderbilt, sitting beside "a lady in a gray flannel suit, with a blue-striped shirt and a green silk cravat. Her cheeks were puffed and shiny, her hair hung loose and colorless, and her eyes were blurred and watery, as though worn by lamentation."

Millay had just come from autographing three hundred and thirty-five sets of the limited edition and thirty-six sets on Japan vellum of the ultra-limited edition of *Wine*. She was cross-eyed with fatigue. They had a round of martinis.

"I have spent the whole morning signing my books," said Miss Millay. "I am utterly exhausted. Just look. My hand is shaking. That's the trouble with being a celebrity. One gets sucked into the whirlpool. One does things that one shouldn't be doing and says things one shouldn't be saying and life grows horribly cheap and perfunctory and vulgar. I should *never* have consented to read my poems in public. It makes them sound so blatant. I feel like a prostitute."

"Not a prostitute surely, Edna dear," said Saxton with alarm.

"Or pretty damn close to it. One feels so pawed over. I keep thinking of Emily Dickinson. All those thousands of slips of paper. Nobody ever pawed *her* over in this cheap, macabre fashion."

"There still was a trace of a prancing charm and a young vulnerability," Prokosch wrote. He felt a sort of

loyalty to Miss Millay which dated back to the exhilarating twenties. *Wine from These Grapes* had just been published and I was sadly disappointed but I still felt an affection for *Second April* and *Fatal Interview*. "The sonnets I loved best," I murmured half guiltily, "were 'Only until this cigarette is ended' and 'Oh, sleep forever in the Latmian cave.' "

She glanced at me quickly with a panic-stricken glitter. "You say *loved*. It's all over, then? Never mind. It's rather a blow but there are worse things that can happen, even to the best of us." . . . Then she plucked a cigarette from a flat silver case and lit it ceremoniously with her freckled fingers.

2

When George Dillon found himself increasingly bogged down in the Baudelaire translations, Edna and Eugen invited him to Steepletop for the summer. Eugen wired the invitation, which George accepted immediately: "It is like you to send the telegram others would just think of sending. In this case your good deed is going to flower and bear fruit—it is as welcome as a rainfall on the dusty hills of Kansas and it has the same effect on my drooping spirit." George had sent Millay several of his translations and asked her to write the introduction to his Baudelaire, if she liked them. Crucially, she agreed.

George's letter to Eugen continued:

> I have never done anything that made me feel so *alone,* so absolutely cut off from the world around me. . . . Your friendly appreciation, and a note from Vincent saying that she will write the introduction, have sufficed to bring back something of the old enthusiastic feeling I had a year ago, and I am determined to finish the book to the best of my ability.

The trouble was, he wrote Vincent, that by then he would probably be good for nothing, "and if I come I shall expect to be treated like an uninteresting old uncle and set off in a corner or under a tree with a book."

There was something wildly disingenuous about this response. George Dillon was twenty-eight to Eugen's fifty-five; Edna Millay was forty-three. Some old uncle! Years later he would tell a mutual friend that "though their hospitality was warm and constant, I didn't go often to Steepletop. . . . they were usually surrounded by much older friends, and I felt somewhat out of it." But by then he was cloaking the intimacy of their relationship. In 1935, no matter how avuncular he may later have claimed to be, when he accepted the invitation he was about to enter their world again. This exquisite fragment of an unpublished and undated poem found among Dillon's papers tells us how he felt about Millay:

> Finding her body woven
> As if of flame and snow
> I thought, however often
> My pulses cease to go,
> Whipped by whatever pain
> Age or disease appoint,
> I shall not be again
> So jarred in every joint,
> So mute, amazed, and taut
> And winded of my breath—
> Beauty being at my throat
> More savagely than death.

It was a lovely summer at Steepletop. Cool green woods led to their farmhouse, its spring-fed pool surrounded by gardens of roses and Japanese irises. Two small stone fountains splashed water, and the grassy paths were overgrown with sweet fern, bordered by pines and fields of blueberries.

Steepletop was not one of the grand dark-shingled Berkshire cottages. It was gay and playful and bohemian, free of the careful formality of Edith Wharton's estate, The Mount, in nearby Lenox. It was a place where swimming suits were not welcome.

Indoors, Vincent and George began work on what was becoming *their* translation. For what had been "entirely George Dillon's book," Edna would write in her preface to the Baudelaire, had in fact become a collaboration. At first she had told herself she was just translating a phrase for fun, then as an exercise she'd translated an entire poem. After that she admonished herself, "you'll go straight back to work on your own book, which is *the most important thing in the world to you,* and you won't even *think* of translating another. This is what I said to myself, but neither of us believed me. . . . I was in for it." This was precisely the phrase she had used in an early letter to Dillon, when she had first been in love with him. "From that day to this moment I have thought of nothing, lived for nothing, but my translations from *Les Fleurs du Mal.*"

George liked to sleep late, while Eugen, up early, bare-chested and in shorts, puttered around the gardens in the morning and whistled for Altair and Ghost to go for a walk. He cooked every meal, tempting feasts with lots of wine, and there were always gin rickeys at cocktail time by the pool. Eugen's hair was thinning in the front now, and a faint bald spot showed up at his crown in the snapshots they took that summer— whereas George's black unruly curls, wet after a swim, were as slick as licorice.

On June 11, there was a very silly sonnet-writing session among Edna, George, and Eugen at Steepletop, a copy of which Edna sent to Arthur Ficke. "Me & George & Ugin had hysterics over this sonnet last night. We shrieked, we rolled on the floor, we stuffed rugs into our mouths. Perhaps you can think up some more. There *are* some more. We just had to stop because we were afraid we were going to die.

> "I was Brynhilde, but am now grown old.
> I saw Valhalla fallen, and Wotan dead.
> My spear is heavier than my arm can hold,
> My wingéd casque a weight upon my head. . . .
> I see around me in a rocky place
> A ring of flame, and hear the voice of him,
> Sieglinde's son, who, roving with a pack
> Of young companions, children of the brave,
> Shouted and plunged and took upon his back
> The crested fire as it had been a wave.
> Oh, laughing boy,—oh, to this moment dear!
> Who seeing me stared and said, 'A woman here?'

Of young companions, bravest of the brave
"   "   "   , in the brook to lave
"   "   "   , none of them a slave,
"   "   "   , hating to behave,
"   "   "   , through the forest grave (nave)
"   "   "   , hunting for a cave,
"   "   "   , in a manner suave,
"   "   "   , boredom off to stave,
"   "   "   , still too young to shave,
"   "   "   , hell about to pave,
"   "   "   , did not stamp or rave
"   "   "   , (one of them called 'Dave')"

But what happened when Edna and George sat in the library upstairs at Steepletop sparring over a word, disagreeing, then suddenly in absolute agreement? Eugen must have felt out of place. No one not engaged in those impossibly strict translations could have hoped to share the enflaming intensity of their labor, their intellectual play, their connection.

On July 23, Eugen left them alone together at Steepletop and wrote to Edna from the Turner Inn in Keene, New Hampshire:

Darling,
    Although we did not make an agreement, I come Friday trusting that we did really make an agreement.—
    I'll leave Monday.—

All my love
Uge

This note implied a lot. Eugen would return, but for a weekend only. When three weeks later he sent her a snapshot of himself, freshly shaven, in a linen suit, looking very well groomed, he looked worried. As well he might be. For once again, Eugen had withdrawn, leaving them alone. On his way to Ragged Island, Maine, Eugen wrote her again:

Darling Freckles,
    I'm so unbelievably happy, that I must write to you. . . . It was blowing a little and the sea was running, but not quite so badly as when we sailed and rowed over. You remember. . . . At 6 p.m. the wind had freshened, white caps all over and dirty clouds to the S.W. . . . An hour later it blew like the devil. . . . A nice little storm, with the breakers making white spray against a black sky way up in the air, and the grass blown flat on the ground, and the Greasy Joan [their skiff] riding sweetly on the hall-off, and I snug in the kitchen looking at "the scenery."—I know this reads like a letter of a 12 year old boy to his mama, but that's the way I feel. . . .

It is funny, but the happier I am the more I want you and long for you
and Christ I long for you. I want to show you so many things. . . . My
warmed over fish chowder is smelling up the whole house, so I guess it is
boiling and I'd better eat it.

He was beginning to sound just as he had in the letters he had written
to her when she'd been in France with Dillon in the summer of 1932—
Eugen, the one who cooks and provides, tempting her with sweet dishes,
with flowers, with the natural world of which he is master. It took him six
more pages to tell her what he really felt:

Love certainly is funny, not to say entertaining.—Here I am happy, oh so
happy, being alone on my beautiful fearful island. . . . and I must write and
long for a red haired freckled unfaithful little bitch with beautiful breasts
and an innocent child's red kitty. . . . This is a crazy letter.

Eugen's excessiveness was a part of his nature. He was stirred by her
unfaithfulness. She seemed to be most alluring to him when she was least
available.

I am crazy with delight of all here, and crazy for you.—Remain my own
darling unfaithful Vince and my darling, Scramoodles and true, after your
own fashion to your own

Skiddlepins.—

Eugen never knew when to stop. He pressed—not like a man who was
sure of himself but like a man who was demonstrating his need and his
sincerity. He insisted. He repeated. It's as if by insisting he could make his
love more true.
And then, finally:

I LOVE YOU.—
Ugin signing off.—
Please, please standbye?—

He was interminable. But he also seemed, this time, to be in control.
One week later, George wrote to Saxton at Harper, using Eugen's stationery with his name and "Steepletop" engraved on the letterhead:
"Herewith the partial manuscript of the greatest verse translation of the
twentieth century." He was even cheeky:

These copies can be treated as carelessly as you like. We will make entirely
new ones for the final manuscript.
We hope that you will still like the poems when you read them to yourself.

Then, as a stunning postscript: "My address for the next two weeks will be in care of Mr. Boissevain, Orr's Island, Maine." They would be all together on Ragged Island.

On the twenty-eighth of August, writing to Saxton from Orr's Island, the post office for Ragged, George and Edna signed the Baudelaire contract. Dillon's own publisher, the Viking Press, had written him a sharp letter. Viking was pleased for him that he was in a "brilliant collaboration" with Edna Millay, and it might well have been natural for him to assume "on account of Miss Millay's longer standing as an author, that the book should go to her publishers, rather than to yours. On the other hand, the project was yours to begin with . . . "; the company reminded him politely that he still owed them his next book.

When George sent this letter to Saxton, he added a note at the bottom. He was not bound to them for the Baudelaire, he said, since there was nothing in his contract about books written in collaboration. He asked that duplicate copies be sent to him, not only of the contracts but of all correspondence and proofs. While it was easier for Harper to write to Edna since they were constantly in touch with her about other matters, "that system is excellent as long as she and I are closely in touch, but after the First of the month we shall not be."

At the end of September, most of their translations were done, but Edna's promised preface was still incomplete, and the biographical note she now felt compelled to write was not yet begun. She planned a week in Paris with Eugen to get both chapters absolutely right and complete.

3

On September 28, Millay received a disturbing letter from her father. He wrote from Kingman, Maine, and he sounded bewildered. "You will be surprised to hear from me and under such conditions," he began. "Matters have gone badly with me for the last few years and I have gotten where I must do something." He explained that he had suffered a stroke during the summer, and though he was improving, the town of Kingman, which owed him money, was bankrupt "and will never be in financial condition in time to be any good to me. I really have no income at all." His friends had tried to help, but he had fallen into debt.

Unless you can see your way clear to help me there is nothing for me but to apply to the state for aid which I am loath to do. My needs are not large; Some seven or eight dollars will take of me weekly after my immediate needs are taken care of me.

Several times in this brief letter he misconstructed his request for help: he meant "take care of me."

> It is quite possible that I may not have to be cared for me very long. . . . and if you feel that you want to help me rather than call on the state, it will make me much happier in my old age.
>
> H. T. Millay

After she helped him, he wrote to her once more: "I want to tell you that what you are doing for me is plenty and I am grateful beyond any I can say. I don't know what I might have or could have done." He signed this letter "Your Father." It was ironic that the small sum Henry Millay asked of his daughter was only a few dollars more than what they had so desperately needed from him in her girlhood.

It was the last letter she would ever receive from her father, who died in December. Eugen traveled alone to Maine to attend to his burial and to gather his few remaining personal possessions. None of his daughters went to the funeral.

Not long after Edna and Eugen left for Paris, George wrote to Saxton to tell him that they had suggested he place some of his translations in magazines. He sounded sure and buoyant. On October 2, Saxton answered with discouraging news: *Harper's Magazine* would have to print several poems to get the full effect of his effort, and there was no space for months to come, "since they have just made a similar program for Miss Millay's *Conversation at Midnight.*" It seems cruel, or maybe just careless, of Edna and Eugen to have recommended something they must have known was unlikely to succeed. George's hopes were thoroughly dashed. There is no evidence that he tried any other publication or that any other magazine took his work.

His correspondence with his new publisher grew sharper after that. On December 30, 1935, Saxton wrote to him with the good news that the Baudelaire led the nonfiction list for Harper's spring books at its sales conference. If Dillon had never before felt diminished by the force of Millay's reputation in relation to his own, he must have felt it now. Saxton continued:

> It has to do with the order of names on the title-page and jacket of the book, and it comes down to this: The whole selling staff is convinced that the appearance of Miss Millay's name in second place . . . will indicate to the bookseller and the public that Miss Millay has only a minor association with the volume; and that the result will be a considerable loss of sales.

The publisher's emphasis was "to be placed on Miss Millay's name, because it is her identification with the book that will increase the orders."

Dillon was to understand that none of this was Saxton's personal viewpoint, "and I am not unmindful of your priority in the Baudelaire project and Miss Millay's wish to recognize this." This had nothing to do with quality or honor or position or priority, he assured him. However: "There can be no question that the use of Miss Millay's name will make a tremendous difference in the fate of the book." If Dillon agreed—and if Millay did—"wire me simply: 'Agree reversing names.' "

In point of fact, Saxton had already delivered the same message to Millay. He was not, he insisted, "unmindful of what you have said in your correspondence about Dillon's priority in the Baudelaire project and your wish to recognize this." But there was no question that the "use of your name will make a tremendous difference in the fate of the book." He had hesitated to put this question before her, "and I know it will be an embarrassing one for you." He assured her that he was not sending a copy of this letter to Dillon, and he asked her simply to wire him AGREE REVERSING NAMES, "and I will put the whole question to Dillon *as a suggestion from this office,* without indicating that you have reached any decision on the question. I can in fact frame a letter to him which I can also send to you at the same moment and ask for your joint reply." But Millay did not agree. George's name would come first.

At the end of November, Edna wrote to Gladys Ficke, telling her that Eugen had found them a house in Florida

> somewhere between Palm Beach and Miami. I am going down tomorrow with the servants. I wanted so much to get over to see you and our darling Artie, but I am so simply exhausted after getting the Baudelaire off to Harpers, that packing—even with somebody else to pack under my direction!—is taking all the strength I have. . . . So I shan't see you, kids, before I go. But I'll see you next summer; and we'll have lots of fun, because Arthur will be well again, and more like his cute, gay old self, and I shan't be working so hard, so perhaps I shall be a bit more like *my* cute, gay old self!

Eugen had found a furnished house near the Branns, their neighbors in Austerlitz, in Delray Beach. It had everything, Edna said, but hot water. The water was supposed to be heated on the roof by the sun, but since they had arrived it had been cold and rainy and foggy. Eugen wrote to Deems Taylor telling him there was nothing to do but collect shells and drink.

Edna and I pick up shells. . . . Quite a number of people pick up shells. We have quite a number of palm trees around our house. Edna likes the noise they make; but I don't. When the wind blows they make quite a lot of noise; Edna likes it. I don't, though. Edna doesn't like the Branns' butler, though. I do, though. He puts lemon-juice in the martinis. I don't like that.

Eugen's postscript was hilarious:

How much money can you lend me until the first week in May? I shall be quite rich again on the first of May, but I'm not very rich right now; in fact, all I have in my pockets is a fifty-cents piece, and I have to keep that to do a trick with. I could misuse two grand. But even one grand would come in and go out very handy. If not that, maybe you could let me have three dollars.

Once they were settled at Delray Beach, Edna's letters to Harper about the production of the Baudelaire began in earnest. By Christmas Day, she told George she was trying to get their final proofs back to Harper in

time to have a nervous breakdown. . . . It is obvious that Harper & Bros. are trying to kill us so that they'll never have to have anything to do with either of us again. You will have noticed that when they give us a week's extension they give the printers a fortnight; it's easy to see who is teacher's pet here. . . . I'm perfectly furious with them.

In a turn at once affectionate and chiding, while thanking him for catching a mistake she'd made, she twitted him for changing "Eldorado" to "El Dorado" in her translation of "Le Voyage":

Poe spelled it Eldorado; and that is probably why Baudelaire spelled it that way. Baudelaire must have read Poe's poem "Eldorado" before he wrote "Le Voyage." I know what an old pedant you are, and what a hopeless Anglophile; but it seems to me that in this particular book, what was good enough for Poe and good enough for Baudelaire ought to be good enough for us.

George sheepishly agreed. He even agreed to the changes she made in the table of contents, and he requested of Harper only two things:

On the page where our books are listed, mine are to be put underneath those of Miss Millay. I think the reason is obvious. It is only in connection with the Baudelaire, and due to the special circumstances of its production, that my name could take even typographical precedence above hers.

But he did ask that in the copyright notice his name "correspond to the order of the names on the title page"; in other words, his name first.

This is a small thing, but it will help in a slight way to substantiate the fact that this particular book was my project: which is the only excuse anyway for what will seem grotesque to everyone who opens the book—I mean the precedence of an obscure name over an illustrious one.

When Millay got the jacket proof, she wired George:

TITLE OF BOOK HEARTBREAKINGLY PEDESTRIAN AND DULL EVERYBODY WILL THINK IT BIOGRAPHY OF BAUDELAIRE ARE YOU AGAINST USING FLOWERS OF EVIL AS TITLE WHY NOT GIVE OURSELVES SAME BREAK OTHERS HAVE HAD. . . . THIS IS EXTREMELY SERIOUS

VINCENT

George answered immediately; he hadn't seen the jacket proof. Millay exploded.

It never occurred to me that the sons-of-bitches wouldn't have sent *you* a proof of the jacket, too. What ails them? Let's clear out and the hell with them. Let's send them a corrected copy of the Bronx and Queens telephone directory and skip. Let's go to the Galapagos and gather boobies' eggs.

In the meantime I am sending on to you the jacket-proof which by mistake, instead of being mailed to Edna Ferber, was mailed to me.

Time was short. And while she told him that she knew he'd been in the advertising business and she hadn't, "I've been buying longer than you've been advertising; and I know that if I went to Brentano's with money to buy just seven books, this book would be the eighth." She asked him to think it over.

You have just one hour before Sharper and Smothers (alias Harper and Brothers) come in with the confession, a fountain-pen, and a piece of lead pipe. . . . What shall the title be?—I suggest "POSTCARDS FROM HAPPY-DUST CHARLIE TO HIS LENOX AVENUE MOLL."

Love and all that,
Vincent

A flurry of wires crossed between them. They settled on the title she had insisted upon, *Flowers of Evil*. George's final letter to Saxton was far more conciliatory than hers had been; he thanked and congratulated Saxton "in your role of third collaborator."

Flowers of Evil was published on April 2, 1936. George Dillon would never publish another book of his own poems.

CHAPTER 32

Two days after publication, in the April 4, 1936, issue of the *Saturday Review,* Mary Colum savaged their Baudelaire. "For some strange reason poets admire themselves more for their feats in translation than for their own original work: Miss Millay has succumbed to this particular illusion and she glows over the performance of herself and Mr. George Dillon," she wrote. Whereas Dillon, she said, had grasped something of the intellectual structure of Baudelaire's mind, he had captured "almost nothing of the emotional structure; Miss Millay gets something of both. The reason that she does not achieve a closer approach to an acceptable rendering is partly because she is a woman." Baudelaire, it will be remembered, was not. Because Millay and Dillon had agreed from the beginning to sign the translations each had done with their own initials and in the rare instances where they had worked on a poem together to sign both sets of initials, they exposed themselves to this sort of criticism.

Edna wired Arthur Ficke from Florida:

LIFE IS BLAH AND ART IS BLEATING, AND THE GRAVE THING GOD ITS GOAL;
ELSE I MIGHT SOME DAY BE MEETING MARY COLUM SOUL TO SOUL

The reviewer for *The New York Times* soon provided balm enough. He wrote that their translation was "incomparable." He called it a "magnificent translation . . . by two poets whom the unquiet shadow of Baudelaire . . . must surely bless."

Twenty-five years later, when George Dillon was revising their Baudelaire for a paperback edition, he told Alix Daniels, "There was no deliberate claptrap, just a lot of innocent bad taste and lack of skill." What had kept the book in print all those years, he knew, was "the lively and imaginative Millay style, and of course it is the charm of her translations (they are wonderfully faithful, too) . . . this, and the fact that she should have written them at all."

—

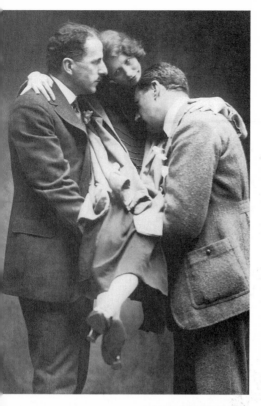

These three shots may have been taken on the day Eugen, Arthur, and Edna lunched together in New York in the spring of 1923. Sharing the pretty maid, Eugen looks like a devoted lover, and Arthur Ficke, with his mustache, like a dapper dan.

Eugen and Edna rent a tiny house at 75½ Bedford Street in Greenwich Village.
(Photo by Jessie Tarbox Beals)

In the spring of 1925, they buy an old farmhouse on three hundred acres in Austerlitz, New York, and call it Steepletop, after a wildflower that grows there.

Soon Cora is helping them restore the place.

She is also cooking and cleaning and taking care of Vincent, who has developed "a headache all the time lately and spots before my eyes, and, as Mother used to say, I don't feel so darned well myself."

Edna St. Vincent
Millay picketing in
April 1927 for the
reprieve of Sacco
and Vanzetti, the
two Italian immi-
grant anarchists
sentenced to death.

Vincent at her
mother's cottage,
Breezy Knoll, in
Camden.

Happier times that summer in Maine with Eugen (above). Norma (left) with her husband, Charles Ellis.

The three sisters: an un-dated snapshot of Edna, Norma, and Kathleen.

Kathleen Kalloch Millay in an undated publicity shot by Arnold Genthe.

Cora Buzzell Millay, 1863–1931.

Cora Millay—spring 1925—posing under an apple tree in Maine.

George Dillon in 1932. He is twenty-six and has just won the Pulitzer Prize for poetry with his second book, *The Flowering Stone*. He is in Paris, where Millay has gone to join him. (AP/Wide World Photos)

On Christmas 1932, Millay began the first of a series of Sunday-night readings of her poems over the air on a nationwide hookup. The first time she heard the recordings played back to her, the first time she'd ever heard herself speak, she asked, "Is that really my voice?" Then, after a pause: "Quite lovely, isn't it?"

When she received an honorary doctorate from New York University in 1937, it was her fifth; she was now one of the most famous women in America.

They raced in their open Cadillac along the pines and fields in their matching racoon coats . . .

. . . or snuggled under quilts in the long winters at Steepletop.

Elegant and debonair, Eugen, an almost perfect husband.

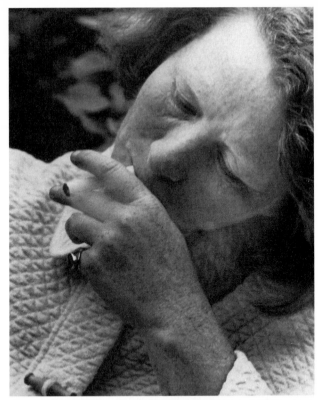

While she was able to retrieve *Conversation at Midnight* from her memory after a fire destroyed her only draft in May 1936, she was beginning to show signs of wear. (Photos by Adolph Altman, courtesy of ASCAP)

At the end of 1940, Millay attended a benefit for United China Relief, to help raise money for Chinese trapped in the war of resistance to Japan. She wrote for the British War Relief, and helped buy an ambulance for the British-American Ambulance Corps.

Steepletop, early 1940s. She was now the chatelaine of seven hundred acres, and she began to look haunted. This photo was taken from a shoot by *Town & Country*.

Edna and Eugen at their mahogany bar, down by the pool at Steepletop in the 1940s, and Edna out on the stoop. (Photos by Jacob Lofman)

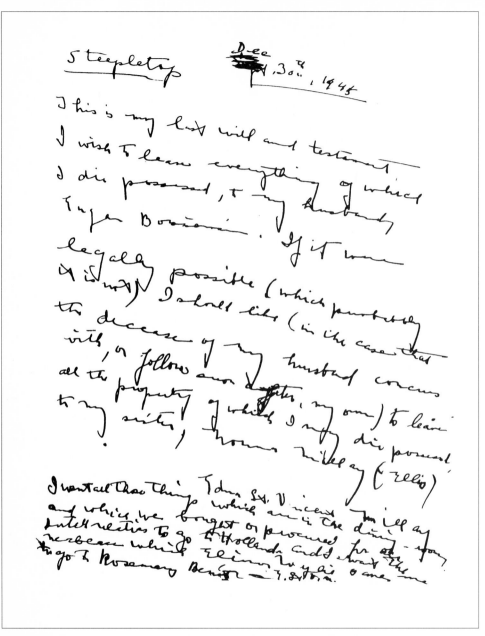

Her will, scribbled on a piece of paper with a shaky hand and dated December 30, 1945.

Two pages from the Drug Notebooks, which began within a week of Kathleen's death in 1943. Entries were recorded meticulously, with daily and hourly notations and complex calculations of dosage. "How am I to give up taking morphine when I need it all the time for one darned thing after another?" she scribbled at the top of the entry for November 12, 1943. "It must be hard enough when it's just a habit!—everybody says it is—everybody says it's impossible, unless you go to a hospital and have nurses injecting insulin and hyoscine into you all day long!" By 1944, Eugen began to keep a record of his addiction, as well as hers.

Norma Millay Ellis, 1893–1986.

Edna and Eugen remained in Florida until May, the month after publication, when Edna returned to writing her verse drama *Conversation at Midnight,* which she had interrupted to work on the Baudelaire with George. On the first of May she wrote, "We start motoring . . . today,—at least, if I stop writing Arthur and start washing my hair. We expect to be at Steepletop by the eighth."

They didn't make it to Steepletop that week. Driving north in their Cadillac, they stopped to visit the islands of Captiva and Sanibel, where the shelling was splendid. They arrived at the Palms Hotel on the beach at Sanibel just an hour or so before sunset. In their eagerness to get to the beach while there was still light, they engaged a room and sent their luggage on ahead. Suddenly Eugen remembered that he'd left the manuscripts under the front seat of the car. He rushed back to the hotel to put them with the rest of their baggage. Millay ran ahead of him onto the beach to search for seashells. Something made her look back. The hotel was engulfed in flames.

They lost everything: a stunning emerald ring, her cherished seventeenth-century copy of Catullus, which was "the only thing that touched me emotionally, the only thing I mourned for. . . . the only thing that could comfort me at all when I got to thinking about it, was to say over and over to myself, 'Desinas ineptire—desinas ineptire, desinas ineptire— . . . et quod vides perisse perditum ducas.' " Which was from the Eighth Lyric of Catullus: "Cease this folly . . . and what you see is lost set down as lost."

They had to drive thirteen hundred miles back to Steepletop in a car whose bushings had burned out, "plodding north at thirty-five, thirty, twenty-five, twenty miles an hour, to the accompaniment of an increasingly interesting populace," swathed in something that had once been a white linen suit, wrapped up in a rug because even her coat was lost in the fire. She was such "a complete mess" that they slunk into hotels in the dark of night only to creep out at daybreak.

But those losses were not the hardest to bear. Norma, who'd read in the newspaper about the fire and the complete loss of Vincent's manuscripts, wrote to her immediately: "Sweetheart. . . . The greatest tragedy would be not that your manuscript was destroyed but that it might never have been written." But since it had been written and she had a superb memory, it was all inside.

> It happened to be a rude fire, baby, but that is none of your business. Forget it. . . . The important thing is that you have a lot of work to do and you have done a lot of work before and are not afraid of it. . . . I love you not only I find because you are my poet and my beloved sister but because I

know you. . . . I have built up quite a life without you but there are certain things I know that are part of the foundation of my life—that are in my blood, and I know you. I can't help you by saying this. . . . that you already know. I am perhaps a little drunk with this day of painting, of poetry, Bourbon and my love for you. Norma.

"It was a major tragedy," Eugen wrote back.

The terrible thing is, that Edna lost the entire Mss. of her new book, which was going to the printer in June.—And the Mss. of practically another book.—I hope she will be able to remember many of them.—But the whole thing has shaken her up quite a bit, and she does not seem to wish to start trying to remember them. . . . but with her vitality and courage, she'll get over it, bye and bye, and be once more interested in her work.— Poor Kid.

In the summer she began the work of remembering the poems and writing new ones. She thought she could have "the Conversation," as she called her play, to Gene Saxton at Harper in time for spring publication, but she had an enormous amount of work still to do, and she was hampered psychologically by knowing it had been completely destroyed.

Under more favourable conditions, since I have a very good memory, I might have been able to recall the whole book,—if, for instance, a copy of it had been in existence somewhere, though at the moment unavailable; or if I had been required to recall it, not knowing that the only copy had been burnt. Conscious, however, that with the exception of a few of the poems which had been published in *Harper's Magazine* the preceding autumn, no line of the book existed anywhere except in my memory, if indeed there, I was handicapped by the strain under which I worked.

That summer Edna and Eugen had a tennis court built up on the top of the field where her little studio from the days of *The King's Henchman* had burned down. It was a first-rate court, with hard red clay laid over pebbles and basalt, better even than the country club courts in Great Barrington, Massachusetts, she bragged a little to George. But she could barely play on it because her arm was hurt: "It hurts my arm to type, too, but not so much. They say what ails my arm is bursitis, which is the same as tennis elbow, or tennis shoulder." As odd as it must have seemed, Eugen had strained his shoulder, practicing hard serves, and had been laid up too.

In a footnote to Millay's published letters, Norma Millay added this note: "The trouble with her arm was the first evidence of serious injury caused by an accident in the summer of 1936 which was to give the poet increasing pain." Eugen was considerably clearer about what had happened in his letter to Charlie:

> We had an accident which might have been serious but happily ended with only great discomfort to Edna. Going around a sharp turn the door of the Station-Wagon flew open and Edna was thrown out. She rolled down an embankment. She had an enormous bump on her head, scratches & bruises all over. And her right arm, which was just getting better, is bad again and she cannot play the piano or write the typewriter. Damn bad luck.—We certainly have had . . . bad luck this year!

In the fall, still locked in struggle with her manuscript, she decided to dedicate *Conversation* to Arthur Ficke and drove over to Hardhack to tell him. Arthur was overwhelmed with pleasure. "On this day, Oct. 24, 1936," he entered in his diary,

> Edna St. Vincent Millay came to see me, and Gladys and Eugen . . . and then Vincent formally asked my permission to dedicate her forthcoming book of poems "To the poet Arthur Davison Ficke." I am dizzy, and in tears. Vince cried a little, too.
>
> It would be hard for an outsider to understand why I am a little dizzy today. Vincent is a fool—and also a great poet. If there is anything that I don't know about her, both as an ass and an angel, then that matter is unknown to anybody, even herself.

He continued in what was his first and only specific acknowledgment of just how close they had been: "Yet in spite of all this, I am deeply stirred by her desire to give public expression to the fact that, for almost twenty-five years, we have been very important to each other—as friends, lovers, colleagues, lonely fellow-sparks in a dark world." That same night he wrote to her quickly:

> My dear—I have always loved you, and I have always felt that your finest poems were surpassed by no poems that have ever been written, anywhere, anytime.
>
> And in the terrific loneliness that is the fate of every poet, I have dreamed sometimes that a little of <u>my</u> work, too, might be remembered. . . . I know of no present assurance that could mean to me as much as the fate that you will dedicate your book to me. I feel as if I had been told—"Rise, <u>Sir</u> Arthur Ficke!" . . . Isn't it funny that you didn't fully understand how deeply I would be moved by your publishing of our "bans."!

The next day, he wrote again:

Miss Millay, Esq:

I shall not easily forget yesterday. I don't know, really, whether you are a better poet than I am: such matters remain among the religious mysteries. But I do know that your reputation as a poet is much greater than mine. I also know that my love for you has been no little or laughable element in my life: it has been a real thing, for many years. I also know that an absurd feeling (which you will understand instantly) makes me wish that my otherwise-futile life might result in a few of my poems entering into the blood-stream of the race. I also know, now, that you really love me, and that you are not ashamed of the fact that I love you. . . . It's just that I'm very proud that you care to record the fact that we have meant something in each other's lives. When, someday, I die, please reread my sonnets to you "Beauty in Exile"—and then, perhaps for the first time, you will fully grasp the fact that I loved you.

I graciously accord you permission to dedicate your forthcoming book to me. It is only by this complete reversal of what I feel that I can say what I mean.

Arcturus

However uncomfortable Edna may have felt, she had loved him, and once he had stood for all she dreamed of. She did dedicate *Conversation* to him, but she trimmed "To the Poet" from her dedication, which read, simply, "To Arthur Davison Ficke."

In mid-January 1937, nine months after the publication of their Baudelaire, Millay called George Dillon from the St. Regis, where she'd dug in to complete *Conversation.* He wrote back immediately:

It was strange to hear your voice last night. Somehow quite in line with this strange and unseasonable January—the Forsythia in bloom, etc. I wonder what prompted your atavistic impulse. Anyway, I'm glad you had it.

In the excitement of hearing your voice again I forgot to say anything about those superb Oregon pears you sent us at Christmas. We did enjoy them immensely.

I was glad to know that you've been writing poems, and wish you could send me some. . . . Today I'll probably spend thinking about you and not doing a damn thing.

How oddly forlorn his letter sounds. How distant they must have become. Imagine sending him fruit at Christmas—a gift for an old relative, for someone with whom the connection is thin. After this note she did write back, but by the close of her letter there was a plaintive sadness to her tone: "I wish you would write me, and tell me how you are and what you are doing. I love you always, even though we never see each other and you never hear from me."

In April, Millay accepted an invitation from New York University to receive an honorary doctorate. In the same letter she was informed of a small dinner being given on her behalf by the chancellor's wife, Mrs. Chase, at their house. Now, one week after having accepted, she learned that on the same evening of the dinner given in her honor by the chancellor's wife, another separate dinner was to be given at the Waldorf-Astoria in honor of the male recipients. Her response to the chancellor of New York University, Harry Woodburn Chase, was exceedingly formal; she said that while she had received from him on April 26 the request that she accept the honorary degree the university wished to bestow upon her—and in the same letter an invitation from the chancellor's wife, Mrs. Chase, to receive her as "guest of honour at a dinner given for a small group of ladies at the Chancellor's house on the evening before Commencement," she'd replied at once, accepting the award. But she had since learned that

> On an occasion, then, on which I shall be present solely for reasons of scholarship, I am, solely for reasons of sex, to be excluded from the company and the conversation of my fellow-doctors. Had I known this in time, I should have declined not only Mrs. Chase's invitation to dinner, but also, had it appeared that my declining this invitation might cause Mrs. Chase embarrassment, the honour of receiving the degree as well.

Now it was too late to do either. She was deeply offended. And she was eloquent. "I beg of you, and of the eminent Council whose representative you are, that I may be the last woman so honoured, to be required to swallow from the very cup of this honour, the gall of this humiliation. Very sincerely yours, Edna St. Vincent Millay."

Cass Canfield, the new president of Harper, escorted Millay to the commencement. He remembered the occasion a little uneasily. He knew nothing of the insult to Millay, only the honor. "Well, I was on the board of directors—a sort of trustee—and of course they knew I was her publisher; and everyone was accompanied, so I was with her. I knew her then almost not at all." In the photographs in the newspapers they are shown striding toward Washington Square Arch together in the bright morning sunlight. Even in heels, Millay barely reaches his shoulder. Her chin is very clearly jutting forward, and she is wearing her own doctor's cap and gown, for by that spring 1937 she had accepted five honorary degrees—from New York University, Tufts, Russell Sage, the University of Wisconsin, and Colby College.

2

Conversation at Midnight was unlike anything she'd ever written. It was an audacious piece of work, intellectually provocative, colloquial, funny, and cloaked in a masculine voice. There wasn't a woman in it. It was also anti-war: "Have pity upon a nervous host, opposed / Not only to fascism, but also to war." *Aria da Capo,* her little gem of a play written two decades earlier, had also been antiwar, but this was not commedia dell'arte; there's not a macaroon or a shepherd in sight. Intellectually compelling, it marked her return to the political stage. The play is built around the sophisticated banter of a group of men—a stockbroker, an advertising executive, a priest, a failed but gifted painter, and Carl, a Communist, who is also a poet—all of whom have gathered in the drawing room of their host, Ricardo's, house:

> It is the room of a wealthy and somewhat eccentric bachelor of considerable culture, who has furnished his quarters to his own liking. The room is at the same time luxurious and faintly shabby. It has a high, rather ornate ceiling. There is an open fire-place with a handsomely carved white marble mantel, surmounted by a huge mirror with an elaborate gilt frame.

His house is on West Tenth Street, just off Fifth Avenue, in the elegant reaches of Greenwich Village, near Washington Square. A butler comes in with a tray of Scotch, Irish, and Bourbon whiskeys, soda and ice, two bottles of claret, and glasses. He leaves, and the conversation opens with Merton, the broker, saying casually, "That was the year I killed five hundred quail."

The play was only somewhat about what Edmund Wilson would call *The American Jitters.* It was impossible between 1936, when Millay began to rewrite what she could remember of *Conversation,* and the fall of 1937, when it was published, not to acknowledge that Europe was again on the brink of war. This was a time when America had made swing king, when Charlie McCarthy, candid cameras, and crossword puzzles were the crazes. *How to Win Friends and Influence People* topped the bestseller list for 1937, along with, for the second year, the immensely popular *Gone with the Wind.* Self-help books and historical fiction swept an America eager to emerge from the Depression and escape from the turmoil in Europe. Since *Wine* was published in 1934, the Nazis seized full power in Germany and began their insidious anti-Semitic campaign. In 1936, the Rome-Berlin Axis was announced as Germany goose-stepped into the Rhineland. A civil war raged in Spain, backed by Hitler's Germany and Stalin's Soviet Union. Anne Morrow Lindbergh's *North to the Orient* remained on the bestseller list for the second year—her name forever linked in the American imagination not only with her husband's historic flight to Paris but with the tragic kidnapping of their baby son. Franklin D. Roosevelt defeated Alf Landon by 523 electoral votes, but even with his New Deal, one fifth of all Americans were unemployed.

The New York Times Book Review put *Conversation at Midnight* on its front page, and the Book-of-the-Month Club took it as an alternate main selection. Millay's popular success was stunning. If mining *Conversation* from her memory had been hard work, publishing it was sheer, insolent fun. The correspondent from the *New York Post* came to Steepletop to interview her. She lifted a glass of champagne with one hand, waved a hunk of coarse sweet Russian black bread with the other, and said, "Here's to my new book. May it comfort my friends and confound my critics!"

She was standing at the little mahogany bar Eugen had rigged up near the swimming pool with her foot hooked roguishly on the brass rail, sipping Pol Roger 1921, when she turned to the reporter again. "Mind you, I hope it will confound MY critics; not THE critics!" she said and smiled at him.

The reporter, Michael Mok, asked his readers if they had any idea what the smile of Edna Millay looked like. "Her face around the luminous sea-green eyes crinkles, hiding the gold flecks of the freckles; she tilts back her head, shaking her bobbed russet hair; she parts her lips, letting her small even teeth glisten in the sun." Millay was once more her high-keyed, caroling self: "The nightingale of the Berkshires has pulled the thorn from her breast." Three years before, when Mok had first met her, she had been disconsolate: "The fist of the world was pounding the door of her ivory tower. It opened a crack. Through it she saw the rise of the Fascist fury, heard the clink of armaments. Hatred again inflamed Europe; fear cowed the innocent. She averted her face." But since then, she had "decided that the only way to fight evil is to come to grips with it." And *Conversation* was her way to settle the score.

"You know me as a passionate pacifist," she told Mok, "but now, sometimes, I'm almost tempted to think that we must arm." Then, in a declaration of what she understood her role as a poet to be, she made her position absolutely clear:

Everything that touches the individual as an individual is matter for poetry, but when the poet becomes a member of the mass, his vein is bound to be exhausted.

The poet can be concerned with what goes on outside, but the moment the outside comes in, dictates to him what pen, what ink, what paper he shall use, what thoughts he shall think, he declines and dies.

I think there might be a great Communist poet, a great Fascist poet. Communism and Fascism are subjects for poetry, but Communism and Fascism will never permit those poems to be written.

I can't imagine myself living, working, in such a world. I should either have to stultify myself or be shot.

The liberty under which this new book of mine comes out is more precious to me than anything anywhere. That's what makes life real.

At this point Eugen, who had been quietly standing behind the bar, coughed and said, "At the rate my Pol Roger is going it would be cheaper to cut this short and take you two in to lunch. But Vincent . . . doesn't bring out a book every day. How about one more glass?"

However, two of Millay's closest friends from the past, Edmund Wilson and John Peale Bishop, did not like *Conversation* at all. Wilson, who had sided with American Communists in the 1932 election and was now considered to be a leftist in New York literary circles, was disappointed because the conflict between the Communist and the stockbroker was really

the conflict between the classless and the class ideal, and Miss Millay has sidestepped this by making the pretenses of both parties ridiculous. For her, the whole upshot of the matter seems to be that both the stockbroker and the radical hanker only after the status of obedient cogs in a smoothly running machine. But is this what they are fighting about in Spain? Miss Millay probably does not really think so, since she has lately contributed to a volume of translations of Spanish poems, for the benefit of the Loyalist cause.

She had also written for the Spanish cause "Say that We Saw Spain Die":

> O splendid bull, how well you fought!
> Lost from the first.
> . . . the tossed, the replaced, the
> watchful *torero* with gesture elegant and spry,
> Before the dark, the tiring but the unglazed eye deploying the
> bright cape,

Which hid for once not air, but the enemy indeed, the authentic
    shape,
A thousand of him, interminably into the ring released . . .
    the turning beast at length between converging colours
    caught.

Save for the weapons of its skull, a bull
Unarmed, considering, weighing, charging
Almost a world, itself without ally.

What Wilson wanted was the lyric girl whose work and self he'd loved almost two decades earlier. At the close of his review he was reduced to lambasting the entire current state of verse in America: "Compare MacNeice and Auden with Yeats and Houseman; Robinson Jeffers with John Masefield; Eliot's *Murder in the Cathedral* with his earlier work. . . . And now Edna St. Vincent Millay, one of the sole surviving masters of English verse, seems to be going to pieces, too." He ended on a note that read like an epitaph: "Yet I miss her old imperial line."

A quarter century later, in 1960, the iconoclastic British critic Kenneth Tynan, writing in *The New Yorker,* had called *Conversation* "the brilliant book of orchestrated debate that is to my mind Miss Millay's highest intellectual achievement." He closed with Carl's lovely, mournful affirmation of life:

Beautiful as a dandelion-blossom, golden in the green grass,
This life can be.
Common as a dandelion-blossom, beautiful in the clean grass, not
    beautiful
Because common, beautiful because beautiful;
Noble because common, because free.

Tynan understood Millay to be a "thinker. . . . a ravaged observer of the human plight," not a "pretty non-combatant, a delicate fashioner of pathetic parlor verse."

CHAPTER 33

While it was important to Millay not to lose the friends to whom she'd once been attached, there were few women among them unless they were the wives of men she and Eugen were close to: Gladys and Arthur, Alyse and Lulu, Mary and Deems. She had very little contact now with either of her sisters. Kathleen had all but disappeared from her life, and Norma was being kept at arm's length. She counted very few writers in her inner circle. Charlie suggested that this was because Eugen picked her friends. Bill Brann, who after a very successful career in advertising now bred and trained Thoroughbreds, and George LaBranche, a stockbroker who raised pheasants on his nearby estate and had written a book on fly fishing, were men with whom Eugen was comfortable, and both lived nearby. Maybe in her wide public fame Millay lost or had never shared that sense of belonging to the same generation that Edmund Wilson prized so highly in his friendships with the men he knew at Princeton: Scott Fitzgerald and John Peale Bishop. Millay didn't see Wilson anymore because of a misunderstanding between them about his portrayal of her as Rita Cavanaugh in his novel *I Thought of Daisy*. It wasn't that she was offended by his characterization of her; she felt the novel was badly written. Whenever he or Bishop reviewed her work, as they just had with *Conversation,* they fell hard on her, judging her work sharply and with a sense of disappointment.

Millay had never entirely lost track of George Slocombe, nor he of her. Since they had last known each other in France, Slocombe had achieved a distinguished international reputation as a journalist. He was now a regular contributor to American publications, among them the New York *Herald Tribune, The Saturday Evening Post, Esquire, Vanity Fair,* and *The Nation.* His stature as a figure in international politics had grown, too. He had been commended by the British government for having initiated the negotiations that had freed Gandhi from imprisonment, which had led to the Pact of Delhi. He had become the foreign editor of the *Evening Standard* in 1932, and he had eleven books to his credit.

On the rare occasions when he had visited America, where he lectured and wrote what he called "my Monday articles" for the *Herald Tribune,* Slocombe and Millay had missed each other. On an impulse, he wrote to her now and said his pieces would be easier to write if he knew she would be reading them. He had just returned from a research trip through Switzerland, Germany, Austria, and Czechoslovakia, "a depressing tour for they are all preparing for war."

Edna asked him to come and stay with them at Steepletop. He accepted immediately. As it turned out, she was holed up at One Fifth Avenue when he arrived. "Darling," he wrote when he left,

> I couldn't say anything to you over the telephone, any more than I can say anything at railway stations. . . . I slept last night for 12 hours and woke up & found it noon, but it took me 2 days to get used to going to sleep earlier

than 3 a.m. I am in the middle of an emotional & spiritual reaction. Perhaps it is leaving you. . . . Darling you cannot imagine how lovely it was to be with you in New York. It gave an air of surprise & wonder to what I feared would be an unimportant if not boring stay. . . . Give my love to Eugen. I am glad he is my friend.

When she called him in California, where his lecture tour had taken him, he said he loved hearing her voice.

This town is too fantastic—so many young girls, so much beauty in sky and landscape, so many handsome white villas under the palms and cypresses, so many neon signs. I asked at a party last night if there were no attractive women of forty-four in Hollywood. Answer: yes but they all try to look like twenty. This town is sex crazy but not in a big way, to use their own crazy language.

In December 1937, he wrote, "Am I going to see you in January? . . . Darling I love you. George."

Early in the spring, George Slocombe went alone to Steepletop to spend a week with Edna and Eugen, "in a lovely & rare intimacy which I think we all loved." He found himself writing poetry there. In one poem he asked Edna what Elinor Wylie had been like. Millay's response was her "Sonnet in Answer to a Question"; she even dated it:

> MARCH 8, 1938.
>
> Oh, she was beautiful in every part!—
> The auburn hair that bound the subtle brain;
> The lovely mouth cut clear by wit and pain,
> Uttering oaths and nonsense, uttering art
> In casual speech and curving at the smart
> On startled ears of excellence too plain
> For early morning!—*Obit.* Death from strain;
> The soaring mind outstripped the tethered heart.
>
> Yet here was one who had no need to die
> To be remembered. Every word she said
> The lively malice of the hazel eye
> Scanning the thumb-nail close—oh, the dazzling dead,
> How like a comet through the darkening sky
> You raced! . . . would your return were heralded.

George Dillon was chosen as editor in chief of *Poetry* magazine after the death of Harriet Monroe. He was only thirty-one, and it looked like the perfect position from which to continue his career, which was now floundering. He wrote asking Millay for a new poem for the magazine. She said she wanted to give him something, but she just couldn't bring herself to send him anything yet. "You say you know that I have some unpublished poems; that's true, I have. But it's not so easy to get at them as it was when you and I were looking through that black note-book together." It wasn't only that *Conversation* had burned up in the fire; she had also lost almost a full manuscript of new poems. "And I'm so exhausted from digging *Conversation at Midnight* piece by piece out of my memory, that I hardly have the heart to start excavations again on another site. I'm pretty sure that I can remember most of the poems when I get around to it; I'm just bored with the whole idea."

As often in her letters to him now, she inquired politely about him: "Please let me know what you are going to do, my dear, and where you are going to be. . . . Have you been writing anything? If you have, I beg you to send me something. Please let me hear from you soon. Don't be unkind, just because I've waited so long to answer you. I'll be better next time. Vincent."

Does anyone ever do better?

2

At the beginning of 1938, Eugen was telling people that Edna was often sick, in bed for days on end. One of her lecture bureaus, Famous Speakers, wrote that it hoped her health had improved so that she might accept an offer for an engagement in Chicago that paid "upward a thousand to fifteen hundred."

She wired Norma, who had heard about her constant illnesses:

DARLING I AM NOT SICK I AM NICE AND WARM AND ALL THAT BUT I AM DOING THE GUGGENHEIMS THEREFORE HAVE NO THOUGHT FOR MAN OR ANGEL ONLY FOR POETS SO LOTS OF LOVE TO MY LITTLE SISTER AND DONT YOU BE FOOLISH SEFE

Was illness an excuse Eugen invented to defend her from the niggling obligations and duties she had no time for? But he persisted, even in a letter to George Dillon. "The reason why you have not heard from her is that she had been sick in bed for the last two months," he wrote to Dillon on December 5, 1937. "She is a little bit better now and doubtless you will hear from her as soon as she has recovered." A month later, he was more specific: "Vincent, who has been sick with the flu for two months, is getting stronger every day, and I hope, will soon be quite recovered." But by the spring he told George that "All we need now to make everything perfect is to have Vincent entirely recovered. . . . She still has a nurse." At the end of May he said he'd forgotten whether or not he'd told him "how sick Vincent has been this winter. . . . It has been a terrible and anxious winter. I have to have a day and a night nurse for her sometime." Eugen took a home movie of her, filmed at Steepletop, sitting in what looks like a wheelchair, facing the camera wearing a beret, her shoulders draped with a shawl, with a private nurse attending her, albeit lighting her cigarette.

In an undated notebook Edna made very detailed, orderly notes for her doctor in Great Barrington: "My birthday yesterday reminded me that I am over forty-five. . . ." It was February 23, 1938, when Edna Millay would have been forty-six.

1. What virtue is there in the old-fashioned spring remedy—said to cleanse the system, particularly the blood—of impurities?
2. a. Is there iron in dandelion greens, boiled, with no water thrown away?
   b. Of what good to the system is the property known as (I don't know how it is spelled) Thoraxicum,—which is found in dandelion greens?
   c. Is there more iron in spinach (particularly the perennial kind, called "Good King Henry") than in boiled dandelion leaves & roots?
3. What virtue as a spring tonic is to be found in an infusion (very strong, dark and bitter) of the leaves and flowers of the plant called "boneset," or "thoroughwort"—Eupatorium perboliatum?
   a. What are the foods considered very bad for persons with a very high blood pressure?
   b. Would not these foods be useful in raising the blood pressure—of a person whose b.p.—like my own—is, for his age, too low? . . .
   c. Might not this low blood pressure, all by itself, account for the fact that to get out of bed, to take a bath, to dress, to arise from a comfortable chair when once seated in it, to do any work at all, whether housework or writing, or getting on a heavy fur coat, hat and gloves, drawing on and clasping the clasps of galoshes, rising and selecting a walking-stick, pulling open a door hard to open, and stepping out into a world of icy, slippery roads, or roads deep under snows and exhausting to proceed along for even the hired man—might not this low blood pressure all by itself account for the fact that I must exert so great an amount of will-power, and of stern discipline of quick, anxious, angry and determined mind over inert and uninterested matter, in order to force myself to do anything at all?
   d. Is "Benzedrine" the only thing which can for a few hours give me a feeling of energy, and the power to do the things I do much desire to do, but am kept from doing by physical, not mental inertia?

e. Would it harm me in any way to take per diem:
6 capsules of Taka-combex;
2 pellets (1 black—the vitamins, and 1 grey, the minerals) of Vi-Syneral?
and 1 injection (a moderate amount) of Betaxin,—which I think is plain Vitamin B1?
f. I think that I am badly in need of minerals,—calcium, iron, iodine, phosphate, etc.

She continued to ask a few more questions, mostly about boosting the calcium in her diet by drinking milk from their Guernsey cows, with lime added to make it easier for her to digest, "(as, I believe, is often done in the case of babies who reject their milk)." She even suggested taking calcium gluconate, which she'd once taken, because, she wrote, "[Note: my bones are soft; my teeth are brittle. Do not these facts indicate a lack of organic calcium?]"

What Millay did not mention in her long list of remedies and complaints was any pain as a result of the automobile accident a year and a half earlier.

There is a puzzling letter in Millay's files from Henry Allen Moe, the president of the Guggenheim Foundation, dated January 1938. He asked Millay not to fret about a loan she'd taken from the foundation: "A delay in payment will make no difference to Senator Guggenheim or to the Foundation." Why she needed the money and why she asked for it was nowhere made clear, but the need was real enough for Eugen to have approached Curtis Hidden Page, a manuscript and rare-books dealer, who offered to buy *Renascence* for three or four hundred dollars, which seemed to Eugen to be too little:

I think if we can't get $800 for it, we should wait for better times. . . . Nobody has money and as for anybody to have money to spend on art, beauty, or fun or other idiotic luxuries, I think we must wait for 1940 when we may see Mr. and Mrs. Roosevelt walk out of the White House unless he leaves it before that, feet first.

At the end of February, Eugen thanked Curtis Hidden Page for his check for $650, "in behalf of ourselves, our grocers, butchers, tailors and candlestick-makers."

Now, the poor girl is hard at work reading two suitcases full of books, Mss., sheet proofs, etc. etc. in order to pick out the people for the Guggenheim Fellowships.—This takes her two months of her precious life every year!—I am trying to make her give it up.—but then she is cursed with a social conscience and a New England conscience at that! I'm glad I was born without that disturbing and useless thing.

In a letter that exists in three drafts, the last (and presumably final) one dated March 18, Millay addressed Mr. Moe and the members of the committee. It is a sorry communication:

> These reports reach you in many instances in an unfinished state; some of them are mere sketches; some of them consist of only a line or two. . . . I had not taken into consideration that I might fall ill and be unable to continue with, and to perfect the work, as I had planned it. . . . I beg you to forgive in this report much material which seems, since I am unable to present it to you in a finished state and in a context which would have explained my use of it, rambling and in some instances extraneous.

By now something was very much the matter: her illness had invaded her working life. Her critical acuity, however, remained untouched. Among her draft papers is a two-page report on a poet whom she recommended that the Guggenheim Foundation turn down:

> He writes nothing but sonnets. He has become so skilled in this form that he writes sonnets easily and naturally; his emotion is accustomed to being penned in this stall, and enters it willingly. This is true of all sonnet writers . . . true of all poets who habitually write ballades; Villon could have made you a ballade while fencing with you. . . . We all make mistakes; we all think at times that we have written a very good poem, when we have, in fact, written an undistinguished one.

With Muriel Rukeyser, whose application she also rejected, her report ran to four pages. When she veered off course somewhat, her veering was always interesting:

> I think I know something about the particular kind of arrogance which Miss Rukeyser impresses me as having. Young women full of energy and ideas, as well as somewhat radical ideals, can have a pretty bad time of it and become pretty angry and discouraged working as under-graduates in any American college. . . . I know that when I was at Vassar, although I felt great respect and admiration for many members of the faculty and still admire and deeply love a few of them, I was constantly being irked by what seemed to me either utter lack of imagination, or merely officious nonsense on the part of some others; and I can see in my mind now that particular walk with which I must have moved about the cam-

pus: a slight swinging of the hips to keep the chip on the shoulder in place.

Rukeyser was writing in "U.S.1" about the horror of the men who had died of silicosis contracted while working in a tunnel in West Virginia, and while Millay found it both "inexcusable and criminal" to permit such mining without safety devices to protect those men, nevertheless "the business of a person who wishes to make a poem about this situation is primarily to write poetry. This section of Miss Rukeyser's book is not poetry. It is an indignant and reiterated statement that this sort of thing is a shocking thing." The work of a poet, she explained, is not the same as the work of a reporter, an agitator, or a reformer; and when Rukeyser broke into prose in the trial section of the case, it was "not even good propaganda for her point."

> If you could make her see that we don't really care at all about her religion, her politics or her morals, that as far as we are concerned, she is free to go tattooed forward, aft and amidships with anchors and mermaids, or to worship the God Bip, and be as anthropophagous as a crocodile; that if her writing should prove to be very high class indeed, we would even try to bail her out for minor munchings, and keep her out of trouble generally, then, perhaps something might really be done.

Again and again in her notes Millay addressed the political orientation of the applicants—and insisted upon the sanctity of the artist's work. She also cautioned the foundation about its direction and, in doing so, revealed her own. She never asked; she insisted.

> My task . . . is made extremely difficult by the fact that my tastes in poetry, as in all the arts, is so catholic. . . . Belonging to no party, no church, having no cause which I would bolster at the expense of good writing, having no axe to grind, my task, as I said, is difficult. Of the six writers I am recommending this year, three are definitely revolutionists, one is definitely a classicist, one is probably mad and the other is doubtless trying to recover from shell-shock. What are you going to do about them? . . . I have come loudly out into the open, and am running the risk of making an utter fool of myself. I think the Guggenheim Foundation cannot properly be administered on any other terms; we may not foster the conservative at the expense of the experimental; the solid at the expense of the slippery; we must take chances; we must incur danger. Otherwise we shall eventually become an organization which gives prizes for acclaimed accomplishment, not fellowships for obscure talent, tangible promise, probable development, and possible achievement.

Later, when her friend the poet Harold Lewis Cook told her he was too intimidated by the august award even to apply for it, she wrote him:

> Listen, toots, nobody who ever had this Guggenheim Fellowship for poetry ever did a darned thing with it. . . . Some people have kept on working just about as they would have worked if they hadn't got it and some people have been entirely dried up by getting it. What has George Dillon done since he wrote those two marvellous first volumes? Nothing except translate (along with me) about half the poems of Baudelaire and become editor of "Poetry: A Magazine of Verse." . . . I have yet to see any person, at least in the Poetry Department, do a darned thing which he told the Guggenheim he was going to do. Most of them have done flat nothing.

By the fall of that year, Eugen phoned Henry Allen Moe to tell him that Miss Millay would be unable to judge poets for the Guggenheim Foundation any longer. He gave no reason.

Whatever her private opinion about George Dillon's lack of productivity, when Dillon again asked for a few poems from her for his magazine, she wired him in Chicago that she could send him six or seven now. He took all of them (adding her "Sonnet in Tetrameter," which she feared might be too "early Millay") for his October 1938 issue. If he had any suggestions to make, she wrote, "for God's sake, make them." And here she struck a note of loneliness: "I have been for a long time without anybody to talk with about my poetry, any other poet I mean." The other poets she knew disliked her new stuff and loathed the work of the new poets she admired. She sounded defensive: "I imagine that, although you like these poems, you might very well have preferred poems less early-Millay in character . . . poems more concerned with, apparently, things going on in the world outside myself today; poems more, if we may still use that old-fashioned word, 'modern.' "

She signed this letter "Love" after she'd told him, "When I think of my reading engagement in Chicago, it makes me happy to remember that you will be there. I think I should feel lonely in Chicago without you."

The next day she wrote to him again to say that she was sending him a photograph for the magazine's Gallery, a Carl Van Vechten photograph in which she is wearing a dark, heavy suit and looks as if she means serious business. She enclosed a handkerchief he'd left at Steepletop. "Probably the others of this kind are all worn out by now and this will come to you almost (but not quite, I am sorry) like a gift."

INTENTION TO ESCAPE FROM HIM

I think I will learn some beautiful language, useless for commercial
Purposes, work hard at that.
I think I will learn the Latin name of every songbird,
    not only in America but wherever they sing.
(Shun meditation, though; invite the controversial:
Is the world flat? Do bats eat cats?) By digging
    hard I might deflect that river, my mind, that
        uncontrollable thing,
Turgid and yellow, strong to overflow its banks in spring, carrying
    away bridges;
A bed of pebbles now, through which there trickles one clear
    narrow stream, following a course henceforth nefast—

Dig, dig; and if I come to ledges, blast.

The poems she sent to George have one thing in common: they have an
intensity that, while not new in her work, had been lacking in the recent
past. They are free verse with very little rhyme; and each is marked by a
sense of overwhelming loss.

THE FITTING

The fitter said, "*Madame, vous avez maigri.*"
And pinched together a handful of skirt at my hip.
"*Tant mieux,*" I said, and looked away slowly, and took my under-lip
Softly between my teeth.

Rip—rip!

Out came the seam, and was pinned together in another place.
She knelt before me, a hardworking woman with a familiar and
    unknown face,
Dressed in linty black, very tight in the arm's-eye and smelling of
    sweat.
She rose, lifting my arm, and set her cold shears against me,—
    snip-snip;
Her knuckles gouged my breast. My drooped eyes lifted to my
    guarded eyes in the glass, and glanced away as from someone
    they had never met.

"*Ah, que madame a maigri!*" cried the *vendeuse,* coming in with dresses
    over her arm.

"*C'est la chaleur,*" I said, looking out into the sunny tops of the horse-
chestnuts—and indeed it was very warm.

I stood for a long time so, looking out into the afternoon, thinking of
the evening and you . . .

While they murmured busily in the distance, turning me, touching
my secret body, doing what they were paid to do.

She very much wanted Dillon to publish "The Fitting." He'd seen it
before in France and had suggested a change she agreed to that was
shrewd—what had been "quiet body" became "secret body" in the next-
to-last line. But in manuscript the poem, which had been written on Jan's
stationery from the Petite Villa Hou'zée, was called "Short Story," and the
body is neither "quiet" nor "secret" but sacred.

CHAPTER 34

T hat summer and fall Eugen worked to make Steepletop shipshape:
hired men came to cable the great old maples that edged their lawns,
and the dark evergreens that skirted the pool as well as the apple trees on
the near end of the blueberry field were pruned and treated, sprayed and
fed. The head gardener was Edna. She spaded and weeded, but she was,
she told a reporter from *Good Housekeeping,*

a bad transplanter. When I find that the hole I've dug for a rosebush is too
small and I have to drag it out and dig some more, or when roots which
I've carefully spread out curl back and slap at me, I become irritated. My
husband will spend hours transplanting one rose. He has infinite patience.
I haven't.

In the hardy garden were beds of oriental poppies and lupine the color
of ink. There were white double-headed peonies, called Festiva Maxima,
and rose beds of hybrid teas whose fragrance lasted into fall. The harebell
seeded itself everywhere, and the wild red columbine, "which I dug up
and brought down in my lap from the top of a mountain near here. Holly-
hocks did well in the rock garden where they no more belonged than they
did in the driveway, where they also thrived."

In September, Eugen had two ornamental wrought-iron washstands
made with elegantly fitted mirrors and marble tops for the pool. At the

end of one secluded alley of evergreens was a fat little marble cherub by Randolph Rogers, done up as an Indian with a quiver of arrows slung over his plump chest. Iron gate hinges were made to match the ornamental washstands, with a drying rack and a hat tree, and Charlie was commissioned to do paintings in automobile paint to weather the outdoors. At the entrance to the garden were two fleshy putti resting on clouds, one blowing a trumpet, the other peering at a cedar waxwing alighted on his finger.

"Tell Charlie," Eugen wrote Norma, "the behind of one of the cupids needs a little rouge and powder." He assured her that the nude that hung over their outdoor bar, which he had christened "Barroom Fanny" (and that looked very like Norma), "came through the winter swell, the tough baby."

The summer was going to be glorious, they insisted to their friends. When Eolo Testi, one of the young men who played cello in their quartet at the Blochs' summer music school in Hillsdale and, as Edna wrote, "sort of lives here," beat the pants off Eugen at tennis, they filmed it. First, a tan Eugen is playing very smartly if a bit stiffly, dressed in white tennis shorts; both men are bare-chested, and Edna officiates perched atop a high wooden stand. Eugen calmly walks to the net, unbuttons his shorts, and steps out of them, handing them over the net to the laughing dark-haired young man who has just trounced him. Edna rushes toward Eugen, smiling, and wraps him in a blanket. That summer of 1938, Edna Millay was voted one of the ten most famous women in America.

On July 13, Edna wrote to Blanche Bloch, who had been giving her piano lessons, asking if the quartet they had often before brought to Steepletop could come again for a dress rehearsal.

"Long before Tanglewood," Blanche Bloch remembered, "we had a music school in Hillsdale, and we would have our rehearsals in the Millay house. Edna never liked to meet people. She was conscious of who she was. And others were conscious of who she was. She would sit in a big hat in the first row.

"We held our dress rehearsals at Steepletop. We rehearsed in the front room, with the two pianos—two members of the quartet lived with them for a while, Dante Bergonzi and Eolo Testi. . . . second violin was Brodus Earle, and Arno Kyam played viola. Boissevain and Ficke and a doctor sponsored the quartet."

Sitting in the garden behind their house, Blanche Bloch recalled that Edna had studied with her for five years. "She was musical. She had the best taste in music. But she had tiny hands and she couldn't play Chopin études. She simply could not do it. She wanted to play only virtuoso pieces, she didn't have enough technique, and I told her that she couldn't. She would say, 'Blanche, play me this! play me that!' She never stopped. I remember that she wanted to play the Rachmaninoff Second—well, we could play it slowly, in half-time."

Alexander Bloch, Blanche's husband, who was a composer and conductor, said, "Sometimes she'd just call up and sing pieces of music, maybe that she'd just heard or that had gone through her mind, and she'd say, 'Allie, what is that?' When I knew, which was not too often, I'd tell her."

Blanche interrupted him: "Edna did exactly what she pleased, when she pleased, and where she pleased. One must remember that about her. And she would just disappear when she wanted to.

"Whereas, Gene—oh, Gene was one of the most charming men. When he laughed, he filled the world with vitality. And he told the most wonderful stories. He had a really rich brother with whom he once carried on about being a sheep rancher—it was something like that—he wrote this brother that he had a great sheep ranch! That was just like him. Well, the brother came over after all this correspondence about feed and breeds, you know, and there was only one sheep! Oh, perhaps they had three.

"After her manuscript was burned in Florida she came to see us. All the newspapers published the story of her loss of manuscripts. We were not at all sure what we were going to say—how could anyone be consoled after such a loss? And do you know what she said? She said, 'O, Florida. O, cold Florida! Could any state be horrida?' Well, we both just roared with laughter—and with relief."

2

Before the publication of *Huntsman, What Quarry?*, her first book of lyric poetry in five years, in May 1939, Millay again began a reading tour. She traveled by train, by car, and, if the train was delayed, very rarely by airplane. She crossed the country as far east as Boston, as far north as Buffalo, as far south as Fort Worth and as far west as Los Angeles. She read in Pittsfield and Albany, then in Cleveland and Dayton, Springfield and Columbus, Danville and Chicago. She went to Indianapolis, Decatur, and Cincinnati. To Huntington, West Virginia, and back either to Cincinnati again or on to Newport-Hamilton/Norwood, Ohio, on the Kentucky border. She read in St. Louis, Tulsa, Denton, Dallas, and Forth Worth; in El Paso, Los Angeles, San Francisco, Albuquerque, Denver, Omaha, Cedar Rapids, and Des Moines. She read in Pittsburgh, Philadelphia, Wilmington, and in some tiny town just above Charlottesville in the center of Virginia, in Raleigh/Durham, and then the long trip back up to Baltimore, New York City, Hartford.

Her only break was when, two weeks into her tour, she took one day off to attend the New England Futurity at Narragansett, where Bill Brann's two-year-old colt won $33,000. She told a reporter in Dayton, Ohio, that when he had won she'd become so excited she couldn't stand up.

" 'I'm crazy about seeing horses run,' she confessed, 'I have studied everything in the English manual but I'm no feminine Bing Crosby yet. I'd like to have a stable of a few horses myself, and perhaps some day my poetry will earn enough to make that possible.' " Eugen commented dryly that the reporter hadn't come to interview her as a jockey.

She read new poems that dealt with the conflicts raging in Europe: "Say that We Saw Spain Die" (which had just been published in *Harper's Magazine*) and a trio of sonnets about China and Japan. "Poets are deeply aware of world conditions," she explained at one lecture. "In fact, they have a tendency more than any other writers to become very world-conscious and you will find much of this reflected in future poetry." She cautioned, however, that it was destructive to move from headlines into verse: "It's dangerous to write immediately one's emotions are stirred, for then one is apt to say things that may be wrong or regretted afterwards."

In Dayton, she was to speak at the dinner meeting of the Nomad Club before her reading. A reporter described first what she was wearing for the reading—"a stunning gown of red velvet, trimmed in gold braid and a black velvet cape"—and then how she looked and moved:

> Hair, amber red, swept back from the poet's forehead, and hung loosely at the nape of her neck; gown, cerise red, molded the body and swept in train along the floor. Flame! and flame, too the emotions of the poet. Could the audience hear her without the microphone? She motioned toward the "monstrosity" with a gesture of scorn.

When she learned that those in the rear could not, "Miss Millay moved toward the microphone, commanding: 'Put that thing on.' Remarking, as though in aside: 'I am simply furious.' " Beginning again, she stopped once more. What was that roaring noise? she asked. The ventilating system. Learning that it couldn't be turned off, "she continued with the finest reading of a poem we have heard voiced by a poet, and we have heard several of the world's great. This was 'Childhood Is the Kingdom Where Nobody Dies.' "

She read from *Figs;* she dramatized portions of *Conversation at Midnight;* and then, as always, she did her child poems from *A Very Little Sphinx.* She put one hand on her hip and glared. She slouched. She squared her shoulders and stuck her chest out. She tossed her head. She peeked up from under her curls. She stamped her foot. She grinned. But whatever she did, she pleased her audience. The best-liked part of her program was often the early poems.

> I know a hundred ways to die.
> I've often thought I'd try one:
> Lie down beneath a motor truck
> Some day when standing by one.
>
> . . .
>
> I know some poison I could drink.
> I've often thought I'd taste it.
> But mother bought it for the sink,
> And drinking it would waste it.

Or, assuming what the newspaper in Ohio called "a childish puckishness that makes one think of A. A. Milne," she said:

> Look, Edwin! Do you see that boy
> Talking to the other boy?
> No, over there by those two men—
> Wait, don't look now—now look again.
> No, not the one in navy-blue;
> That's the one he's talking to.
> Sure you see him? Striped pants?
> Well, he was born in Paris, France.

which brought the house down. But she could change in an instant; looking dreamily into the wings of the stage, she began:

> Wonder where this horseshoe went.
> Up and down, up and down,
> Up and past the monument,
> Maybe into town.
>
> Wait a minute, "Horseshoe,
> How far have you been?"
> Says it's been to Salem
> And halfway to Lynn.
>
> Wonder who was in the team.
> Wonder what they saw.
> Wonder if they passed a bridge—
> Bridge with a draw.
>
> Says it went from one bridge
> Straight upon another.

And suddenly you knew, as her audience in 1938 in Dayton or Cincinnati could not have known, that the source of this poem lay in Millay's own past. We are accompanying her in that carriage driven down a dusty country lane in Massachusetts before the turn of the century, with her grandmother as the horse shies and bolts, throwing her from the careening buggy to her death.

> Says it took a little girl
> Driving with her mother.

These child poems were charged with the energy of family secrets; little explosions of meaning and sharp loss. When Millay stood there, defiantly, all five feet one inch of her, she seemed to become that child—her fishtail train flowing behind her, playing with it, curling it over her arm, tossing it, snapping it like a silk banner behind her. But it was her voice that captured people. That rich, dark, deep contralto always came as a surprise from such a little person. It was the honeyed easy depth, the emotional vibrance of her voice that held her audiences to her. Yet it was odd that this forty-six-year-old woman would still alternate her serious lyrics with her girlish kiddie poems. What was she doing when she tossed her hair back from her face, wiped her mouth with the back of her hand, planted her feet wide apart squarely on the floor, and began?

Last came her new sonnets, which were no longer love songs; they were meditations, as Louise Bogan called them, lamentations, measured mourning for a world that was about to go to war. She dropped her head; then, lifting her face, she ended with a ringing anthem to a freedom that was both personal and political. Women in the audience were heard to catch their breath. The audience was on its feet exploding with applause as she sank to one knee, dragging the train of her gown behind her, then raised her face into the glow and heat of Dayton's applause.

No one had read as she did since Dickens had last toured America. Across the country she read in Masonic temples, at women's clubs, in university lecture halls, and at small colleges. The newspapers said she was "unequalled."

A woman in the audience in Los Angeles who had first heard Millay when she was at Vassar remembered:

She was to give a reading at the Los Angeles Philharmonic—a big place, packed to the top gallery. Bare stage, except for a standing mike. She came out, alone, wearing the usual loose something, green, I think. Standing well away from the mike, she began. Almost at once came cries of "Louder!" "Can't hear!," &, insistently,—"Use the mike!" A crescendo that drowned her out. She stood there, waited while it sank to grumbling, then gestured at the mike & said something like—"I will not tell you my poems thru this mechanical contraption. They come from me to you, direct. Please be entirely silent & I will make you hear me." Oh no! It started up again, as she resumed. Twice. My seat was very near the front, & I never felt such tension. Growing, too. There was resentment in it, then anger, finally real antagonism. I suppose it took 5 minutes, while she stood still and fought them. Scary minutes, for there was a sort of peak when she almost lost them. But she didn't. Somehow they did settle & listen. She said every poem she'd chosen, just with her voice, an hour or so of speaking. Then she turned to go off—& then the house came down. Cheers. People stood up. Some cried. It was a show of guts & stubbornness & pride. And foolishness, I suppose.

Each month of 1938 brought news on the radio and in newspapers of fresh destruction and barbaric violence in Europe. In September, as Millay's tour began, Neville Chamberlain, the British prime minister, journeyed to Munich and along with the premier of France came to an agreement with Hitler about the future of Czechoslovakia and the Sudetenland. There was no representative of the Czech government present. They had made the agreement, they assured their public, to guarantee "peace in our time," a policy called appeasement.

In October, Germany took the Sudetenland. One night in the fall, in November in Berlin, just as the lights went out at bedtime, men in black uniforms or in no uniforms at all began to smash store windows; Jews who had been harassed and provoked and prodded before were that night killed. Their synagogues were set on fire. Hundreds of thousands of merchants' shop windows were shattered: it was Kristallnacht.

Early in her tour she was careful what she said about the war:

I am horrified at what I hear is happening in Germany. . . . I don't believe we can possibly keep apart from the rest of the world. But I don't know enough about it to be wise enough about it to say that these things are true.

All we get is the American viewpoint here and we can't see the other side.

She said that she would like to write a play about democracy versus fascism. She linked her own turning to drama as a "natural progression." Propaganda, she said, was never good art; it wasn't even good propaganda. By the time she reached San Francisco the caption beneath her photograph read, WE MUST FIGHT FOR DEMOCRACY. " 'I used to be a most ardent pacifist,' said Edna St. Vincent Millay at Hotel St. Francis yesterday, 'but my mind has been changed. I am afraid the only hope of saving democracy is to fight for it—not necessarily to be dragged into a war unprepared, but to choose our own time.' "

There were, she said, men in power who were

not human beings in the sense that we have been brought up to understand that term. We have beasts in control of human beings. I am not speaking of the German people themselves, but if we have a wild animal to deal with we cannot be pacifists forever. Whatever we do, we cannot keep aloof from the general world situation; it is silly to think we can.

But she didn't stop there.

Persons who begin writing lyric poetry at a young age are deeply concerned with themselves. . . . As they mature, they begin to grow out of themselves and they feel concern for others. Lyric poets who continue writing lyric poetry are likely to go into a dry rot and just write the same thing over again.

3

Although the relationship between Edna and Kathleen had become strained, Edna and Eugen went to see her in Santa Monica during her tour. Howard had left Kathleen, and although she had tried to write screenplays (she was briefly hired to work on Disney's *Snow White*) in the end all her efforts had failed. She was broke, she was drinking heavily, and her health had deteriorated dangerously. The two sisters spent the afternoon together, and Edna gave her money and said she'd help with the cost of her divorce, if that was what Kathleen wanted. The next Edna heard from her was a collect wire on January 28, 1939:

DEAR SISTER HAVE YOU FORGOTTEN ME SO SOON AGAIN I AM SORRY TO TROUBLE YOU BUT MY FRIENDS REMIND ME THAT I PROMISED AND THREATEN TO TAKE THINGS IN THEIR OWN HANDS AGAIN BECAUSE UNFORTUNATELY I HAVE NEW OBLIGATIONS SINCE PEOPLE KNOW YOU HAVE BEEN HERE AND I AM TOO TROUBLED AND WORRIED PLEASE WIRE ANY ANSWER YOU DESIRE LOVE AS ALWAYS

KATHLEEN

Eugen wrote back quickly: a $100 check had been mailed to her two days before. He asked whether she'd received their first check, sent two weeks before.

Your wire was not entirely clear.—But then we are accustomed to receiving garbled wires as they are telephoned to our house, then taken more or less down and finally reach us. (By the way, our telegrams are more public than a p.c., we don't care, but in case you want to say something you don't want to make public property, I suggest an air-mail letter).—

The way we received the wire it read in part, "unfortunately I have new obligations since people know you have been here."—

In case this is the way you wired it then of course it would seem to mean that you have acquaintances who mistakenly take Edna for a rich woman from whom they can expect money.—Alas, I wish it were true! But we live a fairly hand to mouth existence. She has six people who are dependent on her which has been quite a drain on the old pocket book.—

I know she wants to help you get a divorce if she possibly can.—So when you are ready to do this, let her know, and she'll do what she can. You wrote you thought of going to Reno, because you thought other methods might be unpleasant for Edna.—Don't give that a thought. It won't bother her in the least. Just do it as you want to do it, which I hope will be the least costly way.

There were two pages of rough notes attached to his letter, which while they probably were not sent to Kathleen, give a fairly clear idea of what Eugen was thinking. The first was simply that while Edna wanted "to save you all possible chagrin & unpleasantness she is going to be . . . hard put to find the money." He did not cotton to the implicit threat in her wire. "You must not forget Kathleen, that we have been entirely out of touch with you and you may think that we know something, when in reality we know nothing but that altogether too short visit in December."

Kathleen wrote directly to Edna two days before her birthday:

Dear Sister Edna—(Titter Binny!)
You know, I positively got sentimental the other night . . . the fire was low—and so was I. So—I had the radio on—low, too—and three women were harmonizing—and I remembered those three Millay brats and how they used to sing together—you know, Edna, I think I sometimes miss that more than any other thing in my whole life in the gay days of long ago! Do you ever miss the singing, too?

Then she told her she was feeling better but still worried about money:

I owe the butcher and the baker and the electric light bill—but not so much as I did when I saw you in December. The only trouble was that after you had been seen in these yere parts in that sixteen-cylinder Cadillac I had to pay the back rent. . . . I can't use any excuses now as I could before. I know it is silly—but it does happen to be so.

And while she'd originally told her she needed $500 for her divorce, now she asked for $700, although even "that will not cover all the money for the whole two months there." She needed $500 "now—soon, that is, any time so that I can get things over with before the heat sets in too much—I still have to watch the blood pressure, you know, it mustn't ever get back to two hundred and forty again, or I'll explode or something." She signed herself "Kathleen" with "Wumps" in parentheses beside it. "Love, dear—and of course, I'll pay you back for helping me now over this messy thing—one of these days."

Eugen was beside himself. First it had been a few hundred dollars in California. Then the $500 for her divorce had grown to $700. As early as 1936, in a letter to Norma, Eugen was clear about the reasons for his irritation with Kathleen—she had left unpaid bills in Camden for them to pay, even though she knew "how your mother hated bills in Camden"—but it was the end of his letter that struck home. "I don't think it is very swell of Kathleen, especially since she hates Edna." Now he wrote to her promptly:

> Dear Kathleen:
>
> I am sorry having to write you all the time disappointing letters.—But the fact is that Edna cannot help you to get a divorce, now that you write that it will cost about $1000.—When she saw you you said the cost would be $200.—which she gave you. You had to use this money for something else, and now that it would need another $1000 or thereabouts she cannot do it. Since Howard does not bother or interfere with you at all, might it not be advisable to wait until either you or Edna can comfortably afford it? It seems more reasonable to use the little money that Edna can spare from time to time, for you to rest and get well with.
>
> I am enclosing $100.—This is all we can do just now. I hope it will last you some time.

He went on to write, "If you need later on more [sic], let her know." But in Edna's hand his "If" is changed to "When." "She might be able to give you $50 a month for some time. I hope that you will be able to manage on that." Scrawled on the back, in Eugen's hand, is the following:

> Please try to impress on the people who are bothering you for money that Edna is far from a rich woman and that it is no use for them to harass you.—
>
> I am sorry about that Cadillac which we hired at the hotel for the occasion instead of taking a taxi, a taxi might have cost us . . . less but the larger car was more comfortable and E. was working extremely hard and was very tired.
>
> E. wanted to answer your letter herself but she is hurrying to complete a ms. which must go off to the printer in the next few days.—She sends you her love.

At this point their correspondence stopped as suddenly as it had begun. Kathleen fell silent.

In the spring of that year, Millay had heard from Agnes Yarnall, a young sculptor who'd done a bronze of her head in 1933. She'd read that Edna had been collecting shells when the hotel with her manuscript inside had gone up in flames; now she sent her (among other things) a rare harp shell. When Millay wrote to thank her, she said her own collection was full of gaps, and these shells were rare and stunning. "You were very good to give me this. . . . Perhaps we shall meet again." Now, on tour, Edna and Eugen invited Agnes to come to Cincinnati, where Millay was reading. Years later, Agnes Yarnall tried to recall under what circumstances she'd gone. "There was either a telephone call or a note, and she asked me to join them. . . . I got there before they did. I remember them coming in the late afternoon. On the train, I think. They seemed very tired, both of them. They had a sort of suite, but we were all on the same floor.

"There was this great bond between them, you know—no question about it. And she depended on him—for things like trains and schedules and dates.

"After the reading, we went to their suite. And she was nervous. She was very edgy, pacing. That sort of thing. We were sitting there. And then she did it. I don't think she even knew that I noticed. Then she went into her bedroom and fell asleep.

"Eugen said, 'This happens sometimes, you must not be troubled by it.' I said very little. . . . In the morning, she said quietly to me, 'You don't really have to go, do you? You're disappointed in me. I've made you lose faith in me'—something like that. She sensed it, I suppose. And I said, 'No, I've got to go home to Mother.' Then she gave me the book you have in your hands. And she signed it.

"I don't flourish well in an atmosphere of depression, and I never saw them again. Now you know why. I've never told anyone before. . . . She was destroying herself and, my dear, there is nothing you can do in the face of that but watch. Or refuse to watch."

4

Millay was back at Steepletop for the holidays, and she was nearly at the end of her tour. She had only one more reading to do, an appearance in Worcester: "An old friend," she wrote to George Dillon, "which doesn't bother me much." She told him she'd gone and bought a Walt Kuhn painting: "one of the clown ones, a beauty." The terms were simple: "One

million dollars down and a ball and chain about my ankle for the rest of
my life."

> Darling,
>   It is quaint how much I miss you. It is archaic. It should have gone out
> along with samplers and paintings on china. (But perhaps these have come
> in again, together with herb gardens and uncomfortable furniture.)

She wanted George's reaction to two groups of poems before her final
manuscript went to Harper: "Theme and Variations" and "Sonnets from a
Town in a State of Siege"—"please let me know at once." She tried to
make light of her insistence: "What a stolid yet exuberant letter, rambling
all over the landscape, Tudor, Georgian and Victorian!" In closing, she
again asked him to read the poems "if you have time. Otherwise wire me
that you have no time." When she didn't hear back from him, she wired
him. When, she asked, could she telephone him?

In a handwritten postscript she added that she'd send "Rendezvous"
later; she was not including it at present because it was so badly typed "it
is impossible."

There must have been a good deal of conversation in the house about
these poems. Millay waited ten days to send her December 29 letter off to
George. One day later, on January 9, Eugen (unbeknownst to her) wrote
directly to Dillon about them:

> Vincent told me that she had written you a letter about her new poems. She
> had, however, been postponing sending you her poems . . . she thinks she
> ought to tear them up and that they are no good.
>   I am crazy about them and I think that they are amongst the very best that
> she has written, but then I am not a poet and I am swayed so easily by Vin-
> cent's opinion about all poetry and about her poetry especially, that I am not
> sure enough to advise her. . . . It is in moments like these that I know I must
> fail her, not being a poet and I must look to you to help her. Please do it.
>
> Love,
Ugin

What were these poems that they caused her such uncertainty? Mary
Kennedy, who had known Millay since her marriage to Deems Taylor,
remembered Millay coming to discuss them late one night in her apartment in New York:

> She had come by herself. She'd been drinking, you see. She read me these
> poems to Dillon. They were greatly changed, I believe, when she pub-
> lished them. They were about betrayal . . . not adultery. I did not think,

then, that they were for Eugen, and I do not now. They were about a real betrayal—in other words, it has given me my death wounds. . . . With Edna there were two warring elements and they were never resolved.

Oh, it's heartbreaking! It's vanity! The poetry, she knew. No one could touch her in that. But as a person, you see, as a woman, as a lover. Well . . . She was capable, then, of picking up a barman. I saw her do that! It was the drink. And vanity. Of course, who knows how far it went? Perhaps the barman refused to go with her. Or perhaps they did not go to bed.

Millay sent George Dillon "Rendezvous" and the eight poems that make up "Theme and Variations." These last poems were the ones Mary Kennedy had kept from that night in manuscript. The theme was her sweet ally, love, and its old companion, betrayal, and the variation now was her familiar, pain:

I

Not even my pride will suffer much;
Not even my pride at all, maybe,
If this ill-timed, intemperate clutch
Be loosed by you and not by me,
Will suffer; I have been so true
A vestal to that only pride
Wet wood cannot extinguish, nor
Sand, nor its embers scattered, for,
See all these years, it has not died.

And if indeed, as I dare think,
You cannot push this patient flame,
By any breath your lungs could store,
Even for a moment to the floor
To crawl there, even for a moment crawl,
What can you mix for me to drink
That shall deflect me? What you do
Is either malice, crude defense
Of ego, or indifference:
I know these things as well as you;
You do not dazzle me at all.

Some love, and some simplicity,
Might well have been the death of me.

George did respond. He wrote all over the margins of her typescript. He didn't much like this first one, particularly the last couplet; it seemed "tacked on," he told her. The final poem, the eighth, is elegiac:

> The time of year ennobles you.
> The death of autumn draws you in.
>
> The death of those delights I drew
> From such a cramped and troubled source
> Ennobles all, including you,
> Involves you as a matter of course.
>
> You are not, you have never been
> (Nor did I ever hold you such),
> Between your banks, that all but touch,
> Fit subject for heroic song. . . .
> The busy stream not over-strong,
> The flood that any leaf could dam. . . .
>
> Yet more than half of all I am
> Lies drowned in shallow water here:
> And you assume the time of year.
>
> I do not say this love will last;
> Yet Time's perverse, eccentric power
> Has bound the hound and stag so fast
> That strange companions mount the tower
> Where Lockhart's fate with Keats is cast,
> And Booth with Lincoln shares the hour.
>
> That which has quelled me, lives with me,
> Accomplice in catastrophe.

She had made two brilliant changes between this typescript and what had been her working draft, where she'd written:

> Where Brutus walks in Caesar's thongs
> And Booth with Lincoln shares the hour

Millay cut the reference to Brutus and Caesar and found a more apt poetic assassin in Lockhart. Lockhart, whom very few people other than scholars had heard of, was in his day such a savage critic that he was nicknamed "The Scorpion." When he condemned Keats's *Endymion,* he was accused, by Byron, of having hastened the young, sick poet's death.

Her final couplet is compelling and again far better than it had stood in draft, where she had written, "That which had quelled me, rides with me / Golden, in high catastrophe." But "Golden" and "high" were words that inflated the ending and meant far less than the potency of "Accomplice." "That which has quelled me, lives with me, / Accomplice in catastrophe." For what she was talking about in these poems was her own part in the assassination of her spirit. These, the final lines of the entire sequence, must be the most powerful. They strike not only a ringing close but a true one. And while George Dillon did not take any of the eight poems in "Theme and Variations" for *Poetry* magazine, he did take "Rendezvous":

> Not for these lovely blooms that prank your chambers did I come.
>   Indeed,
> I could have loved you better in the dark;
> That is to say, in rooms less bright with roses, rooms more casual,
>   less aware
> Of History in the wings about to enter with benevolent air
> On ponderous tiptoe, at the cue "Proceed."
> Not that I like the ash-trays over-crowded and the place in a mess,
> Or the monastic cubicle too unctuously austere and stark,
> But partly that those formal garlands for our Eighth Street
>   Aphrodite are a bit too Greek,
> And partly that to make the poor walls rich with our unaided
>   loveliness
> Would have been more chic.
>
> Yet here I am, having told you of my quarrel with the taxi-driver over
>   a line of Milton, and you laugh; and you are you, none other.
> Your laughter pelts my skin with small delicious blows.
> But I am perverse: I wish you had not scrubbed—with pumice, I
>   suppose—
> The tobacco stains from your beautiful fingers. And I wish I did not
>   feel like your mother.

5

On January 11, 1939, Edna read at Clark University in Worcester, Massachusetts, where she'd first read in 1927. She and Eugen were houseguests of the president of the college, Loring Dodd, and his wife, Ruth Dodd. Arriving the afternoon of her reading, she lay down for a nap. Through what was later called "sheer exhaustion," she overslept and didn't reach Clark's lecture hall until considerably after 8:15 P.M., the time at which her performance was scheduled to start.

In a letter she later wrote to Mrs. Dodd but did not send, she remembered walking down the staircase of their house to meet the three of them standing in the hall below her, "my husband's face white and tense with anxiety for me, your husband's face black with anger against me, and your own sweet face twisted a little as if you had just been crying." She remembered, too, stumbling sleepily down the stairs in my long velvet train and my one glass slipper!—or at least it seemed like that, for I had been abruptly awakened from such a happy dream and recalled to a world where people must, with frantic haste, get into their costumes and, dizzy with fatigue, step briskly and brilliantly out onto a stage to perform night after night their difficult and exacting chore.

She told the story like a fairy tale twisted into nightmare. "I had often spent the afternoon preceding my appearance on the stage, and the night following it, in the house of a friend, or even in the house of a stranger, perhaps the president of the University." But she would never do it again. It was too hard on her hosts "and impossibly difficult for me." Lavish dinners were prepared, guests were invited to meet her, "and I always forgot to write beforehand saying that I never ate dinner just before giving a reading." What she required was rest, alone.

Afterward there would be receptions arranged, which she "would be unable to attend because I had to catch, in a hurry, a train for some other city." There had been, that winter of her tour, she wrote, many disappointed hostesses and several angry ones.

She decided never to do that sort of thing again, instead "always to go to a hotel where I should be a care to nobody, upset nobody's arrangements and be, myself, free." Why was she constructing this maze of excuses? She said that her doctor had told her she could not go on this tour without, in addition to her husband "to care for me,"

> also a personal maid to pack and unpack me, and to get me into my costume. . . . she was always there to awaken me from an exhausted slumber, to draw my bath, throw me into it, drag me out of it, dry me off, haul my gown over my head, hook it, button it, snap it, straighten out the train of it, set me down before my dressing table and, holding my head against her shoulder with one hand, with the other hand paint my mouth and brush my lashes with mascara.

While Eugen had dinner downstairs with the Dodds, "I, as naturally as an exhausted animal, crawled into bed and went to sleep." She sounds lifeless, like a mannequin being manipulated.

The *Worcester Telegram* reported the next morning only that "Edna St. Vincent Millay—as vehement, mettlesome and exciting as one of her poems—stirred an audience to an answering mood last night." Edna St. Vincent Millay, they said, "the youthful, provocative figure of last night's performance, is proof of the youthful springs of her genius." In fact, she would never be able to make a national reading tour again.

PART NINE

ADDICTION

CHAPTER 35

The weather was miserable that spring at Steepletop. It was icy cold, and "the trees are hardly in bud and the field mice are still sheltering in my house. I don't blame the poor little brutes," Eugen wrote to Dillon. "I am doing the same myself." But the weather would turn warm, their pool would be swimmable, their tennis court playable, "so what about coming and seeing your little Berkshire friends sometime this summer?" George wasn't to beg off on account of his work because he could keep in touch with his office by telephone. "And you needn't pay for it because, evidently, I needn't pay it, at least I haven't paid the telephone bill for five or six months. I think it's the influence of Roosevelt on the utilities." If Eugen wasn't exactly inveigling George to come, he was certainly trying to make it hard to refuse. But this time, George didn't bite.

That March 1939, Hitler stormed into Prague in an open Mercedes-Benz with bright red Nazi flags snapping on its fenders. Czechoslovakia, dismembered by the Allies in Munich, had fallen. Millay's sonnet "Czecho-Slovakia" became a memorial.

> If there were balm in Gilead, I would go
> To Gilead for your wounds, unhappy land,
> Gather you balsam there, and with this hand,
> Made deft by pity, cleanse and bind and sew
> And drench with healing, that your strength might grow,
> (Though love be outlawed, kindness contraband)

And you, O proud and felled, again might stand;
But where to look for balm, I do not know.
The oils and herbs of mercy are so few;
Honour's for sale; allegiance has its price;
The barking of a fox has bought us all;
We save our skins a craven hour or two.—
While Peter warms him in the servants' hall
The thorns are platted and the cock crows twice.

If she said nothing to George about the increasing anger, even despair, she felt as one country after another in Europe fell under the German boot, there were poems like this one that expressed her outrage directly.

Vincent Sheean, the journalist and author, who was a friend of Dorothy Thompson as well as Millay, remembered Millay's being called a premature anti-Fascist. "And what the hell did that mean?" he said. "There were very pro-Hitler elements here, and there was a great resistance to getting into the war. You know people were saying: You can do business with Hitler! And they meant it."

There were others, of course, who recognized the outrage in Europe— Dorothy Thompson and Anne O'Hare McCormick of *The New York Times* among them—but Millay was a poet, not a newspaperwoman or a columnist or a radio broadcaster. It was Thompson, whom Millay knew from their days together in Budapest, who said that America needed her poets now. "I want to propose to you a conspiracy of poets," she proclaimed, "to offset the innumerable conspiracies which have made this world a nightmare. . . . We need the intuitive imagination of the great poets, to comprehend in even a small way the nature of the forces that are moving the world."

Thompson was lambasting the isolationists, the " 'appeasers,' . . . the America Firsters, and 'the architects of cynicism' in American life." Democracy had to be defended—in France, in Britain, wherever it existed—and there was no place in America now for complacency. Thompson was on the radio for fifteen days and nights at the end of the summer of 1939 as Poland fell and other countries in Europe were invaded. America was, however, still neutral, and most Americans wanted to keep it that way.

In October 1939, Edna took up the cudgels in earnest. She joined a broadcast on WJZ New York on the Herald Tribune Forum. The theme was "The Challenge to Civilization." Mrs. Ogden Reid, co-owner of the newspaper, was the moderator. The basis for the program was the host's belief that there was a solidarity among "civilized people" who were now being challenged by the war in Europe; there was among them "an eagerness for peace." James Conant, the president of Harvard, was the keynote speaker. Edna Millay was the second speaker. When she was introduced, she was called "an American possession . . . contrary to most poets she does not live in an ivory tower. . . . She has been called the greatest woman poet since Sappho."

On the old acetate recordings that were kept, her voice sounds high and rather clipped. There was something frail in it as she warned of the internal peril to America:

> In this country, where freedom of speech is poured so generously into the parched throats of aliens, and of naturalized aliens among whom, as we know, are many whose first allegiance still is to the land of their birth, not to this land, and whose chief concern is to discredit and pull apart, not to support and strengthen, our form of government—there is danger today that the good, average American citizen, fearful of making some indiscreet remark and of helping thus to get his country into war, will become completely tongue-tied.

What we had to fear most, she said, was the menace of the "most loyal and idealistic Communist, and the most loyal and idealistic Fascist." If we love democracy, then "We must love it in England and in France. In Germany we must love it, if only we could find it there"—and here she paused for a long time—"but we have not found it there."

> Why, then, should we be so afraid to say that as regards the war between a Germany whose political philosophy is repugnant to us and an allied Britain and France whose concepts of civilized living are so closely akin to our own that we hope with all our hearts that Great Britain and France may win this war and Germany lose?

We must avail ourselves, she told her audience, "as patriotic American citizens, of this fine free speech of ours." She closed by reading her poem "Underground System" from *Huntsman, What Quarry?*, which had come out in May. It is impossible now not to feel that while Millay was describing the condition in which America found itself, she was also describing her own condition.

That October, Helen Rogers Reid wrote Eugen anxiously, "I can't resist urging you to consider taking Miss Millay to [the] Harkness Pavilion. . . . I have such confidence in the men who work there that I believe they might be able to find the solution to your difficulties." Clearly whatever was troubling Edna was evident to others and no longer a closely guarded secret.

—

In November, in Switzerland, at the sanitarium of Davos-Platz, Llewelyn Powys hemorrhaged. Blood was constantly seeping into his mouth, his temperature was high, and he was no longer well enough to read or to see anyone. When Alyse sent a snapshot showing him lying on his cot outdoors, wrapped in striped woolen shawls, Edna wrote that he looked like that "Darling wicked voluptuous old Pan of a Lulu" whom she and Eugen both loved. In his thin, gaunt face his eyes were as radiant as stars. Alyse wrote to tell them that his curly hair and beard were long and white and "he looks wonderfully beautiful." Edna wrote back at once:

> Lulu, my poor, poor darling, if I wait to write you in ink, a proper letter, that a man out of his happiness dashed down again, with his tired eyes might read, I shall again be so overwhelmed by all I want to say to you, that again as so many times in these past months I shall not write you at all.—And that must not be;
>
> I must say something to you, simply to speak to you, even if I say nothing.
>
> So here I am, half an hour later, just thinking of you, saying nothing.— How senseless to try to say something to give you courage when you have already so much more of that than anybody I know, except Alyse.
>
> —Oh, Lulu, I do so hope that by the time you get this you will be better!
>
> My Love, Edna

But the bleeding would not be stanched. At one point, his breathing heavy, he gasped, "They are dragging me the wrong way." He wanted to be allowed to die. When it was clear that he was very close to the end, he asked for paper and wrote, "Love Life! Love every moment of life that you experience without pain." He died, after an injection of morphine to ease his pain, on December 2, 1939.

"Alyse," Edna wrote, "my dear and lovely Alyse, my heart's friend;—if only I could be with you now, this afternoon, just for the length of time it takes to drink three cups of tea, quietly, saying hardly anything—

"There is nothing that I can write; there would be nothing that I could say. But oh, if only I could be with you, my dear, just for an hour or two."

2

Perhaps it was just as well that George Dillon hadn't come to Steepletop that summer, for Millay was besieged by health problems of her own. In the fall Eugen wrote to George: "Vincent has not been feeling so very well this summer and we are going now once a week to New York to see an eye doctor and an osteopath." She was also in the care of the distinguished Dr. Connie Guion, who had come to Steepletop.

On November 21, 1939, Dr. Guion addressed a letter to Eugen:

> Dear Mr. Boissevain, nurse in charge! and patient!
> This will summarize the discussion which you, Miss Millay & I had together and in twos.
> My findings were
> first—a sore toe: this is an almost-healed blister, covered by a scab about so big. [She drew a picture.] It is not infected nor more tender than normal for such a condition.
> advice: Put over this a felt ring which I am sending, arrange the ring so no pressure comes on the scab. If the shoe hurts, cut out an area of the shoe large enough to relieve pressure.
> Exercise will hasten healing now because it will increase circulation.
> second—a back with curves so [and here she drew a curvy line and arrows]—These are the result of bad posture & will not be altered now. I could find no spot of localized tenderness over the area of pain or erythema.
> I believe the origin of the pain at X above is over-exercise after a too protracted period pulling plantains. I think the pain has resulted in spasm of the muscles of the back. Which results in pain.

For this she prescribed medication, exercise, wet heat, alternating hot baths and cold showers, rubdowns, and putting "on a woolen vest." In a curious addition to her letter she mentioned a "pain killer" Millay was taking that Guion felt increased constipation. But she does not say what the painkiller was. There's nothing about her eyes or her headaches. There are only a sore toe, a backache due to poor posture, constipation, and what she called the "Third Condition—the menopause":

> This underlies the whole picture; it makes the patient more susceptible to pain, less stable nervously and therefore she must use up more nervous energy to control her reactions.
> She has been receiving the right material but too little of it.
> To meet this give her one ampoule of the Progynon daily. It is best given into the muscle. If she leans over the back of a chair & you give it in the upper, outer side of the buttock it will not pain her. Warm the ampoule by putting it in water just about room temperature or hold it in your hand till it is body temperature. It will run easier. I am sending you needles.

She drew a picture of buttocks with dots for "dimples" and an X for where the shot should be administered. She taught Eugen Boissevain exactly how to give his wife an injection accurately, swiftly, and without pain. Actually, he already knew how. And so did Edna.

CHAPTER 36

The week after Edna saw Dr. Connie Guion at Steepletop, she went to New York with Eugen to get new passports. In their passport photos, both look worn, but Edna looks stricken and wary. Eugen checked in to the St. Regis Hotel without her, for on December 1 she entered New York Hospital, where she remained under the care of Dr. Guion for three weeks. Surviving hospital records suggest that her treatment was simple and clear: "This is the first admission of this 47 year old female complaining of pain in the back, headache and blister over left big toe joint."

Her past medical history was not unusual. She had been operated on for what her doctors quaintly called "congenital bands" in 1923, "with no benefit." They noted that she was chronically constipated. Her period had begun early, and was both regular and painful. She'd had two pregnancies that had miscarried very early. She'd had her last period in February, ten months before. She was "Now in menopause—hot flushes, sweats, irritable, unstable emotionally." She had been taking a hormone called Theelin for the past year. Her present illness had begun in the previous July with the weed-pulling episode she'd discussed with Connie Guion. She had constant headaches and back pain. But none of these complaints is sufficient to explain a three-week hospitalization.

Then there is this striking sentence: "Her L.M.D. [local medical doctor] in Pittsfield has prescribed morphine and Dilaudid to be given her by hypodermic by her husband. She has been taking from 0.015 to 0.004 as required by her pain." A usual dose of morphine is 10 to 15 milligrams (this notation appears to be in kilograms). To prescribe both morphine and Dilaudid, an opiate roughly three times more potent than morphine, is peculiar. Even if she were in menopause, she could have been missing periods because of the morphine, which can cause flushing, sweats, and constipation. No explanation is given of what was causing her such pain. Her physical examination revealed little beyond enlargement of her liver, a sign of alcohol damage. Her X rays showed a slight curvature of the spine and early indications of arthritis. She was allowed to roam the hospital freely and was "discharged improved" on December 21.

As it turned out, while Dr. Guion was prescribing injections of Progynon, an estrogen, those were not the only injections she was approving. "Miss Millay's condition," she wrote Eugen later,

was such that she not only required a daily visit but a visit twice a day and a telephone call at bedtime to the night nurse. She was nervous and easily upset. . . . I did not wish to have any discussion by the house officers of the amount of morphine she was taking. To avoid this I signed for it daily and personally ordered the drug.

Dr. Guion must have known that Millay was dependent on morphine. She may have been aware of her increasing use and have kept her in the hospital for both observation and detoxification. If so, it is strange that she continued to sign for such significant doses.

Connie Guion was a highly respected doctor; she was forceful, direct, astute, and used to being obeyed. A doctor who was then a very young intern remembers seeing her talk to patients on rounds: "She'd look them straight in the eye and say, 'You are not sick!' She'd get a glass of warm water and tell them, 'Now, you drink it!' " She was not, however, a person who dealt easily with a temperament like Millay's, and she may have been swayed by her reputation. Ten years Millay's senior, Connie Guion had been a poor, ambitious, gifted girl who had graduated from Wellesley College at twenty-four. Commited to her family, she had put her last two sisters through college before going to medical school. Young women of her generation could not be stopped unless they married young, and Guion never married. In 1932, she was made chief of the General Medical Clinic at New York Hospital, an outpatient clinic for the treatment of the poor— not, perhaps, a first-rate appointment, but an extraordinary appointment for a woman nevertheless.

In one of the notebooks she kept during the late 1930s she made the following notes under "Menopause," which she described as "instability in the vasomotor nervous system and its complications." Under "Treatment" she said the most important element was to establish confidence in the doctor by "understanding the disabling situation." Changes in a woman's body were described as "instability" with "complications," and she understood the situation to be "disabling." Her notes continued in a tone just short of patronizing:

> Never belittle . . . reassure that all symptoms can be relieved.
>> it takes time—
>> trial & error
>> no change in mentality
>> No change in libido
>> Not necessary to get fat or depressed.
>
>> 2. Drugs. . . . If patient has been to many doctors better to give hormones promptly.

This was exactly the period, in the late 1930s and early '40s, when the beneficial effects of estrogen first became known in the medical world.

The doctor who had known Connie Guion as an intern said, "It is not quite clear what the mechanism of the reaction is, but in many women taking small amounts of estrogen can change things around. So the patient is able to think more clearly. And it is also true that by the use of estrogens more patients were able to fight other disturbances, other addictions, even. It was called the hormone of serenity."

But Millay was not taking small amounts. And no one knew the effect of taking estrogen with morphine. Whatever it was, Edna Millay did not become serene.

Eugen had been planning a restful holiday in the British Virgin Islands, on Tortola, where he'd found a remote cottage on Half Moon Bay. There were no cars on the island, and Road Town, the tiny capital, was about fifteen minutes away by skiff. The cottage was brand new. Every room in the house faced the sea, and only a coconut grove separated it from the bay. There were kerosene lamps for reading, candles for dining. Although it was entirely private, simple food was easy to get, and there was plenty of fish, which could be delivered to their door or caught. A cook would come with the house for the princely sum of five dollars a month plus food.

They took it eagerly, sight unseen except for a handful of snapshots showing a room with bookcases, an empty terrace, and the back of a servant with a feather duster. Eugen asked if they could bring their dog, to which the owners immediately agreed. They must also have asked about sand flies and mosquitoes, because the owner wrote that they were eliminated by the prevailing wind "except in rare instances." The house would be ready for them the first week of December. The plan was for Edna to read and rest, regain her strength and her health. Eugen would swim and fish. It sounded idyllic.

The only record of their stay on Tortola is a bill from the small local market where Eugen shopped. Along with basic provisions such as salt, potatoes, onions, and sugar are twenty-eight bottles of gin, vermouth, and whiskey—and a case and a half of beer. They were there thirty days, and they had no guests.

In March 1940, Eugen wrote Norma:

This place has been a total fiasco. Everything is beautiful, the damnest scenery, I mean, and there are no white people on the island who can come and see us, but the house is funny, so uncomfortable, no beds . . . no chairs. And sandflies day AND night. So that is not very good for the back of little Edna. Morphine is the only thing which gives her a little relief.

He thought her back was getting "slowly very slowly better." And the trade winds, which always came in December, they were assured, had not yet come, "So it may come any time, when the sandflies will disappear! When I said that to Edna she said: 'I'm from Missouri, and I wish I had never left.' " Anyway, he wrote, "I am having fun. I have a little sail boat, and I swim and I am extravagantly healthy."

Millay was getting morphine in Tortola. Six months later, Dr. Guion complained to Eugen about his not having paid her bill. Impatient with his excuses, she reminded him, "Furthermore, during January and February I received eight letters from you asking for further advice and medication." Still receiving no payment, she wrote directly to Edna three months later, in December: "During your stay in the Virgin Islands, I cooperated with your husband . . . to see that you were provided with every medicine needed."

Upon their return to Steepletop in March, the bills from their druggist in Great Barrington listed "20 Morphine ¼ gr. 65c"—along with sunflower seeds, Kodak snaps, cigarettes, and Progynon B. In April, there was more morphine. In less than one week in July, they added 125 tablets of Nembutal, a barbiturate, which induces sleep. In high doses, it can give an effect of euphoria, comparable to that of morphine.

2

In January 1939, Edna had signed another contract with Harper for two books, *Huntsman, What Quarry?* (which was being published in May) and an untitled work, with her customary $1,000 advance due on delivery of each manuscript. The higher royalty rate that she had negotiated during the surge of sales after *Wine* was published in late 1934—15 percent, increasing to 20 percent after 5,000 copies had been sold—had remained in place.

She had in the past sometimes drawn against her future royalties by taking advances of $500 or $1,000 and even $2,500 once in 1934, but never as a monthly stipend and always against substantial royalties that had already been earned and were in her account at Harper. She had, in other words, an established practice of requesting money from her publisher in advance of payment. In July 1939, she made what Gene Saxton called a sudden "financial call": She needed $500 immediately, with another $500 on August 1. Then $1,000 was to be paid to her on the fifteenth of August, September, and October.

Although she had already taken $1,000 in March and another $1,000 in June 1939, *Huntsman* had sold 29,000 copies within the first month after publication (plus another 500 copies of an expensive limited edition), so she was still earning a good deal more than she was charging against her account. But then, in the spring of 1940, she asked Harper to provide her with $1,000 a month for twelve months.

In a letter dated April 12, 1940, Gene Saxton explained to her what their predicament would be if she continued to require such a healthy draw. He had gone over her royalty figures carefully. During 1939, the older books had produced $2,426.29 in royalties. *Huntsman, What Quarry?* had earned $13,740.77, making a total for the year of $16,167.06. Coming to 1940, the royalties due from all sources as of May 1, 1940, were $1,665.39.

Harper had already paid her $1,500. In May, it would advance her another $1,000; then $2,500 on June 14 and $1,500 on June 25. She was about to place herself in debt to her publisher. The burden, Saxton told her, "rests upon the publication of a new book within each twelve months." Her older books had had higher earnings in the past, "but practically speaking, it is the new book that carries the load."

He said he was most likely stating the obvious; it was just that if there were no new book forthcoming, "we shall find ourselves in, say, May, 1941 with an unearned royalty debit of approximately $10,000." That wasn't, he assured her, of any great importance, since that debt would immediately be offset by the sales of a new book. "What worries me, however—and I want to raise the point for your consideration—is, what arrangement can be applied beyond the twelvemonth period to furnish funds if at that time no new volume is in sight?" He was multiplying months without income, when "the problem of finances becomes a serious one, as we should, in the end, have reached a total of $18,000 to $20,000." He suggested a $500 or $600 monthly arrangement instead. It would give her a freer hand in preparing a new volume or at least provide for the months following delivery of a new manuscript when it was not yet earning money for her.

Saxton was exceedingly courteous—deferential, even: "We want to meet you as fully as possible, and our only concern is not to have the scheme break down . . . by reason of the sheer weight of the advance." Then, in what was a clear indication of Saxton's conservative nature—he was not, after all, a writer; publishing was his business: "Perhaps I should add also that I realize that I am presenting the picture at its worst."

A pattern was becoming established from which Millay would be unable to escape: she would be indebted to Harper until she published a new book. That book would clear away her indebtedness with a few hundred dollars to spare; then the pattern would begin all over again, just as Saxton had cautioned. From now until the end of her life her publisher would be her banker. The real question was why she needed money so urgently in July 1939 and why she continued to require these monthly sums.

The answer was, in part, Kathleen. Even in Kathleen's first year at Vassar, she had struck a note with her sisters that wasn't simply plaintive, it was accusatory. "I don't care what you are doing!" she had written to them. "You are using me like Hell and I am too tired and too worried to stand it. . . . it wouldn't do your souls any harm to help me by letting me know that you exist and that you are interested in whether I am or not."

By 1926, Kathleen, who had begun to publish well after her sister, was inevitably being compared to her, almost always to her disadvantage: "Were there no Edna St. Vincent Millay, then surely Kathleen Millay, the younger sister . . . would be considered a major poet." This response from the Chicago *Evening Post* continued, "That she hasn't the bravado of her well-beloved sister denotes perhaps a lesser courage. . . . It is delicate, exquisite verse of rare charm and with the wistful quality that characterizes her sister's verse; it lacks, however, the brilliant futile daring that is hers."

The title of the review of Kathleen's first book of poetry in their home state of Maine was "The Other Millay." "There is an apparent kinship between Kathleen's poems and sister Edna's," said the *San Francisco Chronicle*. "Let us hope that between the Millay sisters we do not come to a Shakespeare-Bacon controversy in modern dress and boyish bob—trying to decide which sister wrote the poems of both."

When Edna and Eugen had seen Kathleen in California in December, they had given her money for her divorce. In her subsequent wires and letters it had become clear that she hadn't used the money to divorce Howard Young. In the spring, completely without warning, she moved back to New York City, pleading that there was no work for her on the West Coast. "Look where I am! Isn't it exciting? Just a good old ghost yanked back from the dead to her old stamping ground." But if her letters began in a festive spirit, they inevitably ended by asking for money:

> I realize Edna is not a rich woman, as Ugin continually points out—I never thought she was—and it must be hard on her to have six people dependent on her—I'm sorry she has such a hard time. Anyway, I'll try to get some kind of job soon—no matter what—and be a burden to her no longer.

Letter after letter continued in this vein, telling them how ill she was, how she needed medication, asking for money—"If possible, I wish you could send me sixty dollars this time as it seems I have to have a few prescriptions filled. . . . There's a bad pain setting in all over my body"—and always adding a needling comment about her effort to "not bother you anymore after another month or so," while wishing them a lovely time wherever they had gone to to "get all rested and tanned." Her letters were constant with complaints—it was too hot in the city, she couldn't find work—until July 27, 1939, when she entered New York Hospital, where she remained until mid-August. She had fainted while walking and told the doctors she had had a pain in her heart. They found her story unreliable, and their diagnosis was that she was suffering from chronic alcoholism, high blood pressure, and what they called psychoneurosis.

Kathleen wrote to Edna from the hospital that she was run-down and needed a respite from the New York summer. Edna came to her from Steepletop at once. After their visit, Kathleen wrote to her:

> The doctor insists the thing for me to do is to go to Maine for a month or six weeks—and I must not go alone. Them's her orders. . . . It seems I came much nearer fading out of the picture than I realized—which may have been just as well at the time. Anyway, it takes a long time to get back to anything after all the long and exhausting illnesses I've had all my life— and trouble—trouble—toil and very little else. . . .
>
> Anyway, my love to you both—Ugin was so very sweet yesterday! It was such a relief to see his smiling face—and he made me laugh!

That was August 10. They spoke on the telephone from Steepletop on the thirteenth, although a bad electrical storm made their connection sketchy and Edna could barely hear her sister. Eugen wrote telling Kathleen how much they wanted to help her and to more clearly explain what they could provide. The tone of his letter, while not unfriendly, was stern:

> 14th August 1939
>
> Dear Kathleen: . . .
>
> This is on my mind:
>
> It seems to me most unpleasant for both you and us, if you are put in a position in which you are forced to have to consult us about your immediate plans. I think it would be so much better and more dignified if you knew what financial help Edna can give you and then make your plans accordingly. Now this is what Edna can do.
>
> She will pay the hospital bill, until you leave, which I understand will be tomorrow or Wednesday. She will pay the doctor. (Will you please ask the doctor to send her bill to Edna?) She can then give you $150.—for the first month up to 15th September. This month will be the most expensive. Then $100.—up to 15th October and this will have to cover expenses find-

ing a place in New York, and then $80.—up to 15th November. I fear we will be able to give you but very little after that. . . .

I will see that you get your checks on time, but on the other hand you will have to trim your sails so that you do not get caught in a jam, because that would be unfortunate for you as we would not be able to help you. And that is a fact.—So for your own sake I implore you not to run up any bills for they will not be paid by us. . . . you seem determined to go to Maine and you might run into some embarrassing incidents should you try to get credit there.

It is unfortunate that you are set on going to what is probably the most expensive summer resort in the U.S.A.

Kathleen left the hospital immediately after her telephone conversation with Eugen, *before* his letter to her arrived. When she received it, she wrote directly to Edna:

Please thank Ugin for telling me exactly what you can do. I wanted you to tell me when I saw you but I guess you did not understand. It has been so long since you knew what it was to wonder where tomorrow's food was coming from—and, of course, since Ugin was born to money, he has never known—I suppose neither of you can realize what constant illness and worry can do to me.

Eugen, not Edna, answered her. He said he'd "implored" her not to leave the hospital but "to stay . . . until you had found a place to go to on leaving the hospital." Then he gave up and said she should go to Maine and Edna would pay for the rental of a cottage. Four days later Kathleen wired thanking Ugin for his "nice letter":

HEAT HERE TERRIBLE WOULD LOVE TO LEAVE FOR MAINE . . . SORRY PAID NEW APARTMENT RENT SATURDAY.

But if he could wire her another $100, she could still take a cottage. Eugen exploded in barely controlled anger:

August 23, 1939

Dear Kathleen:
    I just received your wire and I must admit that it is impossible for me to follow your changing plans. However, it is not necessary for me to understand them as you are white and twenty and I am sure you know what you want.

It is unfortunate that you rented an apartment last Saturday, now that a few days later you change your mind and think it preferable to go to Maine. . . . why you should rent an apartment for a month, against your doctors advice, is beyond me. . . .

Now you wire that you need another $100. I am sorry we are not able to give you that; unfortunately, we are unable to do more than we told you we could do.

We are leaving Sunday or Monday at the latest for a prolonged trip, and no mail will be forwarded to us beyond that time, so you will be unable to communicate with us after Saturday.

On the same day, he wrote to Norma in cold fury:

As to Kathleen, I will not give you any news from her. I hate the God damned bitch. She has spoiled my summer and has done everything crazy and difficult that it is possible for a creature to do. She is unmanageable, and I am sure that she is cookoo. She is wily in getting money out of Edna and I am sure that she is trying to suck as much money out of her as she possibly can. However, these are only my own personal opinions. Edna, however, who has been holding out until now, hoping for a come-back from Kathleen and that everything would be straight, admits at last that the evidence goes to show that she has been lied to and double crossed and milked of every penny that can be squeezed out of her. . . . If you are very sensitive to moods and nuances in literature you will have gathered by this time that I am in a bad humor and not to be played with.

It was in this sorry stew of family resentment, illness, and anger that Eugen received, on September 7, 1939, a psychiatric assessment of Kathleen, who had been examined earlier in August at New York Hospital. The psychiatrist wrote that while she was suffering from high blood pressure and alcoholism, she was certain that Edna's fame had damaged her own success as a writer. But far worse was her fixed idea that Vincent had stolen ideas from her and incorporated them into her work. The doctor thought that only a neutral authority could intercede, and he suggested a young woman who was a colleague of Dr. Guion, whom Kathleen had seen and trusted.

Edna's sudden call for money from her publisher was to pay Kathleen's hospital bills—and to pick up far more than medical expenses. Within five months Edna had sent Kathleen more than $1,000 and paid her various medical bills, which amounted to another $500. That both sisters had been hospitalized within months of each other—which Kathleen did not know—in the same hospital was bizarre. But the fierce downward spiral of Kathleen's dependence on Edna and her anger toward her were hardly over.

3

By May 1940, after a series of violent German assaults, Rotterdam was destroyed, Holland had fallen to the Nazis, and the British expeditionary force sent to help France in a last-ditch effort to repulse the German invasion had been pushed to the sea at a spot on the coast called Dunkirk. On June 14, Paris fell to the Nazis, and America's Ambassador Bullitt was reported to be in German "protective custody." Huge black headlines marked the faces of all the newspapers. That morning in June *The New York Times,* the *Herald Tribune,* and the *Daily News* published Edna Millay's stinging attack against isolationism, "Lines Written in Passion and in Deep Concern for England, France and My Own Country." In the *News* the poem was set, incongruously, beside its own isolationist editorial. "Not in years," wrote the wire services, "has a poet sought so directly the ear of so wide a public. . . . In an era in which poets have been accused of having too little to say to the many, Miss Millay suddenly launched her ringing call to arms under the impact of the tragic drama in France."

She asked the American public directly to abandon isolationism, to heed, "the shrieking plea / For help, of stabbed Democracy." The poem was picked up by newspaper after newspaper throughout the United States and Canada, each one commenting that she'd sent it forth from her sickbed in the Berkshires. They said it was a landmark in literary history. They said she had written the first important poem of the second great war.

> Dear Isolationist, you are
> So very, very insular!
> Surely you do not take offense?—. . . .
> 'Tis you, not I, sir, who insist
> You are an Isolationist.
>   · · ·
> No man, no nation, is made free
> By stating it intends to be.
>   · · ·
> (Meantime, the tide devours the shore:
> There are no islands any more.)
>   · · ·
> Oh, build, assemble, transport, give
> That England, France and we may live,
> Before tonight, before too late,
> To those who hold our country's fate
> In desperate fingers, reaching out
> For weapons we confer about,
> All that we can, and more, and now!

. . .

> Let French and British fighters, deep
> In battle, needing guns and sleep,
> For lack of aid be overthrown,
> And we be left to fight alone.

By early fall the poem was retitled "There Are No Islands Any More" and published as a separate booklet of ten pages by Harper. The manufacturer, Haddon Press, offered to do the presswork and binding for free, and the paper manufacturers fell into line. Now all Harper needed, Gene Saxton wrote Eugen, was a statement from Edna, signed by her and printed up front. He suggested that she write

> This poem, written by me in the cause of democracy, has been printed and distributed with my permission, free of royalty, all proceeds from the sale being turned over to the Red Cross or some similar war relief agency.

When the poem caught the eye of the unfortunate Ferdinand Earle, who, broke and unemployed, had written asking for her help and who'd thought Millay was so ill she couldn't utter a word, he was mightily offended. "Once-dear Edna Millay," he wrote her, "Considering that you owe your entire first spectacular successes to my efforts, how shabby, the secretary's indirect reply, to my letter!"

Eugen answered him the next day, explaining that he was not Edna's secretary but her husband:

> As she has been very sick and has recently returned from the hospital I have thought it necessary to relieve her of everything possible, of all worry and all correspondence. For that same reason I am not showing her your last letter, but will show her this letter as soon as she is feeling better and doubtless you will hear from her.
>
> I presume you got angry by seeing a poem written by her and evidently you did not believe my letter. However, you are mistaken. She wrote this poem in a great desire to do something during these difficult and unhappy times. That was something I could not prevent her from doing.
>
> It seems strange to me, that you, a poet yourself, and who has lived in Paris, should be unable to understand that even a person who has been very ill for several months and has only recently returned in an ambulance from a hospital where she has undergone a series of painful operations on the nerves of the dorsal spine and who is in such constant pain that she is obliged to be given hypodermic injections of morphine several times a day—that even a person in such a condition, filled with horror and despair

at the thought that the Nazi Germans are about to march into Paris, might compose the passionate lines which you seem to have read.

Earle was immediately contrite. And Edna answered him herself in August, addressing him, once again, as she had in Camden, as her Dear Editor:

> I am sorry that I was too ill to write you; oh, so sorry that I hurt your feelings. I am still too ill to write you,—even to dictate as I am doing now, . . . that is to say, it is against doctor's orders that I do it. But . . . I cannot bear to have you continue to think me forgetful and ungrateful. I remember too well that day, years ago, when I came back from the pasture carrying a pailful of blueberries which I had picked, and my mother was waiting for me on the doorstep with your letter in her hand. . . . I think of you always with the same affectionate gratitude I felt at the time when you were trying so hard to make the other judges see my poem as you saw it, trying so hard to obtain for me that prize of $500, a fortune then. (Almost a fortune to me now, in fact. Though in the meantime there have been periods when I could have paid $500 for an evening gown. My life has always gone abruptly and breath-takingly up and down, like a roller-coaster!)

She told him she was still far too ill to help him; she had to reserve whatever strength she had for her own work.

> But you, who were the first, outside the little village where I lived, to think my poetry of some consequence, would be the first now, I think, to consider that I should give to it all the strength that I have.
> I am, believe me, with the same grateful heart as on that day long ago when I learned that somebody beside my mother, a person whose name I later learned to be Ferdinand Earle, liked a poem of mine called "Renascence."

It was only in this letter to Ferdinand Earle and in a draft of a letter to George Dillon that Millay explained the apparent cause of her illness:

> . . . for something over a year now I have been very sick,—or, rather, not sick, simply in constant pain, due to an injury to certain nerves in my back referred to by the ten or twelve different doctors & surgeons who have tried to cure the trouble, as nerves 4, 5 & 6 of the dorsal spine—referred to by me as that place up under my right shoulder-blade. The nerve injury is the result, it seems probable, of my having been thrown out of the station-wagon one night—not by the driver, as you are probably thinking, but by the sudden swinging open of the door against which I was leaning; I was

hurled out into the pitch-darkness—a very strange sensation it was, too—
and rolled for some distance down a rocky gully before I was able to grab
at some alders or something & come to a halt. I have had three operations
on these nerves and should be quite well now, I think, if I were not still,
naturally, rather weak.

In her reworked and redated (September 14, 1940) typescript of this letter, she for the first time called the operations unsuccessful.

Professor Irwin Edman of Columbia University reviewed Millay's pamphlet "There Are No Islands Any More," alongside Stephen Vincent
Benét's *Nightmare at Noon* and *The Irresponsibles* by Archibald MacLeish.
While there was no questioning the urgency of the situation or the integrity
of the writers, the critic was meant to be something more than a ther-
mometer measuring excitement and sincerity or even what Edman called
"moral seriousness." All three authors were exemplary, but as works of art
what they had written was questionable. Millay had very clearly subtitled
hers "Lines Written in Passionate and Deep Concern," and most readers,
Edman felt sure, would remember her lines published in what he called
"display form" by newspapers during the crucial days of the fall of France
that past June. He called her work epigrammatic journalism. He didn't like
the white heat of Millay's emotion. "If artists are to become writers of
burning tracts, it seems to be intellectually irresponsible to condemn the
discipline of art because it is not the discipline of a military emergency."

Harper, which had been supportive of her in June, when in ten days it
had deposited $4,000 into her accounts, adding up to an advance from
May 1940 to the end of the year of $10,000, had not expected another
book from her within the year of the publication of *Huntsman*. But then,
neither had she. The urgency, despair, and fury she felt about America's
lack of response to the war, its continuing isolation, found voice in her
work now. Her poems began to run in newspapers around the country;
The New York Times published four sonnets in its Sunday Magazine on
October 13, 1940.

Her champion at Harper, Gene Saxton, understood her need to get the
poems into book form immediately. "The poems themselves are, of
course, of the utmost timeliness, and have great drive and emotion," he
wrote Eugen. "That is why it is so essential to speed the production."
Would she be willing to have Harper rush the book through without
sending her proofs? It would follow her copy absolutely.

Within two weeks of his letter the poems were set in galleys. "Everyone
here has been much moved by the emotional quality of the poems," Sax-

ton wrote, "and there is a mixture of surprise and pleasure in the unexpected arrival of this volume in the autumn list." Her new book, *Make Bright the Arrows,* would be published on November 20.

On November 15, Charles Lindbergh gave his famous—or infamous— "Our Drift Toward War" speech, in which he warned that America was woefully underprepared for war, its defenses inadequate against the Nazis' power. President Roosevelt may have assured the French that America's efforts would be redoubled, promising France "more equipment," but America's Congress remained strongly isolationist. Lindbergh was advocating staying out of Europe's war. He had visited Germany six times between 1936 and 1938 at the invitation of Field Marshal Göring, who had given him Germany's highest medal for distinguished aviation, which he had accepted.

Anne Morrow Lindbergh had written a "Prayer for Peace," which her husband arranged to have published in *Reader's Digest* for Christmas 1939. She had qualms about what she was writing: "I am filled with mistrust and misgivings about it. . . . Will it hurt C? Or help him?" Clearly she knew that her husband was being accused of being pro-Nazi.

The following summer, while Britain was being bombed in a ferocious air war, Anne Lindbergh began to work on an article that was eventually published as a forty-one-page book, *The Wave of the Future.* "I do not 'write' it exactly, I am so full of it. . . . It flows out of me, unmindful of how it is 'written.' "

Charles Lindbergh took his wife's article to New York and showed it to Alfred Harcourt, publisher of her two bestselling books, *North to the Orient* and *Listen! The Wind.* Harcourt was anxious to publish it at once.

That August, Anne Lindbergh explained to her mother, Mrs. Dwight Morrow, who was deeply opposed to the Lindberghs' point of view, that her goal was to give "a moral argument for isolationism . . . because I think it is vital to stay out." She had been "impelled to write it, because of my personal loyalty and desperate feeling of injustice to C., but I wouldn't do it on that alone."

In November 1940, Edna Millay was elected to the American Academy of Arts and Letters. Newspaper reporters in New York interviewed her at her suite at the St. Regis, where she sat, they wrote, "half lost" in a huge chair, her "auburn hair still worn as she wore it when an undergraduate." In the accompanying photographs, she looked unwell. Her hair was flat, her face puffy, her mouth turned down like the rim of a cup. Instead of being dressed for the photographs accompanying the interview, she was wearing a dressing gown.

She was asked by one journalist if she found it odd that the American Academy of Arts and Letters had waited until now to make her a member, since she had been "for 25 years one of America's most distinguished poets."

"After all," she said today . . . "perhaps I wasn't ready for such an honor. Perhaps they thought I wasn't mature enough."

There was a faint twinkle in the little red-haired poet's eyes—eyes somewhat weary from a late celebration, in company with her husband Eugen Boissevain and William Lyon Phelps. . . . "We stayed up very late— and we drank lots of sherry."

She had decided, she told the reporters, to take an apartment in the city "to be closer to the realities, closer to where men and women are giving aid to Britain, trying to aid the oppressed of France and Poland and Norway." She explained that she would become a propagandist for democracy:

If I can write just one poem that will turn the minds of a few to a more decent outlook . . . what does it matter if I compose a bad line or lose my reputation as a craftsman? . . . I used to think it very important to write only good poetry. Over and over I worked it to make it as flawless as I could. What does it matter now, when men are dying for their hopes and their ideals? If I live or die as a poet it won't matter, but anyone who believes in democracy and freedom and love and culture and peace ought to be busy now. He cannot wait for the tomorrows.

When Peter Monro Jack reviewed *Make Bright the Arrows* in *The New York Times Book Review,* he wrote, "Miss Millay was compelled to write this book. Her readers will be compelled to read it." There was no doubt that it was a piece of propaganda, but he reminded them that Milton, Wordsworth, and Rupert Brooke had written propaganda in the heat of war. "Miss Millay may have written more nicely, but she has never written more strongly, with absolute belief and accuracy."

Reviewing her again in the New York *Herald Tribune* Books section, Professor Irwin Edman did not agree: "But it is a sad obligation to report that the tragedy of the present hour has not wrung great poems out of Miss Millay, nor, with the exception of a few sonnets and possibly the opening poem, even notably good ones." He stopped just short of savaging the book. He did like the sonnet "Blue bright September air, with her and there / On the green hills a maple turning red." But he admonished Millay that her arrows could have been made bright only by art: "But it must be poetry, first. . . . That is not true of most of these sincere but sputtering verses."

Millay sent George Dillon the book a few weeks after publication. She cautioned that her new book was "not poems, posters; there are a few good poems, but it is mostly plain propaganda." She added that if "some bright boy reviews it for Poetry, please remind him that I know bad poetry as well as the next one." She thought that by subtitling it "1940 Note-book," she'd made it plain enough "that this book is a book of impassioned propaganda, into which a few good poems got bound up because they happened to be propaganda, too."

Eleven years later Dillon said this was the last letter on the subject of poetry he ever received from Vincent Millay. "It was a book containing several poems I had advised her not to publish. After trying it on two well known critics, who annihilated it, and on two others who refused it, I printed what seemed to me at the time a just and respectful review." Reading it over years later, he realized that the review had been, "in a feminine way, ruthless." While he didn't lose Millay's friendship, "My punishment was that she never sent me her poetry again."

Even her old Vassar friend Charlotte Babcock Sills, to whom she had sent *Make Bright,* was offended by the book. Millay insisted she was adamant about America's *not* getting into the war in Europe, "And if this book had really been the book you took it to be . . . would I have done the insolent and cruel thing which it would have been to send to you and Mac a book of poems trying to incite this country to send American boys into foreign lands to fight?" For the Sillses had three grown sons.

> Have you the slightest conception of what this reputation means to me, who have been building it carefully for more than twenty years, taking a long time, months, sometimes as long as several years before permitting a poem to be published because I felt that in one line of it, one syllable was not as close to perfection as I might be able to make it?
>
> Thus, you see, the dearest thing in life I possess which might possibly be of help to my country, has already gone over the top, in the hope that your sons need never go to war.

But it was a disingenuous defense, and her letter did nothing to mask Millay's own strain.

4

At the end of 1940, a benefit was organized in New York for United China Relief, to which a number of writers were invited to help raise money for Chinese trapped in the war of resistance to Japan. Vincent Sheean was asked by Henry Luce to be the chairman of the dinner given at the Waldorf-Astoria to launch the organization. Writers were invited to sit at the speakers' table, and Edna Millay was asked to recite a poem. When Sheean saw her, he thought she looked like "a stricken deer."

"Edna Millay had come to the dinner in her smallest and most frightened mood. She had been very ill and she had worried immeasurably over Hitler's victories in Europe and the disappearance of so many brave small countries, including Eugen's. The atmosphere at the Waldorf was not favorable to her." Sheean tried to take care of her; the glare of the blue lights was awful. He found her standing behind her chair.

" 'I can't sit with strangers only,' she said in an agonized whisper. 'Please, I must have Eugen sitting beside me. Believe me, it's true. I don't know what will happen if he isn't here. Please, please—otherwise I'll have to go home.' " She was, he remembered, trembling all over. "So I went to Pearl [Buck], and she arranged it that Edna had a place with Eugen beside her at the central table." But in all the commotion of the evening, with some of the speeches broadcast over national networks, Edna's having been asked to recite a poem was forgotten. Sheean was outraged; the next morning he sent her roses, along with a note regretting what had happened.

The Nazis began to bomb Britain in earnest in the summer of 1940, and the merciless pounding continued for months on end. The French Republic was in ashes. In its place, ruling a partitioned France, was the Fascist government of Marshal Henri Pétain, a hero of the First World War.

By now Edna Millay barely left her upstairs rooms at Steepletop. Sometimes she wandered around the house in her robe with the sound of the broadcasts on the radio tormenting her. Sometimes she and Eugen sat crouched beside their Philco, leaning into the pale golden glow of the dial as it broadcast news from the front. She could hardly sleep for pain. In the morning, as soon as she awoke, she held a tiny glass vial shaped like a tear in her hand to warm it, fixed a steel needle into a metal plunger, and shot the colorless liquid directly into her arm or her thigh. Sometimes, then, the pain let go, and she vanished. It was at first dreamy and peaceful and without pain from any source: "Luxe, calme et volupté. . . ."

At the close of her workbook for this year she wrote out the following:

CHART
MISS MILLAY
Dec. 31, 1940

Awoke 7:30, after untroubled night. Pain less than previous day.
7:35—Urinated—no difficulty or distress

7:40—⅜ gr. M.S. hypodermically, self-administered in left upper arm +
profuse bleeding, almost instantly quenched.

7:45 to 8—smoked cigarette (Egyptian) (mouth burns from excessive
smoking)

8:15—thirsty—went to ice-box for glass of water, but no water there. Take
glass of beer instead which do not want. Headache, lassitude and
feeling of discomfort & stuffiness from constipation.

8:20—cigarette (Egyptian)

9:00—"

9:30—Gin Rickey (cigarette)

11:15—Gin Rickey

12:15—Martini (4 cigarettes)

12:45—¼ grain M.S. & cigarette

1.—pain bad & also in lumbar region. no relief from M.S.

She'd been awake ten minutes when she took her first injection of morphine. By noon she'd had a glass of beer, eight cigarettes, and three strong
drinks. But maybe most crucially, this was the first time she wrote in her
own hand that she was injecting the morphine herself. This chart, which
she began on New Year's Eve day, a time for making resolutions, established a pattern of record keeping she would continue as long as she was
addicted. But first she fought that acknowledgment by denying it. She had
help—right at home, where it was now the dead of winter.

CHAPTER 37

At the turn of the year, Edna and Eugen fled Steepletop for New York
and took an apartment at 400 East Fifty-second Street, around the
corner from Margaret Cuthbert. It wasn't only the war effort that brought
Millay to New York; she was far more ill than anyone knew. Margaret
called a young friend of hers, Dorothy Leffler, on New Year's Day 1941,
to ask her a favor: Would she do some work for "Miss Millay who was ill
and needed help badly"? Miss Leffler, who had experience as an assistant
editor at Bobbs-Merrill, was asked to arrange her time so she could spend
part of every day with Millay. No one explained what kind of help Millay
needed or described her illness.

When Leffler arrived the first afternoon, Millay suddenly dictated a
poem to her. "Not having taken dictation in some five years, I had a terrible feeling I might not be able to read my notes and one of Miss Millay's

poems might be lost forever." Fortunately her shorthand held, but although Leffler spent the next four months with her, that was the only time Millay ever dictated anything to her.

Eugen explained that they were in New York so that Edna could receive medical help for an injury to the nerves of her shoulder received in an automobile accident. Edna added that she had never been free of pain since. "While I was with her," Leffler recalled, "Mr. Boissevain would administer shots of some kind several times a day to control the pain."

During those four months she could recall Millay's getting dressed and going out only four or five times. Once was to make the only recording of her reading her own poems for RCA Victor, for which she, strangely, asked Miss Leffler to make the selection. "There was no great ceremony about it. I think I said I hoped she would include a certain poem and she said, 'Why don't you select the poems you'd like me to record.' And I did. She certainly wasn't disinterested nor too ill to make the selection." Once she accompanied Edna and Eugen to Margaret Cuthbert's for cocktails. "That time Miss Millay simply put a coat over her robe, and we took a taxi around the corner to Margaret's apartment."

Margaret, who had known and adored Eugen for years, dropped him a note after drinks that Sunday:

Did I tell you this one—

There was a young girl from Madras
Who had a beautiful ass—
It was not what you think!
Round, firm & pink
But grey—with long ears (or hairs)
And ate grass—

After the limerick, she struck a worried note: "Should Edna drink & take morphine. Doesn't one soothe & one excite? And so counter balance each other? I once took bromide—also did some plain & fancy drinking & almost choked to death."

One afternoon Millay came into the living room fully dressed. "Mr. Boissevain made a great fuss about it," Miss Leffler remembered, and Edna said, "Most men get excited when a woman undresses for them but this is the first time I've known one to get excited because a woman got dressed."

Millay had agreed in November to write a response to Anne Morrow Lindbergh's *The Wave of the Future.* Now, with Miss Leffler's help, she started. She fired off question after question to her assistant: "Find out how many times she uses the title-phrase, either entire or just as The Waves, & copy phrases. Copy Dorothy Thompson's remarks about title, how it was taken from a fascist book or pamphlet." It wasn't only that Millay was distressed by the book, as she told Miss Leffler, because it "supported the fascist point of view; she was especially upset that Mrs. Lindbergh should have written such a book."

The Wave of the Future had been published within weeks of Millay's *Make Bright the Arrows*. Rarely had two books that asked the same question—should America defend her allies, or should she remain isolated from them?—taken such opposing points of view. When Anne Lindbergh wrote about "our world," she defined it as "the world in which we were brought up—the good, the Christian, the democratic, the capitalist world." She suggested it was vanishing through the democracies' lack of moral fiber, in which "the race declined in hardiness," in which there was "dissatisfaction, maladjustment and moral decay." Near the close of her book she admitted, "I do not believe we need to be defended against a mechanized German army invading our shores, as much as against the type of decay, weakness, and blindness into which all the 'Democracies' have fallen since the last war. . . . There is no fighting the wave of the future." Mankind had to learn "not to resist the inevitable push of progress."

In Millay's working notebook of November 1940, she had already begun the handwritten draft of her response. She called it "The Dyke of the Present," a reference to protective land barriers that hold back the sea, "(A reply to Anne Morrow Lindbergh's *The Wave of the Future*)." This draft breaks off after several pages, only to begin again, run on for a few pages more, and stop. Then, in a typescript of roughly fifty pages, she tried again and again to work out what she thought. She wrote that even if Lindbergh's book was "at least for the first twenty of its forty-one pages, lucidly written," the second half was marred by disingenuous sentimentality. Why should we resign ourselves to this approaching wave?

If this wave, whatever it may be, is scheduled to engulf us soon, no matter what we may do, it would seem to me more admirable, more valiant (old-fashioned words, but still with a strong and pleasant herb-like savour about them) to say to the Wave, "Here is my Honour and here is my Individuality: if you want them, come and take them; I give nothing to you." Instead, Mrs. Lindbergh has counselled us, since we cannot avert death, not to conspire against illness.

Why, Millay pressed, hadn't the man who had once done a thing "which declared holiday in all our hearts," a man "we once called 'Lindy,' " why hadn't Charles Lindbergh returned to Field Marshal Göring "his glittering gew-gaws"?

On the last page of notes she made the one statement that may have frozen the completion of her work: "It seems at the outset such a hopeless task to raise one small voice against the many voices lifted in praise of C. & A. Lindbergh, Inc." They were beloved; they were trustworthy; they represented the best in American life. Who would believe Edna Millay's "one small voice" in the face of their public esteem?

"I just don't know why she didn't finish her answer to 'Wave of the Future,' " Dorothy Leffler wrote. "She was very enthusiastic about it when she began it but then simply tired of it. . . . After she stopped working on her answer she never referred to it again."

Millay was in no condition to marshal her response into a coherent essay, and she stopped cold. That April 1941, when she began to record her poems for RCA, even her superb voice seemed to fail her. It sounded thin, uncertain, and forced.

2

By the spring their finances were shot. "Once again I must ask my publishers to come—come running—to my aid," Edna wrote to her editor. She said she had to make it sound facetious or she couldn't go on with the letter. "It seems to me that I never get you finally paid up, with a few hundred dollars to spare, but I have to start right in borrowing from you again." What was particularly infuriating was not only that she was constantly in pain but that she had to lay "one sweet luscious grand after another between the self-complacent and condescending teeth of one officious and inefficient hospital after another."

She tried to assure Gene Saxton that she had finally hit on a cure. She was being treated by a doctor whose doses of everything from what she called "all the tons of calcium gluconate and assorted minerals" and vitamins by the barrel had begun to work. "Every day I get better. One whole day I was almost without pain." The next sentence was stunning for what she acknowledged: "Seldom has the morphine seemed so slow in getting to me; although poor Ugin, who naturally hates like hell to have to give it to me, is quicker with it than the doctor by now." But because of the war, "Eugen has lost everything he had. . . . There is not a penny he can get at. So for the time being it's up to me."

What was cut from her published letters survives in the original:

And as for me, something has just happened in my own personal family affairs—not tragic, just ugly and pathetic and from a financial point of view extremely burdensome to me . . . without the further considerable help of Harpers' *ruinous* to me.

Kathleen had surfaced again, ill, broke, angrily demanding more money.

Millay enclosed a list of her financial needs:

March 11, 1941

As things stand now, I shall be
the debtor of Harper & Bros. on
or about the 20th of May, 1941,
to the amount of $3,500.00
I need immediately   1,000.00
I shall need on Apr. 10   1,000.00
From June up to and
including November
I shall need *per month*
$600, this amounting to   3,600.00
If Harpers' can advance me
this amount as outlined I
shall owe on or about Nov. 20   ———————
                                        9,100.00

(This amount of course minus such
royalties as I may have earned in
the meantime)—E. St. V. M.

Harper met her needs fully. Gene Saxton had only one request: that she work to bring together her *Collected Sonnets*. "We've just had a most enthusiastic session with the salesmen about the 'Collected Sonnets.' What they need most, in their selling, is the authority to say 1) that the volume will have 2 or 3 unpublished Sonnets and 2) a Preface."

In scores of pages in her working notebooks, Millay tried again and again to work out what she wanted to say in a preface. In one fine passage she even tried to define the sonnet:

I did not know then what a sonnet was. I thought, as many people think, and not at all unreasonably, that a sonnet was any kind of short lyric, the word sounds like a diminutive, and informal. What greatness of spirit, what nobility of mood, what austerity, what solemn and serene behaviour, what formal grace and method of procedure as of a ritual most precise and perfect of high ecstasy restrained—what a sonnet could be, what it was meant to be, and what it sometimes even was, I was to learn.

She wrote about the sonnet's development from Petrarch, about the influence of authors she had read when young, of Emerson, Whittier, and Longfellow, for example, whom she had read only for the story,

with the exception of Hiawatha. . . . But I did not know that Longfellow was taken seriously by *anybody* as a poet. Not a line of his ever made my scalp tighten and my hair move upward on my head like the serpent-curls of Medusa. . . . For I never did believe, and never have believed a word he said. . . . And this has always made me feel sad, and, yes, more than a little treacherous, so deeply indebted to him am I for those happy hours in my earliest childhood, long before I could read . . . when my mother, sitting beside my bed after supper, in her black dress with its smoothly fitting bodice and its yoke, collar and cuffs of shining black jet, would read to me from Hiawatha or Evangeline. Sometimes on winter evenings she would read to me, or often recite from memory, for she knew, I think, the whole long poem by heart, the beautiful "Snowbound" of Whittier, and quite unconscious that I was doing so, I learned much of it by heart myself at this time, and still remember it. Until the day, much later, when I discovered for myself the exciting poetry of Emerson, I always considered Whittier by far the best of the New England poets.

Then she would veer off and begin on another tack, with pages of lists of writers who had influenced her—"Shakespeare—yes, Milton—no, Wordsworth—yes, George Meredith—yes, Arthur Ficke—yes, D. G. Rossetti—no (?)"—as well as that poet who "*would* have influenced me if I had read him. Gerard Manley Hopkins—same thing—did not know til circa 1935."

All the pages were akin to these. Millay would set an idea forth only to turn it aside, and no amount of piecing, turning, or recapitulation could make a coherent preface.

One night she stuck this desperate note under Eugen's bedroom door, asking him for help:

Attention
Snig, Esq.
Personal Somewhat
Important Maybe
Please Answer

I've spent so much time & strength writing pieces of prefaces about what I'm going to leave out and why, and what I propose to keep in and why,—that I've had no occasion to look over the book itself, and see *why* I'm omitting what I'm omitting, *if* I am omitting it—or *why* I am retaining, et cet. I've been trying so hard to write twenty different prefaces to this benighted book that I haven't the foggiest notion as to what the book will be composed of or whether or not it is fit to print.—This is where I stand—or, rather, lie prone, Sniggies!—Have you any suggestions?—I'm about baffled!—

> Love,
> me.

She was flummoxed. She knew it, and now so did Eugen, who finally wrote to Gene Saxton in an attempt to explain away her delay. She'd had the galleys since mid-May, and it was now August. In what had become a pattern with them, Eugen cloaked her inability to focus on her work by blaming illness and pain:

> I am sorry having to bring you some bad news.
> Edna will be unable to finish her introduction for her "Collected Sonnets." She has been working at it for several months and has all her material gathered and has written quite a lot of it. But, the last two weeks she has been very sick and unable to do anything. She just has to give up writing it. She is terribly unhappy about it, especially as she was really enjoying writing it. As it is, the physical exertion of writing even a half page makes her back ache so badly that it is impossible for her to continue.
> What she intends to do now is to write short notes or remarks explaining why the sonnets of "Conversation at Midnight" and most of the sonnets in "Make Bright The Arrows" are not included in this collection. This, however, could not be used as an introduction but will have to be added at the end of the book and called NOTES or REMARKS.

Finally Edna called Arthur Ficke for help. "Vincent has been fussing and stewing," Arthur wrote in his journal, "about a preface for her 'Collected Sonnets.' She finally got into a state of despair, and about two weeks ago sent for me to go over and see her. I found, to my horror, that she was trying to produce an elaborate . . . treatise on the sonnet."

Millay agreed to cut the preface. She would take Arthur's advice and write only a note with an explanation of why certain of her sonnets were not there. But she was still in a jam and could not write even this note, when she asked him to take over the whole editing. "So I spent 24 hours correcting the proofs. Yesterday I drove over, and explained all my suggested changes to her, and she accepted them. Last night I transferred the corrections to the publisher's copy of the proofs. And now they can be sent off."

Arthur saved her from her excesses. But he also kept her from publishing passages she'd written about what she thought sonnets were and about her own first literary sources and influences. When he tried to describe her character in his journal, he did not acknowledge his own competitiveness, her addiction, or the terrible pressure she was under because of her sister's needs and accusations. But he did help.

> She is the oddest mixture of genius and childish vanity, open mindedness and blind self-worship, that I have ever known. She lets me, as a fellowcraftsman, dissect her mistakes and scold her and make fun of her, because she feels perfectly safe in the fundamental admiration I have for her best work: but . . . She has built up so enormous an image of herself as the Enchanted Little Faery Princess that she must defend it with her life.

Barely a month before, when Witter Bynner was visiting Edna at Steepletop, Arthur was deeply hurt that Vincent had not invited him and wrote to tell her so:

> You know, Vince, there is a part of my nature which I cannot alter, *an utterly incurable sense of despair.* Perhaps I spread that horror to others; perhaps I blight and discourage you when I come into contact with you. I don't *mean* to do it—but perhaps I do it.

But he had rights in their friendship, too:

> I will not relinquish my right to keep on loving you. I shall not relinquish my rights to remember great poems, great letters, great moments of love. . . . I love you, my dear. I have always loved you. I always shall. One power can stop that—but it is not you.

A week later, on September 4, 1941, Ficke continued his almost obsessive notes about Millay in his private journal. He wrote that while she knew a great deal,

> of recent years, all her critical acumen has been swamped by waves of hysterical emotion. I wonder if perhaps she is having the menopause? . . . doubtless she would rather die than make this admission that she is growing older. She looks very old and worn sometimes: this is partly her illness. My God, I just looked up her age: she was born in 1892, so is only 9 years younger than I am—that is, she is 49. I do not think she realizes that at all.

Critical as he could be, he never doubted the power or the openness of her work:

> Vincent, especially, made girls feel that passion was clean and beautiful. . . . She appeared at a moment when American youth had need of her. . . .

[for] the lesson of beauty that she taught them: for the revolt she expressed was not merely away from a stuffy prison and also toward an open meadow. . . . there was an unmistakable wind of pure dawning in what she did.

Edna Millay was sharply aware of her declining critical reputation—how could she not be?—and of her aging. When Joseph Freeman and his wife were Arthur's weekend guests, Edna summoned Freeman to Steepletop. One of the founders in 1926 of *The New Masses,* Freeman was labeled a Communist, although he insisted, somewhat disingenuously, that he was a poet who happened to be interested in communism. Edna had not seen him since *Conversation,* when she had asked him to be the model for the young Communist, Carl. Freeman described his recollections of their meeting, and of Arthur's plan, sixteen years later in a letter to Floyd Dell:

> On the way to Austerlitz, Arthur explained to me that he was greatly concerned about Edna. She was suffering from *imaginary* backaches and ought to be psychoanalyzed; he had been analyzed and had been greatly benefitted; he had been urging Edna to go to an Analyst—but she refused; what he wanted me to do was to persuade her to go. But why should she listen to me? . . .
>
> At Austerlitz, Gene . . . handed us highballs, then told me that Edna was in her study and wanted to see me *alone.* I don't know why, but this embarrassed me. . . . it seemed to me that anything Edna had to say to me she could say and ought to say in front of Gene and Arthur; and I said so. Gene went in, spoke to Edna and came back: No, she had to see me alone. So I went in and there she was in a big armchair, pale and fragile . . . and her eyes were sad. She asked me to sit down and got to the point at once. Life had become unbearable; she was getting old. . . . She was losing her looks, she was losing her ability to write, her poems are no good any more, the young men no longer fall in love with her, life was not worth living. . . . As she spoke she began to weep—the tears rolled down her hollow cheeks.

Freeman couldn't bear to see a woman cry and began to console her. She was as beautiful as ever. How could young men help falling in love with her? When he told her that if he were young, he would fall in love with her,

> she began to smile and, while she insisted that she had lost her looks and the power to evoke love in young men and her poetic gift, she did not sound as earnest about it as before. . . . here, at her elbow, was her latest group of sonnets—and they were terrible, she could not bear to look at them.

They couldn't be bad, he told her,

and the fact is that for me that afternoon Edna *was* beautiful, and if I were younger, or perhaps simply unattached, I might . . . have fallen in love with her; and even without looking at her sonnets, I knew, knew absolutely they could not be bad. I asked her to read them; she said no, no, she couldn't; you read them. So I read one aloud; she listened with a strange light in her face; it was a beautiful poem and I said so, and tears came into her eyes, this time tears of joy . . . for being a fool, I thought it was more important for the ageless poet to know that her poetry was still beautiful than for the woman of fifty to have young lovers. Now Edna laughed—and now she was ready to read her poems aloud and when she read them they were even more beautiful—and the afternoon sun came in through the window and I was listening to a clear young voice and looking at a young beautiful face. When she was done reading, we kissed—not the kiss of Eros, the kiss of Agapé; warm, loving, and chaste. And she said, the others may come in. Arthur and Gene came in and I could see they were astonished and delighted that Edna was all smiles, all joy; and we had some drinks . . . and Arthur and I kissed Edna and shook hands with Gene and left Steepletop.

As they drove back, Arthur asked if Edna had agreed to go to an analyst. Caught in Edna's spell, Joseph Freeman had completely forgotten his task.

When Rolfe Humphries reviewed Millay's *Collected Sonnets* in *The Nation,* he damned her with faint praise:

Miss Millay's public has grown, unfortunately . . . to include collectors as well as readers; so there is always apt to be some fancy business, now, about her publications. This encourages skeptical criticism, and the fact that the direction of her progress has been from legend to success somewhat confuses discussion of her merit as an artist. If she is not taken quite seriously in this role today, it may be that she was taken too seriously twenty years ago . . . placing her out of her class, over her head, instead of keeping her where she really belonged, with Meredith, say, or as Elizabeth Barrett Browning's naughty younger sister in the parlor, the last of the female Victorians, and in that sense only, the herald of the Coming Woman.

PART TEN

THE DYING FALL

CHAPTER 38

Once there were three sisters, and the eldest, who had always been talented, was now rich and famous. The middle sister was as pretty, lighthearted, and lazy as she was without true ambition. But the youngest sister, while gifted—she had published two novels and three books of poems—sounded too much like her eldest sister for her own good, and nothing went right for her. There was a twist of envy that gnawed and grew in her as if it were malignant, until she became devious and ill.

Now, imagine this scene at Steepletop earlier in their lives. One sister, whose house it was, enters the room like a lion; she tosses her curly red mane, licks the inside of her wrist, draws it carefully over her ears as if it were a paw, and roars. The youngest enters the room like a Model T Ford, batting her eyes like headlights on bright, making a noise like a horn honking. Only one of the three sisters will survive to tell all the stories she knows, and that is the sister who now sits in the room, scooping out Stilton, drinking a scotch and soda while waving an Egyptian cigarette aloft, laughing, singing a snatch of song, and watching. She is the sister who tells the tales: Norma Millay.

In 1940, a friend of Norma's, an ardent collector of first editions and any rare Millayana she could find who had dealt for some years with a bookseller in Greenwich Village, gave Norma disturbing news: the bookseller had received a diary purportedly kept by Norma, Vincent, and Kathleen when they were children in Maine. It had been edited by Kathleen and sent to Macmillan for publication, "and will show," the friend continued, the early influences on Vincent during her formative years—especially the fact that much of Vincent's early poetry was derived from Kathleen whom she discouraged in any projects to write on her own, telling her that since she (Vincent) had had poems accepted by magazines, *she* was obviously the poet of the family and Kathleen would be better off helping her to get her poems in shape than wasting her time trying to write.

Surely, Norma thought, unless the entire story was a fabrication, no one had the right to publish such a diary without Edna Millay's consent.

Norma did not know that as early as 1936, well before any clear rift had opened between Vincent and Kathleen, Kathleen had submitted a peculiar entry to *Who's Who*. It was considerably longer than Edna's, and under "Author," where Kathleen's novels, *Wayfarer* (1926) and *Against the Wall* (1929), had been listed in order of their publication along with her three books of poetry—*The Evergreen Tree, The Hermit Thrush,* and *The Beggar at the Gate*—there followed a puzzling verse entry, *Of All the Animals,* with a 1932 publication date, as well as lists of "fairy stories" with titles and dates. But there is no record anywhere of these works' ever having been published in either magazine form or as books. Kathleen was embellishing— if not outright lying about—her achievements.

By 1940, Eugen no longer tried to conceal his disdain for Kathleen, who continued to ask for money. "You asked me whether I showed your letters to Edna," he wrote on December 12. "No.—Generally I do not.—You two are practically strangers.—in the 18 years I have known Edna, you two have met not more, I should say, than ten times and maybe exchanged 3 letters. I don't see why I should bother her now."

Eugen was interceding for Edna, and it was not helpful to either of the sisters for him to be placed so effectively between them. While his intercession seemed to protect Edna from Kathleen's wrath and jealousy, in fact it only intensified it.

As to myself, I really don't know you at all. I have met you a few times and am now in a lively financial correspondence with you.—But you know, of course, that if it was not for the fact that you are related to E., we, you and I both, would go out of our way to avoid each other.

Furthermore, we have been hearing for many years, reports from several people how you, either drunk or sober, talk about E. behind her back. This of course does not tend to make me either like or respect you and the effect on E. is to make her distrust any expression of friendship from you, although she has always wanted to be friends with you. But now that these reports keep coming in, even after she has done so very much to help you, the situation is even more difficult than ever. . . . Nevertheless for your Mother's sake & for the sake of when you [were] all young girls & used to sing songs together, which she still remembers with happiness, as you wrote sometime ago, you also do, she is very glad indeed to help you to the best of her ability, when you are up against it.

Eugen then wrote to Charlie, telling him to get from Kathleen a mahogany table, which had been Cora's, in exchange for a check for fifty dollars enclosed in his letter, to go toward Kathleen's debts, "that is if the bitch sticks to her word and sells it to us.—

"If she does not sell it then <u>don't</u> give her the check."

But Charlie was not a skillful messenger, and he wobbled. He didn't get the table, and he did give her the fifty dollars. Eugen's next letter to Kathleen showed barely controlled fury:

> I was pleased to hear from Charlie . . . that you are on your feet again and need not sell your table to pay your debts.—That is very good news indeed: now Edna need no longer keep borrowing money to pay your debts and can now stop supporting you.
>
> Charlie told me that you were going to write me all about it, but of course I did not expect to hear from you, as you never yet have written to acknowledge receipt of money from Edna but only to ask for more money or complain that the check you were expecting is a day or two overdue. Under the circumstances I do not understand why Charlie gave you my check for $50.00. But nevermind, you are welcome to it.

Kathleen wrote back a nine-page, single-spaced letter of hurt and recrimination. Not only had Charlie been sent to spy upon her, but she was homeless, hungry, ill, and broke, and Eugen's letter had nearly killed her.

> Silly and sentimental as it may seem to you—(who care nothing for anything but money and forwarding my sister's fame, because it is amusing to shine in the reflected glory and also doesn't take any energy)—difficult as it may be for you to realize . . . I have been very hurt to finally become convinced that my sisters care nothing for me at all. I loved them dearly as we grew up and fully believed they loved me. I worked for them, took care of them when they were ill, and used energy I could ill afford to throw away—as I was always the one who was really sick. . . . Strange as it may seem to you—I do not blame you for any of this. It was obviously quite settled and finished long before any of the family ever met you. You are a puppet floundering about in the midst of the Millays—and will never know what it is all about. They have strange temperaments indeed for the placid mind of a stolid Dutchman. However, it is not my fault I was born into the family, any more than it is your sagacity that made you chance to be born with the proverbial silver spoon in your mouth.

She couldn't stop:

And now you tell me my sister is actually borrowing money in order to live at the St. Regis—which, of course, has always been one of the absolute obligatory necessities and hangouts of poets since time began. And to give ambulances to dying soldiers—*such* charming publicity for any philanthropist, isn't it Eugen? And—incidentally—*only* incidentally—to buy very cheaply the one thing on earth I prize—a beautiful antique table which is the only thing I have from my mother. Of course, Edna has her big estate, and any number of things from mother—practically all the old dishes that had been in the family for years . . . and she's still *borrowing* money!

Her letter went on and on: Vincent had given Norma a piano and Charlie a car, whereas it was she, Kathleen, who had given their mother the cottage in Maine, in which after her mother's death she now owned only a one-third share. If she had to do it over again, she'd keep the cottage in Maine in her own name and simply let her mother use it the rest of her life. "She never had anything, and it was obvious no one else would give her anything—and at least it made her happy at the end of her life and that is what I did it for. Sentimental—? Yes. But not so stickily sentimental as the poem that paid Edna 1000 dollars for the Pulitzer prize!"

Then Kathleen made what she called a business proposition: she would give her sisters the first chance to buy her share in the cottage. She promised that after their business in this purchase was settled she would never try to reach them again, "unless it is necessary for legal reasons."

In the somber, careful draft of Eugen's reply—in which all the corrections and the softening of his language are in Edna's hand—he wrote:

I asked Edna whether she wished to buy your share in the cottage, and she said that she would rather, since you feel as you do about it—that it really belongs to you—give instead her share in it to you.—Norma feels the same way about it, and is also making over her share in it to you, in view of the way you feel about it.

Charlie would have a lawyer draw up a document and give her the keys. He had told Edna about the table, which he had intended to be a surprise present from him. "She told me that she would never want to take that away from you. So that's settled."

Kathleen said his letter had made her very happy. She asked him to thank "both girls for me, and please understand how I mean it when I say I sincerely hope I will never bother you anymore in any way."

A few months earlier, in the spring of 1941, Kathleen had written to a man who had presented himself as the director of the Manuscript Division of the Drake Memorial Museum in Pennsylvania. This same man had written to Edna six months earlier, asking for a longhand manuscript copy of "God's World," which, he said, was at the suggestion of the president of the United States. He had enclosed a copy of a letter from Miss LeHand, secretary to President Roosevelt. Eugen had answered his letter cordially, but nothing had come of it and their correspondence had stopped.

Kathleen, however, had responded vehemently, saying she was destitute. She said it was futile to ask her sister or Eugen for help.

> I have obvious reasons for hating the name under which I was born. It is nothing short of a curse. . . . I live alone. I have no money. . . . I realize there is no reason why one sister should care what happened to another. . . . if only there were no such things as wealthy Dutch brother-in-laws who could tell a million people how much he did for everybody while the everybody in question could only manage to reach a half dozen people . . . with the truth of starvation.

After receiving two such letters from Kathleen, the man wrote to Eugen, enclosing a copy of Kathleen's letter and threatening to publish it if Millay did not write out in longhand the poems he had asked for. Since he was using the mails to threaten and to defraud them, which was a federal offense, Eugen was able to have him arrested. *The New York Times* picked up the story and published Kathleen's accusations against her sister, while adding that the Boissevains had, in fact, been supporting her.

The young man turned out to be an unemployed grocery clerk with an appetite for embezzling and fraud. After this fiasco, there was no further correspondence between the sisters.

2

On June 10, 1942, the German government announced that it had razed the entire Czech village of Lidice to the ground. The village was suspected of sheltering the underground leaders who had assassinated SS-Obergruppenführer Reinhard Heydrich, a man so brutal his nickname was "The Hangman." The Nazis retaliated: they shot to death 173 men and boys, deported 203 women to the Ravensbruck concentration camp, and gassed 81 of the village's 104 children. The rest of the children were sent to orphanages or German families. Then the Nazis set fire to the houses and church until nothing was left standing. "Lidice, they proclaimed, was now forever erased from the map and the memory of the world."

When the outrage of Lidice reached America, Rex Stout, the president of the Writers' War Board, asked Edna Millay, whom he knew from their days in the Village, to write a poem to help ensure that Lidice would never be forgotten. By October she had finished "The Murder of Lidice," a long narrative poem that was broadcast over NBC on October 19 and short-waved to England and Europe. Spanish and Portuguese translations were beamed to South America.

Norma described in a letter to her sister how she had felt as she had waited alone for "The Murder of Lidice" to come on the radio at 10:30 that night: "When Woollcott's voice came on, it was trembling with nervous excitement—that seasoned old dear, too! I knew then that it was going to be something terrific and felt alright and settled back—and it was terrific. It wasn't just radio at all—it was alive."

Praise poured in from around the nation, and Millay's correspondence swelled. She was asked for another poem, to help rally the American public to the war effort on the home front. The Advisory Council of the Writers' War Board then asked her to speak on shortwave for three or four minutes to remind Americans of the English spirit on the second anniversary of the London air blitz.

Meanwhile, some of her friends were deeply critical of her war effort, perhaps none more so than Arthur Ficke, who scolded in his journal:

> Tonight Edna Millay's poem "The Murder of Lidice" is to be read over the radio. I have seen it in its fragmentary stages, when she was all confused about it. . . . I don't know how people manufacture such things. What worries me is that this is *so bad for her,* so utterly false to her real nature. . . .
>
> She has always required the center of the stage—but that was good for her, so long as it was *her own private drama* that was being enacted. As a lyric poet, she was superb, unsurpassable. . . . I cannot, I will not, believe that this war is an ultimate conflict between right and wrong: and though I do not doubt for a moment that we are less horrible than the philosophy and practice of Hitler, still I think we are very horrible: and I will not, I must not, accept or express the hysterical patriotic war-moods of these awful days.

It was astonishing that Millay was able to write at all, given the amount of drugs she was taking. She knew the risk to her reputation of writing propaganda. Even Rex Stout, a writer himself, although of immensely successful mysteries, conceded that she was opening herself up to negative criticism. "Well, of course, if a poet writes something for an intellectual reason, it is a different kind of writing entirely," he said. "We had asked her for a propaganda poem, a piece of propaganda. They're a different genre, and they're bound to be. . . . I think Edna was really bothered by what some goddamned critic wrote about her poem. She shouldn't have been capable of feeling, of reacting to what some literary critic who has never written a creative line in his life says. But she was, of course she was." Her sense of urgency was, in fact, prophetic.

We now know what no one in America knew then: that the Germans had actually filmed their eradication of Lidice as an instructive device, demonstrating to Nazi soldiers how to raze an entire village.

To Hal she later wrote that she was very busy: "yes, of course, writing more verses for my poor, foolish, bewildered, beloved country." But she wrote very little propaganda poetry after "Murder of Lidice." The poem "Not to Be Splattered by His Blood (St. George Goes Forth to Slay the Dragon—New Year's 1942)" had been written well before the outbreak of the war, she told him.

Norma had been in a difficult position in relation to her sister for some time. Kept increasingly at arm's length, she persisted in her attempts to reestablish their connection. "I've gotten a little selfconscious through the years at ringing the lovely Cuthbert from her tea to find out if-and-where you live," she wrote in a birthday letter in 1942. Her uneasiness toward Eugen was evident: "I'd send my love to Gene . . . if this wasn't a bit of business just between us girls. I send my love to you." There was often in her letters, alongside her ambivalence at being cut off, an admiration about which there was no equivocation: "Your sonnets in tetrameter have been very alive in this room over the last month. You are a great poet. And great poetry has great power."

Yet Norma's voice was not always so reassuring. Her concern for her sister's health was very real:

Listen Darlings—you *have* to get to New York City and right away quick. Don't laugh & think of the things in the way of such a move because I love you both & I know what I'm talking about. You'll have deep snow there any minute and you say there is no one there to help you and you are "two sick people." You can't *do* this. . . . (and, darling Gene, there is no reason why you should kill yourself & give out energy you need to help you recover) and if Vincent isn't able to travel normally—listen—really *listen*— before it snows you in—call a hospital in Hudson & get an ambulance with a doctor to *take* you into the city where, if anywhere, you can get help. . . . You understand I don't know your circumstances—I am not being pre- sumptuous, I just know & know terribly and cannot bear it that you must act *at once* & leave Steepletop.

"Your letter was something to lighten the heart," Edna wrote with clear emotion.

[A]lmost nobody it seems ever thinks—thinks deeply and intensely and in complete forgetfulness of himself—of any other person. We are all, or nearly all, of us, so centred in ourselves; we see nothing except as it touches ourselves, what its effect upon us might be. I know almost nobody who is really capable of complete forgetfulness of himself, even for a minute, in the troubles of another.—Which is why your letter, so full of thinking yourself into two other people's lives so empty of yourself, is such a lovely thing.

Do you know Christina Rossetti's "Goblin Market"?—Did we ever read it together?—I forget. It is the story of two sisters, one of whom cannot resist the calling of the goblins in the wood, to come and buy and eat the goblin fruit, and eats it, and goes mad, and is dying of longing to taste it again; and her sister goes to the wood and risks the loss of her own health and life to get some of the goblin's fruit to cure the one who is wasting away to death.

Vincent and Norma had read "The Goblin Market" together when Vincent, who had sent her a copy, had been at Vassar. If Christina Rossetti's poem is an analogy of the relationship between sisters, it was fascinating that Vincent should use it now. Surely it was she who was "dying" of her longing, her addiction to morphine, her appetite for a narcotic. Norma's letter was a response to Vincent's addiction. Vincent passed it off, admiring Norma's selfless concern while ignoring her plea that they get help "before it snows you in."

Who can tell how, privately, she may have taken Norma's warning? There is only one long letter in draft, unsent, written in fury and in haste after Millay had spent two hours at the Austen Riggs Clinic in Stockbridge, Massachusetts:

Me, with my Savile Row riding-breeches. . . . Me with my two Top Flight tennis racquets just *singing* for the court. . . . Me, who never show my face (or perhaps it's my figure) in New York without having at least four attractive men of my acquaintance dialing their 'phones, to take me out. . . . Me, to be stuck in a loony-bin with a contingent of bulging old biddies . . .

Me, with my old clothes by *Worth* and my new clothes by Bergdorf Goodman; me, with my tweeds by Henri's of Bond Street and my hostess gown by Jessie Turner, waddling and hissing out of the dining-room in mad haste . . .

Me, a busy woman like me, with a score of interests and a dozen occupations, me, speaking over short wave to England for the British-American

Ambulance Corps, me, speaking at dinner in the Waldorf ballroom for China Relief, me, up to the neck in work for the Office of Facts & Figures, the Red Cross, and a half dozen other organizations . . . sitting for two solid hours in your damned office . . . all because a little squirt of an M.D. in Great Barrington who wouldn't know whether a baby were coming head-first or feet-first has apparently got it into what he doesn't use in place of a head, that I am a congenital defective with criminal tendencies, an alcoholic, a drug-addict, and a generally undesirable member of our civic group! . . .

If I weren't mad enough to spit, I might be amused enough to laugh, and I dare say by this afternoon I shall be getting a good laugh out of it. . . . And the further insolence of all such institutions,—the unmitigated gall to assert that . . .

Here she breaks off, but the damage is done. Her protest is wildly out of proportion—undermining the impression she's trying to create of a healthy, attractive woman, too sought after, too elegant and revered—to what? "To be stuck in a loony-bin." Her clothes, her reputation, and her occupation with war work make her far too busy to deal with the disturbingly simple questions the young doctor has asked: Why can't she sleep at night? Why can't she remember where she put her hat and coat?

Her defense was to proclaim that the Riggs Foundation made her "sick enough to chuck up." It was "rank insolence." It was "unmitigated gall." It was "absurd." It was also terrifyingly true.

☙ ☙ ☙

When Norma realized that something was very wrong at Steepletop and offered to help, she learned that Eugen had joined Edna in taking morphine. "Gene was to meet me at the train station. I saw him. And it just came over me: What do I do? What does a decent sister do? I thought, will I have to kill him? You know, it just came over me. He couldn't see me. He couldn't even look directly at me. Then I knew. He was on it, too."

Norma described a scene in the front room at Steepletop when Edna threw her arms around her shoulders and said, "Oh, ours was just a childhood love." Norma pried her fingers loose. " 'Oh, sure,' I said to her, 'of course. Just childhood!'

"But there were locks on all the doors now. And there was nowhere we could just quietly sit together and talk without Gene's bursting in!

" 'Come on,' I said to Vincent. 'Let's go somewhere, anywhere, where we can talk.'

" 'We can talk here, sister,' she said. And then she just drifted off somewhere. Where I couldn't reach her. *I* couldn't reach her anymore! Do you understand that? What it means? Then I thought: Well, I could kill him. I could kill Gene."

☙ ☙ ☙

On September 21, 1943, weak and unable to eat, Kathleen entered St. Vincent's Hospital in Greenwich Village. A friend who went with her stayed throughout several hours of consultations and examinations. When the doctors couldn't discover what was wrong with her, they decided to take X rays. As she was being wheeled out of the X-ray room, Kathleen became unconscious. She died without regaining consciousness.

Because the cause of her death was unclear, Kathleen was taken to Bellevue Hospital for an autopsy. Norma, who had tried to talk to Vincent on the telephone about it, wrote to her afterward, "They found there that she died of acute alcoholism which is what is written on the death certificate." They found "her heart was normal," Norma said. "It is wonderful to know that no evil thing had started up again inside her. . . . I find I can't go on from here into other things I want to say—this is a little document that is ended."

The New York Times ran Kathleen's obituary on September 23, under a headline that dealt the final slight: "Kathleen Millay, Sister of the Poet."

The only signal of Edna's response to Kathleen's death came exactly one week later, when she and Eugen began the first of an astonishing series of notebooks. Written primarily in Eugen's hand, they provided a detailed record of the day, month, hour, and dosage of the drugs they were taking. They are among the most troubling and pitiful documents in American literary history.

The first notebook begins on Tuesday, September 28, 1943, and continues to Thursday, November 30. On the first day of their record keeping, "Vince," as Eugen called her, was taking what appears to be a total of 3 grains of morphine, starting at 7 A.M., then at 8:10, 9:20, 9:40, 10:30, 10:45, 12:45, 1, 2:15, 2:30, 3, 4, 5, 6, 7:15, 8:15, 9:30, 10:30, 12, 1, 1:30 A.M., when she finally sleeps. On September 29, she takes 3⅜ grains, the next day 2⅝. If the dosages in 1943 were the same as they are today, 65 milligrams equals 1 grain (an initial 10 milligrams of morphine might reasonably be used to lessen the pain of a cancer patient). Edna Millay was taking an average of 195 milligrams a day.

"Never since I first began taking it have I felt so free of it, both mentally & physically, as today," she noted on October 18 alongside her chart. Eugen's hand added a more sinister note: "during day 4 nembutal lots of codeine." Nembutal is an analgesic barbiturate that makes one sleep. She was taking it as well as morphine; Benzedrine, which is an upper; and codeine, a narcotic for the relief of pain. She was, in other words, taking a cocktail of drugs, some contradictory in their effects but all of which must have left her ravaged.

There are strange notes in her hand: "What happened to that other ⅛ grain? Did it leak out?—they sometimes leak. I feel *sure* I didn't take it. (Later) evidence. It leaked. The codeine hypo did the same thing. They had both been left slanting downward." At the bottom of this page, in an apparent effort to account for the number of drugs she was taking, she wrote that it "is too much, but not discouraging, considering how many different kinds of pain I have."

She was making some attempt to lessen her dependence on morphine. Near the end of October, a Dr. Cassel's name is written in the index for the day before "insulin trial." While the amount of insulin would double and more codeine be added, together with nervosine, which, she wrote, was an "anti-jitters" medication, pints of ginger ale, and more Nembutal, the amount of morphine doesn't seem to lessen.

On November 12, she made the following note to herself:

Awake all night with sore throat:—no *fair!*—Last week it was a burned finger; the week before a sprained knee!—How am I to give up morphine when I need it all the time for one darned thing after another? It must be hard enough when it's just a habit!—everybody says it is—everybody says it's impossible, unless you go to a hospital and have nurses injecting insulin & hyoseine into you all day long!

According to her own notations, Millay was taking drugs the full twenty-four hours of the day. She no longer paused to sleep.

1.—(A.M.)	2	1.45	2
4.—	1	2.50	1
5.30	1	5.00	1+
6.15	1	6.20	1
6.20	2	8.20	1
9.00	2	8.50	2
11.—	1	10.00	2
12.30	2–	10.45	2
		12.15	1
		12.45	1

A few days after this, she fell sick. It may have been then that Eugen called for Norma. On November 6 and 7, he had written in his own notebook, "Misery loss of courage."

—

Norma was unaware of these drug notebooks at that time. When Eugen summoned her to Steepletop that Thanksgiving, she went as quickly as she could. "Gene called me because he needed me," she wrote Vincent afterward,

> and, at first, we were almost getting somewhere—I wish it could have gone on but after a night's sleep he got back in his stride and was belittling and unfriendly. He not only didn't speak to me but couldn't look at me. That was, of course, silly and not very helpful. If ever I saw anyone who needed help he did, and I couldn't help because he wasn't going to let me anymore. He said I mustn't walk in on you anymore because you might be crying—all right—if you were crying that was just when I would care to look in on you—just when I *should* look in. I'm interested in why you must be crying. I'm sure I could *do* something about it. But his old jealousy cropped up.

Here the undated letter—which may never have been sent—broke off without a signature, and another, much longer letter began. Protective of Edna or controlling, Eugen was very much resented by Norma. The postman had just arrived with a letter from Eugen saying that Norma's proposed trip back to Steepletop "for a week, six weeks ago, is not feasible." "Now *there's* a bit of typical Steepletop that gets me into my subject nicely," Norma wrote. Once again, Eugen was fending off a sister. But this sister wanted to help. The crucial thing is that Vincent, while staying offstage and protected, was always at the center of the drama. Norma's letter continued:

> It seemed impossible to me, you see, that you could be up there sick so long and really believe nothing could be done to stop your menopause distresses. You talk of black moods and hot flashes as though nothing could be done about them. That isn't true. . . . Some research was done and a paper made of it for me on menopause and I also have notes on drug habituation.

Norma enclosed four and a half single-spaced pages of notes drawn from medical sources that she listed on the last page as a sort of bibliography, and waited for a reply.

About this time, Norma heard from Ann Eckert, a friend of Kathleen's and the beneficiary of her will. Kathleen had wanted their mother's manuscripts to go to the Morgan Library in New York, and Miss Eckert, who had contacted the library, said it seemed very interested.

Then the little cottage, about which I have had to write to England to Kathleen's husband Howard, she wanted to give to me as you know. I am deeply touched by all this, and deem it the biggest compliment. . . . Perhaps this Spring we could go to Kathleen and plant an Evergreen tree there for her. She loved them so very much.

Norma sent a copy of Eckert's letter to Vincent, along with the letter she had written in reply. In closing, she said she was eager to hear from her sister about her letter "and my plan for you to get helped onto your feet." "I have learned in a general and impersonal way," she wrote, "that many amazingly prominent persons have gone to New York Hospital with the understanding that they didn't wish it to be 'News' and that no bit of knowledge of their presence there has ever leaked out." She assured Vincent that she'd have the personal care of a certain doctor "and be his private patient because the climacteric (do I *kill* you, sister) is his particular field." She said, discreetly, that "anything else that might be bothering you can be cleared up at the same time. . . . I want so to have a very well and strong sister that I hope I'll be hearing from you soon." She was clever enough to send her love "to you and to Gene . . . I hug you both."

Eugen's response was made to Charlie. Norma's letter had bothered Edna considerably, he said, and while she wanted to respond to "certain assertions and opinions of Norma's," she found it difficult to write.

> . . . am writing to you because you are a correspondent after my own heart, who does not like to answer letters, so there is a good chance that this will be the end of this kind of correspondence.
>
> I mentioned several times to Edna to ask her sister Norma to come and help us for a week. She was not very enthusiastic about it because Norma generally spends so much time telling Edna how she must feel about things and what she ought to have done in the past and what she ought to do in the present and the future and tires her so much. I had spoken a couple of times with Norma over the telephone and received a few letters in which she seemed to me to be more mellow and quiet and I made some inquiries from somebody who had seen her last summer sometime and who had told me that she had changed quite a lot. . . . So we took a chance. . . . I telephoned Norma to find out whether she was well enough and strong enough to come here to help us. . . . Then, to my surprise, that same evening she telephoned me back that she was leaving that noon. I did not want her to come just then but I thought it was possible this was the only time she could come and so you both arrived here. The first night everything went well but after you left everything went wrong. I think, through a misunderstanding on Norma's part, she thought she was asked to come here to make a diagnosis of Edna's case and that she came here as

an M.D. and a psychiatrist, whereas, I had hoped she would come here as a mother's helper to cook and help clean the house and look after Edna, none of which she did. She did upset Edna quite a lot by complaining about me and lecturing her on this, that and the other thing.

Whatever Edna may have felt is described only through Eugen's words. He made, in this letter, no effort to disguise his contempt for Norma's feelings. He had asked Norma

not to come barging into Edna's bedroom without knocking. The trouble here is that Norma thinks there is a great intimacy between Edna and herself, which certainly has not been the case for the thirty years that I have known Edna. It is possible that many years ago they were intimate but now the only thing that binds them is the memory of a common childhood several decades ago. If Norma would treat both Edna and myself as acquaintances whom she does not know very well I think that lots of friction would be avoided.

Edna was apparently furious that Norma had consulted doctors without her permission or request. According to Eugen, they had been to "in the last three years by actual count twenty-nine doctors . . . and been to six hospitals," so they knew at first hand any kind of information a doctor could give. "In the meantime, I hope that if we see Norma again it will be on the footing of people who would like to have the other person like them and show their best side the way one does with people you are not very intimate with but would like to have like you."

A copy of this letter, written on Steepletop stationery and dated March 7, 1944, was in the files at Steepletop, left unsigned. Why hadn't Edna interceded on her sister's behalf? For as bossy as Norma could be, there is no doubting her love.

3

If Vincent and Eugen's effort to track their addictions with a close record was intended to diminish their reliance on drugs, they had clearly failed: the notebooks continued with a few breaks until July 24, 1944. On the twenty-seventh, Edna entered Doctors Hospital in New York City under the name of Mrs. Boissevain. Mary Halton was her doctor (she had also been Kathleen's), and Dr. Foster Kennedy, a distinguished neurologist, was called in as attending consultant. The diagnosis was "nervous exhaustion & neuritis." Dr. Halton gave Millay's general medical history:

Patient began to be nervous about 10 years ago—periods became scant & began missing—was treated on and off with ovarian extract—nine years

ago became despondent—began to take some drinks of alcohol bever-
ages—more than ever before—

Eight years ago was thrown out of an automobile—shoulder became
painful—was given much morphine and other sedatives from this time
on—x-rays were negative—nerves were injected with "novocain"—
abdominal pain came on—was operated on "for adhesions."

The pain in the shoulder region had then shifted to her lower back and
was now more generalized. She had come to dislike food, had a poor
appetite, and felt pain when she was nervous. ". . . unable to sleep and
takes morphine and luminal sodium . . . by hypo—also takes nembutal—
Has also taken demerol—is unable to work—"

At this time, she was drinking gin every day, usually mixed with ginger
ale. She was in a terrible state, crying about her inability either to sleep or
to work.

The nurses' reports recorded the agony she was suffering as her dosage
of morphine was reduced from ¼ grain, or 15 milligrams, to ⅙ grain, or 10
milligrams. On August 3, 1944, 5 A.M.: "awakened cheerful. Very happy to
think she only had three doses of morphine." But after an injection at 7
A.M. and another at 11 A.M., thirty minutes later she was crying with pain.
At noon her doctor visited her.

She was given morphine again at 6 P.M., at 8:30, and at 10:15. She was
also given sleeping medication. "Had a much better day," the nurse
reports. "Resting in bed—less depressed today." But she was still complaining of severe pain in her back.

By August 6, she was crying hysterically. "Very much disturbed," the
nurse reports. "Dr. Kennedy visited. Complaining of severe pain running
and staggering about room."

Over the next two weeks she continued to complain about pain and
remained "restless and nervous." Sometimes she seemed disoriented and
confused. She never slept for long. By the end of the third week of August
she was free of morphine. She was still receiving other medication, and
quite a lot of it, but not morphine. Then the nurses' reports pick up again:

August 23, 1944: Rolling about bed—beating with hands. Crying with
pain. Very dramatic in trying to show nurse how intense the pain is. No
effect from medication. Still noisy and complaining of intense pain.

They gave her what was called a sterile hypo, a shot with nothing in it,
a placebo. It had no effect. Then she was given an injection of Luminal, a
barbiturate, and for the first time in her entire hospitalization she slept
from 11 P.M. until 6:35 A.M.

August 28, 1944: 7 p.m. Drowsy & depressed, talks to nurses. "I foolishly tried to run out of the hospital in my nightgown," moaning, "Oh, what a disgrace to be here." "Oh, why did I come here." Very dramatic, said, "When one has sunk so low, even as I there is no hope." Told nurse "You must give me all you can" (sedatives).

On August 29, in the morning, she awakened at four and had hot tea. She was still not sleeping well. She was "elated & noisy—singing." Later in the morning she told the nurse she wanted "something to pull herself together."

She was discharged just under one month later, on September 27. While it looked as if the doctors had managed to wean her from morphine by substituting other drugs, she continued to smoke and drink, and the progress report was ominous: "Patient discharged. Still an alcoholic— initial condition unimproved. Diagnosis—exhaustion????"

Among her notes scribbled in pencil at Steepletop, there's one with the initials "N.Y.R." (New Year's Resolutions?); at the top of the first page, Edna wrote:

1. Care for *Nothing* so much, (after your poetry) as to make You– Know–WHO(m) happy. Put everything from your mind but this, and your work. (And what's more, *keep* everything else but these two things out of your mind!)
2. *Never* mention yourself, if possible to avoid it, *especially* before YOU–KNOW–WHO(m). *Never* bring the conversation round to yourself, *even for a minute, even to illustrate a point,* or in a brief paren- thesis, to show that you understand what YOU–KNOW–WHO is saying. *Never* mention anything from your past, any incident of your childhood. Forget that *you* exist.
3. —Go out of doors EVERY DAY, no matter *What* you are working on, for at least a short walk.

You-Know-Who is Eugen. The relationship between them had turned into a destructive dependence. Now there were other notes, pages of them, with strange drawings of her own face in a grimace, of a heart pierced by an arrow with drops of blood spilling into the text.

Things I *must* do for Eugen, if I truly love him,—and I *do,* more than any- body ever loved anybody.

1. Even if I am suffering TORMENT, speak in a voice with *no hint* of pain, speak in the strong, gay rich voice he loves, the voice of a person vitally interested in things, deeply amused by and full of laughter at other things, even when I don't care *anything* about *anything*. . . . *DON'T WHINE!*—Never, even when you are dying, if you are still conscious, permit yourself to speak in a *SICK VOICE!* CRY AS LITTLE AS *POSSIBLE!* BUT *NEVER* WHINE!!!

The italics and the capitals are all hers. There were the following instructions: to pull herself up by her bootstraps, to disguise her feelings, to smoke and drink very little "When Ugin is in the room"; not to bite her fingernails; to let Eugen find her outdoors "instead of *Still in Bed,* or in your *SPECIAL CHAIR* (Pah!—Old Woman!)" These pages, too, are accompanied by a macabre drawing of her face. It is hideously emblematic of how she feels she must behave toward Eugen. The upper part of the face is masked and blackened in pencil so that only the tip of her nose and a painted grinning slash of mouth show. Across the place where her eyes would be runs the phrase, like a banner, "KEEP THE CORNERS OF YOUR MOUTH *U P* AND *DISGUISE* YOUR F E E L I N G S !" There is also a page, startling to find, labeled *"Advice to Little Nancy"*:

Exercise will-power in *all* things, big or little. Don't become self-indulgent. Don't become sloppy in *anything,* in your thinking, in your dress, in *anything.* Don't fool yourself. If you feel nervous, don't purposely (half-subconsciously) make yourself *more* nervous. Instead, turn your attention at once upon something which interests you. . . . Have a drink, sometimes. *Never* let the other person see you using the hypodermic, or know that you are about to do so, or have just done so.

Never leave the syringe about where you see it.

In February 1945, just before her fifty-third birthday, Millay entered the Hartford Institute of Living to try another cure. Eugen stayed in New York City with Margaret Cuthbert and Alice Blinn, who remembered, "He really got sick and was in the hospital for a few days. We kept that from Edna, of course, and the doctor told us, or told him anyway, that he had a spot on his lung. Did he do anything about it? No, he was busy taking care of Edna. Of course we thought it was tuberculosis."

She also described a scene that confirmed Norma's suspicion: "Eugen took morphine so that he would know what it was like for her to be addicted—so that he would know what she went through trying to stop it. . . ."

"But you know, when he was with us, he came out of the bathroom one morning and he said, 'The only boring thing is, your nose runs while you are shaving. Well, at least Edna doesn't have to shave.' You see, he'd flushed all of it down the toilet! . . .

"Of course he was not addicted for as long a time as Edna was, so perhaps it was easier for him. But there was no fuss about it. He simply stopped.

"Hartford was a disaster. After the Hartford episode, Eugen simply had to get her out of there."

Millay felt incarcerated and was desperate to leave. At first her letters to Eugen, especially one written on Valentine's Day, when he had sent her flowers, seemed resigned to making the best of the situation. But after less than a month, she begged him to get her out.

4

In the summer of 1945, with the war in Europe at last over, Edna and Eugen left for Ragged Island, where they had decided to try their own cure. On the way they planned to spend the night with Tess Adams at her house on Bailey's Island, which faced Ragged. Tess had invited Vincent Sheean and his wife, Dinah, for the weekend they would arrive. Vincent Sheean wrote about their meeting in his book *The Indigo Bunting,* a memoir Cass Canfield persuaded him to write.

"Toward the end of the afternoon the Boissevains arrived from Steepletop in a car loaded down with all sorts of food, pots and pans and other necessities for their stay on Ragged Island," he wrote. They had tea in the great room facing the ocean, where there was always a fire in the immense stone fireplace. "Our conversation was lively, but Edna took very little part in it. She said enough to show that she was with us, although nothing more; she was rather silent and looked very frightened, small, and withdrawn." She was, Sheean wrote, going through a bad time, the worst a writer could go through: "She could not write." Sheean was still too much frightened of her to address any remark in her direction.

Miss Millay was, to put it bluntly, a frightening apparition to many of us. Her temperament was so variable that it was impossible to tell what mood might overwhelm her next. . . . But most of all, I think, the reason why even the most sympathetic stranger was frightened of Edna was that she was herself so terrified. Her terror communicated itself and created terror. I hardly dared to look at her more than once or twice that evening.

Eugen, of course, knew all about this. That is probably why he was so jovial, talkative, and merry at tea and afterward, to save Edna . . . from the pain of speech.

None of them, with the single exception of Eugen, had any true idea what was the matter with her.

Sheean was left alone on the terrace with Edna as the others went off to see about dinner. It was getting dark, the fog was closing in; they were silent while Edna sat looking out to sea. "Then she said, in her deep voice . . . 'Thank you for the roses. They lasted a long time.' " Sheean, startled, had no idea what she meant. He hadn't sent her any roses. In the morning Edna and Eugen left before he was up, leaving word with Tess that they were all invited to visit Ragged Island soon.

Two months later, in September, they did. Eugen picked them up in their motor dory, the *Greasy Joan,* and set out into the open Atlantic, four miles from the coast of Maine. Forty-five minutes later they coasted into anchor at Ragged, where Edna appeared in a white shirt, her dungarees rolled to the knee, as she ran down the rocky path to meet them. Sheean would never forget this sight of her:

> There were circling round and round her head all the way down through the rocks, three sea gulls. She came toward us, as you might say, in a completely legendary manner. . . . She was glowing with health and spirits; her red hair was blown free and her green eyes were shining. She was in every respect different from the mouselike stranger of two months before.

Their house, set on a hill overlooking the rocky little harbor, was simple and bare: a table and chairs, a couple of beds, and books. There was no electricity. They fell asleep when it was dark and rose at first light. Behind the house were woods; out front, a great iron pot for boiling lobsters. "When she thought it was time, it was Edna who tossed the lobsters into the pot. . . . It was the only time I ever saw her do any cooking (if that is cooking)."

She told him she was in trouble: "I haven't been able to write anything at all for a long time. . . . It sometimes seems to me that it is all over—that it will never come again." When Sheean tried to suggest that casting her writing into prose might be a release for her, she said it was difficult. " 'It isn't for me,' she said slowly, as if thinking aloud. 'I'm afraid of it.' "

> Edna spent long periods at a time in the water; she was part mermaid, apparently, and was quite insensible to cold or to fatigue in water; she always swam naked. . . . Eugen was less thoroughly a sea child and during her incredible durations in the water he would be setting lobster pots or bringing in the lobsters, cleaning up the house or repairing nets for fishing. . . . "Nobody ever wears a bathing suit at Ragged Island," she said decisively when we arrived at the harbor. "It's a rule of the island. We think bathing dress of any sort is indecent, and so do the waves and so do the sea

gulls and so does the wind. No bathing dress has been seen on Ragged Island since we came here."

Eugen, naked, looked powerful, the color of mahogany, while Edna was softer, "nut-brown color." "Emerging from the sea at last, dripping and with green eyes ashine, she seemed to have regained some particular strength from the long immersion."

Dinah Sheean had admired Millay's poetry from her childhood and now watched her intently as the poet talked and swam: "She had passed that obvious stage of beauty in a woman's life. Of course there are women of seventy who keep themselves, in a way. She was not like that. She was attractive, certainly. She was a little bit pouchy then. And she didn't bear any signs of making that effort.

"Eugen had the quality of making a woman feel marvelous," Dinah said. "He seemed genuinely to like women. There are not so many who do, you know. Oh, the concentration he had for you. And a sort of warmth." Then Vincent Sheean suddenly remembered the roses. He'd signed the card sending the roses to her five years before, when on the occasion of the China Relief at the Waldorf-Astoria Edna had been forgotten in the melee.

Yet Millay was not in fact well. If she hadn't drunk wine with the Sheeans on Ragged Island, she certainly did when she got home to Steepletop, where she knew Arthur Ficke lay dying of cancer of the throat at Hardhack. Arthur had asked Ugin to tell him "very briefly, on paper" just how much morphine he took per day. "2 grains," Ugin wrote. "At less bad times, how much could you get on with?" Eugen said ½ grain, and while Arthur asked the same two questions of Vincent's dosages, Ugin left those spaces blank. Arthur added, "in my case, the matter of habit-forming is scarcely of importance; for not even the merriest ironic joker would suggest that I shall be alive for a very long time."

It was Arthur's habit to keep a sort of chronology of his life, which he appeared to have begun in 1941 and called his "Memorandum of Dates." For 1945 he noted, "I still very sick. Gladys cooks for me! Death of F. D. Roosevelt. Unconditional surrender of Germany. Back to Hillsdale in May. . . . I grow steadily worse. There is no hope now—and I care less than might be expected."

In October 1945, Edna sent him the letter he had been longing to have from her. She told him that the sonnet he'd asked her about years before in the gun room of the LaBranches' estate—when she'd been so angry with him for having asked her whether or not it had been written to him—*was* his.

> And besides, you sprang the question on me so suddenly . . . that it almost caught me off guard. And I loathe being caught off guard; it makes me furious. (A devil's trick that is of yours, too, Angel-in-all-else.)
>
> Perhaps, also, I didn't want you to know, for sure, how terribly, how sickeningly, in love with you I had been.
>
> And perhaps, also, I was still in love with you, or I shouldn't have cared.
>
> Well, anyway. The sonnet was the one beginning: "And you as well must die, beloved dust." In case you've forgotten. Which you haven't.
>
> Vincie

Arthur Davison Ficke died on November 30, 1945. Standing in the dark, wet day by his grave at Hardhack, Edna recited her poem to him:

> And you as well must die, belovèd dust,
> And all your beauty stand you in no stead;
> This flawless, vital hand, this perfect head,
> This body of flame and steel, before the gust
> Of Death, or under his autumnal frost,
> Shall be as any leaf, be no less dead
> Than the first leaf that fell,—this wonder fled,
> Altered, estranged, disintegrated, lost.
> Nor shall my love avail you in your hour.
> In spite of all my love, you will arise
> Upon that day and wander down the air
> Obscurely as the unattended flower,
> It mattering not how beautiful you were,
> Or how belovèd above all else that dies.

CHAPTER 39

The month after Arthur's death that winter, Edna Millay wrote out what she called her last will and testament. Her hand was wildly uneven and downward-slanting.

> *Steepletop Dec. 30th, 1945* . . . I wish to leave everything of which I die possessed, to my husband, Eugen Boissevain. If it were legally possible (which

probably it is not) I should like (in the case that the decease of my husband concurs with, or follows soon after, my own) to leave all the property of which I may die possessed, to my sister, Norma Millay (Ellis).

Edna St. Vincent Millay

I want all those things which are in the dining-room and which we bought or procured for our Dutch relatives to go to Holland. And I want the necklace which Elinor Wylie gave me to go to Rosemary Benét— E. St. V. M.

Norma thought the phrase that Eugen's death might "concur with" or follow Edna's own suggested they were planning a joint suicide. Things were very dark now at Steepletop, and within six weeks of writing her will, on February 6, 1946, Edna Millay was again admitted to Doctors Hospital for what was called "recurrent depression." She arrived with Eugen, so unsteady on her feet that she staggered. She was unable to undress by herself, and the nurse who helped her noticed the unmistakable odor of alcohol on her breath. She was given Luminal Sodium and Ovaltine when she arrived, a barbiturate and a nice cup of hot chocolate, comforting and sedating. She insisted that Luminal was the only medication that made her sleep, but even with the Luminal she moved restlessly from her bed to her chair and back again, smoking constantly, talking continuously, and drinking steadily—a martini before lunch and another before dinner, as well as a bottle of red wine, which she said the doctor had permitted her.

When Eugen came to visit, there was an observable change in her mood: she was agitated, and she gave way to pouting and tenseness. There was also a good deal of weeping. In his company she seemed reduced to being childish and petulant. She did not talk about her writing or her life, except on the day before her fifty-fourth birthday, which she passed in the hospital. She was awake between 12 and 4:30 A.M., and, considerably agitated, she told a nurse that she'd never get well or rested in the hospital. One of the nurses said her mannerisms were childish and that when she was discouraged she cried, "then she made prompt right-about turn & was all right."

There was no mention of morphine in her medical records or in the nurses' reports, and a month later, on March 8, she was discharged as "symptom free."

That summer, after she emerged from the hospital, Millay revived her lapsed correspondence with Edmund Wilson, who had written years earlier to tell her how much her recordings of her poetry meant to him. She said that his "verdict was like an Imprimatur to me." She told him his letter had come to her while she was in Doctors Hospital, where she was enjoying there a very handsome—and, as I afterwards was told, an all but life-size—nervous breakdown. For five years I had been writing almost nothing but propaganda. And I can tell you . . . there is nothing on this earth which can so much get on the nerves of a good poet, as the writing of bad poetry. Anyway, finally, I cracked up under it.

She did not tell him she had been addicted to morphine. That stigma was too sharp; she admitted only to a breakdown.

It is sheer desperation and pure panic—lest, through my continued silence, I lose your friendship, which I prize. . . . I think, and I think it often, "Where ever he is, there he still is, and perhaps some day I shall see him again, and we shall talk about poetry, as we used to do."

She told him that, having been unable to write during the period of her breakdown, she had begun to memorize great amounts of poetry—long, difficult poems, Matthew Arnold's "Scholar Gypsy," Keats's "The Eve of St. Agnes" and "Lamia," one third of Father Hopkins's poetry, Shelley's "To the West Wind" and "Hymn to Intellectual Beauty"—"Anyway, I have them all now. And what evil thing can ever again even brush me with its wings?"

She began to write again. It was as if a black cloth had been lifted from her, and in the fall of 1946, the spring and summer of 1947, she published "Ragged Island," "To a Snake," and the sonnet "Tranquility at length, when autumn comes," each a fully achieved, masterly poem.

> Tranquility at length, when autumn comes,
> Will lie upon the spirit like that haze
> Touching far islands on fine autumn days
> With tenderest blue, like bloom on purple plums;
> Harvest will ring, but not as summer hums,
> With noisy enterprise—to broaden, raise,
> Proceed, proclaim, establish: autumn stays
> The marching year one moment; stills the drums.
> Then sits the insistent cricket in the grass;
> But on the gravel crawls the chilly bee;
> And all is over that could come to pass
> Last year; excepting this: the mind is free
> One moment, to compute, refute, amass,
> Catalogue, question, contemplate, and see.

Sometimes it was in Eugen's hand, writing for her in her notebooks, that she worked out a sonnet like this superb one:

I will put Chaos into fourteen lines
And keep him there; and let him thence escape
If he be lucky; let him twist, and ape
Flood, fire, and demon—his adroit designs
Will strain to nothing in the strict confines
Of this sweet Order, where, in pious rape,
I hold his essence and amorphous shape,
Till he with Order mingles and combines.
Past are the hours, the years, of our duress,
His arrogance, our awful servitude:
I have him. He is nothing more or less
Than something simple not yet understood;
I shall not even force him to confess;
Or answer. I will only make him good.

The "sweet Order" is of the sonnet, emblematic not only of shapely discipline but of her own terrible struggle.

Edna and Eugen spent that summer on Ragged Island, where she
underwent their own form of therapy, which seemed to consist of spending hours floating in the icy water of the Atlantic. She thrived on it. There
is only this one letter from her to Eugen written then:

> The House, Ragged Island
> September
> You have just gone down to the harbour again. It seems really only a
> moment since we both came up from the harbour, you drenched to the
> skin, I shining and excited almost to—what is the French word?— . . . what
> the hell is it?—anyway, watching it, at a safe distance until you called me to
> help you with the ropes (and what a silly knife you have, it doesn't cut at
> all . . . I could have done better with my teeth). . . . Darling, come up from
> the harbour—the sea is making. . . .
> Don't go out, please.
> We have everything here. There's no need to tackle it. . . .
> Meen Liefje:
>   Ik gaar naar top-side.
>   Misschien slaap ik.
>   Misschien niet.
>   Oy sey nooit t'hius.
> [Dearest:
>   I'm going topside.
>   Maybe I'll sleep.
>   Maybe not.
>   You are never home.]

When they got back to Steepletop, they marked her recovery by hanging the American flag from the windows above the entrance to Steepletop
and sending a snapshot of it to Margaret Cuthbert, as they had promised
they would.

But she had recovered. She was no longer dependent upon morphine,
but she was not entirely well. She continued to drink (there was a small
mountain of whiskey bottles left on Ragged Island); she certainly took far
too many barbiturates; and no one yet knew the destructive interactions
among the sorts of drugs she was relying upon.

Harper, now in the person of Cass Canfield—for Millay's beloved editor,
Gene Saxton, had died suddenly in the summer of 1943—continued to
advance her $250 a month while pressing her for another book. How
about an edition of her collected dramatic works? She refused in a long
letter, explaining, "The effect of writing so much propaganda during the
war—from the point of view of poetry, sloppy, garrulous and uninte-
grated—is to make me more careful and critical of my work even than I
formerly I was, so that now I write more slowly than ever. But there will
be a book."

The following year, 1948, when she was again pressed by her publishers,
and again refused, she teased Harper's distinguished director of production, Arthur Rushmore, whose suggestion that she bring out a volume of

The Love Poems of Edna St. Vincent Millay, containing a 'mellow Foreword in retrospect' in which she confides to the public 'when, where, and
under what impulsion' (the italics are mine [Millay's]) these poems were
written, leaves me strangely cold.

(I did get a grin out of it, though. Pretty hard put to it, weren't you,
dearie, to say it with flowers, and yet say it?)

She didn't doubt that it would, as he said, win her new readers. "People
who never in all their lives, except when in school and under compulsion,
have held a book of poems in their hands, might well be attracted by the
erotic autobiography of a fairly conspicuous woman, even if she did write
poetry." But they were not the readers whose esteem she prized. And even
he, she told him, "with all your exquisite skill, could not make charming
the indelicacy of such a foreword—as you suggest." With wry good humor
she told Canfield, "Trusting, however, in closing, that for one year more it
may be said of me by Harper & Brothers, that although I reject their proposals, I welcome their advances."

Millay was nonetheless vexed by her continued dependence on her publisher for money. As early as July 27, 1944, she had written Cass Canfield, "You can't go on grub-staking me for ever. For that is more or less what it amounts to." All she'd written was war poems with very little about anything else.

> And such as there might be, would not be good, not first-class.
>
> And I can't have that. I can't bring out a book of lyrics, not after all I've written, in which there are just merely here and there a good line. I'd considerably rather die.
>
> But dying is really rather hard, you know. Not for oneself, I mean; that's comparatively easy: just get things all neatened up, and then go ahead and do it. No. It's the other people. They hang on to one so.

But Harper did continue to stake her, and to everyone's delight, in the spring of 1945 there was an Armed Services Edition of her *Lyrics and Sonnets,* with a proposed printing of 140,000 copies.

When Canfield returned to New York from his work for the Office of War Information in France, he wrote to Millay telling her that it had been pointed out that in Sonnet XIV in "Epitaph for the Race of Man," the name Aeolus should be Ixion. "Apparently it was Ixion who, for an insult to Hera, was punished by being tied to a wheel that turned perpetually. Would you want us to make this change?" he innocently asked.

For a woman who insisted to her dearest friends that she was unable to write letters, that it was a disease for which she had invented a word, "epistolaphobia," Millay answered Canfield in an astonishing five-page letter of splendid invective:

> It occurs to me with something of dismay, that, if I were dead—instead of being as I am, alive and kicking, and I said *kicking*—the firm of Harper & Brothers . . . might conceivably, acting upon the advise of a respected friend, alter one word in one of my poems.
>
> This you must never do. Any changes which might profitably be made in any of my poems, were either made by me, before I permitted them to be published, or must be made, if made at all, someday by me. Only I, who know what I mean to say, and how I want to say it. . . . no other person, could possibly lay hands upon any poems of mine in order to correct some real or imagined error without harming the poem more seriously than any faulty execution of my own could possibly have done. . . . I am speaking of poetry composed with no other design than that of making as good a poem as one possibly can make, of poetry written with deliberation and under the sharp eye of an ever-alert self-criticism, of poetry in other words, written with no ulterior motive, such as, for instance, the winning of a world-war to keep democracy alive.

Cass Canfield said he could only offer his "unconditional surrender. My forces are spent and I have no arms left to lay down." But he did tell her with a pride only somewhat less fierce than her own, "I think I need not tell you that this House intends to preserve your poetry as it is; to do otherwise would make us as guilty as an art dealer who tampered with an El Greco painting."

In 1948, Marie Bullock, the founder of the Academy of American Poets, invited Millay to serve on its board of chancellors, assuring her all that would be required of her was one or two brief notes each year. But Millay weighed appointments seriously; she read both the bylaws and the certificate of incorporation very carefully. Then she turned Mrs. Bullock down cold. No one had ever turned the academy down. In a wonderful letter, Millay tried to soften her objections by suggesting to Mrs. Bullock that she "wished you had not, in your earnestness, got yourself all embroiled with a firm of lawyers who in their bossy dustiness have made it so difficult for you to do the beautiful thing you want to do." Mrs. Bullock's husband was the lawyer whose firm had drawn up the bylaws.

Millay's objections were twofold: First, the Fellows who received the $5,000 stipend, generous in those days, had to report their progress in writing three times a year, within thirty days prior to the quarterly payment. Second, no fellowship holder could engage in gainful occupation during the period of the award. That meant that a poet could not teach, edit, or serve in government—even though, clearly enough, a number of chancellors did. It was true, Millay wrote, that five thousand dollars was a lot of money.

> But pottage is pottage, even when it is five thousand dollars worth of pottage. And I can have no part in seducing any poet into accepting this award, under these conditions.
> I think of what Shelley said, in "An Exhortation":
>
> > "Yet dare not stain with wealth or power
> > A poet's free and heavenly mind.
> > . . .
> > Spirits from beyond the moon,
> > Oh, refuse the boon!"

While the academy did amend its bylaws the following year, they retained their spirit—a poet could still not engage in any gainful employment—actually the word used is "occupation"; when in November 1949, badly in debt, Millay was offered the fellowship herself, she declined in no uncertain terms. Her friend the poet Leonora Speyer said she was "a goose." Max Eastman called her a "self-spoilt child," a "martinet and self-indulgent." Later Hal Bynner would say it had been "striking evidence of her cocky Irish integrity."

Edmund Wilson and his wife, Elena, were at the music festival in Tanglewood that summer of 1948. They wrote asking if they might come to call at Steepletop.

Edna and Eugen's living room seemed to Wilson the same as it had been in 1929, the last time he'd been there: the blackened bronze bust of Sappho with the fierce ivory whites of her eyes staring from the entrance corner, the two magnificent dark grand pianos, the ornate golden birds Edna had brought back from their trip to the Orient, "but now the birds were paler, their background was gray; the couches looked badly worn; the whole place seemed shabby and dim."

Another startling thing he noticed, not having seen her in nineteen years, was the change in Edna's relationship to Eugen. "As we drove through the long tunnel of greenery that led to the Steepletop house, I felt, as I had not done before, that Edna had been buried out there." An aging Eugen shuffled out to meet them. "He was greying and stooped. It seemed to me he was in low morale. 'I'll go and get my child,' he said. I did not realize at first that this meant Edna."

When Edna entered the room, he did not recognize her. "She had become somewhat heavy and dumpy, and her cheeks were a little florid. Her eyes had a bird-lidded look that I recognized as typically Irish, and I noticed for the first time a certain resemblance to her mother. She was terribly nervous; her hands shook; there was a look of fright in her bright green eyes." Eugen brought them all martinis, and Wilson sensed that he was managing Edna, babying her. Elena thought Eugen seemed to be shaking Wilson at Millay, "as if I had been a new toy with which he hoped to divert her." Only when the conversation turned to poetry did Edna come to life: she grew excited and intense. She showed him a good deal of the poetry she was then working on. The living room was cluttered with notebooks and drafts, and he "could see that she was just emerging from some terrible eclipse of the spirit. This was, after all, the girl, the great poet, I knew, groping back *in luminis oras* from the night of the underworld."

Wilson wanted his wife to hear Edna recite her own poetry, and he pressed her to do so. "As she did so, the room became so charged with emotion that I began to find it difficult to bear. I could not weep, I did not want her to weep, and . . . I soon insisted upon leaving." It was their last meeting, and while he called her "fatiguing," even now he was not indifferent to her.

> So she was still . . . almost as disturbing to me as she ever had been in the twenties, to which she had so completely belonged—for she could not be a part of my present, and to see her exerted on me a painful pull, as if to drag me up by the roots, to gouge me out of my present personality and to annihilate all that had made it.

He does not tell us that he wrote her again the following year asking to see her, and she refused him. "This is awful," she wrote back, "but I can't see you; I can't see anybody on earth just now; I am working seventy-two hours a day; and I don't dare run the risk of being deflected." This was, she told him, "an ironic and hateful thing; I have so often longed to talk with you. . . . and I know that I shall—as soon as I am able to feel anything at all beyond the periphery of my intense occupation." Then she corrects, quite sharply and confidently, one of his own poems he has sent her in which he used backward rhyming endings. "Don't do it. 'Slag' is a fine word. 'Gals' is cheap, common and indecent. . . . don't for God's sake, use it, in a poem which has so much elegance."

In a letter to Cass Canfield she confided that she'd spent the past seven months writing new poetry, but she'd also written

> after having read a thoughtful review by Lewis Gannett concerning a late book by T. S. Eliot, and, more recently, after reading the brilliant and truly witty, although some times I thought, in some ways overstressed articles by Robert Hillyer in the Saturday Review of Literature, against the awarding of the Bollingen Award to Ezra Pound—a satire in verse against T. S. Eliot.

She called it *The Cult of the Occult,* and it was not simply a satire of Eliot's poem; she made a mockery of what was then the most influential poem of the modernist movement. She said she would give him no footnotes.

> In this collection of poems, of which I think there will be about twenty, to be numbered in roman numerals as was Eliot's "The Waste Land," there is nothing coarse, obscene, as there sometimes is in the work of Auden and of Pound, and nothing so silly as the childish horsing around of Eliot, when he is trying to be funny. He has no sense of humour, and so he is not yet a true Englishman: read some of the verse in Punch. There is, I think, in these poems of mine against Eliot nothing which could be considered abusive: they are merely murderous.

She sent along copies of several of them, to which Canfield replied, "I thought the verses were brilliant satire. They shed a deadly spotlight on the false attitudes and pretentiousness of Eliot and a whole group of writers that imitate him."

2

Norma's relationship with Vincent remained deeply troubled. Well before Wilson's visit, in a letter which she later admitted was "probably not sent," she wrote:

> Dear Kid, Dear Toots, Dear Edna St. Vincent, Dear Flotsam,—this is a thing from your sister Jetsam (or Jettison and Flatson, if you are preference minded) and, as a bit of oily waste or a bobbling bottle of Scotch, there is no telling where this thing will beach. I, cast as Jetsam . . . just don't give a good goddamn. It's such fun just to be going places.
>
> What are the wild waves saying, sister?
>
> Do you think we will make the Jersey coast by nightfall?— . . . The answer (you must have heard) being—"Where do you get this 'we' stuff." . . . Letters are a wonderful invention. It's too bad you don't take to them more. I suppose if one is a perfectionist one has to save the scraps— for bits of colour here and there. Letters are wasteful, I'm afraid.

There are pages of these letters to Vincent, which Norma did not destroy, which she even transcribed and talked about but never sent.

> Oh, little sister, little sister, it is not my fault that you are ill. Why should I take it so entirely upon myself? Life is short anyway—and especially now there is no life to speak of. . . . Though you and I know it is the only thing worth mentioning . . . personal, individual, sensual life. Dear life.

Some letters are typed, even dated, as this one is, "Sunday, August 14th," but with no year given:

> I called you, sister—my biennial checkup on your health and wealth and possibly a clue to your state of mind—any gleanings. Your phone was disconnected, I was informed—no other instrument under the name of EB. listed.
>
> This is impossible. What could it mean? The old clutching—the strangling—the search for air. . . . Was it that you hadn't enough money to pay its upkeep? You have wealthy friends. . . . You could sell something— Gene would part with a cabbage—start a roadside stand—country doughnuts—something!
>
> I couldn't reach you. I—you!

When Norma finally did reach her sister, their telephone conversation got off to a bad start:

> The first thing you say . . . is have I got any lavender for my linens and I answered have I any linen? . . . You were very serious about it—"O you have no linen?" It was almost a symbol of how far apart we are from understanding one another. . . . You have said some of the Goddamndest things to me in the last years and I have let them ride but if you are going back over our early years to try to find reasons for not loving me—let me speak too.

There are pages and pages of these letters, and they all say the same thing: I've lost you. "Sweetheart—sweet freckled heart. . . . how are you?"

In February 1949, Norma finally sent a letter and enclosed a small ring. "When we were young, Mother had given us three silver rings with green scarabs set in each ring," she explained to me, "and inside on the flat part of the band was written, 'Hunk,' 'Sefe,' and 'Wump.' And I sent her my ring, which was our signal that I was in trouble. And she said, 'How nice to have it!' "

Norma had sent Vincent a poem she had written, as well as her ring. Vincent responded on March 2, 1949:

> Hunk:
>   Your little silver ring came on my birthday. I would have written you a letter at once in answer to that, except that I had done something queer to my shoulder—wrenched it, strained it, pulled a ligament—I don't know—one of those things you do when you are so busy doing something that you don't notice what else you're doing—and my shoulder hurt and I couldn't write. I can only type a few lines now, though I'm much better; but I must get some word to you. Not only about the ring, and all that it meant, all that the three rings meant, when the three of us were children—Sefe, Hunk and Wump, and so engraved (Oh, poor little Wumpty-Woons) I can't go on about that—

Wumpty-Woons was Kathleen's family nickname. But Norma was having none of it. "I wanted to *see* her. I was desperately unhappy, but the truth is: I need *you*. Not a letter! Not 'I'm touched when I get it.' She's pretty far removed from the sentiment of the thing, isn't she? She's overcome. Honey, I wanted to be close to her!

"Because it was poetry, I knew she would have to respond. . . . After a while this was the only way I had to reach her." Then Norma showed me her poem:

Of my home beneath the mantle of your wing,
So confidently cradled to your heart
You overlooked, I think, it was not part
Of you, 'Twas I who did the fashioning.
Blest with a sibling in our common seed
and happy as your satellite to soar,
I heard no menace in the ocean's roar,
of the chill above the Mountain took no heed.
'Til flying ever higher in the light
New currents called on you for added skill—
You, sensing an impediment to flight
disclosed my house of down: you wore me still.
As gulls above the rocks will loose their prey
You forced the fingers of your stowaway.

Vincent's letter to Norma had continued:

—I want to write you about your poem, that fine poem you sent me—
later I will—but in the meantime, how many poems as good as that have
you written? Get them together, in case you haven't, work over them in
case you need to in some instances, write more, in case you haven't
enough, bring out a book. There's no doubt at all that you have the talent,
the imagination and the technique. Any publisher would publish the book,
if this poem is a sample of its quality. So get on with it, and don't let anything stop you: you're good.

Love,
Sefe

᠊ᠥ᠎ ᠊ᠥ᠎ ᠊ᠥ᠎

Almost four decades later, Norma sat with her head down, her hands
clasping her brow. She brought her fist down sharply on the kitchen table.
"Imagine having to write a sonnet good enough that she would have to
recognize it—and *me!*" she said. "It's an extraordinary letter of Vincent's,
but I worked hard for that. I had not said, 'This is your sister, Norma, I
want to see you,' but 'Sister, I must see you! I must! If I come up will you
go to a bar with me where we will sit and talk?'

"She would say to me, 'Oh, Sister, we can sit and talk here.'

"I couldn't talk alone with her. Because of Gene. Because Gene would
come bursting into the room, as he'd done before. She said, 'Sister, were
you trying to kill me?'

" 'No, I was just trying to get close to you.' "

It was as if the voices of the sisters were crowding into the room, across time, addressing each other, defending their lives and their choices. Norma broke the intensity of this scene with resolution: "I like myself better as a person than I like her as a person. You can put that down. A writer, to write all the time—you cannot do that without being selfish. Vincent was not self-centered at all. I think she was just naturally selfish. She had to be. She had to guard her time, her . . . oh, what? Her self. And so did Gene."

∽ ∽ ∽

On August 22, 1949, Gene wrote to Norma. Edna, he said, was hard at work writing. "She tells me that she had hoped that you were busy doing the same thing." In closing, he reminded her that they had taken out their telephone more than a year and a half before. He said it was a "noisy and impertinent machine" that they never wanted back. "The outside world, friends and relatives can always reach either of us by letter." Clearly, Norma was someone who inhabited that outside world. Then he told her, "Edna and I are leaving Wednesday for Boston. Edna is taking me to a hospital for an operation." He did not tell her he had lung cancer.

Seven days later, on August 29, 1949, Eugen Jan Boissevain died at Deaconess Hospital in Boston.

CHAPTER 40

> It seems to me that what happened to Edna was as dreadful as what happened to Scott Fitzgerald—though she had more character and more genius. Of course she always pulled herself together . . . but I don't think you ought to try—as people's families so often do—to suppress the tragic aspects because they might be painful or shocking to Edna's more conventional admirers. Her poetry is not the work of a being for whom life could ever have been easy or gone along at a comfortable level. It will always give the lie to any too respectful biography . . . but it will also always be there to make the casualties of her life seem unimportant.
>
> —Edmund Wilson to Norma Millay, January 31, 1952

Norma had not yet received Eugen's letter telling her they were going to Boston for his operation when the telephone rang. "I picked up the phone, and a voice said, 'Boston calling.' Then a little voice said, 'Oh, sister.' It was Vincent. And I said, 'Oh, sister!,' but she didn't reply. There was a long silence. And then I suddenly understood." It was not necessary to say that Eugen had died. "We talked a little bit about poetry. We talked about that sonnet I had written. Vincent said, 'You didn't know?'

" 'Why, no. How could I know?' "

After she hung up, Norma immediately wrote to her:

> Dear, I'm not calling back to say this because you might possibly be asleep and that would be a blessing. . . . Charlie and I would, as you know, love to have you come here. Whatever your plans are you will need rest. . . . We could come get you anywhere and you could be as alone and quiet as you wished here.

Edna hadn't thought Eugen would die. The operation had gone well, although Boston was in the middle of a heat wave that August and there was no air-conditioning in the hospital, which had made his labored breathing even more difficult. They had put him in an oxygen tent and then taken it away because he was doing well. Norma described sitting at the kitchen table at Steepletop after his death: "And Vincent was breathing—she was telling us how she had helped him breathe—she almost took on his illness. He said to her, 'We're going places now.' Then she went back to the hotel to rest. And then they called her." He had had a cerebral hemorrhage.

Tess Adams had received word from Eugen and written back quickly, but not quickly enough, for her letter was delivered to Edna in Boston. "Darling Ugin, I think of you as being as strong as the sea." After all, she wrote as lightly as she could manage, "why does a big guy like you need two lungs?" She asked him to tell Edna she would go to Boston immediately to be with her: "I would vanish except when she wanted a buffer, or a friend." Now it was Tess who drove the grief-stricken Millay back to Steepletop.

Alice Blinn and Margaret Cuthbert arrived the day after Edna returned to Steepletop. They, too, had received a letter from Eugen on August 20 saying he had not been feeling well and had seen a number of doctors who had told him he had cancer in his right lung.

> Very unpleasant. I'll have to be there 4 to 6 weeks. (If the operation is successful.) Terrible for poor Vince. She will be all alone here but she wants to be alone. I am so afraid it will interfere with her work. I hope, if everything goes O.K. to be back before snow flies. . . . my dear love to both of you. And Good Luck to all of us.—Ugin.

Edna was upstairs when the two women arrived, Alice Blinn remembered.

"We were waiting a rather long time for her to come down. I still remember the sound of her coming across the slate hall entranceway. I suppose we were anxious. Then I looked up to see her strike a pose in the doorway. 'Who am I?' " she asked.

" 'You're Henry the Eighth by Holbein,' I said quickly, for that was exactly what she looked like. Then she turned and struck another pose. I said, 'Edna, if I knew you'd read a book I read when we were children I'd say you were the Little Colonel.'

" 'I am! I am, Alice!'

"And, of course, she was so pleased. How we laughed. It was not often, but she could be playful, even then."

It was during this visit, late one night at Steepletop after Eugen's death, that Alice talked with Edna about her need for a will. Who would manage her estate, Alice asked, prepare her manuscripts for publication or for sale?

"She sat very quietly listening to me, and she was very serious, looking up at me with that rather quizzical expression she had. Certainly she listened intently. And then she said, 'Well, Alice, I'm not sure whether Norma isn't the one to do it.'

"And that was it. That was the end of it. I knew she had made her decision. Why she made it, I do not know. I don't think I understood it then nor now, but there was no question that that was the end of the conversation."

When George Dillon heard about Eugen's death from a word dropped in a letter, he quickly wrote to Edna:

> It seems incredible and wrong. I have no details and don't even know where you are but am trying to hope that you will let me know, or tell someone to let me know, if I can do anything whatever to help. This sounds horribly dutiful. It is not. I am free to do whatever you need me for, and it would be what I most want to do.

Then he said what she must have needed to hear: "Please remember that you can count on me. George."

She scribbled a note hastily, in what looks like a drunken scrawl, next to George's address and phone number in Richmond for Mary Herron, the postmistress in Austerlitz, who was helping her with her correspondence: "Mr. George Dillon (or his mother or father). Say that I have been in hospital for two weeks and have just now received his letter. Ask him if he can come to Steepletop for a few days, to be with me and help me.—Edna St. Vincent Millay."

Dillon did not come. He too had fallen ill. He was home from the hospital in mid-October when she telephoned him.

He wrote in reply, "It meant a great deal to me, as you knew it would, to know that Eugen had spoken of me so recently. I always looked upon him as a justification for the human race, and as time has gone on, I realize more and more how incomparable he was." Then he said that while he knew she had courage aplenty, what he hoped was that she would find release in her work.

He said he'd resigned from his editorship of *Poetry:*

> The truth is, I don't react strongly to the poetry now being written. The war output was deplorable . . . I did look for something to turn up after the war. But where is it? (The young people who care about poetry seem to be largely concerned with theory, and not very new or interesting theory, rather than performance.)

He might get a job that would take him back to North Africa, where he had been stationed during World War II. But it was uncertain. He'd let her know. He sounded adrift. George could not have known what very bad shape Millay was in when she returned to Steepletop that September.

Eugen had been dead less than two weeks when Millay entered Doctors Hospital for the third time, on September 11, 1949. The admitting physician was Dr. William Hall Lewis, Jr., who was a friend of her neighbors the LaBranches. "A session occurred in New York at this time," Dr. Lewis recalled, "in late August or early September. Friends of hers who were in the city considered that she should have some attention from them, and also that she should be in a position to have some medical supervision to judge her moods and depressive reactions." They were afraid she could not cope with being alone.

Dr. Lewis's diagnosis was "Acute neurasthenia" aggravated by "Nutritional deficiency" and "Cirrhosis of the liver." "The medication given at this time consisted of more nutritional intake with a modest sedation of barbiturates. Was also given vitamins and liver extract by injection. . . . She required some Sodium Luminal, grains 2, by injection. For relaxation. Also, a nurse is prescribed to be with the patient twenty-four hours for present. Do not leave alone. Medication consisted thereafter of Sodium Luminal or Seconal taken by mouth. She was allowed to have—a note of 9/16/49—wine, one and one-half bottles per twenty-four hours."

She had come in complaining of simple exhaustion. Dr. Lewis said she had apparently been drinking for some time and was worn out. She told the nurse that she "desires large amount of sedation."

It was a bright, sunny day, Dr. Lewis recalled, when the ambulance arrived at Steepletop at eleven o'clock to pick her up and take her to Doctors Hospital. At the last minute Edna decided she would be better off at home. There was a forty-five-minute discussion when the nurse who was to accompany her in the ambulance reported to Dr. Lewis "that a sedative was given to Edna in order for her to make the trip."

The journey was on the Taconic Parkway, which was heavily traveled, especially on a pretty fall Sunday. Once under way Edna suddenly rapped on the partition between her and the driver's seat and requested that the ambulance pull over because "she needed to wee-wee." The shades were drawn for her privacy, and the ambulance men looked straight ahead. After some time Edna reported that she had not been successful and felt she could do better if the shades were raised. Still unable to go, she "requested the driver to whistle. . . . The driver started to whistle as best as he could under the circumstances." The nurse who was with her "did notice that the companion driver was getting more and more red in the back of the neck until he finally exploded in great volumes of laughter." They finally got under way, and she was admitted to the hospital late that afternoon.

"In my discussion with Edna it did not seem that she was unduly depressed. Or showing any suicidal inclinations," Dr. Lewis remembered. "Being accustomed to wine and other alcohol content, it was agreed she could have a liter and a half of wine per day. . . . Later the nurses informed me that she was obtaining one bottle of wine a day from each of four individuals separately who came to call upon her, putting them on the top shelf of the closet in the hospital room. I immediately discussed this with her and . . . she felt that I was inconsiderate in my appreciation of the value of wine . . . it was a beautiful amber and rosy liquid that inspired the literary imagination. I told her that in view of her medical condition and past history it seemed best to have some moderation. . . . She reacted very strongly to that. . . . I was entirely too medical, and I was treating this beautiful liquid of the Gods like a common medicine."

By September 14, she was taking hot tea, grapefruit juice, and claret in the morning. At 3 P.M., the nurse noted that she was "out of bed in chair. Has had very good day. . . . Seems stronger & steadier." Edna was making very definite plans now, and although two friends had called wanting to come and visit her, she'd put them off.

The next morning found her weeping and asking for medication; she said she'd come to rest and to sleep. She'd doze for ten minutes and then awaken weeping. She was smoking and drinking. She complained bitterly about medication and said she "requires 5 or 7 grams, not an 'infant's dose.' " Then she slept fitfully for about five hours, between two and seven.

The next morning she was described as "In biting, fault-finding mood re medication: 'Please don't reason with me.' " Dr. Lewis visited and she told him, "I want to get out and get to work!" At 3:30, she went to the hospital's beauty parlor for a shampoo, but by the evening she was again depressed and weepy. She was afraid she wouldn't be able to sleep, and she drank two thirds of a bottle of wine after supper.

Friday, September 16, 1949: "Patient sitting up, drinking & smoking. Extremely agitated about way she is being treated. Repeats her story of medication & dosage she requires. Wanted gin."

On Sunday the eighteenth she'd been in Doctors Hospital a full week. She was irritated at what she felt to be the indignity of her treatment, asked for various remedies, and then refused them all. Then, in what looked to be a very impatient nurse's hand: "will not try to sleep. ABSOLUTELY WILL NOT COOPERATE." She refused even to lie down and told the nurse that if she did she would suffocate.

By lunchtime that day she was on her feet, and she refused wine for the first time. On Monday she was drinking ginger ale and tea and eating with appetite. She was also beginning to sleep.

While her friends refused to agree with her that she should be allowed to leave the hospital, she was determined to. It had been three weeks since Eugen had died, and she wanted to be at home, alone. Since none of them, not Tess nor Gladys Fiske nor Margaret Cuthbert would drive her, she called Cass Canfield.

Years later, Cass Canfield could no longer recall which of her friends had called him to decide whether she could safely leave the hospital. "The doctor involved wouldn't make the decision, and somehow it fell to me. I thought she should be at her home. After all, that was where she wrote her poems. It was her home and she belonged there, whatever she did."

Canfield remembered stopping on the drive to Steepletop at some inn off Route 22. "We had something to eat. I asked her if she'd like a drink and she said no. We had wine, a quart of wine. I drank perhaps a glass, a glass and a half, and she drank all the rest.

"Yes, I was aware that she might kill herself. But I thought that was up to her in a way."

—

Once she was back at Steepletop, John Pinnie, who had been their hired man since they had bought Steepletop in 1925, stayed on with her to help run the place. The local postmistress, Mary Herron, read and answered the many letters of sympathy that came in after Eugen's death. She also did Millay's bookkeeping, wrote out her checks, helped with her taxes, and cared for her.

Three months after Eugen's death, Cass Canfield asked her to look over William Rose Benét's introduction, written for a special edition of her *Second April* and *The Buck in the Snow,* which Harper was bringing out in a new series. She wrote five pages of detailed critical notes about the introduction, telling Canfield that there were things

> to which I properly, as a person, can object: the too familiar . . . use of the name "*Vincent*" (too familiar for a formal piece of writing . . . Bill Benét has always called me Vincent, as did Elinor Wylie); and the bit of gossip beginning, "I think I know of whom," (which also would prove distracting to the reader, who would say to himself, "This might be juicy, if only I could squeeze it")

because it was marked by bad writing which made her feel "sick and embarrassed." Nevertheless, she asked only that one sentence be altered completely; in its place she wrote:

> In this year Edna St. Vincent Millay married Eugen Jan Boissevain, who rendered to her a devotion—and not only a devotion, but an understanding of the demands of her art—that endured until his death in 1949.

Canfield said it was heartbreaking: her sharp loss ringing through her clear restraint.

Lena Reusch went to clean for Millay after Eugen's death because John Pinnie asked for her help. "He told me she needed someone and asked if I'd work for her every other day. It was Mondays, Wednesdays, and Fridays, I believe. Well, the first thing we did was, we got the dining room all fixed up. That was a mess! Things all over, every which way."

Edna was making plans for the house and thinking ahead to next spring. There were things that had to be done now, before the snowfall. She made a note of instructions for Bill Reusch, Lena's husband, and put it in her bedroom desk for safekeeping.

> Putty up holes where bees get into garage
> Take down old electric-engine house

Put 2 electric lights in woodshed (one of them in laundry closet)
Put wire cover on Incinerator
Plane 2 storm-windows
Plane doors of cupboard in Laundry
Put sash-weights & cords in 2 windows
Put panes in several Windows

Mr. Reusch came and did the carpentry. "Just fixing up different things that needed it. A new cellar door, I remember. She knew what she wanted and how it should be done, and I liked her very well. She could be very concerned about—oh, what? little things to me. And she was funny sometimes. She'd joke. I remember that I had to wax the floor and I asked her where the heavy polisher was to buff it. And she sort of smiled at me and, putting on her socks, she skated and danced across my freshly waxed floor, and did it shine!"

Other local people came to reupholster the couches and make slipcovers. "She wanted something covered in green and white stripes with leaves through it from a sample book she had," one neighbor recalled.

"She always stood straight up, that little bit of a thing. Up straight as a ramrod. After he died I came to call to see what I could do for her. She was standing in her bathrobe at the kitchen door. And she threw this at me right off, 'Did you think I wasn't going on?' Again, that intensity! I didn't know what to say. Then we started making big plans."

No one had wanted her to go home to Steepletop alone. Her friends were very firm; they argued with her. They fought her, in fact. But she needed to have her way. At the turn of the year, in January 1950, five months after Eugen's death, Edna told Norma how she'd managed. She was, she wrote,

stuffing myself with all the best proteins and taking my stinking vitamine capsules and my loathsome Liver-Iron-and Red Bone Marrow Extract. Well, baby, I must go now, and lift a three-inch beefsteak out of the deep-freezer to thaw for my luncheon; and, for my breakfast (I am writing this at 6 A.M.) squeeze the juice from five oranges and one lemon; boil the two eggs which my chickens were boasting about all yesterday afternoon.

She'd made recovery into a game. She had no appetite,

So I hit upon the bright idea of splitting myself into two personalities, one the patient, one the nurse. The nurse, now, cooks my meals, and sees to it that they are not only nutritious, but also appetizing and attractive. And she prepares my medicines with no repugnance. . . . As for the patient, she obediently, and also absent-mindedly, swallows and swallows. . . . Mrs. Somebody-Anybody got her name in this manner: when in Doctors' Hospital, I made known to several friends who visited me there, my decision to return to Steepletop and live here all alone, they were appalled, and begged me not to try it. They all said, "But you *must* have *somebody* with you! You simply *can't* be there without *anybody!*" . . .

When, finally . . . I was here alone, and thought up my pretty schizophrenia; I named my nurse Mrs. Somebody-Anybody. She doesn't know that I called her that; she wouldn't like it. So to her face I call her "Mrs. S.A." She thinks I mean Mrs. Sex-Appeal! And she *bridles,* my dear, she actually *bridles!*

Don't worry about me at all, either of you. To pretend that it is not agony would be silly. But I can cope.

In the spring, when Mary Herron asked her how she was going to bear up without Eugen, she said she was

plenty scared. . . . Shrinking from being hurt too much. Scared the way I used to be as a child, when I had to go to the dentist. In the days before they gave you novocaine.

I have already encountered the first dandelion. I stood and stared at it with a kind of horror. And then I felt ashamed of myself, and sorry for the dandelion. And suddenly, without my doing anything about it at all, my face just crumpled up and cried.

How excited he always was when he saw the first dandelion! And long before the plants got big enough for even a rabbit to find them, he had dug a fine mess, for greens. He used to say "pick dandelions"; and I would say, "Not pick,—dig." And he would say, "Oh, don't scold poor Uge—he does so his best."

Alas, alas, and alas.

When Mary Herron offered to pay for the fresh butter Edna had asked John Pinnie to churn for her, Edna was outraged: "After all that you have done for me, and are constantly doing—no sister could have given me more tender care—"

☙ ☙ ☙

We began to talk about what Norma called "that last time" she and Vincent had seen each other. At some point in the conversation Norma had called Gene "a beautiful animal." Vincent had said, "You, too, Normie?" Then she had fallen to the floor.

"I don't remember what I had said. But it certainly shouldn't have been taken that way. I wish to God I could remember what I said."

Charlie slowly, thoughtfully, interrupted, "You said Gene was a beautiful animal."

"It certainly shouldn't have been taken that way. We would have killed each other. I had gotten where I just wasn't taking anything. Vincent could really look right at you. You see, she took nothing lightly. She was wary. I tried to talk to her, and she left me and went upstairs. She had gone.

"Well, what am I going to do? She was highly sensitized at the time. And Charlie said he'd go up, and pretty soon they were laughing. And I came up, she threw her arms around me—'I want only you, sister. You come back!'

" 'I *am* back,' I said in her arms.—Of course, that's borne out by the little scrap of paper [the will].

"But I couldn't be Gene! She was a nervous wreck. Well, I'm a little more matter-of-fact. Well, dear, I don't know what it is—we're different. I don't know what it was. And I was beginning to see that she could go on. You must remember that we had to earn a living. Then it was a whole year."

❧ ❧ ❧

Millay began to handle all of her own correspondence and not rely on Mary Herron, to whom she'd written, "It's time I stopped being such a baby." She went to work to try to control Oxford University Press's *Book of American Verse*—rather, she attempted, but failed, to limit its desire to anthologize only her very early work and her love poems.

Suddenly it was fall. She wrote to Margaret Cuthbert, inviting them to come anytime after September 1. "When once I have the whole first year behind me, when I can no longer say to myself, 'Only a year ago today he was still alive,'—then, something will have happened." It "might perhaps give me something to lean against for the second year.

"However, I know nothing about it. I am exploring strange and uncharted country. I am the first one that ever lost Eugen."

She'd promised a Thanksgiving poem to *The Saturday Evening Post,* and even though she scrapped the first version with only ten days to go, she managed to find the words she needed and finished it.

It was her first poem to see print since Eugen's death. She wrote to Cass Canfield, "It was going along well, I thought; but as things got worse and worse in Korea, I began to see that it was not the right poem for the occasion. 'What,' I asked myself, 'would a few Indian war-hoops mean, and a neighborly little scalping party,—to a nation dreading and awaiting the atom bomb?' " So she scrapped the first version of the poem "and sat there, scared frozen; the deadline only ten days off; my promise to deliver the poem long ago given to the *Post;* and not an idea in my head. . . . when I got so scared that I was fair frantic, there was nothing to do but relax, and start all over; and so I did. And almost at once the first lines of the new poem came into my head."

> Hard, hard it is, this anxious autumn,
> To lift the heavy mind from its dark forebodings.

"Oh," she told Cass, "I know that I am making a big fuss about a small piece of work—but it is so wonderful to be writing again!" Her point by the close of the poem is one that reverberated in her life:

> the trained hand does not forget its skill . . .
> Strength we have, and courage; an acetylene will.

She thanked Canfield for the money he'd been sending her. She'd been too busy worrying the poem along to have noticed, and then "the August slip came in." It was "a great help to me. And it was kind of you to do it, without even speaking about it."

"She had, don't you see, this clarity of mind," Canfield insisted. "Her verses, her poems were absolutely clear. There was always a clarity in her poems—no matter what she wrote about."

Ragged Island—which a number of her good friends thought she might, even must, sell—she had no intention of letting go. "As soon as I can bear it," she wrote Tess, "I shall go back there." Maybe even the next summer. In August 1950, remembering the August before, she added, "No, my dear. Don't bring me any lobsters. And don't bring me any seaweed."

Often she worked late. To Lena Reusch, her new housekeeper, she left this note:

> This iron is set too high. Don't put it on where it says "Linen"—or it will scorch the linen. Try it on "Rayon"—and then, perhaps on "Woollen." And be careful not to *burn your fingers* when you shift it from one heat to another.
> It is 5:30, and I have been working all night. I am going to bed.
> Goodmorning—
>
> E.St.V.M.

On the morning of Octobert 18, she wired Scribner's that she would give them a quote for the jacket of Rolphe Humphries's translation of the *Aeneid*. Then she settled down before the fire and made pages of small, clear notes in pencil, so unlike the wild, uneven hand with which all those earlier terrifying notes to herself had been written. She read late into the following morning, and, after carefully placing a glass of white wine and the bottle on the staircase, she went upstairs.

She turned the light on in her bedroom and smoked a few cigarettes. Perhaps she'd gone upstairs to take something to help her sleep, a Seconal. But although she was wearing her silk dressing gown and slippers, she didn't go to bed. Instead she walked back to the dark staircase and stood at the top of the narrow wooden stairs in the old house. Something happened. Then she pitched wildly forward, falling, hurtling down the full length of the stairs to the landing. Her neck was broken in the fall.

All the lights were on in the house when John Pinnie came the next morning to do the chores. He put the mail on the kitchen table. "John saw the light on up in her bedroom," Lena Reusch remembered. "He hadn't seen her all day, and he went back into the house. I believe he said to fix the furnace, or maybe it was to lay the fire. Then John saw her. Her feet were down, and she was curled around at the landing of the stairs.

"John ran down to our house, and I sent him right down to . . . our neighbor below, and he called Dr. Wilcox. There was just John and I drove up to the house. And I stayed there until the doctor came. I didn't think about it, or I would have run. Dr. Wilcox and John came, and they put her on the couch. And, oh, my, her slippers fell off."

Dr. Oscar Wilcox, Jr., came to the house and pronounced her dead. He later wrote, "I found her at the foot of the stairway from which she had apparently fallen. . . . She was lying at the foot of the stairway with a sort of dressing gown around her. I did not think she was retiring for the night but coming down stairs perhaps for something."

Her head was resting on some magazines and letters on the landing, where there was a mark of blood and one notebook with the penciled draft of a poem. She had traced a ring around the last three lines:

> I will control myself, or go inside.
> I will not flaw perfection with my grief.
> Handsome, this day: no matter who has died.

In her bedroom at the time of her death there were only two photographs. One was a snapshot of Norma and Kathleen taken in Maine. They are hugging each other and smiling into the camera. They look young and pretty. "I sent this to her in Europe," Norma remembered, "and she said she wanted to get right in between!" The other is in an elegant dark leather pigskin frame with a metal overlay of raised hearts and flowers. A little boy, dressed as a soldier, is standing in velvet breeches, holding a toy sword in his left hand. He is wearing a plumed helmet and a metal breastplate. His dark curls are long and fall below his shoulders, and there is lace on the wrists of his smart jacket and at his throat. He is a stocky boy with sad eyes and a mouth turned down like the rim of a cup. It is signed "Eugen Jan Boissevain."

Edna St. Vincent Millay had survived her beloved cavalier by one year, one month, and twenty days.

ACKNOWLEDGMENTS

I owe a great deal to many people, and I want to thank them here. To those beloved friends who stood by me and believed in my effort to shape this book—Dr. Ellen Reitz Conrad, the Honorable Vesta Svenson, Marga Beth Cibulka, Roberta and Donald Gratz, Shelby White and Leon Levy, who generously took me into their world with travel and laughter and play—my best thanks. And where would I be without the sustaining friendship of Paula Weideger and Henry Lessore, Emily Trafford Berges, Jay Meek, Doron Weber, Charles Ruas and Rob Wynne? Let alone my Virgil, William Josephson, who has led me through every circle of whatever inferno I was caught in, with a clear intelligence and a golden spirit that buoyed my own. Toni Morrison's advice and support and, most crucially, her own model of a continuing literary life have meant the world to me. To Lois Gould: my world would be a lesser place if she were not writing in it.

Vartan Gregorian has been a matchless friend, and I've treasured his guidance. Joni Evans pulled me out of a mess with style and I remain grateful to her. To Lynn Nesbit, who helped me to believe that this biography was first-rate, if only I would finish it. There was nobody, however, who saw with more certainty or who believed in this biography more consistently than Kate Medina—I can't thank her enough. To Pat Goldbitz, who worked tirelessly in my behalf, whether I was in Michigan or Istanbul, my thanks. But it is Joy de Menil whose clear head, hard work, and editorial brilliance helped me to shape this book. She's my wizard, and she's tops.

I am grateful to the Guggenheim Foundation for their early support; to Judith L. Pinch at the Woodrow Wilson Foundation and to the Lila Wallace–Reader's Digest Fund for sending me to teach in Arkansas and South Carolina; to Robert Weisbuch and James A. Winn, who were at the University of Michigan when they hired me; to Dr. Micaela Iovine at the Fulbright Commission in Washington and to Dr. Ersin Onulduran in

Turkey for arranging my stint at Boğaziçi Universitesi in Istanbul, and to Oya Başak and Asli Tekinay for their welcome. My best thanks to Alice L. Birney, American Literature Manuscript Historian at the Library of Congress, and to Vincent Virga, photo editor, for making my life much easier during the researching of this book.

It was in the Frederick Lewis Allan Room at the New York Public Library, and later in The Writers Room, which I helped to found, that I found a refuge in which to write. Donna Brodie and el Staff know how very much I value them. Joellyn Ausanka is simply the best, most helpful and gracious person I have ever worked with; and, thank God, she spells better than I do. But in the end it is my family—Kate and Matthew and Amy and Hester and Evan Dority—whom I treasure. I don't write for them, but they have given me the heart from which I write.

NOTES

These abbreviations are used throughout the footnotes.

ADF	Arthur Davison Ficke
Beinecke	Beinecke Rare Book and Manuscript Library at Yale University
Berg	Berg Collection, The Astor, Lenox and Tilden Foundation, The New York Public Library
CBM	Cora Buzzell Millay
CP	*Collected Poems*
EB	Eugen Jan Boissevain
ESVM	Edna St. Vincent Millay
EW	Edmund Wilson
FE	Ferdinand Earle
GD	George Dillon
HM	Henry Millay
KM	Kathleen Millay
Ls.	*Letters of Edna St. Vincent Millay,* ed. Allan Ross Macdougall (New York: Harper & Brothers, 1952)
LWF	"Lest We Forget" (unpublished diary)
MK	Mitchell Kennerley
n.d.	No date
Newberry	Newberry Library of Chicago
NM	Norma Millay
n.p.	No page
n.y.	No year
PM	Postmark
St. Coll.	Steepletop Collection. The Millay collection of letters, notebooks, manuscripts, and photographs is now at the Library of Congress. During the years of research and writing of this biography, I referred to the various documents as "the Steepletop Collection." Alice Birney, who is the American Literature Manuscript Historian at the Library of Congress, agrees that this name is the most accurate and useful.
UVa	University of Virginia
VC	Vassar College Library

Note to reader: If in the text I have given the date a letter was written, I do not repeat it in the note.

PROLOGUE

xiii "When the Nazis razed . . .": Susan Schweik, *A Gulf So Deeply Cut: American Women Poets and the Second World War* (Madison: University of Wisconsin Press, 1991), p. 62.

xvi "I remember a swamp": ESVM to Esther Root, *Ls.,* p. 176.

CHAPTER 1

3 "a girl who had lived": ESVM, *Collected Sonnets,* "Foreword," p. vii.

4 "Have the baker leave": CBM to ESVM, n.d., c. 1904. St. Coll.

4 "We had one great advantage": NM, typescript, n.d., 1976. St. Coll.

4 "I'm the Queen": ESVM, *Poetical Works,* pp. 53–54.
5 "At night, sometimes": NM, typescript, n.d., 1976. St. Coll.
6 "She was supposed to be": Henry Pendleton, interview with author, October 1976.
6 "We have just": ESVM to *St. Nicholas,* n.d., c. 1906. St. Coll.
7 "When I was fourteen": ESVM, *Ls.,* p. 9.
7 "The Land of Romance," Edward J. Wheeler, *Current Literature,* vol. XLII, no. 4, April 1907, p. 456–57.
9 "She was not like": NM, interview with author, Sept. 8, 1976.

CHAPTER 2

11 "a driving force": Clementine Todd Parsons, *O Rare Red-Head,* unpublished memoir. Much of the information in this chapter and in the next is drawn from two unpublished manuscripts by Edna St. Vincent Millay's aunt Clementine Todd Parsons, *O Rare Red-Head* and *Above the Salt,* in which there are sometimes as many as three versions of the same incident. These manuscripts include quotations from letters written by Cora Millay, as well as from fragments of autobiographical material she sent to her sister.
12 "One unhappy day" and subsequent quotes: CBM, unpublished, undated notes. St. Coll.
14 Among her keepsakes: Cora L. Buzzell, collection of flyers, tickets, programs, 1886. St. Coll.
16 "I was sure I was going to die" and subsequent quotes: diary entries, newspaper clippings, telegrams. St. Coll.
17 But by then: Story of birth of ESVM drawn from Clementine Todd Parsons, *O Rare Red-Head.*

CHAPTER 3

18 In the spring: Clementine Todd Parsons, *O Rare Red-Head,* p. 26.

CHAPTER 4

34 "Abbie . . . must have been": Martha Knight, interview with author, May 4, 1976.
34 "I guess I'm going": ESVM, diary, June 29 [1908]. St. Coll.
35 "For instance . . . giving parties": "X," interview with author, May 6, 1976.
35 "Vincent opened the front door" and subsequent quotes: Ethel Knight Fisher, "Her Girlhood Days," *The Rockland Courier-Gazette,* June 16, 1942, p. 8.
36 "I don't know": ESVM, *The Dear Incorrigibles.*
36 "Now, Muvver": ESVM, *The Dear Incorrigibles.*
36 "Once upon a time": ESVM, *The Dear Incorrigibles.*
37 "To live alone" and subsequent quotes: ESVM, notebook, n.d., pp. 91–94. (Norma Millay's note: "Note Book No. 6. ESTVM. Pieces [mostly discarded] from Foreword to

'Coll Sonnets.' Beginning of 'Radiance rose.' c. 1940?"). St. Coll.
38 "In this case": ESVM, diary, July 19 [1908]. St. Coll.
39 "I think I'll call her": ESVM, diary ("Mammy Hush-Chile"), c. July 1908. St. Coll.
39 "I make two cups": ESVM, diary ("Mammy Hush-Chile"), c. July 1908. St. Coll.
40 "To My Mother": ESVM, *Poetical Works of Vincent Millay,* July 10, 1908, p. 1. St. Coll.
41 "for an hour's stay": CBM to ESVM, March 10, 1909. St. Coll.
42 "In her class": Stella Derry Lenfest, *Yankee,* September 1953, p. 20.
42 "the first big disappointment": ESVM, diary ("Mammy Hush-Chile"), April 17, 1909. St. Coll.
43 "She was absent": Martha Knight, interview with author, May 4, 1976.
44 "Well, she spoke": Jessie Hosmer, interview with author, May 5, 1976.
44 "Oh, Mammy": ESVM, diary ("Mammy Hush-Chile"), Sept. 30, 1909. St. Coll.

CHAPTER 5

44 In October, Vincent won: diary, 1910. Program of *Willowdale* pasted into Millay's "Rosemary" scrapbook. St. Coll.
45 "with my sun-bonnet": ESVM, diary 1910. St. Coll.
46 "send you some more" and subsequent quotes: HM to ESVM, Sept. 16, 22, 29, Nov. 12, Dec. 11, 1909. St. Coll.
46 "I wish I could": HM to ESVM, Dec. 24, 1909. St. Coll.
46 "beautiful Christmas": ESVM to CBM, Dec. 25, 1909. St. Coll.
46 "Dear St. Nicholas": *Ls.,* p. 9
47 "Rosemary," a poem: *Poetical Works,* pp. 61–63.
47 "Mama said today": ESVM, Feb. 24, 1910. Black leather 1910 diary. St. Coll.
47 "I am going": HM to ESVM, March 15, 1910. St. Coll.
47 "The Hotel that was burned": HM to ESVM, March 25, 1910. St. Coll.
48 "She was quite upset": Robert Farr, "What Impact Did Camden Have on the Poet, Vincent Millay?" *Lewiston Journal,* Magazine section, June 8, 1957, p. 1a.
49 "If your father": CBM to ESVM, July 14, 1910. St. Coll.
51 "Schedule": NM, ESVM, KM, n.d. St. Coll.

CHAPTER 6

52 "I am . . . as surely": ESVM, diary ("Mammy Hush-Chile"), April 3, 1911. St. Coll.
52 "Sometimes I'm afraid": "Her Book," August 3, 1911. Edna St. Vincent Millay Papers, Diaries and Notebooks 33. Diary, "Vincent Millay—Her Book," April 1911–January 1913. Library of Congress.
52 "You are strong": ESVM, diary ("Mammy Hush-Chile"), p. 38. St. Coll.
53 "Sometimes I don't mind": "Her Book," July 3, 1911.

54 "It is as if": "Her Book," July 27, 1911.
54 "I cannot stand it": CBM to ESVM, Aug. 3, 1911. St. Coll.
54 "Just a few words": CBM to "My Girls," c. summer 1911, St. Coll.
55 "Where'd you get": ESVM to CBM, Aug. 18, 1911. St. Coll.
55 "We have been": "Her Book," c. Oct. 3, 1911.
57 "I'm getting old": "Her Book," "Monday— 10th."
57 "I do not know": "Her Book," Feb. 11, 1912.

CHAPTER 7

58 "The minute we came in": ESVM, diary, "Sweet & Twenty," unpaged, March 12, [1912].
59 "My dear little daughter": CBM to ESVM, March 3, 1912. St. Coll.
59 "to enjoy his dear girls": CBM to ESVM, March 4, 1912. St. Coll.
59 "He's had pneumonia": *Ls.,* p. 13.
59 "I see Papa twice": *Ls.,* p. 14.
59 "I am glad": CBM to ESVM, March 5, 1912. St. Coll.
60 "Sister Millay": NM to ESVM, n.d., c. March 20, 1912. St. Coll.
61 "because . . . I don't care": "Her Book," March 4, [1912].
61 "And they certainly": ESVM to "Dear Children," St. Patrick's Day [1912]. UVa.
62 "Dear Vincent": CBM to ESVM, March 21, 1912. St. Coll.
63 "Renascence was partly": CBM, typescript, n.d. St. Coll.
63 "If I'd thought": NM, interview with author, Jan. 23, 1979.

CHAPTER 8

63 "You inquire my Books": Emily Dickinson to Thomas Wentworth Higginson, *The Letters of Emily Dickinson,* vol. 2, ed. Thomas H. Johnson (Cambridge, Mass.: Belknap Press of Harvard University Press, 1958), pp. 404–5.
64 Vincent had gone: *Ls.,* p. 307.
64 "E. Vincent Millay, Esq.": *Ls.,* p. 17.
64 "It may astonish you": ESVM to Mitchell Kennerley, July 24, 1912. St. Coll. In *Letters of Edna St. Vincent Millay,* which was published in 1952 and has never been revised, the editor, Allan Ross Macdougall, said that it had been "impossible to find the fifteen or so letters which the young poet, in her excitement over his appreciation and acclaim, wrote to Ferdinand Earle from Camden." Before Earle's death in 1951, the year after Millay's, he wrote that her many letters to him had been stolen. What I have done is to reconstruct her letters from drafts that were kept in the files at Steepletop. Among them only two are in typescript and dated, suggesting they are copies of the letters she actually sent.
65 "Dear and true Poetess!": The Editor to ESVM, Aug. 6, 1912. St. Coll.
65 "I am to some extent": ESVM to "Editor, 'The Lyric Year,' " Aug. 9, 1912. St. Coll.

66 "to reach just such budding": FE to ESVM, Aug. 14, 1912. St. Coll.
66 "But it makes no difference": ESVM to "Mrs. Mitchell Kennerley," c. mid–end August 1912. Pencil draft. St. Coll.
66 "Isn't it dear": CBM to ESVM, n.d., c. August 1912. St. Coll.
67 "Mother said I could go" and subsequent quotes: NM, interview with author, n.d.
69 "If I had known": ESVM, diary, "Sweet & Twenty," "Being The Extraordinary Adventures Of Me In My Twenty-first Year," largely undated, or dates guessed.
69 "I should wager odds": The Editor to ESVM, Sept. 14, 1912. St. Coll.
70 "by betting on": ESVM to FE, n.d., c. late September 1912. St. Coll.
70 "Dear Tom Boy": FE to ESVM, Sept. 29, 1912. St. Coll.
71 *Bursting* to learn": ESVM to FE, n.d., c. late September 1912. St. Coll.
71 "I realize that you": FE to ESVM, n.d., PM Oct. 4, 1912. St. Coll.
71 "Now, to be serious": FE to ESVM, Oct. 4, 1912. St. Coll.
72 "[I]f it will make you": ESVM to FE, n.d., fragment, c. early October 1912. St. Coll.
72 Two days later: FE to ESVM, c. October 1912. St. Coll.
72 "If you could": ESVM to FE, n.d., fragment, c. October 1912. St. Coll.
73 "flame back into silence": FE to ESVM, Oct. 14, 1912. St. Coll.
73 "My Editor": ESVM to "My Editor," Oct. 15, 1912 (draft). St. Coll.
74 "friendships, relations, acquaintance-ships": FE to ESVM, Oct. 25, 1912. St. Coll.
74 "I am asking you": ESVM "To the Patch-Work Letter Man—" Oct. 28, 1912 (draft, date crossed out).
75 "I say: the Prizes": FE to ESVM, Nov. 2, 1912. St. Coll.
76 "This, then": ESVM to FE, Nov. 5, 1912. St. Coll.
76 "What have I done": FE to ESVM, Nov. 15, 1912. St. Coll.
76 "But it didn't get the prize!": ESVM, "Sweet & Twenty," Nov. 14, 1912. She recorded Jessie Rittenhouse's reaction, which Earle had sent her.
76 "The 'Lyric Year' ": Jessie Rittenhouse, review, *The New York Times,* Dec. 12, 1912, reprinted in *The New York Times* (New York: Arno Press, 1969).
77 "You might easily think": Caroline B. Dow to ESVM, Oct. 15, 1912. St. Coll.
77 "I have always wanted": ESVM to Caroline B. Dow, Nov. 18, 1912.
77 "the country life": Caroline B. Dow to ESVM, Dec. 2, 1912. St. Coll.
78 On December 18, 1912: M. L. Burton to ESVM, Dec. 18, 1912. St. Coll.
78 "I have on hand": Caroline B. Dow to ESVM, Jan. 9, 1913. St. Coll.
78 "Isn't this *fierce?*": ESVM to CBM, n.d., c. January 1913. UVa.
78 "Since three of the largest": Caroline B. Dow to ESVM, Jan. 11, 1913. St. Coll.

78 "I would write": Charlotte Bannon to ESVM, Jan. 4, 1913. St. Coll.

78 "I do not want": Charlotte Bannon to ESVM, n.d., PM Jan. 20, 1913. St. Coll.

80 "How did you come by": ADF to ESVM, Dec. 9, 1912. St. Coll.

80 "As to the line": ESVM to ADF, *Ls.,* p. 22.

80 "O, Wonder-child!" ADF to ESVM, Dec. 19, 1912. St. Coll.

80 "Mr. Earle may be extolled": Louis Untermeyer, Chicago *Evening Post,* Friday Literary Review, Dec. 27, 1912, p. 2.

81 "Some people think": "Her Book," Jan. 10, 1913. St. Coll.

CHAPTER 9

87 "buildings everywhere": ESVM to the Millay family, *Ls.,* p. 32.

88 "You see": ESVM to family, Feb. 24, 1913. Berg.

89 "Well, here I am": ESVM, "Sweet & Twenty," Feb. 7, 1913. St. Coll.

89 "Miss Dow": ESVM to CBM, n.d., c. February 1913. St. Coll.

89 "Well, now I've come": ESVM to "Dear Family," n.d., c. February 1913. St. Coll.

89 "O, it seems": CBM to ESVM, Feb. 10, 1913. St. Coll.

89 "I met two": ESVM to "Dear Family," n.d., c. February 1913. St. Coll.

90 "Isn't it perfectly dear": NM to ESVM, n.d., PM Feb. 15, 1913. St. Coll.

90 "Only you, my family": ESVM to family, n.d., c. February 1913. St. Coll.

91 "only rejoiced": CBM to ESVM, Feb. 18, 1913. St. Coll.

91 "Loose in New York!": ADF to ESVM, Feb. 13, 1913. St. Coll.

92 "And in order": LWF, Feb. 15, 1913.

92 "I call her 'Sara' ": ESVM to CBM, PM April 22, 1913. St. Coll.

93 "lovely home": ESVM to family, April 18, 1913. UVa.

93 "Has it ever occurred": ESVM to Louis Untermeyer, April 11, 1913. Lilly Library, Indiana.

94 "Wish I could hear": ESVM, "Sweet & Twenty," Feb. 20, 1913.

94 "I felt that": FE to ESVM, Feb. 25, 1913. St. Coll.

95 "Mr. Earle I saw": ESVM to CBM, n.d. (Cora's hand: "April 22, 1913"). St. Coll.

95 "Witter Bynner is tall": ESVM to family, n.d., c. spring 1913. St. Coll.

95 "just a small party": ESVM, *Ls.,* p. 36.

95 "If I should die": LWF, March 10, 1913.

96 "Did a lot": LWF, March 30, 1913.

97 "I am *dying*": ESVM to NM (postcard), PM March 18, 1913.

97 "I wish I hadn't": ESVM to NM, March 20, 1913, (copy). UVa.

97 "Po' ole Sephus": NM to ESVM, n.d., c. March 1913. St. Coll.

98 "Promise me, please": ESVM to CBM, *Ls.,* p. 37.

98 "I am going crazy": LWF, April 27, 1913.

99 "It isn't anything great": ESVM, *Ls.,* p. 44.

100 "beautifully written": CBM to ESVM, PM May 12, 1913. St. Coll.

100 "because this is the better": ESVM to CBM, PM May 9, 1913. St. Coll.

101 "Yesterday I got an A": ESVM to CBM, May 13, 1913. St. Coll.

102 "Mother should have been": NM, interview with author, n.d.

103 "They are in the *country!*": ESVM to CBM, PM May 16, 1913. St. Coll.

105 "Dearest old neglected Muvver": ESVM to family, n.d., c. late spring 1913. St. Coll.

105 "She had just": George Perry to author, interview, September 1976.

105 "Sister, don't smile": NM, interview with author, Nov. 11, 1973.

106 "Thank you for the statement": Ella McCaleb to Barnard College, June 27, 1913. Barnard College.

106 "Did I fail": Ella McCaleb to ESVM, Aug. 15, 1913. St. Coll.

CHAPTER 10

107 "It's all right": ESVM to "Dear Family," n.d., PM Sept. 11, 1913. St. Coll.

108 "reckoned it as a Failure": Mildred Thompson, July 27, 1951. VC.

108 "my sophomore": ESVM to CBM, Sept. 20, 1913. St. Coll.

108 "I am writing": Agnes Rogers to ESVM, n.d., PM Aug. 21, 1913. St. Coll.

108 "She was one": Agnes Rogers, interview with author, Oct. 24, 1974.

109 "Frank, you've got": Lydia Babbott to author, c. September 20, 1974.

110 "So Vassar College": ADF to ESVM, Dec. 12, 1913. St. Coll.

110 "Don't worry": ESVM to ADF, *Ls.,* pp. 48–49.

111 "I let her lead me": ESVM to "Dear Folks," Oct. 27, 1913. St. Coll.

111 "I heard a masculine": ESVM to NM, Nov. 1, 1913. St. Coll.

111 "They give themselves": ESVM to "Dear Family" (fragment), n.d., c. November 1913. St. Coll.

111 "Catherine can't do": ESVM to NM, n.d., PM Nov. 18, 1913. St. Coll.

112 "Wore my tan satin": LWF, Dec. 12, 1913.

113 "Heaps of fun": Ibid., Dec. 13, 1913.

113 "To think that": ESVM to "Dear 'dored Family," n.d., c. Christmas 1913. St. Coll.

114 "If she's trying": ESVM to "Dear Family," n.d., c. spring 1914. St. Coll.

115 "This I must tell you": ESVM to "Dear Family," n.d., c. April 1914. UVa.

116 "I shall be": CBM to ESVM, April 18, 1914. St. Coll.

116 "Vincent just stood": Helen Sandison, interview with author, May 29, 1975.

117 "Once I taught": Elizabeth Hazelton Haight, *Vincent at Vassar,* p. 1.

117 "& photographs, photographs": ESVM to "Dear Family," Sept. 17, 1914. St. Coll.

118 "Vincent was very definitely": Virginia Kirkus Glick, interview with author, May 1, 1980.

119 "She had this confidence": "X," interview with author, April 23, 1980.

119 "You don't know": ESVM to family, n.d., PM Oct. 12, 1914. St. Coll.

119 "After it was over": ESVM to sisters, Oct. 19, 1914. St. Coll.

120 "dead, worse than": NM to ESVM, n.d., PM Oct. 19, 1914.

120 "two or three": ESVM to family, n.d., PM Oct. 5, 1914. St. Coll.

120 "probably make more": ESVM to sister, Nov. 4, 1914. St. Coll.

121 "Hunk's & my latest": KM to ESVM, n.d., PM Oct. 5, 1914. St. Coll.

121 "Let's have a cup": CBM to ESVM, Feb. 10, 1915. St. Coll.

121 "Why have we not": CBM to ESVM, Feb. 20, 1915. St. Coll.

124 "I think Elaine": KM to ESVM, March 22, 1915. St. Coll.

124 "Girls, I want you": ESVM to family, n.d., PM June 7, 1915. St. Coll.

125 "It won't be long": ESVM to Elaine Ralli, n.d., PM Aug. 25, 1915. Private collection.

126 "My Dear": ESVM to Arthur Hooley, n.d., PM July 31, 1915. St. Coll.

CHAPTER 11

127 "Into a scene": "Pageant of Athena Wonderful Spectacle," Poughkeepsie Eagle, Oct. 11, 1915, p. 164.

127 "Of course you are": Caroline B. Dow to ESVM, n.d., PM Oct. 31, 1915. St. Coll.

128 "You know neither": ESVM to family, Oct. 27, 31, PM Nov. 1, 1915. St. Coll.

130 "Dearest little old sweetheart": Elaine Ralli to ESVM, n.d., PM Dec. 18, 1915. St. Coll.

130 "knew Vincent had dropped her": Catherine Ryan, interview with author, April 23, 1980.

131 "My dear": ESVM to Arthur Hooley, Oct. 6, 1915. St. Coll.

131 "Arthur—Arthur—Arthur—": ESVM to Arthur Hooley, Nov. 15, 1915. St. Coll.

132 "I shall be glad": ESVM to Charles Vale (pseudonym of Arthur Hooley), n.d., PM Dec. 6, 1915. St. Coll.

132 "Wouldn't you just love": ESVM to Charles Vale, n.d., PM Feb. 3, 1916. St. Coll.

132 "Edna—Edna": Arthur Hooley to ESVM, March 1916. St. Coll.

133 "Arthur, promise me": ESVM to Charles Vale, n.d., PM March 13, 1916. St. Coll.

133 "Never mind": ESVM to family, n.d., PM March 13, 1916. St. Coll.

134 "I came down Friday": ESVM to family, n.d., PM March 28, 1916. St. Coll.

136 "another year of": CBM to the girls, Aug. 3, 1916. St. Coll.

136 "She must be made": CBM to ESVM, n.d., c. summer 1916.

136 "You must not think": ESVM to CBM, n.d., PM Aug. 2, 1916. St. Coll.

137 It was late: Charlotte Babcock Sills '17, Vassar Alumnae Magazine, December 1960, pp. 25–26.

137 "The faculty . . . voted": Elizabeth Haight, Vincent at Vassar, p. 14.

138 "I . . . told her": Vassarion, 1967, pp. 51–52.

138 "Dear Mother & Sister": June 6, 1917, Ls., pp. 62–63.

139 "Dear Friends": CBM to Vassar Board, Miss McCaleb, and Dr. MacCracken, June 10, 1917.

140 "You told me once": ESVM to Dr. MacCracken, n.d., c. spring 1917. UVa. Box 8.

140 "But I'm not sleepy": ESVM to Dr. MacCracken, n.d., c. spring 1917. UVa. Box 8.

140 "What are they thinking": CBM to ESVM, June 10, 1917. St. Coll.

140 "but I really did not know": Ella McCaleb to CBM, June 13, 1917. St. Coll.

141 "Tell Mother": Ls., p. 64.

141 "Highly Esteemed": NM to ESVM, June 19, 1917. St. Coll. (Letter not sent.)

142 "Mother—listen": NM to CBM, n.d., June 1917. St. Coll.

142 I found a small green leather case: NM, interview with author, June 14, 1977.

142 "Vincent was free": NM, interview with author, Nov. 22, 1975.

CHAPTER 12

143 "We could have": Ls., pp. 67–68.

144 "You wrote me a beautiful": ESVM to Edith Wynne Matthison, Ls., p. 69.

145 "I am terribly": Edith Wynne Matthison to ESVM, July 27, 1917. St. Coll.

145 "Love me, please": ESVM to Edith Wynne Matthison, July 28, 1917. St. Coll.

145 "I could use": ESVM to Elizabeth Hazelton Haight, July 26, 1917. St. Coll.

145 "My friend at Greenwich": Elizabeth Hazelton Haight to ESVM, July 31, 1917. St. Coll.

146 "heart's desire": Elizabeth Hazelton Haight to ESVM, Aug. 12, 1917.

146 "There were good": Alfred A. Knopf, interview with author, June 8, 1976.

147 "But, oh, the manner": Alfred A. Knopf, interview with author, June 17, 1976.

147 "He is a great big": Ls., p. 73.

147 "Mr. Carpenter, who wrote": Ls., p. 76.

148 "she believes in me": Ls., pp. 76–77. UVa, Barrett College, no. 7115, box nos. 6 and 7.

148 "I came thinking": ESVM to Charlotte Babcock Sills, Oct. 12, 1917. UVa, C. Walker Barrett Collection.

150 "They were great events": Charles Ellis, interview with author, May 10, 1973.

151 "Am sending you": ESVM to NM, Nov. 24, 1917.

152 "She was so pretty": KM to CBM, n.d., PM December 1917. St. Coll.

152 "It may have been": Norma Millay interview with author, May 10, 1973.

152 "It has just come": Edward J. Wheeler to ESVM, Dec. 12, 1917. St. Coll.

153 "I have wondered": Caroline B. Dow to ESVM, n.d., PM April 5, 1918. St. Coll.

154 "Without demur or delay": Millay's relationship with Floyd Dell is based on his book Homecoming: An Autobiography, (New York: Farrar & Rinehart, Inc., 1933), as well as on the two versions of his unpublished essay "Not Roses."

CHAPTER 13

158 "This was said": Floyd Dell, "Not Roses."
159 "I remember her": NM, interview with author, Nov. 20, 1976.
159 "My dear, dear girls": CBM to ESVM and NM, Jan. 8, 1918. St. Coll.
159 "I used to be": CBM to ESVM, Feb. 21, 1918. St. Coll.
160 "Would you mind": ESVM to Harriet Monroe, *Ls.,* p. 85.
161 "A young artist": NM to CBM, c. Feb. 26, 1918. St. Coll.
163 "So we sat darning": NM, interview with author, Nov. 20, 1976.
164 "My time": *Ls.,* p. 133.
164 "Into the golden vessel":The closing lines in her workbook are wildly at odds with this published version. In her draft she wrote:

Love will be ours again as oft before
When hungrily we ate his heavy fruit
And slumbered, & no [illegible/singing?]
    voice upsprang,
Save in his singing is the minstrel mute.
Warm were the waters of the Lesbian
    shore,
And many loved, but Sapho loved & sang.

Anyone can love, but only "Sapho loved & *sang.*"
164 "You will forgive me": ESVM to CBM, n.d., PM March 7, 1918. St. Coll.
165 For the first time: *Art for the Masses,* p. 42.
166 "Don't worry about": ESVM to CBM, n.d., c. spring 1918. St. Coll.
166 "One morning . . . Edna and I": Floyd Dell, "Not Roses . . . ," Newberry, p. 27.
167 "Somebody else had my job": Floyd Dell, *Homecoming,* p. 322.
167 "I want, if possible": W. A. Roberts to ESVM, Sept. 13, 1918. St. Coll.
170 "The only decent thing": Edmund Wilson, *The Shores of Light: A Literary Chronicle of the Twenties and Thirties* (New York: Farrar, Straus and Young, 1951), p. 793.
171 "Dearlings": CBM to ESVM, May 24, 1918. St. Coll.
171 "Edna": KM to ESVM, n.d., PM Oct. 1, 1918. St. Coll.
171 "She was really": Mrs. Bennett Schauffer, interview with author, June 1974.
172 "When the sisters appeared": Malcolm Cowley, interview with author, Sept. 7, 1972.
173 "it really didn't take at all": NM, interview with author, June 4, 1980.
173 "skillful—their harmonies": Max Eastman, *Great Companions: Critical Memoirs of Some Famous Friends* (New York: Farrar, Straus and Cudahy, 1959), pp. 78–79.
174 "it was impossible": W. A. Roberts, "Tiger Lily," p. 10. VC.
176 "I have never": Susan Jenkins Brown to author, June 1974.
177 "We realized now": NM, interview with author, Aug. 11, 1975.
177 "We're not going": ESVM to CBM, *Ls.,* p. 90.
178 "You should see": Alexander Woollcott, *The New York Times,* Dec. 13, 1919, sec. 8, p. 2.

178 But there was more: NM, interview with author, Aug. 4, 1975.
178 "Dearest Girl, My Own": James P. Lawyer to ESVM, n.d., PM Nov. 27, 1919. St. Coll.
178 "God knows, Edna": James P. Lawyer to ESVM, n.d., PM Nov. 28, 1919. St. Coll.
179 "I carry my typewriter": ESVM to CBM. *Ls.,* p. 131.
179 "Jim was a beautiful boy": NM, interview with author, Aug. 4, 1975.
180 "If I can earn": ESVM to NM, n.d., PM Feb. 26, 1920. St. Coll.
180 "I guess my mind": James P. Lawyer to ESVM, n.d., c. winter–spring 1920. St. Coll.
181 "Vincent did care": NM, interview with author, Aug. 4, 1975.
181 "Pity me not": *Vanity Fair,* November 1920.

CHAPTER 14

181 "wherefore I deduce": ESVM to Jessie B. Rittenhouse, April 7, 1920. UVa.
182 "The slender red-haired": Hubertis M. Cummings to EW, Sept. 3, 1960. Beinecke.
182 "Aren't you about ready": MK to ESVM, Dec. 29, 1919. St. Coll.
182 "You, dear, I thought": ESVM to MK, n.d., "New Year's Day" [1920]. Dartmouth College.
182 "There's not a copy": Eighteen years later, Kennerley attached the following note to their correspondence:

I had published "Renascence" in 1917 and had considerable difficulty over two years in giving away the first edition of about 750 copies.
    I printed a second edition of "Renascence" in 1919 which sold very slightly. It was not until 1922–23 that people began to talk about Edna Millay and buy her books.

Kennerley had paid exceedingly little for *Renascence,* and his $25.00 check, which he said "is one of many similar checks which I paid the author on account of 'Renascence' though it was years before the book earned any appreciable sum," was wildly disingenuous. He was of course making a point in his own behalf. But he included only two checks endorsed by her, for July 24, 1918, and January 2, 1920, the latter having been sent to her on the heels of her January 1 letter. Certainly his firm's advertisements for *Renascence*— "Ten books of poems for $5 with a free copy of 'Renascence' by Edna St. Vincent Millay"—were not guaranteed to assuage any author's fears. To make matters even worse, he added: "I have several thousand books of poems in my cellar. Send $5 and I will mail you postpaid, ten different volumes, and a free copy of 'Renascence,' the most beautiful poems ever written by an American." It meant he was giving the book away as a sort of bonus.
183 "Charlie did the sets": NM to author, Oct. 18, 1974.
183 "I was thrilled": Edmund Wilson, *The Shores of Light: A Literary Chronicle of the Twenties and Thirties* (New York: Farrar, Straus and Young, 1952), p. 748.

184 When the war: Edmund Wilson, *The Twenties: From Notebooks and Diaries of the Period,* ed. Leon Edel (New York: Farrar, Straus and Giroux, 1975), p. xxxiv.

185 "Walter, dear": ESVM to Walter Adolphe Roberts, n.d., PM July 14, 1920. VC.

186 "I remember we didn't": William M. Reedy to ESVM, April 10, 1920. St. Coll.

186 "If you will send me": ESVM to MK, n.d., c. spring 1920. Dartmouth College.

186 "Mitchell, dear": ESVM to MK, June 22, 1920. Dartmouth College.

188 "remoteness, mosquitoes": George Cram Cook and Susan Glaspell to ESVM, May 22, 1920. St. Coll.

189 "I don't know how" and *"Please* be decent": EW to ESVM, July 27, 28, 1920. St. Coll.

189 "I don't know what": ESVM to EW, *Ls.,* pp. 98, 99.

189 "I have thought": ESVM to EW, *Ls.,* p. 99.

190 "E.W.": EW's papers. Beinecke.

190 "John Bishop used to say": Wilson, *The Twenties,* p. 59.

190 "I who have broken": Ibid., p. 62.

190 "They gave me dinner": Wilson, *The Shores of Light,* pp. 759–60.

191 "Edna was now": Ibid.

191 "But . . . there was nothing sordid": Ibid., p. 760.

191 "Since there were only": Ibid., p. 764.

192 "One of the younger": Nancy Milford, *Zelda,* p. 78.

192 "From the point of view": ESVM to family, *Ls.,* p. 101.

192 "Who is Edna killing": CBM to NM, Sept. 6, 1920. St. Coll.

193 "Our little house": NM, interview with author, Sept. 16, 1982.

193 "Between John Bishop and me": Wilson, *The Shores of Light,* p. 755.

194 "My dear dear girl": John Peale Bishop to ESVM, n.d., c. spring—summer, 1920. St. Coll.

194 "For god's sake, Edna": John Peale Bishop to ESVM, n.d., PM Oct. 31, 1920. St. Coll.

194 "September 11": Milford, *Zelda,* p. 75.

194 "Bunny Wilson and Edna": Ibid., pp. 77–78.

196 "Dearest beloved Mother": ESVM to CBM, Oct. 20, 1920. St. Coll.

197 "I'll be thirty": Wilson, *The Shores of Light,* p. 766.

197 "botched abortion": NM, interview with author, Sept. 16, 1982.

198 "à deux—à trois": John Peale Bishop to ESVM, n.d., PM Dec. 18, 1920. St. Coll.

198 "sitting on her day bed": Wilson, *The Twenties,* pp. 64–65.

198 "to which she answered": Ibid., p. 769.

199 "Also, I am becoming": ESVM to Witter Bynner, Oct. 29, 1920. St. Coll.

199 "There was something": Wilson, *The Shores of Light,* pp. 752–53.

199 "her own emotions": Ibid., p. 756.

200 "Dearest, beloved Mother": ESVM to CBM, *Ls.,* pp. 105–7.

200 "I shall bid you": CBM to ESVM, Dec. 21, 1920. St. Coll.

200 "My baby!": CBM, journal, Jan. 4, 1921. St. Coll.

201 "Healing": CBM, "Healing," n.d., c. summer 1920. St. Coll.

CHAPTER 15

204 "apropos of divorce": Frank Crowninshield to ESVM, Nov. 5, 1920. St. Coll.

204 "Did you see": ESVM to NM, March 11, 1921. St. Coll.

205 "You know, mother": ESVM to CBM, n.d., PM Jan. 18, 1921. St. Coll.

206 "The other night": CBM to ESVM, Feb. 1, 1921. St. Coll.

206 "so that through them": Walter Fleisher to ESVM, Jan. 21, 1921. St. Coll.

206 "February 13": ESVM to CBM, PM Feb. 13, 1921. St. Coll.

207 "Clem told her": CMB to ESVM, March 24, 1921. St. Coll.

207 "I have a curious feeling": *Ls.,* p. 131.

208 "Dearest Darling Baby Sister": *Ls.,* p. 117.

208 "It is nearly six months": *Ls.,* pp. 118–19.

209 "You told me": ESVM to EW, n.d., c. summer 1921. UVa.

209 "a very first-rate hotel" and following quotes from Wilson: EW to John Peale Bishop, July 3, 1921. Edmund Wilson, *Letters on Literature and Politics, 1912–1972,* Elena Wilson, ed. (New York: Farrar, Straus and Giroux, 1977), pp. 67–68.

CHAPTER 16

210 "The Café du Dôme": George Slocombe, *The Tumult and the Shouting.*

211 "The name I first called": George Slocombe to ESVM, July 20, 1921. St. Coll.

211 "Rise on your legs": *Ls.,* pp. 125–26.

212 "I do hope it is not": *Ls.,* p. 130.

212 "it verged on the sentimental": Edmund Wilson, *The Shores of Light: A Literary Chronicle of the Twenties and Thirties* (New York: Farrar, Straus and Young, 1952), p. 780.

217 "Mother has been": CBM to ESVM, Sept. 27, 1921. St. Coll.

218 "to you what you would": George Slocombe to ESVM, n.d., PM Sept. 23, 1921. St. Coll.

CHAPTER 17

219 "They wear the uniforms": ESVM, Albanian journal, "Tues. 18." c. 1921. St. Coll.

220 "But in spite": *Ls.,* p. 134.

220 "She remained in Rome": John Carter to Allan Ross Macdougall, March 9, 1951. UVa.

220 Just before leaving Rome: Note headed "Rome—Palace Hotel—Sunday—Nov. 13, 1921."

220 "Sweetheart": ESVM to CBM, Nov. 18, 1921. St. Coll.

221 "Whadda you think": ESVM to NM, n.d., PM Nov. 16, 1921. St. Coll.

221 "Now I have two bruvvers!": ESVM to NM, Nov. 13, 1921. St. Coll.

222 "I had thought you lost": George Slocombe to ESVM, Nov. 19, 1921. St. Coll.

222 "Oh, if only": ESVM to ADF, Jan. 25, 1921. UVa.

222 Arthur wrote back: ADF to ESVM, Feb. 14, 1921. St. Coll.

222 "Dear, does Hal know": ESVM to ADF, n.d., PM July 26, 1921. Beinecke.

222 "I must write you" and following quotes from Millay: Ls., pp. 132–133.

I think that no other letter of hers is signed "Edna." And not all my later-acquired wisdom enables me to understand how and why I failed to grasp the full import of this letter, and "smash the world to bits and remould it nearer to the heart's desire."

What I mean is that the signature is obviously a surrender of her proud will—an acceptance of me as the male and herself as the female elements in this strange relationship.

Whether it would have worked out well, I do not know: I do not know. [ADF note, Yale/Beinecke]

223 "Dearest Hal": Dec. 23, 1921. Ls., pp. 139–40.

224 "Dearest Edna": WB to ESVM, Jan. 19, 1922. "16 Gramercy Park, New York City. Shanghai no longer but on a train between Cincinnati and New York."

225 "I smoke too many": Ls., pp. 143–45.

226 "of the fact that you": ADF to ESVM, Feb. 9, March 7, 1922. St. Coll.

227 "Poor boy": Feb. 22, 1922. Ls., p. 146.

227 "I was interviewed": ESVM to family, Feb. 23, 1922. St. Coll.

227 "She was a little bitch": Marian K. Sanders, Dorothy Thompson: A Legend in Her Time, pp. 86–87.

228 "Beloved Sister": Ls., p. 146.

228 "Bon voyage, sweetheart!": ESVM to CBM, March 8, 1922. St. Coll.

CHAPTER 18

229 "mean, monotonous, vicious": George Slocombe to ESVM, Jan. 17, 1922. St. Coll.

229 "My dear": George Slocombe to ESVM, April 16, 1922. St. Coll.

229 "For the first time": John Carter to ESVM, April 2, 1922. St. Coll.

229 "Paris April 1st, 1922": ESVM, Paris notebook, April 1, 1922. St. Coll.

230 "Remember . . . that rainy": Margot Schuyler to Allan Ross Macdougall, Aug. 30, 1951. UVa.

230 "I did call her": Margot Schuyler, interview with author, Dec. 16–17, 1975.

230 "I hope this won't": Margot Schuyler to ESVM, n.d., c. April 1922. St. Coll.

231 "For goodness sake telephone": Margot Schuyler to ESVM, n.d., PM April 19, 1922. St. Coll.

231 "You are most like": ESVM, Paris notebook, April 26, 1922. St. Coll.

232 "and then we all went": CBM to "Dear girls," carbon copy, April 13, 1922. St. Coll.

232 "that wicked": Harold Lewis Cook, interview with author, Sept. 13, 1976.

232 "Dearest Kids": Ls., pp. 150–51.

232 "I saw Bernhardt": CBM to NM, carbon copy, May 29, 1922. St. Coll.

233 "fact that she has": Ls., p. 152.

233 "The idea of loving": Max Eastman, Great Companions: Critical Memoirs of Some Famous Friends (New York: Farrar, Straus and Cudahy, 1959), pp. 83–85.

234 "She dropped into": Dwight Townsend Hutchison, "Recollections of Edna Millay," unpublished ms., n.d., p. 1.

234 "We were sitting": Dwight Townsend Hutchison, telephone interview with author, July 24, 1974.

235 affadavit: Affidavit, June 28, 1922. St. Coll.

235 "Certificat de Coutume," June 28, 1922. St. Coll.

235 "His name was Daubigny!": Margot Schuyler, interview with author, Dec. 16–17, 1975.

237 "The weather had been cold" and subsequent quotes: Dwight Townsend Hutchison, "Recollections of Edna Millay," unpublished ms., n.d., pp. 2–3, 4–5.

238 "I have been sick": ESVM to EW, July 20–22, 1922. Ls., p. 153.

238 "The poet synges": Ls., p. 155.

239 "Mother is wonderful": ESVM to NM, July 21–22, 1922. Ls., pp. 155–57.

239 "Willow Tree" and other quotes about herbs: Culpeper's Complete Herbal (London: W. Foulsham & Co., n.d.).

240 "I cannot say": Dwight Townsend Hutchison, telephone interview with author, July 24, 1974.

240 "Norma": NM, interview with author, Aug. 23, 1976.

241 "Not that I've been sick": ESVM to CBM, n.d., PM Sept. 6, 1922. St. Coll.

241 "I've been such": ESVM to CBM, PM Sept. 11, 1922. St. Coll.

241 "Edna, Doris felt": Jonathan Mitchell, interview with author, December 1975.

242 "just to break": ESVM to NM, Oct. 13, 1922. Ls., p. 161.

242 "It's the greatest": ESVM to NM, Oct. 13, 1922. Ls., p. 162.

243 "A friend of Sefe's": CBM to NM, Nov. 13, 1922. St. Coll.

243 "No, I've never tried": ESVM to NM, Nov. 10, 1922. St. Coll. (Ls., p. 165, but with this cut.)

243 "My God": ESVM to ADF, Ls., p. 169.

244 "And she looked so": Margot Schuyler, interview with author, Dec. 17, 1975.

CHAPTER 19

247 Even Edmund Wilson: Edmund Wilson, Letters on Literature and Politics, p. 106, and The Shores of Light, pp. 770–71.

248 "Figs from Thistles" was the title of a group of poems published in Poetry in June 1918; it became A Few Figs from Thistles when it was published by Frank Shay as a book in 1920.

249 "The houses": Clare Sheridan, *My American Diary,* p. 192.

250 "Eugene and Edna": Floyd Dell, *Homecoming,* p. 308.

250 "As soon as she returned": Jonathan Mitchell, interview with author, December 1975.

251 "that at the meeting": Frank D. Fackenthal to ESVM, April 30, 1923. St. Coll.

251 became the first woman: But because the original awards were in journalism, fiction, playwriting, history, and biography, it was only the second time the prize for poetry was offered. Poetry was not added as a category until 1922.

251 "My mother is on her way": Eleanor Carroll, "Laughing at Life with Edna St. Vincent Millay," "A Fireside Afternoon in Croton Hills with Girl Winner of $1,000 Pulitzer Poetry Prize," New York *Evening Post,* May 19, 1923, n.p. VC.

252 "Dearest Mother": *Ls.,* p. 174.

252 "Darling Mother": *Ls.,* p. 176.

253 I'd just turned: NM and Charlie Ellis, interview with author, summer 1974.

255 "If I die now": Miriam Gurko, *Restless Spirit,: The Life of Edna St. Vincent Millay* (New York: Thomas Y. Crowell Company, 1962), p. 155.

255 "MARRIED YESTERDAY": Eugen Boissevain to Mrs. Charles Boissevain, July 20, 1923. St. Coll.

255 "Dearest Mummie": ESVM to CBM, n.d., PM August 3, 1923.

255 "They not only removed": NM to CBM, n.d., "Croton-on-Hudson/Sunday," PM July 23, 1923. St. Coll.

256 "a beautiful car": CBM to Susan Ricker, July 25, 1923. UVa.

256 "Tess, darling": *Ls.,* p. 176.

CHAPTER 20

257 "Darling Mummie": ESVM to CBM, n.d., PM Oct. 5, 1923. St. Coll.

258 "It is wonderful": ESVM to CBM, Nov. 7, 1923. *Ls.,* p. 177.

258 "Of *course*": ESVM to CBM, Dec. 15, 1923. St. Coll.

258 "Am I a swine?": ESVM to EW, Jan. 8, 1924. *Ls.,* p. 179.

258 "I saw Edna": EW to John Peale Bishop, *Letters on Literature and Politics,* p. 118.

260 "Seated in one corner": *Rochester Democrat and Chronicle,* Feb. 15, 1924, n.p.

260 "I got through": ESVM to EB. *Ls.,* p. 181.

261 "Once a day": ESVM to EB, Feb. 5, 1924. *Ls.,* pp. 184–85.

261 "My emotions": "Dodie's Mother" to ESVM, July 28, 1920. St. Coll.

261 "It might have been": ESVM, notebook, no. 55, p. 104. Library of Congress.

262 "Boys & girls": ESVM notebook, no. 26, n.p. Library of Congress.

263 "The Boissevains": Tom de Booy, interview with author, April 26, 1974.

264 "Dear Mother Millay": EB to CBM, April 18, 1924. St. Coll.

264 "She is doing fine": EB to CBM, n.d., PM May 4, 1924. St. Coll.

264 "The old lady": EB to ADF, n.d., PM May 4, 1924. Beinecke.

264 "then *on foot*": ESVM to CBM, May 4, 1924. St. Coll.

264 "ring for it": ESVM, Japan diary, May 5, 1924. St. Coll.

265 "But . . . the moment": ESVM to CBM, "June 22 (more or less) 1924." *Ls.,* pp. 188–89.

266 "having the most wonderful": ESVM to CBM, July 14, 1924. *Ls.,* pp. 189–90.

266 "gives instructions": EB and ESVM to CBM, Aug. 18, 1924. St. Coll.

267 "We left the hospital": EB to ADF, Oct. 29, 1924. Beinecke.

268 "a teeming family": Hilda von Stockum Marlin, interview with author, Oct. 18, 1980.

CHAPTER 21

271 "I thought she was": Mary Kennedy, interview with author, Sept. 30, 1977.

271 "cropped hair": "Edna St. Vincent Millay Reads Her Poems at Literary Institute," *Christian Science Monitor,* n.p., May 6, 1925.

272 "as a married woman": and subsequent quotes from John Hurd, Jr., "Poets and Writers Flock to Bowdoin for the Round Table of Literature," *Boston Sunday Globe,* May 10, 1925, p. 12.

274 "whose notorious sexual life": Jeffrey Meyers, *Robert Frost, a Biography* (Boston and New York: Houghton Mifflin, 1996), pp. 173, 181–82.

274 "Here we are": ESVM to CBM. *Ls.,* pp. 194–95.

276 "Darling children": EB to ADF, n.d., PM illegible, c. fall 1925. Beinecke.

276 "Darling Artie and Gladdie": ESVM to ADF and Gladys Brown Ficke, n.d., c. fall 1925. Beinecke.

276 "I am speechless": ESVM to ADF, n.d., c. fall 1925. Beinecke.

276 "pretending not": EB to ADF and Gladys Brown Ficke, n.d., c. fall 1925. Beinecke.

277 "who would cure": EB to ADF and Gladys Brown Ficke, n.d., PM Nov. 4, 1925. Beinecke.

277 "Vincent now has": EB to ADF, n.d., c. November 1925. Beinecke.

277 "She looks over": EB to ADF and Gladys Brown Ficke, n.d., PM Nov. 27, 1925. Beinecke.

278 "God, but it": EB to ADF, n.d., no PM, dated December 1925 by Ficke. Beinecke.

278 "We saw the last": EB to ADF and Gladys Brown Ficke, Dec. 30, 1925. Beinecke.

CHAPTER 22

279 "because the workmen": EB to CBM, n.d., c. summer 1925. St. Coll.

279 "All I did": Mrs. Joseph Sobleski, interview with author, October 1984.

279 "We have 12 tons": EB to ADF, Dec. 30, 1925. Beinecke.

279 "Hallelujah! Vincent has": EB to ADF, Jan. 2, 1926. Beinecke.

280 "but I cannot leave": EB to ADF and Gladys Brown Ficke, Feb. 2, 1926. Beinecke.

280 "Vincent says": EB to DT, Jan. 5 [1926]. Deems Taylor Papers.

281 "in the old Saxon style": EB to DT, Jan. 19, 1926. Deems Taylor Papers.

281 "looking at everything": ESVM to FPA, March 2, 1926. Ls., p. 207.

281 "I'm sending this": ESVM to DT, n.d., "(Along in February, snowed in)," c. February 1926. Mary Kennedy Papers.

282 "KINGS MESSENGER ABSOLUTELY": ESVM to DT, May 21 [1926]. Mary Kennedy Collection.

282 "and you will be": EB to DT, June 10, 1926. Mary Kennedy Collection.

283 "I remember that": Mary Kennedy, interview with author, Sept. 30, 1977.

283 "Vincent's illness": CBM to _____, Feb. 8, 1926. St. Coll.

283 "Ugin and I": CBM, diary, March 28, 1926. St. Coll.

283 "Unpleasant here today": CBM, diary, March 29, 1926. St. Coll.

284 "We just received": EB to ADF and Gladys Brown Ficke, n.d., PM March 20, 1926. Beinecke.

284 "take any pictures": EB to ADF, Aug. 9, 1926. Beinecke.

284 "Vincie went on": EB to ADF and Gladys Brown Ficke, n.d., PM Aug. 9, 1926. Beinecke.

285 "Dear, dear": ADF to EB, Aug. 15, 1926. St. Coll.

285 ". . . COME AND SEE": AB to "Eugene Millay," wire, Sept. 7, 1926. St. Coll.

285 "If we have": ESVM to CBM, Dec. 6, 1926. Ls., p. 212.

286 "a box": EB to ADF, "From Steepletop to Santa Fe. Undated. Probably March 1927." c. spring 1927. Beinecke.

286 "You will have to be": ESVM to CBM, Jan. 6, 1927. Ls., p. 213. This letter also tells of Norma's activities: "And Harry Dowd's Mozart opera, La Finta, opens Jan. 17, just a month before mine, & Norma is singing Serpetta,—Folly—she just wrote me. Isn't that thrilling?—If you come to New York for my opening, you can go to hear Norma in La Finta, too!—What a lovely life it is!—Isn't it, darling?"

287 "Mother Darling": KM to CBM, February 1927. St. Coll.

287 "The first rehearsal": ESVM to Deems Taylor. Ls., pp. 214–15.

288 "My Darling": Gladys Brown Ficke to ADF, ADF's typescript, February 1927. Beinecke.

CHAPTER 23

289 "I saw her wince": Edmund Wilson, The Twenties, pp. 348–49.

290 "When one looks back": Edmund Wilson,

"The Muses Out of Work," The New Republic, May 11, 1927, pp. 319–21.

290 "when she and": Elinor Wylie, New York Herald Tribune Books, Feb. 20, 1927, section VII, pp. 1, 6.

290 "very meager, poor": Mrs. E. B. White to author, Oct. 5, 1973.

291 "Edna Millay's father" and subsequent quotes: Griffin Barry, "Vincent," The New Yorker, Feb. 12, 1927.

292 "About that stevedore": ESVM to CBM, n.d., c. February 1927. St. Coll.

292 "everybody worn out": ESVM, diary, March 11, 1927. St. Coll.

292 "I feel a little": ESVM, diary, March 3, 1927. St. Coll.

292 "Today on the front page": ESVM, diary, March 9, 1927. St. Coll.

293 "Now nobody wants": New York Evening Post, March 8, 1927, n.p.

293 selling for $60: Detroit News, Feb. 27, 1927.

293 "Tonight Elinor told Gene": ESVM, diary, April 4–5, 1927. St. Coll.

294 "I gave it to her": ESVM, diary, April 7, 1927. St. Coll.

294 "I wrote Kathleen": ESVM to CBM, May 25, 1927. Ls., p. 220.

295 "Immigrant": Kathleen Millay, The Evergreen Tree (New York: Boni & Liveright, 1927), p. 13.

296 "The Spinner's Song": Ibid., p. 29.

296 "Washington is still": Stanley Olson, Elinor Wylie: A Life Apart (New York: Dial Press, 1979), pp. 285–86.

296 "I wrote a letter": ESVM, typescript, April 18, 1927, p. 20.

296 "It is not": Ls., pp. 216–17.

297 "My darling": Elinor Wylie to ESVM. "May second," n.y., PM May 3, 1927, London. St. Coll.

297 Sacco and Vanzetti: Herbert B. Ehrmann, The Case That Will Not Die, Commonwealth vs. Sacco and Vanzetti (Boston: Little, Brown, 1969), pp. 459–60; Katherine Anne Porter, The Never-Ending Wrong (Boston: Little, Brown, 1977).

297 joined the picket line: Miriam Gurko, Restless Spirit: The Life of Edna St. Vincent Millay (New York: Thomas X. Crowell, 1962), pp. 178–83.

298 "I suggested that": ESVM to Gov. Alvan T. Fuller. Ls., p. 222.

298 "Let us abandon": CP, pp. 230–31.

299 "And know that": Kathleen Millay, The Hermit Thrush (New York: Horace Liveright, 1929), p. 121.

299 "I don't imagine": ESVM to CBM, n.d., c. November 1927. St. Coll.

CHAPTER 24

302 "Eleanor went": ESVM, journal, April 2, 1927. St. Coll.

303 "My darling Elinor" ESVM to Elinor Wylie, Sept. 19, 1928. Beinecke.

306 "Let me add": ESVM to GD, "Saturday, Dec. 15," n.y. (c. Dec. 15, 1928). Alice Baur

Hodges, cousin to George Dillon, kept a group of Millay's letters to him. These letters were, according to Hodges, wrapped in tin foil by Dillon for safekeeping.

307 "incandescent": James Thomas Flexner, conversation with author, c. fall 1974.

307 "Young Phil Hitchborn": Laura Benét to author, Feb. 23, 1977.

307 "Carl Van Doren wept": Mary Kennedy to author.

307 Details of Wylie's funeral: Stanley Olson, pp. 331–32. The poem recited by Edna was "On a Singing Girl" from Wylie's *Black Armour.*

307 "Dear Vincent": William Rose Benét to ESVM, Dec. 20, 1928. St. Coll.

308 "Darling You": ESVM to GD, n.d., PM Dec. 24, 1928. ABH Collection.

309 "And do you think": ESVM to GD, n.d., PM Dec. 29, 1928. ABH Collection.

310 "Vincent is writing": EB to GD, n.d., PM December 1928. ABH Collection.

311 "My darling, forget": ESVM to GD, n.d., "Wednesday," PM Feb. 21, 1929. ABH Collection.

CHAPTER 25

311 "I hope that": ESVM to CBM, July 3, 1930. St. Coll.

311 "She gave me": ESVM, 1930–34 diary, May 17, 1934, p. 19. St. Coll.

312 "Darling, for God's sake": ESVM to GD, Oct. 28, 1930. ABH Collection.

312 "Ugin & I": ESVM to GD, Nov. 18, 1930. ABH Collection.

313 "Darling, I'm sending": ESVM to GD, Nov. 20, 1930. ABH Collection.

313 "Darling": GD to ESVM, n.d., c. 1930. St. Coll.

318 "Handsome, reckless, mettlesome": Malcolm Elwin and John Lane, *The Life of Llewelyn Powys* (London: The Bodley Head, 1946), p. 199.

319 "She in her long": Alyse Gregory, undated diary entry (c. Dec. 19 or 20, 1930). Private collection.

320 "about forty in all": ESVM to CBM, Dec. 10, 1930. St. Coll.

320 "about forty-four": ESVM to NM, Jan. 4, 1931. St. Coll.

321 "present agreement includes": Eugene Saxton to ESVM, April 18, 1928. St. Coll.

321 "sufficiently wearing": CBM to Clementine Todd Parsons, Jan. 12, 1931. Private collection.

322 "I am much better": CBM to Clementine Todd Parsons, Jan. 22, 1931. Private collection.

322 "I am sending": CBM to ESVM, Jan. 30, 1931. St. Coll.

323 "COME MOTHER VERY SICK": Telegram, Feb. 4, 1931. Berg.

323 "Ugin took along": ESVM to KM, Feb. 18, 1931. Berg.

324 "DEAR HOWARD PLEASE": ESVM and NM to Howard Young, telegram.

325 "AM KIND OF INSANE": Telegram, Feb. 13, 1931. Berg.

325 "So, our little": NM, typescript, Feb. 5, 1978.

325 "Steaming black horses": EB to Llewelyn Powys, February 1931. St. Coll.

326 "Vincent and I": NM, interview with author, March 17, 1974.

CHAPTER 26

329 "If you love": *World-Telegram,* scrapbook of clippings re: *Fatal Interview,* n.d., c. March–April 1931. St. Coll.

330 "She was a sunny": "Here's a Charming Double Interview in which Edna St. Vincent Millay, Famed American Poetess, Sees Herself as Her Husband Sees Her," NEA News Service, c. spring 1931.

331 "I had felt sure": ESVM to GD, n.d., c. March 20, 1931. ABH collection.

331 "My darling, your": ESVM to GD, n.d., c. March 26, 1931. ABH collection.

334 ". . . he was dominating": Elizabeth Breuer, "Edna St. Vincent Millay," *Pictorial Review,* Nov. 1931. All Breuer quotations are from this article.

CHAPTER 27

342 "Oh darling": ESVM to GD, n.d., PM Dec. 8, 1931. ABH Collection.

343 "Dear Miss Millay": Henry Allen Moe to ESVM, "2-i-32." St. Coll.

343 "I regretfully assure you" and subsequent quotes: ESVM, draft, Guggenheim report, n.d., c. 1931. St. Coll.

344 "How beautiful is": George Dillon, *The Flowering Stone* (New York: The Viking Press, 1932).

345 "Melodious, intelligent": Percy Hutchison, *The New York Times,* Nov. 22, 1931, p. 24.

345 "Kathleen Millay is primarily": William Rose Benét, *Saturday Review of Literature,* Dec. 5, 1931.

345 "I thought": Susan Jenkins Brown to author, n.d., PM June 25, 1974.

346 "Edna St. Vincent Millay": ESVM, scrapbook. Collected by Corrinne W. Sawyer, Mantor Library, University of Maine, Farmington, Maine. Archives. PS 3525 1495 532.

346 "Darling . . . I will come": GD to ESVM, n.d., PM Feb. 21, 1932. St. Coll.

346 "Darlinks": EB to NM, n.d., PM April 25, 1932. St. Coll.

346 "The Seine": Floyd Dell, "Edna Millay Finds a Cook," New York *Herald Tribune,* March 19, 1933.

348 "I feel strengthened": GD to Frank D. Fackenthal, May 29, 1932. Columbia University.

349 "Along my body": *CP,* p. 631.

349 "Darling Skiddlepins": ESVM to EB, May 17, 1932. St. Coll.

350 "She was a woman": Alix Daniels to author, May 22, 1974.

350 "For instance, one day": Alix Daniels to author, June 21, 1975.

351 ". . . the hyacinths": EB to ESVM, n.d., PM May 23, 1932. St. Coll.

351 "I just must hear": EB to ESVM, n.d., PM May 25, 1932. St. Coll.

352 "Darling Wham-wham": ESVM to EB, May 20, 1932.

352 "I hate not knowing": EB to ESVM, n.d., PM May 26, 1932.

352 "Do I write too often?": EB to ESVM, n.d., PM May 26, 1932.

353 "What ever happens": EB to ESVM, n.d., PM May 26, 1932. St. Coll.

353 "I wore my new": ESVM to EB, May 25, 1932. St. Coll.

354 "I know you love": EB to ESVM, n.d., c. June 11, 1932. St. Coll.

354 "I am ashamed": EB to ESVM, n.d., PM June 2, 1932. St. Coll.

357 "Everything would be": EB to ESVM, n.d., PM June 20, 1932. St. Coll.

CHAPTER 28

359 "Is there any danger": EB to ESVM, n.d., PM June 28, 1932. St. Coll.

361 "DISREGARD LETTER": ESVM to EB, telegram, n.d. St. Coll.

361 "My own sweet darling": EB to ESVM, n.d., PM July 4, 1932. St. Coll.

362 "fresh out of Harvard": Donald Gurney, interview with author, Jan. 28, 1975.

362 "Miss Barney needs": Lucie Delarue-Mardrus to ESVM, June 9, 1932.

362 "We want you": Natalie Clifford Barney to ESVM, June 12, 1932. St. Coll.

363 "Woodblocks won't do": ESVM to Eugene Saxton. Ls., pp. 244–45.

363 Harper brought: Karl Yost, A Bibliography of the Works of Edna St. Vincent Millay (New York: Burt Franklin, 1968). Originally published in 1937 by Harper & Brothers.

363 "It was all very": Mary Kennedy, interview with author, Sept. 30, 1977.

363 "Rachel Berendt read": Donald Gurney, interview with author, Jan. 28, 1975.

364 "Wonderful country!": Allan Ross Macdougall, unpublished memoir.

365 "I didn't know": NM to author, July 20, 1982.

CHAPTER 29

367 "mostly love poems": ESVM to Eugene Saxton, May 12, 1934. UVa.

367 "Poor passionate thing": CP, p. 339.

367 "There were only": Charles Ellis, interview with author, August 4, 1975.

368 "I got a job": Ls., pp. 248–49.

369 A gleeful Tess: Mary Kennedy, interview with author, Sept. 30, 1977.

369 "suppose we shall": ADF diary, Beinecke.

369 "to spend August": Ls., pp. 252–53.

370 "I put it" and subsequent quotes: ESVM to Henry Allen Moe, March 10, 1933. St. Coll.

371 "And it was just": Elizabeth Clark, interview with author, May 8, 1974.

CHAPTER 30

372 "right out on": Ls., p. 251.

375 "Well, my dear": GD to ESVM, n.d., c. spring 1934. St. Coll.

376 "and this although": ESVM, diary, March 16, 1934.

377 "all primed": ESVM, diary, March 26, 1934. St. Coll.

378 "I knew Eugen": Charlotte Boissevain, interview with author, April 30, 1974.

378 "Ugin got very tight": ESVM, diary, March 28, 1934. St. Coll.

378 "The funny little": ESVM, diary, March 30, 1934. St. Coll.

379 "She exercised no": ESVM, diary, April 3, 1934. St. Coll.

379 "Liked some of": ESVM, diary, April 7, 1934. St. Coll.

379 "Well, . . . I can understand": Ibid.

379 "Saw the forty-eight": ESVM, diary, April 9, 1934. St. Coll.

380 "Lulu looking beautiful": ESVM, diary, April 14, 1934. St. Coll.

380 "for the dummy": ESVM, diary, May 12, 1934. St. Coll.

380 "My idea about": ESVM to Eugene Saxton, May 12, 1934. UVa.

381 "I don't believe" and other quotes to end of chapter: Charles Ellis, interviews with author, Aug. 30, 1972; Sept. 4, 1975.

381 "On Thought in Harness": "On Thought in Harness" was published in the Saturday Evening Post on February 24, 1934. Charles Ellis seems to have remembered incorrectly the year he painted Edna St. Vincent Millay.

CHAPTER 31

383 "What marvelous news": ESVM to GD. June 7, 1934. ABH collection.

383 "sold out": EB to NM, Nov. 14, 1934. St. Coll.

384 "My translations are": GD to Alix Daniels, July 13, c. 1934; Oct. 22, c. 1934; n.y.

384 "a steel hand": ABH, interview with author, December 1973.

385 "In reading the name" and subsequent quotes: Horace Gregory, "Edna St. Vincent Millay, Poet and Legend," review of Wine from These Grapes, New York Herald Tribune Books, Nov. 11, 1943.

386 "In her latest book": Louise Bogan, "Conversion into Self," Poetry: A Magazine of Verse, pp. 277–79.

386 "Poetic Strife Begins" and subsequent quotes: New York Post, Dec. 7, 1934, n.p.

387 "like a figure" and subsequent quotes: Frederic Prokosch, Voices, A Memoir (New York: Farrar, Straus and Giroux, 1983), pp. 60–62.

389 "and if I come": GD to ESVM, May 1, n.y., PM 1935. St. Coll.

389 "though their hospitality": GD to Allan Ross Macdougall, Feb. 4, 1951. UVa.

390 "Me & George & Ugin": ESVM to ADF, June 11, 1935.

392 "Herewith the partial": GD to Eugene Saxton, Aug. 20, 1935. Berg.

393 "You will be surprised": HM to ESVM, Sept. 28, 1935. St. Coll.

394 "I want to tell": HM to ESVM, Nov. 15, 1935. St. Coll.

394 "It has to do": Eugene Saxton to GD, Dec. 30, 1935. Berg.

395 "unmindful of what you have said": Eugene Saxton to ESVM, Dec. 27, 1935. St. Coll.

395 "somewhere between Palm Beach": ESVM to Gladys Brown Ficke, *Ls.,* p. 262.

396 "Edna and I pick up": EB to DT, Jan. 14, 1936. Joan Kennedy Taylor collection.

396 "time to have": *Ls.,* p. 263.

396 "Poe spelled it Eldorado": *Ls.,* deleted portion of letter, p. 264.

396 "On the page": GD to Eugene Saxton, Dec. 10, 1935. Columbia University Rare Book and Manuscript Library.

397 "TITLE OF BOOK": ESVM to GD, Jan. 9, 1936. Syracuse University Library.

397 "It never occurred": ESVM to GD, January 1936. Syracuse University Library.

397 "in your role": GD to Eugene Saxton, Feb. 5, 1936. Columbia University Rare Book and Manuscript Library.

CHAPTER 32

398 "For some strange": "Baudelaire in English," *SRL,* April 4, 1936, p. 15.

398 "LIFE IS BLAH": ESVM to ADF, April 20, 1936. UVa.

398 "incomparable": Cuthbert Wright, "Charles Baudelaire's Poems in English Dress," *The New York Times Book Review,* May 3, 1936, pp. 4, 18.

398 "There was no": GD to Alix Daniels, May 15, 1962. Private collection.

399 "We start motoring": ESVM to ADF, May 1, 1936. UVa.

399 "the only thing": *Ls.,* pp. 282, 284–85.

399 "Sweetheart": NM to ESVM, n.d., c. May 1936. St. Coll.

400 "It was a major tragedy": EB to NM, n.d., PM blurred, c. May 1936. St. Coll.

400 "Under more favourable": ESVM, "Foreword," *ConM,* p. vii.

401 "We had an accident": EB to Charles Ellis, n.d., c. fall–winter 1936–37. St. Coll.

401 "On this day": ADF diary, pp. 112–13. Beinecke.

401 "My dear": ADF to ESVM, Oct. 24, 1936. St. Coll.

402 "Miss Millay, Esq": ADF to ESVM, Oct. 26, 1936. St. Coll.

403 "On an occasion": ESVM to Harold O. Voorhis, Secretary of New York University. *Ls.,* pp. 290–91.

403 "Well, I was": Cass Canfield, interview with author, July 11, 1973.

404 five honorary degrees: Two years earlier, Brown University had offered her its "honorary degree of Doctor of Letters" (Clarence A. Barbour to ESVM, May 9, 1935. St. Coll.); she did not reply. On May 6 they wired her; when they still had no word, they tried to telephone only to find she had no telephone. On May 9, 1935, they wrote again. There is no evidence either in her own files, at Steepletop, or in the records at Brown University that she responded. Whatever had

happened, by the following year, 1936, telephones were installed at Steepletop.

405 "Here's to my new book" and subsequent quotes: Michael Mok, "Edna St. Vincent Millay Sings Again," *New York Post,* July 15, 1937, p. 15.

406 who had sided: Edmund Wilson, *The Thirties,* ed. Leon Edel (New York: Farrar, Straus and Giroux, 1980).

406 "the conflict between": Edmund Wilson, "Give That Beat Again," *The Shores of Light,* pp. 681–87.

406 "Say that We Saw": *CP,* p. 377.

407 "the brilliant book": Kenneth Tynan, "Beat Attitudes," *The New Yorker,* Feb. 20, 1960, p. 104.

CHAPTER 33

408 "a depressing tour": George Slocombe to ESVM, Oct. 17, 1936. St. Coll.

408 "Darling": George Slocombe to ESVM, Mar. 29, 1936. St. Coll.

409 "Am I going": George Slocombe to ESVM, Dec. 9, 1937. St. Coll.

409 "in a lovely": George Slocombe to Allan Ross Macdougall, Feb. 8, 1951. UVa.

410 "You say you know": ESVM to GD, Sept. 28, 1937. Syracuse University.

410 "The reason why": EB to GD, Dec. 5, 1937, n.d., c. February 1938; April 27, 1938; May 31, 1938. Syracuse University.

412 "A delay in payment": Henry Allen Moe to ESVM, Jan. 31, 1938. St. Coll.

412 "I think if we": EB to Curtis Hidden Page, Jan. 5, 1938. EB to Page, n.d., c. Feb. 28, 1938. UVa.

413 "These reports reach": ESVM to Henry Allen Moe and Members of the Committee, March 18, 1938 (draft). St. Coll.

413 "He writes nothing": Guggenheim report draft, c. 1938. n.p., n.d.

415 "Listen, toots": ESVM to Harold Lewis Cook, July 6, 1938. *Ls.,* p. 296, plus deleted portion. UVa.

415 By the fall: Henry Allen Moe to EB, Jan. 13, 1939. St. Coll.

415 "for God's sake": ESVM to GD, Sept. 5, 1938. *Ls.,* pp. 300–301.

415 "Probably the others": ESVM to GD, Sept. 21, 1938. *Ls.,* p. 302.

CHAPTER 34

417 "a bad transplanter": *Good Housekeeping,* May 1938.

418 "Tell Charlie": EB to NM, June 2, 1935. St. Coll.

418 Edna wrote to Blanche Bloch: ESVM to BB, July 13, 1938. *Ls.,* p. 299.

418 "Long before Tanglewood" and subsequent quotes: Alexander and Blanche Bloch, interview with author, July 15, 1973.

420 " 'I'm crazy about' ": Dayton *Herald,* Oct. 31, 1938. ESVM, scrapbook. Helen Adair Bruce collection.

422 "She was to give a reading": Anonymous source to author, Dec. 9, 1975.

423 "I am horrified": Helen Adair Bruce, scrapbook, n.p., n.d.
425 "Your wire was not": EB to KM, n.d., c. February 1939. St. Coll.
425 "Dear Sister Edna": KM to ESVM, Feb. 20, 1939. St. Coll.
426 "Dear Kathleen": EB to KM, n.d., c. February 1939. St. Coll.
427 "You were very good": ESVM to Agnes Yarnall, *Ls.,* p. 294.
427 "There was either": Agnes Yarnall, interview with author, Nov. 13, 1974. Agnes Yarnall to author, June 30, 1975.
428 "Darling, It is quaint": ESVM to GD, Dec. 29, 1938. ABH collection.
431 didn't reach Clark's: *The Goddard Biblio Log,* vol. 2, no. 4 (Winter 1972), p. 61.
431 "my husband's face": ESVM to Ruth Dodd, n.d., c. 1941. UVa. (Not sent.)

CHAPTER 35

434 "And what the hell": Vincent Sheean, interview with author, Dec. 19, 1974.
434 "I want to propose": Peter Kurth, *American Cassandra: The Life of Dorothy Thompson* (Boston: Little, Brown, 1990), p. 308.
434 " 'appeasers' ": Ibid., pp. 308–10.
435 "In this country": "Edna St. Vincent Millay Warns of Internal Perils for America," New York *Herald Tribune,* n.p., n.d., c. October 1939. Helen Adair Bruce scrapbook.
435 "I can't resist": Helen Rogers Reid to EB, Oct. 11, 1939. St. Coll.
436 "Lulu, my poor": *Ls.,* p. 306.
436 "They are dragging me": Malcolm Elwin and John Lane, *The Life of Llewelyn Powys* (London: The Bodley Head, 1946), p. 271.
436 "Alyse": *Ls.,* p. 306.
436 "Vincent has not": EB to GD, Sept. 19, 1939.
437 "Dear Mr. Boissevain": Dr. Connie M. Guion to EB, Nov. 21, 1939. St. Coll.

CHAPTER 36

438 "This is the first": New York Hospital, Summary, History No. 252461. Millay, Miss Edna St. Vincent.
439 "She'd look them straight": Dr. Leila Wallice, telephone interview with author, Aug. 1, 1991.
439 "Menopause" notes: New York Hospital—Cornell Medical Center, Medical Archives, Dr. Connie M. Guion, box 3, f. 3, Medical Notes Misc., c. 1937–54.
440 "It is not quite": Dr. Leila Wallice, telephone interview with author, Aug. 1, 1991.
440 "This place has been": EB to NM, n.d., PM March 2, 1940. St. Coll.
441 Nembutal, a barbiturate: Goodman and Gilman, *The Pharmacological Basis of Therapeutics,* 8th ed. (New York: Pergamon Press, 1990), p. 358.
441 "financial call": Eugene Saxton to ESVM, July 12, 1939. St. Coll.
442 During 1939: Royalty statement, Harper & Row, June 30, 1939. St. Coll.

442 "What worries me": Eugene Saxton to ESVM, April 12, 1940. St. Coll.
443 "I don't care": KM to "The Millay Family," n.d., PM Nov. 6, 1918. St. Coll.
443 "Were there no Edna": *Chicago Evening Post Literary Review,* Dec. 9, 1927. St. Coll.
443 "Look where I am!": KM to ESVM and EB, n.d., c. spring 1939. St. Coll.
443 "If possible": KM to ESVM and EB, April 28, 1939. St. Coll.
444 "The doctor insists": KM to ESVM and EB, Aug. 10, 1939. St. Coll.
444 "Dear Kathleen": EB to KM, Aug. 14, 1939. St. Coll.
445 "Please thank Ugin": KM to ESVM, n.d., c. mid-August 1939. St. Coll.
445 "to stay": EB to KM, Aug. 18, 1939. St. Coll.
445 "HEAT HERE TERRIBLE": KM to EB, Aug. 22, 1939. St. Coll.
446 "As to Kathleen": EB to NM, Aug. 23, 1939. St. Coll.
446 she was suffering: S. Bernard Wortis, M.D., to EB, Sept. 7, 1939. St. Coll.
448 "This poem, written": Eugene Saxton to EB, July 9, 1940. St. Coll.
448 "Once-dear Edna Millay": FE to ESVM, June 14, 1940. St. Coll.
448 "As she has been": EB to FE, June 15, 1940. St. Coll.
449 "I am sorry": ESVM to FE, Aug. 3, 1940. *Ls.,* pp. 307–8.
449 " . . . for something over": ESVM to George [Dillon], draft, n.d.
450 Professor Irwin Edman: Irwin Edman, "The Role of the Man of Letters in War Time," New York *Herald Tribune Books,* Sept. 8, 1940. p. 6, IX.
451 He had visited: A. Scott Berg, *Lindbergh* (New York: Berkley Books, 1999), pp. 337, 404–7.
451 "I am filled": Anne Morrow Lindbergh, *War Within and Without* (New York: Harcourt Brace Jovanovich, 1980), p. 68. Nov. 27, 1939.
451 "a moral argument": Ibid., pp. 141–43.
452 "for 25 years": "Edna Millay, Academician, Perfectionist Feels She Must Write Fast Now," *New York Post,* Nov. 16, 1940.
453 "It was a book": GD to Allan Ross Macdougall, Feb. 4, 1951. *Ls.,* pp. 309, 310. UVa.
453 "And if this book": ESVM to Charlotte Babcock Sills, Jan. 2, 1941, *Ls.,* pp. 310–12. Susan Schweik, *A Gulf So Deeply Cut: American Women Poets and the Second World War* (Madison: University of Wisconsin Press, 1991), p. 64.
454 "Edna Millay had come": Vincent Sheean, *The Indigo Bunting: A Memoir of Edna St. Vincent Millay* (New York: Harper & Brothers, 1951), pp. 57–61.

CHAPTER 37

455 "Not having taken": Dorothy M. Leffler to author, May 10, 1976.
456 "Find out how many": Dorothy M. Leffler to author, Feb. 2, 1976.

457 "the world in which" and other quotes by Anne Morrow Lindbergh: Anne Morrow Lindbergh, *The Wave of the Future: A Confession of Faith* (New York: Harcourt, Brace and Company, 1940), pp. 9, 22, 33–35.

458 "Once again": ESVM to Eugene Saxton, March 10, 1941. *Ls.,* pp. 312–13, 314.

458 "Eugen has lost": While Millay is referring to money trapped in occupied Holland, there is no information I could find in either the Boissevain family records in Holland or Millay's collection of papers that Eugen had ever received a regular income from Holland.

459 "We've just had": Eugene Saxton to EB, June 6, 1941. St. Coll.

460 "Shakespeare—yes": ESVM, notebook, no. 50. Library of Congress.

460 "Attention Snig, Esq.": ESVM to EB, n.d., c. summer 1941.

461 "I am sorry": EB to Eugene Saxton, n.d., c. summer 1941. St. Coll.

462 "You know, Vince": ADF to ESVM, n.d., c. summer 1941. St. Coll.

462 "of recent years": ADF, notes, Sept. 4, 1941. Beinecke.

463 "On the way": Joseph Freeman to Floyd Dell, May 18, 1958, pp. 6–14. Newberry.

464 "Miss Millay's public": Rolfe Humphries, "Miss Millay as Artist," *The Nation,* Dec. 20, 1941, p. 644.

CHAPTER 38

465 "and will show": NM to _____, March 22, 1940. St. Coll.

466 "As to myself": This is unsigned and may exist only in draft. St. Coll.

467 "that is if the bitch": EB to Charles Ellis, n.d., c. 1941. St. Coll.

467 "I was pleased": EB to KM, n.d., c. 1941 (draft). St. Coll.

468 "I asked Edna": EB to KM, n.d., c. June 1941. St. Coll.

468 "both girls for me": KM to EB, July 4, 1941. St. Coll.

469 *The New York Times* picked up: *The New York Times,* July 1942, n.p., n.d. St. Coll.

469 "Lidice, they proclaimed": Edna St. Vincent Millay, "Foreword," *The Murder of Lidice* (New York and London: Harper & Brothers, 1942), p. v.

470 "When Woollcott's voice": NM to ESVM, October 28, 1942. St. Coll.

470 "Tonight Edna Millay's poem": ADF, journal, Oct. 19, 1942. Beinecke.

470 "Well, of course": Rex Stout, interview with author, c. spring 1974.

471 the Germans had actually: Susan Schweik, *A Gulf So Deeply Cut: American Women Poets and the Second World War* (Madison: University of Wisconsin Press, 1991), p. 61.

471 "yes, of course": ESVM to Witter Bynner, *Ls.,* p. 316.

471 "Your sonnets": NM to ESVM, Nov. 9, 1942. St. Coll.

471 "Listen Darlings": NM to ESVM and EB, n.d., c. fall 1942.

472 "Your letter was": ESVM to NM, Dec. 3, 1942. St. Coll.

472 "*Me,* with my Savile Row": ESVM, n.d., c. 1942 (draft). St. Coll.

473 "Gene was to meet me": NM, interview with author, Nov. 21, 1976.

474 "They found there": NM to ESVM, n.d., c. September 1943. Typescript with note: "To Vincent. Then I didn't send it, it seems."

476 "for a week": NM to ESVM, c. January–February 1944.

481 "He really got sick": Alice Blinn, interview with author, Nov. 5, 1975.

482 "Toward the end" and other quotes from Sheean: Vincent Sheean, *The Indigo Bunting: A Memoir of Edna St. Vincent Millay* (New York: Harper & Brothers, 1951), pp. 34–55.

484 "She had passed": Dinah and Vincent Sheean, interview with author, Dec. 19, 1974.

485 "And besides": *Ls.,* pp. 322–23.

485 "And you as well": *CP,* p. 579.

CHAPTER 39

486 "verdict was like": ESVM to EW, *Ls.,* p. 333.

487 "It is sheer": ESVM to EW, *Ls.,* p. 334.

488 "The House": *Ls.,* pp. 335–36.

489 "The effect of writing": ESVM to Cass Canfield, *Ls.,* p. 338.

489 "The Love Poems": ESVM to Arthur Rushmore, *Ls.,* p. 348.

489 "Trusting, however": ESVM to Cass Canfield, *Ls.,* p. 347.

490 "You can't go on": ESVM to Cass Canfield, July 27, 1944 (draft). St. Coll.

490 to everyone's delight: Edward C. Aswell to EB, March 8, 1945. St. Coll.

490 "It occurs to me": ESVM to Cass Canfield, *Ls.,* p. 334.

491 "unconditional surrender": Cass Canfield to ESVM, Jan. 16, 1946. St. Coll.

491 Marie Bullock: Mrs. Marie Bullock to author, May 31, 1982.

491 "wished you had not": ESVM to Marie Bullock, *Ls.,* p. 346.

492 "but now the birds": Edmund Wilson, *The Shores of Light,* pp. 783–84.

493 "after having read": ESVM to Cass Canfield, *Ls.,* p. 353, and ms. pages. UVa.

494 "I thought the verses": Cass Canfield to ESVM, July 8, 1949.

494 "Dear Kid": NM to ESVM, July 7, 1948. St. Coll.

494 "Oh, little sister": NM to ESVM, n.d. St. Coll.

495 "Hunk": ESVM to NM, *Ls.,* p. 352.

495 "I wanted to *see* her": NM, interview with author, Sept. 3, 1976.

496 "Imagine having to": NM, interview with author, Jan. 15, 1982.

CHAPTER 40

497 "I picked up": NM, interview with author, Feb. 26, 1977.

498 "Dear, I'm not": NM to ESVM, n.d., c. August 1949. St. Coll.

498 "And Vincent was breathing": NM, interview with author. Feb. 26, 1977.

498 "Darling Ugin, I think of you": Tess Adams to EB, Aug. 25, n.y., c. 1949. St. Coll.

498 "Very unpleasant": EB to "Darlings," n.d., PM Aug. 20, 1949.

499 "We were waiting": Alice Blinn, interview with author, Nov. 5, 1975.

499 "It seems incredible": GD to ESVM, Sept. 21, n.y., c. 1949. St. Coll.

499 "Mr. George Dillon": ESVM to Mary Herron, n.d. UVa.

500 "It meant a great deal": GD to ESVM, Oct. 21, n.y., c. 1949. St. Coll.

500 "A session occurred" and subsequent quotes from Dr. Lewis: Dictation, Dr. William Hall Lewis, Jr., to author. Tape 2, Index 3, June 14, 1975.

502 "The doctor involved": Cass Canfield, interview with author, July 11, 1973.

503 "to which I": UVa.

503 "He told me": Lena Reusch, interview with author, Oct. 4, 1974.

504 "She wanted something": Chester Osborne, interview with author, September 1974.

504 "stuffing myself": ESVM to NM, January 1950. *Ls.,* pp. 363–64.

505 "plenty scared": ESVM to Mary Herron, *Ls.,* pp. 366–67.

505 "that last time": NM, interview with author, Aug. 25, 1975.

506 "It's time I stopped": ESVM to Mary Herron, *Ls.,* p. 366.

506 "When once I have": ESVM to Margaret Cuthbert. *Ls.,* p. 376.

506 "It was going": ESVM to Cass Canfield. *Ls.,* p. 374.

507 "Hard, hard it is": Edna St. Vincent Millay, "Thanksgiving . . . 1950," *The Saturday Evening Post,* November 1950, p. 31.

507 "As soon as": ESVM to Tess Adams. *Ls.,* p. 373.

507 "No, my dear": ESVM to Tess Adams, Oct. 9, 1950. *Ls.,* p. 376.

507 "This iron is set": ESVM to Lena Reusch. *Ls.,* p. 376.

508 "I found her": Dr. Oscar Wilcox, Jr., to author, Dec. 20, 1974. Dr. Wilcox signed the county coroner's death certificate saying the cause of her death was "coronary occlusion." But when he was asked why he'd written that, he simply denied it. "I do not know why she fell. The cause of death which I certified was fracture of cervical spine as a result of a fall down stairs. . . . She did not have a 'stroke' or any evidence of heart attack." Dr. Oscar Wilcox, Jr., to author, April 21, 1975.

ABOUT THE TYPE

This book was set in Bembo, a typeface based on an old-style Roman face that was used for Cardinal Bembo's tract *De Aetna* in 1495. Bembo was cut by Francisco Griffo in the early sixteenth century. The Lanston Monotype Machine Company of Philadelphia brought the well-proportioned letter forms of Bembo to the United States in the 1930s.